THEORIES OF CORPORATE GOVERNANCE

How do we ensure corporations are run for the agreed purpose?
What role can Boards of Directors play?
Are CEOs too powerful and insufficiently accountable?

In the wake of the financial and corporate scandals of recent years, corporate governance increasingly is recognized as being at the heart of understanding how and why businesses are run as they are. But while there are diverse and well-established theories of corporate governance, they are rarely gathered in a coherent and comparative way.

This comprehensive reader brings together the most influential writing in the field, with editorial commentary, to provide a uniquely interdisciplinary resource for students and lecturers that underpins contemporary analysis of corporate governance.

Topics covered include:

- The separation of ownership and control
- How economic activity is organized through firms
- The managerial revolution in business
- Agency, stewardship and stakeholder theory
- Globalization and convergence
- The critique of shareholder value
- Post-Enron analysis.

Structured to provide an introduction and overview of corporate governance from the classical theories to contemporary controversies, this reader functions either as a stand-alone text, or as a companion to *International Corporate Governance*, a textbook also authored by Thomas Clarke. Providing a defining insight into this fast-emerging, and highly controversial field, this is the definitive resource for all those seeking to understand the contemporary corporation.

Thomas Clarke is Director of the Centre for Corporate Governance and Professor of Management at the University of Technology, Sydney.

Theories of Corporate Governance

The philosophical foundations of corporate governance

Edited by

Thomas Clarke

Routledge
Taylor & Francis Group

LONDON AND NEW YORK

First published 2004
by Routledge
2 Park Square, Milton Park, Abingdon, Oxon, OX14 4RN

Simultaneously published in the USA and Canada
by Routledge
270 Madison Ave, New York, NY 10016

Reprinted 2005 (twice), 2007

Transferred to Digital Printing 2008

Routledge is an imprint of the Taylor & Francis Group, an informa business

© 2004 Thomas Clarke editorial matter and selection; the contributors and
Publishers for individual chapters (as specified in Acknowledgements Page).

Typeset in Amasis MT Lt by
Newgen Imaging Systems (P) Ltd, Chennai, India
Printed and bound in Great Britain by
Bell & Bain Ltd, Glasgow

British Library Cataloguing in Publication Data
A catalogue record for this book is available from the British Library

Library of Congress Cataloging in Publication Data
A catalog record for this book has been requested

ISBN 10: 0–415–32308–8 (hbk)
ISBN 10: 0–415–32307–X (pbk)

ISBN 13: 978–0–415–32308–6 (hbk)
ISBN 13: 978–0–415–32307–9 (pbk)

Contents

Foreword

It is a pleasure to be asked to contribute a preface to this magisterial work. Its importance and usefulness lie in the way in which Professor Clarke has selected his material to present a comprehensive survey of the theoretical foundations on which the practice of corporate governance has been, if not always consciously, based. He has done this by allowing those who have played a key part in the thinking on corporate governance to have their say. More than that his excellent Introduction explains how the different governance theories relate to each other and how they have contributed to the development of corporate governance in practice.

Each of the separate theories discussed throws light on some aspect of governance, but is limited to that aspect alone and thus cannot capture the theoretical basis of corporate governance as a whole. The trusteeship model arrives perhaps at the nearest we yet have to a general governance theory, since it addresses the basic question of corporate purpose in relation to society. The Introduction, however, clearly illustrates the difficulty of arriving at any general theory of corporate governance, given the inherent complexity of the subject.

One feature of its complexity is that companies combine economic and social roles. Insights from the social sciences, therefore, have their place alongside those from economics. Governance structures are important, in the sense that they have to be clear and understood to be effective, but their precise forms are less so. What matters in practice is the way in which individuals put these structures to work, so people, their selection and their motives count.

Another feature of complexity is the diversity of governance systems and processes around the world. Forms of corporate governance are shaped nationally by their economic, political and legal backgrounds, by their sources of finance, and by the history and culture of the countries concerned.

Beyond all this, we are studying a process in motion and the practice of corporate governance has developed dramatically in the last two decades. The pace has been set by the introduction of governance codes, first nationally and then internationally. These codes have usually been drawn up in reaction to events and have been composed by practitioners, pressed for time and responding to immediate political and public concerns. Ideally, we would call a halt to codes, laws and regulations in this field to give time for theory to catch up with practical experience and illuminate it. This is a vain hope, but at least this book provides access to the relevant writings on corporate governance, against which to analyse and assess the theoretical foundations on which so much has been built so rapidly.

In addition, to changes in structure and process, the balance of power between the lead players in the corporate field has shifted in the last half-century. At the start, boards of directors were generally weak, executive management was in charge and shareholders were dispersed. Gathering investor pressure on the directors of under-performing companies, however, led to a strengthening of boards at the expense of management. This in turn developed into the present position whereby the concentration of shares in the hands of institutional investors has increased their power in relation to boards and management and, at the same time, drawn attention to their responsibilities in matters of governance. While these specific changes relate to countries where capital is raised through the issue of shares, the balance of power is also shifting in countries where banks are the primary source of corporate finance. Here the focus is now on the governance of banks themselves and in turn on their responsibilities for the governance of the companies which they finance.

The forces driving these changes have been mainly market based, a point which is relevant to the issue of convergence internationally. It leads on, however, to another question of balance, this time the balance between market and statutory regulation. That again is a moving picture, as was demonstrated by regulatory reactions to Enron, and it is one which varies country by country.

A further source of movement and of complexity relates to the wider implications of corporate governance. Governance codes began by focusing on the role of boards of directors, as the bridge between the providers of corporate funds and those who put them to work. Their contribution to better governance was real, but limited to the purposes for which they were designed. National codes were followed by international ones, whose aims were more inclusive. They were designed to encourage investment to flow where it could be most productive by raising national corporate governance standards to acceptable international levels. This chimes with my own view of the overall purpose of corporate governance, which is to align as nearly as possible the interests of individuals, corporations and society.

At whatever level corporate governance is studied and reviewed, there can be no doubt about the value of Professor Clarke's book in bringing together and clarifying the theories which have contributed to, and have relevance for, the development of corporate governance. For students of the subject it is a one-stop shop, which sets corporate governance squarely in its historical and theoretical context. For practitioners and policy-makers it should be compulsory reading.

Sir Adrian Cadbury
May 2004

Acknowledgements

The author and the Publisher would like to thank the following Publishers:

Harvard University Press for permission to reprint Alfred D. Chandler Jr, *The Visible Hand: The Managerial Revolution in American Business*, 484–500, Cambridge, MA: The Belknap Press of Harvard University Press, Copyright 1977 by Alfred D. Chandler Jr.

The Quarterly Journal of Economics for permission to reprint Berle, A., The Impact of the Corporation on Classical Economic Theory. From *The Quarterly Journal of Economics*, 79, 25–40, 1965.

Elsevier for permission to reprint Jensen, M.C. and Meckling, W.H., Theory of the Firm, Managerial Behaviour, Agency Costs and Ownership Structure, *Journal of Financial Economics*, 3, 305–12, 1976.

The Journal of Law and Economics and The University of Chicago for permission to reprint Fama, E. and Jensen, M., Separation of Ownership and Control, from the *Journal of Law and Economics*, 26, 301–26. Copyright 1983 by The University of Chicago, all rights reserved.

Academy of Management Review for permission to reprint Eisenhardt, K.M., Agency Theory: An Assessment and Review. Copyright 1989 by Academy of Management.

Harvard Business School Press for permission to reprint Mace, M., Directors: Myth and Reality. Harvard Business School Press, Boston, MA, 178–207, 1971. Copyright 1971 by the Harvard Business School Publishing Corporation, all rights reserved.

Harvard Business School Press for permission to reprint Lorsch, J. and MacIver, E., Pawns or Potentates: The Reality of America's Corporate Boards, Boston, MA: Harvard Business School Press, 1–15, 1989. Copyright 1989 by the Harvard Business School Publishing Corporation, all rights reserved.

Academy of Management Review for permission to reprint Davis, J.H., Schoorman, F.D. and Donaldson, L., Toward a Stewardship Theory of Management. Copyright 1997 by Academy of Management.

Blackwell Publishing for permission to reprint Hillman, A.J., Cannella, A.A. and Paetzold, R.L., The Resource Dependence Role of Corporate Directors: Strategic Adaptation of Board Composition in Response to Environmental Change. *Journal of Management Studies*, Oxford: Blackwell, 37, 2, March, 235–55, 2000.

Academy of Management Journal for permission to reprint Judge W.Q. Jr and Zeithaml, C.P., Institutional and Strategic Choice Perspectives on Board Involvement in the Strategic Decision Process. Copyright 1992 by Academy of Management.

Academy of Management Review for permission to reprint Jones, C., Hesterly W.S. and Borgatti, S.P., General Theory of Network Governance: Exchange Conditions and Social Mechanisms, 22, 4, October 1997, 911–45. Copyright 1997 by Academy of Management.

Brookings Institution Press for permission to reprint Margaret M. Blair, *Ownership and Control: Rethinking Corporate Governance for the 21st Century*. Copyright 1995, 202–34.

Elsevier for permission to reprint Thomas Clarke, The Stakeholder Corporation: A Business Philosophy for The Information Age. From *Long Range Planning*, 31, 2, 1998, 182–94. Copyright 1998.

Academy of Management Executive for permission to reprint Michael Useem, Corporate Leadership in a Globalising Equity Market. From *Academy of Management Executive*, 12, 43–59. Copyright 1998.

Elsevier for permission to reprint Mauro F. Guillén, Corporate Governance and Globalisation: Is There Convergence Across Countries? From *Advances in International Comparative Management*, 13, 175–204. Copyright 2000.

Taylor and Francis for permission to reprint Rhodes, M. and Apeldoorn, B. van, Capital Unbound? The Transformation of European Corporate Governance. From *Journal of European Public Policy*, 5, 3, September, 406–27. Copyright 1998. http://www.tandf.co.uk/journals.routledge/13501763

Cornell International Law Journal and Douglas M. Branson for permission to reprint The Very Uncertain Prospect of 'Global' Convergence in Corporate Governance. From *Cornell International Law Journal*, 34, 321–62. Copyright 2001.

Taylor and Francis for permission to reproduce Lazonick, W. and O'Sullivan, M., Maximising Shareholder Value: A New Ideology for Corporate Governance. From *Economy and Society*, 29, 1, 13–35, figs 1–6 and table 1. Copyright 2000. http://www.tandf.co.uk

Taylor and Francis for permission to reproduce Ewald Engelen, Corporate Governance, Property and Democracy: A Conceptual Critique of Shareholder Ideology. From *Economy and Society*, 31, 3, August, 391–41. Copyright 2002. http://www.tandf.co.uk

Academy of Management Review for permission to reprint Jeffrey N. Gordon, What Enron Means for the Management and Control of the Modern Business Corporation: Some Initial Reflections. Copyright 2002.

Cornell Law Review for permission to reprint John C. Coffee Jr, What Caused Enron? A Capsule Social and Economic History of the 1990s. From *Cornell Law Review*, 89, 2. Copyright 2004.

Introduction: Theories of Governance – Reconceptualizing Corporate Governance Theory After the Enron Experience

Governance has proved an issue since people began to organize themselves for a common purpose. How to ensure the power of organization is harnessed for the agreed purpose, rather than diverted to some other purpose, is a constant theme. The institutions of governance provide a framework within which the social and economic life of countries is conducted. From the earliest days *corporate governance* has been a subject of some controversy, though the term itself has only emerged recently.

This book sets out to present the competing theoretical explanations of corporate governance that have been developed over time, as new dilemmas of corporate governance have been revealed. The book begins with an examination of the economic foundations of the corporate system, the managerial revolution, and the separation of ownership and control. The dominant position of agency theory in the understanding of corporate governance and the question of managerial hegemony, are considered. The rival stewardship theory is presented, and the external pressures that managers are required to deal with are explored. Contemporary stakeholder theory of the firm is outlined.

Areas of lively theoretical debate are then delved into beginning with theories of the convergence of corporate governance systems around the market-based Anglo-Saxon model. This debate is continued with a focus on the concept of shareholder value, and whether this will become the overwhelming objective of corporations, or whether it represents the projection of a narrow set of ideological interests. Finally there is a theoretical discussion of the lessons of Enron, and what this means for the management and control of the modern corporation. The objective is to introduce the main highlights of the historical corporate governance debate as it unfolded up until the present day, with a selection from the most prominent theories. First though, it is necessary to define more closely the meaning of corporate governance.

DEFINING GOVERNANCE

Corporate governance concerns the exercise of power in corporate entities. The OECD provides a functional definition of corporate governance:

> Corporate governance is the system by which business corporations are directed and controlled. The corporate governance structure specifies the distribution of rights and responsibilities among different participants in the corporation, such as the board, managers, shareholders and other stakeholders, and spells out the rules and procedures for making decisions on corporate affairs. By doing this, it also provides the structure through which the company objectives are set, and the means of attaining those objectives and monitoring performance.

However, corporate governance has wider implications and is critical to economic and social well-being first, in providing the incentives and performance measures to achieve business success, and second, in providing the accountability and transparency to ensure the equitable distribution of the resulting wealth. The significance of corporate governance for the stability and equity of society is captured in the broader definition of the concept offered by Adrian Cadbury (2004): 'Corporate governance is concerned with holding the balance between economic and social goals and between individual and communal goals. The governance framework is there to encourage the efficient use of resources and equally to require accountability for the stewardship of those resources. The aim is to align as nearly as possible the interests of individuals, corporations and society.'

Aligning different interests into forms of productive collaboration is not an easy task, and company directors are 'charged with balancing the sometimes competing interests of a variety of groups that participate in public corporations' (Blair and Stout, 2001: 409). The ongoing nature of corporate governance is indicated by the definition of the Commission on Global Governance (1995: 2) 'A continuing process through which conflicting or diverse interests may be accommodated and co-operative action may be taken.' The dilemmas and contests implied in these definitions, are more fully elaborated in the theories of corporate governance that follow.

THEORIES OF GOVERNANCE

Economic foundations

The development of corporate governance is bound intimately with the economic development of industrial capitalism: different governance structures evolved with different corporate forms designed to pursue new economic opportunities or resolve new economic problems. The first recorded instance of a non-financial company with a diffuse share capital was the Dutch East India Company established in the early seventeenth century 'more than 1,000 investors put their money into it, and were thus rapidly confronted with the key corporate governance issues' (Frentrop, 2003: 46). Financial scandals of epic proportions in the French Mississippi Company and the English South Sea Company in 1720 associated unincorporated joint-stock companies with speculative frenzy (Tricker, 1984: 31). Adam Smith famously took a dim view of the

corporate forms proliferating in the eighteenth century:

> The directors of such joint-stock companies, however, being the managers rather of other people's money than of their own, it cannot well be expected, that they should watch over it with the same anxious vigilance with which the partners in a private copartnery frequently watch over their own. Like the stewards of a rich man, they are apt to consider attention to small matters as not for their master's honour, and very easily give themselves a dispensation from having it. Negligence and profusion, therefore, must always prevail, more or less, in the management of the affairs of such a company.

> (1937: 700)

Inexorably technological advances and the expansion of markets in the nineteenth century increased the scale and complexity of enterprises, and rapidly escalated the need for additional capital. In this context the joint-stock company moved from the margins to the mainstream of economic activity. Investors however remained wary of staking their personal fortunes on the future of unincorporated joint-stock companies with unlimited liability. In the UK incorporation with limited liability was finally granted in 1862, with a surge in company incorporations followed by some early collapses and evidence of fraud (Tricker, 1984: 35). On the continent of Europe a more prescriptive and regulatory approach was adopted, however limited liability was granted in France in 1863. In Germany though the formation of limited companies was permitted in 1884, this was tightly regulated with a mandatory board of supervision, separate from the company's board of directors, to represent and protect the shareholders' interests (Tricker, 1984: 36). Yet it was in the great emerging market of the United States that the corporate form matured earliest towards the colossus it ultimately became:

> This then became the pattern for constructing America's largest enterprises in the twentieth century. Entrepreneurs would found a business, succeed, and make the business grow. Frequently banks would lend capital. Eventually, the successful firm would go public, issuing new stock (or selling the founders' stock) to the public. For some firms, the stock market's role was to raise new capital: for

many others, its role was to provide the founders and their heirs an exit when they wanted to diversify and cash out, often via mergers. Although descendants sometimes took over running the firm from the founders, more frequently hired managers did, and stock dissipated into fragmented holdings as the heirs sold off their inheritance and the managers raised new capital in public markets. For many other firms, the stock market's initial role was neither to raise new capital nor to directly allow for exit when the founders diversified, but to finance the massive mergers at the end of the nineteenth century.

(Roe, 1994: 4)

Chandler's (Chapter 2) influential analysis of the managerial revolution examines how the *visible hand* of management replaced what Adam Smith termed the *invisible hand* of market forces. Capturing economies of scale possible with new technologies required large inputs of capital, beyond the means of individual entrepreneurs. He describes the railroads stretching across the United States, as the first of the large-scale modern enterprises:

Ownership and management soon separated. The capital required to build a railroad was far more than that required to purchase a plantation, a textile mill, or even a fleet of ships. Therefore, a single entrepreneur, family or small group of associates was rarely able to own a railroad. Nor could the many stockholders or their representatives manage it. The administrative tasks were too numerous, too varied, and too complex. They required special skills and training which could only be commanded by a full-time salaried manager. Only in the raising and allocating of capital, in the setting of financial policies, and in the selection of top managers did owners or their representatives have a real say in railroad management.

(Chandler, 1977: 87)

Chandler explains how the fundamental shift towards managers running large enterprises exerted greater influence in determining the size and concentration of US industry than other factors often cited as critical such as the quality of entrepreneurship, the availability of capital or public policy. Multi-unit business enterprise replaced the small traditional enterprise when administrative coordination permitted

greater productivity, lower costs and higher profits than coordination by market mechanism. The advantages of internalizing the activities of many business units within a single enterprise could not be realized until a managerial hierarchy was created. As the multiunit business enterprise grew in size and diversity and as its managers became more professional, the management of the enterprise became separated from its ownership. In making decisions career managers preferred policies that favoured the long-term stability and growth of their enterprises to those that maximized current profits.

Berle and Means work *The Modern Corporation and Private Property* was one of the most influential analyses of the development of corporate governance in twentieth century. They contend that the growing concentration of economic power and an increased dispersion of stock ownership made the public corporation in which a separation of ownership and control had taken place central to economic activity in the United States. In the preface to the 1932 edition of the work, Berle wrote: 'The translation of perhaps two-thirds of the industrial wealth from individual ownership to ownership by the large, publicly financed corporations vitally changes the lives of property owners, the lives of workers, and the methods of property tenure. The divorce of ownership from control consequent on that process almost necessarily involves a new form of economic organisation of society (1967: xli).' Their work influenced legal and economic theory, and the United States law including the creation of the Securities and Exchange Commission (SEC).

Berle and Means suggest that the splitting of the 'atom of property' changed the meaning of property and to apply the traditional meaning of property would mean that the 'bulk of American industry might soon be operated by trustees for the sole benefit of inactive and irresponsible security owners (1967: 311)'. Instead, they argue:

The owners of passive property, by surrendering control and responsibility over the active property, have surrendered the right that the corporation should be operated in their sole interests – they have released the community from the obligation to protect them to the full extent implied in the doctrine of strict property rights. At the same time, the controlling groups, by means of the extension of corporate powers, have in their own interest broken the bars of tradition which require that the corporation be operated solely for the benefit of the owners of passive property. Eliminating the sole interest of the passive owner, however, does not necessarily lay a basis for the alternative claim that the new powers should be used in the interest of the controlling groups. The latter have not presented, in acts or words any acceptable defence of the proposition that these powers should be so used. No tradition supports this proposition. The control groups have, rather, cleared the way for the claims of a group far wider than either the owners or the control. They have placed the community in a position to demand that the modern corporation serve not alone the owners or the control but all society.

(1967: 312)

Berle (Chapter 3) offers a review of the implications of the modern corporation from the vantage point of 1965 when many of the trends he had identified with Means three decades earlier had become more pronounced, despite the reluctance of neoclassical economic theory to acknowledge their existence. Berle's review was published originally in the *Quarterly Journal of Economics*, and takes the form of a debate with an earlier article by Peterson (1965) in the same issue on 'Corporate Control and Capitalism', which attempts to defend a more traditional economic view of the corporation. Berle and Means continued in their insistence of the revolutionary impact of the modern corporation upon economics, but though their work was instrumental in the practical policy achievements of Roosevelt's New Deal (1933–1940) (Nodoushani and Nodoushani, 1999), they had less influence upon neo-classical economics (Lee, 1990).

In the preface to the 1968 edition of *The Modern Corporation and Private Property*, Berle argues, 'The trend toward dominance of that collective capitalism we call the "corporate system" has continued unabated. Evolution of the corporation has made stock-and-security ownership the dominant form by which individuals own wealth representing property devoted to production (as contrasted with property devoted to consumption) . . . Most "owners" own stock, insurance savings and pension claims and the like, and do not manage; most managers (corporate administrators) do not own. The corporate collective holds legal title to the tangible productive wealth of the country – for the benefit of others. The word "revolutionary"

has been justifiably applied to less fundamental change. The United States is no longer anticipating a development. It is digesting a fact' (1967: viii–x). Berle and Means go beyond traditional legal and economic theory, to offer a new concept of the modern corporation that might have served as a foundation for a new theory of corporate governance, however little of this potential was realised by their successors.

Agency theory

The separation of ownership and control and the managerial revolution remained subjects of interest and occasionally of some controversy, but much of the steam left the debate with the long period of post Second World War expansion of the Western economies, the sustained increase in international trade and the unchecked growth of the multinational corporations. Meanwhile neoclassical economics attempted to develop a theory of resource allocation based on market exchange, and neglected the economic analysis of the productive sphere of the economy. A number of later schools of economic thought broke further from the economic ideal of neoclassical economics than the market imperfections approach, and attempted explanations for economic governance based on a new understanding of economic activity and resource allocation. Among these new economic theories of the firm, agency theory became the dominant force in the theoretical understanding of corporate governance in the last decades of the twentieth century.

Agency theory emerged from the seminal papers of Alchian and Demsetz (1972) and Jensen and Meckling (1976) explaining the firm as a nexus of contracts among individual factors of production. Previously classical economics conceived the firm as a single-product entity with a commitment to the maximization of profits, and what went on within the firm was considered to be of subordinate interest to what went on in markets. Agency theory argued economics was able to analyse the workings of the firm by explaining it as a constantly re-negotiated contract, contrived by an aggregation of individuals each with the aim of maximizing their own utility (Learmount, 2002: 3).

As Jensen and Meckling (Chapter 4) argue agency theory rests upon this contractual view of the firm. The essence of the agency problem is the separation of management and finance. Managers raise funds from investors to put them to productive use or to cash out their holdings in the firm. Financiers need the managers specialized human capital to generate returns on their funds. In principle the financiers and managers sign a contract that specifies what the managers do with the funds, and how the returns are divided between them and the financiers. The trouble is future contingencies are hard to forsee and complete contracts are infeasible. The managers and financiers have to allocate residual control rights – the rights to make decisions not foreseen in the contract. Managers end up with substantial residual control rights, and therefore discretion over how to allocate investors funds. From this point of view much of the subject of corporate governance concerns the constraints that managers put upon themselves, or that investors put on managers, to reduce misallocation and thus to induce investors to provide more funds.

Agency theory offers shareholders a pre-eminent position in the firm legitimized not by the idea that they are the firm's owners, but instead its residual risk takers (Alchian and Demsetz, 1972). Fama (1980: 290) emphasizes the irrelevance of ownership:

> Ownership of capital should not be confused with ownership of the firm. Each factor in a firm is owned by somebody. The firm is just the set of contracts covering the way inputs are joined to create outputs and the way receipts from outputs are shared among inputs. In this 'nexus of contracts' perspective, ownership of the firm is an irrelevant concept.

The agency view suggests that shareholders are the 'principals' in whose interest the corporation should be run even though they rely on others for the actual running of the corporation. Fama and Jensen (Chapter 5) propose the separation of decision-making and risk-bearing functions observed in the large corporation occurs in other organizations such as large professional partnerships, financial mutuals and nonprofits:

> We contend that separation of decision-making and risk-bearing functions survives in these organizations in part because of the benefits of specialisation of management and risk bearing but also because of an effective common approach to controlling the agency problems caused by separation of decision-making and risk-bearing functions.

It is claimed shareholders have the right to residual claims because they are the residual risk bearers. As equity investors, shareholders are the only economic actors who make an investment in the corporation without any contractual guarantee of a specific return, it is suggested. As 'residual claimants' shareholders bear the risk of the corporation making a profit or loss, and have an interest in the allocation of corporate resources to make the largest residual possible. Since other stakeholders in the corporation will receive the returns for which they have contracted, the maximization of shareholder value results in superior economic performance, not only for the particular corporation, but for the economy as a whole, it is held. Fama and Jensen argue shareholders are better equipped to bear risk than managers or workers, because they are not tied to the firms in which they hold shares. Shareholders can diversify their investment portfolios to minimize risk. This separation of management and residual risk bearing in the corporation allows optimal risk allocation in the corporate economy.

Since the basis of agency theory is the self-interested utility-maximizing motivation of individual actors, it is assumed that the relationship between shareholders ('principals') and managers ('agents') will be problematic: how is the 'principal' able to prevent the 'agent' from maximizing his own utility (Jensen, 1994)? For agency theorists efficient markets are the solution; consequently the main focus of their approach to corporate governance is the elaboration and facilitation of market mechanisms that can mitigate the agency problem. These include an efficient market for

- corporate control
- management labour
- corporate information.

All of which will ensure management bear the costs of its own misconduct and will therefore create the incentives for self-control (Learmount, 2002: 4).

If this corporate form is based on such inherent dilemmas, why is the form so popular? With a great rhetorical flourish Jensen and Meckling (1976: 330) pose the question more profoundly:

> Why, given the existence of positive costs of the agency relationship, do we find the usual corporate form of organisation with widely diffuse ownership

so widely prevalent? If one takes seriously much of the literature regarding the 'discretionary' power held by managers of large corporations, it is difficult to understand the historical fact of enormous growth in equity in such organisations, not only in the United States, but throughout the world. Paraphrasing Alchian (1968): How does it happen that millions of individuals are willing to turn over a significant fraction of their wealth to organisations run by managers who have so little interest in their welfare? What is even more remarkable, why are they willing to make these commitments purely as residual claimants, i.e. on the anticipation that managers will operate the firm so that there will be earnings which accrue to stockholders?

The idea of the firm as a series of contracts was developed in a different way by new institutional economists (Learmount, 2002: 4). Neoclassical economics sees the market as the only way to organize efficient contracting, and the firm is seen simply as an artefact of constantly re-negotiated contracts; in contrast, new institutional economics conceives the firm to be a discrete, relatively permanent hierarchy that exists as an alternative to contracting in markets. Like neoclassical economics, new institutional economics is concerned with ensuring the efficiency of private contracting, but rather than concentrating on the maximization of profit, the focus is perceived to be the minimization of transaction costs (Coase, 1937; Learmount, 2002: 4; Williamson, 1979, 1985).

Ronald Coase's (1937) transaction cost economics insisted notwithstanding the assumption of neoclassical theory that the allocation of resources is coordinated through a series of exchange transactions on the market, that in the real world a considerable proportion of economic activity is organized in firms. Coase examines the economic explanation for the existence of firms, and why economic activities take place within firms rather than through markets. He explains the nature of firms in terms of the imperfections of markets, and in terms of the transaction costs of market exchange. New institutional economics differs from agency theory in that the corporate governance problems of firms are perceived to proceed from a number of contractual hazards, including

- self-interested opportunism
- information asymmetries

- asset specificity and small numbers bargaining
- the problem of bounded rationality (Williamson, 1984, 1985).

This approach is concerned with discovering internal measures and mechanisms which reduce costs associated with contractual hazards to an efficient level: the external discipline of the market cannot be relied on to mitigate these problems, as it has only 'limited constitutional powers to conduct audits and has limited access to the firm's incentive and resource allocation machinery' (Williamson, 1975: 143). Like neoclassical economics though, the locus of attention remains the shareholder–manager relationship, but in this case it is because shareholders are perceived to 'face a diffuse but significant risk of expropriation because the assets in question are numerous and ill-defined, and cannot be protected in a well-focused, transaction specific way' (Learmount, 2002: 5; Williamson, 1984: 1210).

Kathleen Eisenhardt (Chapter 6) offers a contemporary assessment and review of agency theory, suggesting the theory offers unique insights into information systems, outcome uncertainty, incentives and risk, arguing these are 'novel contributions to organizational thinking, and the empirical evidence is supportive of the theory, particularly when coupled with complementary theoretical perspectives'. Though it has been criticized by organizational theorists as minimalist (Hirsch et al., 1987; Perrow, 1986), Eisenhardt identifies links to mainstream organization perspectives: 'At its roots, agency theory is consistent with the classic works of Barnard (1938) on the nature of cooperative behaviour and March and Simon (1958) on the inducements and contributions of the employment relationship. As in this earlier work, the heart of agency theory is the goal conflict inherent when individuals with differing preferences engage in cooperative effort, and the essential metaphor is that of the contract.'

Agency theory also is similar to political models of organizations Eisenhardt argues, since both perspectives assume the pursuit of self-interest at the individual level and goal conflict at the organizational level (e.g. March, 1962; Pfeffer, 1981). In both perspectives information asymmetry is related to the power of lower order participants (Pettigrew, 1973). 'The difference is that in political models goal conflicts are resolved through bargaining, negotiation, and coalitions – the power mechanisms of political science. In agency theory they are resolved through the coalignment of incentives – the price mechanism of economics.'

Eisenhardt recognizes further similarities between agency theory and the information processing approaches to contingency theory (Chandler, 1962; Galbraith, 1973; Lawrence and Lorsch, 1967). Both perspectives assume that individuals have bounded rationality, and that information is distributed asymmetrically throughout the organization. Both use efficient processing of information as a criterion for choosing among various organizational forms. 'The difference between the two is their focus: in contingency theory researchers are concerned with the optimal structuring of reporting relationships and decision-making responsibilities; whereas in agency theory they are concerned with the optimal structuring of control relationships resulting from these reporting and decision-making patterns.'

The prevalence of agency theory in the governance literature is ascribed by Daily *et al.* (2003: 372) to two factors:

> 'First, it is an extremely simple theory, in which large corporations are reduced to two participants – managers and shareholders – and the interests of each are assumed to be both clear and consistent. Second, the notion of humans as self-interested and generally unwilling to sacrifice personal interests for the interests of others is both age old and widespread . . . Economists struggled with this problem for centuries until Jensen and Meckling (1976) provided their convincing rationale for how the public corporation could survive and prosper despite the self-interested proclivities of managers. In nearly all modern governance research governance mechanisms are conceptualised as deterrents to managerial self-interest.'

From this approach it is assumed the main purpose of corporate governance mechanisms is to provide shareholders with some reassurance that managers will try to achieve outcomes that are in the shareholders' interests (Shleifer and Vishny, 1997). Internal and external governance mechanisms help to bring the interests of managers in line with those of shareholders, including

- an effectively structured board;
- compensation contracts that encourage a shareholder orientation;

- concentrated ownership holdings that lead to active monitoring of executives;
- the market for corporate control that is an external mechanism activated when internal mechanism for controlling managerial opportunism or failure have not worked (Daily *et al.*, 2003; Walsh and Seward, 1990).

As Simon Learmount (2002) argues Anglo-American economic theories of the firm have dominated thinking on corporate governance in much of the world, despite widespread criticisms of their underlying assumptions and propositions that they

- tend to see the firm principally in contractual terms;
- are guided by the assumption of utility-maximizing self-interested human behaviour;
- tend to posit the protection of investor's capital as the 'corporate governance problem'.

While arguably justifiable at the level of market analysis, they are less defensible at the level of the firm itself. Organizational approaches to corporate governance proposed as a counter to economic theories in contrast

- tend to begin with a more complex concept of the firm;
- allow for more positive orientations towards the welfare of others;
- conceive of the governance of companies as routinely involving multiple relationships (Learmount, 2002: 1).

However, whereas economic theories are well-established in academic research and public policy, organizational approaches to corporate governance tend to be less well-developed theoretically, or are relatively embryonic, and as a result have had much less influence on policy development. As Learmount contends, the impact of the hegemonic influence of exclusively economic approaches in corporate governance theorizing has constricted the subject into a restricted form: 'Notwithstanding their inherently distinctive conceptualisations of the "governance problem", the different theories . . . have helped to reify the firm as an economic mechanism, and institutionalise the idea that corporate governance is primarily concerned with the control of managers by shareholders' (Learmount, 2002: 5).

Managerial hegemony

The revelations by Mace (Chapter 7) of the great divide between the myth of the powers and responsibilities of boards of directors, and the reality of their ineffective performance, would confirm the worst fears of the agency theorists. This was the time of the greatest ascendancy of US corporations and executives (of the world's 50 largest corporations in 1959 a total of 44 were based in the US with an 87 per cent share of total revenues (Lazonick, 2002: 2)). Mace analyses how triumphant CEOs controlled the Boards of Directors of the companies they ran. CEOs in the US increased their influence to the point where they were able to determine board membership, to decide what boards did and could not do, controlled the information and professional advice that Boards received, and even determined the compensation package for senior executives. Disclosures of major corporate disasters perennially raise the question, 'where were the board of directors?' But there was a wide gap between what people assume directors are supposed to do, and what they actually were allowed to do. Dysfunctional boards rather than being the rare exception became the norm in the United States. As Boards became trivialized, 'directors were ornaments on the corporate Christmas tree', the era of all-powerful CEOs had arrived.

Lorsch and MacIver (Chapter 8) present a more considered view of the potential power of Boards of Directors, arguing the significance of the board processes that occur for an accurate understanding of the relative influence of the board. To comprehend the reality of corporate governance in any country there is a need to understand the relationship between owners, managers and the board of directors. There was a clear historical progression in the position of boards of directors in the United States from the period of the 1950s/60s when they were becoming increasingly ornamental, to the initial stages of becoming more independent and empowered in response to public concerns particularly regarding the overseas activities of corporations, with the call for boards to have a majority of non-executive directors. Then in the 1980s as the market for corporate control sharply intensified, the focus on the boardroom receded, supplanted by the discipline of capital markets as the rate of mergers, takeovers and acquisitions increased. Finally in the 1990s with the experience of further corporate collapses and market failure, there were increasing pressures from

government, institutional investors and the wider public for more active, independent company boards.

The body of evidence supporting the managerialist thesis has strengthened over time (Herman, 1982; Mizruchi, 1983; Pettigrew, 1992). 'Managers are expected to exercise day-to-day operating control, which gives them an intimate knowledge of the business, putting the board at a disadvantage. In addition to this specialised knowledge, managers in profitable companies are able to finance investments from retained earnings, thus allowing them to weaken the dependence on shareholders for capital (Mizruchi, 1983). This allows them to pursue aims other than profit maximisation' (Stiles and Taylor, 2002: 18–19). Pfeffer (1972: 220) notes that it is an established practice that board members are selected by management. 'In many practical respects, management is, therefore in control of the board.' The managerialist thesis implies passive boards with little input into corporate decision-making, and little influence over the chief executive, therefore with little capacity to represent the interests of shareholders. However, it can be argued that the increased concentration of ownership, and interlocking directorships do provide a powerful check on managerial control (Zeitlin, 1974), and the increasing concentration of ownership in recent years has suggested a constellation of ownership interests capable of constraining managerialism (Scott, 1985; 1997).

Stewardship theory

A very different model of management is presented by stewardship theory. Davis, Schoorman and Donaldson (Chapter 9) take issue with the assumption of agency theory of the self-interested manager rationally maximizing his own economic gain. This individualistic model is predicated on the notion of an in-built conflict of interest between owners and managers. Accordingly opportunistic agents can only be curbed by vigilant monitoring, and incentive schemes based around money, promotions and negative sanctions. But Donaldson (1990: 372) insists 'Students of human behaviour have identified a much larger range of human motives, including needs for achievement, responsibility, and recognition, as well as altruism, belief, respect for authority, and the intrinsic motivation of an inherently satisfying task' (Wood and Bandura, 1989). Stewardship theory holds that there is no conflict of interest between managers and owners, that the optimum governance structure allows coordination of the enterprise to be achieved most effectively, and authorizes managers to act since according to this theory they are not opportunistic agents but good stewards who will act in the best interests of owners (Donaldson and Davis, 1991). Stewardship theory sees a strong relationship between managers' successful pursuit of the objectives of the enterprise, and not only the principal's satisfaction, but also that of other participants in the enterprise collective reward. Davis, Schoorman and Donaldson describe this virtuous circle thus:

> A steward protects and maximises shareholder's wealth through firm performance, because, by so doing, the steward's utility functions are maximised. Given the potential multiplicity of shareholders objectives, a steward's behaviour can be considered organisationally centred. Stewards in loosely coupled, heterogeneous organisations with competing stakeholders and competing shareholders objectives are motivated to make decisions that they perceive are in the best interests of the group. Even in the most politically charged environment, one can assume that most parties desire a viable, successful enterprise. A steward who successfully improves the performance of the organisation generally satisfies most groups, because most stakeholder groups have interests that are well served by increasing organisational wealth.

As a result of this benign view of management, stewardship theory takes a more relaxed view of the need to separate the roles of chairman and chief executive, and favours boards having a majority of specialist executive directors rather than a majority of non-specialist independent directors. However Donaldson and Davis insist this is not an attempt to replace one form of determinism by another, but to introduce a realistic note of contingency in a model based on manager– principal choice: 'Managers *choose* to behave as stewards or agents. Their choice is contingent on their psychological motivations and their perceptions of the situation. Principals also choose to create an agency or stewardship relationship, depending upon their perceptions of the situation and the manager.'

External pressures

The focus of the theories so far examined is largely upon the internal monitoring dilemmas of corporate governance, but there is a coherent stream of theoretical approaches including institutional theory, resource dependence theory and network theory that are concerned with the external challenges of building relationships and securing resources in dynamic environments. If agency theory is about the problem of *control* these externally oriented theories are about the problem of *connection*. As Stiles and Taylor (2002: 17) explain with regard to resource dependency theory, this reveals another dimension of corporate governance acknowledging 'the open systems nature of organisations, transacting with environments, and constrained by networks of interdependencies with other organisations, rather than understanding the behaviour of organisations simply in terms of rational, intentional managerial action'.

Resource dependency theory relates corporate governance to Lawrence and Lorsch's (1967) thesis that successful organizations possess internal structures that match environmental demands. Pfeffer argues company board size and composition are 'rational organisational responses to the conditions of the external environment' (1972: 223). Hillman *et al.* (Chapter 10) highlight how company directors may serve to connect the firm with external resources that help to overcome uncertainty. Coping effectively with uncertainty is essential for organizational survival (Alchian, 1950; Pfeffer and Salancik, 1978; Thompson, 1967). Hillman *et al.* explain 'Uncertainty clouds the organization's control of resources and choice of strategies, and impedes simple day to day functioning. Effective coping with uncertainty leads to power (Pfeffer and Salanick, 1978) and, ultimately, increased survival likelihood (Singh *et al.*, 1986). Thus, by having directors who serve to link the organisation with its external environment, a board may act to reduce uncertainty. But, in the resource-dependence role, directors may do more than reduce uncertainty. Directors also bring resources to the firm, such as information, skills, access to key constituents (e.g. suppliers, buyers, public policy decision makers, social groups) and legitimacy (Gales and Kesner, 1994). The extent to which directors benefit the firm depends on whether their inclusion provides access to valued resources and information, reduces environmental dependency, or aids in establishing legitimacy' (Daily and Dalton, 1994).

Judge and Zeithaml (Chapter 11) contrast two different perspectives on how boards of directors make strategic decisions concerning their external environment. They refer to the increasing external pressures for greater board involvement in corporate strategy coming from the institutional forces of increased legal intervention and regulation, more active pension funds, and the market for corporate control. Institutional and strategic choice perspectives are used to conceptualize board responses to these external pressures. Institutionalization is the process by which organizational structures and processes, and their consequences, come to be taken for granted (Mayer and Rowan, 1997; Zucker, 1987). Much organizational action reflects a pattern of doing things that evolves over time and becomes legitimated within an organization and an environment (Pfeffer, 1982). An influential concept is isomorphism, by which organizations conform to the accepted norms of their populations (DiMaggio and Powell, 1983). Judge and Zeithaml suggest 'The institutional perspective is a relatively deterministic theoretical framework that places great emphasis on environmental norms and the weight of firm history as explanations of organisational actions. Institutional theorists see the use of structures and processes that an environment legitimates as sensible because it implies responsible management, pleases external constituencies, and avoids potential claims of negligence if something goes wrong' (Eisenhardt, 1988).

Taking the opposite tack, the strategic choice perspective focuses on the choices managers make and the actions they take to adapt to an environment (Child, 1972; Hambrick and Finkelstein, 1987). Managers have the ability to learn about, manage, and sometimes create the organization's environment (Hamel and Prahalad, 1994). Judge and Zeithaml state 'The strategic choice perspective emphasises nondeterministic explanations of organisational processes and outcomes (Bourgeois, 1994). Strategic choice theorists acknowledge the influence of the external environment, but their focus is on adaptive responses to that environment.'

Forging social networks is one way of coordinating the production of complex products and services while dealing with demanding environments. Jones et al. (Chapter 12) examine how in many industries such as biotechnology, film, music, financial services, and fashion, coordination is characterized by informal social systems rather than bureaucratic structures within firms and formal contractual relationships between them (Gerlach, 1992; Nohria and Eccles, 1992). This *network governance* constitutes a 'distinct form of coordinating economic activity' (Powell,

1990: 301) that contrasts and competes with markets and hierarchies. Jones et al. identify two key concepts patterns of interaction, and flows of resources that define network governance:

- Patterns of interaction in exchange and relationships

    - patterns of exchange
    - long term recurrent exchange that creates inter-dependencies
    - informal interfirm collaborations
    - reciprocal lines of communication

- Flows of resources between independent legally separate units.

Jones et al. explain 'Network governance involves a select, persistent and structured set of autonomous firms (as well as nonprofit agencies) engaged in creating products or services based on implicit and open-ended contracts to adapt to environmental contingencies and to coordinate and safeguard exchanges. These contracts are socially – not legally – binding.' Network governance appears ideally suited for industries with high levels of demand uncertainty generated by rapid changes in knowledge and technology, with short product life cycles where the rapid dissemination of information is critical. In emerging conditions of hypercompetition where rapid and flexible responses are necessary, the viability of network governance will be increasingly significant.

Stakeholder theory

Stakeholder theory has a historical lineage considerably longer and more substantial than agency theory, though it has had much less impact on thinking and policy concerning corporate governance in recent times (Clarke and Clegg, 2000; Clarkson, 1995; Donaldson and Preston, 1995; Freeman, 1984). Freeman and Reed (1990) define organizations as multilateral agreements between the enterprise and its stakeholders. The relationship between the company and its *internal* stakeholders (employees, managers, owners) is defined by formal and informal rules developed through the history of the relationship. This institutional setting constrains and creates the strategic possibilities for the company. While management may receive finance from shareholders, they depend on employees to fulfil strategic intentions. *External* stakeholders are equally important, and relationships with customers, suppliers, competitors, and special interest groups are also constrained by formal and informal rules. Finally governments and local communities set the legal and formal rules within which businesses must operate (Freeman, 1994; Post *et al.*, 2003).

Corporations should be regarded not as bundles of assets that belong to shareholders, Margaret Blair (Chapter 13) argues but rather as institutional arrangements for governing the relationships between all of the parties that contribute firm-specific assets. This includes not only shareholders, but also long-term employees who develop specialized skills of value to the corporation, and suppliers, customers and others who make specialized investments. If the job of corporate management is to maximize the total wealth created by the enterprise rather than just the value of the shareholders stake, then management must take into account the effect of corporate decisions on all stakeholders in the firm. However stakeholders must be defined specifically as those who have contributed firm-specific assets that are at risk in the enterprise (Blair, 1996).

In practice, executives leading companies and managers operating them have always utilized elements of the stakeholder approach Clarke (Chapter 14) claims. As firm-specific skills become an increasingly important part of the firm's valuable assets, and as corporate constituencies become increasingly alert and demanding, it is likely that corporate managers increasingly will need to adopt stakeholder perspectives however great the apparently countervailing pressure to increase shareholder value. The growing emphasis on customer relations, employee relations, supplier relations, and indeed, investor relations is an indication that managers are having to grapple with the imperative to satisfy the interests of more complex constituencies than shareholder theory would suggest. The conception of the company as a set of relationships rather than a series of transactions, in which managers adopt an inclusive concern for all stakeholders, is much closer to established European and Asian business values, and has been apparent in the behaviour of many of the leading US and UK companies. It represents an important step towards a sense of corporate citizenship – an organization with a mature appreciation of its rights and responsibilities.

Theories of convergence

The outsider system of market based corporate governance that prevails in the United States and United Kingdom characterized by dispersed ownership and the primacy of shareholder value is the dominant force in international corporate governance. Here the principal–agent problems are assumed to be paramount. In Europe a relationship-based system of corporate governance has prevailed, reflecting the rich cultural diversity of the continent, and different corporate history and values. These insider systems are more dependent on loans from banks than the equity market, and tend to have the support of close business networks. Finally there are the family-based corporate structures of the Asia Pacific, again reflecting different cultural traditions and aspirations. Though there is much evidence of convergence of the different regional corporate governance systems around some common international principles, there remains a commitment to diversity of approach in practice (Clarke, 2004a).

The greatest ongoing theoretical debate in corporate governance is whether there is global convergence towards the Anglo-Saxon market based *outsider* model of corporate governance. This trend appeared irresistible in the late 1990s with the apparently miraculous success of the new economy in the United States, however after Enron and the collapse of the National Association of Securities Dealers Automated Quotations (NASDAQ) the virtues of the American system seem less self-evident. Advocacy of the convergence thesis came from the most influential quarters including the G7, OECD and leading Western business schools. Cultural differences were usually acknowledged before being politely dismissed in the face of an inexorable economic logic. For example Nestor and Thompson concede:

There are a wide variety of corporate governance regimes in OECD countries. Over the years, individual economies developed different market mechanisms, legal structures, factor markets and private or public institutions to act as owners or corporate governance principals in the economy. These arrangements might even vary within the same country according to the sector. They are very often the result of institutional, political and social traditions. Understanding and accepting this variety of approaches is a fundamental first step for analysing the impacts of increasing globalisation on national systems.

(Nestor and Thompson, 2000: 2)

Before they move immediately on to insist:

Despite differing starting points, a trend towards convergence of corporate governance regimes has been developing in recent years. Pressures have been rising on firms to adapt and adjust as a result of globalisation. Their products are having to compete directly on price and quality with those produced internationally, which mandates a certain *de facto* convergence of cost structures and firm organisation that, in its turn, might spill-over on firm behaviour and decision-making. But most important, convergence might be the result of globalisation of capital markets: new financial instruments (such as ADRs and GDRs), deeper integration of markets, stronger international competition and the emergence of growth of new financial intermediaries have radically changed the corporate financial landscape in a global way, at least for the larger enterprises. The latter, along with the governments of their countries, are increasingly conscious that, in order to tap this large pool of global financial resources, they need to meet certain governance conditions.

(Nestor and Thompson, 2000: 2)

Michael Useem (Chapter 15) highlights the impact of the internationalization of finance. Institutional investors were constrained by their national boundaries for much of the twentieth century, but they are now discovering an outside world of higher returns and lower risks. Company executives are learning that foreign investors are able to provide more capital at lower cost. The globalization of equity markets is a product of the 1980s. Governments are opening their markets to foreign investors; investors are diversifying their portfolios; and companies are scouting for new holders. In response, firms are restructuring their operations to enhance shareholder returns, redefining management relations with foreign shareholders, and revising management compensation to align with global investor interests. Company executives are mastering new leadership skills for operating in an environment increasingly defined by a relatively small number of large international stockholders.

International investment institutions are pressing for world standards for corporate disclosure and governance.

The OECD *Principles of Corporate Governance* (1999, revised 2004) were intended to assist governments in their efforts to evaluate and improve the legal, institutional and regulatory framework for corporate governance in their countries, and to provide guidance and exchanges for stock exchanges, investors, corporations and other parties with an interest in developing good corporate governance. (Millstein, 2001), who chaired the OECD Business Advisory Group, argues that diversity in governance practices is not inconsistent with the convergence in governance principles. Cultural and institutional differences may relate to particular national environments, but the underlying principles may allow a more fundamental compatibility. The OECD principles are equitable treatment, responsibility, transparency and accountability. If it is accepted that these principles can be upheld and pursued in a variety of institutional contexts in different regions of the world then the OECD principles could be a genuine basis for agreement. However there remains a strong sense that the OECD itself shares the interest in encouraging governance systems throughout the world towards the market based, outsider system (Dignam and Galanis, 1999).

While conventional wisdom suggests that cross-national patterns of corporate governance are converging, or will converge on the Anglo-Saxon capital-market-driven model characterized by a sharp separation between ownership and control, Mauro Guillen (Chapter 16) insists corporate governance models cannot be seen in isolation from the rest of the institutional underpinnings of the economy in question. First, corporate governance systems are embedded in legal traditions that are unlikely to change in the near future. Second, corporate governance models interact in complex ways with other institutional features that are tightly coupled with the ways in which firms compete in the global economy. Third, convergence is unlikely because any process of change in corporate governance, whether induced by globalization or not, is effected by political dynamics whose final outcome is hard to predict. Longitudinal evidence from both advanced and newly industrialized countries shows little convergence over the last twenty years.

Rhodes and van Apeldoorn (Chapter 17) argue against analyses that minimize the role of domestic institutions and understand the contemporary transformation of European capitalism solely in terms of globalization-driven, neoliberal convergence. Although national systems may be driven in a market-liberal direction, this will not mean convergence as domestic elites will be unwilling to undermine their own positions; path-dependence will create formidable pressures for continuity with adjustment rather than abandonment of structures that have delivered efficiency in the past. With regard to international pressures, international competition and the implementation of European monetary are as likely to reinforce existing relationships as they are to break them down, while the new regulatory regime for European economies still permit considerable scope for diversity.

Douglas M. Branson (Chapter 18) argues that the 'one size fits all' approach of convergence advocates is culturally and economically insensitive (often the people who insist on common corporate governance institutions for countries, are the same people who reject common corporate structures and procedures for companies). Value systems in Asia still firmly based on post-Confucianism and tradition are insurmountable barriers to the early importation of US style corporate governance. The dominant forms of ownership in the world remain family ownership and other forms of *embedded* capitalism in which the economy is perceived to be subservient to the society, rather than the opposite. Branson insists the issue of global convergence is of less significance than the growth of the multinational companies, environmental degradation, economic imperialism and other problems associated with globalization. These externalities are a result of managers over-performing in the pursuit of profits, yet the Anglo-Saxon model focuses on the problems of managers underperforming.

Critique of shareholder value

The sharpest intellectual skirmish in the convergence debate has been around whether shareholder value represents the essential corporate objective that will soon be accepted universally. The view of the inevitability of convergence became a rally call for those who think equity markets and the pursuit of shareholder value are the basis of contemporary corporate governance. Henry Hansmann, a professor of law at Yale, and Reinier Kraakman, a professor of

law at Harvard, in their slightly presumptuously titled article, 'The End of History for Corporate Law', have no doubts about identifying with this shareholder ideology:

> Despite very real differences in the corporate systems, the deeper tendency is towards convergence, as it has been since the nineteenth century. The core legal features of the corporate form were already well established in advanced jurisdictions one hundred years ago, at the turn of the twentieth century. Although there remained considerable room for variation in governance practices and in the fine structure of corporate law throughout the twentieth century, the pressures for further convergence are now rapidly growing. Chief among these pressures is the recent dominance of a shareholder-centred ideology of corporate law among the business, government and legal elites in key commercial jurisdictions. There is no longer any serious competitor to the view that corporate law should principally strive to increase long-term shareholder value. This emergent consensus has already profoundly affected corporate governance practices throughout the world. It is only a matter of time before its influence is felt in the reform of corporate law as well.
>
> (Hansmann and Kraakman, 2001: 1)

In fact from 1998 to 2002 in the UK, the other leading exponent of the Anglo-American approach, the possibility of considering other stakeholder interests beyond shareholder value was keenly debated in the Review of Modern Company Law (DTI, 2000). The conclusion was that boards should pursue 'enlightened shareholder value' in which it is by balancing the interests of different stakeholder groups to enhance cooperation between them, that the long-term interests of shareholders are best protected. This review recommended the introduction of a mandatory Operating and Financial Review in which companies account for not only their business performance in financial terms, but give an account of the company's key relationships with employees, customers, suppliers and others on which its success depends, and report on its environmental and social policies and performance. Such changes in UK company law would reflect the fundamental assumptions and often long-established principles in company law and practice in Europe, which have as yet survived the onslaught of shareholder value ideology.

During the US stock market boom in the 1990s there was a widespread belief in the economic benefits of the maximization of shareholder value as *the* principle of corporate governance. Lazonick and O'Sullivan (Chapter 19) offer an analysis of the rise of shareholder value as the driving force of corporate governance in the United States, tracing the transformation of US corporate strategy from the retention of corporate earnings and reinvestment in the business through the 1970s, to one of downsizing of corporate labour forces and enhancing corporate earnings to shareholders over the past two decades. This raises important questions concerning whether shareholder value management orientations can contribute to sustainable enterprise. The rhetoric of shareholder value has become prominent in Germany, France and Sweden in recent years, and been incorporated in the OECD principles of corporate governance. Lazonick and O'Sullivan confront the questions, what does maximizing shareholder value mean, and is it an appropriate principle of corporations in the advanced economies?

Why despite the resilience of national institutions and practices are there increasing signs that national systems of corporate governance are giving way to an idealized American model of shareholder activism and liquid equity markets is explored further by Engelen (Chapter 20). He identifies three claims for shareholder value: the prudential claim for shareholder control and the market allocation of capital of superior efficiency; the functional claim for shareholder control resting on the contribution of risk-carrying capital, and the moral claim based on a liberal doctrine of ownership that grounds exclusive rights in property title holders. Engelen argues that public equity markets are used for specific purposes, but the overwhelming majority of productive investment is financed from the retained earnings of the companies themselves. With regard to ownership he claims, 'In practice, property rights never completely determine concrete ownership relations and the interdependencies they underpin, and hence leave much leeway for political contestation.' Referring to MacPherson's (1973) distinction between exclusive and inclusive definitions of property, he insists liberal legal doctrine that conceptualizes property exclusively as individual or 'private' rights, does not recognize such alternatives.

Post-Enron theories

Any sense that the rest of the world simply needed to learn from the robust, market-based corporate governance systems of the Anglo-Saxon model were rudely dispelled by the spectacular sequence of US corporate crises commencing in 2001 at Enron, WorldCom, Tyco International, Adelphia Communications, Global Crossing, Qwest Communications, Computer Associates, and Arthur Andersen. The collapse of Enron, the largest bankruptcy in US history, led to thousands of employees losing their life savings tied up in the energy company's stock. Federal indictments charged Enron executives with devising complex financial schemes to defraud Enron and its shareholders through transactions with off-the-books partnerships that made the company look far more profitable than it was (Bratton, 2002; Deakin, 2004; McLean and Elkind, 2003; Swartz and Watkins, 2003). WorldCom ironically named one of *Fortune* magazine's most admired global companies in 2002, wrongly listed over $3 billion of its 2001 expenses, and $797 million of its first quarter 2002 expenses as capital expenses, which were not reflected in the company's earnings results. WorldCom agreed to restate all of its earnings results for 2001, as well as those for the first quarter of 2002. The SEC in June 2002 charged WorldCom with massive accounting fraud (Clarke, 2004b). At Tyco tens of millions of dollars in fraudulent bonuses were uncovered, and $13.5 million dollars in unauthorized loans to key Tyco managers.

Gordon (Chapter 21) contends the Enron experience challenges some core beliefs and practices that have underpinned the academic analysis of corporate law and governance, including mergers and acquisitions, since the 1980s: 'These amount to an interlocking set of institutions that constitute "shareholder capitalism" American-style, 2001, that we have been aggressively promoting throughout the world. We have come to rely on a particular set of assumptions about the connection between stock market prices and the underlying economic realities; the reliability of independent auditors, financial standards, and copious disclosure in protecting the integrity of financial reporting; the efficacy of corporate governance in monitoring financial performance; the utility of stock options in aligning managerial and shareholder interests, and the value of employee ownership as both an incentive device as well as a retirement planning tool.'

Coffee (Chapter 22) highlights how Enron exposed the way in which increased market incentives and legal deregulation had led auditors to acquiesce in aggressive accounting methods that often bordered illegality while analysts remained positive in spite of the warning signs. The changes in executive compensation in the 1990s designed to align executive interests with those of shareholders, provided an irresistible incentive to managers to inflate earnings, even if this was not sustainable, as they could bail out before the inevitable reality confronted the shareholders. At a time when the average tenure of CEOs of US corporations was diminishing to between three and four years, the temptation of immense stock options caused many executives to spike the share price, cash in their options, and move on quickly. Meanwhile the markets responded slowly, if at all, to the mounting evidence of overvaluation.

Coffee suggests that 'the explosion of financial irregularity in 2001–2002 was the natural and logical consequence of trends and forces that have been developing for some time. Ironically, the blunt truth is that recent accounting scandals and the broader phenomenon of earnings management are by-products of a system of corporate governance that has indeed made corporate managers more accountable to the market. But sensitivity to the market can be a mixed blessing – particularly when the market becomes euphoric and uncritical. To the extent that the market becomes the master, governance systems that were adequate for a world in which market focuses were weaker must be upgraded in tandem with market developments to protect the market from manipulation and distortion by self-interested managers'.

RECONCEPTUALIZING CORPORATE GOVERNANCE THEORY AFTER THE ENRON EXPERIENCE

The disaster that befell corporate America in 2001–2002 involving a prolonged series of revelations of malfeasance relating to what previously were regarded as leading corporations, resulted in the dramatic intervention of the US Congress and the passing of the Sarbanes–Oxley Act. Government, regulators, professions, institutional investors, individual shareholders, employees and the wider community struggled to comprehend the implications of what had occurred which appeared to seriously undermine

confidence in the security of equity investments, the probity of US executives, and even the fundamentals of market based capitalism (Clarke, 2004b). 'In the period 2000–2002, the New York market suffered the biggest stock market crash in US history compared with GNP. Since early 2000 when it peaked at $15,000 billion, market capitalisation fell by $7,000 billion, i.e. 46 per cent, and those who invested at the top of the market lost half of their investments' (Taylor, 2003: 158. *The Economist*, 7 September 2002).

Figure 1 illustrates the NASDAQ Composite Index and the Standard and Poor's 500 Index for the seven year period 1997 to 2003, the largest speculative hysteria in the history of the world. The verdict of the Federal Reserve Chairman Alan Greenspan, having earlier dismissed the dot-com bubble as 'irrational exuberance', was that in this period of the longest bull market ever 'An infectious greed seemed to grip much of the business community. It is not that human beings have become any more greedy than in generations past. It is that the avenues to express greed have grown enormously' (*New York Times*, 17 July 2002). Yet the people who made money on the way up this speculative rise, were not the same people who lost money on the way down. Insiders including investment bankers, smart money traders, and executives loaded with stock options had time to cash in. For example many executives of the fabulously over-valued telecommunications companies walked away rich, cashing in over US$6 billion in 2000 as they touted the sector's growth potential just as it was about to collapse (*Wall Street Journal*, 12 August 2003). It was the pension funds, insurance funds and mutual funds not only in the United States, but all over the world who were persuaded to invest in the US market, who suffered most of these losses. Trillions of dollars of losses were distributed among the hundreds of millions of people who as a result faced a less secure material future than they had imagined.

As the US market begins the slow process of recovery, some would brazenly claim this tragic experience was further proof of the efficient markets theory, that all financial prices accurately reflect all public information at all times, and that the market had corrected as soon as the relevant information was available. But as Robert Shiller (2000: 203–4) presciently argued at the very peak of the boom

The high market valuations in the stock market have come about for no good reasons. It is a serious

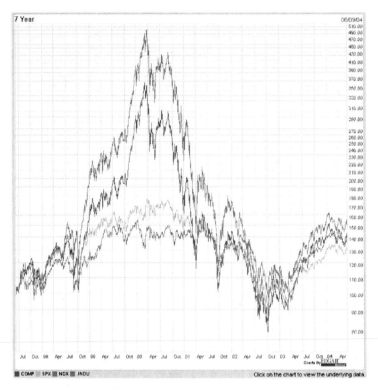

Figure 1 NASDAQ Composite Index and S&P 500 Index 1997–2003.

Source: NASDAQ.

mistake for public figures to acquiesce in the stock market valuations we have seen recently, to remain silent about the implications of such high valuations, and to leave all commentary to the market analysts who specialise in the nearly impossible task of forecasting the market over the short term and who share interests with investment banks or brokerage firms. The valuation of the stock market is an important national – indeed international – issue. All of our plans for the future, as individuals and society, hinge on our perceived wealth, and plans can be thrown into disarray if much of that wealth evaporates tomorrow. The tendency for speculative bubbles to grow and then contract can make for very uneven distribution of wealth. It may even cause many of us, at times, to question the very viability or our capitalist and free market institutions.

Behind these excessive valuations and the inevitable ensuing losses was an unprecedented display of accounting fraud, regulatory failure, executive excess, and avoidable bankruptcy, with the resulting widespread disastrous losses incurred by employees, pension funds, and investors. What was so alarming was that each element of the corporate governance system in these cases appeared to have failed, 'The collapse of Enron has disclosed that every component of the infrastructure of US capitalism was dysfunctional. Companies' accounts were misleading, their auditors conniving, their lawyers conspiring, the ratings agencies asleep, and the regulators inadequate. "Faith in corporate America hasn't been so strained since the early 1900s," claims *Business Week* magazine' (*AFR*, 2002: 24).

In this context Enron could be regarded as illustrative not only of a failed business but of systemic failure:

Enron's business model exemplifies the pathology of the shareholder value system which became dominant in Britain and America in the 1980s and 1990s. The company's focus on short-term stock price appreciation, in part the result of the share options granted to senior management, was the cause of its downfall. It was this which led to the use of special purpose entities to conceal debts and artificially inflate the value of the company's stock. In pursuing an *asset-lite* Strategy at the expense of long-term growth, the company placed itself at risk of implosion once the business cycle turned down, as it happened in the course of 2001. From this perspective, the fate of Enron is less important than the future of the business model that it came to represent. Unless the regulatory framework is adjusted to make this model unattractive, it will only be a matter of time before the same approach is tried again.

(Deakin, 2003: 584)

Enron was not just a dramatic bankruptcy, but symptomatic of a serious malaise in the US corporate system that could be contagious. The Enron factor represents a threat to the international economy of the greatest significance. Fortunately the collapse in stock markets in 2001/2002 though quantitatively the largest crash ever, has not been followed by the crisis in confidence and investment that ushered in the great-depression following the Wall Street crash of 1929. However the viability and the integrity of the outsider market-based system of corporate governance has been called into question, as have the theories that explained and justified it. To fully understand the fundamental nature of these questions a further examination of the Enron phenomenon is required.

Enron

The failure of Enron in 2001 sparked shock waves throughout the United States, revelations that many other leading corporations needed to restate their accounts, a sequence of major bankruptcies, and the passing of the Sarbanes–Oxley Act. The sense of dismay was all the greater since Enron had been portrayed to the public as a model company for the new economy, and the Enron executives were closely networked into the highest reaches of the American political establishment.

Enron was founded in 1985 by chairman Kenneth Lay as a natural gas pipeline company. In the newly deregulated gas industry, Enron pioneered the creation of a market for natural gas. The Gas Bank allowed producers and buyers to trade and hedge gas supplies. Under the direction of CFO (and later briefly CEO) Jeffrey Skilling, Enron expanded into energy sectors in other countries, developing an increasingly

influential role as a trading house for the energy industry. Using this model Enron diversified into electricity, coal, paper, plastics, metal, and then with the establishment of Enron Online, moved into telecommunications bandwidth trading.

Enron secured a reputation for exceeding earnings expectations. However, the market performance of the diversified company began to falter with some major disasters including a public embarrassment in India. In order to sustain the impression of sustained profits growth despite these reversals, a series of special purpose entities were established by CFO Andrew Fastow. Large debts amounting to billions of dollars could be concealed in the financial arrangement that Enron had with the special purpose entities (SPEs). As Enron's share price began to fall, its capacity to hide its losses began to diminish. In October 2001 Enron disclosed non-recurring charges of US$1.1 billion, a reduction in shareholder's equity of US$1.2 billion, and a US$700 million loss, thereby revealing to the market the significance of these shadowy SPE companies. Six weeks later Enron, which had US$62 billion in assets, filed for bankruptcy (Bratton, 2002; Deakin, 2004; McLean and Elkind, 2003; Swartz and Watkins, 2003).

By this time the company was acquiring an unsavoury reputation not only for its accounting fraud, but for the manner of its business operations. The Commodities Futures Trading Commission (CFTC) provided an exemption that limited the regulatory scrutiny of Enron's energy derivatives trading business (a process earlier set in motion by the CFTC chairman Wendy Gramm, who subsequently joined Enron's board) (Swartz and Watkins, 2003: 227). The operations of the energy market that Enron was at the center of caused a series of catastrophic power shortages and blackouts in California in 2000/2001, that seriously harmed the economy of the state (previously the epicentre of the new economy, now apparently unable to resolve one of the most basic problems of the old economy), and similar disruption in other parts of the United States. As Enron took advantage of the newly deregulated California energy market, rolling blackouts began, the first in the state since the Second World War. Before May 2000 electricity prices had averaged US$24–40 per megawatt hour, frighteningly the price then surged to the price cap of $750 per megawatt hour in June:

Entire neighbourhoods saw their power shut of for an hour to two hours at a time – at which point their power was turned back on and another neighbourhood went dark. In just that one month, the total wholesale cost of electricity topped US$3.6 billion, roughly half of what power had cost for all of 1999. The ISO, in search of a solution, lowered the cap on the price it would pay for power generated in California from $750 per megawatt to $500 and finally to $250 ... Small businesses had to shut their doors because they couldn't pay their bills. State officials pleaded with companies and consumers alike to turn down their air conditioners and dim their lights. Schools that had obtained lower rates by signing contracts under which their power supply could be interrupted – never thinking such a thing could happen – had to send students home because their electricity was shut off. Companies with similar contracts had to turn off their air conditioning entirely, even though it was approaching 100 degrees outside ... And Enron was taking full advantage: Belden and his West Coast trading desk were booking profits the likes of which they'd never seen before, some $200 million just between May and August 2000.

(McLean and Elkind, 2003: 271–73)

Enron was accused of manipulating the energy market to its own advantage, causing dramatic increases in the cost of power until the Federal Energy Regulatory Commission was forced to intervene. The essential corporate objective of Enron was to manipulate the rules of the energy market in order to make money: 'Enron filed imaginary transmission schedules in order to get paid to alleviate congestion that didn't really exist. That was called *Death Star*. *Get Shorty* was a strategy that involved selling power and other services that Enron did not have for use as reserves, with the expectation that Enron would never be called upon to supply the power or would be able to buy it later at a lower price. The point of *Ricochet* was to circumvent California's price caps. For instance, Enron exported power from California and brought it back in when the ISO was desperate and had to pay far higher prices. (This strategy was used by all the power traders and was known as "megawatt laundering")' (McLean and Elkind, 2003: 270). As the California state senate committee began its investigation into this crisis, and subpoenaed documents from Enron, the company stonewalled and counter sued, only relenting when it faced contempt charges and financial sanctions.

The real reason Enron was stonewalling was that its lawyers knew full well what the documents would reveal, and they wanted to delay the discovery of *Deathstar* and *Get Shorty* as long as they could – forever if possible. There was another issue the company didn't want to disclose. When the traders closed the books on 2000, Belden's West Coast power division had booked US$460 million in profits. The West Coast gas traders who also benefited from the crisis in California – made $870 million. Enron wasn't just trying to hide this fact from the preying eyes of investigators. It didn't want *anyone* to know how much it had made from trading – even its own investors. After all, it was simply not possible to make that kind of money acting as a logistics company. It could be made only by speculating. To reveal that number would be to reveal the truth.

(McLean and Elkind, 2003: 282)

The California energy disaster was preceded some years earlier by an infamous overseas incident that illustrated the huge ambitions and disturbing amorality of the company. The company became embroiled in a monstrous white elephant energy plant in Dabhol in India, a project that lasted from 1992–7. This was the first step in Enron's grand US$20 billion plan to reshape the energy market of India. However though the company successfully negotiated, and then in some distress renegotiated, a contract with the Maharashtra State Energy Board for a 20 year power purchase from the Enron Dabhol plant, this was at prices there was no possibility of the state ever being able to afford (the *New York Times* calculated that the cost would exceed Maharashtra's entire budget for primary and secondary education). When the US$3 billion project failed, Enron's share of the losses was US$900 million. There was much evidence that many of Enron International's other overseas projects in Europe, South America, the Middle East and Asia worth US$19 billion to the company, were similarly misconceived (Swartz and Watkins, 2003).

The metamorphosis of Enron from an energy infrastructure company, into effectively an investment bank Enron Capital and Trade Resources (ECT) competing in energy trades was complete by the late 1990s. Enron had become 'a virtual hedge fund in the view of some, yet a firm that morphed overnight into its bizarre structure from origins as a stodgy gas pipeline company. The pace of this transition seemingly outdistanced the development of risk management systems and an institutional culture paralleling those of traditional financial firms' (Coffee, 2002: 1404). This became the model for *asset-lite* companies, unencumbered by physical assets and heavily dependent on their intangible assets, in this case the intellectual assets of the Enron traders who developed, competed in, and often controlled the markets they entered.

In summary Enron demonstrates the following failings in corporate governance:

- Systemic failure to disclose to the market significant financial and accounting transactions that substantially impacted on the balance sheet of the company, its reported profitability, debt level, share price and market valuation.
- Systemic failure of transparency that would allow market regulators, investors, creditors and others to understand the financial position of the company.
- Systemic failure of the Chairman, CEO and Board of Directors to exercise their fiduciary responsibilities to investors in ensuring effective financial controls were in place in the company, and effective auditing and reporting procedures completed.
- Systemic conflict of interest on the part of the chief financial officer, and other officers of the company.
- Conflict of interest of the external auditor in receiving extensive consulting as well as auditing fees from Enron, and becoming too closely involved in the management of the company.
- Fundamental failure in the morality and ethical basis of the decision-making of the company, with systemic deception of investors, manipulation of markets, and exploitation of customers.

The limitations of established economic theories

The catastrophe caused by the failure of Enron, could not compare with the damage this company would have caused if it had succeeded. In one sense Enron is a resounding historical proof of the historical validity of agency theory – a classic illustration of how self-interested managers can strip the wealth out of a company, leaving misled shareholders with little if anything of their investments. In another sense if Enron had continued to succeed making ever-rising profits by amoral means, exploiting business strategies that wreaked havoc in the economies they operated

in, then shareholders interests may have been served, with the denial of every other conceivable economic interest as the company continued to hike prices by exercising monopoly power, destabilizing essential energy and other services, creating volatility in markets that undermined the prospects of continuing normal business in other industries, and damaging people's lives as a result. Little attention has been paid in the literature so far to the stakeholder dimensions of the Enron saga. Enron not only betrayed its shareholders, in a more immediate and direct way it betrayed its customers, and in the end, its employees also.

Economic theories that stress the importance of monitoring of management to resolve the agency problem were validated by Enron, where an out-of-control management effectively evaded the monitoring efforts of the Enron board, auditors, regulators and ultimately the market. However agency theory fails on two more serious counts in the effort to understand the Enron experience. First, the assumptions of agency theory concerning the self-interest of managers were behind the policy of aligning managers and shareholders interests by focusing executive incentives on generous stock options. In reality this provided a more powerful incentive to manipulate short-term corporate earnings than to improve long-term performance. By assuming the worst in policy, the worst was brought out in economic behaviour (Learmount, 2002; Moran and Ghoshal, 1996). Second, the relentless emphasis on the importance of shareholder value in recent times has created the conditions for the disconnection of corporations such as Enron from their essential moral underpinnings, encouraging them to concentrate exclusively on financial performance, and to neglect not just the wider stakeholder interests of customers and employees, but the essential interests of the economies and communities in which they operate.

The problem with established economic theories of corporate governance is that they misconceive the irreducible core of corporate governance, at the same time as underestimating the complexity of the phenomenon. If agency theory is useful in highlighting the self-interested economic inclination of agents, it misses the essential basis of trust upon which all human relations are based. At the same time, reducing economic relations to a series of contracts fails to comprehend the complexity of corporate relationships and the need to continually adapt to changing market environments. Why then has agency theory remained the pre-eminent explanation of corporate governance and guide to regulatory policy and law, when it is so clearly one-dimensional in its focus? It could be argued that among the reasons for the prevalence of agency theory is the fact that the dimension it focuses upon is the apparently competing interests of the most powerful players in corporate governance – the executives and major investors – in the dominant Anglo-American economies.

The weaknesses of existing organization theories

Managerialist theory stands up better as an explanation of the shenanigans that masqueraded as management at Enron (Bratton, 2002; McLean and Elkind, 2003; Swartz and Watkins, 2003). Rather than Enron being a unique one-off experience as Coffee claims, Enron was the inevitable result of an era in which Emperor CEOs, all-powerful CFOs, and executives indulged with stock-options the value of which would impress medieval princes, were allowed free rein as long as they delivered improved earnings (and often when they did not). This was an era in which the emphasis was upon money making rather than the morality of how you made it. It was not just the institutions and mechanisms of corporate governance that failed. Indeed Finkelstein and Mooney (2003) show that at Enron, WorldCom, Global Crossing, Qwest and Tyco most of the boxes had been ticked in terms of the majority board representation of outsiders, appropriate board size, splitting the roles of Chairman and CEO, and ensuring directors had a financial stake in the shares of the company). Ethical and professional commitment failed at Enron. Of course Enron had a professional code of ethics also but this did not translate into effective management action.

The tenets of stewardship theory – the capacity and willingness of managers to balance different interests in the professional pursuit of company strategy – would appear to be more than a little challenged by the Enron events. It was in their fundamental failure to uphold their stewardship and fiduciary duties that the Enron executives were most irresponsible. This suggests how far some contemporary executives have moved from the concept of management as a profession, and decision-making as a moral exercise. Perhaps if the principles of stewardship theory were more firmly established in management development, the

practice of them might improve. While monitoring mechanisms are required, the motivation of managers will always determine how necessary they are. Indeed it is the cynical and calculative view of management that helps to legitimate and disseminate the most self-interested behaviour. As Moran and Ghoshal insist unrelenting cynicism can help to engender the management and organization it fears, and a more balanced view of management and organization may be required:

In response perhaps to the earlier over-emphasis on functionalism, theories of today are dominated by a profoundly pessimistic view of organisations, concerned far more about the unintended consequences of organising than about organising for their intended purpose, and by an even more sceptical view of individual–organisation interactions, grounded in the assumption that the human role in organisations is largely passive and frequently pathological. Transaction cost economics is only one example of this bias; the pessimism is just as strong in the assumptions of inertia in population ecology (Hannan and Freeman, 1997), in the faith in isomorphism that has virtually replaced the role of leadership in institutional theory (contrast e.g., DiMaggio and Powell, 1983, and Selznick, 1957), in the denial of any role of organisational purpose and direction in the behavioural theory of the firm (Cyert and March, 1963), and in the all-pervasive concern for shirking opportunism, and inertia in organisational economics (Alchian and Demsetz, 1972; Jensen and Meckling, 1994; Milgrom and Roberts, 1992). The issues these theories highlight are not wrong, and, indeed, these issues have considerably enriched our research agenda. However, collectively, they also have shaped a field of enquiry that is neither realistic nor balanced in its fundamental premises.

(Moran and Ghoshal, 1996: 70)

Utilizing multiple theoretical perspectives

Most existing theories of corporate governance offer a view through a single analytical lens that might offer important insights, but can hardly serve to explain in full the complex and changing phenomena in question. The analysis of Enron clearly calls for the application of a range of theoretical critiques to understand fully the dilemmas involved. Daily *et al.* (2003: 372) in a recent review suggest:

> A multitheoretic approach to corporate governance is essential for recognising the many mechanisms and structures that might reasonably enhance organisational functioning. For example, the board of directors is perhaps the most central internal governance mechanism. Whereas agency theory is appropriate for conceptualising the control/monitoring role of directors, additional (and perhaps contrasting) theoretical perspectives are needed to explain director's resource, service and strategy roles.
>
> (Johnson *et al.*, 1996; Zahra and Pearce, 1989)

In a recent survey of board practice Philip Stiles and Bernard Taylor recommend the explanatory power of a series of theoretical perspectives. The structure of the board, its monitoring of budgets and plans, and its address to performance and targets, all reflect the assumptions of agency theory and transaction cost theory underpinning the control role of the board:

> Consistent with this theme, however, is the finding that boards may actively help companies to unlearn organisational practices that have become dysfunctional (Nystrom and Starbuck, 1984). That is, boards may diagnose new opportunities, select new performance measures, and emphasise certain control systems at the expense of others, in order to bring the organisation to a new focus. This supports the stewardship theory of board activity and suggests that, in certain circumstances, both organisational economics and stewardship theories may be complementary. The combination of what Tricker (1994) calls the conformance and performance roles suggests that multiple theoretical lenses are appropriate. Reinforcing the case for complementary theoretical perspectives is the evidence of boundary-spanning activity on the part of non-executive directors but also of the executive directors, providing support for the resource-dependence view of board activity. Our approach is, therefore, in line with greater calls for reconciliation between economic and organisational perspectives (Eisenhardt, 1989; Judge and Zeithaml, 1992; Kosnik, 1987) and shows that seemingly

contradictory approaches can coexist as theoretical explanations.

> (Stiles and Taylor, 2001: 122–3)

The search for new theoretical perspectives

Though bringing together different theoretical perspectives will strengthen the analysis of corporate governance there will remain significant problems both in terms of the relevance and the explanatory powers of existing theory when faced with a more complex and demanding business world. For too long academic analysis of corporate governance has been marginalized as of little relevance, as Tricker (1994: 2–3) insists, 'The gap between the contributions of theory and what practitioners are interested in seems to be widening. Rigour and relevance should not be mutually exclusive.' The narrowness of existing theory constricts its capacity to understand and explain corporate governance in a way that is meaningful or helpful to others, and often there is little tolerance of fresh ideas, amounting to an 'empirical dogmatism' in the words of Daily *et al.* (2003: 379):

> Researchers too often embrace a research paradigm that fits a rather narrow conceptualisation of the entirety of corporate governance to the exclusion of alternative paradigms. Researchers are, on occasion, disinclined to embrace research that contraindicates dominant governance models and theories (i.e. a preference for independent governance structures) or research that is critical of past research methodologies or findings. This will not move the field of corporate governance forward.

The search for new paradigms of corporate governance is now necessary in the post-Enron era, if theory is to regain relevance and explanatory force.

Trust

Beginning the search for new paradigms of corporate governance the concept of *trust* is a good place to start. 'Trust is of all times. It is pervasive and indispensable.' (Nooteboom, 2002: 1) Trust was at the centre of social and economic activity since the birth of civilization, and before. There are two sides to this, trust on the part of the truster, and trustworthiness on the side of the trustee. Trust involves expectations of the behaviour of others, with regard to business. Sako (1992: 32) defines trust as 'a state of mind, an expectation held by one trading partner about another, that the other behaves or responds in a predictable and mutually expected manner'. Somehow this absolutely essential element to business relationships was sidetracked by the transaction cost economics of Williamson: 'His argument was that if trust does go beyond calculative self-interest it does not add anything to existing economic analysis, and calculative trust seems a contradiction in terms. However, if trust does go beyond calculative self-interest, it necessarily yields blind trust, which is unwise and will not survive in markets, and is best limited to personal relations of friendship and family. This yields a crucial challenge to the notion of trust and its use in economics and business, and demands a coherent response' (Nooteboom, 2002: 6).

The underlying assumption of Williamson's impoverished conception of trust is that humans are self-interested and opportunistic; therefore transaction cost economics must concentrate on constraints and sanctioning mechanisms to enforce trustworthiness. More recent organization research has suggested that as social organizations, the governance of firms might be explored in terms of social relationships including trust (Lane and Bachman, 2001; Learmount, 2002: 14; Tyler and Kramer, 1996). For example, Powell (1990) distinguishes varieties of trust which operate as forms of governance based on cooperation. Production networks such as Silicon Valley or North Italy have developed a cooperative infrastructure depending not simply on geographic proximity but social interaction that attenuates the risks of the individual business units. In another example research and development networks in technology fields engender non-calculative types of trust through sharing ideas and knowledge. In Japanese corporate networks a more calculative trust based on the maintenance of reputation prevails. Finally in the multiple strategic alliances proliferating in every industry, Powell identifies calculative trust as the basis of the agreement.

Trust is a vital component of corporate governance, and the absence of trust is deeply corrosive. As Stiles and Taylor (2001: 23) note, much of the activity of corporate governance revolves around the building of trust: 'A series of studies by Westphal and Zajac has highlighted how the interpersonal influence processes in the board/chief executive relationship can help trust and cooperation develop within the board and help problem-solving and decision-making activity (Westphal and Zajac, 1995; 1997; Zajac and Westphal, 1996).' In their own research on boards Stiles and Taylor (2001: 123–4) indicate how trust and control are not mutually exclusive, 'Underpinning the discussion has been the central role of trust in enhancing both board task performance and board cohesiveness. The model of trust argued for has not been the traditional one of trust and control conceptualised as opposite ends of a continuum. Rather trust and control are interdependent. Because the board operates in complex and uncertain conditions and is often characterised by role conflict the potential for both trust and control to coexist is apparent. Control mechanisms serve to focus members attention on organisational goals, while trust mechanisms promote decision-making and enhance cohesiveness.'

Social capital

As a concept trust has many implications for corporate governance in the relationships between managers and investors, boards and managers, companies and stakeholders. However, it is possible to reconceive the entire governance of corporations around the concept of trusteeship. John Kay insists there is an alternative to the shareholder/agent model of the corporation, which accepts that the large corporation is a social institution not the creation of private contracts. The concept of trusteeship fully encompasses the role of directors who control assets they do not beneficially own:

> The notion that boards of directors are the trustees of the tangible and intangible assets of the corporation, rather than the agents of the shareholders is one which the executives of most German and Japanese companies, and of many British firms, would immediately recognise. The duty of the trustee is to preserve and enhance the value of the assets under his control, and to balance fairly the various claims to the returns which these assets generate . . . The responsibility of the trustees is to sustain the corporation's assets. This differs from the value of the corporation's shares.

The difference comes not only because the stock market may value these assets incorrectly. It also arises because the assets of the corporation, for these purposes, includes the skills of its employees, the expectations of customers and suppliers, and the company's reputation in the community. The objectives of managers as trustees therefore relate to the broader purposes of the corporation and not simply the financial interests of shareholders ... Thus the trusteeship model demands, as the agency model does not, the evolutionary development of the corporation around its core skills and activities because it is these skills and activities, rather than a set of financial claims, which are the essence of the company.

(Kay, 1997: 135)

As with trust, the idea of social capital suggests a radical reconceptualization of corporate governance that the trusteeship model is only one illustration of. Leenders and Gabbay (1999: 3) define organizational social capital as, 'The set of resources, tangible or virtual, that accrue to an organisation through social structure, facilitating the attainment of goals.' Nooteboom (2002: 147) suggests further, 'Social capital entails access to resources in the general sense: markets, materials, components, finance, location, information, technology, capability, legitimisation, credibility, reputation, and trust.' The concept of social capital entails an evaluation of a deeper and more complex set of social relationships of the corporation than the single focus on shareholders. Developing social capital requires an array of skills and investments, forms of value creation and a more general accountability than ever conceived in agency theory.

Knowledge-based business

The increasing salience of intangible assets is another related challenge for corporate governance theory and practice. As the value of intangible assets comes to greatly exceed the value of tangible assets, corporations must transform their measurement and control processes. This argument has particular resonance in knowledge-based companies, and all companies are becoming more knowledge-based 'You would be hard-pressed to find a single organisation of any kind, that has not become more "knowledge intensive",

dependent on knowledge as a source of what attracts customers and clients and on information technology as a means of running the place' (Stewart, 1997: 18). Peter Drucker (1993) more than a decade ago declared the knowledge worker as the single greatest asset. Grant (1997: 452) pursues the argument further, 'If knowledge is the pre-eminent productive resource, and most knowledge is created by and stored within individuals, then employees are the primary stakeholders. The principal management challenge ... is establishing mechanisms by which co-operating individuals can coordinate their activities in order to integrate their knowledge into productive activities.' Charles Handy states why traditional conceptions of principal/agent are no longer appropriate:

The old language of property and ownership no longer serves us in the modern world because it no longer describes what a company really is. The old language suggests the wrong priorities, leads to inappropriate policies, and screens out new possibilities. The idea of the corporation as the property of the current holders of shares is confusing because it does not make clear where the power lies. As such, the notion is an affront to natural justice because it gives inadequate recognition to the people who work in the corporation, and who are, increasingly, its principal assets.

(Handy, 1997: 27)

Stewart (1997: 32) elaborates further, 'A knowledge company is different in many ways ... not only are the assets of a knowledge company intangible, it's not clear who owns them or who is responsible for them. Indeed a knowledge company may not own much in the way of traditional assets at all.' The corporate governance of knowledge-based companies (if they are not partnerships) will be increasingly different from the traditional corporate model, and go beyond existing adaptations in terms of extensive employee stock ownership plans, involving direct questions of control.

Complex adaptive systems?

The increasing knowledge intensity of business, together with the increasingly common network form of enterprise, and proliferating alliance formation, indicate that business is becoming more complex requiring more sophisticated non-hierarchical control mechanisms. Conventional economic theory allows two types of control mechanisms, either a market or hierarchy, neither of which portray the intelligence and reflexivity of the networked enterprise. The idea of a complex adaptive system has some attractions in understanding the emerging business enterprise. A *complex adaptive system* is a system of systems. 'Each component of a complex adaptive system has a degree of independent decision-making, but each is affected to some degree by the actions of the other elements' (Morley, 2000). In Ralph Stacey's (1996) analysis of complex adaptive systems he highlights the importance of interaction in an environment of other complex adaptive systems allowing co-evolution; interaction in an iterative, non-linear manner; discovery through feedback; choice in the identification and selection of feedback information; acting according to the rules in relation to the systems in its environment; discovering the responses its action provokes; using this information to adapt behaviour; and the revision of rules to perform double loop learning.

These traits of complex adaptive systems seem close to the emerging challenges of corporate governance recognized by Bob Monks (1998) as multiplicity, spontaneity, accommodation, adaptation, transcendence and metamorphosis. Reflecting this complexity are broader definitions which see governance as 'self-organising, interorganisational networks characterised by interdependence, resource exchange, rules of the game, and significant autonomy from the state' (Rhodes, 1997: 15; Turnbull, 1997). Stiles and Taylor examine how governing this complexity translates into corporate board practices:

> In broad terms, what we have seen through the empirical data is a view of boards whose members, through a complex interplay of context, individual abilities, and structural conditions, actively negotiate over time their respective roles and the social order of the board as a whole. With the legal duties of the board under describing the de facto operations of board running, and regulations and codes of practice covering only part of board endeavour, ultimately the board's mandate will mean different things to different people, and 'negotiation is needed to achieve order in the context of change' (Hosking, 1996: 342). This has obvious affinities with Gidden's structuration theory which argues for the interdependence of structure and action. As Pettigrew and McNulty (1995: 13) argue: 'the

mobilisation and skilful use of power sources may change the rules of the game and provide a new context for subsequent influence attempts' (Stiles and Taylor, 2001: 123).

A political economy of corporate governance?

Prevailing theories of corporate governance project little of the historical development of the corporate system and surrounding economy, the waves of industrial innovation that have occurred, the social arrangements that have been critical, or the political contests that have been fought. A political economy of corporate governance is necessary for this wider understanding. What is required is a wider conception of the company, its activities and impacts upon the economy, together with some sense of how the wider economy and society impact upon the company in the course of a dynamic co-evolution. In an attempt to address the co-evolution of the phenomena of governance and economy von Tunzelmann (2001: 8) identifies 'three main eras of governance during the industrial era – marked successively by the predominance of markets, corporate hierarchies and then networks – and three industrial revolutions spanning multiple technologies but originating in the successive predominance of labour processes, capital processes and information processes'. He suggests a complex pattern of co-existence, 'National modes of governance are likely to be characterised by complexity, in breadth at least. That is, throughout the industrial era, markets, corporate hierarchies, political hierarchies and networks have coexisted in virtually all countries of at least moderate size. The relative importance of each may have varied from one country to the next at any point in time, but throughout all modes had to find the means to coexist with one another, whether through working together or working alongside each other' (von Tunzelmann, 2001: 14).

From a different perspective William Lazonick and Mary O'Sullivan have commenced work on an economic theory of governance, that addresses more fundamental questions than the theory of the market economy has attempted for some time. They begin with a broader definition of governance than the Anglo-American focus on the institutions that mediate a separation of ownership and control in the corporation, arguing that corporate governance is concerned with the institutions that influence how business corporations allocate resources and returns, specifically, 'A system of corporate governance shapes who makes investment decisions in corporations, what types of investments they make, and how returns from investments are distributed' (Lazonick, 2001; Lazonick and O'Sullivan, 2000; O'Sullivan, 2000). Lazonick contends that the theory of the firm represents the major weakness of the theory of the market economy in the attempt to understand the way in which market economics actually works. The problem with the theory of the firm is that it precludes an analysis of how business enterprises may allocate resources to transform market and technological conditions in ways that generate innovation. 'It is the introduction of a theory of innovative enterprise into a theory of resource allocation that transforms "the market" from being an explanation of economic development to being an outcome of economic development, and that, as a result, transforms our understanding of the roles of organisations and institutions, as well as markets, in determining economic performance' (Lazonick, 2002: 10).

Sustainability?

It is time for the principal–agent problematic to be reinforced with the environment–trustee problematic in both theory and practice. The competitive struggle to grow businesses and accumulate capital (whether measured by shareholder value or not) has disturbed the natural balance of the earth and threatened essential life-support systems. 'The dominant social paradigm sees unlimited human progress resulting from the exploitation of infinite natural resources. In other words, humanity stands apart from nature, at the centre of all life. People's relationships with nature are based on exploitation and control: the natural environment must serve human needs, and organisations are central to the achievement of this end. Management theorists and practitioners must work to improve the efficiency of these organisations. The question is always how to make organisations more efficient, not what they are or what their purpose is. The way to the future, to progress, to growth lies through the domination of nature' (Clarke and Clegg, 2000: 380; Gladwin et al., 1995).

A view rapidly gaining ground is that the way in which economic activity is presently organized and oriented is fundamentally unsustainable. In the past, companies did not recognize or acknowledge the environmental and social effects of their operations,

such as the impacts of releases into water on river systems, or the effects of particular emissions upon human health. The United States Environmental Protection Agency (EPA) (1995: 1) has developed a useful dichotomy – private versus social costs. The term environmental cost has at least two major dimensions: it can refer solely to costs that directly impact a company's bottom line (termed *private costs*) or it can also encompass the costs to individuals, society, and the environment for which a company is not directly accountable (termed *societal costs* by the EPA but typically referred to as externalities). 'Externalities generated by an organisation, although possibly ignored from an accounting perspective, are often recognised as costs by other entities' (ICAA, 2003: 19). Consideration of the range of environmental costs an entity might be encouraged to consider widens the scope of accounting systems, though makes measurement more difficult, and governance more problematic (Dunphy et al., 2003; Gray, 1996; Ong, 2001).

The environmental context in which business must operate in future suggest the following imperatives which all corporations will face, and all corporate governance systems will need to resolve: maintaining a licence to operate via transparency and accountability; generating more value with minimum impact; preserving the natural resource base; doing business in a networked, intelligent, multi-stakeholder world. In summary the challenge is to find means of enduring value creation without social or environmental harm (Clarke and dela Rama, 2003; Elkington, 1997; Hawken et al., 1999).

The Enron test

How would these new, albeit as yet mostly not fully developed, theoretical perspectives explain the Enron phenomenon. From the perspective of trust, the fundamental crime of Enron was a betrayal of trust, not simply towards its investors, but towards its consumers, employees and the communities that it was supposed to serve. Enron was on a short-fuse before the inevitable implosion generated by this lack of trustworthiness. Regarding the concept of social capital, Enron's aggressive accumulation of profit ostensibly in the interests of shareholder value, involved the neglect of the building of social capital that might endure. Enron certainly had become a knowledge-based business, and was keenly aware of the market value of the knowledge it possessed, but illustrates the damage that can be caused when intelligence is not secured by a sense of responsibility. Enron was certainly a prototype of a corporation as a complex adaptive system, both in terms of its own structure and operation, and the fluid and complex external markets it interacted with. However this was a complex adaptive system that was working intelligently to undermine the systems it related to, rather than strengthen them by building productive relationships. From the view of political economy Enron would be an example of how a corporation can shape and distort markets, and manipulate regulations to facilitate this. Finally from the perspective of sustainability, Enron was a corporation not only unsustainable environmentally, but unsustainable as a business.

CONCLUSIONS

Corporate governance has been subjected for too long to the static template of agency theory, and its rigid concern for an outdated conception of property rights that bears little resemblance to how corporations are financed or managed. 'Corporate governance must no longer confine its analysis to the relationship between managers, boards and shareholders. The narrowness of this focus is a major contributing factor to the present round of corporate scandals of which Enron is the most emblematic' (Deakin, 2003: 584). The dynamic complexity of corporate governance can only be conveyed by bringing together a range of theoretical perspectives to assist understanding. This understanding needs to go beyond the immediate mechanisms and institutions of corporate governance, to consider the bigger questions of how corporations allocate resources and returns, and how they contribute to economic development. In turn this requires investigation of the relationships between corporations and the economies and societies in which they exist.

REFERENCES

AFR (2002) US Crisis of Confidence, *Australian Financial Review*, 4/5 May 2002.

Alchian, A. (1950) Uncertainty, Evolution and Economic Theory, *Journal of Political Economy*, 58, 211–21.

Alchian, A. (1968) Corporate Management and Property Rights, in American Enterprise Institute, *Economic Policy and the Regulation of Securities*, Washington DC.

Alchian, A. and Demsetz, H. (1972) Production, Information Costs, and Economic Organisation, *American Economic Review*, 62, 777–95.

Barnard, C. (1938) *The Functions of the Executive*, Cambridge MA: Harvard University Press.

Barney, J.B. (1991) Firm Resources and Sustained Competitive Advantage, *Journal of Management*, 17, 99–120.

Berle, A. and Means, G. (1967) *The Modern Corporation and Private Property*, Harcourt, Brace and World, Inc: New York.

Blair, M.M. (1996) *Wealth Creation and Wealth Sharing: A Colloquium on Corporate Governance and Human Capital*, Washington DC: The Brookings Institute.

Blair, M.M. and Stout, L.A. (2001) Corporate Accountability: Director Accountability and the Mediating Role of the Corporate Board, *Washington University Law Quarterly*, 79, 403–47.

Bourgeois, L.J. (1994) Strategic Management and Determinism, *Academy of Management Review*, 9, 586–96.

Bratton, W. (2002) Enron and the Dark Side of Shareholder Value, *Tulane Law Review*, 76, 1275–361.

Cadbury, A. (2004) Foreword, Stijn Claessens, Corporate Governance and Development, Washington: Global Corporate Governance Forum, Focus 1, 2004.

Chandler, A.D. (1962) *Strategy and Structure*, New York: Doubleday.

Chandler, A.D. (1977) *The Visible Hand*, Cambridge, Massachusetts, Belknap Press.

Child, J. (1972) Organisation Structure, Environment and Performance: The Role of Strategic Choice, *Sociology*, 6, 1–22.

Clarke, T. (2004a) *International Corporate Governance: A Comparative Approach*, London: Routledge.

Clarke, T. (2004b) Cycles of Crisis and Regulation: The Enduring Agency and Stewardship Problems of Corporate Governance, *Corporate Governance – An International Review*, 12, 2, 153–61.

Clarke, T. (2004c) Corporate Governance: Critical Perspectives on Business and Management, Volumes I, II, III, IV, V, London: Routledge.

Clarke, T. and Clegg, S. (2000) *Changing Paradigms: The Transformation of Management Knowledge for the 21st Century*, London: HarperCollins Business.

Clarke, T. and dela Rama, M. (2003) 'The Impact of Socially Responsible Investment on Corporate Social Responsibility', in D. Crowther and L. Rayman-Bacchus (eds), *Perspectives on Corporate Social Responsibility*, Aldeshot: Ashgate.

Clarkson, M.B.E. (1995) A Stakeholder Framework For Analysing and Evaluating Corporate Social Performance, *Academy of Management Review*, 20, 92–117.

Coase, R. (1937) The Nature of the Firm, *Economica*, 4, November, 386–405.

Coffee, J.C. (2002) Understanding Enron: 'It's the Gate-keepers, Stupid', *The Business Lawyer*, 57, August, 1403–20.

Commission on Global Governance (1995) *Our Global Neighbourhood*, New York: Oxford University Press.

Cyert, R.M. and March, J.G. (1963) *A Behavioural Theory of the Firm*, Engelwood Cliffs NJ: Prentice Hall.

Daily, C. and Dalton, D. (1994) Bankruptcy and Corporate Governance: the Impact of Board Composition and Structure, *Academy of Management Journal*, 37, 1603–17.

Daily, C.M., Dalton, D.R. and Cannella, A.C. (2003) Corporate Governance: Decades of Dialogue and Data, *Academy of Management Review*, 28, 3, 371–82.

Deakin, S. (2003) After Enron: An Age of Enlightenment?, *Organisation*, 10, 3, 583–87.

Deakin, S. (2004) Learning From Enron, *Corporate Governance – An International Review*, 12, 2.

Dignam, A. and Galanis, M. (1999) Governing the World: The Development of the OECD's Corporate Governance Principles, *European Business Law Review*, 10, 9–10, September 1994, 396–407.

DiMaggio, P.J. and Powell, W.W. (1983) The Iron Cage Revisited: Institutional Isomorphism and Collective Rationality in Organisational Fields, *American Sociological Review*, 48, 147–60.

Donaldson, L. (1990) The Ethereal Hand: Organisational Economics and Management Theory, *Academy of Management Review*, 15, 3, 369–81.

Donaldson, L. and Davis, J.H. (1991) Agency Theory or Stewardship Theory: CEO Governance and Shareholder Returns, *Australian Journal of Management*, 16, 49–64.

Donaldson, T. and Preston, L. (1995) The Stakeholder Theory of the Corporation: Concepts, Evidence, Implications, *Academy of Management Review*, 20, 65–91.

Drucker, P. (1993) *Post-Capitalist Society*, New York: HarperCollins.

DTI (2000) *Modern Company Law For A Competitive Economy: Developing the Framework*, A Consultation Document from The Company Law Review Steering Group, London: HMSO.

Dunphy, D., Griffiths, A. and Benn, S. (2003) *Organisational Change for Corporate Sustainability*, London: Routledge.

Eisenhardt, K.M. (1988) Agency and Institutional Theory Explanations: The Case of Retail Sales Compensation, *Academy of Management Journal*, 31, 488–511.

Eisenhardt, K.M. (1989) Agency Theory: An Assessment and Review, *Academy of Management Review*, 14, 57–74.

Elkington, J. (1997) *Cannibals with Forks: The Triple Bottom Line of 21st Century Business*, Oxford: Capstone.

Fama, E. (1980) Agency Problems and the Theory of the Firm, *Journal of Political Economy*, 88, 288–307.

Fama, E. and Jensen, M.C. (1985) Separation of Ownership and Control, *Journal of Law and Economics*, 26, 301–26.

Finkelstein, S. and Mooney, A.C. (2003) Not the Usual Suspects: How to Use Board Process to Make Boards Better, *Academy of Management Executive*, 17, 2, 101–13.

Freeman, R.E. (1984) *Strategic Management: A Stakeholder Approach*, Englewood Cliffs NJ: Prentice Hall.

Freeman, R.E. (1994) The Politics of Stakeholder Theory: Some Future Directions, *Business Ethics Quarterly*, 4, 409–22.

Freeman, R.E. and Reed, W.M. (1990) Corporate Governance: A Stakeholder Interpretation, *Journal of Behavioural Economics*, 19, 4, 337–60.

Frentrop, P. (2003) *A History of Corporate Governance 1602–2002*, Brussels: Deminor.

Galbraith, J. (1973) *Designing Complex Organisations*, Reading MA: Addison-Wesley.

Gales, L. and Kesner, I. (1994) An Analysis of Board of Director Size and Composition in Bankrupt Organisations, *Journal of Business Research*, 30, 271–82.

Gerlach, M.L. (1992) The Japanese Corporate Network: A Blockmodel Analysis, *Administrative Science Quarterly*, 37, 105–39.

Gladwin, T.N., Kenelly, J.J. and Krause, T.S. (1995) Shifting Paradigms for Sustainable Development: Implications for Management Theory and Research, *Academy of Management Review*, 20, 4, 874–907.

Grant, R.M. (1997) The Knowledge-Based View of the Firm: Implications for Management Practice, *Long Range Planning*, 30, 3, 450–54.

Gray, R. (1996) Reporting for Sustainable Development, in R. Welford and R. Starkey (eds), *Business and the Environment*, London: Earthscan.

Hambrick, D. and Finkelstein, S. (1987) Managerial Discretion. A Bridge Between Polar Views of Organisational Outcomes, *Research in Organisational Behaviour*, 9, 369–406.

Hamel, G. and Prahalad, C.K. (1994) *Competing for the Future*, Boston MA: Harvard Business School Press.

Handy, C. (1997) The Citizen Corporation, *Harvard Business Review*, 75, 5, 26–8.

Hannan, M.T. and Freeman, J. (1997) The Population Ecology of Organisations, *American Journal of Sociology*, 82, 929–64.

Hansmann, H. and Kraakman, R. (2001) The End of History for Corporate Law, *Georgetown Law Journal*, 89, 439.

Hawken, P., Lovins, A.B. and Lovins, L.H. (1999) *Natural Capitalism: The Next Industrial Revolution*, London: Earthscan.

Herman, E. (1982) *Corporate Control, Corporate Power*, New York: Cambridge University Press.

Hirsch, P., Michaelis, S. and Friedman, R. (1987) 'Dirty Hands' Versus 'Clean Models': Is Sociology in Danger of being Seduced by Economics?, *Theory and Society*, 317–36.

Hosking, D.M. (1996) Negotiated Order, in N. Nicholson (ed), *Encyclopaedic Dictionary of Organisational Behaviour*, Oxford: Blackwell Business.

Huselid, M. (1995) The Impact of Human Resource Management Practices on Turnover, Productivity and Corporate Financial Performance, *Academy of Management Journal*, 38, 635–72.

Institute of Chartered Accountants in Australia (ICAA) (2003) *Environmental Management Accounting*, Melbourne.

Jensen, M.C. (1994) Self-interest, Altruism, Incentives and Agency Theory, *Journal of Applied Corporate Finance*, Summer, 40–55.

Jensen, M.C. and Meckling, W.H. (1976) Theory of the Firm, Managerial Behaviour, Agency Costs and Ownership Structure, *Journal of Financial Economics*, October, 305–60.

Jensen, M.C. and Meckling, W.H. (1994) The Nature of Man, *Journal of Applied Corporate Finance*, 7, 2, 4–19.

Johnson, J.L., Daily, C.M. and Ellstrand, A.E. (1996) Boards of Directors: A Review and Research Agenda, *Journal of Management*, 22, 409–38.

Judge, W.O. and Zeithaml, C.P. (1992) Institutional and Strategic Choice Perspectives on Board Involvement in the Strategic Decision Process, *Academy of Management Journal*, 35, 4, 766–94.

Kay, J. (1997) 'The Stakeholder Corporation', in G. Kelly, D. Kelly and A. Gamble, *Stakeholder Capitalism*, London, Macmillan Press.

Kooiman, J. (1993) *Modern Governance*, London: Sage.

Kooiman, J. (2000) Societal Governance, in J. Pierre, *Debating Governance*, Oxford: Oxford University Press, 138–66.

Kosnik, R. (1987) Greenmail: A Study of Board Performance in Corporate Governance, *Administrative Science Quarterly*, 32, 163–85.

Lane, C. and Bachmann, R. (eds) (2001) *Trust Within and Between Organizations*, Oxford: Oxford University Press.

Lawrence, P. and Lorsch, J. (1967) *Organisation and Environment*, Boston, Division of Research, Harvard School of Business Administration, Harvard University.

Lazonick, W. (2001) Public and Corporate Governance: The Institutional Foundations of the Market Economy, *Economic Survey of Europe*, 2, 59–76.

Lazonick, W. (2002) *American Corporate Economy*, Volume 1, Critical Perspectives on Business and Management, London: Routledge.

Lazonick, W. and O'Sullivan, M. (2000) *Perspectives on Corporate Governance, Innovation and Economic Performance*, Fontainebleau: INSEAD.

Learmount, S. (2002) Theorising Corporate Governance: New Organisational Alternatives, ESRC Centre for Business Research, University of Cambridge, Working Paper no 237.

Leenders, R.Th.A.J. and Gabbay, S.M. (1999) *Corporate Social Capital and Liability*, Dordrecht: Kluwers.

Lee, F.S. (1990) *The Modern Corporation* and Gardiner Mean's Critique of Neoclassical Economics, *Journal of Economic Issues*, XXIV, 3, September 1990, 673–93.

Lorsch, J. and MacIver, E. (1989) *Pawns Or Potentates: The Reality of America's Corporate Boards*, Boston MA: Harvard University Press.

Mace, M. (1971) *Directors: Myth and Reality*, Boston MA: Harvard Business School Press.

McLean, B. and Elkind, P. (2003) *The Smartest Guys In the Room*, London: Viking.

MacPherson, C.B. (1973) *Democratic Theory: Essays in Retrieval*, Oxford: Oxford University Press.

March, J. (1962) The Business Firm as a Political Coalition, *Journal of Politics*, 24, 662–78.

March, J. and Simon, H. (1958) *Organisations*, New York: Wiley.

Mayer, J.W. and Rowan, B. (1997) Institutionalised Organisations. Formal Structures as Myth and Ceremony, *American Journal of Sociology*, 83, 440–63.

Milgrom, P.R. and Roberts, J. (1992) *Economics, Organisation and Management*, Englewood Cliffs NJ: Prentice Hall.

Millstein, I.M. (2001) The Evolution of Corporate Governance in the United States – Briefly Told, Forum for US – Europe Legal – Economic Affairs, Rome, Italy, September 12–15, 2001, 1–22.

Mizruchi, M.S. (1983) Who Controls Whom? An Examination of the Relation Between Management and Boards of Directors in Large American Corporations, *Academy of Management Review*, 8, 426–35.

Monks, R.A.G. (1998) *The Emperor's Nightingale – Restoring the Integrity of the Corporation*, Oxford: Capstone.

Moran, P. and Ghoshal, S. (1996) Theories of Economic Organisation: The Case for Realism and Balance, *Academy of Management Review*, 21, 1, 58–72.

Morley, S. (2000) Redefining Control: Applying Complexity Theory to Corporate Governance, Information Systems Department, London School of Economics and Political Science.

Nestor, S. and Thompson, J.K. (2000) Corporate Governance in OECD Economies: Is Convergence Under Way?, Directorate for Financial, Discal and Enterprise Affairs, Paris: OECD.

Nodoushani, O. and Nodoushani, P.A. (1999) The Debate on Corporate Governance: An Historical Analysis of Berle and Means Contributions, *The Journal of Behavioral and Applied Management*, Summer/Fall, 1, 1, 55–64.

Nohria, N. and Eccles, R.G. (1992) *Networks and Organisations: Structure, Form and Action*, Boston: Harvard Business School Press.

Nooteboom, B. (2002) *Trust: Forms, Foundations, Functions, Failures and Figures*, Cheltenham: Edward Elgar.

Nystrom, P.C. and Starbuck, W.H. (1984) To Avoid Crises, Unlearn, *Organisational Dynamics*, 13, 53–65.

OECD (1999) *Principles of Corporate Governance*, Paris: OECD.

Ong, D.M. (2001) The Impact of Environmental Law on Corporate Governance: International and Comparative

Perspectives, *European Journal of International Law*, 12, 4, 685–726.

O'Sullivan, M. (2000) The Innovative Enterprise and Corporate Governance, *Cambridge Journal of Economics*, 24, 393–416.

Perrow, C. (1986) *Complex Organisations*, New York: Random House.

Peterson, S. (1965) Corporate Control and Capitalism, *Quarterly Journal of Economics*, LXXIX, 1, 1–24.

Pettigrew, A. (1973) *The Politics of Organisational Decision-Making*, London: Tavistock.

Pettigrew, A. and McNulty, T. (1995) Power and Influence in and Around the Boardroom, *Human Relations*, 8, 845–73.

Pfeffer, J. (1972) Siza and Composition of Corporate Boards of Directors: The Organisation and its Environment, *Administrative Science Quarterly*, 17, 218–19.

Pfeffer, J. (1981) *Power in Organisations*, Marshfield MA: Pitman.

Pfeffer, J. (1982) *Organisations and Organisation Theory*, Boston MA: Pitman.

Pfeffer, J. (1994) *Competitive Advantage Through People*, Boston MA: Harvard Business School Press.

Pfeffer, J. and Salancik, G. (1978) *The External Control of Organisations: A Resource Dependence Perspective*, New York: Harper Row.

Post, J., Preston L. and Sachs, S. (2002) Managing the Extended Enterprise: The New Stakeholder View, *California Management Review*, 45, 1.

Powell, W.W. (1990) Neither Market Nor Hierarch: Network Forms of Organisation, in B. Staw and L.L. Cummings (eds), *Research in Organisational Behaviour*, Greenwich CT: JAI Press.

Rhodes, R.A.W. (1997) *Understanding Governance*, Buckingham: Open University Press.

Roe, M.J. (1994) *Strong Managers Weak Owners – The Political Roots of American Corporate Finance*, Princeton: Princeton University Press.

Sako, M. (1992) *Prices, Quality and Trust: Interfirm Relations in Britain and Japan*, Cambridge: Cambridge University Press.

Scott, J.P. (1985) *Corporations, Classes and Capitalism*, London: Hutchison.

Scott, J.P. (1997) *Corporate Business and Capitalist Classes*, Oxford: Oxford University Press.

Selznick, P. (1957) *Leadership In Administration*, Evaston IL: Row Peterson.

Shiller, R.J. (2000) *Irrational Exuberance*, Princeton: Princeton University Press.

Shleifer, A. and Vishny, R.W. (1997) A Survey of Corporate Governance, *Journal of Finance*, 52, 737–83.

Singh, J., House, R. and Tucker, D. (1986) Organisational Change and Organisational Mortality, *Administrative Science Quarterly*, 32, 367–86.

Smith, A. (1937) *The Wealth of Nations*, New York: Modern Library.

Snell, S.A. and Dean J.W. (1992) Integrated Manufacturing and Human Resource Management: A Human Capital Perspective, *Academy of Management Journal*, 35, 467–504.

Stacey, R. (1996) *Complexity and Creativity in Organisations*, San Francisco: Berrett Koehler Publishers.

Stewart, T.A. (1997) *Intellectual Capital: The New Wealth of Organisations*, London: Nicholas Brealey.

Stiles, P. and Taylor, B. (2002) *Boards at Work: How Directors View Their Roles and Responsibilities*, Oxford: Oxford University Press.

Swartz, M. and Watkins, S. (2003) *Power Failure: The Inside Story of the Collapse of Enron*, New York: Doubleday.

Taylor, B. (2003) The Crisis in Corporate Governance, *Corporate Governance: An International Review*, 11, 3.

Thompson, J. (1967) *Organisations in Action*, New York: McGraw Hill.

Tricker, R.I. (1984) *Corporate Governance*, Aldershot: Gower.

Tricker, R.I. (1994) Editorial, *Corporate Governance: An International Review*, 2, 2–3.

Tricker, R.I. (2000) *Corporate Governance: The History of Management Thought*, London: Ashgate Publishing.

Turnbull, S. (1997) Corporate Governance: Its Scope, Concerns & Theories, *Corporate Governance: An International Review*, 5, 4, 180–205.

United States Environmental Protection Agency (EPA), (1995) *An Introduction to Environmental Accounting as a Business Management Tool: Key Concepts and Terms*, Washington DC.

von Tunzelmann, N. (2001) Historical Coevolution of Governance and Technology, *The Future of Innovation Studies*, Eindhoven University of Technology, The Netherlands, 20–23 September.

Walsh, J.P. and Seward, J.K. (1990) On the efficiency of Internal and External Corporate Control Mechanisms, *Academy of Management Review*, 15, 421–58.

Westphal, J.D. and Zajac, E.J. (1995) Defections From the Inner Circle: Social Exchange, Reciprocity and the Diffusion of Board Independence in US Corporations, *Academy of Management Best Papers Proceedings*, 281–5.

Westphal, J.D. and Zajac, E.J. (1997) Defections From the Inner Circle: Social Exchange, Reciprocity and the Diffusion of Board Independence in US Corporations, *Administrative Science Quarterly*, 40, 60–83.

Williamson, O.E. (1975) *Markets and Hierarchies: Analysis and Anti-Trust Implications*, New York: Free Press.

Williamson, O.E. (1979) Transaction-Cost Economics: The Governance of Contractual Relations, *Journal of Law and Economics*, 22, 233–61.

Williamson, O.E. (1984) Corporate Governance, *The Yale Law Journal*, 93, 1197–230.

Williamson, O.E. (1985) *The Economic Institutions of Capitalism*, New York: Free Press.

Wood, R. and Bandura, A. (1989) Social Cognitive Theory of Organisational Management, *Academy of Management Review*, 14, 361–84.

Zahra, S.A. and Pearce, J.A. (1989) Boards of Directors and Corporate Financial Performance: A Review and Integrative Model, *Journal of Management*, 15, 291–334.

Zajac, E.J. and Westphal, J.D. (1996) Director Reputation, CEO-Board Power, and the Dynamics of Board Interlocks, *Administrative Science Quarterly*, 41, 507–29.

Zeitlin, M. (1974) Corporate Ownership and Control: The Large Corporation and the Capitalist Class, *American Journal of Sociology*, 79, 1073–119.

Zucker, L.J. (1987) Institutional Theories of Organisations, in W.R. Scott and J.F. Short (eds), *Annual Review of Sociology*, 13, 443–64.

PART ONE

Economic foundations

INTRODUCTION TO PART ONE

The institutions and processes of corporate governance have evolved with the economic development of industry, with the adaptation of different governance structures to meet the needs of emerging business opportunities and economic constraints. Technological advances and expansion of markets over time considerably increased the scale and complexity of enterprises, rapidly expanded the need for capital, and demanded more sophisticated means of corporate governance. The arrival of the joint-stock company with limited liability provided the foundation for the extensive expansion of industrial capitalism in the later nineteenth century and throughout the twentieth century. From the beginning it became clear that robust mechanisms for corporate governance would require reinforcement by external regulation if investors funds were to be protected; a view strongly upheld in the continental European economies.

It was in the massively growing American economy that the corporate form matured earliest into the vast, complex structures associated with the modern corporation. Chandler (Chapter 2) examines how in this new context the *invisible hand* of Adam Smith's market forces, is replaced by the *visible hand* of management. To capture the economies of scale possible with new technologies and growing markets required large inputs of capital, beyond the means of individual entrepreneurs, leading to the separation of ownership and control. Large scale, multi-unit business enterprises replaced the small traditional enterprise, where administrative coordination permitted greater productivity, lower costs and higher profits than coordination by market mechanisms.

As Berle and Means argued in their work, this divorce of ownership from control involves a new form of economic organization of society in which corporate governance reflects new responsibilities. New conceptions of corporate and managerial responsibility came out of the widespread social and economic upheaval of the early twentieth century. In the United States the Wall Street Crash of 1929, was followed by a new regulatory regime, and when the Great Depression refused to yield, with the intervention of the New Deal. This involved revolutionary changes in government–business relations, and the role of business corporations in a democratic society. The doctrine of *laissez-faire* was abandoned in favour of managerial capitalism and the potential of big business. Berle (Chapter 3) offers a review of the implications of the modern corporation from the vantage point of 1965 when many of the trends he had identified with Means three decades earlier had become more pronounced, despite the reluctance of neoclassical economic theory to acknowledge their existence.

"The Managerial Revolution in American Business"

from The Visible Hand (1977)

Alfred D. Chandler Jr

This study does more than trace the history of an institution. It describes the beginnings of a new economic function – that of administrative coordination and allocation – and the coming of a new subspecies of economic man – the salaried manager – to carry out this function. Technological innovation, the rapid growth and spread of population, and expanding per capita income made the processes of production and distribution more complex and increased the speed and volume of the flow of materials through them. Existing market mechanisms were often no longer able to coordinate these flows effectively. The new technologies and expanding markets thus created for the first time a need for administrative coordination. To carry out this function entrepreneurs built multiunit business enterprises and hired the managers needed to administer them. Where the new enterprises were able to coordinate current flows of materials profitably, their managers also allocated resources for future production and distribution. As technology became both more complex and more productive, and as markets continued to expand, these managers assumed command in the central sectors of the American economy.

GENERAL PATTERNS OF INSTITUTIONAL GROWTH

The significance of the coming of this new function and class for an understanding of American economic history can be pinpointed by briefly summarizing the general patterns of growth. Such a summary demonstrates how historical experience substantiates the general propositions outlined in the introduction to this study. It suggests areas of research for economists concerned with industrial organization and the theory of the firm and for historians concerned with the new class and its growing power in the American economy. Although this summary deals only with the institution in the United States, it can provide a set of ideas for analyzing and explaining its history in other economies as well.

The multiunit business enterprise, it must always be kept in mind, is a modern phenomenon. It did not exist in the United States in 1840. At that time the volume of economic activity was not yet large enough to make administrative coordination more productive and, therefore, more profitable than market coordination. Neither the needs nor the opportunities existed to build a multiunit enterprise. The few prototypes of the modern firm – textile mills and the Springfield Armory – remained single-unit enterprises. The earliest multiunit enterprise, the Bank of the United States, became extremely powerful and, partly because of its power, was short-lived. Until coal provided a cheap and flexible source of energy and until the railroad made possible fast, regular all-weather transportation, the processes of production and distribution continued to be managed in much the same way as they had been for half a millennium. All these processes, including transportation and finance, were carried out by small personally owned and managed firms.

The first modern enterprises were those created to administer the operation of the new railroad and telegraph companies. Administrative coordination of the movement of trains and the flow of traffic was essential for the safety of the passengers and the efficient movement of a wide variety of freight across the nation's rails. Such coordination was also necessary to transmit thousands of messages across its telegraph wires. In other forms of transportation and communication, where the volume of traffic was less varied or moved at slower speeds, coordination was less necessary. There the large enterprise was slower in coming. When steamship and urban traction lines did increase in size, they had little difficulty in adapting procedures perfected by the railroads. And when the development of long-distance technology permitted the creation of a national telephone system, the enterprise that managed it became organized along the lines of Western Union.

The new speed and volume of distribution brought a revolution in marketing. Multiunit enterprises began to coordinate the greatly expanded flows of goods from producers to consumers. The commodity dealers, the large full-line wholesalers, and the new mass retailers (department stores, mail-order houses, and chains) pushed aside the existing commission merchants. The administrative coordination they provided permitted them to lower prices and still make profits higher than those of the merchants they replaced. As time passed, the mass retailers supplanted the wholesalers because they internalized one more set of transactions and so coordinated flows more directly and efficiently.

In production, the first modern managers came in those industries and enterprises where technology permitted several processes of production to be carried on within a single factory or works (i.e. internalized). In those industries, output soared as energy was used more intensively and as machinery, plant design, and administrative procedures were improved. As the number of workers required for a given unit of output declined, the number of managers needed to supervise these flows increased. Mass production factories became manager-intensive. Nevertheless, as long as the output of these factories was distributed efficiently by the new mass marketers, the manufacturing enterprise remained small. Only a score of managers were needed to manage even the largest of the new factories.

On the other hand, where the mass marketers were unable to provide the services needed to distribute the goods in the volume in which they could be produced, the enterprise became large. The modern industrial enterprise began when manufacturers built

their own sales and distribution networks, and then their own extensive purchasing organizations. By integrating mass production with mass distribution, they came to coordinate administratively the flow of a high volume of goods from the suppliers of the raw materials through the processes of production and distribution to the retailer or ultimate consumer.

In all these new enterprises – the railroads, the telegraph, the mass marketers, and the mass producers – a managerial hierarchy had to be created to supervise several operating units and to coordinate and monitor their activities. The railroads, in managing their huge regional systems, and Western Union, in administering its national one, had to recruit large managerial staffs that included several levels of middle managers. On the other hand, in the marketing and the nonintegrated mass producing enterprises and in all but the largest steamship, traction, and utilities companies, the managerial hierarchy remained relatively small. But when an enterprise integrated mass production with mass distribution, its management became even larger than those in transportation and communication.

Once such a hierarchy had successfully taken over the function of coordinating flows, the desire of the managers to assure the success of their enterprise as a profit-making institution created strong pressures for its continuing growth. Such growth normally resulted from two quite different strategies of expansion. One was defensive or negative and stemmed from a desire for security. Its purpose was to prevent sources of supplies or outlets for goods and services from being cut off or to limit entry of new competitors into the trade. The other strategy was more positive. Its aim was to add new units, permitting by means of administrative coordination a more intensive use of existing facilities and personnel. Such positive growth might be considered as productive expansion and negative or defensive growth as nonproductive expansion. One increased productivity by lowering unit costs, the other rarely did.

In the growth of railroad and telegraph enterprises, both positive and negative motives were significant. Expanding the system by building or buying lines into another major commercial center helped to assure fuller use of existing facilities and personnel. This was particularly true if connecting lines were not adequate to handle the full flow of current traffic. Such expansion was also used to prevent a basic source or outlet of traffic from being taken over by a rival road or to prevent a rival from obtaining access to sources of traffic. Once the nation's basic transportation network had been completed, defensive rather than productive growth became the norm. Where lines already existed with capacity to carry current traffic, the building or buying of additional roads resulted almost wholly from defensive measures. The costs of such expansion were far greater than any savings that might be achieved from more efficient coordination of flows. For this reason, the building of the giant systems during the 1880s and 1890s resulted in nonproductive rather than productive expansion of railroad enterprises.

Defensive motives were less significant to the modern marketing enterprises. Because the marketers normally had a number of suppliers, they were rarely threatened by the possibility of having their stocks cut off. Nor was there much opportunity to keep stocks out of competitors' hands. The marketers went into manufacturing only on those relatively rare occasions when processors were unable to provide the goods at the price, quality, and quantity desired. The cost of obtaining expensive manufacturing plants normally outweighed any gains to be achieved by more effective coordination. Nor were there defensive reasons to integrate forward. The wholesalers had little to gain by purchasing their customers, and the retailers were, of course, at the end of the distribution line.

The basic strategy of growth for the mass marketers was, then, one of productive expansion. They expanded by adding new outlets and new lines that permitted them to make more complete use of their centralized buying, goods handling, and administrative facilities. A comparable strategy of productive expansion was carried on in the twentieth century by banks and other financial and service enterprises. They became large, managerial firms by adding new branches or outlets that permitted them to make more intensive use of their centralized services and facilities.

For those manufacturers who moved into mass distribution when they found existing marketers inadequate for their distribution needs, the motives for expansion were both defensive and productive. The initial reasons for building their marketing and then their purchasing organizations were positive; in the beginning the creation of a buying and selling network was essential to insure the administrative coordination needed to keep their production facilities fully employed. Necessary for the mass production and mass distribution of their products, the administrative coordination made possible by obtaining such selling, buying, and transportation facilities provided these enterprises with a powerful barrier to competition.

Integration backwards into the control of materials, on the other hand, tended to be more defensive than productive. It was productive where, as in the case of food and tobacco companies, suppliers were numerous and scattered. Then the creation of an extensive buying network made possible the maintenance of a high-volume flow of perishable or semiperishable products into processing plants. But where supplies were limited or could be easily-controlled by a small number of enterprises, expansion was defensive. Mass producers wanted to have assured control over at least some of the sources of raw or semifinished materials. They also found it advantageous to bar others from access to these supplies. The savings from improved scheduling hardly covered the heavy cost of such investments.

Positive motives appeared and played a larger role than did defensive ones in the *continuing* growth of the large integrated industrial enterprise. Like the marketers, the industrialists continued to set up new branch sales offices at home and abroad. Increases in sales, in turn, brought expansion in manufacturing facilities and enlarged purchasing organizations. These industrial firms also added new lines to make more intensive use of their buying, selling, and processing facilities. Such additions, in turn, required the creation of new facilities. The sale of by-products in markets different from those of the primary line called for the creation of new marketing departments. Lines taken on to make fuller use of a distributing network often required the development of new manufacturing and purchasing units. In time such enterprises found it profitable to produce and market products that made use of only their technological capacities and managerial experience. Such moves into new product lines for new markets were not done to protect their own sources or outlets, or to take preventive action against others. They were to permit the continuing use of existing resources as well as to develop new ones.

Because large integrated industrial enterprises carried on a wider variety of functions over a wider geographical area than did marketing, transportation, and communications enterprises, they had greater potential for continuing growth. The facilities and administrative skills of the railroad and telegraph companies could not be easily transferred to other economic activities. The marketers, with their small investment in and little pressure to buy into manufacturing, remained marketers. Their expansion was limited to the number of outlets that could make effective use of their centralized purchasing and other facilities. Much the same was true of financial firms and a variety of such enterprises.

On the other hand, the large integrated industrial enterprises, with their extensive marketing, manufacturing, purchasing, raw-materials producing, transportation, and research facilities, had a wider variety of resources that could be transferred to the production and distribution of other products for other markets. The executives in these large managerial hierarchies were trained in different types of economic activity and so were better equipped to take on the manufacture and sale of new products in new markets than were those in enterprises that carried out only one basic function – finance, marketing, transportation, or communication. Moreover, because the large integrated industrial had more and different types of operating units than other kinds of business enterprises, the likelihood that units might be underutilized was greater. It was rare for all units in such an enterprise to be operating at the same speed and capacity. Such disequilibrium provided constant pressure for the growth of the firm.[1] Whether the enterprise was pushed by the need to use existing physical and human resources or pulled by the coming of new markets that might use its facilities, it tended to move into areas where existing demand and technology created the needs and opportunities for administrative coordination. Such productive expansion was inherently more profitable than defensive expansion, and so set the direction in which the enterprise grew. And the distance the enterprise moved in this direction was closely related to the nature of its resources, the skills of its managers, and the transferability of these resources and skills to new products, services, and markets.

In those industries where administrative coordination of mass production and mass distribution was profitable, a few large vertically integrated firms quickly dominated. Concentration and oligopoly appeared as a consequence of the need for and the profitability of administrative coordination. Where markets and technology did not give the manufacturing or processing enterprises a competitive advantage, large mass retailers came increasingly to coordinate flows. Because of the number and complexity, of these flows, many small suppliers and distributors, including brokers and freight forwarders, continued to fill-in and even-out the flows. Their functions, however, supplemented, and were integrated into, the larger economy by the coordinating activities of the mass producers and mass marketers.

Although administrative coordination has been a basic function in the modernization of the American economy, economists have given it little attention. Many have remained satisfied with Adam Smith's dictum that the division of labor reflects the extent of the market. Like George Stigler, they see the natural response to improved technology and markets as one of increasing specialization in the activities of the enterprise and vertical disintegration in the industries in which these enterprises operate.[2] Such an analysis has historical validity for the years before 1850 but has little relevance to much of the economy after the completion of the transportation and communication infrastructure. Besides ignoring the historical experience, such a view fails to consider the fact that increasing specialization must, almost by definition, call for more carefully planned coordination if volume output demanded by mass markets is to be achieved.

Economists have also often failed to relate administrative coordination to the theory of the firm. For example, far more economies result from the careful coordination of flow through the processes of production and distribution than from increasing the size of producing or distributing units in terms of capital facilities or number of workers. Any theory of the firm that defines the enterprise merely as a factory or even a number of factories, and therefore fails to take into account the role of administrative coordination, is far removed from reality.

In addition, administrative coordination helps to account for a significant segment of what economists have defined as a residual, that is, the proportion of output that cannot be explained by the growth of input. Certainly the speed and regularity with which goods flow through the processes of production and distribution and the way these flows are organized affect the volume and unit cost. Until economists analyze the function of administrative coordination, the theory of the firm will remain essentially a theory of production. The institution through which the factors of production are combined, which coordinates current flows, and which allocates resources for future economic activities in major sectors of the economy deserves more attention than it has yet received from economists.

THE ASCENDANCY OF THE MANAGER

Historians as well as economists have failed to consider the implications of the rise of modern business enterprise. They have studied the entrepreneurs who created modern business enterprise, but more in moral than in analytical terms. Their concern has been more whether they were exploiters (robber barons) or creators (industrial statesmen). Historians have also been fascinated by the financiers who for brief periods allocated funds to transportation, communication, and some industrial enterprises and so appeared to have control of major sectors of the economy. But they have paid almost no notice at all to the managers who, because they carried out a basic new economic function, continued to play a far more central role in the operations of the American economy than did the robber barons, industrial statesmen, or financiers. When they have looked at the development of the American economic system, historians have been more concerned about the continuing of family (i.e. entrepreneurial) capitalism or of financial capitalism than about the spread of managerial capitalism.

At the beginning of this century the American economic system still included elements of financial and family capitalism. Managerial capitalism was not yet fully dominant. Where the initial cost of facilities was high, as was the case with the railroad, the telegraph, urban traction lines, and other utilities, investment bankers and other financial intermediaries who had played a major role in raising funds for the enterprise continued to participate in decisions on the allocation of resources for the future. Where, as was the case with the mass marketers, initial capital costs were low and high volume output generated funds for expansion, the entrepreneurs who created the firm and their families continued to have a say in top management decisions. But by 1917 representatives of an entrepreneurial family or a banking house almost never took part in middle management decisions on prices, output, deliveries, wages, and employment required in the coordinating of current flows. Even in top management decisions concerning the allocation of resources, their

power remained essentially negative. They could say no, but unless they themselves were trained managers with long experience in the same industry and even the same company, they had neither the information nor the experience to propose positive alternative courses of action.

The relationship between ownership and management within the integrated industrial firm reflected the way in which it became large. The experience of those that expanded initially by building an extensive marketing and purchasing organization paralleled that of the mass marketers. Because internally generated funds paid for the facilities and financed continued growth, the founder and his family retained control. Even when the enterprise went to the money markets for funds to supplement retained earnings for expansion, the family continued to own a large minority and nearly always controlling share of its stock.

Nevertheless, members of the entrepreneurial family rarely became active in top management unless they themselves were trained as professional managers. Since the profits of the family enterprise usually assured them of a large personal income, they had little financial incentive to spend years working up the managerial ladder. Therefore, in only a few of the large American business enterprises did family members continue to participate for more than two generations in the management of the companies they owned.

The descendants of the founders of and early investors in such industrial enterprises continued to reap the profits of successful administrative coordination. Indeed, the majority of American fortunes came from the building and operation of modern business enterprises. These families remain the primary beneficiaries of managerial capitalism, but they are no longer involved in the operation of its central institution. By mid-twentieth century few had any direct say in the decisions concerning current flows and future allocations so essential to the operation of the American economy.

A comparable pattern occurred in those industrial enterprises that grew large through merger rather than through internal growth. The financiers who provided or arranged to obtain funds to rationalize and centralize production and to create new marketing and purchasing organizations remained on the boards of consolidated industrial enterprises. They rarely, however, had as strong an influence on the boards of directors of industrial enterprises as they had on the boards of railroad companies. The capital needed for the initial reorganizations was less than that required for railroad system-building, and the profits for internal financing generated by these industrials was higher. In a few of the largest and best-known mergers – General Electric, United States Steel, International Harvester, and Allis Chalmers – outside directors from the financial community outnumbered insiders taken from management. But on the boards of a much greater number of food, machinery, chemical, oil, rubber, and primary metals enterprises, outside financiers were very much in the minority. Their influence was significant only when the enterprise decided to go to the money markets to supplement retained earnings. With a few notable exceptions, such as United States Steel, managers soon came to command those enterprises where financiers were originally influential. Financial capitalism in the United States was a narrowly located, short-lived phenomenon.

By mid-century even the legal fiction of outside control was beginning to disappear. A study of the 200 largest nonfinancial companies in 1963 indicates that in none of these firms did an individual, family, or group hold over 80 percent of the stock.[3] None were still privately owned. In only 5 of the 200 did a family or group have a majority control by owning as much as 50 percent of the stock. In 26 others a family or group had minority control by holding more than 10 percent of the stock (but less than 50) or by using a holding company or other legal device. In 1963, then, 169 or 84.5 percent of the 200 largest nonfinancial companies were management controlled. In 5 of these firms families did still have influence, but because they were professional, full-time salaried executives, not because of stock they held. Thus by the 1950s the managerial firm had become the standard form of modern business enterprise in major sectors of the American economy. In those sectors where modern multiunit enterprise had come to dominate, managerial capitalism had gained ascendancy over family and financial capitalism.

As the influence of the families and the financiers grew even weaker in the management of modern business enterprise, that of the workers through representatives of their union increased. Union influence, however, directly affected only one set of management decisions – those made by middle managers relating to wages, hiring, firing, and conditions

of work. Such decisions had only an indirect impact on the central ones that coordinated current flows and allocated resources for the future.

Except on the railroads, the influence of the working force on the decisions made by managers of modern business enterprises did not begin until the 1930s. Before then craft unions had some success in organizing the workers in such labor-intensive skilled trades as cigar, garment, hat, and stove marking, shipbuilding, and coal mining – trades in which modern business enterprise rarely flourished. They organized the workers in the shops of small, single-unit, owner-managed firms into local, city, and state unions. These regional organizations were represented in a national union which was, in turn, loosely affiliated with other craft unions in the American Federation of Labor.

The craft unions, however, made little effort to unionize those industries where administrative coordination paid off. Workers in the mass production industries, where the large modern industrial enterprises clustered, were primarily semiskilled and unskilled workers. Those industries employed few skilled craftsmen. With the coming of the modern factory, the plant manager and his staff took over from the foreman the decisions concerning hiring, firing, and promotion, as well as those on wages, hours, and conditions of work. As the enterprise grew, such decisions were placed in the hands of middle management. Policy matters were determined by executives in new personnel departments housed in the central office. And until the 1930s, these middle managers were rarely forced to consider seriously the demands of labor unions to represent the workers in making such decisions.

Even with the strong support of the Roosevelt administration, the American Federation of Labor was unable to meet the challenge of organizing the mass production industries.[4] The success of such an organizing drive required the restructuring of its unions along industrial – plant and enterprise – rather than geographical – city and state – lines. In addition, the craft unions had difficulty in devising a program that appealed to the semi-skilled and the unskilled workers and still met the needs of their skilled members. Only in 1936 after the creation of the Committee for Industrial Organization, after its split from the A F of L, and after the resulting "civil war" in the ranks of labor, did the mass production industries begin to be extensively unionized. Only then did the managers of large enterprises in the automobile, machinery, electrical, chemical, rubber, glass, and primary metals industries begin to share their decisions with representatives of their working forces.

Even so, union leaders, during the great organizing drives of the late 1930s and immediately after Second World War, rarely, if ever, sought to have a say in the determination of policies other than those that directly affected the lives of their members. They wanted to take part only in those concerning wages, hours, working rules, hiring, firing, and promotion. Even the unsuccessful demand "to look at the company's books" was viewed as a way to assure union members that they were receiving a fair share of the income generated by the company. The union members almost never asked to participate in decisions concerning output, pricing, scheduling, and resource allocation.

A critical issue over which labor and management fought in the years immediately after Second World War was whether the managers or the union would control the hiring of workers. With the passage of the Taft–Hartley Act of 1947, the managers retained control over hiring, a prerogative that has never been seriously challenged since. And since that time the unions have made few determined efforts to acquire more of "management's prerogatives."

The actions of government officials, particularly those of the federal government, have had an increasingly greater impact on managerial decisions than have those of the representatives of workers, owners, or financiers. By and large, however, their impact has been indirect. They have helped to shape the environment in which management makes its decisions, but, except in time of war, these officials have only occasionally participated in the making of the decisions themselves. And since the market has always been the prime factor in management decisions, the government's most significant role has been in shaping markets for the goods and services of modern business enterprise.

Prior to the depression and Second World War, the impact of the state and federal government on the modern corporation was primarily through taxes, tariffs, and regulatory legislation. Taxes remained low until the war and had a minimal impact on the direction and rate of growth of the modern managerial enterprises and the sectors they administered. Tariffs, which protected all industries, were of more help in maintaining small-unit, competitive enterprises than

in assisting those that exploited the economies of speed and sold their products on a global scale. Antitrust legislation and, since its founding in 1914, the Federal Trade Commission have continued to discourage monopoly and encourage oligopoly. The Federal Reserve Board, formed in 1914, has affected the interest rates and money markets and therefore the managers' financial environment. The wave of regulatory legislation passed during the New Deal reduced the choices open to management in transportation, communications, and utilities enterprises. However, except in the issuance of securities, the new legislation placed few limitations on the discretionary power of mass marketers and mass producers to coordinate flows and allocate resources.

The government's role in the economy expanded sharply in the 1930s and 1940s. With the coming of Second World War, the federal government became for the first time a major customer of American business enterprise. Before that time, except for a brief period during First World War, government buyers, including the military forces, provided only a tiny market for the food, machinery, chemical, oil, rubber, and primary metal companies that made up the roster of American big business. The suggestion that the *rise* of big business has any relation to government and military expenditures (or for that matter to monetary and fiscal policies) has no historical substance. Only during and after the Second World War did the government become a major market for industrial goods. In the postwar years, that market has been substantial, but it has been concentrated in a small number of industries, such as aircraft, missiles, instruments, communication equipment, electronic components, and shipbuilding.[5] Outside these industries, output continues to go primarily to non-government customers.

Far more important to the spread and continued growth of modern business enterprise than direct purchases has been the government's role in maintaining full employment and high aggregate demand. Again, it was only after Second World War that the government inaugurated any sort of systematic policy to maintain demand and thereby support the mass market. One reason the federal government took on this responsibility was that the depression clearly demonstrated the inability of the private sector of the economy to maintain continuing growth of a complex, highly differentiated mass production, mass distribution economy. In the 1920s, the new corporate giants had begun to calibrate supply with demand. They had no way, however, of sustaining aggregate demand or of reviving it if it fell off. In the middle and later part of the decade, when national income stopped growing, the larger firms maintained existing output or cut back a bit. When the 1929 stock market crash dried up credit and further reduced demand, they could only roll with the punches. As demand fell, these enterprises cut production, laid off workers, and canceled orders for supplies and materials. Such actions further reduced purchasing power and with it aggregate demand. The very ability to effectively coordinate supply with demand intensified the economic decline. The downward pressure continued relentlessly. In less than four years, the national income was slashed in half. The 1931 forecasts of General Motors and General Electric for 1932, for example, were horrendous. At best they might have operated at about 25 percent of capacity.

The only institution capable of stopping this economic descent was the federal government. During the 1930s, it began to undertake this role, but with great reluctance. Politicians and government officials moved hesitantly. And managers and businessmen, those who had the most to gain, were among the most outspoken critics of the few moves that were made. Until the recession of 1937, President Franklin D. Roosevelt and Secretary of the Treasury Henry Morgenthau still expected to balance the budget and bring to an end government intervention in the economy. Roosevelt and his cabinet considered large-scale government spending and employment a temporary expedient. When Roosevelt decided in 1936 that, despite high unemployment, the depression was over, he reduced government expenditures. National income, production, and demand immediately plummeted. By then, a few economists and government officials and still fewer business managers began to see more clearly the relationship between government spending and the level of economic activity. Nevertheless, the acceptance of the government's role in maintaining economic growth and stability was still almost a decade away.

During Second World War attitudes changed. The mobilization of the war economy brought corporation managers to Washington to carry out one of the most complex pieces of economic planning in history. That experience lessened ideological anxieties about the government's role in stabilizing the economy. Then the fear of postwar recession and consequent return of mass unemployment brought support for legislation to commit the federal government to maintaining full employment and aggregate demand. While a few managers and businessmen favored such legislation, most continued to oppose what they considered government interference in the processes of business. The Employment Act of 1946 passed only through the concerted efforts of liberal and labor groups.[6] By the 1950s, however, businessmen in general and professional managers in particular had begun to see the benefits of a government commitment to maintaining aggregate demand. They supported the efforts of both Democratic and Republican administrations during the recessions of 1949, 1957, and 1960 to provide stability through fiscal policies involving the building of highways and shifting defense contracts.

In carrying out these policies, the government officials had no intention of replacing the managers as the coordinators of current demand and allocators of resources for the future. They acted only when the activities of the corporate managers failed to maintain full employment and high demand. The federal government became a coordinator and allocator of last resort.

In the United States, neither the labor unions nor the government has taken part in carrying out the basic functions of modern business enterprise as it has been defined in this study. They had had as little *direct* say as the representatives of the owners or financiers in decisions coordinating current flows and allocating resources for future production and distribution. Such decisions remain market-oriented. They continued to reflect the managers' perceptions of how to use technology and capital to meet their estimates of market demand.

The appearance of managerial capitalism has been, therefore, an economic phenomenon. It has had little political support among the American electorate. At least until the 1940s, modern business enterprise grew in spite of public and government opposition. Many Americans – probably a majority – looked on large-scale enterprise with suspicion. The concentrated economic power such enterprises wielded violated basic democratic values. Their existence dampened entrepreneurial opportunity in many sectors of the economy. Their managers were not required to explain or be accountable for their uses of power.

For these reasons the coming of modern business enterprise in its several different forms brought strong political reaction and legislative action. The control and regulation of the railroads, of the three types of mass retailers – department stores, mail-order houses, and the chains – and of the large industrial enterprise became major political issues. In the first decade of the twentieth century, the control of the large corporation was, in fact, the paramount political question of the day. The protest against the new type of business enterprise was led by merchants, small manufacturers, and other businessmen, including commercial farmers, who felt their economic interests threatened by the new institution. By basing their arguments on traditional ideology and traditional economic beliefs, they won widespread support for their views. Yet in the end, the protests, the political campaigns, and the resulting legislation did little to retard the continuing growth of the new institution and the new class that managed it.

THE UNITED STATES: SEED-BED OF MANAGERIAL CAPITALISM

Modern business enterprise has appeared in all technologically advanced market economies. Comparable protests, even stronger ideological and political opposition, has not prevented its emergence and spread in Western Europe and Japan. In recent years the same type of multiunit enterprises, using comparable administrative procedures and organizational structures, have come to dominate much the same type of industries as in the United States.[7] In these industries a new managerial class has become responsible for coordinating current flows of goods and services and allocating resources for future production and distribution. The study of the past history and present operations of modern business enterprise in Europe and Japan provides as significant a challenge to economists and historians as the analysis of the American story.

In Europe and Japan, however, the new institution appeared in smaller numbers and, at least until after Second World War, spread more slowly than it did in the United States. Because it came slower and later, its builders and administrators have often looked to the American experience for models and precedents. Therefore one of the most significant questions for economists and historians studying modern business enterprise in its international setting is to explain why the institution appeared so quickly and in such profusion in the United States.

An obvious, though still untested, reason why the United States became the seed-bed for managerial capitalism was the size and nature of its domestic market. In the second part of the nineteenth century the American domestic market was the largest and, what is more important, the fastest growing market in the world. In 1880, the nation's national income and its population were one and a half times those of Great Britain. By 1900, they were twice the size of Britain's and, by 1920, three times the size.[8] As Simon Kuznets's carefully drawn data reveal, the rate of growth of the American population and national product was consistently much higher than that of other technologically advanced nations – France and Germany, as well as Britain – during the years between the American Civil War and First World War.

The American market was not only larger and faster growing than in these other nations; it was also more homogeneous. Income distribution appears to have been less skewed than in other nations. Markets were less defined by class lines than they were in Europe. The newness of the American market – much of which had been unsettled wilderness a few decades earlier – also meant that business enterprises were new and business arrangements had not had time to become routinized and rigid.

The existence of such a fast-growing, homogeneous, open market did more than encourage the rise of mass marketers. It hastened the adoption of new technologies. This market stimulated the rapid spread of fundamental innovations – the railroad, the telegraph, and the new coal technologies in the furnace, foundry, and refining industries. It then encouraged Americans to pioneer in the machinery and organization of mass production. They developed machinery (often based on European innovations) to mass produce a wide variety of products. Of even more importance, they were the first to manufacture standardized machines by mass production methods.

Smaller and slower growing domestic markets in Western Europe and Japan lessened the interest of manufacturers in adopting new mass production techniques and also reduced the incentive to build large marketing and purchasing organizations. In Britain and France producers continued to rely on middlemen to handle their more traditional wares, which in turn were produced in a more traditional craft fashion. Where large, integrated enterprises did appear, they remained small enough to be managed at the top by a small number of owners. So the entrepreneurial enterprise and with it family capitalism continued to flourish. In Germany and Japan, where the integration of production and distribution was more common, smaller markets and cash flows reduced the opportunity to rely on internal financing and so increased the dependence on outside financiers – the large banks in Germany and the major financial groups (the Zaibatsu) in Japan. Managers continued to share top management decisions with financiers. There financial capitalism continued to hold sway.

Cultural and social differences also may have played a role in delaying the coming of the large managerial enterprise and with it managerial capitalism. Legal differences based on cultural values were of particular significance. The Sherman Act by prohibiting cartels of small family firms hastened the growth of big business in the United States. In Europe a family firm federated with other family firms, through holding companies in Britain or through cartels in Germany, to assure continuing profit. Even when European firms merged into integrated holding companies, they did so primarily for the defensive purpose of assuring outlets and supplies. Such companies remained essentially federations that employed neither middle nor top managers to coordinate flows of goods or allocate resources. Owners or their representatives made decisions on price, output, and coordination at weekly or monthly conferences. In the United States, such federations were illegal. The Sherman Act and its interpretation by the courts provided a powerful pressure that did not exist elsewhere to force family firms to consolidate their operations into a single, centrally operated enterprise administered by salaried managers.

In Europe, class distinctions may have made a difference. Families identified themselves more closely with the firm that provided the income with which to maintain their status more than did families in the United States. In those large enterprises that did integrate mass production and mass distribution and in which the owners hired middle managers to coordinate flows, the family continued to dominate top management. Often the family preferred not to expand the enterprise if it meant the loss of personal control.

Since Second World War, such restraints have diminished, and the spread of managerial enterprise has accelerated within Western Europe and Japan. The war and postwar needs have encouraged the adoption of new mass production technology.

Domestic markets have grown rapidly as gross national output rose and as income became more equitably distributed. The coming of the European Economic Community further enlarged markets. Laws against monopoly and restrictive business practices have discouraged the continuance of holding companies and cartels of family firms. Class distinctions have blurred. Large enterprises with salaried top as well as middle managers have grown in size and increased in numbers. They have clustered in much the same industries as in the United States – those in which administrative coordination pays the best. With the spread of modern managerial business enterprise in Europe and Japan, all the paraphernalia of professional management has appeared – the associations, the journals, the training schools, and the consultants.[9]

Such comparisons between the development and operation of modern multiunit enterprise at home and abroad are only tentative. Much more information is needed to test these suggested hypotheses. Nevertheless, readily available data underline the central importance of administrative coordination and allocation to modern technologically advanced, urban, industrial market economies and emphasize the value of further study of the institution and class of managers.

The comparative approach is surely the proper one for such a continuing work in the history of modern business enterprise. Describing and analyzing the history of the new institution and the ways in which it has carried out its basic functions in different nations can help to define the organizational imperatives of modern economies and reveal much about the ways in which cultural attitudes, values, ideologies, political systems, and social structure affect these imperatives. As important, such studies can provide clues to ways to answer a critical issue of modern times. They may suggest how narrowly trained managers, who must administer the processes of production and distribution in complex modern economies, can be made responsible for their actions – actions that have far-reaching consequences.

NOTES

1 Edith T. Penrose, *The Theory of the Growth of the Firm* (New York, 1959), chap. 5.
2 George Stigler, "The Division of Labor Is Limited by the Extent of the Market," *Journal of Political Economy*, 59: 185–193 (June 1951).

3 Robert J. Larner, "Ownership and Control in the 200 Largest Non-Financial Corporations, 1929 and 1963," *American Economic Review*, 56:777–787 (Sept. 1966). Larner's later book, *Management Control and the Large Corporation* (New York, 1970) expands his survey to cover almost all the 500 largest companies. There he finds the same basic patterns of management control as he did for the 200 largest. A rebuttal to Larner–Philip J. Burch's *The Managerial Revolution Reassessed: Family Control in America's Large Corporations* (Lexington, Mass., 1972) – does little to contradict the hypothesis that the managers operate the central sectors of the American economy. By using the criteria that 4–5 percent of stock means control, Burch finds that of the 200 largest firms on *Fortune*'s list of 500 largest industrials in 1965, 43 percent were probably management controlled, 17.5 percent were possibly family controlled, and 39.5 percent were probably family controlled. Under the possibly family controlled category, he lists, for example, Standard Oil of New Jersey, Socony Mobil, Standard of California, and Standard Oil of Indiana as possibly controlled by the Rockefeller family (the last with the Blaustien family), although there were no Rockefellers on the board or among the top and middle managers. Burch gives little indication how a "family, group of families, or some affluent individual," who holds 4–5 percent of the stock affects the decisions in that enterprise that coordinate flows and allocate resources, except to point out that in a large percentage of family firms, family members have over the years "served in major executive capacities." These are not defined but clearly include serving on the board of directors. What Burch's data does show is that wealthy Americans invest in the securities of large corporations, that some families of the entrepreneurs who helped to found a company still retained as much as 5 percent of the stock in those companies, and that members of those families often have jobs in that enterprise. Burch helps to document the fact that wealthy families, particularly those of the founders of modern business enterprises, are the beneficiaries of managerial capitalism, but gives little evidence that these families make basic decisions concerning the operations of modern capitalistic enterprises and of the economy in which they operate.

4 The paragraphs on labor organization and the coming of the commitment to maintaining aggregate demand follow those in Alfred D. Chandler, Jr., "The Role of Business in the United States: A Historical Essay," *Daedalus*, 98: 35–38 (Winter 1969).

5 *Report of President's Committee on the Impact of Defense and Disarmament* (Washington, DC, 1965), chap. 1, reprinted in James L. Clayton, *The Economic Impact of the Cold War* (New York, 1970), pp. 54–64. Of the eighty-one largest industrials in 1960, only twelve were among the twenty-five largest military contractors during the 1960s. Of these, four aircraft companies and General Dynamics had from 57 to 88 percent of sales in military contracts. Sperry-Rand sold 35 percent of its output to the government. Three electrical and electronic companies (General Electric, Westinghouse, and RCA) sold from 13 to 19 percent of their output to the government. (In addition, IT&T and AT&T, which is not on the list, made 19 and 9 percent respectively of their sales to the military.) Of the remaining three, IBM sold 7 percent to the military, General Motors 3 percent, and Ford's Philco Division 3 percent. The list of 81 companies is from Alfred D. Chandler, Jr., "The Structure of American Industry in the Twentieth Century," *Business History Review*, 43: 297–298 (Autumn 1969) and the list of leading contractors is in Clayton, *Economic Impact of the Cold War*, table 12, p. 44. For the impact of military spending on industrial research and development see Clayton, pp. 147–164.

6 See Stephen K. Bailey, *Congress Makes a Law* (New York, 1950), chaps. 2, 5.

7 See Leslie Hannah, ed. *Management Strategy and Business Development: An Historical and Comparative Study* (London, 1976); Herman Daems and Herman van der Wee, eds., *The Rise of Managerial Capitalism* (The Hague, 1974); Keiichiro Nakagawa, *Strategy and Structure of Big Business* (Tokyo, 1976); Derek F. Cannon, *The Strategy and Structure of British Enterprise* (Boston, 1973); Robert J. Pavan, *Strutture Strategie delle Imprese Italiane.* (Bologna, 1976); G.P. Dyas, "The Strategy and Structure of French Enterprise," Ph.D. diss., Harvard Business School, 1972; and H.I. Thanheiser, "The Strategy and Structure of German Industrial Enterprise," Ph.D. diss., Harvard Business School, 1972.

8 Simon Kuznets, *Economic Growth of Nations: Total Output and Production Structure* (Cambridge, Mass., 1971), pp. 38–40, and W.S. and E.S. Woytonsky, *World Population and Production* (New York, 1973), pp. 383–385.

9 Alfred D. Chandler, Jr., "The Development of Modern Management Structure in the U.S. and the U.K.," in Hannah, ed., *Management Strategy and Business Development*, chap. 1, briefly reviews the British experience.

"The Impact of the Corporation on Classical Economic Theory"*

from Quarterly Journal of Economics (1965)

Adolf A. Berle

In 1932 the thesis was presented by myself and Gardiner C. Means that the growth and functioning of large corporations introduced certain elements not adequately taken into account by classical economic theory.

One such element was the shift of management function away from entrepreneurial "capitalist" owners and to administrators; another, that there was in process an inevitable alteration in the position of shareholders, changing the traditional logic of property as respects "ownership" of these corporations. As these trends continued, the shift would have increasingly greater effect.

Continued observation thereafter indicated increasing intrusion of at least three other developments: (a) the competitive process was changing in quality, impact and effect; desire for market-power increasingly was becoming the controlling consideration; (b) formation and control over application of capital was increasingly ceasing to be individual and (where not carried on by the state) was increasingly becoming a function of the large corporations. Capital formation itself was increasingly effected by corporations through price rather than through personal savings, in view of corporate capacity to include as part of its price not only depreciation allowances but also an item of profit not designed for distribution to stockholders; and (c) finally, the role of the stock and securities markets as sources and allocators of capital was declining, notably in the case of risk-capital and markets for equity stocks.

As corollary, large corporations increasingly would come to be regarded, and to regard themselves, as part of a political-economic system rather than as classical merchant adventurers.

Properly, these propositions are now reviewed by economists. So, of course, they should be. Particularly, the neoclassical school of economic thought rejects the idea that any change in theory is required by current phenomena.

To this writer, the neoclassically oriented critiques of the propositions mentioned above seem not to take adequate account of the factual results of the flood-tide of institutional development that carries the bulk of the burgeoning industrial evolution. Scant heed is paid to the vast (the word is used advisedly, not rhetorically) changes in productive and commercial processes. Too little attention is paid to the changes in quantity, quality, content and distribution of the resulting ownership interests. In neoclassical theoretical analysis, there has been a natural, though unhappy, tendency to use classical economic terms and phrases (accurate when used to describe conditions of half a century ago) as though their then-content accurately describes today's processes.

No one denies that the bases of the present system are "capitalist" in origin. But to assume from that historical fact that "capitalism" is the same system as that prevailing, let us say in 1900, is about as relevant as to assume that a modern motorcar is essentially the same as a fringed surrey because both have four wheels and transport passengers. Still less is it sound to conclude (as does Professor Peterson)[1] that merely because the American economy is mainly dependent on "voluntary, self-supporting private enterprise," that fact "largely precludes serious departure from the other principal features of capitalism as traditionally viewed." That proposition involves an attempt to maintain that "capitalism" as classically understood has not evolved to the point of change, despite the huge volume of factual, technical and statistical evidence to the contrary.

The writer does not hold himself responsible (despite Peterson's inclusion of them) for all projections, deductions, speculations which have been drawn from the phenomena of corporate development by a growing number of observers and commentators, though all are interesting, some are important, and few can be safely ignored. This essay deals merely with the salient points of Peterson's neoclassical thesis. These appear to be as follows:

1   No significant alteration has occurred in the location of managerial responsibility or in the ownership-control thereof, requiring change either in economic theory or its application.
2   In any case, the fundamental of capitalism remains unchanged: the motivation and practice of corporations remains that of profit-maximization, and they remain controlled by competition and cognate market forces so that significant intrusion of social motive is and must be of negligible effect.
3   No significant change has occurred in the institution of "property" as represented by stock held by stockholders, and the stock markets in substantial measure retain their capital allocation function.

His conclusion appears to be that investment, production and distribution, and the position of ownership are all motivated, carried on and maintained in the traditional way. For neoclassical economists, business remains as usual. Given the facts, I think they are wrong.

PRELIMINARY: SOME MEASURABLE FACT-PHENOMENA

As preliminary, it is not inapposite to call attention to a few statistically measurable phenomena in all three fields. If stereo-types of economics, musty or otherwise, are being demolished, their destruction has been accomplished by observable fact rather than by "wayward" commentators.

Size and scope of large corporate activities[2]

For the year 1963, the 500 largest industrial corporations had combined sales of $245 billions; these accounted for about 62 per cent of all manufacturing sales in the United States. (The largest of these 500, General Motors, accounted for $16,500,000,000; the smallest, $86 millions.) Surrounding most of the giants is a penumbra of nominally independent but actually captive, or dependent, or market-controlled companies whose market decisions and behavior move more or less along lines determined by the central large-scale corporation. This multiplying factor does not show up in the figure given. Few fair-minded scholars would deny that big corporations dominate the manufacturing scene. Obviously, in greater concentration, large corporations even more markedly dominate the transportation, public utility and communications industries.

In all the 500 largest corporations (there are a handful of atypical exceptions such as Du Pont, Ford, Time, Inc., and some smaller oil companies) and a number of the smaller corporations (whose market percentage is relatively statistically small), "control" is atomized among large stockholder lists ranging from a minimum of several thousand to a maximum of more than a million. This process of atomization is not complete, but it is continuously going forward.

Distribution of ownership[3]

The total number of individual stockholders is estimated at between 17 and 20 million individuals (more probably the lower figure). In addition, financial institutions (pension trust funds, mutual investment funds, fire insurance companies and others) have substantial holdings of stock; these are held for a far larger number of individuals who derive income or other benefits through these institutional conduits. An extremely rough estimate of the number of these individuals would add not less than 25 million more to the figure (this is a drastic underestimate) though they appear as pension trust beneficiaries, etc., and not as individual stockholders.

Change in wealth-holding[4]

The over-all change in the property system forecast more than thirty years ago has gone far towards reality. At the close of 1963, total personally-owned wealth in the United States was estimated by the economic department of the First National City Bank (on the basis of Federal Reserve and National Bureau of Economic Research statistics) at $1,800 billions. The largest item, $550 billion, consisted of corporate stock. The other items were: $200 billion of life insurance company reserves, United States securities, corporate bonds and the like; and $375 billion of liquid assets such as cash and bank deposits. These three items total about $1,125 billion – just under two-thirds of the total personally-owned wealth. (The balance consisted of owner-occupied homes and personally-owned durables.) *Nearly one-third of all personally-owned property, apparently, now consists of stock, representing ownership of the corporate system.* More, indeed, if the individually-owned indirect holdings of stocks, bonds and securities, held chiefly through pension rights and fiduciary institutions, are included. Further, if anyone cares to follow the statistics over the past two decades, it will be apparent not only that personally-owned wealth has absolutely increased, but also that the elements of its make-up have undergone a major change as stock increasingly replaces personally-owned "things." The word "revolutionary" in its current, rather weakened, sense is not inapplicable to that change.

Source of and power over capital

Finally, though Peterson pays disproportionately little heed to this, a more striking shift has occurred in the method of accumulating and the decisions governing the application of, capital. More than 60 per cent (probably converging in 1965 toward 65 per cent) of all capital entering industrial corporations is internally generated by accumulating depreciation allowances and undistributed profits – both items being produced by charging to the consumer prices sufficient to permit such accumulations. Another 20 per cent of such capital is derived from bank credit extended directly by commercial banks or industrial corporations, presumably in anticipation of such accumulation. Only the balance – not more than 20 per cent at best – and probably closer this year to

15 per cent – is derived from personal "savings." These conceivably might be material for classical risk-taking, decision-making or other capitalist application by their owners. Factually, they are not. They go overwhelmingly into intermediate institutions such as savings banks which perform this function, and are not applied to risk-capital investment. So much of this item as goes into equity or risk capital operations is largely devoted to a single group of industries – communications (such as AT&T) and public utilities; in these industries rate regulation does not permit accumulation of capital through price to the same extent as in the case of nonregulated industries.

Against this background of facts, the neoclassical critique must be tested. The facts themselves cannot seriously be questioned. Meticulous scholarship might change the figures by a few billions or an insignificant percentage. The problem is whether change from an aggregate of small-scale individual family-or-ownership-directed enterprise into the conditions indicated by these and like facts entails change or modification of classical economic theory. Since economic theory is in preponderant measure dependent upon assumed motivations, to maintain an unchanged theory must involve assumption that the motivations and possibilities of action thereon are substantially similar under present conditions as those prevailing before its development.

Peterson feels there is "slender base" for assuming any change. It may properly be suggested that there is even slenderer base for assuming these motivations or possibilities of action thereon have remained the same.

THE SHIFT FROM "CAPITALIST" CONTROL

It would seem today merely whimsy to deny that decision-making control had shifted, away from the "entrepreneur group" of owners who manage, protect and maximize their profits and capital, into the hands of more or less professional corporate administrators. So much so, in fact, that space need not be wasted on extended argument. Any other result (state ownership aside) would be impossible. Save in the diminishing number of enterprises whose founding adventurer or his family still holds an aggregate block of stock sufficient to dislodge a management if they are displeased, stockholders physically cannot, and by law are not permitted, to enter the decision-making process. Further, save in exceptional circumstances (the AT&T may be one such), corporations as a rule do not need and often do not want to have recourse to their stockholders for additional capital. It is maintained, with truth, that the opinions of stockholders do have influence; that stockholders at meetings can raise "pertinent and sometimes embarrassing questions, sometimes with devastating effect"[5] and that they constitute a substantial special public, some of whom at least scrutinize the management. Yet sporadic and only occasionally effective use of this scrutiny does not add up to "control" or anything approaching it. At best, the scrutiny is a variety of post-audit. This is an instance of an old word ("control"), apt in the days of plutocratic 1890's, used by neoclassicists in quite different sense as applied to the discontinuous, occasional, quasi-political corporate processes of corporate government today. Practically its entire content now is that stockholders like to see dividends and market values rise, and, disliking the contrary, complain, seek to find the causes, on extremely rare occasions organize changes, when there is trouble.

In considerable personal experience, the writer has not encountered any situations in which a direct decision to apply (or withhold) capital from a given development, or to enter or refrain from entering a new field, has been decided by stockholders. One need not jump to the conclusion that the administrators of corporations are therefore "irresponsible." But again their responsibility differs in content. They are responsible to the impersonal institutional collective known as "the company"; they are secondarily responsible to the direct desire of stockholders at any given moment to enhance their immediately tangible take or to have losses explained. Stockholders act like an unorganized, usually inert, political constituency. They are a "field of responsibility"—far, indeed, from an entrepreneurial controlling force.

Nor has the situation been materially changed by the practice of endeavoring to make corporation administrators into stock owners through option or other plans. More often than not these plans are endeavors to soften the impact of income taxes or spread out the high pay of productive years to take care of the administrator's declining years. Rare indeed is the corporate administrator who decides a corporate problem differently because he has ownership of or option to buy a block of his company's shares.

THE IMMUTABILITY OF CLASSICAL ECONOMIC PRINCIPLES[6]

Less impressive is Peterson's second proposition, namely, that since our economy is dependent on "voluntary self-supporting private enterprise," this fact "precludes departure from its other principal features."[7]

The proposition must be interpreted broadly; as it stands, it is merely bizarre. The American economy was perhaps more dependent on "voluntary self-supporting private enterprise" in the days when monopolies were tolerated than it now is. Private enterprises voluntarily (and enthusiastically) moved into and endeavored to create monopoly situations and to free themselves from competitive restraints (to which we must later pay a little attention). The proposition has to be clarified by adding "under a competitive system." Within limits, addition of the phrase is justified. A powerful structure of antitrust law, Federal trade administration, Department of Justice enforcement, and supporting legal rules in many fields does maintain a version of the competitive system.

Peterson argues, accurately, that under the system "private" (in the sense of non-statist) enterprise must constantly pay attention to obtaining revenue greater than its costs and will seek as great a margin of revenue over costs as can be got. The argument thus runs that the primary object of a corporation must and can only be to maximize its profits, since it is constrained by the forces of competitive conditions. It may not, indeed it cannot, therefore, allow itself luxury of expenditures for social purposes beyond an insignificant margin when profits are healthy. Broadly this is true; but again, the conceptions applying have changed their content.

Competition

Let us begin with "competition." The first object of competition in the case of large-scale units is to establish that degree of market control, or of equilibrium with other units selling in its markets, so that satisfactory profits may be reaped. One result is the prevalent phenomenon of the "administered price" whose behavior, we are learning, differs considerably from classical patterns. This is not the content of older, classically-described competition. It may, but frequently does not, mean selling in the highest market or buying in the lowest. Sometimes it means pricing to assure entry into, or continued holding of, a particular market sector, though at the time higher prices may be available elsewhere. It may, and very often does, mean low profit or non-profit to increase a market sector, or to fend off some large opponent ambitious to take over. More often its motive is to maintain equilibrium in a market satisfactorily shared with a few colleague-competitors. One may refer to the excellent study by Ralph Cassady, Jr. entitled, *Price Warfare in Business Competition: A Study in Abnormal Competitive Behavior.*[8] The subtitle is accurate. Price competition, beyond the narrowest margin, commonly is abnormal behavior; it breaks out when equilibrium is disturbed or threatened; then it partakes of the nature of an international conflict.

"Competition" at present thus is more often determined by considerations of market-power than by those brought to mind by the ancient word. Normally, a state of price equilibrium reasoned satisfactory to all hands is reached, leaving marginal areas only in which the struggle for a customer (or alternatively, the struggle to buy supplies) can be carried on. Most of the time a "live and let live" policy prevails, tacitly, lest there be violation of antitrust laws. The full competitive battery is unmasked only when a new-comer seeks to upset the equilibrium, barging into a reasonably occupied field, or a companion company becomes dangerously aggressive. In great areas, this rarely happens. Factually, if the antitrust laws and state scrutiny were withdrawn, the competitive system would cease to exist in all major lines within a very few years.

Unhappily also for Peterson's argument, a vast sector of the American economy is not, even theoretically, within the classical economic system. Most of wages, all transport, all communication, all utilities, most agricultural products, petroleum and great sectors of metals operate under a system of fixed, not competitive prices, and of regulated monopoly, or of legally-maintained competition. The enterprises involved are *soi-disant*, private and voluntary; they are actually vast collectives. They are expected to be self-supporting; they are not state-owned; but where not licensed monopolies, they are not in full degree competitive and their markets are in large measure guaranteed; the number of economic forces bearing on them is vastly reduced. Behavior of large-scale enterprise, under these conditions cannot on the empirical evidence available, be fairly assimilated to the "market place behavior" posited by the old theory. There are, it is true, elements of similarity. They are under a degree of restraint, partly by market forces, often by state action. But the impact, the degree, and the results of these restraints have changed.

Maximization of profit

Maximization of profit, it is said, is the prime driving force of corporations now as always in the case of business. Agreed.

Classic (and neoclassical) theory assumes that this fact excludes possibility of significant use of the corporate assets and mechanism for social purposes. Both indeed add that such use not only cannot but should not be made. The corporation's significance is thus limited to that of a profit-seeking unit, having the same motivations and acting in the same way as the classical entrepreneur–businessman. Fundamentally a good deal of this is true. Inaccuracy in using the general concept as guide to assumed motivations and behavior of the corporation arises from the changed state of fact. Maximization of profit in the case of giant corporations not only may, but usually does, mean acting quite differently from the small-scale firm; thus the content of the phrase has changed.

Ably-run corporations think of themselves as perpetual, as dependent on maintaining long-range position and as responsible for meeting market demands (which they hope to increase) for an unlimited future. Their policies thus require and include long-range planning, for periods of five to twenty years ahead. At any given moment, they will sacrifice a portion of immediate profit for long-range position. This takes many forms: tieing up capital to assure future source of supply, foregoing immediate profit for better position in any given market; hazarding resources in experimental operations (some of great size) whose profit potential is undemonstrated, campaigning for a changed tax-position – to take only a few. Of course, they hope the policies adopted will eventually "pay off" in revenue dollars, or in added percentage of market, or otherwise, but the time-dimension is changed. On any given occasion this may mean not buying in the cheapest market and not selling in the dearest; not taking immediate opportunity, but seeking the distant rainbow. And so on ad infinitum. Though the profit motive is regnant, it is modified in application, timing and direction by all manner of companion considerations.

Not least among these considerations is a lively appreciation by corporate administrators of the capacity of the state to step in when public dissatisfaction (wholly unconnected with their profits) threatens intrusion through political process. Most really large corporations can, immediately, take measures diminishing costs – for example, transferring, or consolidating company-owned towns, and abandonment of same, dropping overboard unpromising lines of activity, breaking substantial competitors, retiring older employees, but are restrained from doing so by considerations of general welfare or public relations. Clearly they expect their ultimate situation to be better than if they pursued the last dollar of profit. One need not, therefore, deny that a form of "profit maximization" is involved. But the results, market-wise, substantially modify the uncomplicated predictions of classical economists. Elaboration here is impossible: the situations are at once too varied and too fundamental. Enough to say that, when a certain size and degree of market control has been attained, crude following of classically assumed patterns would probably involve the corporation in difficulties with the public, with labor, with the antitrust laws, with legislative and executive authority – though they could make immediate gains. Refusing them is, perhaps, profit maximization – but reinterpreted in the light of modern reality.

Corporate size and concentration is here a powerful, probably a determinative, element. Size extends business decisions from the purely economic into fields of social movement carried on by political action and reaction. An individual trader need think only of himself. A collective trader whose stockholders number hundreds of thousands and whose customers run in millions must think politically as well. Rudimentary political science as well as market economics must be taken into account. Every modern state has assumed responsibility in whole or in part for general economic conditions, and for tolerability of those conditions for most, if not all, its citizens. For a large corporation, the premises on which the state will act and what action it can and is likely to take can never be ruled out.

This suggests that the "Instruction in Elementary Economics" contemplated by Peterson must take in much more territory than that envisaged in his paper.[9] It must do more than "take account of the choices, of all people among all goods, of the scarcities of all resources, of all alternative ways of using them," and

must endeavor to enlarge the corporation's "worm's eye view" of the forces bearing on it. Factually many, perhaps most, corporate administrators do take elaborate account of these forces, and often maintain expensive staffs for that precise purpose. Most of them realize that at any given moment the "choices of all people" may be determined by monopsonic policies of government (as in defense industries), by power-relations with labor, by currency and credit factors determined by the Federal Reserve Board, even by currents of public thought. The corporate operations may include working out price and wage relationships under the guidance of the Secretary of Labor or even the White House; currents of future need in national defense; plans to supply shifting population; relationships with the Department of Interior or the Department of Agriculture to assure supply; maintenance of regional economic stability in conjunction with local authorities-to name only a few. All of which suggest that the elements of economic "control" posited by classicists and neoclassicists need considerable elaboration.

While necessity of this reappraisal is at least partly a consequence of the size of the corporation, it also results from a modern political-economic factor which now is constant and must never be overlooked. In most developed (and a good many underdeveloped) countries of the world – and certainly in the United States – public opinion and political processes no longer tolerate the results flowing from pursuit of the purely economic and competitive processes to their logical end. The community more often than not prefers continuous employment and stability to the minor price-advantage tossed out by competition. Political action will be invoked against unduly low wages, against undersupply of an essential product, against unemployment, perhaps even against oppressive price fluctuations. In blunt, the state, energized by democratic processes, is always a factor, actual or potential. The "entire range of alternatives on the other side of the market in which it sells and buys"[10] are only some and not necessarily the most determinative elements in the supposed "controls" relied on by classical and neoclassical theory.

This brings us to a brief observation on the progress of the "corporate conscience." (To economists, the phrase is oddly romantic: to lawyers, it is ancient and familiar history and therefore by them better understood. Because a corporation is an artificial legal, and not a human being it was held in old common law courts to have no "soul" and therefore no "conscience"; it could not validly take an oath; it was not amenable to moral considerations, and so forth.) Corporations are composed of and managed by men. Each member of the administrative group does have a conscience and thus consensus does influence corporate action. In substantial measure, as Peterson rightly says, the "corporate conscience" does have a great deal to do with performing the supply function well, with honesty, upright dealing, and observance of applicable laws. But these same managers have also absorbed the idea that corporations (for better or worse) are also held responsible by an appreciable sector of opinion for some at least of the social conditions proceeding from their operations – also that, if offensive, these conditions may bring into action the powerful machinery of the state. If corporate managers do not themselves know this, their public relations departments tell them so. The "corporate conscience" may be little more than a lively appreciation of possible consequences either of direct violation of ethics or of social results not tolerable to the community, but it is nonetheless real for all that. Where there is a superior management, its "conscience" transcends this, anticipating rather than remedying deficiencies. Deliberate sacrifice of the firm's long-run prosperity is, to be sure, highly unlikely if not unethical. But one result of a corporate conscience may be the devising of means or even the seeking of governmental or other measures – for example, pension trust funds or even (as in the case of oil) stabilization arrangements – making possible attainment of the desired conditions without that sacrifice. Of this sort of corporate activity there is a very great deal. The law indeed goes farther – it approves and encourages a limited amount of direct corporate philanthropy – though this is less important perhaps than other areas in which the "corporate conscience" has come to be an active force.

STOCKHOLDERS DERIVE WHAT INFLUENCE THEY HAVE FROM SOCIAL-POLITICAL, NOT FROM ENTREPRENEURIAL, FACTORS

The place of the stockholders as residual recipient of profits deserves a final word. Here classical (and neoclassical) theory reaches romantic heights. It insists on having owner-risk-taking entrepreneurs. The

seventeen million stockholders are nominated for the role – no other candidates presenting themselves in the corporate spectrum. Ironically, the facts refuse to write the appropriate script. This writer, believing that control function has shifted away from "ownership," sees little necessity for maintaining the fiction of "owner-entrepreneurship" in the corporate picture, or even substantial reason for having the institution. In any case, willy-nilly, we have not got it. To the contrary, we have, essentially a new form of property.

Desire to discover an "owner-entrepreneurship" or "risk-taking" function in stockholders is basically (I think) an emotional desire to find some functional justification for having stockholders at all. A couple of generations ago, they pulled their weight in the economic boat because they saved, and invested their savings, at hazard of risk and with hope of profit in productive enterprise: in other words, supplied risk-capital. They also chose, supervised, contributed to, and controlled management. This justified their existence in classical theory. Solid argument could be made for it. As of today, it is probably true that stockholders have saved (or have inherited past savings). But, as we have noted, these savings no longer are a major source of capital. At best, not over 2 or 3 per cent (often less) of new risk-capital actually entering industrial enterprise in each year is supplied from this source. In overwhelmingly large part, personal savings devoted to buying of stock are used, not to furnish capital to enterprise but to buy out the holdings of some prior stockholder. Nym buys General Motors stock from Bardolph, who bought it from Pistol, who bought it at 10,000 removes from the heirs of Sir John Falstaff – who did, in fact, invest some money in an original issue of common stock of General Motors at its birth. Nym's purchase is still, quaintly, called "investment" – the word having, as usual, changed its content.

The only facts we know are that Nym's money never did get to General Motors and never will; further, that a half-century having elapsed, Nym's purchase no longer has crucial connection with maintaining General Motors' capacity to acquire new capital by selling new issues of stock. An element of such connection is present – especially in the public utility industry – but so tiny as to be almost invisible. Factually, the stock buying and selling processes carried on through the exchanges have sentimental rather than functional connection with General Motors. Nym's "risk-taking" is the risk of the stock market price fluctuations, completely different from the risk Sir John Falstaff may have taken when he paid good money into the treasury of the nascent motor car enterprise. It is almost, though not wholly, true that the process is completely independent. The relation is about that of the buyer of a sweepstake ticket to the owner of a race horse whose performance determines the lottery prize – little more. No real reason exists to believe that the entire stock exchange process releases significant amounts of capital for true investment in enterprise, though there may, of course, be a small slop-over margin. Commonly, however, when Nym buys Bardolph's General Motors stock, Bardolph does not finance a new enterprise with the proceeds. He turns around and buys Standard Oil of New Jersey – and so on in millions of transactions.[11]

Dr Paul Harbrecht has been considering a theory that the stock markets have developed a separate, more or less closed, system of property-holding and exchange, and that this system is essentially independent from the actual productive process. Prima facie, there is a good deal of evidence to support the theory. Since, as we have seen, the corporation does not need the stockholders' savings, and the stockholder has no management function – merely vague and occasional quasi-political influence – the classical justification for him as source of capital, or as investment risk-taker, let alone as entrepreneur– manager, simply disappears. He toils not, neither does he spin. He merely expects dividends from capital operation, and an unearned increment of value as the corporation compounds the return on withheld profits ploughed back into the business.

Justification of the stockholder's position, if there is one, therefore, must be found oustide classical or neoclassical economic theory. I believe there is such justification though the base is politico-social rather than economic. There are solid values in having men and families attend to their own problems and develop their own lives. That requires that they should have a form of wealth – giving them capacity to choose their ways of consumption, and their manner of living, and power to make their own application of such wealth to their own conception of life. Passive property, like stock, does enable men to do this. Yet it is at once apparent that this justification is valid only in direct ratio as stock is widely distributed among the entire population – ideally, among all of it. As such distribution goes forward, there is measurable

addition to the capacity for self-determination of each holder. Further, as the entire organism of the American economy expands, and as capital values increase, an increasing number of Americans – ideally, all of them – become joint heirs of the system's productivity.

That this distribution is gradually occurring is evident. Thirty years ago only a tiny number of Americans held this form of property (or, for that matter, any income-producing property at all). Today, as we see, 17 millions or more hold some of it directly. Tens of millions more hold it indirectly. The distribution is still not good; 1 per cent of the population of the United States still holds a wholly lop-sided preponderance of it. Yet, quite clearly, progress is being made – though more progress has to be made if the vanished economic justification for such property is to be adequately replaced by its only visible alternative – the social justification.

Simultaneously, one notes, the stock markets, save in vestigial trace, have ceased to be allocators of risk-capital and have become allocators of passive property – irrational, but conceivably capable of development into social institutions no less useful than the great life insurance companies and savings banks.

I do not see, therefore, that Peterson's third point stands up, or indeed that his observations are really relevant to the problem in hand. The supine stockholder is protected by an elaborate system of law – chiefly administrative. Indeed he is (and ought to be) very well satisfied with his position. Until, of course, some revolutionary rises to ask him why he should be permitted to have it, especially if a great many others do not. Then it might be remembered that in great parts of the world, including the fascist as well as communist countries and to some extent semi-socialist Britain, his position has been eliminated overnight (as in Russia) or vastly reduced (as in Nazi Germany) or taken over (as in Britain) or sometimes quietly eroded.

Where the stockholder is maintained in his position – as the United States is endeavoring to do – the fact is not proof of the "deep-rootedness" of "traditional capitalism." Rather it results from tenacious holding of an American ideal of individual capacity to choose his own way of life, and of a system giving individuals enough disposable wealth to implement their choice, and from realization that for these ends this form of distributed wealth, however supine and passive, is a useful if not an essential tool.

NOTES

* As example, see, among other recent books, Robin Marris, *The Economic Theory of Managerial Capitalism* (New York: Free Press of Glencoe, 1964). Peterson, S. (1965) Corporate Control and Capitalism, *The Quarterly Journal of Economics*, Vol LXXIX, No. 1, February, pp 1–24.

1 Peterson (1965: 9).

2 *Fortune*, LXIX (July 1964), p. 179.

3 New York Stock Exchange estimates. These are the results of sampling surveys; a certain caution is indicated. The estimates do, I think, give fair indication of the order of magnitude.

4 See first National City Bank (New York), *Monthly Economic Letter*, July 1964, p. 78.

5 Peterson (1965: 22).

6 Classical economists equate economic laws to laws of physical science: men will always act in the same way under the same conditions. Specifically, they will seek to use their labor and their savings or capital to obtain the greatest available profit.

Let us assume this is true. Even on that assumption, at least two powerful variables at once appear.

What is "available" will be determined by the surrounding structure of law and mores.

Interest on loaned money, for example, was not generally available under the medieval system.

Mid-twentieth century development has erected a whole structure of mores and laws precluding, forbidding or endeavoring to prevent results of the competitive system in great areas. The community apparently regards these results as so undesirable (or possibly, so costly) that it is prepared to risk higher prices rather than endure them. It is impossible not to conclude that the available choices are restricted and, even with a self-interest motivation, they have changed.

"Profit" depends on desire. Under medieval mores it was likely as not to include progress toward salvation in the next world; this is why savings were perhaps more often applied to building cathedrals and churches than to constructing profit-making installations.

The argument is made more extensively in my book, *The American Economic Republic* (New York: Harcourt, Brace & World, Inc., 1963).

Neoclassical economics, even if it accepts as immutable the classical premise, must take account of two major variations: (a) that huge institutions are different from individuals and that choices available to individuals within large institutions differ from those available to individual owner-entrepreneurs; and (b) that the mores, politics, and systems of laws built thereon demand results which do not logically flow from the competitive system, certainly as carried on by large institutions, and which shift the application of the self-interest theory.

To the classicist, any interference with his "natural laws" is assumed to invite disaster. In America at least these disasters seem not to have occurred and there is no substantial evidence that they will.

7 Peterson (1965: 9).

8 Occasional Paper No. 11, Bureau of Business and Economic Research, Graduate School of Business Administration, Michigan State University (East Lansing, Mich., 1963).

9 Peterson (1965: 13).

10 Peterson (1965: 13).

11 The argument has been fully made and need not be repeated. See Berle, "Modern Functions of the Corporate System," *Columbia Law Review*, LXII (1962), 433.

PART TWO

Agency theory

INTRODUCTION TO PART TWO

In the long period of economic growth and prosperity following the Second World War, controversy concerning the managerial revolution subsided, as multinational corporations consolidated their position in the global economy. Neoclassical economic theory continued with the attempt to develop a theory of resource allocation based on market exchange, and neglected the productive sphere of the economy. In the effort to provide a more adequate explanation of economic activity new theories of the firm were elaborated, including agency theory that became by default the dominant force in the theoretical understanding of corporate governance in the last decades of the twentieth century.

Agency theory explained the firm as a nexus of contracts among individual factors of production. Classical economics had conceived the firm as a single product entity with a commitment to the maximization of profits, and the operation of the firm was considered of less interest compared to the operation of markets. Agency theory examined the workings of the firm as a constantly re-negotiated contract by many individuals each with the aim of maximizing their own utility. Jensen and Meckling argue (Chapter 4) the essence of the agency problem is the separation of management and finance. Managers end up with substantial residual control rights, and discretion over how to allocate investors' funds. From this viewpoint, corporate governance essentially concerns the constraints that are applied to managers to minimize misallocation of funds.

Agency theory offers shareholders the pre-eminent position in the firm, not as the firm's owners, but as the residual risk takers. This view suggests shareholders are the *principals* in whose interest the corporation should be run even though they rely on others to do this. Fama and Jensen (Chapter 5) propose that this separation of decision-making and risk-bearing functions observed in the large corporation occurs in many other forms of organization. Since the basis of agency theory is the self-interested utility-maximizing individual, it is assumed the relationship between shareholders and managers will inevitably be problematic, as the principals attempt to prevent their agents from maximizing their own utility.

Kathleen Eisenhardt (Chapter 6) offers a contemporary assessment of agency theory, identifying links to mainstream organization perspectives, though agency theory has often been criticized by organization theorists as minimalist. Drawing parallels with political models of organization, and contingency approaches, she emphasizes the contribution of agency theory to the understandings of information asymmetry, risk, control and incentives in organizational life. However, other organizational and management theorists have explained the prevalence of agency theory in terms of its simplicity, reducing the complexity and dilemmas of large corporations to the relationship of just two participants – managers and shareholders, and assuming the interests of each are clear and consistent. Other conceptions of the firm allow for a wider range of orientations and relationships, creating a more complex but more realistic series of problems for corporate governance.

"Theory of the Firm: Managerial Behavior, Agency Costs and Ownership Structure"

from Journal of Financial Economics (1976)

Michael C. Jensen and William H. Meckling

INTRODUCTION AND SUMMARY

Motivation of the paper

In this chapter we draw on recent progress in the theory of (1) property rights, (2) agency, and (3) finance to develop a theory of ownership structure[1] for the firm. In addition to tying together elements of the theory of each of these three areas, our analysis casts new light on and has implications for a variety of issues in the professional and popular literature such as the definition of the firm, the "separation of ownership and control", the "social responsibility" of business, the definition of a "corporate objective function", the determination of an optimal capital structure, the specification of the content of credit agreements, the theory of organizations, and the supply side of the completeness of markets problem.

Our theory helps explain the following:

1 why an entrepreneur or manager in a firm which has a mixed financial structure (containing both debt and outside equity claims) will choose a set of activities for the firm such that the total value of the firm is less than it would be if he were the sole owner and why this result is independent of whether the firm operates in monopolistic or competitive product or factor markets;

2 why his failure to maximize the value of the firm is perfectly consistent with efficiency;

3 why the sale of common stock is a viable source of capital even though managers do not literally maximize the value of the firm;

4 why debt was relied upon as a source of capital before debt financing offered any tax advantage relative to equity;

5 why preferred stock would be issued;

6 why accounting reports would be provided voluntarily to creditors and stockholders, and why independent auditors would be engaged by management to testify to the accuracy and correctness of such reports;

7 why lenders often place restrictions on the activities of firms to whom they lend, and why firms would themselves be led to suggest the imposition of such restrictions;

8 why some industries are characterized by owner-operated firms whose sole outside source of capital is borrowing;

9 why highly regulated industries such as public utilities or banks will have higher debt equity ratios for equivalent levels of risk than the average non-regulated firm;

10 why security analysis can be socially productive even if it does not increase portfolio returns to investors.

Theory of the firm: an empty box?

While the literature of economics is replete with references to the "theory of the firm", the material generally subsumed under that heading is not a theory of the firm but actually a theory of markets in which firms are important actors. The firm is a "black box" operated so as to meet the relevant marginal conditions with respect to inputs and outputs, thereby maximizing profits, or more accurately, present value. Except for a few recent and tentative steps, however, we have no theory which explains how the conflicting objectives of the individual participants are brought into equilibrium so as to yield this result. The limitations of this black box view of the firm have been cited by Adam Smith and Alfred Marshall, among others. More recently, popular and professional debates over the "social responsibility" of corporations, the separation of ownership and control, and the rash of reviews of the literature on the "theory of the firm" have evidenced continuing concern with these issues.[2]

A number of major attempts have been made during recent years to construct a theory of the firm by substituting other models for profit or value maximization; each attempt motivated by a conviction that the latter is inadequate to explain managerial behavior in large corporations.[3] Some of these reformulation attempts have rejected the fundamental principle of maximizing behavior as well as rejecting the more specific profit maximizing model. We retain the notion of maximizing behavior on the part of all individuals in the analysis to follow.[4]

Property rights

An independent stream of research with important implications for the theory of the firm has been stimulated by the pioneering work of Coase, and extended by Alchian, Demsetz and others.[5] A comprehensive survey of this literature is given by Furubotn and Pejovich (1972). While the focus of this research has been "property rights",[6] the subject matter encompassed is far broader than that term suggests. What is important for the problems addressed here is that specification of individual rights determines how costs and rewards will be allocated among the participants in any organization.

Since the specification of rights is generally effected through contracting (implicit as well as explicit), individual behavior in organizations, including the behavior of managers, will depend upon the nature of these contracts. We focus in this chapter on the behavioral implications of the property rights specified in the contracts between the owners and managers of the firm.

Agency costs

Many problems associated with the inadequacy of the current theory of the firm can also be viewed as special cases of the theory of agency relationships in which there is a growing literature.[7] This literature has developed independently of the property rights literature even though the problems with which it is concerned are similar; the approaches are in fact highly complementary to each other.

We define an agency relationship as a contract under which one or more persons (the principal(s)) engage another person (the agent) to perform some service on their behalf which involves delegating some decision-making authority to the agent. If both parties to the relationship are utility maximizers there is good reason to believe that the agent will not always act in the best interests of the principal. The *principal* can limit divergences from his interest by establishing appropriate incentives for the agent and by incurring monitoring costs designed to limit the aberrant activities of the agent. In addition in some situations it will pay the *agent* to expend resources (bonding costs) to guarantee that he will not take certain actions which would harm the principal or to ensure that the principal will be compensated if he does take such actions. However, it is generally impossible for the principal or the agent at zero cost to ensure that the agent will make optimal decisions from the principal's viewpoint. In most agency relationships the principal and the agent will incur positive monitoring and bonding costs (non-pecuniary as well as pecuniary), and in addition there will be some divergence between the agent's decisions[8] and those decisions which would maximize the welfare of the principal. The dollar equivalent of the reduction in welfare experienced by the principal due to this divergence is also a cost of the agency relationship, and we refer to this latter cost as the "residual loss".

We define *agency costs* as the sum of:

1 the monitoring expenditures by the principal[9]
2 the bonding expenditures by the agent
3 the residual loss.

Note also that agency costs arise in any situation involving cooperative effort (such as the co-authoring of this chapter) by two or more people even though there is no clear cut principal–agent relationship. Viewed in this light, it is clear that our definition of agency costs and their importance to the theory of the firm bears a close relationship to the problem of shirking and monitoring of team production which Alchian and Demsetz (1972) raise in their chapter on the theory of the firm.

Since the relationship between the stockholders and manager of a corporation fit the definition of a pure agency relationship, it should be no surprise to discover that the issues associated with the "separation of ownership and control" in the modern, diffuse ownership corporation are intimately associated with the general problem of agency. We show below that an explanation of why and how the agency costs generated by the corporate form leads to a theory of the ownership (or capital) structure of the firm.

Before moving on, however, it is worthwhile to point out the generality of the agency problem. The problem of inducing an "agent" to behave as if he were maximizing the "principal's" welfare is quite general. It exists in all organizations and in all cooperative efforts – at every level of management in firms,[10] in universities, in mutual companies, in cooperatives, in governmental authorities and bureaus, in unions, and in relationships normally classified as agency relationships such as those in the performing arts and the market for real estate. The development of theories to explain the form which agency costs take in each of these situations (where the contractual relations differ significantly), and how and why they are born, will lead to a rich theory of organizations which is now lacking in economics and the social sciences generally. We confine our attention in this chapter to only a small part of this general problem – the analysis of agency costs generated by the contractual arrangements between the owners and top management of the corporation.

Our approach to the agency problem here differs fundamentally from most of the existing literature.

That literature focuses almost exclusively on the normative aspects of the agency relationship; that is, how to structure the contractual relation (including compensation incentives) between the principal and agent to provide appropriate incentives for the agent to make choices which will maximize the principal's welfare given that uncertainty and imperfect monitoring exist. We focus almost entirely on the positive aspects of the theory. That is, we assume individuals solve these normative problems and given that only stocks and bonds can be issued as claims, we investigate the incentives faced by each of the parties and the elements entering into the determination of the equilibrium contractual form characterizing the relationship between the manager (i.e. agent) of the firm and the outside equity and debt holders (i.e. principals).

Some general comments on the definition of the firm

Ronald Coase (1937) in his seminal paper on "The Nature of the Firm" pointed out that economics had no positive theory to determine the bounds of the firm. He characterized the bounds of the firm as the range of exchanges over which the market system was suppressed, and resource allocation was accomplished instead by authority and direction. He focused on the cost of using markets to effect contracts and exchanges and argued that activities would be included within the firm whenever the costs of using markets were greater than the costs of using direct authority. Alchian and Demsetz (1972) object to the notion that activities within the firm are governed by authority, and correctly emphasize the role of contracts as a vehicle for voluntary exchange. They emphasize the role of monitoring in situations in which there is joint input or team production.[11] We sympathize with the importance they attach to monitoring, but we believe the emphasis which Alchian–Demsetz place on joint input production is too narrow and therefore misleading. Contractual relations are the essence of the firm, not only with employees but with suppliers, customers, creditors, etc. The problem of agency costs and monitoring exists for all of these contracts, independent of whether there is joint production in their sense; that is, joint production can explain only a small fraction of the behavior of individuals associated with a firm. A detailed examination of these issues is left to another discourse.

It is important to recognize that most organizations are simply *legal fictions*[12] *which serve as a nexus for a set of contracting relationships among individuals.* This includes firms, non-profit institutions such as universities, hospitals and foundations, mutual organizations such as mutual savings banks and insurance companies and co-operatives, some private clubs, and even governmental bodies such as cities, states and the Federal government, government enterprises such as TVA, the Post Office, transit systems, etc.

The private corporation or firm is simply one form of *legal fiction which serves as a nexus for contracting relationships and which is also characterized by the existence of divisible residual claims on the assets and cash flows of the organization which can generally be sold without permission of the other contracting individuals.* While this definition of the firm has little substantive content, emphasizing the essential contractual nature of firms and other organizations it focuses attention on a crucial set of questions – why particular sets of contractual relations arise for various types of organizations, what the consequences of these contractual relations are, and how they are affected by changes exogenous to the organization. Viewed this way, it makes little or no sense to try to distinguish those things which are "inside" the firm (or any other organization) from those things that are "outside" of it. There is in a very real sense only a multitude of complex relationships (i.e. contracts) between the legal fiction (the firm) and the owners of labor, material and capital inputs and the consumers of output.[13]

Viewing the firm as the nexus of a set of contracting relationships among individuals also serves to make it clear that the personalization of the firm implied by asking questions such as "what should be the objective function of the firm", or "does the firm have a social responsibility" is seriously misleading. *The firm is not an individual.* It is a legal fiction which serves as a focus for a complex process in which the conflicting objectives of individuals (some of whom may "represent" other organizations) are brought into equilibrium within a framework of contractual relations. In this sense the "behavior" of the firm is like the behavior of a market; that is, the outcome of a complex equilibrium process. We seldom fall into the trap of characterizing the wheat or stock market as an individual, but we often make this error by thinking about organizations as if they were persons with motivations and intentions. . . .[14,15]

ACKNOWLEDGMENTS

An earlier version of this chapter was presented at the Conference on Analysis and Ideology, Interlaken, Switzerland, June 1974, sponsored by the Center for Research in Government Policy and Business at the University of Rochester, Graduate School of Management. We are indebted to F. Black, E. Fama, R. Ibbotson, W. Klein, M. Rozeff, R. Weil, O. Williamson, an anonymous referee, and to our colleagues and members of the Finance Workshop at the University of Rochester for their comments and criticisms, in particular G. Benston, M. Canes, D. Henderson, K. Leffler, J. Long, C. Smith, R. Thompson, R. Watts, and J. Zimmerman.

NOTES

1 We do not use the term "capital structure" because that term usually denotes the relative quantities of bonds, equity, warrants, trade credit, etc., which represent the liabilities of a firm. Our theory implies there is another important dimension to this problem – namely the relative amounts of ownership claims held by insiders (management) and outsiders (investors with no direct role in the management of the firm).

2 Reviews of this literature are given by Peterson (1965), Alchian (1965, 1968), Machlup (1967), Shubik (1970), Cyert and Hedrick (1972), Branch (1973), Preston (1975).

3 See Williamson (1964, 1970, 1975), Marris (1964), Baumol (1959), Penrose (1958), and Cyert and March (1963). Thorough reviews of these and other contributions are given by Machlup (1961) and Alchian (1965).

Simon (1955) developed a model of human choice incorporating information (search) and computational costs which also has important implications for the behavior of managers. Unfortunately, Simon's work has often been misinterpreted as a denial of maximizing behavior, and misused, especially in the marketing and behavioral science literature. His later use of the term "satisficing" [Simon (1959)] has undoubtedly contributed to this confusion because it suggests rejection of maximizing behavior rather than maximization subject to costs of information and of decision-making.

4 See Meckling (1976) for a discussion of the fundamental importance of the assumption of resourceful, evaluative, maximizing behavior on the part of individuals in the development of theory. Klein (1976) takes an approach similar to the one we embark on in this chapter in his review of the theory of the firm and the law.

5 See Coase (1937, 1959, 1960), Alchian (1965, 1968), Alchian and Kessel (1962), Demsetz (1967), Alchian and Demsetz (1972), Monsen and Downs (1965), Silver and Auster (1969), and McManus (1975).

6 Property rights are of course human rights, that is, rights which are possessed by human beings. The introduction of the wholly false distinction between property rights and human rights in many policy discussions is surely one of the all time great semantic flimflams.

7 Cf. Berhold (1971), Ross (1973, 1974a), Wilson (1968, 1969), and Heckerman (1975).

8 Given the optimal monitoring and bonding activities by the principal and agent.

9 As it is used in this chapter the term monitoring includes more than just measuring or observing the behavior of the agent. It includes efforts on the part of the principal to "control" the behavior of the agent through budget restrictions, compensation policies, operating rules etc.

10 As we show, the existence of positive monitoring and bonding costs will result in the manager of a corporation possessing control over some resources which he can allocate (within certain constraints) to satisfy his own preferences. However, to the extent that he must obtain the cooperation of others in order to carry out his tasks (such as divisional vice presidents) and to the extent that he cannot control their behavior perfectly and costlessly they will be able to appropriate some of these resources for their own ends. In short, there are agency costs generated at every level of the organization. Unfortunately, the analysis of these more general organizational issues is even more difficult than that of the "ownership and control" issue because the nature of the contractual obligations and rights of the parties are much more varied and generally not as well specified in explicit contractual arrangements. Nevertheless, they exist and we believe that extensions of our analysis in these directions show promise of producing insights into a viable theory of organization.

11 They define the classical capitalist firm as a contractual organization of inputs in which there is "(a) joint input production, (b) several input owners, (c) one party who is common to all the contracts of the joint inputs, (d) who has rights to renegotiate any input's contract independently of contracts with other input owners, (e) who holds the residual claim, and (f) who has the right to sell his contractual residual status."

12 By legal fiction we mean the artificial construct under the law which allows certain organizations to be treated as individuals.

13 For example, we ordinarily think of a product as leaving the firm at the time it is sold, but implicitly or explicitly such sales generally carry with them continuing contracts between the firm and the buyer. If the product does not perform as expected the buyer often can and does have a right to satisfaction. Explicit evidence that such implicit

contracts do exist is the practice we occasionally observe of specific provision that "all sales are final."

14 This view of the firm points up the important role which the legal system and the law play in social organizations, especially, the organization of economic activity. Statutory laws sets bounds on the kinds of contracts into which individuals and organizations may enter without risking criminal prosecution. The police powers of the state are available and used to enforce performance of contracts or to enforce the collection of damages for non-performance. The courts adjudicate conflicts between contracting parties and establish precedents which form the body of common law. All of these government activities affect both the kinds of contracts executed and the extent to which contracting is relied upon. This in turn determines the usefulness, productivity, profitability and viability of various forms of organization. Moreover, new laws as well as court decisions often can and do change the rights of contracting parties ex post, and they can and do serve as a vehicle for redistribution of wealth. An analysis of some of the implications of these facts is contained in Jensen and Meckling (1976) and we shall not pursue them here.

15 This reading is pp. 305–12 of the original Jensen and Meckling (1976: 305–60).

REFERENCES

Alchian, A.A., 1965, The basis of some recent advances in the theory of management of the firm, *Journal of Industrial Economics*, November, 30–44.

Alchian, A.A., 1968, Corporate management and property rights, in: *Economic policy and the regulation of securities* (Washington, DC: American Enterprise Institute).

Alchian, A.A. and Demsetz, H., 1972, Production, information costs, and economic organization, *American Economic Review* LXII, 5, 777–95.

Alchian, A.A. and Kessel, R.A., 1962, Competition, monopoly and the pursuit of pecuniary gain, in: *Aspects of labor economics* (Princeton, NJ: National Bureau of Economic Research).

Baumol, W.J., 1959, *Business behavior, value and growth* (New York: Macmillan).

Becker, G.S. and Stigler, G.J., 1972, Law enforcement, corruption and compensation of enforcers, unpublished paper presented at the Conference on Capitalism and Freedom, October.

Benston, G., 1977, The impact of maturity regulation on high interest rate lenders and borrowers. *Journal of Financial Economics* 4, no. 1.

Berhold, M., 1971, A theory of linear profit sharing incentives, *Quarterly Journal of Economics* LXXXV, August, 460–82.

Branch, B., 1973, Corporate objectives and market performance, *Financial Management*, Summer, 24–29.

Coase, R.H., 1937, The nature of the firm, *Economica*. New Series, IV, 386–405. Reprinted in: *Readings in price theory* (Irwin, Homewood, IL) 331–51.

Coase, R.H., 1959, The Federal Communications Commission, *Journal of Law and Economics* II, October, 1–40.

Coase, R.H., 1960, The problem of social cost, *Journal of Law and Economics* III, October, 1–44.

Coase, R.H., 1964, Discussion. *American Economic Review* LIV, no. 3, 194–97.

Cyert, R.M. and Hedrick, C.L., 1972, Theory of the firm: Past, present and future; An interpretation. *Journal of Economic Literature* X, June, 398–412.

Cyert, R.M. and March, J.G., 1963, *A behavioral theory of the firm* (Englewood Cliffs, NJ: Prentice-Hall).

Demsetz, H., 1967, Toward a theory of property rights, *American Economic Review* LVII, May, 347–59.

Furubotn, E.G. and Pejovich, S., 1972, Property rights and economic theory: A survey of recent literature, *Journal of Economic Literature* X, December, 1137–62.

Jensen, M.C. and Meckling, W.H., 1976, Theory of the firm: managerial behavior, agency costs and ownership structure, *Journal of Financial Economics*, Elsevier.

Klein, W.A., 1976, Legal and economic perspectives on the firm, unpublished manuscript (Los Angeles, CA: University of California).

Machlup, F., 1967, Theories of the firm: Marginalist, behavioral, managerial, *American Economic Review*, March, 1–33.

Marris, R., 1964, *The economic theory of managerial capitalism* (Glencoe, IL: Free Press of Glencoe).

McManus, J.C., 1975, The costs of alternative economic organizations, *Canadian Journal of Economics* VIII, August, 334–50.

Meckling, W.H., 1976, Values and the choice of the model of the individual in the social sciences, *Schweizerische Zeitschrift für Volkswirtschaft und Statistik*, December.

Monsen, R.J. and Downs, A., 1965, A theory of large managerial firms, *Journal of Political Economy*, June, 221–36.

Penrose, E., 1958, The theory of the growth of the firm (New York: Wiley).

Peterson, S., 1965, Corporate control and capitalism, The *Quarterly Journal of Economics* LXXIX, no. 1, 1–24.

Preston, L.E., 1975, Corporation and society: The search for a paradigm, *Journal of Economic Literature* XIII, June, 434–53.

Ross, S.A., 1973, The economic theory of agency: The principals problems, *American Economic Review* LXII, May, 134–39.

Ross, S.A., 1974a, The economic theory of agency and the principle of similarity, in: M.D. Batch *et al.*, eds, *Essays on economic behavior under uncertainty* (North-Holland, Amsterdam).

Shubik, M., 1970, A curmudgeon's guide to microeconomics, *Journal of Economic Literature* VIII, June, 405–34.

Silver, M. and Auster, R., 1969, Entrepreneurship, profit and limits on firm size, *Journal of Business* 42, July, 277–81.

Simon, H.A., 1955, A behavioral model of rational choice, *Quarterly Journal of Economics* 69, 99–118.

Williamson, O.E., 1964, *The economics of discretionary behavior: Managerial objectives in a theory of the firm* (Englewood Cliffs, NJ: Prentice-Hall).

Williamson, O.E., 1970, *Corporate control and business behavior* (Englewood Cliffs, NJ: Prentice-Hall).

Williamson, O.E., 1975, *Markets and hierarchies: Analysis and antitrust implications* (New York: The Free Press).

Wilson, R., 1968, On the theory of syndicates, *Econometrica* 36, January, 119–132.

Wilson, R., 11969, La decision: Agregation et dynamique des orders de preference, Extrait Paris: Editions du Centre National de la Recherche Scientifique, 288–307.

"Separation of Ownership and Control"

from Journal of Law and Economics (1983)

Eugene F. Fama and Michael C. Jensen

INTRODUCTION

Absent fiat, the form of organization that survives in an activity is the one that delivers the product demanded by customers at the lowest price while covering costs.[1] Our goal is to explain the survival of organizations characterized by separation of "ownership" and "control" – a problem that has bothered students of corporations from Adam Smith to Berle and Means and Jensen and Meckling.[2] In more precise language, we are concerned with the survival of organizations in which important decision agents do not bear a substantial share of the wealth effects of their decisions.

We argue that the separation of decision and risk-bearing functions observed in large corporations is common to other organizations such as large professional partnerships, financial mutuals, and nonprofits. We contend that separation of decision and risk-bearing functions survives in these organizations in part because of the benefits of specialization of management and risk-bearing but also because of an effective common approach to controlling the agency problems caused by separation of decision and risk-bearing functions. In particular, our hypothesis is that the contract structures of all of these organizations separate the ratification and monitoring of decisions from initiation and implementation of the decisions.

RESIDUAL CLAIMS AND DECISION PROCESSES

An organization is the nexus of contracts, written and unwritten, among owners of factors of production and customers.[3] These contracts or internal "rules of the game" specify the rights of each agent in the organization, performance criteria on which agents are evaluated, and the payoff functions they face. The contract structure combines with available production technologies and external legal constraints to determine the cost function for delivering an output with a particular form of organization.[4] The form of organization that delivers the output demanded by customers at the lowest price, while covering costs, survives.

The central contracts in any organization specify (1) the nature of residual claims and (2) the allocation of the steps of the decision process among agents. These contracts distinguish organizations from one another and explain why specific organizational forms survive. We first discuss the general characteristics of residual claims and decision processes. We then present the major hypotheses about the relations between efficient allocations of residual claims and decision functions. The analysis focuses on two broad types of organizations – those in which risk-bearing and decision functions are separated and those in which they are combined in the same agents. We analyze only private organizations that depend on voluntary contracting and exchange.

Residual claims

The contract structures of most organizational forms limit the risks undertaken by most agents by specifying either fixed promised payoffs or incentive payoffs tied to specific measures of performance. The residual risk – the risk of the difference between stochastic inflows of resources and promised payments to agents – is borne by those who contract for the rights to net cash flows. We call these agents the residual claimants or residual risk bearers. Moreover, the contracts of most agents contain the implicit or explicit provision that, in exchange for the specified payoff, the agent agrees that the resources he provides can be used to satisfy the interests of residual claimants.

Having most uncertainty borne by one group of agents, residual claimants, has survival value because it reduces the costs incurred to monitor contracts with other groups of agents and to adjust contracts for the changing risks borne by other agents. Contracts that direct decisions toward the interests of residual claimants also add to the survival value of organizations. Producing outputs at lower cost is in the interests of residual claimants because it increases net cash flows, but lower costs also contribute to survival by allowing products to be delivered at lower prices.

The residual claims of different organizational forms contain different restrictions. For example, the least restricted residual claims in common use are the common stocks of large corporations. Stockholders are not required to have any other role in the organization; their residual claims are alienable without restriction; and, because of these provisions, the residual claims allow unrestricted risk sharing among stockholders. We call these organizations *open* corporations to distinguish them from *closed* corporations that are generally smaller and have residual claims that are largely restricted to internal decision agents.[5]

The decision process

By focusing on entrepreneurial firms in which all decision rights are concentrated in the entrepreneur, economists tend to ignore analysis of the steps of the decision process. However, the way organizations allocate the steps of the decision process across agents is important in explaining the survival of organizations.

In broad terms, the decision process has four steps:

1 initiation – generation of proposals for resource utilization and structuring of contracts;
2 ratification – choice of the decision initiatives to be implemented;
3 implementation – execution of ratified decisions; and
4 monitoring – measurement of the performance of decision agents and implementation of rewards.

Because the initiation and implementation of decisions typically are allocated to the same agents, it

is convenient to combine these two functions under the term *decision management*. Likewise, the term *decision control* includes the ratification and monitoring of decisions. Decision management and decision control are the components of the organization's decision process or decision system.

FUNDAMENTAL RELATIONS BETWEEN RISK-BEARING AND DECISION PROCESSES

We first state and then elaborate the central complementary hypotheses about the relations between the risk-bearing and decision processes of organizations.

1 Separation of residual risk-bearing from decision management leads to decision systems that separate decision management from decision control.
2 Combination of decision management and decision control in a few agents leads to residual claims that are largely restricted to these agents.

The problem

Agency problems arise because contracts are not costlessly written and enforced. Agency costs include the costs of structuring, monitoring, and bonding a set of contracts among agents with conflicting interests. Agency costs also include the value of output lost because the costs of full enforcement of contracts exceed the benefits.[6]

Control of agency problems in the decision process is important when the decision managers who initiate and implement important decisions are not the major residual claimants and therefore do not bear a major share of the wealth effects of their decisions. Without effective control procedures, such decision managers are more likely to take actions that deviate from the interests of residual claimants. An effective system for decision control implies, almost by definition, that the control (ratification and monitoring) of decisions is to some extent separate from the management (initiation and implementation) of decisions. Individual decision agents can be involved in the management of some decisions and the control of others, but separation means that an individual agent does not exercise exclusive management and control rights over the same decisions.

The interesting problem is to determine when separation of decision management, decision control, and residual risk-bearing is more efficient than combining these three functions in the same agents. We first analyze the factors that make combination of decision management, decision control, and residual risk-bearing efficient. We then analyze the factors that make separation of these three functions efficient.

Combination of decision management, decision control, and residual risk-bearing

Suppose the balance of cost conditions, including both technology and the control of agency problems, implies that in a particular activity the optimal organization is noncomplex. For our purposes, *noncomplex* means that specific information relevant to decisions is concentrated in one or a few agents. (Specific information is detailed information that is costly to transfer among agents.)[7] Most small organizations tend to be noncomplex, and most large organizations tend to be complex, but the correspondence is not perfect. For example, research oriented universities, though often small in terms of assets or faculty size, are nevertheless complex in the sense that specific knowledge, which is costly to transfer, is diffused among both faculty and administrators. On the other hand, mutual funds are often large in terms of assets but noncomplex in the sense that information relevant to decisions is concentrated in one or a few agents. We take it as given that optimal organizations in some activities are noncomplex. Our more limited goal is to explain the implications of noncomplexity for control of agency problems in the decision process.

If we ignore agency problems between decision managers and residual claimants, the theory of optimal risk-bearing tells us that residual claims that allow unrestricted risk sharing have advantages in small as well as in large organizations.[8] However, in a small noncomplex organization, specific knowledge important for decision management and control is concentrated in one or a few agents. As a consequence, it is efficient to allocate decision control as well as decision management to these agents. Without separation of decision management from decision control, residual claimants have little protection against opportunistic actions of decision agents, and this lowers the value of unrestricted residual claims.

A feasible solution to the agency problem that arises when the same agents manage and control important decisions is to restrict residual claims to the important decision agents. In effect, restriction of residual claims to decision agents substitutes for costly control devices to limit the discretion of decision agents. The common stocks of closed corporations are this type of restricted residual claim, as are the residual claims in proprietorships and partnerships. The residual claims of these organizations (especially closed corporations) are also held by other agents whose special relations with decision agents allow agency problems to be controlled without separation of the management and control of decisions. For example, family members have many dimensions of exchange with one another over a long horizon and therefore have advantages in monitoring and disciplining related decision agents. Business associates whose goodwill and advice are important to the organization are also potential candidates for holding minority residual claims of organizations that do not separate the management and control of decisions.[9]

Restricting residual claims to decision makers controls agency problems between residual claimants and decision agents, but it sacrifices the benefits of unrestricted risk sharing and specialization of decision functions. The decision process suffers efficiency losses because decision agents must be chosen on the basis of wealth and willingness to bear risk as well as for decision skills. The residual claimants forgo optimal risk reduction through portfolio diversification so that residual claims and decision-making can be combined in a small number of agents. Forgone diversification lowers the value of the residual claims and raises the cost of risk-bearing services.

Moreover, when residual claims are restricted to decision agents, it is generally rational for the residual claimant–decision makers to assign lower values to uncertain cash flows than residual claimants would in organizations where residual claims are unrestricted and risk-bearing can be freely diversified across organizations. As a consequence, restricting residual claims to agents in the decision process leads to decisions (e.g. less investment in risky projects that lower the costs of outputs) that tend to penalize the organization in the competition for survival.[10]

However, because contracts are not costlessly written and enforced, all decision systems and systems for allocating residual claims involve costs. Organizational survival involves a balance of the costs of alternative decision systems and systems for allocating residual risk against the benefits. Small noncomplex organizations do not have demands for a wide range of specialized decision agents; on the contrary concentration of specific information relevant to decisions implies that there are efficiency gains when the rights to manage and control decisions are combined in one or a few agents. Moreover, the risk sharing benefits forgone when residual claims are restricted to one or a few decision agents are less serious in a small noncomplex organization than in a large organization, because the total risk of net cash flows to be shared is generally smaller in small organizations. In addition, small organizations do not often have large demands for wealth from residual claimants to bond the payoffs promised to other agents and to purchase risky assets. As a consequence, small noncomplex organizations can efficiently control the agency problems caused by the combination of decision management and control in one or a few agents by restricting residual claims to these agents. Such a combining of decision and risk-bearing functions is efficient in small noncomplex organizations because the benefits of unrestricted risk sharing and specialization of decision functions are less than the costs that would be incurred to control the resulting agency problems.

The proprietorships, partnerships, and closed corporations observed in small scale production and service activities are the best examples of classical entrepreneurial firms in which the major decision makers are also the major residual risk bearers. These organizations are evidence in favor of the hypothesis that combination of decision management and decision control in one or a few agents leads to residual claims that are largely restricted to these agents.

We analyze next the forces that make separation of decision management, decision control, and residual risk-bearing efficient – in effect, the forces that cause the classical entrepreneurial firm to be dominated by organizational forms in which there are no decision makers in the classical entrepreneurial sense.

Separation of decision management, decision control, and residual risk-bearing

Our concern in this section is with the organizational forms characterized by separation of decision management from residual risk-bearing – what the literature on open corporations calls, somewhat imprecisely, separation of ownership and control. Our hypothesis is that all such organizations, including large open corporations, large professional partnerships, financial mutuals, and nonprofits, control the agency problems that result from separation of decision management from residual risk-bearing by separating the management (initiation and implementation) and control (ratification and monitoring) of decisions. Documentation of this hypothesis takes up much of the rest of the chapter.

Specific knowledge and diffusion of decision functions

Most organizations characterized by separation of decision management from residual risk-bearing are *complex* in the sense that specific knowledge relevant to different decisions – knowledge which is costly to transfer across agents – is diffused among agents at all levels of the organization. Again, we take it as given that the optimal organizations in some activities are complex. Our theory attempts to explain the implications of complexity for the nature of efficient decision processes and for control of agency problems in the decision process.

Since specific knowledge in complex organizations is diffused among agents, diffusion of decision management can reduce costs by delegating the initiation and implementation of decisions to the agents with valuable relevant knowledge. The agency problems of diffuse decision management can then be reduced by separating the management (initiation and implementation) and control (ratification and monitoring) of decisions.

In the unusual cases where residual claims are not held by important decision managers but are nevertheless concentrated in one or a few residual claimants, control of decision managers can in principle be direct and simple, with the residual claimants ratifying and monitoring important decisions and setting rewards.[11] Such organizations conform to our hypothesis, because top-level decision control is separated from top-level decision managers and exercised directly by residual claimants.

However, in complex organizations valuable specific knowledge relevant to decision control is diffused among many internal agents. This generally means that efficient decision control, like efficient decision management, involves delegation and diffusion of decision control as well as separation of decision management and control at different levels of the organization. We expect to observe such delegation, diffusion, and separation of decision management and control below the top level of complex organizations, even in those unusual complex organizations where residual claims are held primarily by top-level decision agents.

Diffuse residual claims and delegation of decision control

In the more common complex organizations, residual claims are diffused among many agents. Having many residual claimants has advantages in large complex organizations because the total risk of net cash flows to be shared is generally large and there are large demands for wealth from residual claimants to bond the payoffs promised to a wide range of agents and to purchase risky assets. When there are many residual claimants, it is costly for all of them to be involved in decision control and it is efficient for them to delegate decision control. For example, some delegation of decision control is observed even in the large professional partnerships in public accounting and law, where the residual claimants are expert internal decision agents. When there are many partners it is inefficient for each to participate in ratification and monitoring of all decisions.

Nearly complete separation and specialization of decision control and residual risk-bearing is common in large open corporations and financial mutuals where most of the diffuse residual claimants are not qualified for roles in the decision process and thus delegate their decision control rights to other agents. When residual claimants have no role in decision control, we expect to observe separation of the management and control of important decisions at all levels of the organization.

Separation and diffusion of decision management and decision control – in effect, the absence of a classical entrepreneurial decision maker – limit the power of individual decision agents to expropriate the interests of residual claimants. The checks and balances of such decision systems have costs, but they also have important benefits. Diffusion and separation of decision management and control have benefits because they allow valuable knowledge to be used at the points in the decision process where it is most relevant and they help control the agency problems of diffuse residual claims. In complex organizations, the benefits of diffuse residual claims and the benefits of separation of decision functions from residual risk-bearing are generally greater than the agency costs they generate, including the costs of mechanisms to separate the management and control of decisions.

Decision control in nonprofits and financial mutuals

Most organizations characterized by separation of decision management from residual risk-bearing are complex. However, separation of the management and control of decision contributes to the survival of any organization where the important decision managers do not bear a substantial share of the wealth effects of their decisions – that is, any organization where there are serious agency problems in the decision process. We argue below that separation of decision management and residual risk-bearing is a characteristic of nonprofit organizations and financial mutuals, large and small, complex and noncomplex. Thus, we expect to observe separation of the management and control of important decisions even in small noncomplex nonprofits and financial mutuals where, ignoring agency problems in the decision process, concentrated and combined decision management and control would be more efficient.

Common general features of decision control systems

Our hypothesis about the decision systems of organizations characterized by separation of decision management and residual risk-bearing gets support from the fact that the major mechanisms for diffusing and separating the management and control of decisions are much the same across different organizations.

Decision hierarchies

A common feature of the diffuse decision management and control systems of complex organizations (e.g. large nonprofit universities as well as large open corporations) is a form of decision hierarchy with higher level agents ratifying and monitoring the decision initiatives of lower level agents and evaluating their performance.[12] Such hierarchical partitioning of the decision process makes it more difficult for decision agents at all levels of the organization to take actions that benefit themselves at the expense of residual claimants. Decision hierarchies are buttressed by organizational rules of the game, for example, accounting and budgeting systems, that monitor and constrast the decision behavior of agents and specify the performance criteria that determine rewards.[13]

Mutual monitoring systems

The formal hierarchies of complex organizations are also buttressed by information from less formal mutual monitoring among agents. When agents interact to produce outputs, they acquire low-cost information about colleagues, information not directly available to higher level agents. Mutual monitoring systems tap this information for use in the control process. Mutual monitoring systems derive their energy from the interests of agents to use the internal agent market of organizations to enhance the value of human capital.[14] Agents choose among organizations on the basis of rewards offered and potential for development of human capital. Agents value the competitive interaction that takes place within an organization's internal agent market because it enhances current marginal products and contributes to human capital development. Moreover, if agents perceive that evaluation of their performance is unbiased (i.e. if they cannot systematically fool their evaluators) then they value the fine tuning of the reward system that results from mutual monitoring information, because it lowers the uncertainty of payoffs from effort and skill. Since the incentive structures and diffuse decision control systems that result from the interplay of formal hierarchies and less formal mutual monitoring systems are also in the interests of residual claimants, their survival value is evident.

Boards of directors

The common apex of the decision control systems of organizations, large and small, in which decision agents do not bear a major share of the wealth effects of their decisions is some form of board of directors. Such boards always have the power to hire, fire, and compensate the top-level decision managers and to ratify and monitor important decisions. Exercise of these top-level decision control rights by a group (the board) helps to ensure separation of decision management and control (i.e. the absence of an entrepreneurial decision maker) even at the top of the organization.[15]

THE SPECTRUM OF ORGANIZATIONS

Introduction

Organizations in which important decision agents do not bear a major share of the wealth effects of their decisions include open corporations, large professional partnerships, financial mutuals, and nonprofits. We are concerned now with analyzing the data each of these organizations provides to test the hypothesis that separation of decision management functions from residual risk-bearing leads to decision systems that separate the management and control of decisions.

To motivate the discussion of specific organizational forms, we also outline a set of more specialized propositions to explain the survival value of the special features of their residual claims. These more specialized hypotheses about the survival of specific organizational forms in specific activities are developed in our paper "Agency Problems and Residual Claims."[16]

Open corporations

Unrestricted common stock residual claims

Most large nonfinancial organizations are open corporations. The common stock residual claims of such organizations are unrestricted in the sense that stockholders are not required to have any other role in the organization, and their residual claims are freely alienable. As a result of the unrestricted nature of the residual claims of open corporations, there is almost complete specialization of decision management and residual risk-bearing. Even managers who own substantial blocks of stock, and thus are residual risk bearers, may elect to sell these shares.

Unrestricted common stock is attractive in complicated risky activities where substantial wealth provided by residual claimants is needed to bond the large aggregate payoffs promised to many other agents. Unrestricted common stock, with its capacity for generating large amounts of wealth from residual claimants on a permanent basis, is also attractive in activities more efficiently carried out with large amounts of risky assets owned within the organization rather than rented. Moreover, since decision skills are not a necessary consequence of wealth or willingness to bear risk, the specialization of decision management and residual risk-bearing allowed by unrestricted common stock enhances the adaptability of a complex organization to changes in the economic environment. The unrestricted risk sharing and diversification allowed by common stock also contributes to survival by lowering the cost of risk-bearing services.

Control of the agency problems of common stock

Separation and specialization of decision management and residual risk-bearing leads to agency problems between decision agents and residual claimants. This is the problem of separation of ownership and control that has long troubled students of corporations. For example, potential exploitation of residual claimants by opportunistic decision agents is reflected in the arguments leading to the establishment of the Securities and Exchange Commission and in the concerns of the modern corporate governance movement. Less well appreciated, however, is the fact that the unrestricted nature of common stock residual claims also allows special market and organizational mechanisms for controlling the agency problems of specialized risk-bearing.

The stock market

The unrestricted alienability of the residual claims of open corporations gives rise to an external monitoring device unique to these organizations – a stock market that specializes in pricing common stocks and transferring them at low cost. Stock prices are visible signals that summarize the implications of internal decisions for current and future net cash flows. This external monitoring exerts pressure to orient a corporation's decision process toward the interests of residual claimants.

The market for takeovers

External monitoring from a takeover market is also unique to the open corporation and is attributable to the unrestricted nature of its residual claims.[17] Because the residual claims are freely alienable and separable from roles in the decision process, attacking managers can circumvent existing managers and the current board to gain control of the decision process, either by a direct offer to purchase stock (a tender offer) or by an appeal for stockholder votes for directors (a proxy fight).

Expert boards

Internal control in the open corporation is delegated by residual claimants to a board of directors. Residual claimants generally retain approval rights (by vote) on such matters as board membership, auditor choice, mergers, and new stock issues. Other management and control functions are delegated by the residual claimants to the board. The board then delegates most decision management functions and many decision

control functions to internal agents, but it retains ultimate control over internal agents – including the rights to ratify and monitor major policy initiatives and to hire, fire, and set the compensation of top level decision managers. Similar delegation of decision management and control functions, at the first step to a board and then from the board to internal decision agents, is common to other organizations, such as financial mutuals, nonprofits, and large professional partnerships, in which important decision agents do not bear a major share of the wealth effects of their decisions.

However, the existence of the stock market and the market for takeovers, both special to open corporations, explains some of the special features of corporate boards, in particular: (1) why inside manager board members are generally more influential than outside members, and (2) why outside board members are often decision agents in other complex organizations.[18]

Since the takeover market provides an external court of last resort for protection of residual claimants, a corporate board can be in the hands of agents who are decision experts. Given that the board is to be composed of experts, it is natural that its most influential members are internal managers since they have valuable specific information about the organization's activities. It is also natural that when the internal decision control system works well, the outside members of the board are nominated by internal managers. Internal managers can use their knowledge of the organization to nominate outside board members with relevant complementary knowledge: for example, outsiders with expertise in capital markets, corporate law, or relevant technology who provide an important support function to the top managers in dealing with specialized decision problems.

However, the board is not an effective device for decision control unless it limits the decision discretion of individual top managers. The board is the top-level court of appeals of the internal agent market,[19] and as such it must be able to use information from the internal mutual monitoring system. To accomplish this and to achieve effective separation of top-level decision management and control, we expect the board of a large open corporation to include several of the organization's top managers. The board uses information from each of the top managers about his decision initiatives and the decision initiatives and performance of other managers. The board also seeks information from lower level managers about the decision initiatives and performance of top managers.[20] This information is used to set the rewards of the top managers, to rank them, and to choose among their decision initiatives. To protect information flows to the board, we expect that top managers, especially those who are members of the board, can effectively be fired only with consent of the board and thus are protected from reprisals from other top managers.

The decision processes of some open corporations seem to be dominated by an individual manager, generally the chief executive officer. In some cases, this signals the absence of separation of decision management and decision control, and, in our theory, the organization suffers in the competition for survival. We expect, however, that the apparent dominance of some top managers is more often due to their ability to work with the decision control systems of their organizations than to their ability to suppress diffuse and separate decision control. In any case, the financial press regularly reports instances where apparently dominant executives are removed by their boards.

Corporate boards generally include outside members, that is, members who are not internal managers, and they often hold a majority of seats.[21] The outside board members act as arbiters in disagreements among internal managers and carry out tasks that involve serious agency problems between internal managers and residual claimants, for example, setting executive compensation or searching for replacements for top managers.

Effective separation of top-level decision management and control means that outside directors have incentives to carry out their tasks and do not collude with managers to expropriate residual claimants. Our hypothesis is that outside directors have incentives to develop reputations as experts in decision control. Most outside directors of open corporations are either managers of other corporations or important decision agents in other complex organizations.[22] The value of their human capital depends primarily on their performance as internal decision managers in other organizations. They use their directorships to signal to internal and external markets for decision agents that (1) they are decision experts, (2) they understand the importance of diffuse and separate decision control, and (3) they can work with such decision control systems. The signals are credible when the direct payments to outside directors are small, but there is substantial devaluation of human capital when internal decision control breaks down and the costly last resort process of an outside takeover is activated.

Professional partnerships

Mutual monitoring, specific knowledge, and restricted residual claims

The residual claims of professional partnerships in activities such as law, public accounting, medicine, and business consulting are restricted to the major professional agents who produce the organization's services. This restriction increases the incentives of agents to monitor each other's actions and to consult with each other to improve the quality of services provided to customers. Such mutual monitoring and consulting are attractive to the professional agents in service activities where responsibility for variation in the quality of services is easily assigned and the value of professional human capital is sensitive to performance. The monitoring and consulting are likely to be effective when professional agents with similar specialized skills agree to share liability for the actions of colleagues.

In both large and small partnerships, individuals or small teams work on cases, audits, and so forth. Because of the importance of specific knowledge about particular clients and circumstances, it is efficient for the teams to make most decisions locally. At this level, however, decision management and decision control are not separate. To control the resulting agency problems, the residual claims in professional partnerships, large and small, are restricted to the professional agents who have the major decision-making roles. This is consistent with our hypothesis that combination of decision management and control functions leads to restriction of residual claims to the agents who both manage and control important decisions.

Large professional partnerships

The partners in large professional partnerships are diffuse residual claimants whose welfare depends on the acts of agents they do not directly control. Thus, these organizations provide a test of our hypothesis that separation of residual risk-bearing and decision management induces decision systems that separate the management and control of important decisions. The major decision control devices of large professional partnerships are similar to those of other organizations with diffuse residual claims. For example, residual claimants in large partnerships delegate to boards the ratification and monitoring of important decisions above the level of individual cases and audits. Moreover, the sharing of liability and residual cash flows among important decision agents (the partners) ensures that large partnerships have strong versions of the mutual monitoring systems that we contend are common to the decision control systems of complex organizations.

The boards of large partnerships have special features that relate to the restriction of the residual claims to important internal agents. The residual claimants are experts in the organization's activities, and they observe directly the effects of actions taken by the board of managing partners. Thus, unlike the stockholders of open corporations, the residual claimants in large partnerships have little demand for outside experts to protect their interests, and their boards are composed entirely of partners.

The board is involved in decisions with respect to the management of the partnership, for example, where new offices should be opened, who should be admitted to the partnership, and who should be dismissed. The board is also involved in renegotiating the shares of the partners. Here, as in other decisions, the boards of large partnerships combine the valuable specific knowledge available at the top level with information from partner–residual claimants. The role of the board is to develop acceptable consensus decisions from this information. Thus, the boards of large professional partnerships are generally called committees of managing partners rather than boards of directors. The idea is that such committees exist to manage agency problems among partners and to study and determine major policy issues in a manner that is less costly than when performed jointly by all partners.

Since the residual claims in a large professional partnership are not alienable, unfriendly outside takeovers are not possible. Inside takeovers by dissident partners are possible, however, because the managing boards of these organizations are elected by the partner–residual claimants.

Financial mutuals

A common form of organization in financial activities is the mutual. An unusual characteristic of mutuals is that the residual claimants are customers, for example, the policyholders of mutual insurance companies, the depositors of mutual savings banks, and the shareholders of mutual funds. Like the diffuse stockholders of large nonfinancial corporations, most of the diffuse depositors, policyholders, and mutual fund

shareholders of financial mutuals do not participate in the internal decision process. Thus, financial mutuals provide another test of our hypothesis that substantial separation of decision management and residual risk-bearing leads to decision systems that separate the management and control of decisions.

The control function of redeemable claims

For the purpose of decision control, the unique characteristic of the residual claims of mutuals is that they are redeemable on demand. The policyholder, depositor, or shareholder can, on demand, turn in his claim at a price determined by a prespecified rule. For example, the shareholder of an open-end mutual fund can redeem his claim for the market value of his share of the fund's assets, while the whole life or endowment insurance policyholder, like the shareholder of a mutual savings bank, can redeem his claim for its specified value plus accumulated dividends.

The decision of the claim holder to withdraw resources is a form of partial takeover or liquidation which deprives management of control over assets. This control right can be exercised independently by each claim holder. It does not require a proxy fight, a tender offer, or any other concerted takeover bid. In contrast, customer decisions in open nonfinancial corporations and the repricing of the corporation's securities in the capital market provide signals about the performance of its decision agents. Without further action, however, either internal or from the market for takeovers, the judgments of customers and of the capital market leave the assets of the open nonfinancial corporation under the control of the managers.

The board of directors

Like other organizations characterized by substantial separation between decision management and residual risk-bearing, the top-level decision control device in financial mutuals is a board of directors. Because of the strong form of diffuse decision control inherent in the redeemable residual claims of financial mutuals, however, their boards are less important in the control process than the boards of open nonfinancial corporations. The reduced role of the board is especially evident in mutual savings banks and mutual funds, which are not complex even though often large in terms of assets. Moreover, the residual claimants of mutuals show little interest in their boards and often do not have the right to vote for board members.[23] Outside board members are generally chosen by internal managers. Unlike open corporations, the boards of financial mutuals do not often impose changes in managers. The role of the board, especially in the less complex mutuals, is largely limited to monitoring agency problems against which redemption of residual claims offers little protection, for example, fraud or outright theft of assets by internal agents.

Nonprofit organizations

When an organization's activities are financed in part through donations, part of net cash flows is from resources provided by donors. Contracts that define the share of residual claimants in net cash flows are unlikely to assure donors that their resources are protected from expropriation by residual claimants. In a nonprofit organization, however, there are no agents with alienable rights in residual net cash flows and thus there are no residual claims. We argue in "Agency Problems and Residual Claims" that the absence of such residual claims in nonprofits avoids the donor–residual claimant agency problem and explains the dominance of nonprofits in donor-financed activities.[24]

The absence of residual claims in nonprofits avoids agency problems between donors and residual claimants, but the incentives of other internal agents to expropriate donations remain. These agency problems between donors and decision agents in nonprofits are similar to those in other organizations where important decision managers do not bear a major share of the wealth effects of their decisions. Our hypothesis predicts that, like other organizations characterized by separation of decision management from residual risk-bearing, nonprofits have decision systems that separate the management (initiation and implementation) and control (ratification and monitoring) of decisions. Such decision systems survive in donor nonprofits because of the assurances they provide that donations are used effectively and are not easily expropriated.

Nonprofit boards

In small nonprofits delegation of decision management to one or a few agents is generally efficient. For example, in nonprofit cultural performing groups, an artistic director usually chooses performers, does the primary monitoring of their outputs, and initiates and implements major decisions. Nevertheless, the important decision agents in these organizations are chosen, monitored, and evaluated by boards of directors. Boards with similar decision control rights are common to other small nonprofits characterized by concentrated decision management, such as charities, private museums, small private hospitals, and local Protestant and Jewish congregations. Boards are also observed at the top of the decision control systems of complex nonprofits, such as private universities, in which both decision management and decision control are diffuse.

Although their functions are similar to those of other organizations, nonprofit boards have special features that are due to the absence of alienable residual claims. For example, because of the discipline from the outside takeover market, boards of open corporations can include internal decision agents, and outside board members can be chosen for expertise rather than because they are important residual claimants. In contrast, because a nonprofit lacks alienable residual claims, the decision agents are immune from ouster (via takeover) by outside agents. Without the takeover threat or the discipline imposed by residual claimants with the right to remove members of the board, nonprofit boards composed of internal agents and outside experts chosen by internal agents would provide little assurance against collusion and expropriation of donations. Thus, nonprofit boards generally include few, if any, internal agents as voting members, and nonprofit boards are often self-perpetuating, that is, new members are approved by existing members. Moreover, nonprofit board members are generally substantial donors who serve without pay. Willingness to provide continuing personal donations of wealth or time is generally an implicit condition for membership on nonprofit boards. Acceptance of this condition certifies to other donors that board members are motivated to take their decision control task seriously.

The Roman Catholic church

To our knowledge the only nonprofit organization that is financed with donations but lacks a board of important continuing donors with effective decision control rights is the Roman Catholic church. Parish councils exist in local Catholic churches, but unlike their Protestant and Jewish counterparts, they are only advisory. The clerical hierarchy controls the allocation of resources, and the papal system does not seem to limit the discretion of the Pope, the organization's most important decision agent.

Other aspects of the contracts of the Catholic clergy in part substitute for the control of expropriation of donations that would be provided by more effective donor-customer constraints on decisions. For example, the vows of chastity and obedience incorporated into the contracts of the Catholic clergy help to bond against expropriation of donations by avoiding conflicts between the material interests of a family and the interests of donor-customers. In addition, the training of a Catholic priest is organization-specific. For example, it involves a heavy concentration on (Catholic) theology, whereas the training of Protestant ministers places more emphasis on social service skills. Once certified, the Catholic priest is placed by the hierarchy. He cannot offer his services on a competitive basis. In exchange for developing such organization-specific human capital, the Catholic priest, unlike his Protestant and Jewish counterparts, gets a lifetime contract that promises a real standard of living. The organization-specific nature of the human capital of the Catholic clergy and the terms of the contract under which it is employed act as a bond to donor-customers that the interests of the Catholic clergy are closely bound to the survival of the organization and thus to the interests of donor-customers.

Although Protestantism arose over doctrinal issues, the control structures of Protestant sects – in particular, the evolution of lay councils with power to ratify and monitor resource allocation decisions – can be viewed as a response to breakdowns of the contract structure of Catholicism, that is, expropriation of Catholic donor-customers by the clergy. The evolution of Protestantism is therefore an example of competition among alternative contract structures to resolve an activity's major agency problem – in this case monitoring important agents to limit expropriation of donations.

There is currently pressure to allow Catholic priests to marry, that is, to drop the vow of chastity from their contracts. We predict that if this occurs, organizational survival will require other monitoring and bonding mechanisms, for example, control over allocation of resources by lay councils similar to those observed in Protestant and Jewish congregations.

The private university and decision systems in complex nonprofits

In complex nonprofits we observe mechanisms for diffuse decision control similar to those of other complex organizations. For example, large private universities, like large open corporations, have complicated decision hierarchies and active internal agent markets with mutual monitoring systems that generate information about the performance of agents. Again, however, the decision control structures of complex nonprofits have special features attributable to the absence of alienable residual claims.

For example, a university's trustees are primarily donors rather than experts in the details of education or research. In ratifying and monitoring decision initiatives presented by internal decision agents (presidents, chancellors, provosts, etc.), and in evaluating the agents themselves, boards rely on information from the internal diffuse decision system – for example, reports from faculty senates and appointments committees – and on external peer reviews.

Moreover, the structure of internal diffuse decision control systems is a more formal part of a university's contract structure (its charter or by-laws) than in large for-profit organizations such as open corporations. For example, unlike corporate managers, university deans, department heads, provosts, and presidents are generally appointed for fixed terms. The end of a contract period activates a process of evaluation, with search committees chosen according to formal rules and with rules for passing their recommendations on to the board. A more formal structure of diffuse decision management and control is helpful to trustees who do not have specialized knowledge about a university's activities. It also helps to assure donors that the absence of discipline from an outside takeover market is compensated by a strong system for internal decision control.

SUMMARY

The theory developed in this chapter views an organization as a nexus of contracts (written and unwritten). The theory focuses on the contracts that (1) allocate the steps in an organization's decision process, (2) define residual claims, and (3) set up devices for controlling agency problems in the decision process. We focus on the factors that give survival value to organizational forms that separate what the literature imprecisely calls ownership and control.

The central hypotheses

An organization's decision process consists of decision management (initiation and implementation) and decision control (ratification and monitoring). Our analysis produces two complementary hypotheses about the relations between decision systems and residual claims:

1 Separation of residual risk-bearing from decision management leads to decision systems that separate decision management from decision control.
2 Combination of decision management and decision control in a few agents leads to residual claims that are largely restricted to these agents.

Combination of decision management and control

When it is efficient to combine decision management and control functions in one or a few agents, it is efficient to control agency problems between residual claimants and decision makers by restricting residual claims to the decision makers. This proposition gets clear support from the proprietorships, small partnerships, and closed corporations observed in small-scale production and service activities. These organizations are all characterized by concentrated decision systems and residual claims that are restricted to decision agents.

Separation of residual risk-bearing from decision management

The role of specific knowledge

In contrast, most of the organizations characterized by separation of residual risk-bearing from decision management are complex in the sense that specific information valuable for decisions is diffused among many agents throughout the organization. Thus in a complex organization separation of residual risk-bearing from decision management arises in part because efficient decision systems are diffuse. Benefits from better decisions can be achieved by delegating decision functions to agents at all levels of the organization who have relevant specific knowledge, rather than allocating all decision management and control to the residual claimants. Control of the agency problems of such diffuse decision systems is then achieved by separating the ratification and monitoring of decisions (decision control) from initiation and implementation (decision management). The efficiency of such decision systems is buttressed by incentive structures that reward agents both for initiating and implementing decisions and for ratifying and monitoring the decision management of other agents.

The role of diffuse residual claims

In most complex organizations, residual claims are diffused among many agents. When there are many residual claimants, it is costly for all of them to be involved in decision control. As a consequence there is separation of residual risk-bearing from decision control, and this creates agency problems between residual claimants and decision agents. Separation of decision management and decision control at all levels of the organization helps to control these agency problems by limiting the power of individual agents to expropriate the interests of residual claimants. Thus diffusion and separation of decision management and control have survival value in complex organizations both because they allow valuable specific knowledge to be used at the points in the decision process where it is most relevant and because they help control the agency problems of diffuse residual claims.

Common features of decision control systems

What we call separation of residual risk-bearing from decision management is the separation of ownership and control that has long bothered students of open corporations. We argue that separation of decision and risk-bearing functions is also common to other organizations like large professional partnerships, financial mutuals, and nonprofits. Moreover, our central hypothesis about control of the agency problems caused by separation of residual risk-bearing from decision management gets support from the fact that the major mechanisms for separating decision management and decision control are much the same across organizations.

The common central building blocks of the diffuse decision control systems of complex organizations of all types are formal decision hierarchies in which the decision initiatives of lower level agents are passed on to higher level agents, first for ratification and then for monitoring. Such decision hierarchies are found in large open corporations, large professional partnerships, large financial mutuals, and large nonprofits. Formal decision hierarchies are buttressed by less formal mutual monitoring systems that are a by-product of interaction that takes place to produce outputs and develop human capital.

The common apex of the decision control systems of organizations, large and small, in which decision agents do not bear a major share of the wealth effects of their decisions is a board of directors (trustees, managing partners, etc.) that ratifies and monitors important decisions and chooses, dismisses, and rewards important decision agents. Such multiple-member boards make collusion between top-level decision management and control agents more difficult, and they are the mechanism that allows separation of the management and control of the organization's most important decisions.

ACKNOWLEDGMENTS

This chapter is a revision of parts of our earlier paper, The Survival of Organizations (September 1980). In the course of this work we have profited from the comments of R. Antle, R. Benne, F. Black, F. Easterbrook, A. Farber, W. Gavett, P. Hirsch, R. Hogarth, C. Holderness, R. Holthausen, C. Horne, J. Jeuck, R. Leftwich, S. McCormick, D. Mayers, P. Pashigian, M. Scholes, C. Smith, G. Stigler, R. Watts, T. Whisler, R. Yeaple, J. Zimmerman, and especially A. Alchian, W. Meckling, and C. Plosser. Financial support for Fama's participation is from the National Science Foundation. Jensen is supported by the Managerial Economics Research Center of the University of Rochester.

NOTES

1 Armen A. Alchian, Uncertainty, Evolution and Economic Theory, 58 *J. Pol. Econ.* 211 (1950), is an early proponent of the use of natural selection in economic analysis. For a survey of general issues in the analysis of organization, see Michael C. Jensen, Organization Theory and Methodology, 50 *Accounting Rev.* (1983).

2 Adam Smith, *The Wealth of Nations* (Cannan ed. 1904) (1st ed. London 1776); Adolf A. Berle and Gardiner C. Means, The Modern Corporation and Private Property (1932); Michael C. Jensen and William H. Meckling, Theory of the Firm: Managerial Behavior, Agency Costs and Ownership Structure, 3 *J. Financial Econ.* 305 (1976).

3 See Jensen and Meckling, note 2.

4 See Michael C. Jensen and William H. Meckling, Rights and Production Functions: An Application to Labor-managed Firms and Codetermination, 52 *J. Bus.* 469 (1979).

5 The terms "public corporation" and "close corporation," which are common in the legal literature, are not used here. "Closed corporation" seems more descriptive than "close corporation." The term "public corporation" best describes government-owned corporations such as Amtrak and the TVA. In contrast, what we call "open corporations" are private organizations.

6 This definition of agency costs comes from Jensen and Meckling, see note 2.

7 Specific information is closely related to the notions of "information impactedness" and "bounded rationality" discussed in Oliver E. Williamson, *Markets and Hierarchies: Analysis and Antitrust Implications* (1975) and The Modern Corporation: Origins, Evolution, Attributes, 19 *J. Econ. Literature* 1537 (1981). Friedrich A. von Hayek, The Use of Knowledge in Society, 35 *Am. Econ. Rev.* 519 (1945) uses specific information to discuss the role of markets in complex economies. see also Thomas Sowell, *Knowledge and Decisions* 13–14 (1980). Our analysis of the relations between specific information and efficient decision processes owes much to ongoing work with William Meckling.

8 See, for example, Kenneth J. Arrow, The Role of Securities in the Optimal Allocation of Risk-Bearing, 31 *Rev. Econ. Stud.* 91 (1964); or Eugene F. Fama, *Foundations of Finance* chs. 6 and 7 (1976).

9 In contrast, the analysis predicts that when venture equity capital is put into a small entrepreneurial organization by outsiders, mechanisms for separating the management and control of important decisions are instituted.

10 These propositions are developed in Eugene F. Fama and Michael C. Jensen, Organizational Forms and Investment Decisions (Working Paper No. MERC 83-03, Univ. Rochester, Managerial Economics Research Center 1983).

11 See Armen A. Alchian and Harold Demsetz, Production, Information Costs, and Economic Organization, 62 *Am. Econ. Rev.* 777 (1972).

12 See Max Weber, *The Theory of Social and Economic Organization* (1947); Peter M. Blau, *Bureaucracy in Modern Society* (1956); Herbert A. Simon, The Architecture of Complexity, *Proc. Am. Philosophical Soc'y* 106, p. 467 (1962); and the titles by Williamson, see note 7. The historical development of hierarchies in open corporations is analyzed in Alfred D. Chandler, *The Visible Hand* (1977); and Alfred D. Chandler and Herman Daems, *Managerial Hierarchies* (1980).

13 The separation of decision management from decision control that we emphasize reflected in the auditing profession's concern with allocating operating and accounting responsibility to different agents. For instance, it is recommended that an agent with responsibility for billing should not have a role in receiving or recording customer payments. See, for example, Charles Horngren, Cost Accounting: A Managerial Emphasis ch. 27 (1982); Howard P. Stettler, Auditing Principles chs. 4 and 8 (1977).

14 See Eugene F. Fama, Agency Problems and the Theory of the Firm, 88 *J. Pol. Econ.* 288 (1980).

15 Decision functions can be delegated in two general ways: (1) joint delegation to several agents (as in a committee), or (2) partitioning and delegation of the parts to different agents. Boards of directors are examples of the former approach; decision hierarchies are examples of the latter.

16 Eugene F. Fama and Michael C. Jensen, Agency Problems and Residual Claims, *Journal of Law and Economics*, 26, 327–49 (1983).

17 Monitoring from the takeover market is emphasized in Henry Manne, Mergers and the Market for Corporate Control, 73 *J. Pol. Econ.* 110 (1965).

18 See Edward S. Herman, *Corporate Control, Corporate Power* ch. 2 (1981), for data on the characteristics of corporate boards.

19 See Fama, note 14.

20 For example, Horngren, see note 13, at 911, describes the role of the audit committee of the board (generally composed of outside board members) as a collector and conduit of information from the internal mutual monitoring system: "The objective of the audit committee is to oversee the accounting controls, financial statements, and financial affairs of the corporation. The committee represents the full board and provides personal contact and communication among the board, the external auditors, the internal auditors, the financial executives, and the operating executives."

21 See Herman, note 18, at ch. 2.

22 Ibid.

23 See Edward S. Herman, Conflict of Interest in the Savings and Loan Industry, in A Study of the Savings and Loan Industry 789 (Irwin Friend ed. 1969), for documentation of such lack of interest. For example, he describes situations where in more than a decade only four depositors in total attended the annual meetings of two savings and loan associations and other situations where management did not even bother to collect proxies.

24 Fama and Jensen, Agency Problems and Residual Claims, in *J. of L&E* (1983). See Henry B. Hansmann, The Role of Nonprofit Enterprise, 89 *Yale L. J.* 835 (1980), for a general discussion of nonprofits.

BIBLIOGRAPHY

Alchian, Armen A. "Uncertainty, Evolution and Economic Theory." *Journal of Political Economy* 58, 3 (June 1950): 211–21.

Alchian, Armen A. and Demsetz, Harold. "Production, Information Costs, and Economic Organization." *American Economic Review* 62, 5 (December 1972): 777–95.

Arrow, Kenneth J. "The Role of Securities in the Optimal Allocation of Risk-Bearing." *Review of Economic Studies* 31, 86 (April 1964): 91–6.

Berle, Adolf A. and Means, Gardiner C. *The Modern Corporation and Private Property*. New York: Macmillan Publishing Co., 1932.

Blau, Peter M. *Bureaucracy in Modern Society*. New York: Random House, 1956.

Chandler, Alfred D., Jr. *The Visible Hand*. Cambridge, MA: Harvard University Press, 1977.

Chandler, Alfred D., Jr. and Daems, Herman. *Managerial Hierarchies*. Cambridge, MA: Harvard University Press, 1980.

Fama, Eugene F. *Foundations of Finance*. New York: Basic Books, 1976.

Fama, Eugene F. "Agency Problems and the Theory of the Firm." *Journal of Political Economy* 88, 2 (April 1980): 288–307.

Fama, Eugene F. and Jensen, Michael C. "Agency Problems and Residual Claims." *Journal of Law and Economics* 26 (June 1983): 327–49.

Fama, Eugene F. and Jensen, Michael C. "Organizational Forms and Investment Decisions." Managerial Economics Research Center Working Paper no. MERC 83-03. Rochester, NY: University of Rochester, Graduate School of Management, 1983.

Hansmann, Henry B. "The Role of Nonprofit Enterprise." *Yale Law Journal* 89, 5 (April 1980): 835–901.

Hayek, Freidrich A. "The Use of Knowledge in Society." *American Economic Review* 35, 4 (September 1945): 519–30.

Herman, Edward S. "Conflict of Interest in the Savings and Loan Industry". In *A Study of the Savings and Loan Industry*, edited by Irwin Friend. Washington, DC: Federal Home Loan Board, 1969.

Herman, Edward S. *Corporate Control, Corporate Power*. Twentieth Century Fund Study. New York: Cambridge University Press, 1981.

Horngren, Charles. *Cost Accounting: A Managerial Emphasis*. Englewood Cliffs, NJ: Prentice-Hall, Inc., 1982.

Jensen, Michael C. "Organization Theory and Methodology." *Accounting Review* 50, 2 (April 1983): 319–39.

Jensen, Michael C. and Meckling, William H. "Theory of the Firm: Managerial Behavior, Agency Costs and Ownership Structure." *Journal of Financial Economics* 3, 4 (October 1976): 305–60.

Jensen, Michael C. and Meckling, William H. "Rights and Production Functions: An Application to Labor-Managed Firms and Codetermination." *Journal of Business* 52, 4 (October 1979): 469–506.

Manne, Henry. "Mergers and the Market for Corporate Control." *Journal of Political Economy* 73, 2 (April 1965): 110–20.

Simon, Herbert A. "The Architecture of Complexity." *Proceedings of the American Philosophical Society* 106 (December 1962): 467–82.

Smith, Adam. *The Wealth of Nations*. 1776. Edited by Edwin Cannan, 1904. Reprint. New York: Modern Library, 1937.

Sowell, Thomas. *Knowledge and Decisions*. New York: Basic Books, 1980.

Stettler, Howard P. *Auditing Principles*. Englewood Cliffs, NJ: Prentice-Hall, Inc., 1977.

Weber, Max. *The Theory of Social and Economic Organization*, edited by T. Parsons. Glencoe, IL: Free Press, 1947.

Williamson, Oliver E. *Markets and Hierarchies: Analysis and Antitrust Implications*. New York: Free Press, 1975.

Williamson, Oliver E. "The Modern Corporation: Origins, Evolution, Attributes." *Journal of Economic Literature* 19, 4 (December 1981): 1537–68.

"Agency Theory: An Assessment and Review"

from Academy of Management Review (1989)

Kathleen M. Eisenhardt

One day Deng Xiaoping decided to take his grandson to visit Mao. "Call me granduncle," Mao offered warmly. "Oh, I certainly couldn't do that, Chairman Mao," the awe-struck child replied. "Why don't you give him an apple?" suggested Deng. No sooner had Mao done so than the boy happily chirped, "Oh thank you, Granduncle." "You see," said Deng, "what incentives can achieve."

("Capitalism," 1984: 62)

Agency theory has been used by scholars in accounting (e.g. Demski and Feltham, 1978), economics (e.g. Spence and Zeckhauser, 1971), finance (e.g. Fama, 1980), marketing (e.g. Basu *et al.*, 1985), political science (e.g. Eisenhardt, 1985, 1988; Kosnik, 1987), and sociology (e.g. Eccles, 1985; White, 1985). Yet, it is still surrounded by controversy. Its proponents argue that a revolution is at hand and that "the foundation for a powerful theory of organizations is being put into place" (Jensen, 1983: 324). Its detractors call it trivial, dehumanizing, and even "dangerous" (Perrow, 1986: 235).

Which is it: grand theory or great sham? The purposes of this chapter are to describe agency theory and to indicate ways in which organizational researchers can use its insights. The paper is organized around four questions that are germane to organizational research. The first asks the deceptively simple question, What is agency theory? Often, the technical style, mathematics, and tautological reasoning of the agency literature can obscure the theory. Moreover, the agency literature is split into two camps (Jensen, 1983), leading to differences in interpretation. For example, Barney and Ouchi (1986) argued that agency theory emphasizes how capital markets can affect the firm, whereas other authors made no reference to capital markets at all (Anderson, 1985; Demski and Feltham, 1978; Eccles, 1985; Eisenhardt, 1985).

The second question is, What does agency theory contribute to organizational theory? Proponents such as Ross (1973: 134) argued that "examples of agency are universal." Yet other scholars such as Perrow (1986) claimed that agency theory addresses no clear problems, and Hirsch and Friedman (1986) called it excessively narrow, focusing only on stock price. For economists, long accustomed to treating the organization as a "black box" in the theory of the firm, agency theory may be revolutionary. Yet, for organizational scholars the worth of agency theory is not so obvious.

The third question is, Is agency theory empirically valid? The power of the empirical research on agency theory to explain organizational phenomena is important to assess, particularly in light of the criticism that agency theory is "hardly subject to empirical test since it rarely tries to explain actual events" (Perrow, 1986: 224). Perrow (1986) also criticized the theory for being unrealistically one-sided because of its neglect of potential exploitation of workers.

The final question is, What topics and contexts are fruitful for organizational researchers who use agency theory? Identifying how useful agency theory can be to organizational scholars requires understanding the situations in which the agency perspective can provide theoretical leverage.

The principal contributions of the paper are to present testable propositions, identify contributions of the theory to organizational thinking, and evaluate the extant empirical literature. The overall conclusion is that agency theory is a useful addition to organizational theory. The agency theory ideas on risk, outcome uncertainty, incentives, and information systems are novel contributions to organizational thinking, and the empirical evidence is supportive of the theory, particularly when coupled with complementary theoretical perspectives.

ORIGINS OF AGENCY THEORY

During the 1960s and early 1970s, economists explored risk sharing among individuals or groups (e.g. Arrow, 1971; Wilson, 1968). This literature described the risk-sharing problem as one that arises when cooperating parties have different attitudes toward risk. Agency theory broadened this risk-sharing literature to include the so-called agency problem that occurs when cooperating parties have different goals and division of labor (Jensen and Meckling, 1976; Ross, 1973). Specifically, agency theory is directed at the ubiquitous agency relationship, in which one party (the principal) delegates work to another (the agent), who performs that work. Agency theory attempts to describe this relationship using the metaphor of a contract (Jensen and Meckling, 1976).

Agency theory is concerned with resolving two problems that can occur in agency relationships. The first is the agency problem that arises when (a) the desires or goals of the principal and agent conflict and (b) it is difficult or expensive for the principal to verify what the agent is actually doing. The problem here is that the principal cannot verify that the agent has behaved appropriately. The second is the *problem of risk sharing* that arises when the principal and agent have different attitudes toward risk. The problem here is that the principal and the agent may prefer different actions because of the different risk preferences.

Because the unit of analysis is the contract governing the relationship between the principal and the agent, the focus of the theory is on determining the most efficient contract governing the principal–agent relationship given assumptions about people (e.g. self-interest, bounded rationality, risk aversion), organizations (e.g. goal conflict among members), and information (e.g. information is a commodity which can be purchased). Specifically, the question becomes, Is a behavior-oriented contract (e.g. salaries, hierarchical governance) more efficient than an outcome-oriented contract (e.g. commissions, stock options, transfer of property rights, market governance)? An overview of agency theory is given in Table 1.

The agency structure is applicable in a variety of settings, ranging from macrolevel issues such as regulatory policy to microlevel dyad phenomena such as blame, impression management, lying, and other expressions of self-interest. Most frequently, agency theory has been applied to organizational phenomena such as compensation (e.g. Conlon and Parks, 1988; Eisenhardt, 1985), acquisition and diversification strategies (e.g. Amihud and Leve, 1981), board relationships (e.g. Fama and Jensen, 1983; Kosnik, 1987), ownership and financing structures (e.g. Argawal and Mandelker, 1987; Jensen and Meckling, 1976), vertical integration (Anderson, 1985; Eccles, 1985), and innovation (Bolton, 1988; Zenger, 1988). Overall, the domain of agency theory is relationships that mirror the basic agency structure of a principal and an agent who are engaged in cooperative

Key idea	Principal–agent relationships should reflect efficient organization of information and risk-bearing costs
Unit of analysis	Contract between principal and agent
Human assumptions	Self-interest Bounded rationality Risk aversion
Organizational assumptions	Partial goal conflict among participants Efficiency as the effectiveness criterion Information asymmetry between principal and agent
Information assumption	Information as a purchasable commodity
Contracting problems	Agency (moral hazard and adverse selection) Risk sharing
Problem domain	Relationships in which the principal and agent have partly differing goals and risk preferences (e.g. compensation, regulation, leadership, impression management, whistle-blowing, vertical integration, transfer pricing)

Table 1 Agency theory overview.

behavior, but have differing goals and differing attitudes toward risk.

AGENCY THEORY

From its roots in information economics, agency theory has developed along two lines: positivist and principal–agent (Jensen, 1983). The two streams share a common unit of analysis: the contract between the principal and the agent. They also share common assumptions about people, organizations, and information. However, they differ in their mathematical rigor, dependent variable, and style.

Positivist agency theory

Positivist researchers have focused on identifying situations in which the principal and agent are likely to have conflicting goals and then describing the governance mechanisms that limit the agent's self-serving behavior. Positivist research is less mathematical than principal–agent research. Also, positivist researchers have focused almost exclusively on the special case of the principal–agent relationship between owners and managers of large, public corporations (Berle and Means, 1932).

Three articles have been particularly influential. Jensen and Meckling (1976) explored the ownership structure of the corporation, including how equity ownership by managers aligns managers' interests with those of owners. Fama (1980) discussed the role of efficient capital and labor markets as information mechanisms that are used to control the self-serving behavior of top executives. Fama and Jensen (1983) described the role of the board of directors as an information system that the stockholders within large corporations could use to monitor the opportunism of top executives. Jensen and his colleagues (Jensen, 1984; Jensen and Roeback, 1983) extended these ideas to controversial practices, such as golden parachutes and corporate raiding.

From a theoretical perspective, the positivist stream has been most concerned with describing the governance mechanisms that solve the agency problem. Jensen (1983: 326) described this interest as "why certain contractual relations arise." Two propositions capture the governance mechanisms which are identified in the positivist stream. One proposition is that outcome-based contracts are effective in curbing agent opportunism. The argument is that such contracts coalign the preferences of agents with those of the principal because the rewards for both depend on the same actions, and, therefore, the conflicts of self-interest between principal and agent are reduced. For example, Jensen and Meckling (1976) described how increasing the firm ownership of the managers decreases managerial opportunism. In formal terms,

> *Proposition 1*: When the contract between the principal and agent is outcome based, the agent is more likely to behave in the interests of the principal.

The second proposition is that information systems also curb agent opportunism. The argument here is that, since information systems inform the principal about what the agent is actually doing, they are likely to curb agent opportunism because the agent will realize that he or she cannot deceive the principal. For example, Fama (1980) described the information effects of efficient capital and labor markets on managerial opportunism, and Fama and Jensen (1983) described the information role that boards of directors play in controlling managerial behavior. In formal terms,

> *Proposition 2*: When the principal has information to verify agent behavior, the agent is more likely to behave in the interests of the principal.

At its best, positivist agency theory can be regarded as enriching economics by offering a more complex view of organizations (Jensen, 1983). However, it has been criticized by organizational theorists as minimalist (Hirsch *et al.*, 1987; Perrow, 1986) and by microeconomists as tautological and lacking rigor (Jensen, 1983). Nonetheless, positivist agency theory has ignited considerable research (Barney and Ouchi, 1986) and popular interest ("Meet Mike," 1988).

Principal–agent research

Principal–agent researchers are concerned with a general theory of the principal–agent relationship, a theory that can be applied to employer–employee, lawyer–client, buyer–supplier, and other agency relationships (Harris and Raviv, 1978). Characteristic of formal theory, the principal–agent paradigm involves careful specification of assumptions, which are followed by logical deduction and mathematical proof.

In comparison with the positivist stream, principal–agent theory is abstract and mathematical and, therefore, less accessible to organizational scholars. Indeed, the most vocal critics of the theory (Hirsch et al., 1987; Perrow, 1986) have focused their attacks primarily on the more widely known positivist stream. Also, the principal–agent stream has a broader focus and greater interest in general, theoretical implications. In contrast, the positivist writers have focused almost exclusively on the special case of the owner–CEO relationship in the large corporation. Finally, principal–agent research includes many more testable implications.

For organizational scholars, these differences provide background for understanding criticism of the theory. However, they are not crucial. Rather, the important point is that the two streams are complementary: Positivist theory identifies various contract alternatives, and principal–agent theory indicates which contract is the most efficient under varying levels of outcome uncertainty, risk aversion, information, and other variables described below.

The focus of the principal–agent literature is on determining the optimal contract, behavior versus outcome, between the principal and the agent. The simple model assumes goal conflict between principal and agent, an easily measured outcome, and an agent who is more risk averse than the principal. (Note: The argument behind a more risk averse agent is that agents, who are unable to diversify their employment, should be risk averse and principals, who are capable of diversifying their investments, should be risk neutral.) The approach of the simple model can be described in terms of cases (e.g. Demski and Feltham, 1978). The first case, a simple case of complete information, is when the principal knows what the agent has done. Given that the principal is buying the agent's behavior, then a contract that is based on behavior is most efficient. An outcome-based contract would needlessly transfer risk to the agent, who is assumed to be more risk averse than the principal.

The second case is when the principal does not know exactly what the agent has done. Given the self-interest of the agent, the agent may or may not have behaved as agreed. The agency problem arises because (a) the principal and the agent have different goals and (b) the principal cannot determine if the agent has behaved appropriately. In the formal literature, two aspects of the agency problem are cited. *Moral hazard* refers to lack of effort on the part of the agent. The argument here is that the agent may simply not put forth the agreed-upon effort. That is, the agent is shirking. For example, moral hazard occurs when a research scientist works on a personal research project on company time but the research is so complex that corporate management cannot detect what the scientist is actually doing. *Adverse selection* refers to the misrepresentation of ability by the agent. The argument here is that the agent may claim to have certain skills or abilities when he or she is hired. Adverse selection arises because the principal cannot completely verify these skills or abilities either at the time of hiring or while the agent is working. For example, adverse selection occurs when a research scientist claims to have experience in a scientific speciality and the employer cannot judge whether this is the case.

In the case of unobservable behavior (due to moral hazard or adverse selection), the principal has two options. One is to discover the agent's behavior by investing in information systems such as budgeting systems, reporting procedures, boards of directors, and additional layers of management. Such investments reveal the agent's behavior to the principal, and the situation reverts to the complete information case. In formal terms,

Proposition 3: Information systems are positively related to behavior-based contracts and negatively related to outcome-based contracts.

The other option is to contract on the outcomes of the agent's behavior. Such an outcome-based contract motivates behavior by coalignment of the agent's preferences with those of the principal, but at the price of transferring risk to the agent. The issue of risk arises because outcomes are only partly a function of behaviors. Government policies, economic climate, competitor actions, technological change, and so on, may cause uncontrollable variations in outcomes. The resulting outcome uncertainty introduces not only the inability to preplan, but also risk that must be borne by someone. When outcome uncertainty is low, the costs of shifting risk to the agent are low and outcome-based contracts are attractive. However, as uncertainty increases, it becomes increasingly expensive to shift risk despite the motivational benefits of outcome-based contracts. In formal terms,

Proposition 4: Outcome uncertainty is positively related to behavior-based contracts and negatively related to outcome-based contracts.

This simple agency model has been described in varying ways by many authors (e.g. Demski and Feltham, 1978; Harris and Raviv, 1979; Holmstrom, 1979; Shavell, 1979). However, the heart of principal–agent theory is the trade-off between (a) the cost of measuring behavior and (b) the cost of measuring outcomes and transferring risk to the agent.

A number of extensions to this simple model are possible. One is to relax the assumption of a risk-averse agent (e.g. Harris and Raviv, 1979). Research (MacCrimmon and Wehrung, 1986) indicates that individuals vary widely in their risk attitudes. As the agent becomes increasingly less risk averse (e.g. a wealthy agent), it becomes more attractive to pass risk to the agent using an outcome-based contract. Conversely, as the agent becomes more risk averse, it is increasingly expensive to pass risk to the agent. In formal terms,

Proposition 5: The risk aversion of the agent is positively related to behavior-based contracts and negatively related to outcome-based contracts.

Similarly, as the principal becomes more risk averse, it is increasingly attractive to pass risk to the agent. In formal terms,

Proposition 6: The risk aversion of the principal is negatively related to behavior-based contracts and positively related to outcome-based contracts.

Another extension is to relax the assumption of goal conflict between the principal and agent (e.g. Demski, 1980). This might occur either in a highly socialized or clan-oriented firm (Ouchi, 1979) or in situations in which self-interest gives way to selfless behavior (Perrow, 1986). If there is no goal conflict, the agent will behave as the principal would like, regardless of whether his or her behavior is monitored. As goal conflict decreases, there is a decreasing motivational imperative for outcome-based contracting, and the issue reduces to risk-sharing considerations. Under the assumption of a risk-averse agent, behavior-based contracts become more attractive. In formal terms,

Proposition 7: The goal conflict between principal and agent is negatively related to behavior-based contracts and positively related to outcome-based contracts.

Another set of extensions relates to the task performed by the agent. For example, the programmability of the task is likely to influence the ease of measuring behavior (Eisenhardt, 1985, 1988). *Programmability* is defined as the degree to which appropriate behavior by the agent can be specified in advance. For example, the job of a retail sales cashier is much more programmed than that of a high-technology entrepreneur. The argument is that the behavior of agents engaged in more programmed jobs is easier to observe and evaluate. Therefore, the more programmed the task, the more attractive are behavior-based contracts because information about the agent's behavior is more readily determined. Very programmed tasks readily reveal agent behavior, and the situation reverts to the complete information case. Thus, retail sales clerks are more likely to be paid via behavior-based contracting (e.g. hourly wages), whereas entrepreneurs are more likely to be compensated with outcome-based contracts (e.g. stock ownership). In formal terms,

Proposition 8: Task programmability is positively related to behavior-based contracts and negatively related to outcome-based contracts.

Another task characteristic is the measurability of the outcome (Anderson, 1985; Eisenhardt, 1985). The simple model assumes that outcomes are easily measured. However, some tasks require a long time to complete, involve joint or team effort, or produce soft outcomes. In these circumstances, outcomes are either difficult to measure or difficult to measure within a practical amount of time. When outcomes are measured with difficulty, outcome-based contracts are less attractive. In contrast, when outcomes are readily measured, outcome-based contracts are more attractive. In formal terms,

Proposition 9: Outcome measurability is negatively related to behavior-based contracts and positively related to outcome-based contracts.

Finally, it seems reasonable that when principals and agents engage in a long-term relationship, it is likely that the principal will learn about the agent (e.g. Lambert, 1983) and so will be able to assess behavior more readily. Conversely, in short-term agency relationships, the information asymmetry between principal and agent is likely to be greater, thus making outcome-based contracts more attractive. In formal terms,

> *Proposition 10*: The length of the agency relationship is positively related to behavior-based contracts and negatively related to outcome-based contracts.

AGENCY THEORY AND THE ORGANIZATIONAL LITERATURE

Despite Perrow's (1986) assertion that agency theory is very different from organization theory, agency theory has several links to mainstream organization perspectives (see Table 2). At its roots, agency theory is consistent with the classic works of Barnard (1938) on the nature of co-operative behavior and March and Simon (1958) on the inducements and contributions of the employment relationship. As in this earlier work, the heart of agency theory is the goal conflict inherent when individuals with differing preferences engage in cooperative effort, and the essential metaphor is that of the contract.

Agency theory is also similar to political models of organizations. Both agency and political perspectives assume the pursuit of self-interest at the individual level and goal conflict at the organizational level (e.g. March, 1962; Pfeffer, 1981). Also, in both perspectives, information asymmetry is linked to the power of lower order participants (e.g. Pettigrew, 1973). The difference is that in political models goal conflicts are resolved through bargaining, negotiation, and coalitions – the power mechanism of political science. In agency theory they are resolved through the coalignment of incentives – the price mechanism of economics.

Agency theory also is similar to the information processing approaches to contingency theory (Chandler, 1962; Galbrath, 1973; Lawrence and Lorsch, 1967). Both perspectives are information theories. They assume that individuals are boundedly rational and that information is distributed asymmetrically throughout the organization. They also are efficiency theories; that is, they use efficient processing of information as a criterion for choosing among various organizing forms (Galbrath, 1973). The difference between the two is their focus: In contingency theory researchers are concerned with the optimal structuring of reporting relationships and decision-making responsibilities (e.g. Galbraith, 1973; Lawrence and Lorsch, 1967), whereas in agency theory they are concerned with the optimal structuring of control relationships resulting from these reporting and decision-making patterns. For example, using contingency theory, we would be concerned with whether a firm is organized in a divisional or matrix structure. Using agency theory, we would be concerned with whether managers within the chosen structure are compensated by performance incentives.

The most obvious tie is with the organizational control literature (e.g. Dornbusch and Scott, 1974). For example, Thompson's (1967) and later Ouchil's (1979) linking of known means/ends relationships and crytallized goals to behavior versus outcome control is very similar to agency theory's linking task programmability and measurability of outcomes to contract form (Eisenhardt, 1985). That is, known means/ends relationships (task programmability) lead to behavior control, and crytallized goals (measurable outcomes) lead to outcome control. Similarly, Ouchi's (1979) extension of Thompson's (1967)

Assumption	Perspective				
	Political	Contingency	Organization control	Transaction cost	Agency
Self-interest	X			X	X
Goal conflict	X			X	X
Bounded rationality		X	X	X	X
Information asymmetry		X		X	X
Preeminence of efficiency		X	X	X	X
Risk aversion					X
Information as a commodity					X

Table 2   Comparison of agency theory assumptions and organizational perspectives.

framework to include clan control is similar to assuming low goal conflict (Proposition 7) in agency theory. Clan control implies goal congruence between people and, therefore, the reduced need to monitor behavior or outcomes. Motivation issues disappear. The major differences between agency theory and the organizational control literature are the risk implications of principal and agent risk aversion and outcome uncertainty (Propositions 4, 5, 6).

Not surprisingly, agency theory has similarities with the transaction cost perspective (Williamson, 1975). As noted by Barney and Ouchi (1986), the theories share assumptions of self-interest and bounded rationality. They also have similar dependent variables; that is, hierarchies roughly correspond the behavior-based contracts, and markets correspond to behavior-based contracts, and markets correspond to outcome-based contracts. However, the two theories arise from different traditions in economics (Spence, 1975): In transaction cost theorizing we are concerned with organizational boundaries, whereas in agency theorizing the contract between cooperating parties, regardless of boundary, is highlighted. However, the most important difference is that each theory includes unique independent variables. In transaction cost theory these are asset specificity and small numbers bargaining. In agency theory there are the risk attitudes of the principal and agent, outcome uncertainty, and information systems. Thus, the two theories share a percentage in economics, but each has its own focus and several unique independent variables.

CONTRIBUTIONS OF AGENCY THEORY

Agency theory reestablishes the importance of incentives and self-interest in organizational thinking (Perrow, 1986). Agency theory reminds us that much of organizational life, whether we like it or not, is based on self-interest. Agency theory also emphasizes the importance of a common problem structure across research topics. As Barney and Ouchi (1986) described it, organization research has become increasingly topic, rather than theory, centered. Agency theory reminds us that common problem structures do exist across research domains. Therefore, results from one research area (e.g. vertical integration) may be germane to others with a common problem structure (e.g. compensation).

Agency theory also makes two specific contributions to organizational thinking. The first is the treatment of information. In agency theory, information is regarded as a commodity: It has a cost, and it can be purchased. This gives an important role to formal information systems, such as budgeting, MBO, and boards of directors, and informal ones, such as managerial supervision, which is unique in organizational research. The implication is that organizations can invest in information systems in order to control agent opportunism.

An illustration of this is executive compensation. A number of authors in this literature have expressed surprise at the lack of performance-based executive compensation (e.g. Pearce et al. 1985; Ungson and Steers, 1984). However, from an agency perspective, it is not surprising since such compensation should be contingent upon a variety of factors including information systems. Specifically, richer information systems control managerial opportunism and, therefore, lead to less performance-contingent pay.

One particularly relevant information system for monitoring executive behaviors is the board of directors. From an agency perspective, boards can be used as monitoring devices for shareholder interests (Fama and Jensen, 1983). When boards provide richer information, compensation is less likely to be based on firm performance. Rather, because the behaviors of top executives are better known, compensation based on knowledge of executive behaviors is more likely. Executives would then be rewarded for taking well-conceived actions (e.g. high risk/high potential R&D) whose outcomes may be unsuccessful. Also, when boards provide richer information, top executive are more likely to engage in behaviors that are consistent with stockholders' interests. For example, from an agency viewpoint, behaviors such as using greenmail and golden parachutes, which tend to benefit the manager more than the stockholders are less likely when boards are better monitors of stockholders' interests. Operationally, the richness of board information can be measured in terms of characteristics such as frequency of board meetings, number of board subcommittees, number of board members with long tenure, number of board members with managerial and industry experience, and number of board members representing specific ownership groups.

A second contribution of agency theory is its risk implications. Organizations are assumed to have uncertain futures. The future may bring prosperity, bankruptcy, or some intermediate outcome, and that future is only partly controlled by organization members. Environmental effects such as government regulation, emergence of new competitors, and technical innovation can affect outcomes. Agency theory extends organizational thinking by pushing the ramifications of outcome uncertainty to their implications for creating risk. Uncertainty is viewed in terms of risk/reward trade-offs, not just in terms of inability to preplan. The implication is that outcome uncertainty coupled with differences in willingness to accept risk should influence contracts between principal and agent.

Vertical integration provides an illustration. For example, Walker and Weber (1984) found that technological and demand uncertainty did not affect the "make or buy" decision for components in a large automobile manufacturer (principal in this case). The authors were unable to explain their results using a transaction cost framework. However, their results are consistent with agency thinking if the managers of the automobile firm are risk neutral (a reasonable assumption given the size of the automobile firm relative to the importance of any single component). According to agency theory, we would predict that such a risk-neutral principal is relatively uninfluenced by outcome uncertainty, which was Walker and Weber's result.

Conversely, according to agency theory, the reverse prediction is true for a new venture. In this case, the firm is small and new, and it has limited resources available to it for weathering uncertainty: The likelihood of failure looms large. In this case, the managers of the venture may be risk-averse principals. If so, according to agency theory we would predict that such managers will be very sensitive to outcome uncertainty. In particular, the managers would be more likely to choose the "buy" option, thereby transferring risk to the supplying firm. Overall, agency theory predicts that risk-neutral managers are likely to choose the "make" option (behavior-based contract), whereas risk-averse executives are likely to choose "buy" (outcome-based contract).

EMPIRICAL RESULTS

Researches in several disciplines have undertaken empirical studies of agency theory. These studies, mirroring the two streams of theoretical agency research, are in Table 3.

Results of the positivist: stream

In the postivist stream, the common approach is to identify a policy or behavior in which stockholder and management interests diverge and then to demonstrate that informatioon systems or outcome-based incentives solve the agency problem. That is, these mechanisms coalign managerial behaviors with owner preferences. Consistent with the positivist tradition, most of these studies concern the separation of ownership from management in large corporations, and they use secondary source data that are available for large firms.

One of the earliest studies of this type was conducted by Amihud and Lev (1981). These researchers explored why firms engage in conglomerate mergers. In general, conglomerate mergers are not in the interests of the stockholders because, typically, stockholders can diversify directly through their stock portfolio. In contrast, conglomerate mergers may be attractive to managers who have fewer avenues available to diversify their own risk. Hence, conglomerate mergers are an arena in which owner and manager interests diverge. Specifically, these authors linked merger and diversification behaviors to whether the firm was owner controlled (i.e. had a major stockholder) or manager controlled (i.e. had no major stockholder). Consistent with agency theory arguments (Jensen and Meckling, 1976), manager-controlled firms engaged in significantly more conglomerate (but not more related) acquistions and were more diversified.

Along the same lines, Walking and Long (1984) studied managers' resistance to takeover bids. Their sample included 105 large US corporations that were targets of takeover attempts between 1972 and 1977. In general, resistance to takeover bids is not in the stockholders' interests, but it may be in the interests of mangers because they can lose their jobs during a takeover. Consistent with agency theory (Jensen and Meckling, 1976), the authors found that managers who have substantial equity positions within their firms (outcome-based contracts) were less likely to resist takeover bids.

The effects of market discipline on agency relationships were examined in Wolfson's (1985) study of the relationship between the limited (principals and general (agent) partners in oil and gas tax and agency affects were combined in order to assess why the limited partnership governance form survived in this setting despite extensive information advantages and divergent incentives for the limited partner. Consistent with agency arguments (Fama, 1980), Wolfson found that long-run reputation effects of the market coaligned the short-run behaviors of the general partner with the limited partners' welfare.

Kosnik (1987) examined another information mechanism for managerial opportunism, the board of

Author(s)	Research stream	Sample	Agency variables	Companion theory	Dependent variables	Results
Amihud and Lev (1981)	Positivist	309 *Fortune* 500 firms	Manager vs. owner controlled	None	Conglomerate mergers and diversification	Support
Walking and Long (1984)	Positivist	105 US firms	Management's equity and options	Shareholder welfare and other controls	Managerial resistance to takeover bid	Support
Anderson (1985)	Principal–agent	159 sales districts in 13 electronics firms	Importance of nonselling activities, length of selling cycle, and difficulty evaluating sales performance	Transaction cost	Representative vs. corporate sales force	Mixed
Eisenhardt (1985)	Principal–agent	54 retail stores	Information systems, cost of outcome measurement, and outcome uncertainty	Organizational control	Salary vs. commission	Support
Eccles (1985)	Principal–agent	150 interviews in 13 chemical, electronics, heavy machinery, and machine component firms	Decentralization	Equity	Type of transfer price	Inductive model
Wolfson (1985)	Positivist	39 oil and gas limited partnerships	General partner's track record	Tax effects	Share price	Support

Study	Type	Sample	Independent variables	Alternative theory	Dependent variables	Result
Agrawal and Mandelker (1987)	Positivist	209 major corporations	Executive stock holdings	None	Acquisitions diverstitures, and debt/equity ratio	Support
Kosnik (1987)	Positivist	110 major corporations targeted for greenmail	Proportion of outside directors, equity held by outside directors, and outside directors with executive experience	Hegemony	Payment of greenmail (yes/no)	Mixed
Eisenhardt (1988)	Principal–agent	54 retail stores	Job programmability, span of control, and outcome uncertainty	Institutional	Salary vs. commission	Support
Conlon and Parks (1988)	Principal–agent	40 dyads	Monitoring	Institutional	Perfomance-contingent compensation	Support
Barney (1988)	Positivist	32 Japanese electronics firms	Employee stock ownership	Size and growth controls	Cost of equity	Support
Singh and Harianto (in press)	Positivist	84 *Fortune* 500 firms	Managerial stock ownership and takeover threat	Managerialist	Golden parachute contracts	Support

Table 3 Summary of agency theory studies.

Note: This set of studies was developed through contracting other agency researchers, scanning journals, and following up referenced articles. Although the list is not exhaustive, it includes many of the relevant studies.

directors. Kosnik studied 110 large US corporations that were greenmail tergets between 1979 and 1983. Using both hegemony and agency theories, she related board characteristics to whether greenmail was actually paid (paying greenmail is considered not in the stockholders' intersts). As predicted by agency theory (Fama and Jensen, 1983), boards of companies that resisted greenmail had a higher proportion of outside directors and a higher proportion of outside directors executives.

In a similar vein, Argawal and Mandelker (1987) examined whether executive holdings of firm securities reduced agency problems between stockholders and management. Specifically, they studied the relationship between stock and stock option holding of executives and whether acquistion and financing decisions were made consistent with the interests of stockholders. In general, managers prefer lower risk acquisitions and lower debt financing (see Argawal and Mandelker, 1987, for a review). Their sample included 209 firms that participated in acquisitions and diverstitures between 1974 and 1982. Consistent with agency ideas (e.g. Jensen and Meckling, 1976), executive security holdings (outcome-based contract) were related to acquisition and financing decisions that were more consistent with stockholder interest. That is, executive stock holdings appeared to coalign managerial preferences with those of stockholders.

Singh and Harianto (1989) studied golden parachutes in a matched sample of 84 Fortune 500 firms. Their study included variables from both agency and managerialist perspectives. Consistent with agency theory (Fama and Jensen, 1983; Jensen and Meckling, 1976), the authors found that golden parachutes are used to coalign executive interests with those of stockholders in takeover situations, and they are seen as an alternative outcome-based contract to executive stock ownership. Specifically, the authors found that golden parachutes were positively associated with a higher probability of a takeover attempt and negatively associated with executive stock holdings.

Finally, Barney (1988) explored whether employee stock ownership reduces a firm's cost of equity capital. Consistent with agency theory (Jensen and Meckling, 1976), Barney argued that employee stock ownership (outcome-based contract) would coalign the interests of employees with stockholders. Using efficient capital market through a lower cost of equity. Although Barney did not directly test the agency argument, the results are consistent with an agency view.

In summary, there is support for the existence of agency problems between shareholders and top executives across situations in which their interests diverge – that is, takeover attempts, debt versus equity financing, acquisitions, and divestitures, and for the mitigation of agency problems (a) through outcome-based contracts such as golden parachutes (Singh and Harianto, 1989) and executive stock holdings (Argawal and Mandelker, 1987; Walking and Long, 1984) and (b) through information systems such as boarda (Kosnik, 1987) and efficient markets (Barney, 1988; Wolfson 1985). Overall, these studies support the positivist propositions described earlier. Similarly, laboratory studies by Dejong and colleagues (1985), which are not reviewed here, are also supportive.

Results of the principal–agent stream

The principal–agent stream is more directly focused on the contract between the principal and the agent. Whereas the positivist stream lays the foundation (i.e. that agency problems exist and that various contract alternatives are available), the principal–agent stream indicates that most efficient contract alternative in a given situation. The common approach in these studies is to use a subset of agency variables such as task programmability, information systems, and outcome uncertainty to predict whether the contract is behavior- or outcome-based. The underlying assumption is that principals and agents will choose the most efficient contract, although efficiency is not directly tested.

In one study, Anderson (1985) probed vertical integration using a transaction cost perspective with agency variables. Specifically, she examined the choice between a manufacturer's representative (outcome-based) and a corporate sales force (behavior-based) among a sample of electronics firms. The most powerful explanatory variable was from agency theory: the difficulty of measuring outcomes (measured by amount of nonselling tasks and joint team sales). Consistent with agency predictions, this variable was positively related to using a corporate sales force (behavior-based contract).

In other studies, Eisenhardt (1985, 1988) examined the choice between commission (outcome-based) and salary (behavior-based) compensation of salespeople in retailing. The original study (1985) included only agency variables, while a later study (1988) added additional agency variables and institutional theory predictions. The results supported agency theory predictions that task programmability, information systems (measured by the span of control), and outcome uncertainty variables (measured by number of competitors and failure rates) significantly predict the salary versus commission choice. Institutional variables were significant as well.

Conlon and Parks (1988) replicated and extended Eisenhardt's work in a laboratory setting. They used a multiperiod design to test both agency and institutional predictions. Consistent with agency theory (Harris and Raviv, 1978), they found that information systems (manipulated by whether or not the principal could monitor the agent's behavior) were negatively related to performance-contingent (outcome-based) pay. They also found support for the institutional predictions.

Finally, Eccles (1985) used agency theory to develop a framework for understanding transfer pricing. Using interviews with 150 exectives in 13 large corporations, he developed a framework based on notions of agency and fairness to presecribe the conditions under which various sourcing and transfer pricing alternatives are both effeicient and equitable. Prominent in his framework is the link between decentralization (arguably a measure of task programmability) and the choice between cost (behavior-based contract) and market (outcome-based contract) transfer pricing mechanisms.

In summary, there is support for the principal–agent hypotheses linking contract form with (a) information systems (Conlon and Parks, 1988; Eccles, 1985; Eisenhardt, 1985), (b) outcome uncertainty (Eisenhardt, 1985), (c) outcome measureability (Anderson, 1985; Eisenhardt, 1985), (d) time (Conlon and Parks, 1988), and (e) task programmability (Eccles, 1985; Eisenhardt, 1985). Moreover, this support rests on research using a varity of methods including questionnaires, secondary sources, laboratory experimentrs and interviews.

RECOMMENDATIONS FOR AGENCY THEORY RESEARCH

As argued above, agency theory makes contributions to organization theory, is testable, and has empirical support. Overall, it seems reasonable to urge the adoption of an agency theory perspective when investigating the many problems that have a principal–agent structure. Five specific recommendations are outlined below for using agency theory in organizational research.

Focus on information systems, outcome uncertainty, and risk

McGrath *et al.* (1981) argued that research is a knowledge accrual process. Using this accrual criterion, next steps for agency theory research are clear: *Researchers should focus on information systems, outcome uncertainty, and risk*. These agency variables make the most unique contribution to organizational research, yet they have received little empirical attention (Table 3). It is important that researchers place emphasis on these variables in order to advance agency theory and to provide new concepts in the study of familiar topics such as impression management, innovation, vertical integration, compensation, strategic alliances, and board relationships.

Studying risk and outcome uncertainly is particularly opportune because of recent advances in measuring risk preferences. By relying on the works of Kahneman and Tversky (1979), MacCrimmon and Wehrung (1986), and March and Shapira (1987), the organizational researcher can measure risk preference more easily and realistically. These techiniques include direct measures of risk preference such as lotteries and indirect measures using demographic characteristics such age and wealth and payoff characteristics such as gain versus loss. (See March Shapira, 1987, for a review.)

Key on theory-relevant contexts

Organizational theory usually is explored in settings in which the theory appears to have greatest relevance. For example, institutional and resource dependence theories were developed primarily in large, public bureaucracies in which efficiency may not have been a pressing concern. The recommendation here is to take the same approach with agency theory: *Key on theory-relevant contexts*.

Agency theory is most relevant in situations in which contracting problems are difficult. These include situations in which there is (a) substantial goal cónflict between principals and agents, such that agent opportunisms is likely (e.g. owners and managers, managers and professionals, suppliers and buyers); (b) sufficient outcome uncertainty to trigger the risk implications of the theory (e.g. new product innovation, young and small firms, recently deregulated industries); and (c) unprogrammmed or team-oriented jobs in which evaluation of behaviors is difficult. By emphasizing these contexts, researchers can use agency theory where it can be most rigorously tested. Topics such as innovation and settings such as technology-based firms are particularly attractive because they combine goal conflict between professionals and managers, risk, and jobs in which performance evaluation is difficult.

Expand to richer contexts

Perrow (1986) and others have criticized agency theory for being excessively narrow and having few testable implications. Although these criticisms may be extreme, they do suggest that research should be undertaken in new areas. Thus, the recommendation is *to expand to a richer and more complex range of contexts*.

Two areas are particularly appropriate. One is to apply the agency structure to organizational behavior topics that relate to information asymmetry (or deception) in cooperative situations. Examples of such topics are impression management (Gardner and Martinko, 1988), lying and other forms of secrecy (Sitkin, 1987), and blame (Leatherwood and Conlon, 1987). Agency theory might contribute an overall framework in which to place these various forms of self-interest, leading to a better understanding of when such behaviors will be likely and when they will be effective.

The second area is expansion beyond the pure forms of behavior and outcome contracts as described in this article to a broader range of contract alternatives. Most research (e.g. Anderson, 1985; Eisenhardt, 1985, 1988) treats contracts as a dichotomy: behavior versus outcome. However, contracts can vary on a continuum between behavior and outcome contracts. Also, current research focuses on a single reward, neglecting many situations in which there are multiple rewards, differing by time frame and contract basis. For example, upper level managers usually are compensated through multiple rewards such as promotions, stock options, and salary. Both multiple and mixed rewards (behavior and outcome) present empirical difficulties, but they also mirror real life. The richness and complexity of agency theory would be enhanced if researchers would consider this broader spectrum of possible contracts.

Use multiple theories

A recent article by Hirsch *et al.* (1987) eloquently compared economics with sociology. They argued that economics is dominated by a single paradigm, price theory, and a single view of human nature, self-interest. In contrast, the authors maintained that a strength of organizational research is its polyglot of theories that yields a more realistic view of organizations.

Consistent with the Hirsch *et al.* arguments, the recommendation here is *to use agency theory with complementary theories*. Agency theory presents a partial view of the world that, although it is valid, also ignores a good bit of the complexity of organizations. Additional perspectives can help to capture the greater complexity.

This point is demonstrated by many of the empirical studies reviewed above. For example, the Singh and Harianto (1989) and Kosnik (1987) studies support agency theory hypotheses, but they also use the complementary perspectives of hegemony and managerialism. These persepectives emphasize the power and political aspects of golden parachutes and greenmail, respectively. Similarly, the studies by Eisenhardt (1988) and Conlon and Parks (1988) combine institutional and agency theories. The institutional emphasis on tradition complements the efficiency emphasis of agency theory, and the result is a better understanding of compensation. Other examples include Anderson (1985), who coupled agency and transaction cost, and Eccles (1985), who combined agency with equity theory.

Look beyond economics

The final recommendation is *that organizational researchers should look beyond the economics literature*. The advantages of economics are careful developement of assumptions and logical propositions (Hirsch *et al.*, 1987). However, much of this careful theoretical development has already been accomplished for agency theory. For organizational researchers, the payoff now is in empirical research, where organizational researchers have comparative advantage (Hirsch *et al.*, 1987). To rely too heavily on economics with its restrictive assumptions such as efficient markets and its single-perspective style is to risk doing second-rate economics without contributing first-rate organizational research. Therefore, although, it is appropriate to monitor developments in economics, it is more useful to treat economics as an adjunct to more mainstream empirical work by organizational scholars.

CONCLUSION

This chapter began with two extreme positions on agency theory – one arguing that agency theory is revolutionary and a powerful foundation (Jensen, 1983) and the other arguing that the theory addresses no clear problem. is narrow, lacks testable implications, and is dangerous (Perrow, 1986). A more valid perspective lies in the middle. Agency theory provides a unique, realistic, and empirically testable perspective on problems of cooperative effort. The intent of this paper is to clarify some of the confusion surrounding agency theory and to lead organizational scholars to use agency theory in their study of the broad range of principal–agent issues facing firms.

ACKNOWLEDGMENTS

The author thanks Paul Adler, Michele Bolton, Philip Bromiley, Jim Hodder, William Ouchi, Gerald Salancik, Kaye Schoonhoven, and Robert Sutton for their comments and suggestions.

REFERENCES

Anderson, E. (1985) The salesperson as outside agent of empolyee: A transaction cost analysis. *Marketing Science*, 4, 234–54.

Amihud, Y. and Lev, B. (1981) Risk reduction as a managerial motive for conglomerate mergers. *Bell Journal of Economics*, 12, 605–16.

Argawal, A. and Mandelker, G. (1987) Managerial incentives and corporate investment and financing decisions. *Journal of Finance*, 42, 823–37.

Arrow, K. (1971) *Essays in the theory of risk bearing*. Chicago: Markham.

Barnard, C. (1983) *The functions of the executive*. Cambridge, MA: Harvard University Press.

Barney, J. (1988) *Agency theory, empolyee stock ownership and a firm's cost of equity capital*. Unpublished working paper, Texas A&M University, College Station TX.

Barney, J. and Ouchi, W. (Eds) (1986) *Organizational economics*. San Francisco, CA: Jossey-Bass.

Basu, A., Lal, R., Srinivasan, V., and Staelin, R. (1985) Salesforce compensation plans: An agency theoretic perspective. *Marketing Science*, 4, 267–91.

Berle, A. and Means, G. (1932) *The modern corporation and private property*. New York: Macmillan.

Bolton, M. (1988) *Organizational miming: When do late adopters of organizational innovations outperform pioneers?* Paper presented at the meeting of the Academy of Management, Anaheim, CA.

Burt, R. (1979) A structural theory of interlocking corporate directorates, *Social Networks*, 1, 415–35.

Capitalism in the making. (1984, April 30) *Time*, 62.

Chandler, A. (1962) *Strategy and structure*. New York: Doubleday.

Colon, E. and Parks, J. (1988) The effects of monitoring and tradition on compensation arrangements: An experiment on principal/agent dyads. In F. Hoy (Ed.), *Best papers proceedings* (191–5). Anaheim, CA: Academy, of Management.

Cyert, R. and March, J. (1963) *A behavioral theory of the firm*. Englewood Cliffs, NJ: Prentice-Hall.

Dejong, D., Forsythe, R., and Uecker, W. (1985) Ripoffs, lemons and reputation formation in agency relationships: A laboratory market study. *Journal of Finance*, 50, 809–20.

Demski, J. (1980) *A simple case of indeterminate financial reporting*. Working paper, Stanford University.

Demski, J. and Feltham, G. (1978) Economic incentives in budgetary control systems. *Accounting Review*, 53, 336–59.

Dornbusch, S. and Scott, W.R. (1974) *Evaluation and the exercise of authority*. San Francisco, CA: Jossey-Bass.

Eccles, R. (1985) Transfer pricing as a problem of agency. In J. Pratt and R. Zeckhauser (Eds), *Principals and agents: The structure of business* (151–86). Boston, MA: Harvard Business School Press.

Eisenhardt, K. (1985) Control: Organizational and economic approaches. *Management Science*, 31, 134–49.

Eisenhardt, K. (1988) Agency and institutional explanations of compensation in retail sales. *Academy of Management Journal*, 31, 488–511.

Fama, E. (1980) Agency problems and the theory of the firm. *Journal of Political Economy*, 88, 288–307.

Fama, E. and Jensen, M. (1983) Separation of ownership and control. *Journal of law and economics*, 26, 301–25.

Galbrath, J. (1973) *Designing complex organizations*. Reading MA: Addison-Wesley.

Gardner, W. and Martinko, M. (1988) Impression management; An observational study linking audience characteristics with verbal self presentaions. *Academy of Management Journal*, 31, 42–65.

Gausch, J. and Weiss, A. (1981) Self-selection in the labor market. *American Economic Review*, 71, 275–84.

Harris, M. and Raviv, A. (1978) Some results on incentive contracts with application to education and employment, health insurance, and law enforcement. *American Economic Review*, 68, 20–30.

Harris, M. and Raviv, A. (1979) Optimal incentive contracts with imperfect information. *Journal of Economic Theory*, 20, 231–59.

Hirsch, P. and Friedman, R. (1986) Collaboration or paradigm shift? Economic vs. behavioral thinking about policy? In J. Pearce and R. Robinson (Eds), *Best papers proceedings* (31–5). Chicago: Academy of Management.

Hirsch, P., Michaels, S., and Friedman, R. (1987) "Dirty hands" versus "clean models": Is sociology in danger of being seduced by econmics? *Theory and Society*, 317–36.

Holmstrom, B. (1979) Moral hazard and observability. *Bell Journal of Economics*, 10, 74–91.

Jensen, M. (1983) Organization theory and methodology. *Accounting Review*, 56, 319–38.

Jensen, M. (1984) Takeovers: Folklore and science. *Harvard Business Review*, 62(6), 109–21.

Jensen, M. and Meckling, W. (1976) Theory of the firm: Managerial behavior, agency costs, and ownership structure. *Journal of Financial Economics*, 3, 305–60.

Jensen, M. and Roeback, R. (1983) The market for corporate control: Empirical evidence. *Journal of Financial Economics*, 11, 5–50.

Kahneman, D. and Tversky, A. (1979) Prospect theory: An analysis of decisions under risk. *Econometrica*, 47, 263–91.

Kosnik, R. (1987) Greenmail: A study in board performance in corporate gioverance. *Administrative Science Quarterly*, 32, 163–85.

Lambert, R. (1983) Long-term contracts and moral hazard *Bell Journal of Economics*, 14, 441–52.

Lawrence, P. and Lorsch, J. (1967) *Organization and environment*. Boston, MA: Division of research, Harvard Business School.

Leatherwood, M. and Conlon, E. (1987) Diffusibility of blame: Effects on persistence in a project. *Academy of management Journal*, 30, 836–48.

MacCrimmon, K. and Wehrung, D. (1986) *Taking risks: The management of uncertainty*. New York: Free Press.

March, J. (1962) The business firm as a political coalition *Journal of Politics*, 24, 662–78.

March, J. and Shapira, Z. (1987) Managerial perspectives on risk and risk taking. *Management Science*, 33, 1404–18.

March, J. and Simon, H. (1958) *Organizations*. New York: Wiley.

McGrath, J., Martin, J., and Kukla, R. (1982) *Judgement calls in research*. Beverly Hills, CA: Sage.

Meet Mike Jensen, the professor of merger mania. (1988, February 8) *Business Week*, 66–7.

Mitnick, B. (1986) *The theory of agency and organizational analysis*. Unpublished working paper, University of Pittsburgh.

Ouchi, W. (1979) A conceptual framework for the design of organizational control mechanisms. *Management Science*, 25, 833–48.

Pearce, J., Stevenson, W., and Perry, J. (1985) Managerial compensation based on organizational performance: A time series analysis of the effects of merit pay. *Academy of Management Journal*, 28, 261–78.

Perrow, C. (1986) *Complex organizations*. New York: Random House.

Pettigrew, A. (1973) *The politics of organizational decision making*. London: Tavistock.

Pfeffer, J. (1981) *Power in organizations*. Marshfield, MA: Pittman.

Pfeffer, J. and Salancik, G. (1974) Organizational decision making as a ploitical process: The case of a university budget. *Administrative Science Quarterly*, 19, 135–51.

Ross, S. (1973) The economic theory of agency: The principal's problem. *American Economic Review*, 63, 134–9.

Shavell, S. (1979) Risk sharing and incentives in the principal and agent relationship. *Bell Journal of Economics*, 10, 53–73.

Singh, H. and Harianto, F. (1989) Management-board relationships, takeover risk and the adoption of golden parachutes: An empirical investigation. *Academy of Management Journal*, 32(1), 7–24.

Sitkin, S. (1987) *Secrecy in organizations: The limits of legitimate information control*. Working paper, University of Texas, Austin.

Spence, A.M. (1975) The economics of internal organizations: An introduction. *Bell Journal of Economics*, 6, 163–72.

Spence, A.M. and Zeckhauser, R. (1971) Insurance, Information, and individual action. *American Economic Review*, 61, 380–7.

Thompson, J. (1967) *Organizations in action*. New York: McGraw-Hill.

Ungson, G. and Steers, R. (1984) Motivation and politics in executive compenstion. *Academy of Management Review*, 9, 313–23.

Walker, G. and Weber, D. (1984) A transaction cost approach to make-or-buy decisions. *Administrative Science Quarterly*, 29, 373–91.

Walking, R. and Long, M. (1984) Agency theory, managerial welfare, and takeover bid resistance. *The Rand Journal of Economics*, 15, 54–68.

White, H. (1985) Agency as control. In J. Pratt and R. Zeck hauser (Eds), *Principals and agents: The structure of busines* (187–214). Boston: Harvard Business School Press.

Williamson, O. (1975) *Markets and hierarchies: Analysis and antitrust implications*. New York: Free Press.

Wilson, R. (1968) On the theory of syndicates. *Econometrica*, 36, 119–32.

Wolfson, M. (1985) Empirical evidence of incentive problems and their mitigation in oil and gas shelter programs. In J. Pratt and R. Zeckhauser (Eds), *Principals and agents: The structure of business* (101–26). Boston, MA: Harvard Business School Press.

Zneger, T. (1988) *Agency sorting, agent solutions and diseconomies of scale: An empirical investigation of empolyment contracts in high technology R&D*. Paper presented at the meeting of the Academy of Management, Anaheim, CA.

PART THREE

Managerial hegemony

INTRODUCTION TO PART THREE

The revelations by Mace (Chapter 7) concerning the difference between the myth and reality of the powers and responsibilities of company boards of directors would confirm the fears of agency theorists. The ineffective performance of directors revealed in the companies investigated by Mace suggests that they were incapable of adequately representing any interest. This was an era of the 1960s' ascendancy of corporate executives, when powerful CEOs selected and controlled the boards of directors of the companies they ran. Mace outlines how CEOs in the United States were able to determine board membership, to decide what boards could and could not do, controlled the information and professional advice the board received and determined the compensation of senior executives, including, often, themselves. When corporations fail, the question always arises, 'Where were the board of directors?' However, there is a wide gap between what directors are supposed to do, what people generally assume directors do, and what they are actually allowed to do in practice. Mace catalogues how dysfunctional boards rather than being exceptional, became normal in the United States.

A more considered and contemporary view of the potential power of boards of directors is presented by Lorsch and MacIver (Chapter 8) who emphasize the importance of understanding board processes to assess the relative influence of the board. They suggest, to comprehend the essential reality of corporate governance in any country, it is necessary to understand the relationship between owners, managers and the board of directors. They chart a progression in the power of boards of directors in the United States, from the time that Mace described when they were becoming increasingly ornamental, to the early stages of becoming more independent and empowered in response to public concerns regarding the activities of corporations, particularly in their overseas operations. Then in the 1980s as the market for corporate control intensified, the focus on the boardroom receded, supplanted by the discipline of capital markets as the rate of mergers, takeovers and acquisitions increased. Finally, in the 1990s, with an increasing incidence of corporate collapse and market failure in the context of a constantly changing and developing market environment, there were increasing pressures from government, institutions and the public for more active and independent boards.

"Directors: Myth and Reality"

from Harvard Business School Press (1971)

Myles L. Mace

Boards of directors have been part of our business scene for over 150 years, but their functions have not been clearly defined and generally accepted through practice in the management of corporations. The provisions of the general corporation law, "The business of a corporation shall be managed by a board of at least three directors," and hundreds of judicial opinions written on legal issues involving directors, provide no consistent and useful definitions of what directors' functions are. There is an abundance of business literature attempting to define appropriate roles for boards, but these efforts, while slightly less general than the phrase "shall manage," do not describe with useful precision what boards should do.

As I served on and worked with boards of directors, it became clear that there was a considerable gap between what directors in fact do and what the business literature said they should do. My research work and this report were efforts to determine what directors really do and to measure the gap between the myths of business literature and the realities of business practice.

WHAT DIRECTORS DO

In most companies boards of directors serve as a source of advice and counsel, serve as some sort of discipline, and act in crisis situations if the president dies suddenly or is asked to resign because of unsatisfactory management performance.

Advice and counsel

It was found that most presidents and outside board members agree that the role of directors is largely advisory and not of a decision-making nature. Management manages the company, and board members serve as sources of advice and counsel to the management. Also most presidents exploit the sources of advice represented on the board, both at board meetings and outside as well. And some thoughtful presidents, when selecting new members of the board to fill vacancies, identify the particular sets of desired qualities or areas of advice – general or specialized – which the presidents believe will add something to their management decisions.

Since typically directors do not devote substantial amounts of time to the affairs of the companies they serve, their advice cannot be of the sort which requires lengthy and penetrating analysis. Accustomed, however, to dealing with top management problems involving sums of money and financial implications of considerable magnitude, directors, within the time constraints, can provide useful inputs to presidents willing to listen.

Outside directors were found to be especially helpful in the advisory role where their general or specialized backgrounds and experiences could be applied to the specific management problems of the company served. For example, if new loans are to be negotiated, or if new financing is to be arranged, these are the kinds of problems commonly faced by those on the board, and their judgments on interest rates or terms are useful to the president. Or if the management of a company's pension plan is under review, the experience of other top executives is another bit of useful evidence for the president working for a solution. And if a new plant location, domestic or abroad, is involved in a request for a capital appropriation, members of the board with similar recent experience can often suggest useful and sometimes new factors bearing on the decision to commit large amounts of capital to a specific location. Occasionally, but not frequently, the advice and counsel of a board member leads to a reconsideration or a modification of a management's commitment or decision. Occasionally, but very rarely, the advice and counsel of a board member may lead to a reversal of a management commitment or decision.

Some sort of discipline

A second role performed by boards of directors is serving as some sort of discipline for the president and his subordinate management. The president and his subordinates know that periodically they must appear before a board made up largely of their peers. It was found that even in those situations where managements know from previous experience that members of the board will not ask penetrating, discerning, and challenging questions, considerable care is taken in preparing figures and reports for board meetings. Something in the way of discipline results simply from the fact that regular board meetings are held.

Presidents and other members of management, in describing the discipline value of boards, indicated that the requirement of appearing formally before a board of directors consisting of respected, able people of stature, no matter how friendly, causes the company organization to do a better job of thinking through their problems and of being prepared with solutions, explanations, or rationales.

The discipline value of boards was found to serve as an administrative device for presidents to use in establishing standards of performance for work done by subordinates. With capital appropriations on the agenda for the next board meeting, many presidents remind functional or divisional managers that market and financial justifications have to be carefully organized and documented so that there will be no possibility of embarrassing questions from board members.

As an element of the discipline concept described by those interviewed, some used the phrase "corporate conscience." The board of directors is regarded as the guardian to assure, and to represent to the outside world, that the president and his subordinates do not engage in what might be regarded by outsiders as unconscionable conduct. The establishment of a compensation and stock option committee, for example, consisting entirely of outside directors with the president serving as an *ex officio* member, is assurance, at least theoretically, that compensation policies and practices do not exceed the appropriate bounds of reasonableness.

Usually the symbols of corporate conscience are more apparent than real, and presidents with complete powers of control make the compensation policies and decisions. The compensation committee, and the board which approves the recommendations of the compensation committee, are not in most cases decision-making bodies. These decisions are made by the president, and in most situations the committee and board approval is perfunctory. The president has de facto powers of control, and in most cases he is the decision maker. The board does, I believe, tend to temper the inclinations of presidents with de facto control, and it does contribute to the avoidance of excesses. Thus it serves the important role of a corporate conscience.

Decision-making in crisis situations

There are two crisis situations where the role of the board of directors is more than advisory. First, if the president dies suddenly or becomes incapacitated, the board has the responsibility to select his successor. In some cases the selection process is largely controlled by the deceased president who has discussed with board members what he wanted them to do "if he is hit by a truck some day." In other instances board members and presidents have neglected to consider the problem of succession. Only when confronted with the unexpected death of the president have they been propelled into a decision-making function. But the board is there – legally constituted to pick a successor and to ensure the continuity of an entity organized to operate in perpetuity.

The drama and trauma that develop when a board of directors has thrust upon it unexpectedly the complete de facto powers of control were illustrated during many of the interviews. The dynamics of the assumption of all or part of the de facto powers of control by individual directors and combines of directors is worthy, in my judgment, of a separate study.

The second crisis situation in which the board of directors performs a decision-making role is when leadership and performance of the president are so unsatisfactory that a change must be made. Here the president is asked to resign – an important decision. And then the board must decide upon a successor – an equally important decision.

I have concluded that generally boards of directors do not do an effective job of evaluating or measuring the performance of the president. Rarely are standards or criteria established and agreed upon by which the president can be measured other than the usual general test of corporate profitability, and it is surprising how slow some directors are to respond to years of steadily declining profitability. Since directors are selected by the president, and group and individual loyalties have been developed through working together, directors are reluctant to measure the executive performance by the president carefully against specific standards. Directors base their appraisals largely on data and reports provided by the president himself. Also, top executives serving as outside directors, being exceedingly busy men, typically do not devote the time to pursue through further inquiry any concerns they may deduce from the data presented to them as directors, even when the concern might extend to the performance of the president.

In those situations where mounting and persuasive evidence leads individual directors or groups of directors to a conclusion that the president is unsatisfactory, it was found that one of three courses of action is usually followed:

(1) *Hire a management consultant.* Periodic management audits by consulting firms appear to be increasingly common and accepted by top executives even in highly successful enterprises. Employing consultants to identify problems at the president's level and to recommend changes, it was found, is used as a means of handling discreetly the unpleasant task of communicating to a president that he is inadequate.

(2) *Resign from the board.* This is the most common and typical response of directors who suspect or conclude that the president is unsatisfactory. Resignation from boards for plausible reasons such as conflict of interest enables a director to avoid facing the ultimate and inevitably unpleasant task of acting to replace a president. In addition, with public disclosure of an apparently reasonable basis for a resignation, typically there is no embarrassment to the company or to the believed-to-be-inadequate president.

(3) *Ask the president to resign.* Most boards of directors and most individual directors are intensely reluctant to face the unpleasant conclusion that the president of the company must be terminated. While sometimes the unpleasantness is avoided by hiring outside consultants or by resigning from the board, there are some situations in which board members who have procrastinated in taking any action find themselves obligated to face the task of asking the president to resign. These situations were found to be relatively rare.

In these cases where the board assumed an important decision-making role by asking for the president's resignation, I found that board members were impressive in their ability and their willingness to assume top corporate responsibilities measured by any set of standards. For the most part the outside directors remained on the board and devoted more than casual amounts of time to the company in distress. Many directors expressed regret for not having responded to the symptoms of weakness they had seen earlier, now more recognizable than before. Finally having faced the issue of the president's shortcomings, however, they stayed on the board even though it would have been less embarrassing not to be identified with a company with top management problems. They gave more of their time to the affairs of the ailing company, and they acted as responsible corporate citizens by assuming for the interim the de facto powers of control held previously by the president.

WHAT DIRECTORS DO NOT DO

The business literature describing the classical functions of boards of directors typically includes three important roles: (1) establishing basic objectives, corporate strategies, and broad policies; (2) asking discerning questions; and (3) selecting the president.

Establishing objectives, strategies, and policies

I found that boards of directors of most large and medium-sized companies *do not* establish objectives, strategies, and policies, however defined. These roles are performed by company managements. Presidents and outside directors generally agreed that only management can and should have these responsibilities.

The determination of a company's objectives, strategies, and direction requires considerable study of the organization's strengths and weaknesses and its place in the competitive environment, careful, time-consuming, penetrating analysis of market opportunities, and a matching of the organizational capacities to meet and serve the changing requirements of the market. And the market, for more and more companies, includes opportunities abroad, thus adding another complicating dimension of analysis. The typical outside director does not have time to make the kinds of studies needed to establish company objectives and strategies. At most he can approve positions taken by management, and this approval is based on scanty facts and not time-consuming analysis.

Giving operational meaning to a set of defined corporate objectives is usually achieved by allocating or re-allocating corporate capital resources. Statements of objectives and strategies are merely products of an analytical exercise until steps are taken to modify or redirect the company's activities through new allocations of corporate capital. The managements of a few companies, it was found, do not accept the idea that boards can or should be involved in the process of capital appropriations, even in an advisory capacity. Accordingly, studies and approvals of capital appropriations are made at management levels and not at the level of the board of directors.

In most companies the allocation of capital resources, including the acquisition of other enterprises, is accomplished through a management process of analysis resulting in recommendations to the board and in requests for approval by the board. The minimum dollar amounts which require board approval and the amount of analytical supporting data accompanying the requests vary among companies. Approval by boards in most companies is perfunctory, automatic, and routine. Presidents and their subordinates, deeply involved in analysis and decision-making prior to presentation to the board, believe in the correctness of their recommendations and almost without exception they are unchallenged by members of the board. Rarely do boards go contrary to the wishes of the president.

In a few instances boards of directors do establish objectives, strategies, and major policies, but these are exceptions. Here the president wants the involvement of directors and not only allows but insists on full discussion, exploration of the issues, agreement, and decision by the board along with the president.

Asking discerning questions

A second classical role ascribed to boards of directors is that of asking discerning questions – inside and outside the board meetings. Again it was found that directors *do not*, in fact, do this. Board meetings are not regarded as proper forums for discussions arising out of questions asked by board members. It is felt that board meetings are not intended as debating societies.

Many board members cited their lack of understanding of the problems and the implications of topics that are presented to the board by the president, and to avoid "looking like idiots" they refrain from questions or comments.

Presidents generally do not want to be challenged by the questions of directors, especially if subordinates of the president are on the board or attending the meeting. It was found that most presidents profess that they want questions asked by interested members of the board, but I concluded that while they say this and even go to some trouble to make directors feel that they are free to do so, actually the presidents do not want questioning or comment. The unsophisticated director may learn from experiencing rebuffs that presidents do not want penetrating, issue-provoking questions but only those which are gentle and supportive and and an affirmation that the board approves of him. Many presidents stated that board members should manifest by their queries, if any, that they approve of the management. If a director feels that he has any basis for doubts and disapproval, most of the presidents interviewed believe that he should resign.

The lack of active discussion of major issues at typical board meetings and the absence of discerning questions by board members result in most board meetings resembling the performance of traditional and well-established, almost religious, rituals. In most companies it would be possible to write the minutes of a board meeting in advance. The format is always the same, and the behavior and involvement of directors are completely predictable – only the financial figures are different.

Not many exceptions to this were found. A few presidents do, in fact, want discerning, challenging questions and active discussion of important issues at the board meetings. They think of the board as accountable and responsible to the company's owners. There are also a few directors who do in fact ask discerning questions notwithstanding the desires of the president.

Typical garden-variety outside directors, selected by the president and generally members of a peer group, do not ask questions inside or outside of board meetings. However, directors who serve on corporate boards of companies because they own or represent the ownership of substantial shares of stock generally do, in fact, ask discerning questions. Their willingness to query presidents is in part a manifestation of the split in the de facto powers of control of the companies. The large stockholder–directors are not usually on the board because the president wants them there, but because, through cumulative voting procedures, they can force their way onto the board.

Directors as described in the literature represent the stockholders. Yet typically they are actually selected by the president and not by the stockholders. Accordingly the directors are on the board because the president wants them there. Implicitly, and frequently explicitly, the directors in point of fact represent the president. But a large stockholder–director is not selected by the president and does not therefore represent the president; rather he represents himself and an interest more likely to be consistent with that of the other stockholders. The attitude of the large stockholder–director generally is: "This is my money – these are my assets." The attitude of the outside non-stockholder–director usually is: "This is somebody else's money – these are not my assets." These differing attitudes with regard to stock ownership often are manifested in the extent to which discerning questions are asked of the president by the directors.

Selecting the president

A third classical role usually regarded as a responsibility of the board of directors is the selection of the president. Yet it was found that in most companies directors do not in fact select the president except under the two crisis situations cited earlier. In some situations formal or informal committees of outside members of boards are charged with the responsibility of evaluating candidates inside the management for the presidency. But generally these committees have no more control over the naming of the president than do similar committees charged with identifying and recommending the names of candidates for board membership. In both committee situations the president with de facto powers of control essentially makes the decisions. The administrative use by the president of board committees to evaluate candidates for his successor in the presidency gives the selection process an appearance of careful evaluation and objectivity. But in most cases the decision as to who should succeed the president is made by the president himself.

Certainly the president knows the key members of his organization better than anyone else. He has worked with them closely and typically over considerable periods of time. He has observed them under various conditions of stress and he, far better than anyone else on the board, can judge and predict which of the inside candidates can best fit the essentially unique set of job requirements of the company's presidency.

Board members with relatively brief exposure to company executives – whether on the board or not – base their appraisals necessarily on very inadequate evidence. When insiders appear before the board for presentations of their divisional operations, for example, or to explain a request for a large capital appropriation, the setting is artificial and synthetic. Executives, aware that the process of evaluation is going on, rehearse their appearances to communicate to the board that they have the capacities and skills needed for the presidency. And the most that outside directors can conclude from such an exposure is: "The executive gave a well-organized presentation, he answered questions well, he spoke well, and he handled himself well."

Boards of directors were found to serve in an advisory role in the selection of a new president – in their capacity as a sort of corporate conscience. The process of electing a new president requires a vote by the board, and the president generally observes the amenities of corporate good manners by discussing his choice with individual members prior to the meeting. Rarely does a board of directors reject a candidate for the presidency who is recommended by the president.

THE POWERS OF CONTROL IN THE CORPORATION

What boards of directors do is determined in large part by the location of the powers of control of the company, and by how the holders of the powers of control choose to exercise those powers.

In the small family company the ownership of the stock and the management are identical. The powers of control are in the family owners, and what the board of directors does is determined by the owners. In my earlier study it was found that the board usually consists of the father (the founder), his wife, and the family attorney. The owner–managers of some small companies add outside directors to multiply the inputs to policy-making, policy implementation, and day-to-day operating problems. The primary function of the outside directors is to provide a source of advice and counsel to the family owner–managers, and they do not serve in a decision-making role except in the case of the unforeseen death of the dominant family owner–manager. Even then, the real decision typically is made by his heirs. They have the authority to manage the enterprise, and the board is at most a legally required body which can be used for advice and counsel on management or family problems. The family owners determine what the board does or does not do.

At the opposite end of the spectrum is the large, widely-held corporation in which typically the president and members of the board own little stock. Here the *de jure* powers of control are dispersed among thousands of owners – stockholders who are generally unorganized as owners, and essentially unorganizable. And yet the president, in the absence of control or influence by the owners of the enterprise, typically does have the de facto powers to control the enterprise, and with these powers of control it is the president who, like the family owner–managers in the small company, determines in large part what the board of directors does or does not do.

Between these two corporate situations there are many variations and combinations of centres of control, or ownership influences on control, of the company. Complete de facto control by the professional manager–president may be diminished or influenced by the presence on the board of a person who owns, or represents the ownership of, a substantial block of stock. In this case the president's de facto powers of control in determining what the board does or does not do may be affected by what the owners or owner–representatives regard as appropriate functions of board members. This may constitute a challenge to the president. It was found that many directors who own, or represent the ownership of, substantial numbers of shares of stock take a deep interest in the operations of the company, spend considerable time in learning the business, and insist on being involved in major company decisions. The degree of the president's de facto powers of control in these cases is affected by the involvement of company stock owners.

Some directors who own or represent the ownership of large numbers of shares were found to be passive, compliant, and not involved in major company problems, and the president's complete powers of control are not diminished or influenced. Analysis of the situations where substantial stockholdings are represented on the board produced no factors which make possible any reliable prediction of whether the stockholder-director will take an active and involved question-asking role. There is some evidence that if the owner of the stock had come into possession of it through his own efforts, such as an entrepreneur developing his own business and then selling it to a larger company for its shares, the acquired entrepreneur will take a very active role as a director of the acquiring company. If the outside director with large stockholdings is a second or third generation heir of an entrepreneur, his involvement as an active director is less likely.

Another situation where the president of a large or medium-sized company was found not to possess the full and complete de facto powers of control is where a retired president stays on as a member of the board. Then typically the outside board members have been selected and invited to the board by the retired president, not the new president. A similar complication of relationships was found to exist in the situation following the sudden death of the president where his successor is designated by the board of directors. The new president holds his position because the directors selected him – directors who were themselves selected by his predecessor. While the new president is demonstrating his capacities to head the enterprise, the outside directors generally share the powers of control of the company. In both cases, with the passage of time, and the designation by the new president of new directors who are *his* directors, the complete powers of control will flow back into the office of the president.

The dynamics of the distribution and flow of powers of control between and among the directors and the president is an appropriate and worthy area for further research. Generally it was found that when the president and the directors own only a little stock, the president possesses and exercises the complete powers of control of the enterprise.

In addition to the location of the powers of control, an important factor affecting what boards of directors do and do not do is *how* the powers of control are exercised by the holders of these powers.

It was found that most presidents are completely aware of their powers of control, but they choose to exercise them in a moderate manner acceptable to their peers on the board. The president communicates to *his* board members that he does indeed control the enterprise, and while this is usually done discreetly, it is understood and accepted by the directors. Many of them, as presidents of their own companies with board members of their own, thoroughly understand the existence and location of the powers of control.

Most presidents think of their directors essentially as a source of advice and counsel, both at the board meetings and outside the meetings. The topics on which advice and counsel are provided, of course, lie within the discretion of the president who determines what items appear on the board meeting agenda and who picks the circumstances under which he chooses to seek the assistance of directors outside the periodic board meetings. Most presidents are willing, it was found, to listen to, and to take into account, the constructive advisory suggestions of directors.

The cases where presidents are described as exercising their de facto powers of control in a moderate manner include most of the situations studied. A few cases were found, however – and these were dramatic exceptions – in which the manner of the president can be characterized as that of a tyrant. A few presidents regard their board as an unnecessary legal appendage and board meetings as bothersome interruptions of their busy day-to-day management of the company. Such presidents may try to reduce the number of time-wasting board meetings by having them quarterly rather than monthly. They may also, for example, make top management changes without concurrence by, or even coordination with, the board. Their disrespect for the board and board functions flaunts their powers of control rather unpleasantly.

Outside directors of tyrant-led companies stated that their willingness to continue in completely meaningless roles as directors is attributable to "my long-standing friendship with the president, for whom I have the greatest admiration," or, "This is a very large and successful company and there is a certain amount of prestige in being identified with it as a director," or "The perquisites are great; where else can I get a free winter vacation in the Caribbean, great duck hunting in the fall, and a company jet which picks me up for every board meeting?"

This tyrannical exercise of the powers of control by presidents was found to exist in a relatively few situations, and an equally small fraction of cases were found in which the president's manner was at the other extreme. Some presidents, but not many, are completely aware that they have de facto powers of control and that they can behave in their relationships with their board in any manner that they elect, but they choose to include the board as a major and important element in the management structure. Such a president accepts the classical concept that the board does indeed represent the stockholders and as the president he is only one man in the total organization; and he wants the involvement of outside directors in determining objectives, asking discerning questions, and appraising and evaluating his performance as president. In these situations usually the only insiders on the board are the president and the chairman. Of all the companies studied over the years, including the last two of full-time intensive field research, only a relatively small minority of instances were encountered where the president felt this way.

OTHER FACTORS AFFECTING WHAT BOARDS OF DIRECTORS DO

The way directors are selected

Directors are generally selected and invited to serve on the board by the president of the company. In some instances a nominating committee of the board is created to identify, screen, and recommend candidates for board membership. It was found, though, that even with the presumed objectivity of a committee of outside directors, the decision as to new members is made by the president.

Again it should be noted that if one or more existing directors own or represent the ownership of substantial stock, the president's de facto power to select new directors may be challenged. In these cases the stock-owning directors are interested in adding new directors of *their* choice, and the president is interested in new directors of *his* choice. Discussion and negotiation inevitably result in some sort of agreement on who should be added, and the balance of power issue continues.

The stockholders, of course, unless their holdings are substantial enough to assure representation on the board through the provisions of cumulative voting or to result in an invitation by the president to serve, play no part in the selection of directors to fill vacancies or in the nomination of directors' names to be included in the annual proxy statement.

Interview discussions on the topic of who makes a good director indicated that presidents in selecting directors for their companies regard the titles and prestige of candidates as of primary importance. Candidates are usually chosen who are in positions equal to those of the other board members, in companies of prestige equivalent to that of the company to be served. If existing board members are chairmen and presidents of companies or senior partners of leading financial or legal firms, potential board members with lesser titles are rarely considered. Newly elected company presidents and newly elected university presidents and deans of graduate schools, it was found, were surprised by the sudden influx of invitations they received to become board members of large and prestigious companies.

In addition to the qualifications of prestige titles in prestige institutions – both business and academic – outside directors are selected who are known as noncontroversial, friendly, sympathetic, congenial, and understanders of the system. Boat-rockers and wave-makers generally are not the choice of presidents with de facto powers of control and with freedom of choice as to who should serve on their boards.

While most presidents prefer to include on their boards only those who have appropriate titles and positions, there are a few presidents who believe that the requirement of prestige titles is not important. They want board members who will participate in the management of the company. Not surprisingly, these presidents are the same ones who want board members who will help establish corporate objectives, ask discerning questions, and evaluate the performance of the president.

Motivations for serving as directors

The fact that the top executives of companies, academic officials, and leading partners of financial institutions and law firms are exceedingly busy people makes it unlikely that they can become deeply involved in another company's problems. They are successful in their respective areas of primary activity because they pay the price of almost complete devotion to the enterprises for which they are responsible. The top position of virtually all business organizations is a time-consuming responsibility. The result is that most top executives devote only nominal amounts of time to serving as directors of other companies.

The principal forces found to motivate business executives to accept board membership are: (1) the opportunity to learn through exposure to other companies' operations something of value that might be useful in their own situations; and (2) the intangible prestige value of identification with well-known and prestigious companies, executives, and other directors.

With few exceptions, top executives who serve as directors of other companies are extraordinary men. The competitive process by which men get promoted through the various levels of business and other large organizations generally provides highly qualified leaders of enterprises. They have demonstrated capacities, skills, and abilities to head significant companies, and they have the qualities to serve as outstanding directors of other enterprises. What they do as directors, however, is determined by the company president with control over their selection. Most presidents do not want outside directors to become involved in their companies, and the selection of busy top executives of equally prestigious organizations insures that by the nature of their positions they will not have time to give more than nominal attention to the affairs of the company served as a director.

* * * * *

During my last twenty-five years of involvement and study of boards of directors, two critically important issues concerning board membership were identified, and executives who were interviewed during the current field research were asked to comment on them: (1) Should inside full-time employees, other than the chairman of the board and the president, serve on the board of directors? (2) Should members of investment banking firms serve as directors of other companies?

THE ISSUE OF INSIDE DIRECTORS

I found that most presidents, even with complete de facto powers of control, prefer to have substantial numbers of insiders on their boards of directors. Very few presidents with whom I have discussed the inside/outside directors' issue believe or follow the practice of having all outsiders on the board (other than the chairman or the president). Most of those interviewed had one or more retired former company executives on their boards, but in all cases they counted them as outsiders when calculating the inside/outside director ratio.

Many reasons were given for having substantial numbers of insiders on the board of directors:

1 Insiders on the board are available for comment on the operations and problems for which they are responsible. If questions arise during a board meeting with regard to, say, a capital appropriation, the interested vice president-director can respond, thus expediting the processing of capital appropriations requiring board approval.
2 Board membership is said to be good for morale, not only of the insiders on the board, but also of their subordinates whose aspirations can appropriately include future board membership for themselves.
3 Membership on the board constitutes a form of intangible compensation – a reward.
4 Insiders serving as directors are exposed to broader management points of view, thus contributing to their growth as executives. Value is found in having insiders learn through personal experience how the management process works at board level.
5 By having key insiders on the board, outside directors, working with them, will be able to evaluate them in terms of their abilities to serve as president should the incumbent president die unexpectedly.

I believe that the reasons given for having insiders other than the chairman and the president on the board are largely rationalizations and specious. Most of the objectives cited can be accomplished through other means. The reason insiders are on boards of directors is that their presidents want them there. If the president with de facto control perceives the functions of the board to be a source of advice and counsel and some sort of discipline, but a decision-making body only in the event of a crisis, then the proportion of inside/outside directors is academic and essentially irrelevant. In these cases the presence of insiders only reduces the number of sources of outside advice. But for the president this is counterbalanced by the presence at meetings of a core of presumed-to-be-loyal supporters.

If the president perceives the role of the board to be the fulfillment of the three functions listed above, but if in addition he wants the board to represent the stockholders' interests by determining objectives, strategies, and policies, asking discerning questions, and selecting, evaluating, and measuring the president's performance – then it is apparent that there should be no insiders on the board other than the chairman and the president. The logical extension of this conclusion is, of course, that the board should be made up entirely of outsiders, and that the chairman and the president should not be on the board themselves.

No instances were found among the companies studied where all directors were outsiders.

THE ISSUE OF INVESTMENT BANKERS AS DIRECTORS

During the last decade there has been increasing discussion among interested participants and observers as to whether investment bankers should serve on boards of directors. Partners of investment banking firms constitute one of the larger sources of directors. My discussions with top executives, both before and during the two-year field research period, indicated clearly that the issue is regarded as timely and important. It was observed also that most of those interviewed expressed firm convictions as to whether investment bankers should or should not serve on boards. Rarely was there a middle ground.

It was found that investment bankers, by the nature of their business, are regarded as extremely valuable members of boards. On financial matters, investment bankers provide a complementary and a supplementary source of knowledge to the financial expertise within the company. Experienced investment bankers, involved on a daily basis, are aware of money rates nationally and internationally, money terms, and market conditions, and they can evaluate the market's reaction to proposed moves by the company. This kind of current substantive financial intelligence is regarded by most presidents as essential.

In addition, investment bankers, through exposure to many different companies in many different industries and regions, bring to company presidents and company boards of directors what one president described as "a treasury of information." Bankers, as they practice their profession, are collectors of information – they learn the problems faced and approaches followed by presidents of a substantial number of other companies. Thus investment bankers as directors were described as "great pollenizers" – they lift ideas from one company and deposit them in other companies.

But it was acknowledged by corporate presidents as well as by partners of investment banking firms that the essential professional financial skills and the general management pollenizing knowledge are available to company presidents whether representatives of investment banking firms are on the boards or not. Investment firms provide professional services the value of which does not depend upon board membership.

Two persuasive reasons for not having investment bankers on boards were found:

(1) An investment banker on a board generally restricts the president to the professional services of that one firm. A representative of a certain investment banking firm on a company's board serves as a signal to the outside world that a firm–client relationship exists. The result is that other bankers with potentially useful financial services are discouraged from approaching the president of the apparently captive company. This finding was also confirmed by investment bankers who were interviewed. It was generally agreed that their primary reason for serving as company directors is a business-getting device, and if they do not get the financial services business, there is no purpose in being on the company board.

Not only do investment banking firms differ with regard to their relative expertise among the many areas of operations, but also one investment firm will vary from time to time with regard to its staff expertise in a certain area. Thus the president of a company restricted to the services of one investment banking firm with changing qualifications is not necessarily able to procure the best professional services available at the time when they are needed.

It was also quite common to find company presidents referring to "the seat" of a certain investment firm on their board, and observing that over the years the firm continued to be represented even though its representatives changed.

Some presidents and investment bankers stated that presidents are not necessarily limited to the services of one investment banking firm if a representative is on the board. It was found, however, that generally the presence of a banker on a board results in that firm, and only that firm, providing whatever investment services are purchased by the company.

(2) A second reason – and I believe far more important – for not having investment bankers on boards is that if they represent a firm which does investment counseling, employs brokers, or controls or advises mutual funds, the investment banker–director has an absolute, real, and disqualifying conflict of interest. As a director, the banker has access to information not available at the same time to the public or to others in the financial community, and information on companies and their operations is an essential ingredient in the function of investment banking firms.

Investment bankers are sensitively aware of the conflicts of interest resulting from their board memberships, and banking firms generally establish a structure of paper rules of procedure and practice intended to separate valuable inside information secured by one partner from use by another partner in, say, the investment counseling area of the firm. These rules, in my judgment, are patently artificial and generally meaningless. It would be unreal to expect investment banking partners with a mutual interest in their firm's profits not even to talk with each other. Investment bankers, to carry that load of conflict without ever breaching the faith, would have to be more honest than people!

In addition to the conflict of interest arising out of information received as an insider, the investment banker–director has another form of conflict when he identifies a company for acquisition and participates in the negotiations resulting in acquisition. The professional and usually highly competent services of an investment banker in finding companies worthy of acquisition, and then in serving as an adviser on the financial terms of a contract to acquire a company, certainly deserve appropriate fees for the services performed. Typically the fees charged for professional work on acquisitions are a function of the monetary size of the acquisition, and also typically the payment of fees is contingent upon the completion of the acquisition – no acquisition, no fee. If a partner of an investment banking firm is a director of the acquiring company, the conflict of interest is apparent and real. Obviously the interests of his firm will be served through the fees paid for professional services if the identified candidate for acquisition is purchased. Some situations were found where the investment banker–director refrained from voting at the board meeting either on the acquisition or on the fees to be paid to his firm. This in my judgment is a meaningless gesture, in that the banker representative as a director is in a position of influence on the board of directors – an arm's-length relationship is inherently impossible.

I conclude that representatives of investment banking firms should not serve as members of corporate boards of directors.

BOARDS OF DIRECTORS IN FAMILY COMPANIES

This report has been concerned largely with what boards of directors of large- and medium-sized companies in fact do. Reference was made earlier to the balance of powers of control in those situations where the de facto powers of the president were challenged or diminished by owners or representatives of owners of large blocks of stock. There is another distinctive group of companies known as family companies in which members of the boards of directors were found to have similar but different roles from those of directors in other companies.

The singular difference in family companies is that boards of directors operate in a working environment complicated by the psychological implications of family members working in the same organization – with and against each other. Members of a family bring into the business conflicts, rivalries, guilt feelings, ambitions, loyalties, prides, resentments, and interrelationships which are quite different from the characteristics of typical nonfamily companies.

Family members with *de jure* powers of control – or de facto powers if shares have been sold or traded to owners outside the family – determine what the boards of directors do or do not do. Board members, it was found, may be in the position of having to serve as arbitrators and conciliators on issues arising among family members in the company. These issues, many times with emotional extras added to the usual problems encountered in business operations, are amenable to compromise and solution by alert and discreet board members. It was found also that in most family company situations directors serve as sources of advice primarily to the family, and

secondarily to the president if he is not a member of the family. Family owners generally want advice and counsel from directors bearing on, for example, the monitoring and measuring of the performance of the company president if he is not a family member, or on whether or how to sell the enterprise to which of several potential corporate acquirers. The controlling owners also seek advice and counsel on the same subjects as those for nonfamily companies.

Boards of directors serve as some sort of discipline for the president, but especially for nonfamily subordinates in the organization. But in contrast to large- and medium-sized companies, boards generally do not select a successor if the president dies unexpectedly or is found to be unsatisfactory. This type of decision typically is made by members of the family who own or have inherited the ownership of the enterprise.

It was found also that in most family companies boards of directors do not determine corporate objectives, strategies, or general policies. Nor do they ask discerning questions or evaluate the president if he is a family member. If he is not a family member but a professional manager, the owners in control want appraisals of the president by board members but reserve for themselves the decision-making power to terminate his employment.

Two unique problem areas confront directors of family companies:

(1) The inability of fathers in control of family enterprises to be objective in appraising the capacities, skills, and motivations of their sons – This is probably true of most fathers, but the frailty is especially relevant when the sons are candidates for the presidency of a family business organization. And this presents an especially uncomfortable dilemma for the outside director when the family in control owns a relatively small percentage of the stock and the balance is publicly owned.

(2) The use of company assets by controlling family members – Some family companies serve as legal vehicles for the provision of personal services, conveniences, and luxuries to family members at company expense. When the enterprise is owned completely by the family, the only other real party of interest and concern is the Internal Revenue Service, and its task turns on whether the costs are appropriate business expenses. But when the family company includes as stockholders people outside the family,

another party of interest and concern is present. And the director has a problem: "Do I represent the family stockholders, or do I represent all the stockholders?"

The general conclusions on what directors do in most family companies must include mention of a few exceptional family companies where boards of directors do in fact determine objectives, strategies, and general policies; ask discerning questions; evaluate and measure the performance of the president whether he is a member of the family or not; provide advice and counsel; serve as some kind of discipline; and select and elect the president. These situations are rare.

SUMMARY OF FINDINGS

In a final summary of my study of directors, I found that in large- and medium-sized companies where the president and board members own only a few shares of stock:

1 Presidents with de facto powers of control select the members of the boards.
2 Presidents determine what boards do and do not do.
3 Directors selected are usually heads of equally prestigious organizations with primary responsibilities of their own.
4 Heads of businesses and financial, legal and educational organizations are extremely busy men with limited motivation and time to serve as directors of other organizations.
5 Most boards of directors serve as advisors and counselors to the presidents.
6 Most boards of directors serve as some sort of discipline for the organization – as a corporate conscience.
7 Most boards of directors are available to and do make decisions in the event of a crisis.
8 A few boards of directors establish company objectives, strategies, and broad policies. Most do not.
9 A few boards of directors ask discerning questions. Most do not.
10 A few boards evaluate and measure the performance of the president and select and de-select the president. Most do not.

QUESTIONS POSED BY THESE FINDINGS

These conclusions pose questions and challenges to all those who are interested in business:

▨ If this is what directors do,

 – what, if anything, needs to be done?
                              should be done?
                                      by whom?

▨ If this is what directors do,

 – is it enough?

▨ If the roles of the board are defined as:
 to provide advice and counsel;
 to serve as some sort of discipline;
 to serve as a decision-making body in the event of a crisis;

 – don't we need a new set of laws redefining the legal responsibilities of directors?

▨ If the roles of boards are defined so as to serve these three functions and
 to determine objectives, strategies, and policies;
 to ask discerning questions;
 to evaluate and measure the president's performance;
 to select and de-select the president.

 – shouldn't directors spend a great deal more time as directors?
 – is it possible to find competent men and women with the time and motivation to accept directorships with these requirements?
 – should the president select directors charged with evaluating and measuring his own performance?
 – do directors represent the president who selects them, or the stockholders who had nothing to do with their selection?
 – who should select directors?

▨ Do investor–stockholders need a board of directors "to manage" the company?
▨ If directors are needed to comply with legal requirements, why not have a board comprised of insiders only?
▨ Should not the board consist of all outsiders, and serve as a layer of management to which the president reports but of which he is not a member?
▨ What *should* boards of directors do?

"Pawns or Potentates: The Reality of America's Corporate Boards"

from Harvard Business School Press (1989)

Jay W. Lorsch and Elizabeth MacIver

Boardroom – the word alone conjures up visions of power, wealth, and privilege in the minds of most Americans. Almost every publicly owned corporation in America has a boardroom, impressively designed and furnished in a fashion that does nothing to undermine the popular view. The boardroom's core, the symbol of its power, is a massive, highly polished table around which the directors are presumed to make the decisions that govern the corporation and affect the wealth of its owners – the shareholders – and the livelihood of its employees.

This symbol of power seems as appropriate to the company's employees, including many of its managers, as it does to the general public who invest their savings, directly or indirectly, through mutual or pension funds in the shares of the companies. This perception of the role and the power of the board of directors meshes, too, with the traditional legal view of corporate governance.

Directors, however, are less sanguine about their power and capacity to govern. While they don't see themselves as pawns of management, as did their predecessors of a decade ago, they acknowledge a number of constraints on their ability to govern in a timely and effective manner. Such constraints include their own available time and knowledge, a lack of consensus about their goals, and the superior power of management, particularly the CEO-chairman.[1] These are the major conclusions of our research into corporate governance in US publicly owned companies, an investigation prompted by the obvious malaise of US business performance over the past decade.

Accusatory fingers have pointed in many directions but, to date, few have questioned the role of those ultimately legally responsible for the health of America's corporations – their boards of directors. Some have blamed top management's shortsightedness and rigidity for the decline of entire industries, such as automobile, consumer electronics, and steel, and for the ills of major companies within these industries.[2] Others have laid the blame on the high wages and lack of productivity of US workers.[3] Still others have diagnosed the problem as a lack of coherent US industrial policy and business-government cooperation like that which is found in Japan and other Pacific-rim countries.[4] While these possibilities and many others may have merit, what is most striking in the debate is the almost universal exclusion from consideration or censure of that major symbol of American corporate power – the board of directors.[5]

In addition, despite directors' close involvement with the wave of unfriendly takeovers and related mergers, the restructurings and leveraged buyouts, few observers have questioned their role in allowing the market value of their companies' equities to become low enough to make the takeover game so attractive to raiders. The resulting changes in the corporate portrait are significant, some might say staggering. Of the "400" companies listed in *Standard & Poor's* in 1977, 157 had disappeared by 1987. Of that vanished number, 109 had been acquired or had merged, and the rate of such activity has been accelerating. As Fruhan reports, "The dollar value of mergers between 1985 and 1987 exceeded $520 billion – ten times the value of mergers between 1975 and 1977."[6] From 1983 to 1987, he adds, nearly 30 percent of the market value of US companies evaporated through acquisition or merger.[7]

Another, more subtle change has emerged in the shift of company ownership from individual stockholders to institutions. It is difficult to pinpoint the exact percentage of shares of publicly owned companies held by institutions, but we can state that it's as high as 66 percent and in the case of some large companies exceeds 70 percent.[8] Again, understanding how directors deal with this challenge seemed important.

We wanted to learn how current corporate governance practices were contributing to any or all of these changes and challenges, and which difficulties, if any, were inhibiting directors in dealing with events and issues confronting US companies in the past decade. We wanted to know how directors view their role and their responsibility as corporate governors in a changing landscape, how well they feel they are governing, and what are the barriers to more effective governance.

In describing our findings and proposing ideas for improvement, we do not want to convert the management-and-worker bashing of the early 1980s into bashing the board. Blaming everything on the directors would be both unfair and untrue. That so many directors of major corporations gave us their time, candor, and insights indicates their own concerns about their role.

Phrases such as "Made in America" and "The American Way" rang a little less boldly in the 1980s. In business and economic terms, we are no longer the undisputed envy of the world's other industrial nations, nor are we the unquestioned role model to which under- and undeveloped nations aspire. The decline was real and, at least in part, measurable – less certain are the causes and, more important, the cures. We believe this study may illuminate some of the ways in which directors are factors for both good and ill, and how some of the impediments to more effective governance might be removed.

PREVIOUS STUDIES

We began our research mindful of earlier studies of corporate governance.[9] In 1971, for example, Mace described board membership as more of an accolade than an obligation, calling directors "ornaments on a corporate Christmas tree."[10] Directors were usually

chosen from the corporation's executives, both retired and active, from more indirectly related sources such as lawyers and bankers, and from successful friends and acquaintances of the CEO – a sort of "old boys' club," with the protection of shareholder interests and evaluation of top management secondary to the role of advising the CEO.

Corporate boards today are very different from the old elitist corps of overseers with limited responsibility. Not only the challenges of the 1980s, but also events of the 1970s, when directors' conduct was scrutinized in cases where corporations engaged in foreign corrupt practices and made questionable political contributions, have forced changes in the composition and the functioning of boards. Such unsavory activities as bribing foreign officials to keep out competition and paying employees phony "bonuses" that were, after taxes, illegally donated to political candidates[11] prompted critical reports from the American Law Institute (ALI) and the Business Roundtable, adding weight to the forces for change.[12]

A majority of directors now come from outside the corporation, the number of board committees to facilitate the directors' work has risen, and directors today view their role and their responsibilities with a seriousness and an involvement that were often lacking fifteen or more years ago. The following three directors speak for almost everyone we interviewed:

In the early years, being invited to join a board was a sign of respect . . . some people served on a lot of boards because the duties were minimal. We weren't given much information before a meeting and even attendance wasn't essential. If you went, it was to listen to management describe its plans. But now that the courts hold directors liable if they don't uphold the business judgment rule, directors have begun to ask for information so they can make informed decisions. They have to be more responsible now – they can't go on 18 boards now, because it's too dangerous.

Directors today don't want colleagues like the old ones who rubber-stamped management's decisions. You don't want to share responsibilities – or liabilities – with people who don't pull their own weight or do their homework.

Directors are more forward nowadays. There's no more of the good-old-boy club meeting atmosphere, because of the directors' responsibility and liability. They don't assume something is correct simply because the CEO said it. They want proof he's right. I'm on seven boards, and the directors question deeply at every meeting I attend.

While the functioning of boards has unquestionably improved, our study indicates that further innovations are needed if directors are to be effective governors. Earlier studies were predicated on an historical legal view of the directors' roles and the boards' functioning – a unidimensional, even simplistic, perspective crediting directors with complete understanding of their legal accountability and duties, freedom from other pressures impinging on their responsibilities, and presuming their legal authority powerful enough to permit them to govern. Modern directors, however, reveal a different reality – one in which the ability to carry out their legally defined responsibilities is often impeded: one shaped not only by the job's legal specifications, but by the directors' psychological reasons for serving, by limits on their time, by their understanding of their accountabilities, and by relationships among themselves and with the CEO-chairman. While the real directors' world differs from outside perceptions of it, both are imbedded in the historical legal perspective. Thus, understanding that perspective is important.

THE HISTORICAL LEGAL PERSPECTIVE

The concept of the corporation as a legal entity came to the United States with the merchant adventurers' associations that brought commerce to the American colonies from England.[13] The Elizabethan view of the corporation as an artificial entity created by legal fiat was echoed in US law by Chief Justice Marshall in 1819 in the Dartmouth College case, when he stated, "The corporation is an artificial being, invisible, intangible, and existing only in the contemplation of the law."[14] Under the Constitution the right to incorporate was vested in the states as one of their sovereign powers, a right so strictly adhered to that the railroads, for example, found it necessary to incorporate in each state where they operated.

The idea for a board of directors also had its roots in colonial enterprises, which were governed by a council of peers. Benjamin Franklin and Alexander Hamilton built on the idea to create boards of directors for their eighteenth-century enterprises. As Vance points out, two centuries after Alexander Hamilton established "the first real American corporation," the statement of

purpose he gave for directors sounds remarkably modern: "the affairs of the company are to be under the management of 13 directors."[15] The phraseology is similar to that of the General Corporation Law of the State of Delaware, where about 50 percent of publicly owned corporations are incorporated: "The business and affairs of every corporation organized under this chapter shall be managed by or under the direction of a board of directors...."[16]

As commerce expanded in the late eighteenth and early nineteenth centuries, various states vied to have companies domiciled in their jurisdictions, courting them through the creation of the most liberal laws applying to directors. In this context, "liberal" meant that directors would not be held to the same tight standards as trustees, the so-called prudent man rule. Instead, directors were expected to exercise the duty of loyalty and the duty of care, and their conduct was judged according to the business judgment doctrine. In spite of the evolution of corporate law and legal variations among the states, these principles still remain at the heart of directors' responsibilities in all jurisdictions.[17] For this reason we want to explain them briefly, even though readers with a legal background will recognize that they are the bare bones of a director's legal position and that the business-judgment rule is still evolving, particularly in Delaware. Our advice to our director readers, as in all legal matters, is: When in doubt, consult your corporate counsel.

The duty of loyalty is best exemplified when a director who serves on the boards of two companies finds he or she has a conflict between the interests of the two. In such an instance, the court would apply a fairness test in which the director must establish his actions as being appropriately diligent, which is the duty of care. Duty of care, therefore, means using due diligence. Practically, this means the director has an obligation to find out everything that he can that bears on the decision in question. When no conflict is involved, the courts will not interfere with the decisions of the board as long as due care has been exercised, under the business judgment doctrine.[18] However, the business judgment doctrine does not apply when there is a conflict of interest. Nor does it apply when the duty of care has not been exercised, or when there is a breach of the duty of loyalty. In such instances, the courts base their judgment on whether the directors have been intrinsically fair.

In gathering the information needed to exercise business judgment, directors are entitled to rely on their own officers as well as experts. This is one reason why prior studies have placed emphasis on the creation and utilization of committees, and on the availability of information to directors. The board is also protected in delegating to others, although there are specific decisions that cannot be delegated: for example, matters related to dividends, the right to sell the corporation, and mergers and acquisitions.

The capacity to delegate and the fact that the "corporation shall be managed by or under the direction" of the board means that one potentially controversial point between managers and directors is the question of the board's activities and decisions compared to those of management. This matter has become particularly important as there have been calls for more active directors. Both the Business Roundtable and the ALI have addressed the potential problem by recommending what the duties of directors should be. The Business Roundtable specifies that directors have the following duties:

1 Overseeing of management and board selection and succession.
2 Reviewing the company's financial performance and allocating its funds.
3 Overseeing corporate social responsibility.
4 Ensuring compliance with the law.[19]

The ALI provides a different approach to management oversight, but not an incompatible list.

1 Elect, evaluate and, where appropriate, dismiss the principal senior executives.
2 Oversee the conduct of the corporation's business, with a view to evaluation on an ongoing basis, whether the corporation's resources are being managed in a manner consistent with enhancing shareholder gain, [within the law, within ethical considerations, and while directing a reasonable amount of resources to public welfare and humanitarian purposes].
3 Review and approve corporate plans and actions that the board and principal senior executives consider major and changes in accounting principles that the board or principal senior executives consider material.
4 Perform such other functions as are prescribed by law, or assigned to the board under a standard of the corporation.

The board . . . should also have power to

1 Make recommendations to shareholders.
2 Initiate and adopt major corporate plans, commitments, and actions, and material changes in accounting principles and practices; instruct any committees, officers, and employees; and review the actions of any committee, officer, or other employee.
3 Act as to all other corporate matters not requiring stockholder approval.[20]

While both groups use the term oversight, the meaning differs. The ALI's position is that it's impossible for directors to "manage" the corporation, as the Delaware law stipulates, in the limited time they have. Therefore, directors should carry out oversight of management only through review and evaluations. If management is not performing effectively, the directors should replace it. The Business Roundtable believes directors can be realistically involved in setting broad policy directions by working with the CEO and other top managers, and can play the role envisioned in the Delaware statute. This argument is further clouded by the fact that not all lawyers agree with the ALI's position. Moreover, the difference of opinion has had little impact on how managers and directors actually view their role.

However, two underlying assumptions stand out in the Business Roundtable and the ALI statements. First is the premise that the legal authority provided in Delaware, or for that matter in other states, is adequate for directors to carry out these duties. The Business Roundtable was quite specific on this point: "Political models are not relevant to an organization whose principal function is the provision of goods and services; which must perform this function subject to the discipline of the marketplace and competition, and which is already subject to a host of external constraints, legal, social and political."[21] It is easy to understand why an association of CEOs, the most powerful voices in their companies, would take this position and argue for an organization "which is cohesive, not divided, and which is fast moving, responsive, and flexible rather than bound by excessive bureaucratic regulations or formalities, either internal or external."[22]

Such statements are seductive and seem appropriate to the dynamic business climate of the 70s and 80s. They also reflect the preference of these corporate leaders for an organization with no added constraints on their ability to lead. Their jobs are highly complicated and, as the Roundtable argument suggests, their decisions are already constrained by a web of market and other forces.[23] While one can empathize, it is clear the Roundtable is implicitly arguing that directors have no barriers to exercising their legal authority. In recent personal conversations with representatives of the Business Roundtable who are concerned with corporate governance, we found them explicit on this point. The directors, most of whom are also CEOs of companies, feel there are major impediments to carrying out their duties.

The second underlying assumption stands out most clearly in the ALI list of duties – directors are accountable to the shareholders. Their duty is to protect shareholders' interests and provide an adequate return on their investment. Such an assumption is consistent with Delaware court decisions that have ruled that directors are fiduciaries in relation to the corporation and its shareholders, not as individuals, but as a class.[24] In this regard, too, Delaware has been historically consistent with the laws of the other states.

From this perspective, the directors' duties are clear, at least in legal theory. Perhaps in more halcyon times, when the shareholders were individuals, such as the proverbial "little old lady from Peoria," it was also clear in reality. But in an era of institutional ownership, leveraged buyouts, and unfriendly takeovers, understanding who the shareholders are and where their real interests lie is even more difficult. Further, corporations are a fundamental institution in our society and economy. They have many other stakeholders: customers, employees, governments, lenders, suppliers, and communities. According to Delaware law, if directors look out for the long-term interests of shareholders they will also be deemed to have taken care of the corporations' other stakeholders. However, in recent years, in response to unfriendly takeovers, seventeen states, not including Delaware, have enacted laws empowering directors to consider stakeholders other than the shareholders.[25]

The key tenets of the traditional legal perspective, then, are that directors are legally responsible for the management of the corporation; that they are expected to exercise the duties of loyalty, care, and good business judgment. Their primary accountability is to shareholders, although there has been change in this regard in states other than Delaware. These principles are the foundation upon which the structure of corporate governance is built. However,

the data gathered from directors indicate that this structure has some significant shortcomings. This conclusion is due less to inherent flaws in the traditional legal foundation than to the fact that this perspective doesn't recognize many of the human and managerial realities directors encounter as they try to govern.[26]

THE DIRECTOR'S REALITY

From the directors' perspective, their legal authority to manage the corporation is a clear mandate, but problems arise as they try to act upon that authority. To understand their difficulty, we need a closer look at the concept of governance. In a corporation, as in the public arena, governing involves the exercise of authority or power toward a particular end. Thus, to govern effectively, directors must have enough power to influence the course of corporate direction, a power that is, at the least, slightly greater than the power of those the directors are to govern – the company's top managers and the employees who report to them.

As obvious as this may seem, we say it with some trepidation, recognizing that for many readers, "power" is an emotionally charged term, conjuring up images of struggles and fights for control. We use the term not in that sense, but to convey the very essence of a process of governance – to be able to govern one must have the power to make decisions and to enforce their execution. The exercise of power may be subtle and unobtrusive, as it is in most corporations, but it must be exercised if there is to be true governance.

Previous discussions of corporate governance have avoided references to the concept of power, preferring to stress the need for outside directors to be independent. However, independence means freedom from unresolvable conflicts of interests with other companies (the duty of loyalty), and autonomy vis-à-vis management. In our view, being a truly independent director means having sufficient power to govern.

In the corporate boardroom, there are multiple sources of power, of which the directors' legal authority is just one. Others are the confidence to express one's ideas and views, knowledge and information about the matter under discussion, and control over the agenda and the discussion process. There is power in unity, too, whenever a majority of the board stands firmly behind a particular position.

But essentially, directors are at a disadvantage when these sources of boardroom power are realistically considered. The CEO-chairman usually has greater knowledge and information and controls both the meeting agenda and the discussion process. Often, he has been instrumental in selecting the other directors. In truth, other than their legal mandate, the directors' only power advantage is their capacity to act as a group by reaching a consensus, but doing this requires group cohesion and time for discussion, often scarce commodities in the typical boardroom.

The directors, in essence, gain the power to govern through the consent of the governed, which may sound like a laudable democratic objective but which is inconsistent with the intent of corporate law. Fortunately, on most boards, in normal times, the CEO-chairman tries not to sabotage his or her board's effectiveness. In time of crisis, however, the implicit understanding between the CEO-chairman and the directors can collapse like a house of cards, particularly when the views of the two sides are in conflict.

Another power constraint directors face, is a confusion among them about the exact definition of their accountability and the reasons for that confusion. Given the importance of public corporations in American society, we also examine the desirability of holding to a traditional legal perspective that expects directors to devote a majority of attention to shareholders.

While there is concern, from the legal perspective, with the division of responsibility between directors and managers, in actuality, the two parties have worked out a mutually satisfactory modus operandi. The problem is that directors can have difficulty mustering sufficient power to carry out their self-defined responsibilities, which include the most important tasks of selecting, evaluating, rewarding, and, if necessary, removing the CEO.

Obviously, there are two aspects to the power imbalance, one being the lack of director power, while on the opposite side are the factors that give the chairman-CEO so much influence. We identify a CEO's power sources relative to that of the directors in the normal conduct of the corporation affairs, then recapitulate the directors' power constraints and assess the balance of power between directors and CEOs in normal times.

The normal power relationship between the chairman-CEO and the directors is the springboard from which directors must act in times of crisis. We explore how board members deal with both internally and externally caused crises, and those that occur suddenly and dramatically, as well as those that emerge more gradually. While there are variations in how difficult the directors' problems are in each situation, there is a common theme. When boards had to act without CEO support, or in opposition to the CEO, lack of power inhibited them, delaying their ability to act. Further, a successful resolution depended upon the serendipitous emergence of a leader from among the outside directors. The obvious question is, What happens on boards where the directors are not so lucky? In our view, the present governance system leaves too much to chance, and allows crises to drag on longer than is good for any of the stakeholders. As we have seen, too many corporations simultaneously having crises causes problems for the whole economy.

THE NEED FOR CHANGE

This concern, along with a recognition that more effective governance means more relative power for directors, leads us to recommend several basic changes in the current system of corporate governance. These innovations will require changes in state laws and in the bylaws of corporations, as well as in the rules governing stock exchanges.

Being pragmatic, we recognize that such changes will be difficult to achieve and slow in coming. We also understand that many CEOs and many directors, whether CEOs or not, may feel the changes are too extreme. For those reasons, we also propose a more modest set of recommendations – "changes within the system" – that we believe would do much to place directors in a better position to govern, and that could be implemented by the CEOs and directors of any company, within their present legal authority. . . .

NOTES

1 The two positions are held by the same person in about 80 percent of US public companies.

2 William J. Abernathy and Robert H. Hayes, "Managing Our Way to Economic Decline," *Harvard Business Review* (July–August 1980), pp. 67–77.

3 Ezra J. Vogel, *Japan as Number One* (Cambridge, Mass.: Harvard University Press, 1976), pp. 131–157.

4 George C. Lodge, *The American Disease* (New York: Alfred A. Knopf, 1984), p. 279.

5 An exception to this statement is by Arch Patton and John C. Baker, "Why Directors Won't Rock the Boat,"

Harvard Business Review (November–December 1987), pp. 10–18. They blame directors for the fact that US companies have not been able to compete in world markets, pointing out that "12 out of 21 leading manufacturing industries in the United States have run to the federal government for protection."

6 William E. Fruhan, Jr., "Corporate Raiders! Head 'Em off at Value Gap,'" *Harvard Business Review* (July–August 1988), p. 63.

7 Ibid., p. 64.

8 Our own analysis of company ownership of the *S&P's* 400 in 1987 indicated institutional ownership of more than 50 percent. Peter Drucker in "Management and the World's Work," *Harvard Business Review* (September–October 1988), p. 71, and in private conversation reports that pension funds alone own more than two-thirds of the equity of America's 1,000 largest companies, and this does not include mutual funds, trust funds, and so forth. Samuel M. Loescher of Indiana University, in an address to the American Economics Association meeting, December 28, 1987, seemed to reconcile our analysis with Drucker's, pointing out that "pension funds are estimated to own 50 percent of the common stock of *S&P* 500 corporations." He went on to point out that if one includes institutional investors that commingle in their portfolios tax-deferred 401K and IRA contributions of individuals, then pension funds own 65 percent of the common stock of these companies.

9 See, for example, Charles A. Anderson and Robert W. Anthony, *The New Corporate Directors* (New York: John Wiley, 1986); Stanley C. Vance, *Corporate Leadership, Boards, Directors, and Strategy* (New York: McGraw-Hill, 1983); and James C. Worthy and Robert D. Neushel, *Emerging Issues in Corporate Governance* (Evanston, IL.: Northwestern University Press, 1983).

10 Myles Mace, *Directors: Myth and Reality* (Boston, MA: Division of Research, Harvard Business School, 1971).

11 Business Roundtable, *The Role and Composition of the Board of Directors of Large Publicly Owned Corporations* (New York, 1978); and the American Law Institute, *Principles of Corporate Governance: Analysis and Recommendation, Tentative Drafts* (Philadelphia, PA 1983).

12 George C. Greanias and Duane Windsor, eds., *The Foreign Corrupt Practices Act: Anatomy of a Statute* (Lexington, MA: Lexington Books, 1982).

13 Vance, *Corporate Leadership*, p. 2.

14 *Dartmouth College v. Woodward*, 1819.

15 Vance, *Corporate Leadership*, p. 5.

16 *Delaware General Corporation Law Annotated Franchise Tax Law Uniform Limited Partnership Act.* As of February 2, 1988 (Englewood Cliffs, NJ: Prentice-Hall Legal and Financial Service, 1988).

17 Further, these principles are at the core of the American Bar Association's "Model Business Corporation Act."

18 While our description focuses on the laws of Delaware, because of its importance as a state of incorporation, the laws of other states are largely consistent with this point. See the American Bar Association Model Corporation Act.

19 Business Roundtable, *The Role and Composition of the Board of Directors of Large Publicly Held Corporations*, p. 3.

20 American Law Institute, *Principles of Corporate Governance: Analysis and Recommendation*, Draft 2 (Philadelphia, April 13, 1984), pp. 66–67.

21 Business Roundtable, *The Role and Composition of the Board of Directors*, p. 25.

22 Ibid.

23 The impact of such constraints was demonstrated in Gordon Donaldson and Jay W. Lorsch, *Decision Making at the Top* (New York: Basic Books, 1983).

24 *Delaware General Corporation Law*, p. 141.3.

25 James A. Hanks, "Recent Legislation on D&O Liability Limitation," *The Business Lawyer* (August 1988) lists: Arizona, Idaho, Illinois, Indiana, Kentucky, Maine, Minnesota, Missouri, Nebraska, New Mexico, New York, Ohio, Pennsylvania, and Wisconsin. James P. Melican, senior vice president and general counsel for International Paper Company, added in private correspondence, January 1989, Connecticut, Louisiana, and Tennessee.

26 The data about the directors' reality was gathered in several ways. First, 100 outside directors of *Standard & Poor's* 400 companies were randomly selected to be interviewed. Of those, about 80 agreed to be, and were, interviewed. Additionally several legal experts were also interviewed for their viewpoint; similarly, a number of British CEOs were interviewed to get their perspectives on US boards as compared to their own. Questionnaires were sent to 3,000 of the directors of these companies, and the response rate was 31 percent. The *S&P's* 400 companies were selected because we wanted to focus on manufacturing companies because of the difficulties these companies have had in the 1970s and 1980s. However, the *Standard & Poor's* list also included some service companies. Finally, about 35 other directors and CEOs were interviewed in the development of the four cases.

PART FOUR

Stewardship theory

INTRODUCTION TO PART FOUR

Stewardship theory presents a very different model of management to agency theory. Davis, Schoorman and Donaldson (Chapter 9) contest the assumption of agency theory of the self-interested manager rationally maximizing his own economic gain. The highly individualistic model of agency theory is predicated on the notion of an inherent conflict of interest between owners and managers. Accordingly, opportunistic agents can only be curbed by vigilant monitoring and incentive schemes based around money, promotions and sanctions. Stewardship theory acknowledges a larger range of human motives including orientations towards achievement, altruism and the commitment to meaningful work. Stewardship theory maintains there is no inherent conflict of interest between managers and owners, and that optimum governance structures allow coordination of the enterprise to be achieved most effectively. Managers should be authorized to act since according to stewardship theory they are not opportunistic agents but good stewards who will act in the best interests of owners.

Stewardship theory recognizes a strong relationship between managers' pursuit of the objectives of the enterprise, the owners' satisfaction, and the satisfaction of other participants in the enterprise reward. Davis, Schoorman and Donaldson suggest that as managers maximize shareholders wealth through raising the performance of the firm, they serve their own purposes. Managers balance competing shareholders' and stakeholder objectives, making decisions in the best interests of all.

With this more favourable view of management, stewardship theory is not convinced of the benefits of boards having a majority of external independent directors rather than specialist executive directors. However, this introduces an element of choice in corporate governance arrangements under which both managers and owners can choose to have either agency or steward relationships, contingent upon their assessment of the motivations of each other, and the situation of the enterprise.

"Toward a Stewardship Theory of Management"

from Academy of Management Review (1997)

James H. Davis, F. David Schoorman and Lex Donaldson

Organization theory and business policy have been strongly influenced by agency theory, which depicts top managers in the large modern corporation as agents whose interests may diverge from those of their principals, the shareholders, where both parties are utility maximizers (Jensen and Meckling, 1976). According to agency theory, losses to the principal resulting from interest divergence may be curbed by imposing control structures upon the agent. Although agency theory appears to be the dominant paradigm underlying most governance research and prescriptions, researchers in psychology and sociology have suggested theoretical limits of agency theory (Hirsch *et al.*, 1987; Perrow, 1986). In particular, assumptions made in agency theory about individualistic utility motivations resulting in principal–agent interest divergence may not hold for all managers. Therefore, exclusive reliance upon agency theory is undesirable because the complexities of organizational life are ignored. Additional theory is needed to explain relationships based upon other, noneconomic assumptions (Doucouliagos, 1994).

Although agency theory addresses manager–principal interest divergence, additional theory is needed to explain what, if anything, causes interests to be aligned. Stewardship theory has been introduced as a means of defining relationships based upon other behavioral premises (Donaldson and Davis, 1989, 1991). Stewardship theory defines situations in which managers are not motivated by individual goals, but rather are stewards whose motives are aligned with the objectives of their principals. Because stewardship theory is relatively new, its theoretic contribution has not been adequately established. Previously,

researchers have contrasted agency and stewardship theories (e.g. Donaldson and Davis, 1989, 1991, 1994; Fox and Hamilton, 1994), but failed to examine the psychological and situational underpinnings of stewardship theory. Clear understanding of the characteristics of the manager and of the situation are essential to understanding manager–principal interest convergence. Although the assumptions underlying stewardship theory have been discussed in general terms (e.g. Donaldson, 1990), as yet, no author has attempted to define the theory of stewardship in terms of its underlying assumptions and mechanisms. Finally, previous research seems to be based upon one-bestway thinking, that is, stewardship theory is correct and agency theory is incorrect (Donaldson and Davis, 1991). Research is needed that shows where stewardship theory fits in the theoretic landscape, relative to agency theory, rather than opposed to it.

In this study, we make three contributions to previous stewardship research. First, we provide a much more detailed description of stewardship theory, its language, definitions of terms, and units of analysis. Second, we explore the psychological and situational mechanisms that motivate stewards to behave pro-organizationally. Finally, we do not assume that agency theory is wrong or inferior to stewardship theory, as previous researchers have stated. We attempt to reconcile the differences between stewardship and agency by describing the conditions under which each is necessary. By articulating stewardship theory in contrast with agency theory, the boundaries within which each of these two theories applies can be charted. In these ways, we hope to contribute to the growing body of stewardship research.

The relationship between stockholders and the manager of a firm has been described as the "pure agency relationship," because it is associated with the separation of ownership and control (Jensen and Meckling, 1976). Therefore, in this research, we focus primarily on upper level managers. We begin with a brief description of agency theory, its origins, underlying assumptions, and theoretical limits. Stewardship theory will then be described along with its terminology, scope, assumptions, and limits. The psychological and situational factors that explain manager–principal interest alignment are discussed. A framework for agency and stewardship theories is provided, through which the interaction of personal characteristics of the manager and the characteristics of the situation are discussed. Through this framework we suggest the theoretical limits of agency and stewardship and avenues for future research.

AGENCY THEORY

At the heart of agency theory are assumptions of man[1] that can be traced to 200 years of economic research. The model of man underlying agency theory is that of a rational actor who seeks to maximize his or her individual utility (Jensen and Meckling, 1976). Both agents and principals in agency theory seek to receive as much possible utility with the least possible expenditure. Thus, given the choice between two alternatives, the rational agent or principal will choose the option that increases his or her individual utility.

The advent of the modern corporation created a separation between ownership and control of wealth (Berle and Means, 1932). Even though owners would prefer to manage their own companies and reap the maximum utility for themselves, this is impossible because of the capital requirements of the modern corporation (Berle and Means, 1932). Corporations grow beyond the means of a single owner, who is incapable of meeting the increased economic obligations of the firm. As a result, the modern corporation typically has multiple owners, each intent on maximizing his or her investment in the enterprise.

Owners become principals when they contract with executives to manage their firms for them. As an agent of the principals, an executive is morally responsible to maximize shareholder utility; however, executives accept agent status because they perceive the opportunity to maximize their own utility. Thus, in the modern corporation, agents and principals are motivated by opportunities for their own personal gain. Principals invest their wealth in companies and design governance systems in ways that maximize their utility. Agents accept the responsibility of managing a principal's investments (wealth), because they perceive the possibility of gaining more utility with this opportunity than by accepting other opportunities.

If the utility functions of self-serving agents and principals coincide, there is no agency problem; both agents and principals enjoy increases in their individual utility. Agency costs are incurred by the principals when the interests of principals and agents diverge, because given the opportunity, agents will rationally maximize their own utility at the expense of their principals. The chance that agents do not share the same interests and utility choices as their principals is substantial. According to agency theory, it is difficult for principals to know *ex ante* which agents will self-aggrandize, and so it is prudent for the principals to limit potential losses to their utility (Williamson, 1985). The objective in agency theory then is to reduce the agency costs incurred by principals by imposing internal controls to keep the agent's self-serving behavior in check (Jensen and Meckling, 1976).

Walsh and Seward (1990: 444) argued that "if a firm's managers entrench themselves with the sole objective of ensuring their own power, prestige, and perquisites, the organization is likely to lose sight of its competitive environmental position and will fail." If the internal control mechanisms suggested by agency theorists fail, more expensive, external control mechanisms (e.g. acquisitions, divestitures, and ownership amendments) will emerge to control self-serving managers (Walsh and Seward, 1990). Because of the expense of the external mechanisms to the principal's utility, internal mechanisms are generally preferred (Walsh and Seward, 1990).

To protect shareholder interests, minimize agency costs and ensure agent–principal interest alignment, agency theorists prescribe various governance mechanisms. Two mechanisms that have received substantial literary attention are alternative executive compensation schemes and governance structures (e.g. Demsetz and Lehn, 1985; Jensen and Meckling, 1976). Financial incentive schemes provide rewards and punishments that are aimed at aligning principal–agent interests. If managers receive compensation that is subject to the successful completion of shareholder objectives (e.g. long-term rewards tied to firm performance), they will be motivated to behave in a manner consistent with stockholders' interests. Such incentive schemes are particularly desirable when the agent has a significant informational advantage and monitoring is impossible. A second mechanism aimed at bringing agents' behavior into alignment with their principals' interests is governance structure. Boards of directors keep potentially self-serving managers in check by performing audits and performance evaluations. Boards communicate shareholders' objectives and interests to managers and monitor them to keep agency costs in check. Outside (nonmanagement) board leadership and membership are desirable to ensure that proper management oversight occurs. Controlling governance mechanisms are prescribed, because agency theorists assume that agent–principal interests may diverge and that given the opportunity the agent will maximize his or her individual utility at the expense of the principal's utility. Although the divergence of interests between the agent and principal may differ to varying degrees, the model of the agent remains as inherently opportunistic, in that there is an ever-present possibility of opportunism, unless it is curbed through controls; moreover, because controls are imperfect, some opportunism will remain.

Agency theorists in no sense specify total control of the agent. If control were total, then the agent would have no discretion and the firm would be owner-managed. The crux of agency theory is that principals delegate authority to agents to act on their behalf. It is this delegation that allows agents to opportunistically build their own utility at the expense of the principals' utility (wealth). Thus, agency theorists specify an intermediate condition of control, that is, first delegation and then controls to minimize the potential abuse of the delegation (Jensen and Meckling, 1976).

The application of agency control does not imply that all managers' decisions will result in increased wealth for principals; it implies only that the managers will strive to attain outcomes favorable for the principals. There are many reasons other than poor motivation for agents' failing to deliver high performance for their principals (e.g. low ability, lack of knowledge, and poor information). Agency theorists are not as concerned with those failings as they are with those resulting from motivational problems.

The limits and boundaries of agency theory are determined by its model of man. Where individualistic, self-serving executive motivation is assumed, shareholders desirous of minimizing the risks associated with perceived nonalignment of principal–agent utility functions should implement agency prescriptions. However, this model has its critics. Jensen and Meckling (1994) criticized this model of man as being a simplification for mathematical modeling and an unrealistic description of human behavior. Doucouliagos (1994) argued that labeling all motivation as self-serving does not explain the complexity of human action. Frank (1994) suggested that this model of man does not suit the demands of a social existence. Hirsch et al. (1987) said that in exchange for simplicity and elegance in their models, economists engage in a some-what broad-brush approach that may reduce empirical verisimilitude and engender less than robust policies. In short, agency theory assumptions limit its generalizability.

Agency theory provides a useful way of explaining relationships where the parties' interests are at odds and can be brought more into alignment through proper monitoring and a well-planned compensation system. Additional theory is needed to explain other types of human behavior, and this is found in literature beyond the economic perspective. To that end, stewardship theory will now be described.

STEWARDSHIP THEORY

Stewardship theory has its roots in psychology and sociology and was designed for researchers to examine situations in which executives as stewards are motivated to act in the best interests of their principals (Donaldson and Davis, 1989, 1991). In stewardship theory, the model of man is based on a steward whose behavior is ordered such that pro-organizational, collectivistic behaviors have higher utility than individualistics, self-serving behaviors. Given a choice between self-serving behavior and pro-organizational behavior, a steward's behavior will not depart from the interests of his or her organization. A steward will not substitute or trade self-serving behaviors for cooperative behaviors. Thus, even where the interests of the steward and the principal are not aligned, the steward places higher value on cooperation than defection (terms found in game theory). Because the steward perceives greater utility in cooperative behavior and behaves accordingly, his or her behavior can be considered rational.

According to stewardship theory, the behavior of the steward is collective, because the steward seeks to attain the objectives of the organization (e.g. sales growth or profitability). This behavior in turn will benefit principals such as outside owners (through positive effects of profits on dividends and share prices) and also principals who are managerial super-ordinates, because their objectives are furthered by the stewards. Stewardship theorists assume a strong relationship between the success of the organization and the principal's satisfaction. A steward protects and maximizes shareholders' wealth through firm performance, because, by so doing, the steward's utility functions are maximized.

Given the potential multiplicity of shareholders' objectives, a steward's behavior can be considered organizationally centered. Stewards in loosely cou-pled, heterogeneous organizations with competing stakeholders and competing shareholder objectives are motivated to make decisions that they perceive are in the best interests of the group. Even in the most politically charged environment, one can assume that most parties desire a viable, successful enterprise. A steward who successfully improves the performance of the organization generally satisfies most groups, because most stakeholder groups have interests that are well served by increasing organizational wealth. Therefore, a pro-organizational steward is motivated to maximize organizational performance, thereby satisfying the competing interests of shareholders.

This explanation does not imply that stewards do not have necessary "survival" needs. Clearly, the steward must have an income to survive. The differ-ence between the agent and the principal is how these needs are met. The steward realizes the trade-off between personal needs and organizational objectives and believes that by working toward orga-nizational, collective ends, personal needs are met. Hence, the steward's opportunity set is constrained by the perception that the utility gained from pro-organizational behavior is higher than the utility that can be gained through individualistic, self-serving behavior. Stewards believe their interests are aligned with that of the corporation and its owners. Thus, the steward's interests and utility motivations are directed to organizational rather than personal objectives.

Stewardship theorists argue that the performance of a steward is affected by whether the structural situ-ation in which he or she is located facilitates effective action. If the executive's motivations fit the model of man underlying stewardship theory, empowering governance structures and mechanisms are appropri-ate. Thus, a steward's autonomy should be deliber-ately extended to maximize the benefits of a steward, because he or she can be trusted. In this case, the amount of resources that are necessary to guarantee

pro-organizational behavior from an individualistic agent (i.e. monitoring and incentive or bonding costs) are diminished, because a steward is motivated to behave in ways that are consistent with organiza-tional objectives. Indeed, control can be potentially counterproductive, because it undermines the pro-organizational behavior of the steward, by lowering his or her motivation (Argyris, 1964). The essential assumption underlying the prescriptions of steward-ship theory is that the behaviors of the executive are aligned with the interests of the principals.

Previously, stewardship theorists have focused on enabling structures for upper managers (Donaldson and Davis, 1989, 1991, 1994; Fox and Hamilton, 1994). For example, Donaldson and Davis (1991) argued that, for CEOs who are stewards, their pro-organizational actions are best facilitated when the corporate governance structures given them high authority and discretion. Structurally, this situation is attained more readily if the CEO chairs the board of directors. Such a structure would be viewed as dys-functional under the agency theory model of man. However, under the stewardship model of man, stew-ards maximize their utility as they achieve organiza-tional rather than self-serving objectives. The CEO-chair is unambiguously responsible for the fate of the corporation and has the power to deter-mine strategy without fear of countermand by an outside chair of the board. Thus, stewardship theo-rists focus on structures that facilitate and empower rather than those that monitor and control.

Given the advantage of stewardship to principals, why isn't there always a steward relationship, rather than an agency relationship? The answer lies in the risks that the principals are willing to assume. In the governance contract between owners and executives, owners must decide how much risk they are willing to assume with their wealth. Risk-averse owners will most likely perceive that executives are self-serving and will prefer agency governance prescriptions. Implementing stewardship governance mechanisms for an agent would be analogous to turning the hen house over to the fox. Agency prescriptions can be viewed as the necessary costs of insuring principal utility against the risks of executive opportunism. From this perspective, a better question might be why would an owner ever take the risks of stewardship governance prescriptions?

Previously, empirical researchers have attempted to validate either agency theory or stewardship theory as a "one best way" to corporate governance, assuming that all managers are either stewards or agents. The results of these studies have resulted in mixed findings; thus, there is the need for both agency theory and stewardship theory explanations of management (Donaldson and Davis, 1994). For example, several researchers found that the agency prescription of independent board leadership (i.e. a nonexecutive board chair) is associated with higher firm performance (e.g. Berg and Smith, 1978; Daily and Dalton, 1994; Rechner and Dalton, 1991). Other researchers found that stewardship's executive-chaired boards have significantly higher corporate performance (e.g. Donaldson and Davis, 1989, 1991; Finkelstein and D'Aveni, 1994). Still others suggest there is no significant difference in firm performance between executive- and outsider-chaired boards (e.g. Chaganti *et al.*, 1985; Molz, 1988). Empirical evidence is similarly mixed with respect to other governance dimensions (Donaldson and Davis, 1994). The mixed support for agency and stewardship theories suggests a need to reconcile these differences. To this end we now move to a discussion of the situational and psychological mechanisms underlying the agency and stewardship models of man.

FACTORS THAT DIFFERENTIATE BETWEEN AGENCY AND STEWARDSHIP THEORIES

There are a number of dimensions on which agency theory assumptions differ from the assumptions of stewardship theory and thereby serve to differentiate the theories. These dimensions can be characterized broadly as either psychological factors of situational factors, and they are discussed in this section.

Psychological factors

The fundamental difference between agency and stewardship theories with respect to psychological factors can be traced to the historical debates regarding the "model of man" described previously in this article. According to agency theory, man is rooted in economic rationality. In an interesting response to the work of Simon (1957a,b), Argyris (1973a: 253) challenged this view of economic man as simplistic regarding human behavior and argued for a "more complex and humanistic model of man" in order to

increase the explanatory power and relevance of organizational theory. The model of man advocated by Argyris, characterized as "self actualizing man," has its roots in the early work of McGregor (1960) and the later work of Maslow (1970). This model is based on the view that humans have a need to grow beyond their current state and reach higher levels of achievement and that the assumptions of the economic view of man limit people from attaining their full potential. Argyris argued that when humans are placed in organizations that are designed on this economic view, they tend to suppress their level of aspirations, thereby creating a self-fulfilling prophecy. He further argued that for those individuals who are unable to suppress their aspirations, frustration with the organizational structures may lead to withdrawal and aggressive behaviors. The model of man described by Argyris is essentially the model of stewardship theory, and many of the predictions regarding the differences in the two theories of governance can be traced back to the basic arguments of the Simon–Argyris debate.

In this chapter, we focus on the specific differences that are most relevant to the distinctions between agency and stewardship theories. These differences are reflected in the assumptions about motivation, identification, and use of power in the context of the hierarchical relationship addressed in both theories.

Motivation

The major distinction between agency and stewardship theories is the focus on extrinsic versus intrinsic motivation. In agency theory, the focus is on extrinsic rewards: tangible, exchangeable commodities that have a measurable "market" value. These extrinsic rewards from the basis for the reward systems that represent the control mechanisms of agency theory. For example, a principal may create a piecework incentive system to protect him- or herself from a self-serving agent. Similarly, medical insurance, 401k savings, and retirement plans may be instituted as a control mechanism to reduce the likelihood of turnover. Each of these rewards has a quantifiable value in terms of dollars that is recognized by both parties. In contrast, in stewardship theory, the focus is an intrinsic rewards that are not easily quantified. These rewards include opportunities for growth, achievement, affiliation, and self-actualization. Subordinates in a stewardship relationship are reinforced by these intrinsic, intangible rewards and are motivated to work harder on behalf of the organization. The bases for this distinction can be found in most of the established theories of motivation, but they are particularly apparent in the need theories. In a stewardship relationship, the focus would be on the higher order needs of Maslow's hierarchy (1970), on Alderfer's growth need (1972), and on the achievement and affiliation needs of McClelland (1975) and McGregor (1966).

A related model of worker motivation, the job characteristics model, was proposed by Hackman and Oldham (1975, 1976, 1980). These authors argued that three psychological states (experienced meaningfulness of work, experienced responsibility for outcomes, and knowledge of the actual results) mediate the relationship between task characteristics and internal work motivation. In order to facilitate the attainment of these psychological states, they advocated the redesign of jobs to increase skill variety, task identity, task significance, autonomy, and feedback. All of these factors are related to increasing the opportunity for growth and responsibility for the worker. This model of work motivation is consistent with the assumptions of stewardship theory that increasing the internal work motivation would lead to higher levels of performance as well as satisfaction with work. It is interesting to note that in their model Hackman and Oldham (1975, 1976, 1980) argued that the growth need strength of the worker is a moderator of the effectiveness of this model, suggesting that there are some workers for whom the assumptions of the stewardship model may not fit.

In a more recent approach to the study of intrinsic motivation, Manz (1986, 1990) developed a theory of self-leadership. According to Manz, "self-leadership is a comprehensive self-influence perspective that concerns leading oneself towards performance of naturally motivating tasks as well as managing to do work that must be done but is not naturally motivating" (1990: 589). Self-efficacy, self-determination, and feelings of purpose are characterized as being critical determinants of intrinsic motivation. He argued that self-leadership involves a belief in one's work that extends beyond the formal reward system and relates to the importance of shared organizational vision. These views are consistent with the motivational assumptions of stewardship theory.

One other group of motivational theories that present a unique perspective on the comparison between agency and stewardship assumptions is social comparison theories or equity theories (Adams, 1965; Cosier

and Dalton, 1983). Although the basic premise of an exchange agreement that is a part of equity theory is more reminiscent of the economic view of man, the distinction between the perspectives is apparent in the social comparison that is assumed. In agency theory, there is an economic- or class-related separation between the principal and the agent. In developing an equitable work arrangement for the agent, the principal considers the fair market wage for the agent and arranges the compensation structure accordingly. The comparison for the agent in determining the "fairness" of the situation is with respect to other agents in similar contexts. In stewardship theory, the principal is a part of the collective and the basis of comparison would include the principal. Thus, according to stewardship theory, the principal would expect to be accountable to the collective for his or her contributions as much as the steward may be qualitatively different and not easily quantifiable, the comparison and mutual accountability are expected.

Proposition 1: People who are motivated by higher order needs are more likely to become stewards in principal–steward relationships than are people who are not motivated by higher order needs.

Proposition 2: People who are motivated by intrinsic factors are more likely to become stewards in principal–steward relationships than are people who are motivated by extrinsic factors.

Identification

Identification occurs when managers define themselves in terms of their membership in a particular organization by accepting the organization's mission, vision, and objectives (Kelman, 1958; Mael and Ashforth, 1992), producing a satisfying relationship (O'Reilly, 1989; Sussman and Vecchio, 1982). Through identification, an organization becomes an extension of the steward's psychological structure (Brown, 1969). An identifying manager interprets comments about the organization as referring also to himself or herself (i.e. he or she takes the comments personally). Identification allows managers vicariously to take credit for organizational successes and to experience frustration for organizational failures (e.g. Katz and Kahn, 1978; Turner, 1981). Because managers vicariously take credit for organizational successes, identification can increase the work-related satisfaction described previously (e.g. Atkinson, 1957).

FOUR

A number of authors have found that managers who identify with organizations attribute organizational success to themselves (e.g. Salancik and Meindl, 1984; Staw, *et al.*, 1983), and this attribution contributes to the individual's self-image and self-concept (Kelman, 1961; Sussman and Vecchio, 1982). This view of organizational identification is consistent with stewardship theory.

In several studies, researchers argued that managers may externalize organizational problems to avoid blame (e.g. D'Aveni and MacMillan, 1990; Staw *et al.*, 1983). When managers externalize attribution for organizational shortcomings, they no longer identify with the organization. In their effort to avoid incriminating evidence, self-serving managers may make organizational problems worse, because they avoid accepting responsibility and making decisions that may rectify the problems (D'Aveni and MacMillan, 1990). This type of manager falls within the domain of agency theory.

A manager who identifies with an organization will thereby work toward the organization's goals, solve its problems, and overcome barriers that are preventing the successful completion of tasks and assignments (Bass, 1960). When individuals identify with their organizations, they more readily engage in cooperative, altruistic, and spontaneous un-rewarded citizenship behaviors (e.g. Mowday *et al.*, 1982; O'Reilly and Chatman, 1986; Smith *et al.*, 1983). Therefore, managers who identify with their organization are motivated to help it succeed and should be empowered to perform their jobs because this will enable them to use their initiative to promote the success of their organization and their principles.

A concept that is closely related to identification is organizational commitment. Porter *et al.* (1974) defined organizational commitment as the strength of the individual's identification with and involvement in a particular organization. They also developed the organizational commitment questionnaire, which is the most widely used measure of organizational commitment. In more recent work, Mayer and Schoorman (1992: 672) characterized organizational commitment as a multidimensional construct consisting of continuance commitment, which represents the desire to remain in the organization, and value commitment, which is the "belief in and acceptance of the goals of the organization." This latter concept of value commitment is more closely related to the notion of identification, and it is an important component of the psychological profile of a steward. In

agency theory, value commitment would not have economic utility and would not be a relevant part of the exchange agreement.

Proposition 3: People who have high identification with the organization are more likely to become stewards in principal–steward relationships than are people who have low identification with the organization.

Proposition 4: People who are high in value commitment are more likely to become stewards in principal–steward relationships than are people who are low in value commitment.

Use of power

Power is an important aspect of the relationship between a principal and a manager. A number of researchers have found that managers receive satisfaction from, and are motivated by, the use of power (e.g. McClelland, 1970, 1975; McClelland and Burnham, 1976). McClelland and Burnham (1976) defined the power motive as a psychological need to influence others toward the accomplishment of valid and accepted organizational goals. Managers who have a high need for power tend to "influence or direct other people; express opinions forcefully; enjoy the role of leader and may assume it spontaneously" (Steers and Black, 1994: 148).

The types of power used in the context of the relationship help to differentiate principal–agent relationships from principal–steward relationships. In the most widely cited typology of power bases, French and Raven (1959) described power in terms of coercive, legitimate, reward, expert, and referent power. In a compatible but simpler typology, the five bases of power are reduced to institutional or organizational power and personal power (Gibson *et al.*, 1991). Institutional power is defined as being vested in the principal by virtue of his or her position in the organization. Thus, termination of organizational membership would terminate the individual's power. The coercive, legitimate, and many aspects of reward power described by French and Raven (1959) could be characterized as institutional power. In agency theory, institutional power is the basis of influence in the context of the principal–agent relationship. In this theory, reward power and legitimate power are used. Appropriate incentive systems and recognition of authority of the principal are combined to create the required level of control in the relationship. Coercive power represents the more severe method of agent control and is often present in a more subtle form through the threat of termination of employment. Personal power, an inherent part of the individual in the context of the interpersonal relationship, is not affected by position. Expert and referent power are characterized as personal power; referent power works through identification of one person with another person. Personal power is developed over time in the context of the relationship and is not affected by the formal roles in the organization. Although slower to develop, personal power can be sustained over longer periods of time. Personal power is the basis of influence in a principal–steward relationship. The choice of the type of power used is a function of the personal characteristics of the individual and the prevailing organizational culture. Certain organizational cultures facilitate the use of institutional power and therefore predispose members to principal–agent relationships. These organizational cultures will be considered next as situational factors.

Proposition 5: People who are more likely to use personal power as a basis for influencing others are more likely to become stewards in principal–steward relationships than are people who use institutional power.

Situational factors

Management philosophy

In the early debates between Argyris and the advocates of the economic model of man, one of the critical points of contention was whether organizational theory should be focused on descriptive or normative models of the organization. Simon (1957a,b, 1973) and others (e.g. Cyert and March, 1963) argued that the economic model, and therefore implicitly the agency theory assumptions, were the predominant basis of relationships in organizations. They cited numerous examples of behavior by both principals and agents to support this claim. In contrast, Argyris (1973a,b) argued that the management philosophy of most organizations was based on economic assumptions and that this became a self-fulfilling prophecy regarding the nature of relationships that would develop. He advocated the development of normative models of organization based on self-actualizing assumptions in order to create an organizational culture that supported the development of stewardship types of relationships. The position advocated by Argyris (1973a,b) was similar to the arguments advanced earlier by McGregor (1960) in his discussion of Theory Y management and by Likert (1961) in his comparison of System 4 management with more control-oriented systems. The common message in each of these theories is that the assumption about the model of man drives the development of management philosophies and management systems, which then serve to produce behavior in the organization that is consistent with the assumptions. Each of these theorists advocated the development of normative models of organization and a break from the traditional management philosophies in order to facilitate the self-actualizing behaviors that are consistent with stewardship theory.

More recently, Walton (1980, 1985) advocated what he called a high-commitment management philosophy. This approach to management was characterized as being highly participative and consisting of open communication, empowerment of workers, and the establishment of trust. Lawler (1986, 1992) elaborated on this view by contrasting the management philosophies he described as *control-oriented* versus *involvement-oriented*. According to Lawler, the control-oriented approach is based on a management philosophy that the thinking and controlling part of the work must be separated from the doing part of the work. In contrast, involvement-oriented approaches emphasize self-control and self-management and do not create a separation among thinking, controlling, and doing the work. The key assumption in involvement-oriented approaches is that when employees are given challenges and responsibility they will develop self-control of their behavior. Lawler (1986, 1992) characterized the control-oriented approaches as a mature philosophy of management that flourished in the 1960s and 1970s largely because the competitive advantages of organizations in the United States were not based on their management philosophies. He characterized the involvement-oriented approach as a newer approach that is still not as widely adopted as the control-oriented approach. Although Lawler advocated the adoption of an involvement-oriented management philosophy as the merging dominant approach, he made this argument through a contingency model.

When short-term cost control and productivity are important issues, the control-oriented approach produces better results. However, he argued that this approach could not be sustained in the long term because of inherently faulty assumptions about the motivation of workers. Thus, when labor costs are low and unemployment is high, the control-oriented approach may work well, because turnover due to employee dissatisfaction will be minimal and replacement costs are low. In contrast, in an uncertain environment, with high labor costs, a focus on long-term effectiveness and quality through self-inspection, or the involvement-oriented approach, has significant advantages. The arguments in favor of the involvement-oriented approach as the dominant management philosophy of the future are based on observations that the environment is changing in ways that make control-oriented approaches less viable.

One important difference between the two management philosophies is in their orientation to risk. We have already noted that in unstable, uncertain environments the involvement-oriented approach is more effective, but in stable environments, the control-oriented approach is best. When control-oriented management encounters an uncertain or risky situation, it manages the risk through the implementation of greater controls. For example, if the product design becomes more complicated, the organization may introduce a quality control unit to inspect the finished parts for defects. As workers feel less motivated because of boring jobs, more supervisors would adopt the control-oriented solution. In contrast, in the involvement-oriented approach, the means of dealing with increased uncertainty and risk is through more training, empowerment, and ultimately trust in workers. In the quality example, workers would be given additional training on the complex product and given the responsibility for self-inspection of quality. If the jobs were boring, they would be redesigned to be more challenging and therefore more motivating.

The issue of trust is a critical aspect of the high-commitment or involvement-oriented management philosophy. Work by Mayer et al. (1995) defined trust as a willingness to be vulnerable in the context of a relationship. Control-oriented systems are designed to avoid vulnerability and therefore to avoid the need to trust. Another important aspect of trust is that it occurs in the context of a relationship, and it is most likely to occur when the relationship is based on personal power (respect and expertise). In a control-oriented approach, the relationships are generally transactional in nature or are based on institutional power.

The key point of this discussion is that the management philosophy of an organization creates a context in which the choice of agency or stewardship relationships is made by principles and managers. A control-oriented management philosophy is more likely to produce choices of agency theory relationships, whereas an involvement-oriented management philosophy is more likely to produce stewardship theory relationships. This view is completely consistent with the observations of Argyris (1973) that the design of organizations based on economic assumptions creates a self-fulfilling prophecy of producing behavior that is consistent with the assumptions. If we follow this reasoning, evolution of the involvement-oriented management philosophy into a more dominant model will lead to be emergence of behavior that is more consistent with stewardship theory.

> *Proposition 6*: People who are in an involvement-oriented situation are more likely to become stewards in principal–steward relationships than are people who are in a control-oriented situation.

Culture

Individualism–collectivism

There are also aspects of culture that may influence the choice between agency and stewardship relationships. In his pioneering work on cultural differences, Hofstede (1980, 1991) described the dimension of individualism–collectivism. Individualism is characterized as the emphasis of personal goals over group goals. Collectivists subordinate their personal goals to the goals of the collective (Triandis, 1995; Triandis et al., 1993). Hofstede (1980) found that nations and regions of the world can be described according to the orientation on this individualism–collectivism dimension. For example, individualism is a cultural pattern found in the United States, Canada, and Western Europe. Collectivism is common in Asia, South America, and Southern Europe. Although much of this research was focused on the cultural pattern of a nation, there is distinctive variation within nations (Triandis, 1995, 1990). The generally accepted view is that the national culture predisposes members of that culture to either a collectivist or an individualistic orientation. However, the extent of this influence varies among individuals, and the effects of other experiences shape the ultimate orientation of each person.

Several specific differences between individualists and collectivists are relevant to the choice between agency and stewardship theory relationships. In collectivist cultures, the self is defined as a part of the group. One's group memberships (e.g. family, university, and organization) are an important statement of identify and achievement. In collectivist cultures individuals are usually addressed by family names, whereas in individualistic cultures "first" or given names are preferred. Success is defined in terms of the success of the group. Collectivists have a very positive attitude toward harmony in groups, avoiding conflict and confrontation. Individualists see confrontation as an opportunity to "work things out" and to communicate more directly. Collectivists prefer long-term relationships and will frequently take a longer time and expend greater effort to "get to know" someone prior to a business transaction. The development of the relationship is an important first step in business dealings, which often depend on a "handshake" or trust. Individualists are more short-term oriented, conduct business independently of personal relationships, use a cost-benefit analysis (economic model) to evaluate the business exchange, and will reduce the risks of doing business by signing a contract.

It should be apparent from the preceding discussion that collectivist culture are more conducive to the emergence of stewardship relationships and that collectivists are more likely to initiate a principal–steward relationship. Individualistic cultures would appear to facilitate agency relationships.

Proposition 7: People in a collectivist culture are more likely to develop principal–steward relationships than are people who are in an individualistic culture.

Power distance

A second dimension developed by Hofstede (1980, 1991) to characterize the cross-cultural differences that is particularly relevant to the agency-stewardship distinction is the concept of power distance. Power distance is generally defined as "the extent to which

less powerful members of institutions and organizations within a country expect and accept that power is distributed unequally" (Hofstede, 1991: 28). According to Hofstede (1980, 1991), in certain cultures, relatively large differences in power among members are accepted and tolerated more than they are in other cultures. In a culture with high power distance, there is an acceptance that less powerful members will be dependent on more powerful members and privileges and status symbols are both expected and popular. Class and caste systems are an accepted part of this culture. In lower power distance cultures, inequalities are minimized, independence of the less powerful is valued and encouraged, and status and class symbols are frowned upon (Hodgetts and Luthans, 1993). The concept of power distance has its roots in the family structure and is pervasive in the institutions that socialize members of the culture (e.g. school, church, and social organizations). In high power distance cultures, children are expected to be obedient to their parents; respect for parents and elders is considered a basic virtue (Hofstede, 1991). In such cases, children are "looked after" and allowed to be dependent for a longer period of time, and, in turn, children treat parents and grandparents with formal deference even through adulthood. In contrast, in low power distance cultures, children are treated as equals, are encouraged to be independent at an early age, and relationships are not related to status or role. Formal respect and deference are seldom shown. This pattern of difference is also observed in organizational life. In high power distance cultures, organizations are centralized, and they include large differences in authority, salary, and privileges between those at the top and those at the bottom. In lower power distance cultures, organizations are decentralized, there is more consultation in decision-making, and the differences in salary and perquisites are minimized. Similar to the discussion of the individualism-collectivism dimension. Hofstede (1980, 1991) and others (e.g. Triandis, 1995) have argued that although the national culture creates a predisposition to either high or low power distance, there can be considerable variance in power distance across organizations and individuals in the same country.

High power distance cultures are conducive to the development of agency relationships, because they support and legitimize the inherent inequality between principal and agent. This idea is especially true in the context of work, because the development of hierarchies, of layers of supervision (as control mechanisms), and of inequalities in rewards and status may lead the agents to "ideologically reject the boss's authority completely, while in practice they will comply" (Hofstede, 1991: 35). This characterization by Hofstede is similar to the predictions regarding the self-serving agent described in agency theory. Low power distance cultures are more conducive to the development of stewardship relationships, because their members place greater value on the essential equality of the principal and the manager. This orientation encourages the development of relationships between principals and managers that are an essential part of stewardship theory.

Proposition 8: People in a low power distance culture are more likely to develop principal–steward relationships than are people who are in a high power distance culture.

Although the individualism–collectivism and power distance dimensions are not perfectly correlated, there appears to be a pattern of relationships that make the predictions regarding the cultural antecedents of stewardship theory somewhat complicated. For example, the United States is generally regarded as an individualistic culture with low power distance. Individualism would suggest a predisposition to agency theory, whereas low power distance would predict more stewardship theory outcomes. Similarly, Japan is a high power distance, collectivist culture, leading to similarly conflicting predictions. The apparent contradictions in predictions suggested by these variables may provide a valuable explanation for the process by which agency and stewardship relationships develop. For example, we might expect that members of a collectivist culture would move very quickly to establish an organizational structure that is conducive to the development of stewardship relationships (e.g. flat decentralized, and team based), but they would have difficulty developing the truly participative, challenging style of trusting interpersonal relationships because of high power distance. This is a common characterization of Japanese attempts to develop high-involvement management philosophies. In contrast, in the United States, we might expect to encounter great resistance to the restructuring of organizations into flatter, more decentralized, team-based units, but once this restructuring is accomplished, we would expect the members to function well as a high-involvement team.

	Agency theory	*Stewardship theory*
Model of man	Economic man	Self-actualizing man
Behavior	Self-serving	Collective serving
Psychological mechanisms		
Motivation	Lower order/economic needs (physiological, security, economic)	Higher order needs (growth, achievement, self-actualization)
	Extrinsic	Intrinsic
Social comparison	Other managers	Principal
Identification	Low value commitment	High value commitment
Power	Institutional (legitimate, coercive, reward)	Personal (expert, referent)
Situational mechanisms		
Management philosophy	Control oriented	Involvement oriented
Risk orientation	Control mechanisms	Trust
Time frame	Short term	Long term
Objective	Cost control	Performance enhancement
Cultural differences	Individualism	Collectivism
	High power distance	Low power distance

Table 1 Comparison of agency theory and stewardship theory.

The conflict that is suggested by the cultural dimensions is not limited to culture. It is certainly conceivable that some of the psychological mechanisms may suggest one theory, whereas other mechanisms may suggest the alternate. We might also expect the possibility of a mismatch between the management philosophy and the psychological characteristics of the managers. Although the specific interactions of these antecedents in the prediction of stewardship versus agency relationships is very intriguing, we believe it is beyond the scope of this article. The further development of this model in terms of the more specific predictions would be a logical next step regarding the empirical testing of the main effects specified in this model.

The discussion so far has focused on the core issues underlying agency and stewardship theories. A summary of the primary differences between the two theories is shown in Table 1. The primary difference lies in the assumptions about human nature. According to agency theory, people are individualistic, utility maximizers. According to stewardship theory, people are collective self-actualizers who achieve utility through organizational achievement.

THE CHOICE BETWEEN AGENCY AND STEWARDSHIP RELATIONSHIPS

In the preceding sections, we presented a model suggesting that there are psychological and situational factors that predispose individuals to agency and stewardship approaches to relationships. As we discussed, many authors argued that humans prefer growth, responsibility, and self-actualization and advocated an involvement-oriented management philosophy and trust as a mechanism for dealing with risk. Although many of these researchers contended that these motivations are universally shared by all people, we frame these issues as a model in which the psychological and situational characteristics of the principal and manager are antecedents of their choice between agency and stewardships relationships. (The position that there is one best choice for psychological [e.g. self-actualizing assumptions] or situational [e.g. a universally dynamic environment] reasons would represent a special case of the model.)

The choice between agency and stewardship relationships is similar to the decision posed by a prisoner's dilemma. First, it is a decision made by both parties to the relationship. The psychological characteristics of each party predisposes each individual to make a particular choice. Second, the situational characteristics have an influence on the choice. The management philosophy may have a significant impact on the choice by both parties. The cultural background (collectivism and power distance) of each party will also affect the choice. Finally, the expectation that each party has of the other will influence the choice between agency and stewardship. A longer history of these parties dealing with each other will provide more data to guide these expectations.

The nature of the dilemma is illustrated in Figure 1. When both the principal and the manager choose an agency relationship, the result is a true principal–agency relationship that is likely to achieve the expectations of each. The agency relationship is designed to minimize potential losses to each party. The manager's psychological profile fits that of the agent, and, thus, he or she will use any discretion to the disadvantage of the organization and principals. Such a manager requires a controlling situation to hold his or her opportunistic tendencies in check. The presence of controls in this case constitutes a fit and ensures that the agency costs are minimized. Thus, both parties have similar expectations of the relationship, and costs are controlled.

When both the principal and the manager choose a stewardship relationship, the results is a true principal–steward relationship that is designed to maximize the potential performance of the group. In this

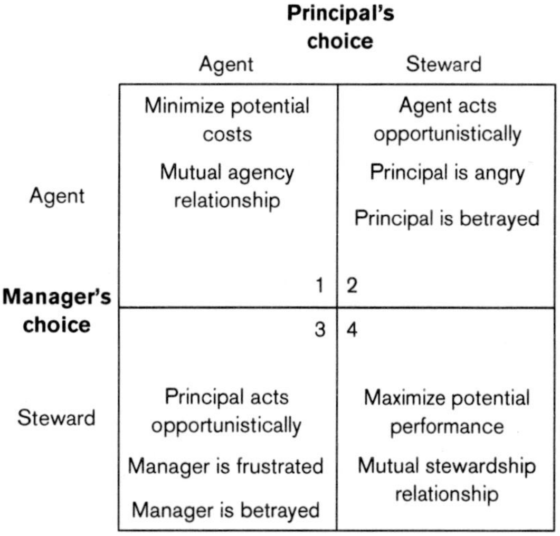

		Principal's choice	
		Agent	Steward
Manager's choice	Agent	Minimize potential costs Mutual agency relationship 1	Agent acts opportunistically Principal is angry Principal is betrayed 2
	Steward	3 Principal acts opportunistically Manager is frustrated Manager is betrayed	4 Maximize potential performance Mutual stewardship relationship

Figure 1 Principal–manager choice model.

situation, the manager has the psychological profile of a steward and thus gains utility from fulfilling the purposes and objectives of the organization. Likewise, the principal chooses to create a stewardship situation that is involvement-oriented and empowering. The mutual gains resulting from this state of fit are high.

The dilemma occurs because there is the possibility of a different choice by each party. If the principal chooses an agency relationship and the manager chooses a steward relationship, the result is likely to be a very frustrated manager who feels betrayed by the principal. When stewards are controlled as if they were agents, they cannot enjoy the types of internal rewards they desire (i.e. growth, achievement, or self-actualization), and as a result, they may engage in antiorganizational behaviors (Argyris, 1964). The application of control may create disenfranchised employees, because principals, rather than those persons actually doing the work, assume the responsibility of deciding and orchestrating firm procedures. Managers in controlling, less trusting climates may not have the opportunity to behave as stewards and therefore may experience decreased feelings of self-worth, self-responsibility, and self-control (Argyris, 1964) and have less desire to behave as stewards. In this situation, the workplace becomes depersonalized, and the manager may begin to view him- or herself as an interchangeable unit. In such environments, employees may resort to antagonistic adaptive activities such as absenteeism and turnover (Fleishman and Harris, 1962; James et al., 1992); theft and vandalism; poor workmanship; slow-downs; stealing; causing waste (Argyris, 1964; James et al., 1992); and demanding better financial compensation, benefits, and working conditions (Herzberg et al., 1959).

If the principal chooses a steward relationship and the manager chooses an agency relationship, the manager acts opportunistically and takes advantage of the principal. A manager whose psychological profile fits that of an agent will behave as a "fox in the henhouse" and will seek to satisfy his or her personal utility at the expense of the organization and the principal. The situation created by the principal empowers the agent to work only to serve him- or herself. Thus, the psychological profile of the manager is out of harmony with the situation, or attempt to remove the manager.

In Table 1, we presented a comparison of the characteristics of agency and stewardship theories. Because of the apparent dominance of stewardship theory one would ask why it would not be adopted by everyone. We believe the answer is in the level of risk that is acceptable to each individual and his or her willingness to trust the other party. Although the highest joint utility is in the principal–steward relationship, in which both parties choose the steward relationship (Cell 4), the least risk of betrayal (losses) is in the principal–agent relationship (Cell 1), in which both parties choose the agency relationship. It is easy to see from this illustration that when each party has an individualistic orientation, the best choice (regardless of the choice of the other person) is an agency relationship. Thus, when two individualistic parties are involved, the inevitable choice is an agency relationship. Only in a collectivist orientation, when both parties subordinate their personal goals to that of the collective, will they evaluate the joint utility and mutually choose a stewardship relationship.

> *Proposition 9*: If a mutual stewardship relationship exists, potential performance of the firm is maximized.

> *Proposition 10*: If a mutual agency relationship exists, potential costs of the firm are minimized.

> *Proposition 11*: If a mixed-motive choice exists, the party choosing stewardship is betrayed, and the party choosing activity is opportunistic.

FUTURE RESEARCH

We have attempted to sketch a broad outline of the psychological and situational processes that are presently somewhat neglected in contemporary management theory and that provide the underpinnings of stewardship theory. More fine-grained analyses are needed, which would include more detailed theory construction, the examination of new variables, and empirical testing. In the future, researchers should inquire into the stewardship mechanisms identified in this article and examine their relative importance, their interactions, and the situational contingencies that affect them.

For our theory, we adopted the simplifying assumption of a choice of agency versus stewardship relationships at a single point in time (i.e. on trial once in a relationship). This assumption was necessary as a first step in establishing the contrast between agency and stewardship theories and for the development of the framework for the choice model. Although this simplification could be viewed as a limitation of our theory, the incorporation of the dynamic aspects of the theory were determined to be beyond the scope of this chapter. Clearly, the role of a long-term relationship is central to the choice of stewardship roles. One of the important implications of the theory of stewardship presented here is that if a mixed-motive choice is made and one party is betrayed, the inevitable progression of the relationship is toward an agency model. Researchers should explore the choice of agency versus stewardship relationships over time, incorporating variables that capture the dynamic nature of principal–manager relationships.

In developing a model of the choice between agency and stewardship theories, we have specified the psychological and situational antecedents of the choice in terms of direct main effects. However, we have not ruled out the possibility that even among the variables identified in this chapter there are likely to be more complex interactions and dynamic effects over time that determine the eventual choice. For example, in an organization that has a high-involvement culture, managers may change over time and learn to value the growth opportunities presented by the job; thorough increased value commitment and identification, managers may develop and use more personal power. Thus, the argument is that there may be an interaction effect between the organization's philosophy and the psychological variables, and in a long-term model, there may be a direct effect of the situation (philosophy) on the psychological factors. This argument is consistent with Argyris's (1964) views regarding the self-fulfilling prophecy created by organizational philosophy and structure. Researchers should explore these potential interactions.

An interesting implication of the theory is related to the cultural variables and the process of implementation of structural changes in organizations. As we noted previously, there appear to be several national cultures in which the values for individualism, collectivism, and power distance would lead to opposite predictions regarding the propensity for stewardship relationships. A more fine-grained examination of these variables may suggest that the impact of the cultural variables may be felt at different stages in the process of implementing structural change. Consider the example of an organization that is changing its traditional hierarchical structure to one that is flatter, more decentralized, more participative, and therefore more conducive to stewardship types of relationships. (In terms of our model, this would be represented as a change from a control-oriented philosophy to an involvement-oriented philosophy.) In the United States (high individualism, low power distance), we might expect this process to meet greater resistance as a firm moves toward collective action, but once such a structure is in place, the participants move rapidly to develop a highly participative environment where there is greater equality. In contrast, in Japan (low individualism, high power distance) we might expect such changes to proceed more smoothly as members accept the team concept, but progress beyond that point might meet great resistance in the absence of "leaders" who provide direction for the teams. Although these scenarios are speculative, they illustrate the richness of these issues as avenues for future research.

Another potential area for future research would include the relationships among theories about trust in organizations, risk-taking behaviour, and stewardship. There has been much interest in the development of models of organizational trust (e.g. Chiles and McMackin, 1996; Hosmer, 1995; Mayer et al., 1995). It should be clear in this chapter that stewardship theory and the choices of stewardship relationships in organizations rely heavily on the trust between the principal and managers as well as the perceived risks. As we noted previously, Mayer and colleagues (1995: 712) defined trust as "the willingness to be vulnerable." This definition of trust is the antithesis of the basic premise of agency theory, which could be restated as "the unwillingness to be vulnerable." We believe there is much to be learned from exploring the relationships among trust and stewardship in organizations.

Finally, the stewardship theory presented here could be integrated into contemporary thinking regarding leadership in organizations. Are charismatic leaders more likely to develop principal–steward relationships? Are transactional leaders following the agency model? Also, is leadership a dyadic process (Liden et al., 1993; Scandura and Schriesheim, 1994)? When considered in the context of stewardship theory, this issue has very interesting implications. According to our theory, the choice of stewardship relationships is made one relationship at a time, and the success of the relationship is a function of the mutual choice by two parties in the relationship. This idea implies that any one principal could have both agency and stewardship relationships with multiple managers at the same time and that managers could have both agency and stewardship relationships with different principals. Each of these issues deserves further investigation.

CONCLUSIONS

We use agency theory to help researchers to understand the conflicts of interest that can arise between principals and agents, the resulting potential problems of opportunism, and the structures that evolve to contain it, such as supervision and incentives. However, organizational relationships may be more complex than those analyzed through agency theory. The propositions of agency theory may not apply in all situations. An alternative model of managerial motivation and behavior is stewardship theory, which is derived from psychological and sociological traditions. Our research adds to the understanding of stewardship theory by describing its terminology and theoretical contribution.

We extend previous stewardship theory research by defining several of the psychological and sociological characteristics that are antecedents to principal–steward relationships. Managers whose needs are based on growth, achievement, and self-actualization and who are intrinsically motivated may gain greater utility by accomplishing organizational rather than personal agendas. Likewise, managers who identify with their organizations and are highly committed to organizational values are also more likely to serve organizational ends. Finally, situations in which the managerial philosophy is based on involvement and trust and the culture is based on collectivism and low power distance generally result in principal–steward relationships.

We also add to previous stewardship research by examining a model based on manager–principal choice rather than determinism. According to our model, managers choose to behave as stewards or agents. Their choice is contingent on their psychological motivations and their perceptions of the situation. Principals also choose to create an agency or stewardship relationship, depending upon their perceptions of the situation and the manager. If either the manager or the principal perceives that the other party will behave in an activity manner (defect), it is in his or her best interest to behave in an agency fashion, and the organization receives a suboptimal return on its investment. If both parties choose to develop a stewardship relationship (cooperate), the organization realizes the maximum reward. Unlike previous researchers, who assumed that managers are predisposed to act like stewards or agents, we base our research on choice rather than on determinism.

Finally, we suggest future avenues for stewardship theory research. We describe a need for more fine-grained analysis of the proposed psychological and situational factors. Through such research, management scholars can come to a clearer understanding of these and other variables that may influence principal–manager relationships. We also argue that more dynamic modeling is necessary to understand how time and prior decisions affect future relationships. We call for research on the interactions among the psychological mechanisms and situational factors and the relationship between trust and risk that each party is willing to assume. In short, a variety of theoretical and empirical projects are needed to help researchers to fully understand stewardship theory.

ACKNOWLEDGMENTS

We thank Edward Conlon, Robert Vecchio, Robert House, and Robert Wood for their helpful comments during the preparation of this chapter.

NOTE

1 By *man* we mean the nongender-specific reference to human beings in general.

REFERENCES

Adams, J.S. 1965. Injustices in social exchange. In L. Berkowitz (ed.), *Advances in experimental social psychology.* 267–99. New York: Academic Press.

Alderfer, C.P. 1972. *Existence, relatedness, and growth: Human needs in organizational settings.* New York: Free Press.

Argyris C. 1964. *Integrating the individual and the organization.* New York: Wiley.

Argyris, C. 1973a. Organization man: Rational and self-actualizing. *Public Administration Review*, 33 (July/August): 354–57.

Argyris, C. 1973b. Some limits of rational man organizational theory. *Public Administration Review*, 33 (May/June): 253–67.

Atkinson, J.W. 1957. Motivational determinants of risk-taking behavior. *Psychological Review*, 64: 359–72.

Bass, B.M. 1960. *Leadership, psychology, and organizational behavior.* New York: Harper.

Berg, S.V. and Smith, S.K. 1978. CEO and board chairman: A quantitative study of dual vs. unitary board leadership. *Directors and Boards.* 3(1): 34–9.

Berle, A. and Means, G. 1932. *The modern corporation and private property.* New York: Macmillan.

Brown, M.E. 1969. Identification and some conditions of organizational involvement. *Administrative Science Quarterly*, 14: 346–55.

Chaganti, R.S., Mahajan, V., and Sharma, S. 1985. Corporate board size, composition and corporate failures in retailing industry. *Journal of Management Studies*, 22: 400–17.

Chiles T.H. and McMackin, J.F. 1996. Integrating variable risk preferences, trust, and transaction cost economics. *Academy of Management Review*, 21: 73–99.

Cosier, R.A. and Dalton, D.R. 1983. Equity theory and time: A reformulation. *Academy of Management Review*, 8: 311–19.

Cyert, R.M. and March, J.G. 1963. *A behavioral theory of the firm*. Englewood Cliffs, NJ: Prentice Hall.

Daily, C.M. and Dalton, D.R. 1994. Bankruptcy and corporate governance: The impact of board composition and structure. *Academy of Management Journal*, 37: 1603–17.

D'Aveni, R.A. and MacMillan, I.C. 1990. Crisis and the content of managerial communications: A study of the focus of attention of top managers in surviving and failing firms. *Administrative Science Quarterly*, 35: 634–57.

Demsetz, H. and Lehn, K. 1985. The structure of corporate ownership: Theory and consequences. *Journal of Political Economics*, 93: 11–55.

Donaldson, L. 1990. The ethereal hand: Organizational economics and management theory. *Academy of Management Review*, 15: 369–81.

Donaldson, L. and Davis, J.H. 1989. *CEO governance and shareholder returns: Agency theory or stewardship theory*. Paper presented at the annual meeting of the Academy of Management, Washington, DC.

Donaldson, L. and Davis, J.H. 1991. Stewardship theory or agency theory: CEO governance and shareholder returns. *Australian Journal of Management*, 16: 49–64.

Donaldson, L. and Davis, J.H. 1994. Boards and company performance—Research challenges the conventional wisdom. *Corporate Governance: An International Review*, 2: 151–60.

Doucouliagos, C. 1994. A note on the volution of homo economicus. *Journal of Economics Issues*, 3: 877–83.

Finkelstein, S. and D'Aveni, R.A. 1994. CEO duality as a double-edged sword: How boards of directors balance entrenchment avoidance and unity of comand. *Academy of Management Journal*, 37: 1079–108.

Fleishman, E.A. and Harris, E.F. 1962. Patterns of leadership behavior related to employee grievances and turnover. *Personnel Psychology*, 15: 43–56.

Fox, M.A. and Hamilton, R.T. 1994. Ownership and diversification: Agency theory or stewardship theory. *Journal of Management Studies*, 31:69–81.

Frank, R.H. 1994. *Microeconomics and behavior*. New York: McGraw-Hill.

French, J.R.P. and Raven, B. 1959. The bases of social power. In D. Cartwright (ed.), *Studies in social power*, 150–167. Ann Arbor, MI: University of Michigan Institute for Social Research.

Gibson, J.L., Ivancevich, J.M., and Donnelly, J.H. 1991. *Organizations*. Homewood, IL: Irwin.

Hackman J.R. and Oldham, G.R. 1975. Development of the job diagnostic survery. *Journal of Applied Psychology*, 60: 159–70.

Hackman, J.R. and Oldham, G.R. 1976. Motivation through the design of work: Test of a theory. *Organizational Behavior and Human Performance*, 15: 250–79.

Hackman, J.R. and Oldham, G.R. 1980. *Work redesign*. Reading, MA: Addison-Wesley.

Herzberg, F., Mausner, B., and Snyderman, B.B. 1959. *The motivation to work*. New York: Wiley.

Hirsch, P., Michaels, S., and Friedman. R. 1987. "Dirty hands" versus "clean models." *Theory and Society*, 16: 317–36.

Hodgetts, R.M. and Luthans, F. 1993. U.S. multinationals' compensation strategies for local management: Cross-cultural implications. *Compensation and Benefits Review*, 25: 42–8.

Hofstede, G. 1980. *Culture's consequences: International differences in work-related values*. Beverly Hills, CA: Sage.

Hofstede, G. 1991. *Cultures and organizations: Software of the mind*. London: McGraw-Hill.

Hofstede, G. 1993. Cultural constraints in management theories. *Academy of Management Executive*, 7(1): 81–90.

Hosmer, L.T. 1995. Trust: The connecting link between organizational theory and philosophical ethics. *Academy of Management Review*, 20: 379–403.

James, L.R., Demaree, R.G., Mulaik, S.A., and Ladd, R.T. 1992. Validity generalization in the context of situational models. *Journal of Applied Psychology*, 77: 3–14.

Jensen, M.C. and Meckling, W.H. 1976. Theory of the firm: Managerial behavior, agency costs and ownership structure. *Journal of Financial Economics*, 3: 305–60.

Jensen, M.C. and Meckling, W.H. 1994. The nature of man. *Journal of Applied Corporate Finance*, 7(2): 4–19.

Katz, D. and Kahn, R.L. 1978. *The social psychology of organizations* (2nd edn.). New York: Wiley.

Kelman, H.C. 1958. Compliance, identification, and internalization: Three processes of attitude change. *Journal of Conflict Resolution*, 2: 51–60.

Kelman, H.C. 1961. Processes of opinion change. *Public Opinion Quarterly*, 25: 57–78.

Lawler, E.E. 1986. *High involvement management*. San Francisco, CA: Jossey-Bass.

Lawler, E.E. 1992. *The ultimate advantage*. San Francisco, CA: Jossey-Bass.

Liden, R.C., Wayne, S.J., and Dean, S. 1993. A longitudinal study on the early development of leader-member exchange. *Journal of Applied Pschology*, 78: 662–74.

Likert, R. 1961. *New patterns of management*. New York: McGraw-Hill.

McClelland, D.C. 1970. The two faces of power. *Journal of International Affairs*, 24: 29–47.

McClelland, D.C. 1975. *Power: The inner experience*. New York: Irvington.

McClelland, D.C. and Burnham, D.H. 1976. Power is the great motivator. Harvard Business Review, 54(2): 100–10.

McGregor, D. 1960. *The human side of the enterprise.* New York: McGraw-Hill.

McGregor, D. 1966. *Leadership and motivation.* Cambridge, MA: MIT Press.

Mael, F. and Ashforth, B.E. 1992. Alumni and their alma mater: A partial test of the reformulated model of organizational identification. *Journal of Organizational Behavior*, 13: 103–23.

Manz, C.C. 1986. Self-leadership: Toward an expanded theory of self-influence processes in organizations. *Academy of Management Review*, 11: 585–600.

Manz, C.C. 1990. Beyond self-managing work teams: Toward self-leading teams in the workplace. In R. Woodman and W. Pasmore (eds), *Research in organizational change and development*, 273–99. Greenwich, CT: JAI Press.

Maslow, A.H. 1970. *Motivation and personality.* New York: Harper and Row.

Mayer, R.C. and Schoorman, F.D. 1992. Predicting participation and production outcomes through a two-dimensional model of organizational commitment. *Academy of Management Journal*, 35: 671–84.

Mayer, R.C., Davis, J.H., and Schoorman, F.D. 1995. An integrative model of organizational trust. *Academy of Management Review*, 20: 709–34.

Molz, R. 1988. Managerial domination of boards of directors and financial performance. *Journal of Business Research*, 16: 235–49.

Mowday, R., Porter, L., and Steers, R. 1982. *Organizational linkages: The psychology of commitment, absenteeism, and turnover.* New York: Academic Press.

O'Reilly, C. 1989. Corporations, culture and commitment: Motivation and social control in organizations. *California Management Review*, 31(4): 9–25.

O'Reilly, C. and Chatman, J. 1986. Organizational commitment and psychological attachment: The effects of compliance, identification, and internalization on prosocial behavior. *Journal of Applied Psychology*, 71: 492–99.

Perrow, C. 1986. *Complex organizations: A critical essay.* New York: McGraw-Hill.

Porter, L.W., Steers, R.M., Mowday, R.T., and Boulian, P.V. 1974. Organizational commitment, job satisfaction, and turnover among psychiatric technicians. *Journal of Applied Psychology*, 5: 603–09.

Rechner, P.L. and Dalton, D.R. 1991. CEO duality and organizational performance: A longitudinal analysis. *Strategic Management Journal*, 12: 155–60.

Salancik, G.R. and Meindl, J.R. 1984. Corporate attributions as strategic illusions of management control. *Administrative Science Quarterly*, 29: 238–54.

Scandura, T.A. and Schriesheim, C.A. 1994. Leader-member exchange and supervisor career mentoring as complementary constructs in leadership research. *Academy of Management Journal*, 37: 1588–602.

Simon, H.A. 1957a. *Administrative behavior* (2nd edn). Glencoe, IL: Free Press.

Simon, H.A. 1957b. *Models of man.* New York: Wiley.

Simon, H.A. 1973. Organization man: Rational or self-actualizing? *Public Administrator Review*, 33 (July/August): 346–53.

Smith, C.A., Organ, D., and Near, J. 1983. Organizational citizenship behavior: Its nature and antecedents. *Journal of Applied Psychology*, 68: 653–63.

Staw, B.M., McKechnie, P.L., and Puffer, S.M. 1983. The justification of organizational performance. *Administrative Science Quarterly*, 28: 582–600.

Steers, R.M. and Black, J.S. 1994. *Organizational Behavior.* New York: HarperCollins.

Steers, R.M. and Porter, L.W. 1991. *Motivation and work behavior.* (5th ed.). New York: McGraw-Hill.

Sussman, M. and Vecchio, R.P. 1982. A social influence interpretation of worker motivation. *Academy of Management Review*, 7: 177–86.

Triandis, H.C. 1990. Cross-cultural studies of individualism and collectivism. In J.J. Berman (ed.), *Nebraska symposium on motivation*, 37: 41–134. Lincoln, NE: University of Nebraska Press.

Triandis, H.C. 1995. *Individualism and collectivism.* Boulder, CO: Westview.

Triandis, H.C., Dunnette, M., and Hough, I.M. (eds). 1993. Cross-cultural studies. *Handbook of industrial and organizational psychology*, Vol. 4. Palo Alto, CA: Consulting Psychologists.

Turner, J.C. 1981. The experimental social psychology of intergroup behavior. In J.C. Turner and H. Giles (eds), *Intergroup behavior*, 66–101. Chicago, IL: University of Chicago Press.

Walsh, J.P., Seward, J.K. 1990. On the efficiency of internal and external corporate control mechanisms. *Journal of Management Review*, 15: 421–58.

Walton, R.E. 1980. Establishing and maintaining high-commitment work systems. In J.R. Kimberly, R.H. Miles, and Associates (eds), *The organizational life cycle: Issues in the creation, transformation, and decline of organizations.* 208–90. San Francisco: Jossey-Bass.

Walton, R.E. 1985. From control to commitment in the workplace. *Harvard Business Review*, 63(2): 76–84.

Williamson. O.E. 1985. *The economic institutions of capitalism: Firms, markets, relational contracting.* New York: Free Press.

PART FIVE

External pressures

INTRODUCTION TO PART FIVE

The focus of the theories examined so far has been upon the internal monitoring dilemmas of corporate governance. However, there is a stream of theoretical approaches that focuses upon the external challenges of corporate governance in terms of building relationships and securing resources. Resource dependence theory, institutional theory and network theory are all interested in the external relations of corporations. Resource dependency theory highlights the interdependencies of organizations rather than viewing them simply in terms of management intentions. Hillman, Cannella and Paetzold (Chapter 10) examine how company directors may serve to connect the firm with external resources that help to overcome uncertainty, and provide access to relationships with suppliers, buyers, public policy makers and other social groups.

Judge and Zeithaml (Chapter 11) contrast the institutional and strategic choice perspective on how boards of directors respond to their external environment. The institutional perspective sees the structures and processes that an environment legitimates from history and experience as the taken-for-granted way forward. In contrast the strategic choice perspective emphasizes the choices managers make and the actions they take to adapt to their environment. Managers have the ability to learn about, manage and sometimes even create the environment of the organization.

Forging social networks is one way of coordinating the production of complex products and services while dealing with demanding environments. Jones, Hesterly and Borgatti (Chapter 12) examine how in many industries such as film, music, finance and fashion, coordination is characterized by informal social systems rather than bureaucratic structures. It could be argued that this *network* governance is a distinct economic activity, contrasting and competing with markets and hierarchies. Autonomous firms engage in open-ended social contracts adapting to environmental contingencies and engaging in productive exchanges. Network governance is suited for industries with high levels of demand uncertainty, short product life cycles, and where the rapid dissemination of information is critical.

'The Resource Dependence Role of Corporate Directors: Strategic Adaptation of Board Composition in Response to Environmental Change'

from Journal of Management Studies (2000)

Amy J. Hillman, Albert A. Cannella Jr and
Ramona L. Paetzold

INTRODUCTION

Boards of directors have received considerable attention recently, both in practitioner and academic venues. A large body of literature examines the agency role of directors, referring to the governance function in which directors serve shareholders by ratifying the decisions of managers and monitoring the implementation of those decisions (Baysinger and Butler, 1985; Baysinger and Hoskisson, 1990; Daily and Dalton, 1994a,b; Fama and Jensen, 1983; Goodstein and Boeker, 1991; Lorsch and MacIvor, 1989; Mizruchi, 1983; Tushman and Romanelli, 1985). The agency role has also been termed the control role of boards by Johnson *et al.* (1996), the management control model (Boyd, 1990; Drucker, 1981; Mace, 1971), and the corporate control role (Pearce and Zahra, 1992; Zahra and Pearce, 1989), all of which focus on the important monitoring and governance function of boards.

Another distinct role that directors play is that of providing essential resources or securing those resources through linkages to the external environment (Boyd, 1990; Daily and Dalton, 1994a,b; Gales

and Kenser, 1994; Johnson *et al.*, 1996; Pearce and Zahra, 1992; Pfeffer, 1972; Pfeffer and Salancik, 1978; Zahra and Pearce, 1989). Resource dependence theory proposes that corporate boards are a mechanism for managing external dependencies (Pfeffer and Salancik, 1978), reducing environmental uncertainty (Pfeffer, 1972) and reducing the transaction costs associated with environmental interdependency (Williamson, 1984). According to Pfeffer and Salancik (1978), boards are 'vehicles for co-opting important external organizations' (p. 167).

Much of the research on boards has examined board composition (Barnhart *et al.*, 1994; Bathala and Rao, 1995; Boyd, 1990; Daily and Dalton, 1994a,b; Daily and Schwenk, 1996; Gales and Kesner, 1994; Johnson *et al.*, 1996; Pearce and Zahra, 1992; Weisbach, 1988). However, most of this work has used a traditional agency method of classifying directors (e.g. insiders and outsiders; or insiders, independent outsiders, and outsiders who have some form of dependence on the firm) regardless of whether the role of interest is agency or resource dependence. In this paper, we assert that because the two roles of directors, agency and resource dependence are theoretically and practically distinct, the salient attributes and characteristics used to examine board composition should similarly be distinct. Specifically, we posit that the common insider and outsider definitions (and the several variants of outsiders used in previous literature) are appropriate in studying the agency role, but are less valuable in understanding the resource dependence role. One objective of this paper is to present a taxonomy for classifying directors that reflects the resource dependence role as distinct from the agency role.

After presenting the resource dependence taxonomy we explore the role of resource dependence by examining the changing nature of board composition in an industry undergoing a major environmental change. If, as Pfeffer (1972) asserts, a board's composition reflects the firm's external dependencies, we would expect to see strategic changes in board composition as a firm's environment changes significantly. The environmental change we study here is the deregulation of a highly regulated industry: US air travel. Under regulation, airlines' major uncertainties arose from federal regulators, who influenced everything from flight schedules to maintenance requirements to ticket pricing. However, this also meant that federal regulations created many certainties for the industry in that many aspects of the external environment were controlled or strongly influenced by regulators. Therefore, the airlines' major dependency in the environment was the regulatory body. After US deregulation in 1978, the major uncertainties began to shift toward non-regulatory sources, such as competitors and consumers, thus increasing the number and scope of environmental dependencies and prompting the firms to alter their board structures to better align them with the new dependencies.

DIRECTOR ROLES: AGENCY VERSUS RESOURCE DEPENDENCE

As noted earlier, much of the literature on board composition has focused on the agency role of the board of directors. In this role, directors act as fiduciaries of shareholders, serving to alleviate or reduce the problems associated with the separation of ownership and control in public corporations by acting to ensure that the actions of managers serve the interests of shareholders (Fama and Jensen, 1983; Jensen and Meckling, 1976). For example, when the strategies of incumbent managers are ineffective, directors are expected to take action, replacing managers if necessary to improve performance. This line of reasoning asserts that directors who are insiders, either managers or employees of the firm, are more inclined to side with management interests in the tension caused by the separation of ownership and control. On the other hand, outsiders, or directors who are not current or past owners or employees of the firm, may better protect the interests of shareholders because they can be more dispassionate in their evaluation of ongoing strategies.

More recently, however, scholars have questioned the ability of the insider/outsider distinction to capture the independence of outside directors (Daily and Dalton, 1994b). For example, MacAvoy et al. (1983), Baysinger and Butler (1985) and Weisbach (1988) classify directors as outside, inside or grey, with grey directors being those directors who are not employees or managers, but who may not be independent of current management because of business dealings with the company or family relationships with management. Grey directors are similar to the affiliated directors category used by Barnhart et al. (1994), Pearce and Zahra (1992) and Johnson et al. (1996) in reference to directors who have some affiliation with the corporation, officers of firms that do business with the corporations, relatives of an officer, former executives, employees or consultants. Yet another refinement of the outsider category is used by Daily and Dalton (1994a,b, 1995) who identify independent directors, referring to those directors who were appointed to a board prior to the incumbent chief executive officer's appointment. These refinements, regardless of the varying labels and measurement methods, are attempts to gauge director willingness to uphold shareholder interests even when doing so would threaten incumbent management or ongoing strategies. This distinction becomes salient because dependent or inter-dependent directors, even though they are not employees of the firm, may have been co-opted by management and therefore be less effective in upholding shareholder interests.

Despite the various categories used to disaggregate outside directors into truly independent and dependent categories, these classification schemes are based on the underlying logic of the agency role: that manager and shareholder interests may diverge and the board is a mechanism for aligning those interests through the monitoring and ratifying of management decisions. Essentially, the agency role boils down to monitoring – agency problems are best alleviated by having objective directors who are not dependent on the firm for employment, sales or other benefits. However, when one examines the other role of directors, the resource dependence role, agency-based classification schemes seem less appropriate.

The resource dependence role of directors is theoretically distinct from the agency role although directors may perform both roles simultaneously (Johnson et al., 1996). In the resource dependence role, directors serve to connect the firm with external factors which generate uncertainty and external dependencies. In order to survive, organizations must cope effectively with uncertainty (Alchian, 1950; Pfeffer and Salancik, 1978; Thompson, 1967). Uncertainty clouds the organization's control of resources and choice of strategies, and impedes simple day-to-day functioning. Effective coping with uncertainty leads to power (Pfeffer and Salancik, 1978) and, ultimately, increased survival likelihood (Singh et al., 1986). Thus, by having directors who serve to link the organization with its external environment, a board may act to reduce uncertainty.

But, in the resource dependence role, directors may do more than reduce uncertainty. Directors also bring resources to the firm, such as information, skills, access to key constituents (e.g. suppliers, buyers, public policy decision makers, social groups), and legitimacy (Gales and Kesner, 1994). The extent to which directors benefit the firm depends on whether their inclusion provides access to valued resources and information, reduces environmental dependency, or aids in establishing legitimacy (Daily and Dalton, 1994a). Some support has been found in previous research for the effectiveness of boards in resource acquisition (Boeker and Goodstein, 1991; Zald, 1969). In addition, support has been found for the assertion that directors may enhance the reputation and credibility of their firms (Daily and Schwenk, 1996; Hambrick and D'Aveni, 1992).

One potential result of linking the firm with external environmental factors and reducing uncertainty is a reduction in transaction costs associated with the firm's external linkages. For example, having an outsider director who possesses regulatory expertise or knowledge may not only reduce uncertainty through a gain in information and expertise, but may also reduce the transaction costs associated with the regulatory agency. Information supplied by this director

about the bidding process for government contracts, the appropriate personnel to contact, or influence over proposed regulation may actually reduce the costs of transactions between regulators and the firm, giving the firm a cost advantage over rivals. Thus, in addition to the benefits of reduced uncertainty and easier acquisition of resources, directors may also reduce the transaction costs associated with the inter-dependencies between the firm and various institutions in the environment (Williamson, 1984).

One of the basic propositions of resource dependence theory is that the need for environmental linkage is a direct function of the levels and types of dependence facing an organization. Thus, using the classification scheme of insiders and outsiders, one might reason that as environmental dependencies and environmental uncertainty increase, the need for external linkages increases and more outsiders would be needed on the board. Therefore, the theory predicts a relationship between the degree of uncertainty or dependency and the composition of the board as measured by the number or proportion of outside directors or the size of the board. This relationship was confirmed by Pfeffer and Salancik (1978), Pennings (1980), Boyd (1990) and Gales and Kesner (1994). But, at this level of classification, all we can assert from these findings is that firms facing different levels of uncertainty and environmental dependency will tend to have different sizes of boards or mixes of outsiders and insiders, or, that across time as environments change, board size or the ratio of outsiders to insiders will vary.

While these results confirm some of the logic behind the resource dependence role of the board, they cannot explain how board composition will vary other than in size or in outsider to insider ratios. Because each director, especially each outside director, brings different linkages and resources to a board, resource dependence theory would also suggest that underlying patterns of board composition more finely grained than an insider/outsider distinction will be observed. Pfeffer's (1972) original work in this area indicated that outside directors are heterogeneous and he finds systematic differences across environments for directors representing financial institutions. However, this further distinction among outside directors has not been adopted by other researchers. In the following section we discuss an expanded classification scheme for outside directors to better understand their resource dependence role.

ROLES OF INDIVIDUAL DIRECTORS AS ENVIRONMENTAL LINKS

As discussed above, each director brings to the organization unique attributes (Kesner, 1988; Kosnik, 1990). By observing these attributes, we can predict what kinds of resources a given director is likely to bring to the board. Aside from maturity, leadership and analytical judgement, which are expected of all directors, differences among directors are perhaps most visible in terms of their individual experience or occupational attributes (Baysinger and Butler, 1985). These differences reflect the heterogeneity of resources such as expertise, skill, information and the potential linkages to other external constituencies. This line of reasoning corresponds to that used by Hambrick and Mason (1984) in their discussion of the linkage between the characteristics of executives and the strategies and decisions the executives derive and implement, and is also similar to that of Westphal and Zajac (1997) who use the personal experiences of executives to predict what kinds of initiatives they will support as outside directors.

In terms of a firm's need for resources from the external environment, some general groups of expertise and linkages may be identified. First, inside directors serve on boards largely to provide firm-specific information (Fama and Jensen, 1983). Thus, while each inside director may have specific types of expertise as well as specific relationships or linkages with environmental contingencies, the primary resource each provides is internally focused. Outside directors, however, primarily provide resources needed to deal with external factors. Pfeffer and Salancik (1978) assert that there are four primary benefits that result from environmental linkages such as boards: (1) provision of specific resources, such as expertise and advice from individuals with experience in a variety of strategic areas; (2) channels for communicating information between external organizations and the firm; (3) aids in obtaining commitments or support from important elements outside the firm; and (4) legitimacy (Pfeffer and Salancik, pp. 145 and 161). We see these four primary benefits relating to specific areas of resource needs that may be met by including outsiders on a board. We developed a taxonomy of directors by linking Pfeffer and Salancik's list of benefits with some commonly observed characteristics of directors among large public corporations. Table 1 provides an overview of a resource dependence taxonomy. This

taxonomy has been largely influenced by the work of Baysinger and Zardkoohi (1986) yet differs in terms of theoretical underpinnings and category definition.[1] In the first column, we provide the descriptive label we used for the class of director. The second column outlines the kinds of resources and linkages which the director is expected to bring to the board, and the third column identifies the characteristics of directors who would fall under the category. We have included insiders as the first row, though the bulk of our discussion emphasizes outside directors. Each category of director is discussed separately here.

Insiders

These are directors who serve currently or have served in the past as active managers, employees or owners of the firm. This definition is consistent with prior research that has divided the board into insiders and outsiders cited in our earlier review. While insiders may have varying attributes that could supply valuable resources from the external environment, this role is not a primary rationale behind their directorship. As such, we view insiders as supplying the board with information about the firm itself and about its competitive environment, and we group all insiders together. We note, however, that future research on directors as resource providers could unpack the insider category. For example, many large firms provide director positions for the chief financial officer and the general council, positions requiring very specific and identifiable expertise.

Business experts

These are similar to Baysinger and Zardkoohi's (1986) decision controllers. They are directors who are active or retired executives in other for-profit organizations, and directors who serve on other large corporate boards. These directors bring expertise and knowledge to the firm as a result of their experience in internal decision making in other firms. Because these directors serve as executives in other organizations, they bring a working knowledge of strategic decision-making and internal firm operations. As such, they may serve as sounding boards for executives, providing advice and council on internal operations (Mace, 1971). Further, their experience

Director category label	Areas of resource needs provided	Types of directors in category
Insiders	Expertise on the firm itself as well as general strategy and direction	Current and former officers of the firm
	Specific knowledge in areas such as finance and law	
Business experts	Expertise on competition, decision making and problem solving for large firms	Current and former senior officers of other large for-profit firms
	Serve as sounding boards for ideas	
	Provide alternative viewpoints on internal and external problems	Directors of other large for-profit firms
	Channels of communication between firms	
	Legitimacy	
Support specialists	Provide specialized expertise on law, banking, insurance and public relations	Lawyers
	Provide channels of communication to large and powerful suppliers or government agencies	Bankers (commercial and investment)
	Ease access to vital resources, such as financial capital and legal support	Insurance company representatives
	Legitimacy	Public relations experts
Community influentials	Provide non-business perspectives on issues, problems and ideas	Political leaders
	Expertise about and influence with powerful groups in the community	University faculty
	Representation of interests outside competitive product or supply markets	Members of clergy
	Legitimacy	Leaders of social or community organizations

Table 1 The resource dependence roles of directors.

outside the firm permits them to supply alternative viewpoints on internal issues, providing executives with valuable information about how other firms deal with similar problems and concerns.

Aside from their role in internal operations, another important role of business experts derives from expertise which is directly relevant to the market or competitive environment that the firm faces. Business experts may facilitate effective evaluation of management proposals, in part, by providing valuable advice as strategies are formulated (Fama and Jensen, 1983; Johnson et al., 1996). This category of directors is best suited to meet the need of expertise in and linkages to critical interdependence in the competitive environment. We add that directors of this category, as well as all other categories, serve to build legitimacy for the firm. Legitimacy is not the emphasis of our taxonomy, in that each type of director provides

some type of legitimacy for the organization, but a business expert's in providing legitimacy would be assessed by noting the prestige associated with the director's work experiences or other affiliations.

Support specialists

These are similar to Baysinger and Zardkoohi's (1986) decision supporters. They are directors who provide expertise and linkages in specific, identifiable areas that support the firm's strategies but do not form the foundation on which the strategy is built. These individuals provide support for senior management in areas requiring specialized expertise such as capital markets, law, insurance and public relations. As such, their role is primarily to meet the need for specialized expertise and linkages to support organizations outside the firm's product markets, such as financial institutions, law firms, public relations firms and so forth.

Support specialists are differentiated from business experts in that they lack general management experience. Rather, these individuals bring specific expertise and/or access and information about environmental contingencies and provide support for the competitive strategy of the firm. Support specialists may directly help to secure commitment from external organizations, as described by Pfeffer and Salancik (1978). For example, having a member of a financial institution serving as a director may communicate that the firm is in need of capital and that the needs and concerns of capital suppliers are important to the firm. This could represent the first step toward securing essential capital resources. As with all of our categories, support specialists may also provide legitimacy to the firm in the symbolic value of having such support function expertise represented on the board.

Community influentials

These are similar to Baysinger and Zardkoohi's (1986) symbolic directors. They are directors with experience and linkages relevant to the firm's environment beyond competitor firms and suppliers. Community influentials include directors who possess knowledge about or influence over important non-business organizations, and includes retired politicians, university or other institutional representatives, and officers of social organizations. The resources supplied by community influentials do not stem from direct experience in controlling other large organizations operating in similar environments, but rather from knowledge, experience and connections to community groups and organizations (Baron, 1995), such as social interest groups or movements, or other community constituencies that may impact or be impacted by the firm's operations and strategic choices. These directors can provide valuable non-business perspectives on proposed actions and strategies. Their expertise and influence with community forces can help the firm to avoid costly missteps when its actions might inadvertently conflict with the interests of these groups. Essentially, community influentials serve as vehicles of co-optation for the organization (Pfeffer and Salancik, 1978) in

that they are included on a board of directors 'as a means of averting threats to its stability or existence' (Selznick, 1965: 13). Like other classes of directors, community influentials serve to legitimate the firm, and the level of prestige associated with a community influential director could be used to measure the extent to which he or she brings legitimacy to the firm.

CHANGES IN THE ENVIRONMENT AND THE BOARD OF DIRECTORS AS AN ENVIRONMENTAL LINK

Changes in the environment are often associated with changes in corporate strategy. Theorists have long argued that organizations respond to changes in their environments by initiating strategic change (Child, 1972; Pfeffer and Salancik, 1978; Singh et al., 1986; Tushman and Romanelli, 1985). Empirical research has provided evidence to support the theory that changes in a firm's environment such as shifts in regulatory (Meyer, 1982; Smith and Grimm, 1987) and technological environments (Pugh, 1981) motivate important strategic changes in organizations. Mizruchi (1983) noted that a company's board is in a position to establish the parameters within which strategic decision making occurs. Goodstein and Boeker (1991) argued that the composition and control emphasis of a board of directors will motivate management toward the adoption of specific strategies. As the board of directors may intervene in strategy and decision-making arenas, the board will actively be involved in any significant changes in strategy (Tushman and Romanelli, 1985). Thus, a change in the environment leads to a change in corporate strategy, which in turn may be facilitated through a change in the composition of the board of directors.

As mentioned above, resource dependence theory asserts that as a firm's external environment changes, so does the need for linkages with that environment. Therefore, the composition of the board may be strategically altered in order to provide the benefits of reduced uncertainty for firms in a different environment *and* to facilitate strategic change. Also, if directors act to link the firm with its external environment and the environment shifts significantly, the effectiveness of linkages may need to be re-evaluated.

In order to study patterns of board composition across different environments, however, we must specify the environments of interest. As noted earlier, this paper is an attempt to further our understanding of the resource dependence role of directors by using a more fine-grained approach, one that should reveal patterns in board composition and strategic adaptation of such composition across environmental conditions. That is, while the four categories developed above capture the central resources and linkages that contribute to the resource dependence role, the relative need for directors in each category will vary based on the environment.

One environmental transition that makes it possible to study the resource dependence role of directors and board composition across environments is the change from regulation to deregulation (Lang and Lockhart, 1990; Mahon and Murray, 1981; Spiller, 1983). Here, regulation refers to economic regulation defined by Mahon and Murray (1981) as regulation directly affecting the competitive dynamics of a specific industry by limiting competitor exit and entry, setting prices or services, and imposing constraints on rivalry. When such an industry is faced with deregulation, firms are confronted with a need for strategic change. Under regulation, firms are limited in the strategies available to them (Smith and Grimm, 1987). Prices and market entry and exit are heavily influenced or even dictated by regulators. In addition, regulatory agencies typically attempt to ensure adequate but not excessive profits. As a result, the incentive to be internally efficient may be reduced for regulated firms because the regulators often serve to decouple the link between internal efficiency and profitability (Smith and Grimm, 1987).

Regulation also shifts some decision-making and planning functions away from managers and toward public officials and shifts managerial emphasis away from customers and toward the regulatory body. Under regulation, the regulatory agency serves a buffering role, ensuring a stable environment and making strategic planning less necessary (Mahon and Murray, 1981). For example, regulatory boards attempt to protect consumers by setting prices and other operational standards. In addition, the financing of regulated firms is often less risky than that for unregulated firms as the oversight mechanisms and price and profit controls set by regulators are established and stable. As the environment changes from regulation to deregulation, new sources of uncertainty arise as firms are no longer protected from competition. When regulation is removed, firms must re-evaluate strategic decisions

and directions, so the change in environmental conditions will eventually lead to changes in strategy. Firms in the newly deregulated environment have no history of competitive interaction and are accustomed to more of a friendly rivalry. They do not know how to read each other's moves and destructive competition is likely to result (Gimeno, 1994). When the environment changes, the old links between the environment and the organization may no longer be satisfactory and therefore these links must be redefined, renegotiated or terminated (Mahon and Murray, 1981). For example, Lang and Lockhart (1990) argue that as an industry is deregulated, a change in board interlocks may be expected as a result of environmental change. We would agree that a change is needed, but what specific changes does resource dependence theory predict?

The argument advanced by Pfeffer (1972) and reasserted here is that the composition of the board of directors should reflect a firm's external environment. Both Pfeffer (1972) and Baysinger and Zardkoohi (1986) tested this proposition by examining (cross-sectionally) firms in different environmental contexts. If the composition of boards is a reflection of the external environment, then, as a firm's environment changes, board composition should change as well. In addition, if directors serve to reduce environmental uncertainty, the importance of individual attributes will be differentially affected by changes in the environment. Therefore, as a firm experiences a significant change in its external environment, the pattern of board composition should correspondingly change as well. We discuss the implications of deregulation for each of the four categories of directors listed in Table 1.

Insiders

Regulatory agencies control many important strategic issues faced by regulated firms. For example, market entry, exit, prices and profit levels are often determined by regulatory agencies and these decisions substantially impact the competitive environment that regulated firms confront. Because regulatory agencies exert a great influence over factors such as these, the shift to deregulation implies that the firms must establish internal mechanisms to deal with issues formerly handled by regulators. Therefore, the need for decision making by boards among regulated firms is less than that among unregulated firms because many strategic options are precluded or restricted for regulated firms.

Inside directors serve to provide firm-specific information to the board (Jensen and Meckling, 1983). Resource dependency theory would hold that the primary duty of insiders serving on the board of directors is to supply this information to the board (or, in the case of regulation, to the regulatory agency), not to serve as linkages to environmental dependencies (Pfeffer, 1972). We are not disputing the role of insiders as linkages to the external environment. However, given that insiders' primary role is that of insider information provision, we argue that on the margin the provision of information, not external linkages, is the most important phenomena to examine here. Given insiders' primary role, one would expect that, under regulation, inside decision makers will take on an increasingly important role as information providers. This role, however, becomes diminished with deregulation as the need for external linkages takes on increased importance. Under deregulation it will still be necessary for insiders to provide information to the board, but the need for external linkages suggests insiders will be less important. Most directors serve a fixed term of office, which complicates somewhat the process of strategically aligning particular director roles. It is likely that many firms will wait until director terms expire or directors retire, and then will replace out-going directors with those who are better able to serve in the desired role. When replacements occur, the intended improvement with the external environment should occur. Therefore,

Hypothesis 1: Under regulation, there is a greater likelihood of replacements to the board of directors being inside decision makers than under deregulation.

Business experts

Regulatory oversight is posited to also alter the role of business experts on the board of directors. Because so many functions of regulated firms are dictated by the regulatory agency and the competitive environment is tightly controlled, the number of business expert directors needed to help make strategic decisions is reduced. Smith and Grimm (1987) argue that

after deregulation many competitive strategic actions become available to firms. Business experts, having broad experience with decision making in other organizations, can provide expertise and judgement concerning strategic actions and options. Given that firms faced with an environmental change such as deregulation usually initiate strategic change in order to better conform to the newly altered competitive environment, business experts take on an increased importance. Mahon and Murray (1981) similarly contend that different skills are needed by deregulated firms relative to regulated firms and that general managers, or firm representatives with managerial or decision-making experience in deregulated environments, will be more important to firms under deregulation.

Hypothesis 2: Under deregulation, there is a greater likelihood of replacements to the board of directors being business experts than under regulation.

Support specialists

As a result of regulatory oversight under regulation, the role of decision support directors, such as lawyers and bankers, may differ from that under deregulation. People with specialized skills in regulation and control, such as lawyers, will be important under regulation to help the firm comply with regulatory mandates and understand regulatory procedures (Mahon and Murray, 1981). When firms dispute or challenge regulatory rulings, it is typically accomplished through the legal system. Also, regulatory mandates are often written in the same form and style as legislation, and support specialists with legal expertise can aid greatly in interpreting the rulings and explaining them to other directors. Finally, legal expertise can be very important prior to the issuance of new regulations, when regulators propose changes and request comments. At this stage, legal expertise can be used to actually shape new regulations prior to their becoming law. However, in a deregulated environment support specialists who are lawyers may be less important.

The need for support specialists with financial expertise, on the other hand, may be less straightforward. Lang and Lockhart (1990) argue that financial pressures increase sharply with deregulation and report more interlocks with financial institutions among unregulated firms as compared to regulated ones. However, in the time period of our study, financial markets in the USA were becoming much more competitive and efficient. The days of relationship banking are over in the USA and while airline financing may be more risky under deregulation than regulation, during our time period it is unlikely that this will affect the need for financial representatives on boards. Instead of having long-term relationships with financial institutions, capital market transactions are becoming much less a matter of who you know. Thus, we would assert that while financing becomes more challenging without the guaranteed profit margins of regulation, deregulated firms will not experience an increased need for members of financial institutions on their boards. We are not asserting that the need for this subgroup as directors is diminished as the environment moves to deregulation, but merely that the need is not increased. Therefore, we propose the following:

Hypothesis 3: Under regulation, there is a greater likelihood of replacements to the board of directors being support specialists than under deregulation.

Community influentials

These directors help to assure that the interests of stakeholders without an active voice in corporate affairs are not abused or ignored. When the environment facing a firm is deregulated, overall uncertainty increases. Lang and Lockhart (1990) find empirical support for an increase in uncertainty faced by airlines as a result of deregulation. Competitive forces sharpen, prices are no longer fixed, profits are no longer guaranteed, and uniform services and standards are no longer regulated. Therefore, more elements of the environment are uncertain, causing higher transaction costs and an increased need for co-optation.

As a result, the firm will have an increased need for directors who may be able to co-opt factors in the deregulated environment. Individuals with community influence, access or prestige (e.g. politicians, university representatives, members of social groups) will become increasingly important to the firm, not only for their information and potential access, but also for the legitimacy they may lend to the organization. Regulation is, at its most basic level, a tie with

the government – a link to legitimacy. The regulatory agency provides security for shareholders and consumers through direct oversight. Once this is removed, the firm will need to regain the loss in legitimacy caused by the absence of the regulatory agency.

One might argue that community influential directors with expertise or connections with the regulatory agency would be extremely valuable as environmental links under regulation. This certainly may be the case, but with the increase in overall uncertainty that accompanies deregulation, we would expect the importance of community influentials to increase overall after deregulation. That is not to say that these members are unimportant during regulation, but rather that, on the margin, deregulation will increase the scope of uncertainty that community influentials may lend expertise and/or access to in the environment. Therefore,

Hypothesis 4: Under deregulation, there is a greater likelihood of replacements to the board of directors being community influentials than under regulation. . . .[2]

NOTES

1 Our taxonomy is fundamentally different from Baysinger and Zardkoohi's (1986) in that it is based on resource dependence theory. As such, we value differential resources and linkages brought by each distinct type of director and categorize them based on these differing resources. Because of this theoretical underpinning, we do not use Baysinger and Zardkoohi's category labels in our taxonomy although operationally they are somewhat similar.
2 This reading is pp. 235–46 of the original Hillman, Cannella and Paetzold (2000: 235–55).

REFERENCES

Agresti, A. (1990). *Categorical Data Analysis*. New York: John Wiley.
Alchian, A. (1950). 'Uncertainty, evolution, and economic theory'. *Journal of Political Economy*, 58: 211–21.
Barnhart, S., Marr, W. and Rosenstein, S. (1994). 'Firm performance and board composition: some new evidence'. *Managerial and Decision Economics*, 15: 329–40.
Baron, D. (1995). 'Integrated strategy: market and nonmarket components'. *California Management Review*, 37: 47–65.

Bathala, C. and Rao, R. (1995). 'The determinants of board composition: an agency theory perspective'. *Managerial and Decision Economics*, 16: 59–69.

Baysinger, B. and Butler, H. (1985). 'Corporate governance and the board of directors: performance effects of changes in board composition'. *Journal of Law, Economics, and Organization*, 1: 101–24.

Baysinger, B. and Hoskisson, R. (1990). 'The composition of boards of directors and strategic control: effects on corporate strategy'. *Academy of Management Review*, 15: 72–87.

Baysinger, B. and Zardkoohi, A. (1986). 'Technology, residual claimants and corporate control'. *Journal of Law, Economics, and Organization*, 2: 339–44.

Boeker, W. and Goodstein, J. (1991). 'Organizational performance and adaption: effects of environment and performance on changes in board composition'. *Academy of Management Journal*, 34: 4, 805–26.

Boyd, B. (1990). 'Corporate linkages and organizational environment: a test of the resource dependence model'. *Strategic Management Journal*, 11: 419–30.

Child, J. (1972). 'Organizational structure, environment and performance: the role of strategic choice'. *Sociology*, 6: 1–22.

Cook, T. and Campbell, D. (1979). *Quasi-experimentation: Design and Analysis Issues for Field Settings*. Boston, MA: Houghton Mifflin.

Daily, C. and Dalton, D. (1994a). 'Corporate governance and the bankrupt firm: an empirical assessment'. *Strategic Management Journal*, 15: 643–54.

Daily, C. and Dalton, D. (1994b). 'Bankruptcy and corporate governance: the impact of board composition and structure'. *Academy of Management Journal*, 37: 1603–17.

Daily, C. and Dalton, D. (1995). 'CEO and director turnover in failing firms: an illusion of change?'. *Strategic Management Journal*, 16: 393–400.

Daily, C. and Schwenk, C. (1996). 'Chief executive officers, top management teams, and boards of directors: congruent or countervailing forces?'. *Journal of Management*, 22: 185–208.

Drucker, P. (1981). *Toward the Next Economics, and Other Essays*. New York: Harper & Row.

Fama, E. and Jensen, M. (1983). 'Separation of ownership and control'. *Journal of Law and Economics*, 26: 301–38.

Fienberg, S. (1980). *The Analysis of Cross-classified Categorical Data*. Cambridge, MA: MIT Press.

Gales, L. and Kesner, I. (1994). 'An analysis of board of director size and composition in bankrupt organizations'. *Journal of Business Research*, 30: 271–82.

Gimeno, J. (1994). 'Multipoint competition, market rivalry, and firm performance: a test of the mutual forbearance hypothesis in the US airline industry, 1984–1988'. Unpublished dissertation, Purdue University.

Goodstein, J. and Boeker, W. (1991). 'Turbulence at the top: a new perspective on governance structure changes and strategic change'. *Academy of Management Journal*, 34: 306–30.

Hambrick, D. and D'Aveni, R. (1992). 'Top team deterioration as part of the downward spiral of large corporate bankruptcies'. *Management Science*, 38: 1445–66.

Hambrick, D. and Mason, P. (1984). 'Upper echelons: the organization as a reflection of its top managers'. *Academy of Management Review*, 9: 193–206.

Hillman, A.J., Cannella, A.A. and Paetzold, R.L. (2000). 'The resource dependence role of corporate directors: strategic adaptation of board composition in response to environmental change'. *Journal of Management Studies*, 37, 2: 235–55.

Jensen, M.C. and Meckling, W.H. (1976). 'Theory of the firm: managerial behavior, agency costs, and ownership structure'. *Journal of Financial Economics*, 3, 4: 305–60.

Jensen, M.C. and Meckling, W.H. (1983). 'Corporate governance and "economic democracy": an attack on freedom'. In Huizenga, C.J. (ed.), *Corporate Governance: A Definite Explanation of the Issues*, UCLA Extension, UCLA.

Johnson, J., Daily, C. and Ellstrand, A. (1996). 'Boards of directors: a review and research agenda'. *Journal of Management*, 22: 409–38.

Kesner, I. (1988). 'Directors' characteristics and committee membership: an investigation of type, occupation, tenure, and gender'. *Academy of Management Journal*, 31: 499–508.

Kosnik, R. (1990). 'The effects of board demography and directors' incentives on corporate greenmail decisions'. *Academy of Management Journal*, 33: 129–50.

Lang, J. and Lockhart, D. (1990). 'Increased environmental uncertainty and changes in board linkage patterns'. *Academy of Management Journal*, 33: 106–28.

Lorsch, J. and MacIvor, E. (1989). *Pawns or Potentates: The Reality of America's Corporate Boards*. Boston, MA: Harvard Business School Press.

MacAvoy, P., Canter, S., Dana, J. and Peck, S. (1983). 'ALI proposals for increased control of the corporation by the board of directors'. In *Statement of the Business Round-table on the American Law Institute's Proposed Principles of Corporate Governance and Structure*. New York: Business Roundtable.

Mace, M. (1971). *Directors: Myth and Reality*. Boston, MA: Harvard Business School Press.

Mahon, J. and Murray, E. (1981). 'Strategic planning for regulated companies'. *Strategic Management Journal*, 2: 251–62.

Meyer, A. (1982). 'Adapting to environmental jolts'. *Administrative Science Quarterly*, 27: 515–37.

Mizruchi, M. (1983). 'Who controls whom? An examination of the relation between management and boards of directors in large American corporations'. *Academy of Management Review*, 8: 426–35.

Pearce, J. and Zahra, S. (1992). 'Board composition from a strategic contingency perspective'. *Journal of Management Studies*, 29: 411–38.

Pennings, J. (1980). *Interlocking Directorates: Origins and Consequences of Connections Among Organizations' Board of Directors*. San Francisco, CA: Jossey-Bass.

Pfeffer, J. (1972). 'Size and composition of corporate boards of directors'. *Administrative Science Quarterly*, 21: 218–28.

Pfeffer, J. and Salancik, G. (1978). *The External Control of Organizations: A Resource Dependence Perspective*. New York: Harper & Row.

Pugh, D. (1981). 'The Aston Program of research: retrospect and prospect'. In Van de Ven, A. and Joyce, W. (eds), *Perspectives on Organizational Design and Behavior*. New York: John Wiley.

Selznick, P. (1965). *TVA and the Grassroots*. New York: Harper & Row.

Singh, J., House, R. and Tucker, D. (1986). 'Organizational change and organizational mortality'. *Administrative Science Quarterly*, 32: 367–86.

Smith, K. and Grimm, C. (1987). 'Environmental variation, strategic change, and firm performance: a study of railroad deregulation'. *Strategic Management Journal*, 8: 363–76.

Spiller, P. (1983). 'The differential impact of airline regulation on individual firms and markets: an empirical analysis'. *Journal of law and Economics*, 26: 655–87.

Tabachnick, B. and Fidell, L. (1989). *Using Multivariate Statistics*. New York: HarperCollins.

Thompson, J. (1967). *Organizations in Action*. New York: McGraw Hill.

Tushman, M. and Romanelli, E. (1985). 'Organizational evolution: a metamorphosis model of convergence and reorientation'. In Cummings, L. and Staw, B. (eds), *Research in Organizational Behavior*. Greenwich, CT: JAI Press, 171–22.

Weisbach, M. (1988). 'Outside directors and CEO turnover'. *Journal of Financial Economics*, 20: 431–60.

Westphal, J. and Zajac, E. (1997). 'Defections from the inner circle: social exchange, reciprocity, and the diffusion of board independence in US corporations'. *Administrative Science Quarterly*, 42: 161–83.

White, M., Tansey, R., Smith, M. and Barnett, T. (1993). 'Log-linear modeling in personnel research'. *Personnel Psychology*, 46: 667–86.

Williamson, O. (1984). 'Corporate governance'. *Yale Law Journal*, 93: 1197–229.

Zahra, S. and Pearce, J. (1989). 'Boards of directors and corporate financial performance: a review and integrative model'. *Journal of Management*, 15: 291–344.

Zald, M. (1969). 'The power and functions of boards of directors: a theoretical synthesis'. *American Journal of Sociology*, 74: 97–111.

"Institutional and Strategic Choice Perspectives on Board Involvement in the Strategic Decision Process"

from Academy of Management Journal (1992)

William Q. Judge Jr and Carl P. Zeithaml

In recent years, external pressure for greater corporate accountability has intensified. Proxy fights are spreading (Dobrzynski, 1988), and shareholder suits against corporate officers and directors are increasing at a 10 percent annual rate (Glaberson and Powell, 1985). As Nussbaum and Dobrzynski argued, "The tight hold professional managers have on the corporation is slipping. Investors are no longer passive. Outside directors are asserting themselves. Other stakeholders – from employees to communities – want a voice. The internal power is beginning to shift" (1987: 102–103).

Increasingly, the pressure for greater accountability in corporate decision-making has focused on board involvement in the strategic decision-making process. Power (1987) observed that institutional investors are pressuring boards to challenge managements' strategic leadership. Galen (1989) reported that the courts are increasingly supporting shareholder efforts to get boards more involved. Furthermore, Weidenbaum (1985) argued that the best defense against corporate raiders is increased board involvement in the strategic decision process.

Some evidence suggests that boards are responding to these external pressures with greater involvement and less passivity. For instance, Heidrick and Struggles (1990) reported that directors are increasingly involved in determining and monitoring the strategic directions of firms. Similarly, a *Business Week* cover story suggested, "Quietly, many boards are asserting themselves – redirecting strategy here, vetoing an investment there" (Dobrzynski, 1989: 66). Worthy and Neuschel (1984) flatly stated that a major increase has occurred in recent years in the duties, power, and responsibilities of corporate boards.

Other evidence, however, indicates that some organizations are resisting increased board involvement in the strategic decisions. For example, Lorsch (1989) found that directors wanted to get more involved but are constrained from doing so. Mace (1986) concluded that boards never get involved in strategic decisions unless faced with a crisis. Whisler (1984) reported that one of the universal "rules of the game" is that boards do not get too involved in setting strategy. Similarly, Patton and Baker (1987) argued that board members continue to refuse to "rock the boat" and get involved.

Because board involvement is such a complex phenomenon, we suspected that no one theoretical perspective could adequately capture the process. As a result, this study used two different, and sometimes conflicting, perspectives to describe and explain board involvement in the strategic decision-making process – the strategic choice perspective (Child, 1972) and the institutional perspective (Meyer and Rowan, 1977). With these two complementary perspectives, we hoped to provide a more comprehensive view of board involvement in the strategic decision process. In sum, the purpose of this study was to advance and test relationships predicted by these two perspectives to better explain why and how boards get involved in the strategic decision process.

EXTERNAL PRESSURES FOR BOARD INVOLVEMENT

Although numerous external pressures exist for greater board involvement, researchers have increasingly recognized three institutional forces as catalysts for change. First, because a board is a legal entity governed by state law, the court system greatly affects board behavior. In general, increasing litigation has been directed at boards. For example, it has been estimated that 1 in 20 boards was sued in the 1960s; 1 in 9 was sued in the following decade; and, in the 1980s, 1 in 5 confronted a lawsuit (Kesner and Johnson, 1990). This trend was highlighted by a landmark ruling, known as the Trans-Union case, in which directors were found to be negligent in their involvement in the strategic decision process and were held personally responsible for the damages (Glaberson and Powell, 1985). As a result, directors perceive themselves as having a growing exposure to legal action, often because of insufficient involvement in strategic decision-making (Galen, 1989).

Pension funds are a second institutional force pressurizing boards to get more involved. In 1970, pension funds owned 17.5 percent of all publicly traded stock. In 1985, they controlled over 33 percent of all public stock, and that figure is projected to increase to 50 percent by the year 2000 (Heard, 1987). Due to the increasing size of pension funds, their managers can no longer sell a firm's stock when they become disenchanted with its top management without a potentially adverse effect on the selling price. As a result, they are waging proxy fights to pressure boards to increase their oversight and involvement (Dobrzynski, 1988).

The market for corporate control is a third major institutional force pressurizing boards to become more involved. During the 1980s, hostile takeover activity was at an all-time high (Bhagat et al., 1989). According to agency theory, hostile takeovers discipline inefficiently run firms by removing control from incumbent executives and directors or threatening to take control (Fama and Jensen, 1983). Thus, hostile takeovers represent a form of corporate governance that substitutes for ineffective board oversight (Brickley and James, 1987). In sum, both real and potential threat of unwanted takeovers pose significant external pressure for greater board involvement.

BOARD RESPONSE TO EXTERNAL PRESSURES

Currently, little conclusive evidence exists regarding how boards in corporate America have responded to these and other pressures for greater involvement in strategic decision-making. For example, the authors of most studies of board involvement have speculated about board behavior by examining decisions for which the board is directly responsible, such as those concerning golden parachutes (Cochran et al., 1985), greenmail (Kosnik, 1987), and top management compensation (Kerr and Bettis, 1987).[1] Although a few field studies have directly examined board involvement (e.g. Henke, 1986; Pearce and Zahra, 1991; Tashakori and Boulton, 1983), these survey studies have suffered from very low response rates (15–21 percent) and are suspect because they only surveyed a single rater in each organization. In sum, researchers simply do not know what boards' roles are in the strategic decision-making process, nor do we know what influences that involvement.

As discussed previously, we used two prominent theoretical perspectives in this research, the institutional and strategic choice perspectives, to conceptualize board response to external pressures. Interestingly, advocates of each perspective view board response in very different ways, and the hypothesized antecedents of that response vary accordingly. Consequently, we begin with a general description of each perspective and then proceed to specific explanations and predictions regarding board strategic role.

The institutional perspective

The institutional perspective addresses the issue of how and why organizational structures and processes come to be taken for granted and the consequences of this institutionalization process (Meyer and Rowan, 1977; Selznick, 1949, 1957; Zucker, 1987). The key idea behind institutionalization is that much organizational action reflects a pattern of doing things that evolves over time and become legitimated within an organization and an environment (Pfeffer, 1982). Therefore, organizational practices can be predicted and explained by examining industry traditions and firm history (Eisenhardt, 1988).

Although there are several different schools of thought within this perspective (Scott, 1987), much of the institutional literature focuses on the concept of isomorphism, whereby organizations conform to the accepted norms of their populations (DiMaggio and Powell, 1983; Rowan, 1982). In effect, an environment legitimates certain ways of organizing. For example, Hirsch (1975) found that industry "gatekeepers" had a major impact on organizational structure and effectiveness. Similarly, Tolbert and Zucker (1983) found that city governments adopted certain organizational structures and processes more than others more because the environment legitimated those structures and processes than because organizational actors took autonomous actions.

However, institutional theorists do recognize that some organizations resist or avoid conforming to external pressures. They explain this resistance in terms of founding conditions and firm history. In other words, a new firm adopts practices common at its time of founding, and this "imprinting" becomes a major influence on the rest of the organization's life (Stinchcombe, 1965). Over time, those practices become the standard way of doing things. Numerous researchers have observed the inertial effects of founding conditions (e.g. Boeker, 1989; Eisenhardt, 1988; Tolbert and Zucker, 1983).

In sum, the institutional perspective is a relatively deterministic theoretical framework that places great emphasis on environmental norms and the weight of firm history as explanations of organizational norms and the weight of firm history as explanations of organizational actions. Institutional theorists see the use of structures and processes that an environment legitimates as sensible because it implies responsible management, pleases external constituencies, and avoids potential claims of negligence if something goes wrong (Eisenhardt, 1988). Given the relatively deterministic assumptions underlying institutional theory, it offers unique explanations and predictions for board behavior that have not yet been explored empirically.

The strategic choice perspective

The strategic choice perspective (Andrews, 1986; Child, 1972) focuses on the actions organizational members take to adapt to an environment as an explanation for organizational outcomes. Its proponents argue that purposeful actions abound in organizations and that organizational members have substantial leeway in shaping their own fates. As such, the perspective focuses attention on individuals and groups within organizations to explain organizational processes. This focus on behavior assumes that organizational actors possess the discretion to act of their own free will (Hambrick and Finkelstein, 1987).

In their landmark study, Miles and Snow identified three fundamental characteristics of the strategic choice perspective. They concluded that this perspective "(1) views managerial or strategic choice as the primary link between organization and environment; (2) focuses on management's ability to create, learn about, and manage the organization's environment; and (3) encompasses the multiple ways that organizations respond to environmental conditions" (1978: 263).

As with the institutional perspective, a number of schools exist within the strategic choice perspective. These schools vary with respect to their conception of the degree and type of deliberateness by which strategies are formed (Mintzberg, 1990). Although it was beyond the scope of this study to address the conflicting viewpoints of these various schools of thought, we noted that most strategy scholars have agreed that for specific strategic decisions, there is first a formation, or prechoice, phase of strategic activity, followed by an evaluation, or postchoice, phase (Fredrickson, 1983). Therefore, researchers have generally accepted a two-phase model of the strategic choice process and given primacy to internal explanations for variations in strategy formation, such as the characteristics of a firm's upper echelon.

In sum, the strategic choice perspective emphasizes nondeterministic explanations of organizational processes and outcomes (Bourgeois, 1984). Strategic choice theorists acknowledge the influence of the external environment, but their focus is on adaptive responses to that environment. In its broadest sense, this perspective represents an evolving, relatively nondeterministic paradigm, or "meta-model," for explaining how organizations adapt to environmental forces (Ansoff, 1987).

An integration of the two perspectives

The two perspectives of interest operate under different theoretical assumptions, but proponents of each appear to be moving closer together. For example, Oliver (1991) argued that institutionalists need to recognize the willful, adaptive behavior some organizations demonstrate. Furthermore, recent empirical work employing the institutional framework has shown that organizations do not passively adapt to their environments (e.g. Covaleski and Dirsmith, 1988; Kurke, 1987; Powell, 1987).

Similarly, strategic choice theorists are recognizing institutional aspects of the strategic decision process. For example, Fredrickson and Iaquinto (1989) characterized the strategic decision process as inertial. Also, Huff (1982) identified industry influences on strategy reformulation and implied that examination of just strategic decision makers was overly narrow. Most recently, Hitt and Tyler (1991) found that industry characteristics significantly influence the strategic decision process.

In summary, these two perspectives appear to offer complementary views of the strategic decision-making process. As Hrebiniak and Joyce (1985) argued, the interaction of deterministic and nondeterministic perspectives must be studied to fully understand organizational behavior. Recognizing this complementarity, Neilsen and Rao described the institutional and strategic aspects of board involvement in the strategic decision-making process to illustrate the "strategy-legitimacy nexus." Therefore, both perspectives may prove to be useful for providing a comprehensive view of board behavior (1987).

HYPOTHESES

In this study, we defined board involvement as the overall level of participation of board members in making nonroutine, organization-wide resource allocation decisions that affect the long-term performance of an organization. This definition excludes strategic activities by senior managers acting purely as corporate officers rather than as board members. Although senior managers are highly involved in strategy formation both in and out of the board context, the focus of this study was on their involvement as board members.

Organizational age and board involvement

An organization's age is the number of years elapsed between its founding and the present. Organizational age has proven to be a particularly powerful construct in institutional literature. Numerous studies have

shown that it affects organizational processes (e.g. Boeker, 1989; Eisenhardt, 1988; Tolbert and Zucker, 1983). Although the impact of organizational age on board behavior has not yet been empirically studied, the institutional perspective suggests that it influences this process as well.

According to the institutional perspective, founding conditions have a major effect on organizational processes (Zald, 1969). Because organizations change slowly, those founded chronologically earlier than others in different environmental conditions are expected to yield different behaviors than those founded later (Hannan and Freeman, 1984). Several empirical studies support this view. For example, Eisenhardt (1988) found that organizational age was a major predictor of compensation practices in the retail shoe industry. She reasoned that founding conditions were different early in the industry's life cycle than they were later and that this difference led older and younger organizations to adopt different practices. Also, Tolbert and Zucker (1983) found that city governments founded before the institutional environment legitimized civil service reform had more autonomy in choosing their organizational structures than younger city governments.

Because older organizations were formed at a time when external pressures to involve boards in strategy were weaker than they are now, these organizations may demonstrate more resistance to increasing board involvement. In contrast, younger organizations may be more susceptible or open to external pressures for greater board involvement (Hannan and Freeman, 1984). In sum, the institutional perspective predicts that organizational age will be negatively associated with board involvement in the strategic decision process because older organizations were formed at a time when external pressures for board involvement were low, and inertia prevents the organizations from adapting to the new situation (Fredrickson and Iaquinto, 1989).

Hypothesis 1: Organizational age is negatively related to board involvement in the strategic decision-making process.

Level of diversification and board involvement

An organization's level of diversification can be conceptualized as the extent to which it is simultaneously active in many distinct businesses (Pitts and Hopkins,

1982). As a result of the increasing diversification of the largest organizations (Bettis and Prahalad, 1983), this variable has become a central topic of organizational research. Although a rich and growing tradition of research addresses level of diversification, very little is known about its relationship to organizational processes (Ramanujam and Varadarajan, 1989). Recent research in the institutional literature reveals that level of diversification does affect organizational processes (D'Aunno et al., 1991).

From an institutional perspective, current industry norms influence organizational processes through isomorphism (DiMaggio and Powell, 1983). Several studies, for example, have demonstrated how organizations conform, or become isomorphic, to industry rules or expectations (Huff, 1982; Tolbert, 1985). Thus, the traditional institutional explanation of organizational structure and process focuses on environmental social norms. This explanation is relatively straightforward until one considers the fact that many of today's organizations compete in multiple industries, and hence, multiple institutional environments with varying isomorphic norms.

Advocates of the institutional perspective have argued that diversification to a certain extent dilutes the pressures of environmental isomorphism by making an organization less dependent on any one particular industry (DiMaggio and Powell, 1983). Oliver (1991) explained that activity in multiple environments usually leads to "constituent multiplicity," a term she defined as the number of conflicting constituent expectations exerted on an organization. This multiplicity, she argued, dilutes environmental pressures for a certain way of operating. Consequently, the pressures of environmental isomorphism may be less focused for diversified organizations.

Therefore, the institutional perspective suggests that external pressures for board involvement will be more divergent for diversified organizations than for nondiversified ones. Given this divergence of external pressures, diversified organizations may be freer to ignore pressures for change (Oliver, 1991). In sum, the institutional perspective predicts that an organization's level of diversification will be negatively associated with board involvement because isomorphic pressures should be more diffuse for diversified firms than for nondiversified ones.

Hypothesis 2: An organization's level of diversification is negatively related to board involvement in the strategic decision-making process.

Insider representation and board involvement

The proportion of insider representation on a board is undoubtedly the most widely studied variable in the corporate governance literature. Researchers have generally defined insiders as board members who are current or former employees of a firm or who are otherwise closely affiliated with the firm (Cochran et al., 1985). In recent years, external stockholders have put increasing pressure on firms to reduce the numbers of inside directors on their boards under the assumption that outsiders provide more objective oversight of the strategic decision process than insiders. For example, Heidrick and Struggles (1990) reported that the proportions of insiders on the boards of the largest US corporations steadily decreased throughout the 1980s from 31 percent to an average of 21 percent in 1989.

Unfortunately, observers of this trend have largely speculated about the impact of insider representation on board behavior, and the empirical results have been equivocal (Zahra and Pearce, 1989). Fortunately, the strategic choice perspective offers theoretical insights into this relationship by focusing more intensively on organizations' internal group dynamics than the institutional perspective. Strategic choice advocates have argued that insiders contribute valuable insights and information to boardroom discussions and hence allow boards to be more involved in the strategic decision process (Baysinger and Hoskisson, 1990). As a result, a balance between informed discussants of strategy and objective monitors of strategic behavior emerges (Rosenstein, 1987).

This internal balance argument has some empirical support in the literature. For example, Ford (1988) found that insider representation was positively associated with board involvement in the strategic decision process for Inc. 500 firms. Also, Tashakori and Boulton (1983) found that higher proportions of insiders on boards were associated with greater board participation in the strategic planning process. Furthermore, insider representation was found to be positively associated with the innovativeness of strategies (Hill and Snell, 1988) and amounts of strategic change (Goodstein and Boeker, 1991) and negatively related to the incidence of golden parachutes in *Fortune* 500 firms (Cochran et al., 1985). More recently, Baysinger et al. (1991) found that insider representation was positively related to the level of corporate R&D spending. Each of these studies has suggested that boards were more effective and involved when insiders were better represented because there may have been better information flows within the boardrooms. In sum, according to the strategic choice perspective, insider representation on a board may be positively related to board involvement.

Hypothesis 3: Insider representation is positively related to board involvement in the strategic decision-making process.

Board size and board involvement

Board size is simply the number of members a board has. Although many studies have examined this structural variable (Zahra and Pearce, 1989), results have been largely equivocal. Once again, theorists have speculated about the variable's impact, but no empirical study has directly examined its actual effect within a theoretical framework. Thus, we turned to the group dynamics literature for an explanation of this relationship.

Previous research on group decision-making has shown that large groups may experience low motivation (Herold, 1979) and problems with coordination and organization (Hackman and Morris, 1975). Thus, as group size increases, the level of members' participation often decreases (Gladstein, 1984).

Several researchers have noted the negative impact of too large a board on board involvement. For example, Herman (1981) reported that large Fortune 500 boards were too cumbersome to conduct effective discussions. Similarly, Kovner (1985) found that large hospital boards were generally ineffective in making strategic decisions in a timely fashion. Other observers (e.g. Lauenstein, 1977; Reed, 1978) have noted that oversized boards slow down decision-making and reduce individual commitment. Thus, board largeness may inhibit effective participation by board members in the strategic decision process because of its negative impact on group dynamics.

Hypothesis 4: Board size is negatively related to board involvement in the strategic decision-making process.

Board involvement and financial performance

Perhaps the most controversial issue surrounding board strategic role concerns board involvement and its impact on the financial performance of organizations (Zahra and Pearce, 1989). Clearly, many issues influence financial performance, such as competitive intensity and organizational size, but the incremental impact of board behavior on organizational size, but the incremental impact of board behavior on organizational performance is unclear. For the fifth and final hypothesis, we used the strategic choice perspective to predict and explain this relationship.

According to the strategic choice perspective, strategic decision makers seek to optimize their firms' financial performance (Hambrick and Mason, 1984). A fundamental assumption of this perspective is that organizational strategy and its processes affect financial performance (Miles and Snow, 1978). All else being equal, better-managed organizations are assumed to achieve higher levels of financial performance.

Andrews (1986) contended that boards are important and neglected strategic resources within firms. The primary basis for this argument is that increased board involvement forces managers to check their assumptions and do their homework before advancing strategic proposals. In addition, outside directors bring an objectivity to the decision-making process that can help to challenge narrow thinking, escalating commitment, and weak analysis (Baysinger and Hoskisson, 1990). These researchers have suggested a positive relationship between board involvement and the financial performance of an organization.

This proposition has some empirical support. Studying the banking industry, Pearce (1983) found that the attitudes of board members were associated with different levels of bank profitability. Also, Pearce and Zahra (1991) found that board involvement for *Fortune* 500 firms was positively related to firm performance after controlling for industry at the two-digit Standard Industrial Classification (SIC) level. Similarly, Baysinger and Butler (1985) concluded that boards affect financial performance when they found that decreases in insider representation were associated with increases in financial performance. Furthermore, Lynch (1979) studied two organizations over two and a half years and observed increasing sales and profitability in the aftermath of increasing

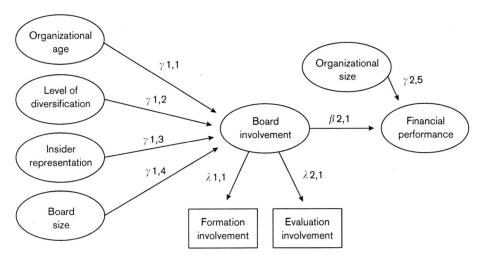

Figure 1 Model of board involvement in the strategic decision-making process.

board involvement in the strategic decision process. Given these preliminary findings, we expected a positive relationship between board involvement and organizational performance because involved boards increase diversity of opinion in the strategy formation process and oversight and objectivity in the strategy evaluation process.

Hypothesis 5: Board involvement in the strategic decision-making process is positively related to an organization's financial performance.

Figure 1 graphically depicts the theoretical relationships examined in this study. As was discussed previously, strategic choice can be conceptualized as occurring in two major phases: the formation phase, when pre-choice direction-seeking activities occur, and the evaluation phase, when postchoice monitoring activities occur. Consequently, board involvement can be conceptualized as involvement in one or both of these phases of the decision-making process. In summary, this study examined four potential antecedents and the financial effect of board involvement in the strategic decision-making process. . . .[2]

ACKNOWLEDGMENTS

We wish to thank Alex Miller, Bill Wooldridge, Christine Oliver, Brian Boyd, and Gerald Fryxell for their helpful comments on earlier drafts of this manuscript. This research was made possible by financial support from the Kenan Institute for Private Enterprise, University of North Carolina at Chapel Hill.

NOTES

1 A golden parachute is a controversial top management perquisite that allows a covered manager to voluntarily resign and collect substantial remuneration. Greenmail transactions are also controversial. Greenmail refers to when a company privately buys back a block of stock from a dissident stockholder who poses an explicit or potential threat to top management's control position.
2 This reading is pp. 766–75 of the original Judge and Zeithaml (1992: 766–94).

BIBLIOGRAPHY

Andrews, K.R. 1986. *The concept of corporate strategy* (2nd edn), Homewood, IL: Irwin.

Ansoff, H.I. 1987. The emerging paradigm of strategic behavior. *Strategic Management Journal*, 8: 501–15.

Bagozz, R.P., Yi, Y., and Philips, L.W. 1991. Assessing construct validity in organizational research. *Administrative Science Quarterly*, 36: 421–58.

Baysinger, B.D. and Butler, H.N. 1985. Corporate governance and the board of directors: Performance effects of changes in board composition. *Journal of Law, Economics, and Organization*, 1(1): 101–24.

Baysinger, B.D. and Hoskisson, R.E. 1990. The composition of boards of directors and strategic control: Effects on corporate strategy. *Academy of Management Review*, 15: 72–81.

Baysinger, B.D., Kosnik, R.D., and Turk, T.A. 1991. Effects of board and ownership structure on corporate R&D strategy. *Academy of Management Journal*, 34: 205–14.

Bentler, P.M. and Bonett, D.G., 1980. Significance tests and goodness of fit in the analysis of covariance structures. *Psychological Bulletin*, 88: 588–606.

Bettis, R.A. and Prahalad, C.K. 1983. The visible and invisible hand: Resource allocation in the industrial sector. *Strategic Management Journal*, 4: 27–43.

Bhagat, S.A., Shleifer, A., and Vishny, R.W. 1989. *The aftermath of hostile takeovers*. Working paper no 276, Center for Research in Security Prices, University of Chicago.

Boeker, W. 1989. Strategic change: The effects of founding and history. *Academy of Management Journal*, 32: 489–515.

Bourgeois, L.J. 1984. Strategic management and determinism. *Academy of Management Review*, 9: 586–96.

Brickley, J.A. and James, C.M. 1987. The takeover market corporate board composition, and ownership structure: The case of banking. *Journal of Law and Economics*, 30: 161–80.

Chatterjee, S. and Blocher, J.D. 1991. *The continuous measurement of firm diversification: Is it really robust?* Paper presented at the annual Academy of Management meetings, Miami, FL.

Child, J. 1972. Organization structure, environment and performance: The role of strategic choice. *Sociology*, 6: 1–22.

Cochran, P.L., Wood, R.A., and Jones, T.B. 1985. The composition of boards of directors and incidence of golden parachutes. *Academy of Management Journal*, 28: 664–71.

Cohen, J. and Cohen, P. 1983. *Applied multiple regression/correlation analysis for the behavioral sciences* (2nd edn) Hillsdale, NJ: Lawrence Erlbaum Associates.

Covaleski, M.A. and Dirsmith, M.W. 1988. An institutional perspective on the rise, social transformation, and fall of a university budget category. *Administrative Science Quarterly*, 33: 562–87.

D'Aunno, T., Sutton, R.I., and Price, R.H. 1991. Isomorphism and external support in conflicting institutional environments: A study of drug abuse treatment units. *Academy of Management Journal*, 34: 636–61.

DiMaggio, P. and Powell, W. 1983. The iron cage revisited Institutional isomorphism and collective rationality in organizational fields. *American Sociological Review*, 48: 147–60.

Dobrzynski, J. 1988. Whose company is it, anyway? *Business Week*, April 25, 60–1.

Dobrzynski, J. 1989. Taking charge. *Business Week*, July 3, 66–71.

Economic Information Systems, 1985. *Establishment database*. New York: Dialogue System.

Eisenhardt, K.M. 1988. Agency- and institutional-theory explanations: The case of retail sales compensation. *Academy of Management Journal*, 31: 488–511.

Fama, E. and Jensen, M. 1983. Separation of ownership and control. *Journal of Law and Economics*, 26: 301–25.

Ford, R.H. 1988. Outside directors and the privately owner firm: Are they necessary? *Entrepreneurship Theory and Practice*, 13(1): 49–57.

Fredrickson, J.W. 1983. Strategic process research: Questions and recommendations. *Academy of Management Review*, 8: 565–74.

Fredrickson, J.W. and Iaquinto, A. 1989. Inertia and creeping rationality in strategic decision processes. *Academy of Management Journal*, 32: 516–42.

Galen, M. 1989. A seat on the board is getting hotter. *Business Week*, July 3, 72–3.

Glaberson, W. and Powell, W. 1985. A landmark ruling that puts board members in peril. *Business Week*, March 18, 56–7.

Gladstein, D. 1984. Groups in context: A model of task group effectiveness. *Administrative Science Quarterly*, 23: 1–39.

Goodstein, J. and Boeker, W. 1991. Turbulence at the top: A new perspective on governance structure changes and strategic change. *Academy of Management Journal*, 34: 306–30.

Graeff, C.L. 1980. Some methodological issues concerning comparative hospital studies. *Academy of Management Review*, 5: 539–48.

Hackman, J.R. and Morris, C.G. 1975. Group tasks, group interaction process, and group performance effectiveness: A review and proposed integration. In L. Berkowitz (Ed.), *Advanced in experimental social psychology*, 8: 45–99. New York: Academic Press.

Hambrick, D. and Finkelstein, S. 1987. Managerial discretion: A bridge between polar views of organizational outcomes. *Research in Organizational Behavior*, 9: 369–406.

Hambrick, D. and Mason, P. 1984. Upper echelons. The organization as a reflection of its top managers. *Academy of Management Review*, 9: 193–206.

Hannan, M.T. and Freeman, J. 1984. Structural inertia and organizational change. *American Sociological Review*, 49: 149–64.

Harrigan, K. 1983. Research methodologies for contingency approaches to business strategy. *Academy of Management Review*, 8: 398–405.

Harris, M.M. and Schaubroeck, J. 1990. Confirmatory modeling in organizational behavior/human resource management. Issues and applications. *Journal of Management*, 16: 337–60.

Harrison, J.R. 1987. The strategic use of corporate board committees. *California Management Review*, 30(1): 109–25.

Heard, J. 1987. Pension funds and contests for corporate control. *California Management Review*, 29(2): 89–100.

Heidrick and Struggles, Inc. 1990. *The changing board*. Chicago: IL. Heidrick and Struggles, Inc.

Henke, J.W. 1986. Involving the directors in strategic planning. *Journal of Business Strategy*, 7(2): 87–95.

Herman, E. 1981. *Corporate control, corporate power*. New York: Cambridge University Press.

Herold, D.E. 1979. The effectiveness of work groups, In S. Kerr (Ed.), *Organizational behavior:* 95–118. Columbus, OH: Grid Publishing.

Hill, C.W.L. and Snell, S.A. 1988. External control, corporate strategy, and firm performance in research-intensive industries. *Strategic Management Journal*, 9: 577–90.

Hirsch, P.M. 1975. Organizational effectiveness and the institutional environment. *Administrative Science Quarterly*, 20: 327–44.

Hitt, M.A. and Tyler, B.B. 1991. Strategic decision models: Integrating different perspectives. *Strategic Management Journal*, 12: 327–51.

Hrebiniak, L.G. and Joyce, W.F. 1985. Organizational adaptation: Strategic choice and environmental determinism. *Administrative Science Quarterly*, 30: 336–49.

Huber, G.P. and Power, D.J. 1985. Retrospective reports of strategic-level managers. Guidelines for increasing their accuracy. *Strategic Management Journal*, 6: 171–80.

Huff, A.S. 1982. Industry influences on strategy reformulation. *Strategic Management Journal*, 3: 119–31.

Information Access Company, 1987. *Ward's Business Directory*. Belmont, CA: Information Access Company.

James, L.R., Mulaik, S.A., and Brett, J.M. 1982. *Casual analysis: Assumptions, models and data*. Beverly Hills, CA: Sage.

Joreskog, K. and Sorbom, D. 1984. *LISREL VI: User's guide* (3rd edn), Mooresville, IN: Scientific Software.

Judge, W.Q. and Zeithaml, C.P. 1992. Institutional and strategic choice perspectives on board involvement in the strategic decision process. *Academy of Management Journal*, 35(4): 766–94.

Keats, B.W. and Hitt, M.A. 1988. A causal model of linkages among environmental dimensions, macro-organizational characteristics, and performance. *Academy of Management Journal*, 31: 570–98.

Kerr, J. and Bettis, R.A. 1987. Boards of directors, top management compensation, and share-holder returns. *Academy of Management Journal*, 20: 645–64.

Kesner, J.F. and Johnson, R.B. 1990. An investigation of the relationship between board composition and shareholder suits. *Strategic Management Journal*, 11: 327–36.

Kohls, J. 1985. Corporate board structure, social reporting and social performance. *Research in Corporate Social Performance and Policy*, 7: 165–89.

Kosnik, R.D. 1987. Greenmail: A study of board performance in corporate governance. *Administrative Science Quarterly*, 32: 163–85.

Kovner, A.R. 1985. Improving the effectiveness of hospital governing boards. *Frontiers of Health Services Management*, 2(1): 4–33.

Kurke, L.B. 1987. Does adaptation preclude adaptability? Strategy and performance, In L.G. Zucker (Ed.), *Institutional patterns and organizations*: 199–222. Cambridge, MA: Ballinger.

Lauenstein, M. 1977. Preserving the impotence of the board. *Harvard Business Review*, 55(4): 36–8, 42, 46.

Lorsch, J.W. 1989. *Pawns or potentates: The reality of America's corporate boards*. Boston, MA: Harvard University Graduate School of Business Administration.

Lynch, J. 1979. *Activating the board of directors: A study of the process of increasing board effectiveness*. Unpublished dissertation, Boston, MA: Harvard University Graduate School of Business Administration.

McDonald, R.P. and Marsh, H.W. 1990. Choosing a multivariate model: Noncentrality and goodness of fit, *Psychological Bulletin*, 107: 247–55.

Mare, M.L. 1986. *Directors: Myth and reality*. Boston, MA: Harvard University Graduate School of Business Administration.

March, J.G. and Simon, H. 1958. *Organizations*. New York: Wiley.

Mever, A.D. 1982. Adapting to environmental jolts. *Adminisrative Science Quarterly*, 27: 515–537.

Mever, J.W. and Rowan, B. 1977. Institutionalized organizations: Formal structure as myth and ceremony. *American Journal of Sociology*, 83: 440–63.

Miles, R.E. and Snow, C.C. 1978. *Organizational strategy, structure, and process*. New York: McGraw-Hill.

Mintzberg, H. 1979. An emerging strategy of direct research. *Administrative Science Quarterly*, 24: 582–89.

Mintzberg, H. 1990. Strategy formation: Schools of thought, In J.W. Fredrickson (Ed.), *Perspectives on strategic management:* 105–236. New York: Harper & Row.

Moody's Investors Service, Inc. 1987. *Moody's industrial manual*. New York: Moody's Investors Service, Inc.

Moody's Investors Service, Inc. 1987. *Moody's OTC industrial manual*. New York: Moody's Investors Service, Inc.

Neilsen, E.H. and Rao, M.V.H. 1987. The strategy-legitimacy nexus: A thick description. *Academy of Management Review*, 12: 523–33.

Nunnally, J.C. 1967. *Psychometric theory*. New York: McGraw-Hill.

Nussbaum, B. and Dobrzynski, J. 1987. The battle for corporate control. *Business Week*, May 18: 102–9.

Nystrom, P.C. and Starbuck, W.H. 1984. To avoid organizational crises, unlearn. *Organizational Dynamics*, 13(1): 53–65.

Oliver, C. 1991. Strategic responses to institutional processes. *Academy of Management Review*, 16: 145–79.

Palepu, K. 1985. Diversification strategy, profit performance, and the entropy measure. *Strategic Management Journal*, 6: 239–55.

Patton, A. and Baker, J. 1987. Why won't directors rock the boat? *Harvard Business Review*, 65(6): 10–18.

Pearce, J.A. 1983. The relationship of internal and external orientations to financial measures of strategic performance. *Strategic Management Journal*, 4: 297–306.

Pearce, J.A. and Zahra, S.A. 1991. The relative power of CEOs and boards of directors Associations with corporate performance. *Strategic Management Journal*, 12: 135–53.

Perrow, C. 1985. Review essay. Overboard with myth and symbols. *American Journal of Sociology*, 91: 151–5.

Pitts, R.A. and Hopkins, H.D. 1982. Firm diversity: Conceptualization and measurement. *Academy of Management Review*, 7: 620–9.

Pfeffer, J. 1982. *Organizations and organization theory*. Boston: Pitman.

Powell, W.W. 1987. Institutional effects on organizational structure and performance, In L.G. Zucker (Ed.), *Institutional patterns and organizations:* 115–36. Cambridge, MA: Ballinger.

Power, C. 1987. Shareholders aren't rolling over anymore. *Business Week*, April 27: 32–3.

Ramanujam, V. and Varadarajan, P. 1989. Research on corporate diversification: A synthesis. *Strategic Management Journal*, 10: 523–51.

Reed, S.F. 1978. On the dynamics of group decision making in high places. *Directors and Boards*, 3(4): 40–56.

Rosenstein, J. 1987. Why don't US boards get more involved in strategy? *Long Range Planning*, 20(3): 30–4.

Rowan, B. 1982. Organizational structure and the institutional environment: The case of public schools. *Administrative Science Quarterly*, 27: 259–79.

Scott, W.R. 1987. The adolescence of institutional theory. *Administrative Science Quarterly*, 32: 493–511.

Selznick, P. 1949. *TVA and the grass roots*. Berkeley, CA: University of California Press.

Selznick, P. 1957. *Leadership in administration*. New York: Row, Peterson.

Shearson Lehman Brothers. 1987. *Analysis of diversified firms*. New York: Shearson Lehman Brothers.

Standard and Poor's. 1987. Health care current analysis. In *Standard and Poor's industry surveys*, 155(18): H1–H28. New York: Standard and Poor's.

Stinchcombe, A. 1965. Social structure and organizations, In J.G. March (Ed.), *Handbook of organizations:* 142–93. Chicago, IL: Rand McNally.

Tashakori, A. and Boulton, W.R. 1983. A look at the board's role in planning. *Journal of Business Strategy*, 3(2): 64–70.

Tolbert, P.S. 1985. Resource dependence and institutional environments: Sources of administrative structure in institutions of higher education. *Administrative Science Quarterly*, 20: 229–49.

Tolbert, P.S. and Zucker, L.G. 1983. Institutional sources of change in the formal structure of organizations: The diffusion of civil service reforms. 1880–1935. *Administrative Science Quarterly*, 23: 22–39.

U.S. Department of Commerce. *U.S. Industrial Outlook*, 1987, Washington, DC: U.S. Department of Commerce.

Wedenbaum, M. 1985. The best defense against the raiders. *Business Week*, September 23, 21.

Whisler, T.L. 1984. *The rules of the game: Inside the corporate board room*, Homewood, IL: Dow Jones-Irwin.

Worthy, J. and Neuschel, R. 1984. *Emerging issues in corporate governance*. Chicago, IL: North-western University Press.

Zahra, S.A. and Pearce, J.A. 1989. Boards of directors and corporate financial performance: A review and integrative model. *Journal of Management*, 15: 291–334.

Zald, M. 1969. The power and functions of boards of directors: A theoretical synthesis. *American Journal of Sociology*, 75: 97–111.

Zucker, L.G. 1987. Institutional theories of organizations, In W.R. Scott and J.F. Short (Eds), *Annual review of sociology*, 13: 443–64. Palo Alto, CA: Annual Reviews.

"A General Theory of Network Governance: Exchange Conditions and Social Mechanisms"

from Academy of Management Review (1997)

Candace Jones, William S. Hesterly and Stephen P. Borgatti

Many industries increasingly are using network governance – coordination characterized by informal social systems rather than by bureaucratic structures within firms and formal contractual relationships between them – to coordinate complex products or services in uncertain and competitive environments (Piore and Sabel, 1984; Powell, 1990; Ring and Van de Ven, 1992; Snow *et al.*, 1992). This type of governance has been observed in such industries as semiconductors (Saxenian, 1990), biotechnology (Barley *et al.*, 1992), film (Faulkner and Anderson, 1987), music (Peterson and Berger, 1971), financial services (Eccles and Crane, 1988; Podolny, 1993, 1994), fashion (Uzzi, 1996, 1997), and Italian textiles (Lazerson, 1995; Mariotti and Cainarca, 1986). Although network governance is widely acknowledged and is seen as producing important economic benefits, "The mechanisms that produce these benefits are vaguely specified and empirically still incipient" (Uzzi, 1996: 677). This vague specification lacks clarity on what network governance is, when it is likely to occur, and how it helps firms (and nonprofit agencies) resolve problems of adapting, coordinating, and safeguarding exchanges.

A synthesis of transaction cost economics (TCE) and social network theory can resolve this vague specification of network governance in multiple ways. TCE provides a comparative framework for assessing alternative governance forms (Williamson, 1994), and it allows us to go beyond descriptive observations of where network governance has occurred and identify the conditions that predict where network governance is likely to emerge. Prior work within the TCE framework has shown that relational contracting is the basis for an alternative governance form between markets and hierarchies (Eccles, 1981; Jarillo, 1988; Mariotti and Cainarca, 1986). These studies, although important, rarely define network governance and do little to show how network governance resolves fundamental problems of adapting, coordinating, and safeguarding exchanges. In addition, these studies most often focus on exchange dyads rather than on the network's overall structure or architecture. By examining exchanges between dyads, "without reference to the nature of other ties in the network or how they fit together" (Wellman, 1991: 35–36), these studies cannot show adequately how the network structure influences exchanges.

Synthesizing TCE and social network theory also advances our understanding of transaction costs and governance.[1] Although the social context, referred to as "structural embeddedness," surrounding economic exchange has been recognized as critical since Granovetter's (1985) widely cited critique was published, it has not been integrated into the TCE framework. "Embeddedness refers to the fact that economic action and outcomes . . . are affected by actors" dyadic (pairwise) relations *and* by the structure of the overall network of relations' (Granovetter, 1992: 33). As Williamson (1994: 85) acknowledges, "[N]etwork relations are given short shrift," partly because of TCE's preoccupation with dyadic relations.

We integrate social context into the TCE perspective by explaining how social mechanisms influence the costs of transacting exchanges. Specifically, we show that exchange conditions characterized by needs for high adaptation, high coordination, and high safeguarding influence the emergence of structural embeddedness. We also show how structural embeddedness provides the foundation for social mechanisms, such as restricted access, macrocultures, collective sanctions, and reputations, to coordinate and safeguard exchanges in network governance. We move beyond recent work on embeddedness by explaining how structural embeddedness arises and provides a foundation for social mechanisms to coordinate and safeguard exchanges. Finally, we show how social mechanisms interact to create an exchange system where coordination and cooperation among autonomous parties for customized exchanges is not only possible but probable.

By integrating TCE and social network theory, we provide a simple, yet coherent, framework for identifying the conditions under which network governance is likely to emerge and the social mechanisms that allow network governance to coordinate and safeguard customized exchanges simultaneously in rapidly changing markets.

The article is organized as follows. First, we review the literature defining network governance and provide our own definition. Second, we identify conditions for network governance and explore why networks, rather than markets or hierarchies, are employed. Third, we explain how structural embeddedness arises out of exchange conditions and provides the foundation for social mechanisms used in network governance. In addition, we specify how key social mechanisms enhance coordination and reduce behavioral uncertainty among exchange parties. These social mechanisms in network governance reduce transaction costs, gaining comparative advantage over markets and hierarchies, which enables network governance to emerge and thrive. Finally, we suggest future directions for research on network governance.

WHAT IS NETWORK GOVERNANCE?

Definitions in the literature

The terms "network organization" (Miles and Snow, 1986), "networks forms of organization" (Powell,

1990), "interfirm networks," "organization networks" (Uzzi, 1996, 1997), "flexible specialization" (Piore and Sabel, 1984), and "quasi-firms" (Eccles, 1981) have been used frequently, and somewhat metaphorically, to refer to interfirm coordination that is characterized by organic or informal social systems, in contrast to bureaucratic structures within firms and formal contractual relationships between them (Gerlach, 1992: 64; Nohria, 1992). We call this form of interfirm coordination "network governance."[2] Network governance constitutes a "distinct form of coordinating economic activity" (Powell, 1990: 301), which contrasts (and competes) with markets and hierarchies.

A number of scholars have offered definitions (see Table 1), typically using different terms and providing partial definitions. These definitions cluster around two key concepts: (1) patterns of interaction in exchange and relationships and (2) flows of resources between independent units. Those scholars who emphasize the first concept focus on lateral or horizontal patterns of exchange (Powell, 1990), long-term recurrent exchanges that create interdependencies (Larson, 1992), informal interfirm collaborations (Kreiner and Schultz, 1993), and reciprocal lines of communication (Powell, 1990). Some highlight patterned relations among individuals, groups, and organizations (Dubini and Aldrich, 1991); strategic long-term relationships across markets (Gerlach and Lincoln, 1992); and collections of firms using an intermediate level of binding (Granovetter, 1994). Those who emphasize the second concept focus on flows of resources (Powell, 1990) between nonhierarchical clusters of organizations made up of legally separate units (Alter and Hage, 1993; Miles and Snow, 1986, 1992; Perrow, 1992), and they underscore the independence of interacting units.

Our own definition includes elements from all of these definitions and is intended to be more complete and specific than its predecessors.

Proposed definition of network governance

Network governance involves a select, persistent, and structured set of autonomous firms (as well as nonprofit agencies) engaged in creating products or services based on implicit and open-ended contracts to adapt to environmental contingencies and to coordinate and safeguard exchanges. These contracts are socially – not legally – binding.[3]

Reference	Term	Definition of network governance
Alter and Hage, 1993	Interorganizational networks	Unbounded or bounded clusters of organizations that, by definition, are nonhierarchical collectives of legally separate units
Dubini and Aldrich, 1991	Networks	Patterned relationships among individuals, groups, and organizations
Gerlach and Lincoln, 1992	Alliance capitalism	Strategic, long-term relationships across a broad spectrum of markets
Granovetter, 1994, 1995	Business groups[a]	Collections of firms bound together in some formal and/or informal ways by an intermediate level of binding
Kreiner and Schultz, 1993	Networks	Informal interorganizational collaborations
Larson, 1992	Network organizational forms	Long-term recurrent exchanges that create interdependencies resting on the entangling of obligations, expectations, reputations, and mutual interests
Liebeskind et al., 1996	Social networks	Collectivity of individuals among whom exchanges take place that are supported only by shared norms of trustworthy behavior
Miles and Snow, 1986, 1992	Network organizations	Clusters of firms or specialized units coordinated by market mechanisms
Powell, 1990	Network forms of organization	Lateral or horizontal patterns of exchange, independent flows of resources, reciprocal lines of communication

Table 1   Differing terms and definitions for network governance.

Note
a Not all business groups are characterized by networks of cooperation (1995: 102).

We use the term "select" to indicate that network members do not normally constitute an entire industry. Rather, they form a subset in which they exchange frequently with each other but relatively rarely with other members. For example, in human service agencies, Van de Ven et al. (1979) found three clusters of agencies having more connections within cluster than between, and they found that each cluster employed different patterns of coordination to achieve distinct goals.

By "persistent" we mean that network members work repeatedly with each other over time. For analytical purposes, we think of working together over time as a sequence of exchanges that are facilitated by the network structure and that, in turn, create and re-create the network structure. In this sense network governance is a dynamic process of organizing, rather than a static entity.

We use "structured" to indicate that exchanges within the network are neither random nor uniform but rather are patterned, reflecting a division of labor, and we use the phrase "autonomous firm" in order to highlight the potential for each element of the network to be legally independent. However, we do not exclude business units that may share common ownership or that may directly invest in each other.

Finally, we use the phrase "implicit and open-ended contracts" to refer to means of adapting, coordinating, and safeguarding exchanges that are not derived from authority structures or from legal contracts. To be sure, formal contracts may exist between some pairs of members, but these do not define the relations among all of the parties. For example, in a film project both the cinematographer and the editor may have contracts with the studio, but these contracts do not specify the relationship between the two subcontractors. Yet the task before them requires these and many other pairs to work together closely in a complicated dance of mutual adjustment and communication. Thus, network governance is composed of autonomous firms that operate like a single entity in these tasks requiring joint activity; in other domains these firms often are fierce competitors. To enhance cooperation on shared tasks, the network form of governance relies more heavily on social coordination and control, such as occupational socialization, collective sanctions, and reputations, than on authority or legal recourse.

Many scholars commonly cite the film industry as an example of network governance (Hirsch, 1972; Meyerson *et al.*, 1996; Miles and Snow, 1986; Powell, 1990; Reich, 1991). Here, film studios, producers, directors, cinematographers, and a host of other contractors join, disband, and rejoin in varying combinations to make films. Network governance comprises a select subset of film studios and subcontractors. The seven major film studios repeatedly use and share among their films an elite set of subcontractors who constitute 3 percent (459 of the 12,400) of those registered in guilds (Jones and Hesterly, 1993). Persistence is indicated by the fact that this network

governance has been in use and thriving since the mid 1970s (Ellis, 1990: 437–439). Structured relations among subcontractors and film studios are based on a division of labor: film studios finance, market, and distribute films, whereas numerous subcontractors with clearly defined roles and professions (e.g. producer, director, cinematographer, and editor) create the film.

EXCHANGE CONDITIONS FOR NETWORK GOVERNANCE

Our goal is to provide a framework explaining why network governance emerges and thrives. To do so we integrate TCE and social network theories. We see governance forms, similar to TCE, as "mechanism[s] for exchange" (Hesterly *et al.*, 1990: 404). In the TCE perspective three exchange conditions – uncertainty, asset specificity, and frequency – determine which governance form is more efficient. Environmental uncertainty triggers adaptation, which is the "central problem of economic organization," because environments rarely are stable and predictable (Williamson, 1991: 278). Asset-specific (or customized) exchanges involve unique equipment, processes, or knowledge developed by participants to complete exchanges. This intensifies coordination between parties. Customization combined with uncertainty requires safeguarding exchanges to reduce behavioral uncertainty, which can range from honest disagreements to opportunism[4] (Hesterly and Zenger, 1993). Frequency is important for three reasons. First, frequency facilitates transferring tacit knowledge in customized exchanges, especially for specialized processes or knowledge. Second, frequent interactions establish the conditions for relational and structural embeddedness, which provide the foundation for social mechanisms to adapt, coordinate, and safeguard exchanges effectively. Third, frequent interactions provide cost efficiency in using specialized governance structures (Williamson, 1985: 60).

Many of our arguments are based on TCE logic. For a governance form to emerge and thrive, it must address problems of adapting, coordinating, and safeguarding exchanges more efficiently than other governance forms (Williamson, 1991). Less efficient modes of organizing are at a comparative disadvantage and will not be selected in the long run. However, we move beyond TCE in three ways. First, we identify the specific forms of uncertainty and asset specificity that give rise to network governance. Second, we

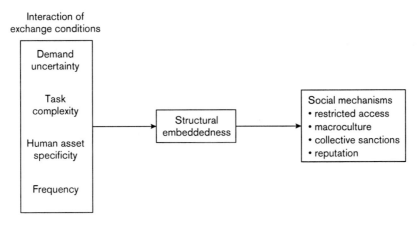

Figure 1 How interaction of exchange conditions leads to structural embeddedness and social mechanisms in network governance.

extend TCE by incorporating task complexity (Powell, 1990; Powell *et al.*,1996) into the explanation of governance form; this is important because it moves the theory beyond a dyadic focus. Third, we show how Williamson's notion of frequency, which is underspecified and underdeveloped in TCE, provides a link with social network constructs of relational and structural embeddedness (Granovetter, 1985, 1992; Uzzi, 1996, 1997). Based on TCE and Powell's work (1990), we identify four conditions necessary for network governance to emerge and thrive (see Figure 1): (1) demand uncertainty with stable supply, (2) customized exchanges high in human asset specificity, (3) complex tasks under time pressure, and (4) frequent exchanges among parties comprising the network. We discuss these in greater detail next.

Product demand uncertainty with stable supply

"Environmental uncertainty" (also called "state uncertainty") refers to the inability of an individual or organization to predict future events (Milliken, 1987). The source of this uncertainty can come from suppliers, customers, competitors, regulatory agencies, unions, or financial markets (Miles and Snow, 1978). Understanding the sources of uncertainty is important, since these influence what governance form is used to coordinate and safeguard exchanges. Research on environmental uncertainty and governance form shows that even modest levels of supply uncertainty, combined with predictable product demand, entice firms to integrate vertically (Helfat and Teece, 1987),

whereas customer demand uncertainty makes vertical integration for firms risky owing to obsolescence (Balakrishnan and Wernerfelt, 1986; Mariotti and Cainarca, 1986) or seasonality (Acheson, 1985).

Under conditions of demand uncertainty, firms disaggregate into autonomous units, primarily through outsourcing or subcontracting (Mariotti and Cainarca, 1986; Robins, 1993; Snow *et al.*, 1992; Zenger and Hesterly, 1997). This *decoupling* (Aldrich, 1979: 325–326) increases flexibility – the ability to respond to a wide range of contingencies – because resource bundles, now exchanged or rented rather than owned, can be reallocated cheaply and quickly to meet changing environmental demands. For example, the network structure of the textile industry in Prato, Italy, enhanced the textile firms' ability to respond quickly to changes in fashion (Piore and Sabel, 1984: 215). In Japanese automobile *keiretsu*, decoupling enhanced organizational flexibility as parties learned from one another what reduced lead-time and improved quality for new models (Nishiguchi, 1994).

We find network governance in industries with high levels of demand uncertainty but a relatively stable supply of labor; these include the film, fashion, music, hightechnology, and construction industries. Demand uncertainty is generated by unknown and rapid shifts in consumer preferences, which is exemplified in the film industry, where, it is unclear what makes a film a hit with an audience. "Who knows what the public wants to see? . . . I defy anyone to tell me up front how much a picture is going to make – or how much it is going to lose," says David Picker, who, as President of United Artists, was in charge of the studio's movie selection (Baker and Firestone, 1972: 29–30).

Demand uncertainty also is generated by rapid changes in knowledge or technology, which results in short product life cycles and makes the rapid dissemination of information critical (Barley *et al.*, 1992; Garud and Kumaraswamy, 1993; Powell and Brantley, 1992; Robertson and Langlois, 1995). In high-technology industries, such as biotechnology and semiconductors, new products and technologies leap frog prior products and technologies, leaving participants scrambling to catch up.

Finally, demand uncertainty is generated by seasonality, which makes vertical integration inefficient, as in the construction (Stinchcombe, 1959) and Maine lobster industries (Acheson, 1985). In Maine lobster trapping, seasonal fluctuations and wide swings in market prices make predicting both catches and revenues difficult. The region relies on a network structure of small firms and individual fishermen rather than vertically integrated firms (Acheson, 1985). In essence, demand uncertainty with stable supply provides conditions amenable to networks and markets but inimical to hierarchies.

Customized exchanges high in human asset specificity

Customized (or asset-specific) exchanges create dependency between parties. For example, if a buyer decides not to purchase the customized product or service, the seller cannot sell or transfer the product or service easily to another (Williamson, 1985). The customization of products or services increases demands for coordination between parties. It also raises concerns about how to safeguard these exchanges, since customizing products or services makes both seller and buyer more vulnerable to shifts in markets. Customization in conjunction with demand uncertainty increases behavioral uncertainty in two ways: (1) parties may disagree about what the initial customized exchange involved, or (2) they may disagree about whether the parties will fulfill their initial, agreed-upon obligations now that circumstances have changed. With customized goods or services, exchange parties may try to reduce their dependency on one another. For example, in the mechanical engineering region of Lyons, both clients and subcontractors devised methods to reduce dependency stemming from customized investments; these methods included restricting sales and having clients purchase specialized tools or dies (Lorenz, 1988).

Customization of products or services is common among firms in a network (Miles and Snow, 1992: 55). This form of customization involves human asset specificity (e.g. culture, skills, routines, and teamwork acquired through "learning-by-doing"; see Williamson, 1985) because it is derived from participants' knowledge and skills, as in semiconductors (Saxenian, 1990), movies (Faulkner, 1987), construction (Stinchcombe, 1959), and process and product improvements in the auto industry (Dyer, 1994; Nishiguchi, 1994).

Customized exchanges with high levels of human asset specificity require an organizational form that enhances cooperation, proximity, and repeated exchanges to transfer effectively tacit knowledge among parties. Cooperation among exchange parties is necessary, for parties must work together to gain tacit knowledge. Since "assets" may quit the exchange or reduce their efforts, they are more dependent upon one another's cooperation to complete the exchange (Coff, 1993). Proximity facilitates transferring tacit knowledge through such an "information-rich" medium as face-to-face communication (Lengel and Daft, 1988; Nohria and Eccles, 1992). In the auto industry resident engineers who are employed by one firm but work at another firm enhance the transfer of knowledge and routines that improve product and process quality (Dyer, 1994; Nishiguchi, 1994). Repeated exchanges allow tacit knowledge, which cannot be assimilated in short-term interactions, to be assimilated over time. Pisano, in his study of the biotechnology industry, found that "knowledge about a particular partner and how to collaborate with that partner represents important relationship-specific capital . . . [which] . . . becomes deeper for collaborative arrangements encompassing multiple projects than for those involving a single project" (1989: 116). Customized exchanges with high levels of human asset specificity are not effectively coordinated by market mechanisms and require either hierarchies or networks.

Demand uncertainty pushes firms toward disaggregation, whereas customized, human asset-specific exchanges intensify the need for coordination and integration among parties. Network governance balances these competing demands by enhancing the rapid dissemination of tacit knowledge across firm boundaries. In Silicon Valley, networks facilitated the rapid deployment of tacit knowledge across semiconductor firms, spurring new innovations and markets, creating new ventures, and generating revenues 10 times that of non-networked Route 128 firms (Saxenian, 1994).

Complex tasks under intense time pressure

"Task complexity" refers to the number of different specialized inputs needed to complete a product or service. Task complexity creates behavioral interdependence (Pfeffer and Salancik, 1978: 41) and heightens the need for coordinating activities. Differing specialists and inputs may result from an increased scope of activities, number of business functions needed, number of products created, or number of different markets served (Killing, 1988). Task complexity coupled with time pressures makes coordinating through a series of sequential exchanges unfeasible. These time pressures are due to the need to reduce lead-time in rapidly changing markets, such as semiconductors, computers, film, and fashion, or to the need to reduce costs in highly competitive markets, such as automobiles and architecture. Task complexity in conjunction with time pressures has led to team coordination, where diversely skilled members work simultaneously to produce a good or service (Faulkner and Anderson, 1987; Goodman and Goodman, 1976; Van de Ven et al., 1976). Teams coordinate activities through mutual adjustment (horizontal information flows and group meetings), which speeds information sharing among parties and reduces the time to complete complex tasks (Clark and Fujimoto, 1989; Imai et al., 1985).

Network governance facilitates integrating multiple autonomous, diversely skilled parties under intense time pressures to create complex products or services. The need for speeding products and services to markets is a critical condition for networks (Powell, 1990). For example, in the film industry the approximate time for film production went from 2 years in the 1950s to 6 weeks in the 1970s (Jones and DeFillippi, 1996). Using networks and team coordination in the auto industry to enhance organizational capabilities (e.g. informal and frequent communication between up stream-downstream production units and between work levels) gave the Japanese a competitive advantage over Europeans and Americans, who used sequential coordination (Clark and Fujimoto, 1989: 43). The reduced lead times and reduced costs in the Japanese auto industry were substantial: 17 hours to assemble a car for the Japanese, versus 25 and 37 hours for Americans and Europeans, respectively (Clark and Fujimoto, 1989). Coriat (1995) argues that automotive firms across the globe are moving toward network governance in an effort to achieve product variety under intense time pressures.

Frequent exchanges among parties

"Frequency" concerns how often specific parties exchange with one another. Although frequent exchange is identified by Williamson (1985) as an important determinant of governance, it is typically "set aside" (1985: 293) in TCE. Because specialized governance structures are costly, they are used only with recurring exchanges (Williamson, 1985: 60). We suggest, however, that frequent exchanges not only justify but enable using interfirm networks as an alternative governance form. Frequency allows human asset specificity to develop from learning-by-doing (Williamson, 1991: 281) and to "deepen" through continued interaction; this creates exchanges where the "identity" of the other matters (Williamson, 1991: 282) and enhances the transfer of tacit knowledge among parties.

Frequency also transforms the orientation that parties have toward an exchange and the amount of informal control that can be exerted over exchanges. Even Williamson notes, "Repeated personal contacts across organizational boundaries support some minimum level of courtesy and consideration between the parties [and] discourage[s] efforts to seek a narrow advantage in any particular transaction" (1975: 107). Reciprocity "transforms a unilateral supply relationship into a bilateral one" (Williamson, 1985: 191) and creates the perception of a similar "destiny" with greater "mutual interest" (Williamson, 1985: 155). In addition, the frequency of dyadic exchanges allows informal control through embeddedness. Embeddedness explains how dyadic exchanges and the overall structure of relations influence economic action and outcomes (Granovetter, 1992). Williamson agrees and argues, "Individual aggressiveness is curbed by the prospect of ostracism among peers, in both trade and social circumstances" (1975: 107–108). Thus, TCE logic is not antithetical to social network notions of embeddedness.

Granovetter (1992) identifies two aspects of embeddedness: relational and structural. Relational embeddedness captures the quality of dyadic exchanges – the degree to which exchange parties consider one another's needs and goals (Granovetter, 1992) and the behaviors exchange parties exhibit, such as trust, confiding, and information sharing (Uzzi, 1997). Uzzi's (1996, 1997) recent work provides a rich description as well as measures for illuminating the behavioral and attitudinal orientations of exchange parties in primarily dyadic exchanges or members' relational embeddedness.

Structural embeddedness – the network's overall structure or architecture – and how it influences behavior is not described by Uzzi, however. Structural embeddedness provides "more efficient information spread about what members of the pair are doing, and thus better ability to shape that behavior" (Granovetter, 1992: 35). Thus, structural embeddedness focuses on social control. This notion of structural embeddedness is akin to Williamson's notion of "atmosphere," which also emphasizes social control by facilitating "informal group influences" (1975: 99), group disciplinary actions, and stronger informal infrastructure (1975: 104).

The importance of frequency and reciprocity and how they allow informal control over exchanges provides important common ground between TCE and social network theorists, although this common ground is rarely recognized by either. However, a point of difference is that although a social network perspective often takes social structures as a given, TCE is interested in identifying the conditions giving rise to alternative governance forms and the social mechanisms that are employed within them. "A successful social analysis," suggests Aldrich, "cannot take social structures as given, but rather must be able to account for their origins and their persistence" (1982: 282). Even Granovetter notes, "Finally, I should add that the level of causal analysis adopted in the embeddedness argument is a rather proximate one. I have had little to say about what broad historical or macrostructural circumstances have led systems to display the social-structural characteristics they have" (1985: 506). We suggest that by integrating TCE with social network theory, we can enhance our understanding of the origins and persistence of structural embeddedness and social mechanisms that allow network governance to emerge and thrive. . . .[5]

ACKNOWLEDGMENTS

We thank Susan Jackson, the former *AMR* Editor; Jim Walsh, a former Consulting Editor; and five anonymous reviewers for their insights, suggestions, and comments, which helped us to improve the manuscript substantially. We also thank our colleagues Charles Kadushin, Benyamin Lichtenstein, Aya Chacar, Steve Tallman, and Anoop Madhok for their comments on earlier drafts.

NOTES

1 Our approach reflects "the increasing points of contact between the two disciplines" (Winship and Rosen, 1988: SI) of economics and sociology. Some scholars question whether the gulf between economics and sociology can or even should be bridged (Swedberg, 1990). We believe that much is to be gained by drawing from both disciplines. Swedberg's observation about the possibilities for combining the perspectives is true for understanding network governance: "What is happening today is very significant: *the border line between two of the major social sciences is being redrawn, thereby providing new perspectives on a whole range of very important problems, both in the economy and in society at large*" (Swedberg, 1990: 5, emphasis in original).

2 The term "network governance" is used, rather than "network organization," because many scholars in management define "organization," either implicitly or explicitly, as a single entity. "Governance" more accurately captures the process and approach to organizing among firms that we discuss here.

3 We thank an anonymous reviewer for insights and suggestions on our definition.

4 Ghoshal and Moran (1996) argue that assuming opportunism is dangerous because it leads to mechanisms that may create more opportunism (the self-fulfilling prophecy). Although we agree with much of Ghoshal and Moran's argument (e.g. we clearly agree that the scope of governance issues should be broader than opportunism), it is not clear to us that their critique applies to our article. First, we do not employ the assumption of opportunism in the strictly narrow way (i.e. self-interest seeking with guile) often either used by or ascribed to Williamson. Instead, we use the term "behavioral uncertainty," which includes unexpected variance in performance and understandings and is more consistent with the broader characterization of opportunism espoused by Alchian and Woodward: "It [opportunism] includes honest disagreements . . . [between] honest, ethical people who disagree about what event transpired and what adjustment would have been agreed to initially had the event been anticipated" (1988: 66). This is clearly a different concept from the one Ghoshal and Moran critique or the strong-form assumption that has occasionally been ascribed to TCE: "the serious presumption that all action is . . . opportunistic" (Hirsch *et al.*, 1990: 89). A second reason why we question whether Ghoshal and Moran's essay applies to our article is that their focus is on the unintended consequences of formal mechanisms that are used to counter opportunism. Our article is clearly about informal mechanisms. For further exploration of the debate on the role of opportunism in organizations, see Barney, 1990, versus Donaldson, 1990, and Hill, 1990; Conner and Prahalad, 1996, versus Foss, 1996; Ghoshal and Moran, 1996, versus Williamson, 1996;

Hirsch et al., 1990, versus Hesterly and Zenger, 1993; and Kogut and Zander, 1996, versus Foss, 1996.

5 This reading is pp. 911–923 of the original Jones, Hesterly and Borgatti (1997: 911–945).

REFERENCES

Abrahamson, E. and Fombrun, C.J. 1992. Forging the iron cage: interorganizational networks and the production of macro-culture. *Journal of Management Studies*, 29: 175–194.

Abrahamson, E. and Fombrun, C.J. 1994. Macrocultures: determinants and consequences. *Academy of Management Review*, 19: 728–755.

Acheson, J.M. 1985. The Maine lobster market: between market and hierarchy. *Journal of Law, Economics and Organization*, 1: 385–398.

Alchian, A.A. and Woodward, S. 1988. The firm is dead; long live the firm: a review of Oliver E. Williamson's *The Economic Institutions of Capitalism*. *Journal of Economic Literature*, 26: 65–79.

Aldrich, H.E. 1979. *Organizations and environments*. Englewood Cliffs, NJ: Prentice-Hall.

Aldrich, H.E. 1982. The origins and persistence of networks: a comment. In P. Marsden and N. Lin (Eds), *Social structure and network analysis:* 281–295. Beverly Hills, CA: Sage.

Alter, C. and Hage, J. 1993. *Organizations working together*. Newbury Park, CA: Sage.

Axelrod, R. 1984. *The evolution of cooperation*. New York: Basic Books.

Axelrod, R. 1985. An evolutionary approach to norms. *American Political Science Review*, 80: 1055–1111.

Bach, S. 1935. *Final cut*. New York: Onyx.

Baker, F. and Firestone, R. (Eds). 1972. *Movie people*. New York: Douglas Book Corp.

Balakrishnan, S. and Wernerfelt, B. 1986. Technical change, competition, and vertical integration. *Strategic Management Journal*, 9: 347–359.

Balio, T. 1987. *United Artists: The company that changed the film industry*. Madison, WI: University of Wisconsin Press.

Barley, S.R., Freeman, J., and Hybels, R.C. 1992. Strategic alliances in commercial biotechnology. In N. Nohria and R. Eccles (Eds), *Networks and organizations:* 311–347. Boston, MA: Harvard Business School Press.

Barney, J.B. 1990. The debate between traditional management theory and organizational economists: substantive differences or intergroup conflict? *Academy of Management Review*, 15: 382–393.

Becker, H.S. 1982. *Art worlds*. Berkeley, CA: University of California Press.

Bhide, A. and Stevenson, H. 1992. Trust, uncertainty and profit, *The Journal of Socio-Economics*, 21: 191–208.

Blau, P.M. 1977. *Inequality and heterogeneity*. New York: Free Press.

Bolton, M.K., Malmrose, R., and Ouchi, W.G. 1994. The organization of innovation in the United States and Japan: Neoclassical and relational contracting. *Journal of Management Studies*, 31: 653–679.

Bryman, A., Bresnen, M., Beardsworth, A.D., Ford, J., and Keil, E.T. 1987. The concept of the temporary system: The case of the construction project. In N. Di Tomaso and S.B. Bacharach (Eds), *Research in the sociology of organizations:* 253–283. Greenwich, CT: JAI Press.

Burt, R.S. 1992. *Structural holes: The social structure of competition*. Cambridge, MA: Harvard University Press.

Burt, R.S. and Knez, M. 1995. Trust and third-party gossip. In R. Kramer and T. Tyler (Eds), *Trust in organizations: Frontiers of theory and research*: 68–69. Thousand Oaks, CA: Sage.

Camerer, C. and Vepsalainen, A. 1988, The economic efficiency of corporate culture. *Strategic Management Journal*, 9: 115–126.

Clark, K.B. and Fujimoto, T. 1989. Lead time in automobile product development: explaining the Japanese advantage. *Journal of Engineering and Technology Management*, 6: 53.

Coff, R.W. 1993. *Corporate acquisitions of human-assets-intensive firms: how buyers mitigate uncertainty*. Paper presented at the annual meeting of the Academy of Management, Atlanta. GA.

Conner, K.R. and Prahalad, C.K. 1996. A resource-based theory of the firm: knowledge versus opportunism. *Organization Science*, 7: 477–501.

Contractor, F. and Lorange, P. (Eds). 1988. *Cooperative strategies in international business*. Lexington, MA: Lexington Books.

Coriat, B. 1995. Variety, routines and networks: the metamorphosis of Fordist firms. *Industrial and Corporate Change*, 4: 205–228.

Daft, R.L. and Lewin, A.Y. 1993. Where are the theories for the "new" organizational forms? An editorial essay. *Organization Science*, 4: i–v.

Dawes, R.M. 1930. Social dilemmas. *Annual Review of Psychology*, 31: 169–193.

DiMaggio, P.J. and Powell, W.W. 1983. The iron cage revisited: institutional isomorphism and collective rationality in organizational fields. *American Sociological Review*, 48: 147–160.

Donaldson, L. 1990. The ethereal hand: organizational economics and management theory. *Academy of Management Review*, 15: 369–381.

Dubini, P. and Aldrich, H. 1991. Personal and extended networks are central to the entrepreneurial process. *Journal of Business Venturing*, 6: 305–313.

Dyer, J.H. 1994. Dedicated assets: Japan's manufacturing edge. *Harvard Business Review*, 72(6): 174–178.

Dyer, J.H. and Ouchi, W.G. 1993. Japanese-style partnerships: giving companies a competitive edge. *Sloan Management Review*, 35(1): 51–63.

Eccles, R.G. 1981. The quasifirm in the construction industry. *Journal of Economic Behavior and Organization*, 2: 335–357.

Eccles, R.G. and Crane, D.B. 1988. *Doing deals: investment banks at work*. Boston, MA: Harvard Business School Press.

Ellis, J.C. 1990. *A history of film* (3rd edn). Englewood Cliffs, NJ: Prentice-Hall.

Faulkner, R.R. 1987. *Music on demand: composers and careers in the Hollywood film industry*. New Brunswick, NJ: Transaction Books.

Faulkner, R.R. and Anderson, A.B. 1987. Short-term projects and emergent careers: evidence from Hollywood. *American Journal of Sociology*, 92: 879–909.

Foss, N.J. 1996. Knowledge-based approaches to the theory of the firm: some critical comments. *Organization Science*, 7: 470–476.

Friedkin, N.E. 1982. Information flow through strong and weak ties in interorganizational social networks. *Social Networks*, 3: 273–285.

Gargiulo, M. 1993. Two-step leverage: managing constraint in organizational politics. *Administrative Science Quarterly*, 38: 1–19.

Garud, R. and Kumaraswamy, A. 1993. Changing competitive dynamics in network industries: an exploration of Sun Microsystems' open systems strategy. *Strategic Management Journal*, 14: 351–369.

Gerlach, M.L. 1992. The Japanese corporate network: a blockmodel analysis. *Administrative Science Quarterly*, 37: 105–139.

Gerlach, M.L. and Lincoln, J.R. 1992. The organization of business networks in the United States and Japan. In N. Nohria and R.G. Eccles (Eds), *Networks and organizations: structure, form, and action:* 491–520. Boston, MA: Harvard Business School Press.

Ghoshal, S. and Moran, P. 1996. Bad for practice: a critique of transaction cost theory. *Academy of Management Review*, 21: 13–47.

Gomes-Casseres, B. 1994. Group versus group: how alliance networks compete. *Harvard Business Review*, 4: 62–74.

Goodman, R.A. and Goodman, P.L. 1976. Some management issues in temporary systems: a study of the professional development and manpower – the theater case. *Administrative Science Quarterly*, 21: 494–500.

Gordon, G.C. 1991. Industry determinants of organizational culture. *Academy of Management Review*, 16: 396–415.

Granovetter, M.S. 1973. The strength of weak ties. *American Journal of Sociology*, 78: 1360–1380.

Granovetter, M. 1982. The strength of weak ties: a network theory revisited. In P. Marsden and N. Lin (Eds), *Social structure and network analysis:* 105–130. Beverly Hills, CA: Sage.

Granovetter, M. 1985. Economic action and social structure: the problem of embeddedness. *American Journal of Sociology*, 91: 481–510.

Granovetter, M. 1992. Problems of explanation in economic sociology. In N. Nohria and R.G. Eccles (Eds), *Networks and organizations: structure, form, and action*: 25–56. Boston, MA: Harvard Business School Press.

Granovetter, M. 1994. Business groups. In N.J. Smelser and R. Swedberg (Eds), *The handbook of economic sociology*. 453–475. Princeton, NJ: Princeton University Press.

Granovetter, M. 1995. Coase revisited: business groups in the modern economy. *Industrial and Corporate Change*, 1: 93–130.

Gulati, R. 1995. Social structure and alliance formation patterns: A longitudinal analysis. *Administrative Science Quarterly*, 40: 619–652.

Gulati, R., Khanna, T., and Nohria, N. 1994. Unilateral commitments and the importance of process in alliances. *Sloan Management Review*, 35(3): 61–69.

Helfat, C.E. and Teece, D.E. 1987. Vertical integration and risk reduction. *Journal of Law, Economics and Organization*, 3: 47–67.

Helper, S. 1991. How much has really changed between, U.S. automakers and their suppliers? *Sloan Management Review*, 32(4): 15–28.

Hesterly, W.S., Liebeskind, J., and Zenger, T.R. 1990. Organizational economics: an impending revolution in organization theory. *Academy of Management Review*, 15: 402–420.

Hesterly, W.S. and Zenger, T.R. 1993. The myth of a monolithic economics: fundamental assumptions and the use of economic models in policy and strategy research. *Organization Science*, 4: 496–510.

Hill, C.W.L. 1990. Cooperation, opportunism, and the invisible hand: implications for transaction cost theory. *Academy of Management Review*, 15: 500–513.

Hirsch, P.M. 1972. Processing fads and fashions: an organization-set analysis of cultural industry systems. *American Journal of Sociology*, 77: 639–659.

Hirsch, P.M., Friedman, R. and Koza, M.P. 1990. Collaboration or paradigm shift?: caveat emptor and the risk of romance with economic models for strategy and policy research. *Organization Science*, 1: 87–98.

Huberman, B.A. and Hogg, T. 1995. Communities of practice: Performance and evolution. *Computational & Mathematical Organization Theory*, 1(1): 73–92.

Imai, K., Nonaka, I., and Takeuchi, H. 1985. Managing the new product development process: how Japanese companies learn and unlearn. In K.B. Clark, R.H. Hayes, and C. Lorenz (Eds), *The uneasy alliance*: 337–375. Boston, MA: Harvard Business School Press.

Jarillo, J.C. 1988. On strategic networks. *Strategic Management Journal*, 9: 31–41.

Jones, C. 1996. Careers in project networks: the case of the film industry. In M. Arthur and D. Rousseau (Eds), *The boundaryless career*. 53–75. New York: Oxford University Press.

Jones, C. and DeFillippi, R.J. 1996. Back to the future in film: Combining industry- and self-knowledge to meet career challenges of the 21st century. *Academy of Management Executive*, 10(4): 89–104.

Jones, C. and Hesterly, W.S. 1993. *Network organization: An alternative governance form or a glorified market?* Paper presented at the annual meeting of the Academy of Management, Atlanta, GA.

Jones, C., Hesterly, W.S., and Borgatti, S.P. 1997. A general theory of network governance: exchange conditions and social mechanisms. *Academy of Management Review*, 22(4): 911–945.

Kadushin, C. 1976. Networks and circles in the production of culture. *American Behavioral Scientist*, 19: 769–784.

Kaufman, H. 1960. *The forest ranger*. Baltimore: John Hopkins University Press.

Kent, N. 1991. *Naked Hollywood*. New York: St. Martin's Press.

Killing, J.P. 1988. Understanding alliances: the role of task and organizational complexity. In F. Contractor and P. Lorange (Eds), *Cooperative-strategies in international business:* 55–68. Lexington, MA: Lexington Books.

Kogut, B. and Zander, U. 1996. What firms do? Coordination, identity, and learning. *Organization Science*, 7: 502–518.

Kollock, P. 1994. The emergence of exchange structures: An experimental study of uncertainty, commitment and trust. *American Journal of Sociology*, 100: 313–345.

Kreiner, K. and Schultz, M. 1993. Informal collaboration in R&D: the formation of networks across organizations. *Organization Studios*, 14: 189–209.

Larson, A. 1992. Network dyads in entrepreneurial settings: a study of the governance of exchange relationships. *Administrative Science Quarterly*, 37: 76–104.

Laumann, E.O., Marsden, P.V., and Prensky, D. 1983. The boundary specification problem in network analysis. In R.S. Burt and M. J. Minor (Eds), *Applied network analysis:* 18–34. Newbury Park, CA: Sage.

Lazerson, M. 1995. A new phoenix?: modern putting-out in the Modena knitwear industry. *Administrative Science Quarterly*, 40: 34–59.

Lengel, R.H. and Daft, R.L. 1988. The selection of communication media as an executive skill. *Academy of Management Executive*, 2: 225–232.

Liebeskind, J.P., Oliver, A.L., Zucker, L., and Brewer, M. 1996. Social networks, learning, and flexibility: sourcing scientific knowledge in new biotechnology firms. *Organization Science*, 7: 428–443.

Light, D. Jr. 1979. Surface data and deep structure: Observing the organization of professional training. *Administrative Science Quarterly*, 24: 551–559.

Lorenz, E.H. 1988. Neither friends nor strangers: informal networks of subcontracting in French industry. In D. Gambetta (Ed.), *Trust: making or breaking cooperative relations*, 194–210. New York: Basil Blackwell.

Macauley, S. 1963. Non-contractual relations in business: A preliminary study. *American Sociological Review*, 28: 55–67.

McMillan, J. 1990. Managing supplier incentives systems in Japanese and U.S. industry. *California Management Review*, 32(4): 38–55.

Mariotti, S. and Cainarca, G.C. 1986. The evolution of transaction governance in the textile-clothing industry.

Journal of Economic Behavior and Organization, 7: 354–374.

Mayhew, B. 1968. Behavioral observability and compliance with religious proscriptions on birth control. *Social Forces*, 47: 60–70.

Meyerson, D., Weick, K.E., and Kramer, R.M. 1996. Swift trust and temporary groups. In R.M. Kramer and T.R. Tyler (Eds), *Trust in organizations: frontiers of theory and research*, 166–195. Thousand Oaks. CA: Sage.

Miles, R.E. and Snow, C.C. 1978. *Organizational strategy, structure, and process*. New York: McGraw-Hill.

Miles, R.E. and Snow, C.C. 1986. Organizations: new concepts for new forms. *California Management Review*, 28(3): 62–73.

Miles, R. E. and Snow, C.C. 1992. Causes of failures in network organizations. *California Management Review*, 34(4): 53–72.

Milliken, F.J. 1987. Three types of perceived uncertainty about the environment: state, effect, and response uncertainty. *Academy of Management Review*, 12: 133–143.

Nishiguchi, T. 1994. *Strategic industrial sourcing: the Japanese advantage*. New York: Oxford University Press.

Nohria, N. 1992. Is network perspective a useful way of studying organizations? In N. Nohria and R.G. Eccles (Eds), *Networks and organizations: structure, form, and action*, 1–22. Boston, MA: Harvard Business School Press.

Nohria, N. and Eccles, R.G. 1992. Face-to-face: making network organizations work. In N. Nohria and R.G. Eccles (Eds), *Networks and organizations: structure, form, and action*, 288–308. Boston, MA: Harvard Business School Press.

Olson, M. 1971. *The logic of collective action: Public goods and a theory of groups* (2nd ed.). Cambridge, MA: Harvard University Press.

Parkhe, A. 1993. Strategic alliance structuring: A game theoretic and transaction cost examination of interfirm cooperation. *Academy of Management Journal*, 36: 794–829.

Perrow, C. 1986. *Complex organizations: A critical essay* (2nd ed.). New York: Random House.

Perrow, C. 1992. Small firm networks. In N. Nohria and R.G. Eccles (Eds), *Networks and organizations: structure, form, and action*, 445–470. Boston, MA: Harvard Business School Press.

Peterson, R.A. and Berger, D.G. 1971. Entrepreneurship in organizations: evidence from the popular music industry. *Administrative Science Quarterly*, 10: 97–106.

Pfeffer, J. and Leblebici, H. 1973. Executive recruitment and the development of interfirm organizations. *Administrative Science Quarterly*, 18: 449–461.

Pfeffer, J. and Salancik, G.R. 1978. *The external control or organizations*. New York: Harper & Row.

Phillips, M.E. 1994. Industry mindsets: exploring the cultures of two macro-organizational settings. *Organization Science*, 5: 384–402.

Piore, M.J. and Sabel, C.F. 1984. *The second industrial divide*. New York: Basic Books.

Pisano, G.P. 1989. Using equity participation to support exchange: evidence from the biotechnology industry. *Journal of Law, Economics, and Organization*, 51: 109–126.

Podolny, J. 1993. A status-based model of market competition. *American Journal of Sociology*, 98: 829–872.

Podolny, J. 1994. Market uncertainty and the social character of economic exchange. *Administrative Science Quarterly*, 39: 458–483.

Powell, W.W. 1990. Neither market nor hierarchy: network forms of organization. In B. Staw and L.L. Cummings (Eds), *Research in organizational behavior:* 295–336. Greenwich, CT: JAI Press.

Powell, W.W. and Brantley, P. 1992. Competitive cooperation in biotechnology: learning through networks? In N. Nohria and R.G. Eccles (Eds), *Networks and organizations: structure, form, and action*, 366–394. Boston, MA: Harvard Business School Press.

Powell, W.W., Koput, K. and Smith-Doerr, L. 1996. Interorganizational collaborations and the locus of innovation: networks of learning in biotechnology. *Administrative Science Quarterly*, 41: 116–145.

Provan, K.G. and Gassenheimer, J.G. 1994. Supplier commitment in relational contract exchanges with buyers: A study of interorganizational dependence and exercised power. *Journal of Management Studies*, 31: 55–68.

Putnam, R.D. 1993. *Making democracy work: Civic traditions in modern Italy*. Princeton, NJ: Princeton University Press.

Reddy, N.M. and Rao, M.V.H. 1990. The industrial market as an interfirm organization. *Journal of Management Studies*, 27: 43–59.

Reich, R.R. 1991. *The work of nations*. New York: Alfred Knopf.

Ring, P.S. and Van de Ven, A.H. 1992. Structuring cooperative relationships between organizations. *Strategic Management Journal*, 13: 483–498.

Robertson, P.L. and Langlois, R.N. 1995. Innovation, networks, and vertical integration. *Research Policy*, 24: 543–562.

Robins, J.A. 1993. Organization as strategy: restructuring production in the film industry. *Strategic Management Journal*, 14: 103–118.

Saxenian, A. 1990. Regional networks and the resurgence of Silicon Valley. *California Management Review*, 33(1): 89–112.

Saxenian, A. 1994. *Regional advantage: Culture and competition in Silicon Valley and Route 128*, Cambridge, MA: Harvard University Press.

Schroeder, D.A. 1995. An introduction to social dilemmas. In D.A. Schroeder (Ed.), *Social dilemmas: Perspectives on individuals and groups*. 1–15. Westport, CT: Prager.

Snow, C.C., Miles, R.E., and Coleman, H.J. Jr. 1992. Managing 21st century network organizations. *Organizational Dynamics*, 20(3): 5–20.

Squire, J.E. (Ed.). 1983. *The movie business book*. Englewood Cliffs, NJ: Prentice-Hall.

Stinchcombe, A.L. 1959. Bureaucratic and craft administration of production: a comparative study. *Administrative Science Quarterly*, 4: 168–187.

Swedberg, R. 1990. *Economics and sociology*. Princeton, NJ: Princeton University Press.

Thomas, L.G. 1996. The two faces of competition: dynamic resourcefulness and hypercompetitive shift. *Organization Science*, 7: 221–242.

Tolbert, P.S. and Zucker, L.G. 1983. Institutional sources of change in the formal structure of organizations: the diffusion of civil service reforms. *Administrative Science Quarterly*, 23: 22–39.

Uzzi, B. 1996. The sources and consequences of embeddedness for the economic performance of organizations: the network effect. *American Sociological Review*, 61: 674–698.

Uzzi, B. 1997. Social structure and competition in interfirm networks: the paradox of embeddedness. *Administrative Science Quarterly*, 42: 35–67.

Van de Ven, A.H., Delbecq, A., and Koenig, R.H. 1976. Determinants of coordination modes within organizations. *American Sociological Review*, 41: 322–338.

Van de Ven, A.H., Walker, G., and Liston, J. 1979. Coordination patterns within an interorganizational network. *Human Relations*, 32; 19–36.

Van Maanen, J. and Barley, S.R. 1984. Occupational communities: culture and control in organizations. In B. Staw and L.L. Cummings (Eds), *Research in organizational behavior:* 287–365. Greenwich, CT: JAI Press.

Volberda, H.W. 1996. Toward the flexible form: how to remain vital in hypercompetitive environments. *Organization Science*, 7: 359–374.

Wellman, B. 1991. Structural analysis: from method and metaphor to theory and substance. In B. Wellman and S.D. Berkowitz (Eds), *Social structures: a network approach*: 19–61. Cambridge, England: Cambridge University Press.

Williamson, O.E. 1975. *Markets and hierarchies: Analysis and antitrust implications*. New York: Free Press.

Williamson, O.E. 1985. *The economic institutions of capitalism: Firms, markets and relational contracting*. New York: Free Press.

Williamson, O.E. 1991. Comparative economic organization: the analysis of discrete structural alternatives. *Administrative Science Quarterly*, 38: 269–296.

Williamson, O.E. 1994. Transaction cost economics and organization theory. In N.J. Smelser and R. Swedberg (Eds), *The handbook of economic sociology*, 77–107. Princeton. NJ: Princeton University Press.

Williamson, O.E. 1996. Economic organization, the case for candor. *Academy of Management Review*, 21: 48–57.

Winship, C. and Rosen, S. 1988. Introduction: sociological and economic approaches to the analysis of social structure. *American Journal of Sociology*, 94(Supplement): S1–S17.

Zenger, T.R. and Hesterly, W.S. 1997. The disaggregation of U.S. corporations: selective intervention, high-powered incentives, and molecular units. *Organization Science*, 8: 209–222.

PART SIX

Stakeholder theory

INTRODUCTION TO PART SIX

Stakeholder theory has a historical lineage, practical applications, and intellectual appeal more substantial than agency theory, and yet has had much less impact on thinking and policy concerning corporate governance in recent times. Stakeholder theory defines organizations as multilateral agreements between the enterprise and its multiple stakeholders. The relationship between the company and its *internal* stakeholders (employees, managers, owners) is framed by formal and informal rules developed through the history of the relationship. This institutional setting constrains and creates the strategic possibilities for the company. While management may receive finance from shareholders, they depend upon employees to fulfil the productive purpose and strategic intentions of the company. *External* stakeholders (customers, suppliers, competitors, special interest groups and the community) are equally important, and also are constrained by formal and informal rules that businesses must respect.

Rather than conceiving of the company as a bundle of assets that belongs to shareholders, Margaret Blair (Chapter 13) argues corporations may be conceived as institutional arrangements for governing the relationships between all of the parties that contribute firm-specific assets. This includes not only shareholders, but also long-term employees who develop specialized skills of value to the corporation, and suppliers, customers and others who make specialized investments. If the job of management is to maximize the total wealth of the enterprise rather than just the value of the shareholders stake, then management must take into account the effect of corporate decisions on all stakeholders in the firm.

Company executives have always utilized elements of the stakeholder approach insists Clarke (Chapter 14). As firm-specific skills become an increasingly important part of the firm's valuable assets, and as corporate constituencies become increasingly alert and demanding, it is likely that managers will increasingly need to adopt stakeholder perspectives however great the countervailing pressures are to increase shareholder value. The growing emphasis on employee relations, customer relations, supplier relations, and indeed investor relations is an indication that managers are having to grapple with the imperative to satisfy the interests or more complex constituencies than agency theory or shareholder value would suggest. The conception of the company as a set of relationships rather than a series of transactions, in which managers adopt an inclusive concern for all stakeholders, is much closer to established European and Asian business values, and has been apparent in the behaviour of many leading US and UK companies.

"Ownership and Control: Rethinking Corporate Governance for the Twenty-First Century"

from The Brookings Institution (1995)

Margaret M. Blair

WHOSE INTERESTS SHOULD CORPORATIONS SERVE?

The finance and market myopia views of the central problem of corporate governance start from an assumption that the appropriate social purpose of corporations is to maximize shareholder return. They differ only over how best to achieve this goal. Finance model advocates believe that shareholder interests are best served by policies and actions that maximize share price in the short run because they accept the central maxim of finance theory: that the price of a share of stock today fully reflects the market's best estimate of the value of all future profits and growth that will accrue to that company. Thus they advocate an unfettered market for corporate control and other reforms that enhance the power of shareholders. Market myopia advocates, however, question whether today's stock price is a reliable enough guide to the future value and returns from the company's investments to be the exclusive focus of managerial attention. They fear that pressures from the financial markets impart a bias in managerial judgments against managing for the long term.

A third point of view is occasionally voiced in the corporate governance debates. This view has two distinct incarnations, but both versions start from the premise that corporations do not exist solely to provide returns to shareholders. Instead, they must serve a larger social purpose. The more familiar version of this idea holds that corporations should be "socially responsible" institutions, managed in the public interest.

This idea was popular among consumer advocates, environmentalists, and social activists in the 1960s, 1970s, and early 1980s and was used in the 1980s by some corporate executives as an argument in support of policies that would inhibit takeovers or give companies more defenses against them. The idea never had much theoretical rigor to it, failed to give clear guidance to help managers and directors set priorities and decide among competing socially beneficial uses of corporate resources, and provided no obvious enforcement mechanism to ensure that corporations live up to their social obligations. As a result of these deficiencies, few academics, policymakers, or other proponents of corporate governance reforms still espouse this model.

Nonetheless, the idea that corporations should have some social purpose beyond maximizing returns to shareholders survives, and a new view about what this purpose should be is just beginning to emerge among the leading thinkers about corporate governance issues. It is that corporations exist to create wealth for society.[1] According to this view, the goal of corporate governance mechanisms and the responsibilities of corporate directors are to see that the firm maximizes wealth creation. In some instances this broad goal may be equivalent to maximizing returns to shareholders, but that will not always be the case.

To those who believe that corporations must serve some larger social purpose, governance reform proposals from the finance and market myopia camps might do damage to this larger social purpose if they tilt too strongly toward compelling corporate executives and their boards of directors to focus exclusively on maximizing shareholder returns.

RECONSIDERING AN OLD QUESTION

Whether it is in the public interest for widely held corporations to be run exclusively for shareholders is an old question. Although seemingly forgotten by most advocates of the finance model, a major issue that Berle and Means originally raised was whether shareholders in widely held companies should be given the same legal rights and protections as owners of other kinds of property. Their answer was no. Because shareholders could not adequately undertake all the responsibilities that ownership of, say, real property normally implies, Berle and Means wrote, they should not necessarily be given all of the rights normally associated with ownership.

> The property owner who invests in a modern corporation so far surrenders his wealth to those in control of the corporation that he has exchanged the position of independent owner for one in which he may become merely recipient of the wages of capital.
> . . . The owners of passive property, by surrendering control and responsibility over the active property, have surrendered the right that the corporation should be operated in their sole interest, – they have released the community from the obligation to protect them to the full extent implied in the doctrine of strict property rights. At the same time, the controlling groups, by means of the extension of corporate powers, have in their own interest broken the bars of tradition which require that the corporation be operated solely for the benefit of the owners of passive property.[2]

Nonetheless, Berle and Means were careful not to imply that corporate management should be free to run companies in their own interest.

> Eliminating the sole interest of the passive owner, however, does not necessarily lay a basis for the alternative claim that the new powers should be used in the interest of the controlling groups. The latter have not presented, in acts or words any acceptable defense of the proposition that these powers should be so used. No tradition supports that proposition. The control groups have, rather, cleared the way for the claims of a group far wider

than either the owners or the control. They have placed the community in a position to demand that the modern corporation serve not alone the owners or the control but all society.[3]

Finance model advocates often cite Berle and Means as their most important intellectual ancestors, but, curiously, they have ignored or dismissed as trivial the key question of whose interests corporations should serve. Moreover, proponents of the finance model have so dominated the debate over corporate governance in recent years that those who might have raised the question have largely been silenced or have been driven to make circuitous arguments that soft-pedal or sidestep the question.[4] By the early 1990s, for example, it had become quite unfashionable for corporate executives to talk about their jobs in any terms other than maximizing shareholder value. Similarly, in his critique of the US system of capital allocation and corporate governance, Michael Porter never explicitly challenges the notion that corporations should be driven by the goal of maximizing value for shareholders. Instead, he refers repeatedly to the "divergence of interests between owners and corporations" and the need to align the goals of investors with those "of the corporation" or to align the goals of management or employees with those "of the corporation."[5]

For these kinds of arguments to make sense, we must think carefully about who and what the corporation is, what goals it should have, and whose interests it should serve. These questions can be asked as legalistic or descriptive ones: What does the law say? Or they can be asked as questions of public policy: What *should* the law say?

WHAT THE LAW SAYS

From its earliest evolution, corporate law has always been a bit schizophrenic about the right to form corporations.[6] On one hand, the right to incorporate was viewed as a simple extension of property rights and the freedoms of association and contract on the part of property owners. Under this "inherence" theory, the right to incorporate is inherent in the right to own property and write contracts. It follows that corporations should be legal extensions of their "owners" in the sense that they should have all the same rights and responsibilities as the individuals who own their equity.

The earliest corporations were "joint stock companies," which in the seventeenth and eighteenth centuries were set up for limited durations to accomplish specific tasks.[7] They were mechanisms for amassing capital to finance trading expeditions, for example, or to finance the construction of roads or canals. The joint stock companies were typically owned by a relatively small group of wealthy people who exercised close control over them.

But from the beginning, these joint stock companies and their successors, first the "trusts" (which were really holding companies), and, ultimately, modern corporations, required some sort of grant or charter from the state to exist.[8] These charters were granted in part because the projects to be undertaken were believed to be in the public interest. Under the "concession" theory, corporations owe their existence to a special concession from the state. This theory considers corporations to be separate entities from the owners of their equity, with a separate right to own and dispose of property, to enter into enforceable contracts, and to engage in business transactions. But their rights and responsibilities are defined and limited by the state and are not equivalent to those of the individuals who own their equity.

For complex historical reasons, the corporate form was used in the nineteenth century much more extensively in the United States than it was in other countries. So corporate law was more fully developed at an earlier date here than elsewhere. The earliest corporations were not granted perpetual life, nor were equity holders granted limited liability, but by the 1820s, most states had passed general incorporation acts that granted both of these features. By the middle of the 1800s, most states permitted the formation of corporations "for any legal purpose" and imposed no limitations on their accumulations of wealth and property. Thus, the right to form corporations became available to all individuals (a fact that supports the inherence view), but corporations themselves had characteristics that were not available to individuals and that only the state could grant (a fact that supports the concession view).

The "property conception" of the corporation

Before the rise of the large, multiunit, modern business enterprise in the late 1800s, "owners managed and managers owned," as professor Alfred D. Chandler, Jr., put it.[9] Although the notion existed that corporations were special entities with some public purpose

aspects, there was no real question in the law about who should have control over corporations and in whose interest they should be run. William T. Allen, chancellor of the state of Delaware, notes that a leading corporation law treatise of the mid-1800s regarded corporations as "little more than limited partnerships, every member exercising through his vote an immediate control over the interests of the body."[10] He further notes that the law had not yet established with certainty that the state even had the right to impose taxes on corporations (separately from taxing their shareholders), and that shareholder liability was not limited to the extent that it is today.

The Pujo Committee report of 1913 detailed the loss of control by shareholders as corporations grew and shareholdings became more dispersed, but by 1919, the law still held that corporations were supposed to be run for the benefit of the stockholders.[11] That point was made crystal clear in a famous case before the Michigan Supreme Court, *Dodge* v. *Ford Motor Co.* The Dodge brothers had sued Ford Motor Co., complaining that Henry Ford suspended dividend payments, choosing instead to retain $58 million in profits to be used to expand the business and lower the price of its products. As shareholders, the Dodge brothers wanted Ford to pay out some of those accumulated profits instead and asserted that, because shareholders owned the enterprise, they could force directors to pay out the profits. The Michigan Supreme Court agreed:

A business corporation is organized and carried on primarily for the profit of the stockholders. The powers of the directors are to be employed for that end. The discretion of directors is to be exercised in the choice of means to attain that end, and does not extend to a change in the end itself, to the reduction of profits, or to the nondistribution of profits among stockholders in order to devote them to other purposes.[12]

According to Allen, this decision is "as pure an example as exists" of what he calls the "property conception of the corporation." Allen's property conception, which conforms closely to my finance model, is based on an inherence view of the corporation, a view that in modern times has been associated with the "Chicago School" of law and economics (much of the theoretical basis and analytical techniques used to defend this position was largely developed at the

University of Chicago). Central to the property conception is the treatment of the corporation as a "nexus of contracts," through which the various participants arrange to transact with each other.[13] In this conception, assets of the corporation are the property of the shareholders, and managers and boards of directors are viewed as agents of shareholders, with all the difficulties of enforcement associated with agency relationships, but with no legal obligations to any other stakeholders. Under this view, "the rights of creditors, employees, and others are strictly limited to statutory, contractual, and common law rights," Allen says.[14]

The "social entity conception"

The property conception of the corporation held sway in US corporate law throughout the 1800s and early part of the 1900s. But with the separation of ownership from control, the development of sophisticated securities markets, and the emergence of a class of professional managers who viewed themselves as "trustees" of great institutions, a competing view began to take hold. "It was apparent to any thoughtful observer that the American corporation had ceased to be a private business device and had become an institution," Berle wrote in the preface to *The Modern Corporation and Private Property*.[15] Similarly, historian Dow Votaw noted that "the buccaneers of the late nineteenth century gave way to the more statesmanlike professional managers of the twentieth. The aggressive, profit- and power-seeking individualist was replaced by the arbitrator and diplomat whose motivations included organization survival, professional reputation, and equitable balancing of interests, as well as profit-making. The modern corporation has been aptly described as a 'constellation of interests' rather than the instrument of the acquisitive individual."[16]

Allen calls this view the "social entity conception," noting that the purpose of the corporation is seen as "not individual but social." As he puts it:

> Contributors of capital (stockholders and bondholders) must be assured a rate of return sufficient to induce them to contribute their capital to the enterprise. But the corporation has other purposes of perhaps equal dignity: the satisfaction of consumer wants, the provision of meaningful employment

opportunities and the making of a contribution to the public life of its communities. Resolving the often conflicting claims of these various corporate constituencies calls for judgment, indeed calls for wisdom, by the board of directors of the corporation. But in this view, no single constituency's interest may significantly exclude others from fair consideration by the board.[17]

This idea, of course, is a direct descendent of the point Berle and Means made in the conclusion to their work in 1932. To be sure, Berle was concerned about the potential for corporate managers to abuse the powers implied in this conception. "Now I submit," he wrote in a later essay, "that you cannot abandon emphasis on 'the view that business corporations exist for the sole purpose of making profits for their stockholders' until such time as you are prepared to offer a clear and reasonably enforceable scheme of responsibilities to someone else."[18]

Until the 1980s the social entity conception of the corporation was never given official legal sanction, although many social activists and several business leaders adopted the idea.[19] As the modern corporation grew in size and power after Second World War, the central concern of legal scholars was not so much whether corporations should or should not be run primarily for shareholders, and certainly not whether the separation of ownership from control would make corporations inefficient or uncompetitive. Rather, the concern was about who should control the vast economic, political, and social power of these large and powerful wealth-generating machines and how that power should be restrained. "It is not enough that the great corporation be a paragon of efficiency and production," Votaw wrote in 1965, expressing a view quite typical of the era.

> The large corporations are the possessors of substantial amounts of this power, and properly so. Without it they could not perform the tasks society demands of them. In a free society, however, we cannot leave the subject there. Power, in either private or public hands, raises difficult questions: How much power? In whose hands? Power for what purposes? To whom are the wielders of power responsible? What assurances are there that the power will be used fairly and justly? and, Is there machinery by which the power and the method of its exercise can be made responsive to the needs of society?[20]

SIX

Votaw noted that the political legitimacy of the corporation was challenged during the Depression, when it appeared that this power was not being used responsibly. But then "the corporation . . . performed brilliantly during World War II" and "the performance of the corporate system since the war has also been very good, as a whole, [producing] rising prosperity and standards of living." As a result, he said, "issues of legitimacy moved into the background."[21]

Questions of legitimacy faded in part because corporations were assuming more and more responsibilities as social institutions. By the late 1960s and early 1970s, corporate responsiveness to a broad group of stakeholders had become accepted business practice (for pragmatic reasons if nothing else).[22] Consumer advocates and religious and political groups that wanted to influence corporate behavior bought token shareholdings so that they could introduce resolutions and vote on important corporate policies. They also staged boycotts and waged publicity campaigns. Although no corporation ever went so far as to, say, elect Ralph Nader to the board of directors, many of them created public affairs offices, added consumer hotlines, gave research grants to universities and other special research institutes, contributed to charity, agreed to divest from South Africa, and engaged much more directly in political dialogue. They also gave their employees paid leave to engage in public service activities and participated in community development programs. Wages were still rising rapidly during this period, and large corporations were increasing the noncash benefits they gave their employees, such as health insurance, pensions, education and training support, and vacation and sick leave. In addition to paying relatively high taxes, they also became significant supporters of public institutions such as theaters, parks, schools, museums, and hospitals. Most companies looked upon such "socially responsible" behavior as a way to improve the general business climate.

The law moved to accommodate the social entity view by protecting companies that engaged in such activities, even when these activities were clearly not directly related to maximizing profits for shareholders. The courts, for example, generally upheld corporations that had made donations to museums or hospitals or had otherwise expended corporate resources on community-enhancing activities against challenges from shareholders. By the 1970s, in fact, forty-eight states had passed laws "explicitly providing that chartered corporations could give to charities without specific charter provision."[23] A clever legal device was developed to justify these kinds of activities without conceding that directors did not have a primary duty to maximize wealth for shareholders. The courts held that, while it might divert shareholder wealth in the short run, responding to the needs and interests of other stakeholders was good for shareholders "in the long run," because the good health and well-being of the communities in which companies operate was considered important for business. "The law papered over the conflict in our conception of the corporation by invoking a murky distinction between long-term profit maximization and short-term profit maximization," Allen writes. "The long-term/short-term distinction preserves the form of the stockholders-oriented property theory, while permitting, in fact, a considerable degree of behavior consistent with a view that sees public corporations as owing social responsibilities to all affected by its operation."[24]

Breakdown of accommodation

For nearly half a century, this practical accommodation in the law worked. These activities were seldom challenged by shareholders, but when they were, they were successfully defended as being beneficial to shareholders in the long run. And, until the 1970s, it appeared that shareholders were benefiting – along with employees and communities – from the broad social role that most large corporations played. An investment made in the Standard & Poor's composite companies in 1945 would have yielded a compound annual rate of return of 7.59 percent by 1972, compared to an average annual yield on high-rated corporate bonds during this same period of about 4.30 percent.[25]

The "in the long run" device for reconciling the goal of maximizing value for shareholders with a more broadly defined goal of social responsibility for corporations broke down in the 1980s for three reasons, according to Allen: the rise of global competition; internationalization of financial markets; and the emergence of the hostile takeover. To these a fourth should be added: the collapse in stock market returns in the 1970s, followed by the rise in the cost of capital in the early part of the 1980s.

The rise of global competition contributed to an irregular but steady erosion of corporate profitability in the post-War decades, especially in the manufacturing sector. Meanwhile, the investment options overseas were expanding, and, by the early 1980s the real return on bonds and other, safer investments in the United States had climbed to new heights. Together, these changed the expectations of the financial markets about the return that corporations should provide, and the resulting discontent among investors opened the way for hostile takeovers and leveraged restructuring.[26]

The emergence of tender offers and hostile takeovers shattered the uneasy "in the long run" legal device for reconciling the property conception and the social entity conception. To shareholders who had been offered an immediate 35 or 40 percent premium to tender their shares, the possibility that the company might perform better as an independent entity "in the long run" seemed irrelevent. Even in terms of evaluating more ordinary business decisions, the extraordinarily high cost of capital that prevailed in the 1980s greatly weakened the defense for expenditures that would show returns only in the long run. At discount rates of 10–15 percent, the return on investments of any kind, whether in new plants and equipment or in community relations, must be much higher and come in much faster than it must at discount rates of 5–10 percent.[27]

The legal response to the breakdown of the accommodation between shareholder wealth maximization and corporate social responsibility has not been completely worked out. Throughout the 1980s, for example, the American Law Institute worked to develop a new consensus statement on principles of corporate governance. Reflecting the political dominance of the "finance model," or "property conception" of that decade, early drafts were strident in tone, asserting that corporations should absolutely and unequivocally be treated as the property of shareholders, that the goal of the corporation should be to maximize value for shareholders, and that the well-being of shareholders should take precedence in every corporate decision. The tone was softened considerably in the final document, which states that the objective of corporations should be "the conduct of business activities with a view to enhancing corporate profit and shareholder gain." In so doing, the document said, corporations "may devote a reasonable amount of resources to public welfare, humanitarian, educational, and philanthropic purposes." Nonetheless, this document still insists that shareholder interests should

dominate and that directors should consider nonshareholder constituencies only when "competing courses of action have comparable impact on shareholders."[28]

At the state level, the rejection of the strict property conception (at least in the context of takeovers) was much more explicit. At least twenty-seven states have passed laws since 1985 that specifically make it legal for (and in at least one state, require) directors to consider other interests in addition to shareholders when making major business decisions, mainly in deciding whether to accept or fight a tender offer. (Two states, Pennsylvania and Ohio, had such a law before 1985.)[29] Typically, these statutes require directors to consider the "best interests of the corporation" as a whole, and then identify a specific set of stakeholders, including employees, creditors, suppliers, and the community in general in addition to shareholders, whose interests are considered tied to the corporation. "States saw a different side of the rampant takeover activity – the social responsiblity side – and began to question whether attaining takeover benefits for shareholders was as consistent with other important interests as economic and legal orthodoxy presumed," says law professor Alexander C. Gavis.[30]

Steven M.H. Wallman, an SEC commissioner who helped to draft the original "corporate constituency" law passed in Pennsylvania in 1983 and its amendment in 1990, defines the corporation's interest as "enhancing its ability to produce wealth indefinitely . . . [including] both profit from today's activities and expected profit from tomorrow's activities."[31] This wealth-producing language is not in the statutes, but Wallman's subsequent explication of what it means for directors to act "in the interest of the corporation" suggests that these laws, if interpreted and applied as Wallman believes they should be, could provide a legal basis for a new conception of the proper goals of corporate governance.[32] Linking the interests of the various constituencies to the interest of the corporation, he asserts, "resolves much of the tension that would otherwise exist from competing and conflicting constituent demands."[33] Defining the interests of the corporation in terms of maximizing the wealth-producing potential of the enterprise as a whole also provides the beginning of a way to resolve the long-term, short-term conflict, as well as a basis for deciding which corporate constituencies matter under what circumstances.

Many legal scholars, policy analysts, and others have sharply criticized these corporate constituency laws. Their only application is in the takeover context, critics say (because the "business judgement rule" still applies in other contexts). In this context, their effect is to give corporate executives and directors carte blanche to do whatever they want, the critics say, because almost any decision can be justified on the grounds that it benefits or protects some constituency. Thus, finance model advocates and even some market myopia advocates disparage these laws as no more than knee-jerk reactions by state legislatures to try to protect management and workers in their states from the threat of hostile takeovers.

The state of Delaware, where more than half of the Standard & Poor's 500 corporations are incorporated, has not passed such a statute, but the decision of the Delaware Supreme Court in *Paramount Communications* v. *Time Inc.* in 1989 was widely interpreted as giving similar leeway to management of Delaware-chartered firms. It did so, however, by again invoking the "long-term/short-term" distinction rather than by directly addressing the question of whose interests should take precedence. In that case, the board of directors of Time Inc. thwarted a takeover bid by Paramount Communications by quickly executing a tender offer for Warner Communications. Paramount's initial cash offering price represented about a 40 percent premium over the price at which Time's stock had been trading just before Paramount's offer, and Paramount later raised the bid, with the higher bid representing a 60 percent premium. But for months (indeed, years) before the Paramount bid, Time had been negotiating a stock-for-stock merger with Warner Communications and had announced a merger plan a few months before the Paramount offer was made. The Delaware Supreme Court refused to stop Time from proceeding with the tender offer for Warner, even though, in taking that action, Time's board foreclosed any opportunity for Time shareholders to accept the Paramount offer or even to vote on the merger with Warner. "The fiduciary duty to manage a corporate enterprise includes the selection of a time frame for achievement of corporate goals," the court ruled. "That duty may not be delegated to the stockholders. ... Directors are not obliged to abandon a deliberately conceived corporate plan for a short-term shareholder profit unless there is clearly no basis to sustain the corporate strategy."[34] Allen, who wrote the chancery court opinion in the case, later wrote that the ruling "might be interpreted as constituting implicit acknowledgement of the social entity conception."[35]

Four years later, in a case again involving Paramount Communications, the Delaware Supreme Court appeared to shift its stance again, this time toward placing more weight on getting the highest value for shareholders, regardless of the effect on management's carefully laid long-range strategic plans. In this case Paramount was negotiating a merger agreement with Viacom when Paramount CEO Martin Davis learned that QVC Network was interested in acquiring Paramount. In response, Paramount put together a deal with Viacom to exchange Paramount shares for a mix of Viacom stock and cash that was estimated to be worth about $70 per Paramount share, and that gave Viacom an option to buy 19.9 percent of the stock of Paramount if the Paramount-Viacom deal were canceled for any of a number of reasons, including an acquisition of Paramount by some other bidder. The options included several unusual features that would be highly disadvantageous to QVC if it proceeded with a tender offer. Nonetheless, QVC did proceed, offering $80 a share for 51 percent of Paramount's stock and filing suit to have the stock option agreement invalidated.

In contrast to its assessment of the facts in the earlier case, the Delaware Supreme Court ruled that Paramount was embarking on a plan to sell control of Paramount and that Paramount's board was therefore obligated to consider all offers in order to get the best price for the company. "The pending sale of control implicated in the Paramount-Viacom transaction required the Paramount Board to act on an informed basis to secure the best value reasonably available to the stockholders," the court ruled.[36]

Technically, the difference between these two cases hinged on whether the defendant directors (Time's board in the first case, and Paramount's board in the second) had put their companies up for sale when they announced merger plans. But in the first case, the court seemed to give directors considerable leeway to reject takeover bids in order to protect long-range strategic plans, and in the second case, the court seemed to sharply circumscribe the types of long-range plans that would be so protected. Thus it remains unclear whether directors of companies incorporated in Delaware can consider the effect of a takeover decision on stakeholders other than just shareholders.[37]

So far, no stakeholder has tested the limits of the "corporate constituency" laws by attempting to enforce his or her claim to consideration in the courts.[38] Unless and until these laws are overturned, however, they give formal legal sanction to the idea that corporations have social purposes in addition to providing profits for shareholders.

WHAT SHOULD THE LAW SAY?

Although the law has still not resolved the issue unequivocally, the belief that the primary goal of corporate endeavors should be to maximize value for shareholders still dominates the public policy debates and has largely been accepted even by corporate executives who not long before tended to resist that idea.[39] Three theoretical arguments are typically given for why it is in society's interest that corporations should be run for shareholders and why shareholders, in turn, should be given control.

Shareholders as "owners"

The first of these arguments holds that shareholders should have the right to control corporate resources and ensure that they are used to their own benefit because they are the "owners." The right to control private property is an essential part of what it means to own something, and ownership rights are a vitally important social norm and important for efficiency reasons.

By now, that argument – that shareholders own the corporation, so therefore they should be able to exercise control over it – should have been put safely to rest. It is simply circular logic. Shareholders own equity, and the question is what control rights ought to accompany that kind of claim against the company. The de facto separation of equity ownership from control, Votaw noted, changed the whole legal concept of property, at least with respect to corporations.

Property consists of a bundle of rights which the owner of property posesses with regard to something – rights to possess, use, dispose of, exclude others, and manage and control. The corporate concept divides this bundle of rights into several pieces. The stockholder gets the right to receive some of the fruits of the use of property, a fractional residual right in corporate property, and a very limited right of control. The rights to possess, use, and control the property go to the managers of the corporation.[40]

When property rights have been broken up in this way, trying to identify one party as the "owner" is neither meaningful nor useful. "To assume that we can know who property owners are, and to assume that once we have identified them their rights follow as a matter of course, is to assume what needs to be decided," Joseph William Singer wrote in an essay on whether steelworkers have any legitimate property rights in the plant where they work.[41]

Building on the idea of property as a bundle of rights, Thomas Donaldson and Lee E. Preston argue that the various property rights that societies grant are generally based on some underlying concept of justice, especially distributive justice. Notions of distributive justice, in turn, are based on some socially constructed notion of who has what moral interest in the use of the asset – for example, who has contributed what effort or made what sacrifice, who has what need, or who has made what prior agreement about the uses of the asset. In modern corporations, by definition, all stakeholders have some stake or moral interest in the affairs of corporations, Donaldson and Preston observe and conclude that "the normative principles that underly the contemporary pluralistic theory of property rights also provide the foundation for the stakeholder theory as well."[42]

Management accountability

The second argument for why it is in the public interest to operate corporations for shareholders holds that, as a normative matter, corporate executives should not be allowed to make arbitrary decisions to use other people's property for their own interest or even for what they believe to be in the public interest. Managers must be held accountable to someone. Diffusing this responsibility among many groups of stakeholders means, in practice, that managers are accountable to no one.

Ronald Coase has argued that, if property rights are clearly established and if all parties can contract freely over the use of resources, then those resources will be used efficiently.[43] According to Coase, it makes no difference (from an efficiency standpoint) whether the factory owner has the right to pollute or the townspeople have the right to clean air. If the property rights are clearly established, the various parties can write a contract in which the townspeople pay the factory owner not to pollute or the factory owner pays the townspeople for the right to pollute. In either case, the process of contracting will determine a socially optimal "price" for polluting, and the factory owner will end up spending the right amount on pollution abatement equipment.[44]

But even if one agreed in principle that clearly established property rights would be socially useful, establishing completely clear "property" rights in complex organizations such as corporations is impossible in practice, in part because the concept of "property" is so complex and multifaceted. The question is which of the many "control" rights should be assigned to shareholders, which given to other stakeholders, and which left to managers.

Nonetheless, if managers do not themselves bear the full costs of their decisions and if they are not held accountable to someone for something, they will be accountable to no one, and they will have few incentives to use resources under their control efficiently.

Versions of this argument were often heard in the debates of the late 1960s and early 1970s about the "social responsibilities" of business. In its simple version, it says that performance is easier to monitor if only one dimension of performance, such as profits (or, in their capitalized form, share value) is measured. In more sophisticated versions, the argument is concerned about private uses of power. As Friedrich A. Hayek puts it, "the tendency to allow and even to impel the corporations to use their resources for specific ends other than those of a long-run maximization of the return on the capital placed under their control . . . tends to confer upon them undesirable and socially dangerous powers."[45]

The central point here is the need for mechanisms to ensure that management is accountable for its decisions. Managers should be held accountable precisely because they are managing assets that are not their own and because they do not personally bear all of the costs of their decisions. But this argument fails to make the case that the objective of managers should be to maximize share value; it therefore also fails to make the case that the shareholders should necessarily be given greater control rights.

The third public interest argument used to justify assigning control rights to shareholders is that shareholders are the residual claimants.[46] They receive the residual gain and bear the residual risk associated with the corporate enterprise, this argument goes, and they therefore have the best incentive to monitor.

To the extent that this is true, maximizing value for shareholders is, equivalent to maximizing the social value of corporations, and it follows that it would be socially optimal to give control rights to shareholders to ensure that share value is maximized.

At first glance, this argument would seem to be the same as saying that the shareholders should monitor because it is their money that is being managed. But saying that it is the shareholders' money does not resolve the underlying questions about the meaning of "ownership" in this case. Ronald Gilson and Mark Roe make the distinction clear: "Equity has governance rights because the holder of the residual profits interest has the best incentive to reduce agency costs; the right to control rests with those who stand to gain the most from efficient production."[47] Previously, Gilson had held that the "description of shareholders as the 'owners' . . . derives . . . from the need for those holding the residual interest in corporate profits to have the means to displace management which performs poorly. . . . This position is based on matters other than a preconception of the rights associated with 'ownership'; indeed, if the statute did not provide for shareholders, we would have to invent them."[48] This argument is the product of a long and somewhat arcane scholarly effort to explain large enterprises in a way consistent with neoclassical economic theory. In very simplified terms, the theory that has been developed goes as follows: team production is often much more efficient than individual production. But, because it is sometimes hard to tell who is responsible for what portion of the output produced by teams, individual team members might try to shirk. Team production thus requires that someone serve as monitor to be sure that no one shirks. What keeps the monitor from shirking? The monitor enters into contracts with all of the other input providers to pay each of them according to their opportunity cost (i.e. what they could get if they sold their services or materials to the next highest bidder), and the monitor receives all of the extra value created by the enterprise, over and above these costs. In other words, the monitor bears the residual risk and receives the residual gain.[49]

In a small, entrepreneurial firm, this monitor is the owner–manager. But who bears the residual risk and receives the residual gain in large, widely held corporations? Scholars who have worked on these questions of organizational theory have generally assumed that it is the shareholders.[50] From that assumption, they have argued that hierarchical decision-making and oversight by boards of directors were institutional arrangements developed as substitutes for direct monitoring by shareholders.[51] And, from that argument, they conclude that boards of directors should represent the interests of shareholders above all other competing interests.

In the idealized model of a corporation described by these scholars, institutional and legal arrangements that direct as much of the oversight and control responsibilities as possible to shareholders or to their representatives make impeccable sense. But shareholders were long ago granted limited liability, which, of course, shifted some of the residual risk onto creditors and others. Moreover, the risks that shareholders bear can largely be diversified away by holding the shares as part of a balanced portfolio. Finally, shareholders generally have unrestricted rights to sell their shares, which means that shareholders, perhaps more than any of the other stakeholders in firms, have the option to "exit" if they are dissatisfied with the performance of the firm. Thus, the notion that shareholders bear all of the residual risk seems doubtful on its face.[52]

For it to be strictly true that shareholders receive all of the residual gain and bear all of the residual risk, the suppliers of all other inputs into the corporate enterprise would have to be compensated by means of "complete" contracts (i.e. contracts that specify exactly what is to happen in all circumstances). These contracts would have to compensate other input providers at their social opportunity cost (including compensation for any explicit, predictable risk they were bearing). If such arrangements were, indeed, the norm, it would not make any difference to employees, lenders, materials and equipment suppliers, dealers, communities, or other stakeholders if a corporation suffered losses and had to go out of business. That is because the inputs supplied by these other parties could be readily redeployed at the same price or wages they had commanded in their service to the corporation or because the providers of these inputs were compensated in advance for any losses they might incur at such time.[53]

Curiously, although this assumption about the allocation of risk and rewards in the corporate enterprise would appear patently wrong, it is almost never challenged outright. In fact, among true believers in the finance model, this assumption is dogma. But labor economists have long noted that workers in large corporations, especially in certain industries, earn higher wages and benefits than do workers with comparable skills and comparable jobs who are self-employed or who work for small entrepreneurial firms.[54] This differential would suggest that some of the residual gains from team production in large corporations are being shared with workers. Neoclassical economists have argued that apparent labor market differentials can be explained by unmeasured differences in labor quality and working conditions. An alternative view is that firms may, in some circumstances, pay higher wages to improve motivation, morale, and job stability, to make recruiting easier, and to encourage employees to develop special skills that may be valuable only to that employer. In other words, the higher productivity justifies the cost of paying wages above the competitive rate. Either way, the residual gain from team production is being shared with workers. And, as the next chapter shows, sharing the residual gain with workers necessarily implies that these workers are sharing in the residual risk associated with the ability of the enterprise as a whole to continue to generate those gains.[55]

It is easy to see why the assumption that shareholders are the residual claimants is so important to those who maintain that shareholders should have control. If other stakeholders could be shown to share in the residual gains and risks, their interest in being able to exercise some control over corporations would be significantly legitimized.

Despite the empirical weakness of the assumption that shareholders receive all of the residual gain and bear all of the residual risk, the underlying point of the finance model argument is quite important – corporations are more likely to be managed in ways that maximize social value if those who monitor and control firms receive (at least some of) the residual gain and bear (some of) the residual risk, and, conversely, if those who share in the residual gains and risks are given the access and authority they need to monitor. Put more simply, corporate resources should be used to enhance the goals and serve the purposes of all those who truly have something invested and at risk in the enterprise. Those parties, in turn, should be given enough of the control rights to ensure that corporate resources are used to those ends. If control rights could be allocated in this way, all of the participants would have an incentive to see that the total size of the pie is maximized, and any one stakeholder group would have trouble increasing the value of its stake simply by pushing costs and risks onto other stakeholders.

In short, it is possible to reject the simplistic finance model or property conception of the corporation to the extent that it implies that directors' only duty is to maximize value for shareholders, and still retain the compelling logic that private control of private property leads to the most efficient use of society's resources. I argue that the view of corporations as wealth-creating machines, with a social purpose of maximizing wealth, provides a clear basis for thinking about how control rights to that machine should be allocated. My conclusions differ from those of most finance model advocates, however, because I make a much more general assumption about what the source of value creation is, and who it is that bears the risk and receives the gains in most corporations today.

The primitive model of corporations in which shareholders are seen as earning all the returns and bearing all the risk is a throwback to an earlier time when the typical corporation owned and operated a canal, a railroad, or a big manufacturing plant. Entrepreneurial investors put up the financial capital, which was used to build or buy the railroad, canal, or factory and to make initial payments to hired managers. The managers, in turn, arranged to buy raw materials and energy, hire labor, oversee production or manage the operations, and (in the case of the factory) ship the goods to market. The proceeds from the sale of those goods was used to meet payroll (including the manager's salary), pay taxes, buy more raw materials, keep the machinery in working order and pay off any loans, and all of these inputs were acquired at the going market rate. Anything left over after that was "profit," and it seemed reasonable and appropriate that the profits belonged to the initial investors (shareholders), who were the only parties with significant assets tied up and at risk in the enterprise. These assets consisted of some inventories and receivables, the entrepreneurial know-how of the owner–manager, and, most, the canal, the roadbed and railcars, or the factory.[56]

For enterprises that fit this model, it may be a reasonable approximation of the truth that the capital investments and the entrepreneurial efforts of the investor are the sources of the wealth and that shareholders capture all of that wealth and bear all the associated risk. For firms that look like this, corporate governance arrangements that provide for them to be run for shareholders and that accordingly give as much control to shareholders as possible, serve to encourage wealth creation by fostering and protecting investments in physical capital and entrepreneurial effort.

But in the 1990s, fewer and fewer publicly traded corporations actually look like the factory model. Much of the wealth-generating capacity of most modern firms is based on the skills and knowledge of the employees and the ability of the organization as a whole to put those skills to work for customers and clients. Even for manufacturing firms, physical plant and equipment make up a rapidly declining share of the assets, while a growing share consists of intangibles (some recognized on the books and given an accounting value, some not) such as patent rights, brand reputation, service capabilities, and the ability to innovate and get the next generation product to market in a timely manner.[57]

It is commonplace to hear chief executives of major corporations say "our wealth is in our people."[58] Although such lines are probably not taken seriously nearly as often as they are said, there are important economic reasons why they should be taken seriously. Moreover, the idea that the wealth of a corporation is in its people has important implications for corporate governance arrangements.

NOTES

1 A few of the leading lawyers and management specialists active in corporate governance reform issues have begun describing corporate goals in these terms. Drucker (1991a: 112) argues that institutional owners of German and Japanese companies "do not attempt to maximize shareholder value or the short-term interest of any one of the enterprise's 'stakeholders'. Rather they *maximize the wealth producing capacity of the enterprise* [emphasis in the original]." Similarly, Millstein (1992: 42) writes about the role that "knowledgeable and diligent ownership *(relationship investing)* can play in causing corporations to better *maximize their wealth producing capacity in the global economy* [emphasis added]."
2 Berle and Means (1932: 3, 355).
3 Berle and Means (1932: 355–56).
4 An exception was an essay by Epstein (1986: 3) that at least acknowledged the question. "Out of this bitter debate [the 1980s takeover battles] emerged a sharp divergence of views on the purpose of the corporation in the American system of capitalism. Whereas many

shareholders thought of it in terms of its profitability, corporate management tended to define it in terms of service to the community, suggesting that their corporations were 'institutions', much like museums or hospitals, that served a public interest as well as the private interest of shareholders." Epstein goes on to defend a view that companies should be run for shareholders and that shareholders should be given more control. Thus Epstein's piece supports my fundamental point about the dominance of the finance model.

5 See, for example, Porter (1992: 20).

6 The section that follows draws heavily on an article by William T. Allen, chancellor of the state of Delaware. See Allen (1992). I have credited Allen where I have taken his arguments directly. See also Votaw (1965: chap. 1) for an informative essay on the evolution of the corporate form.

7 The first joint stock company was formed in 1555, but the form was rarely used before the 1600s. See Votaw (1965: 13–17).

8 The original trusts were voluntary associations of small companies that each agreed to turn their stock over to a common board of trustees, in exchange for trust certificates of equal value, so that the operations of the companies could be managed in common. Their purpose was to formalize the otherwise unenforceable agreements among companies to fix prices or control supply. The trust form came under attack by state and federal courts, and, in response, the state of New Jersey passed a generalized incorporation law permitting the formation of holding companies. The Standard Oil Trust and the other well-known "trusts" of the late 1800s and early 1900s were actually holding companies. See Chandler (1977: 318–20).

9 Chandler (1977: 9).

10 Allen (1992: 8).

11 Report of the Committee Appointed Pursuant to House Resolution 429 and 504 to Investigate the Concentration of Control of Money and Credit, House Report 1593, 62d Cong. 3d sess. Government Printing Office, 1913, as cited in Herman (1981: 7).

12 204 Mich. 459, 170 N.W. 668 (1919), cited in Allen (1992: 10).

13 Jensen and Meckling (1976: 305–60).

14 Allen (1992: 10).

15 Berle and Means (1932: v).

16 Votaw (1965: 28).

17 Allen (1992: 15).

18 Berle (1932). The Berle essay was one of a series of essays in a scholarly debate between Berle and Professor E. Merrick Dodd. Despite his apparent interest in the idea of the corporation as a social institution as expressed in the conclusion to The Modern Corporation and Private Property, Berle argued that giving corporate executives too much power "might be

unsafe, and in any case it hardly affords the soundest base on which to construct the economic commonwealth which industrialism seems to require" (1372). Dodd, by contrast, argued that the law was moving in the direction of viewing the corporation as "an economic institution which has a social service as well as a profit-making function." See Dodd (1932: 1148).

19 In 1946 Frank Abrams, then chairman of Standard Oil Company of New Jersey, described the role of the modern manager as maintaining "an equitable and working balance among the claims of the various directly interested groups – stockholders, employees, customers, and the public at large." See Rostow (1960). In 1978 directors of Control Data Corp. gave formal recognition to the view of corporations as social entities in its proxy statement to shareholders, urging them to pass several amendments to the company's articles of incorporation that would require the board to consider the effect of any takeover proposal on the company's employees and other "stakeholders." "The Board is mindful and supportive . . . of the growing concept that corporations have a social responsibility to a wide variety of societal segments which have a stake in the continued health of a given corporation," the proxy letter stated. See Control Data Corp. Proxy Statement, May 3, 1978, p. 4.

20 Votaw (1965: 87).

21 Votaw (1965: 102).

22 Accepted, at least, by most business leaders. Economists and legal scholars of the Chicago School railed against such behavior, however. For example, Milton Friedman wrote that "businessmen who talk this way are unwitting puppets of the intellectual forces that have been undermining the basis of a free society these past decades." See Milton Friedman, "The Social Responsibility of Business Is to Increase Its Profits," New York Times Magazine, September 13, 1970, p. 33.

23 See Herman (1981: footnote 40, p. 401). Herman cautions that "corporate largess for purposes not readily reconciled with profit-effectiveness is still subject to legal challenge" (p. 256).

24 Allen (1992: 16–17).

25 These calculations are unadjusted for inflation. The difference between the return earned by bondholders and that earned by stockholders over the period may simply be an appropriate level of compensation for the additional risk borne by stockholders. There is no way to measure how much shareholders should be paid for risk. One can only measure how much more they, in fact, earned on high risk investments relative to lower risk investments. The point here is only that shareholders shared in the wealth creation by large corporations, as they should have.

The end date for this analysis was not chosen at random. By 1974 the S&P 500 average had fallen by

24 percent, wiping out all of the gains it had seen in the previous ten years (and reminding investors that investing in stocks did entail some significant risks). This loss in value was not fully regained until 1980. Many observers believe this poor performance by the stock market in the 1970s helped set the stage for the battles for corporate control in the 1980s.

26 This hypothesis about the cause of highly leveraged corporate restructuring activity in the 1980s was first presented in Blair and Litan (1990) and is a major thesis of several essays in Blair (1993).

27 Based on a survey of 228 Fortune 1000 firms conducted in 1990 and 1991, Poterba and Summers (1991) estimate that corporate executives use an average real (inflation-adjusted) "hurdle rate" of 12.2 percent to evaluate investments. More recently, the *Wall Street Journal* reported that corporations were setting very aggressive hurdles on return on investment – some as high as 20 percent – for capital spending planned for 1994. See Fred R. Bleakley, "As Capital Spending Grows, Firms Take a Hard Look at Returns From the Effort," *Wall Street Journal*, February 8, 1994, p. A2.

28 The American Law Institute (1994: 55, 405).

29 See Wallman (1993) for a list of the states with corporate constituency laws.

30 Gavis (1990: 1461).

31 Wallman (1991: 170).

32 In private correspondence with the author September 7, 1993, Wallman took pains to distinguish his "wealth-producing notion" of the duty of boards and the role of corporations from the "social responsibility model."

33 Wallman (1991: 170).

34 See Supreme Court of the State of Delaware, *Paramount Communications, Inc. v. Time Inc.*, 571 A.2d 1140–1155 (Delaware 1990).

35 Allen (1992: 20).

36 See Supreme Court of Delaware, *Paramount Communications Inc. v. QVC Network Inc.*, 637 A.2d 34 (Del. 1994).

37 Takeover lawyer Martin Lipton says that the two cases "can be summarized as holding that under Delaware law the objective of the corporation is the *long-term* growth of shareholder value; assuming the board of directors has used due care (followed reasonable procedures) and did not have a conflict of interest, the board may prefer *long-term* goals over *short-term* goals except when the decision is to sell control of the corporation or to liquidate it in which case the board must use reasonable efforts to get the best value obtainable for the shareholders. Under this standard the board has the right to invest for the *long-term* in people, equipment, market share and financial structure even though the financial markets do not recognize (or overly discount) the future value and even though the board's strategy results in

elimination of dividends and reduction in market price of the stock. Also under this standard, the board has the right to 'just say no' to a premium takeover bid. However, the board does remain subject to shareholder control and the shareholders have the right at least once a year to replace at least some of the directors who have followed a strategy or taken a position disliked by the shareholders [emphasis in original]." Private correspondence with the author, April 5, 1994.

38 "Case law interpreting nonshareholder constituency statutes appears to be nonexistent," says Gavis, who suggests that states with these laws have relatively little corporate activity in them. See Gavis (1990: 1446). But some of the laws include language intended to rule out, or at least discourage, such enforcement action. See Sommer (1991b: 46). Such provisions reinforce the view of some legal scholars and observers who believe that the statutes were intended to protect management, not to give other stakeholders access or standing to make specific claims against corporations.

39 Lazonick (1992: 467, 469) argues that corporate executives have been co-opted by this finance-oriented view because they have risen to the tops of their organizations in an era that rewarded financial market performance more than innovative activity or growth in market share and because their own compensation is now, more than ever, tied to stock price performance.

40 Votaw (1965: 96–97).

41 Singer (1988: 637–38).

42 Donaldson and Preston (1995).

43 Coase (1960: 15–16).

44 The information requirements are quite severe for this hypothesis to hold, however, and the difficulties in enforcing contracts could easily be insurmountable.

45 Hayek (1985: 100).

46 This is the cornerstone of the corporate governance arguments made by Easterbrook and Fischel (1991). Shareholders hold voting rights, as opposed to bondholders, management, or employees, they argue, because shareholders are the residual claimants on firm income and are therefore willing to pay most for voting rights. When a firm is in distress, shareholder incentives become skewed and other constituents receive voting rights. "The fact that voting rights flow to whichever group holds the residual claim at any given time strongly supports our analysis of the function of Voting rights," they wrote (p. 405). See also Easterbrook and Fischel (1983).

47 Gilson and Roe (1993: 887).

48 Gilson (1981: 34).

49 See Alchian and Demsetz (1972), who wrote the classic article that marked the beginning of the development of this view of corporations.

50 In nearly all of the finance literature and much of management and economics literature, shareholders are

assumed, without question, to play this role. A few organizational theorists and labor economists interested in the problems introduced by firm-specific investments in human capital have come to appreciate that shareholders are generally not the only residual risk-bearers, and that the assumption that they are is not inconsequential. But the implications of this fact for efficient corporate governance have not yet been acknowledged or studied by finance theorists nor have they been formally acknowledged in the law.

51 Fama and Jensen (1983) made this argument in their now classic article.

52 Finance specialists have long understood that the value of a company's equity can be increased by shifting some of the risk onto debt holders. Wallman (1991: 178) provides an easy-to-understand example. In this case, maximizing value for the shareholders is clearly not equivalent to maximizing social value. But finance model advocates tend to assume away the implications of this insight for corporate governance by asserting that creditors can write contracts that prohibit the managers of the firm from shifting more risk onto them than they initially bargain for.

53 Fama and Jensen (1983: 302–3) assert (but do not demonstrate empirically) that "the contract structures of most organizational forms limit the risks undertaken by most agents by specifying either fixed promised payoffs or incentive payoffs tied to specific measures of performance. The residual risk – the risk of the difference between stochastic inflows of resources and promised payments to agents – is borne by those who contract for the rights to the net cash flows . . . . Moreover, the contracts of most agents contain the implicit or explicit provision that, in exchange for the specified payoff, the agent agrees that the resources he provides can be used to satisfy the interests of residual claimants . . . . Having most uncertainty borne by one group of agents, residual claimants, has survival value because it reduces the costs incurred to monitor contracts with other groups of agents. Contracts that direct decisions toward the interests of residual claimants also add to the survival value of organizations."

54 See, for example, Dunlop (1988: 56).

55 This last point is probably not obvious, but it arises from the fact that the workers have made firm-specific investments in human capital as part of the process of wealth creation in the enterprise.

56 "How can residual-claimant, central-employer–owner demonstrate ability to pay the other hired inputs the promised amount in the event of a loss?" Alchian and Demsetz ask. "He can pay in advance, or he can commit wealth sufficient to cover negative residuals. The latter will take the form of machines, land, buildings, or raw materials committed to the firm." See Alchian and Demsetz (1972: 791). Historians Galambos and Pratt

(1988: 20) note also that most of the technology that was the source of added value in early factories was embodied in the capital – the physical plant and equipment – and that the employer–owner was often an engineer who was largely responsible for technical decisions about plant design or addition of new equipment.

57 A rough measure of this is the share of the market value of assets accounted for by property, plant, and equipment (PP&E). I calculated these numbers using data on all manufacturing and mining firms listed in Compustat for which the relevant information was available. In 1982 PP&E accounted for 62.3 percent of the market value of mining and manufacturing firms; by 1991, PP&E accounted for only 37.9 percent of the market value.

58 A quick review of interviews with twelve CEOs (on many topics) in recent issues of the *Harvard Business Review* produced the following quotes: "Our employees aren't just agents for the company, they are the company," – Robert F. McDermott, CEO of USAA. "A company is not bricks and mortar or money and finance. It's people;" and "profit is in the hands of employees," – Frederick C. Crawford, CEO of TRW; "If the people on the front line really are the keys to our success, then the manager's job is to help those people that they serve. That goes against the traditional assumptions that the manager is in control," – Robert Haas, CEO of Levi Strauss & Co.

REFERENCES

Alchian, A.A. and H. Demsetz. 1972. Production, information costs and economic organization. *American Economic Review*. December, 62: 777–95.

Allen, W.T. 1992. Our schizophrenic conception of the business corporation. *Cardozo Law Review*. 14 (2): 261–81.

American Law Institute. 1994. *Principles of corporate governance: analysis and recommendations*. Accepted final draft. Philadelphia, PA.

Berle, A.A. Jr. 1932. For whom corporate managers are trustees: a note. *Harvard Law Review*. 45: 1365–72.

Berle, A.A. and G.C. Means. 1932. *The modern corporation and private property*. New York: Commerce Clearing House, Inc.

Blair, M.M. 1993. *The deal decade: what takeovers and leveraged buyouts mean for corporate governance*. Washington, DC: Brookings Institution, p. 390.

Blair, M.M. and R.E. Litan. 1990. Corporate leverage and leveraged buyouts in the eighties. In J.B. Shoven and J. Waldfogel (eds). *Debt, taxes and corporate restructuring*. Washington, DC: Brookings Institution, 43–80.

Bleakley, F.R. 1994. As capital spending grows, firms take a hard look at returns from the effort. *Wall street Journal*. February 8, p. A2.

Chandler, A.D. 1997. *The visible hand: the managerial revolution in American business.* Belknap: Harvard University Press.

Coase, R.H. 1960. The problem of social cost. *Journal of Law and Economics.* October, 3: 1–44.

Dodd, E.M. Jr. 1932. For whom corporate managers are trustees. *Harvard Law Review.* 45: 1145–63.

Donaldson, T. and L.E. Preston. 1995. The stakeholder theory of the corporation: concepts, evidence, implications. *Academy of Management Review.* January, 20: 65–91.

Drucker, P.F. 1991a. Reckoning with the pension fund revolution. *Harvard Business Review.* March–April, 69: 106–14.

Dunlop, J.T. 1988. Labor markets and wage determination: then and now. In B. Kaufman (ed.) *How labor markets work: reflections on theory and practice.* Lexington, MA: Lexington Books, 47–88.

Easterbrook, F.H. and D.R. Fischel. 1983. Voting in corporate law. *Journal of Law and Economics.* January, 26: 395–427.

——. 1991. *The economic structure of corporate law.* Cambridge, MA: Harvard University Press.

Epstein, E.J. 1986. *Who owns the corporations? Management vs. Shareholders.* New York: 20th Century Fund-Priority Press Publications.

Fama, E.F. and M.C. Jensen. 1983. Separation of ownership and control. *Journal of Law and Economics.* 26, June, 301–25.

Friedman, N. 1970. The social responsibility of business is to increase its profits. *New York Times Magazine.* September 13, p. 33.

Galambos, L. and J. Pratt. 1988. *The rise of the corporate commonwealth: United States business and public policy in the 20th Century.* New York: Basic Books.

Gavis, A.C. 1990. A framework for satisfying corporate directors responsibilities under state nonshareholder constituency statues: the use of explicit contracts. *University of Pennsylvania Law Review.* 138: 1456–97.

Gilson, R.J. 1981. A structural approach to corporations: the case against defensive tactics in tender offers. *Stanford Law Review.* 33 (5): 819–91.

Gilson, R.J. and M.J. Roe. 1992. Comparative Corporate Governance: Focusing the United States – Japan Inquiry, Memorandum Prepared for Center for Economic Policy and Research Conference, Stanford University.

Gilson, R.J. and M.J. Roe. 1993. Understanding the Japanese keiretsu: overlaps between corporate governance and industrial organization. *Yale Law Journal.* January, 102 (4): 871–906.

Hayek, F.A. 1985. The corporation in a democratic society: in whose interest ought it and will it be run? In M. Anshen and G.L. Bach (eds) *Management and Corporations.* 99–117. Westport, CT: Greenwood Press.

Herman, E.S. 1981. *Corporate control, corporate power.* New York: Cambridge University Press.

Jensen, M.C. and W.H. Meckling. 1976. Theory of the firm: managerial behaviour, agency costs and ownership structure. *Journal of Financial Economics.* 3, October, 305–60.

Lazonick, W. 1992. Controlling the market for corporate control: the historical significance of managerial capitalism. *Industrial and Corporate Change.* 1 Oxford University Press.

Millstein, I.M. 1992. The evolving role of institutional investors in corporate governance. *Corporate Governance Today – and Tomorrow: The Thoughts of Seven Leading Players.* Washington, DC: Investor Responsibility Research Center, 35–66.

Porter, M.E. 1992. *Capital choices: changing the way America invests in industry.* Research report presented by the Council on Competitiveness and cosponsored by Harvard Business School. Washington, DC.

Poterba, J.M. and L.H. Summers. 1991. Time horizons of American firms: new evidence from a survey of CEOs. Unpublished manuscript.

Singer, J.W. 1988. The reliance interest in property. *Stanford Law Review.* February, 40: 615–751.

Sommer, A.A. Jr. 1991. Whom should the corporation serve? The Berle-Dodd debate revisited sixty years later. *Delaware Journal of Corporate Law.* 16 (1): 33–56.

Rostow, E.V. 1960. To whom and for what ends is corporate management responsible? In E.S. Mason (ed.) *The Corporation in Modern Society.* Harvard University Press, 47–71.

Votaw, D. 1965. *Modern corporations.* Englewood Cliffs, NJ: Prentice-Hall.

Wallman, S.M.H. 1991. The proper interpretation of corporate constituency statutes and formulation of director duties. *Stetson Law Review.* 21: 163–92.

——. 1993. Corporate constituency laws. In M.M. Blair and G. Uppal (eds) *The Deal Decade Handbook.* Washington, DC: Brookings Institution, 31–3.

'The Stakeholder Corporation: A Business Philosophy for the Information Age'

from Long Range Planning (1998)

Thomas Clarke

SUMMARY

Interest in stakeholder approaches to strategic management is growing around the world but at the same time top management's concern with shareholder value has never been greater. Managers in all kinds of firms are faced with the dilemma of how to satisfy the competing claims of shareholders and the other stakeholders. The consequences are evident everywhere as shareholders grow rich and unemployment increases. This chapter examines the stakeholder theory and its potential for solving management's dilemma.

INTRODUCTION

Different economic systems, business strategies and management practices compete, co-exist and sometimes co-operate. As Tricker has noted corporate governance systems are in a state of transition in every industrial country, the greatest impelling force being the internationalisation of capital markets. A likely outcome is increased diversity within an overall trend towards convergence (Tricker, 1994; Clarke and Bostock, 1994). A discernible trend is the increasing influence of Anglo-Saxon shareholder value based approaches to corporate governance, including among European and Asian companies, which formally have sustained stakeholder or collective conceptions of governance (Figure 1). Simultaneously there has been a revival of interest in stakeholder approaches in both the USA and the UK, partly influenced by the evident industrial strength of German and Japanese companies, but also drawing upon indigenous inclinations towards developing a more durable business system.

Business leaders are being called upon to face in two apparently different directions at once, a feat some are happy to attempt to accomplish, but which leaves others looking for an alignment of strategies and values that is more convincingly consistent. The paradox of contemporary management is

1 In response to the excesses of the 1980s a renewed emphasis upon business values, the integrity of companies and the responsibility of business executives. Also a sense that the short term orientation and narrow focus upon financial performance is ultimately self defeating, relative to the longer horizons and deeper commercial

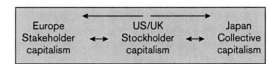

Figure 1 Convergence and divergence of governance systems.

relationships of competitors not subjected to these narrow performance indicators prevails. Finally the wider social and environmental responsibilities and the part played in the community by business enterprise is once again on the agenda.

2   In the context of global competition, international investment patterns and the aggressive growth of mergers and acquisitions, a reinvigorated sense of the significance of releasing shareholder value. (In 1988 at the height of the merger and acquisition activity of this period in the USA $355 billion of corporate assets were involved, in the first eight months of 1997 a total of $639 billion was in play. Worldwide there was a similar growth in acquisition activity to $600 billion in 1989 and $1300 billion estimated in 1997) (*Financial Times*, 10 October 1997).

The New York based take-over expert Martin Lipton suggests that, 'Unlike the financially motivated, highly leveraged bust-up takeovers of the 1980s, most of the current mergers are soundly financed, strategically motivated and will result in better products and services at lower, real prices' (*Financial Times*, 10 October 1997). If this logic is marginally more convincing than it was in the 1980s, it is still easier to square with the conception of the company as a bundle of assets than a set of stakeholder interests. Reflecting on an earlier phase in the corporate battleground, Peacock and Bannock suggested, 'Compared with the slow process of internal growth, which requires detailed planning, trial and error, recruitment of personnel, product development, investment in plant perhaps with long lead times, the building of relationships with suppliers, the establishment of marketing strategies and channels of distribution, an acquisition that can be pushed through in a matter of weeks or months is fast indeed' (Peacock and Bannock, 1991).

Commenting on the intended sale at the end of 1997 of Rolls-Royce Motor Cars by Vickers, to a German car manufacturer, John Harvey-Jones a former chairman of ICI argued, 'The same people who tell us ownership doesn't matter are those who tell us the sole role of business is to reward shareholders. Despite attempts to broaden board responsibilities to balance the interests of investors, employees, customers, suppliers and community (jobs I believed I was doing) the prevalent view still seems to be that shareholder interests are the sole driver' (*The Observer*, 2 November 1997).

Though ascendant in financial circles the shareholder view of the firm has only occasionally enjoyed a strong voluntary commitment from industrial managers who have to wrestle with the more practical concerns of running a business. A more broadly based stakeholder conception of the objectives of companies has a long intellectual lineage beginning with the pioneering work of Berle and Means.

BERLE AND MEANS

Berle and Means were the first to explore the structural and strategic implications of the separation of ownership and control. Berle wrote in the preface of *The Modern Corporation and Private Property* that 'it was apparent to any thoughtful observer that the American corporation had ceased to be a private business device and had become as institution' (Berle and Means, 1932). The dispersal of equity ownership of companies raises a number of governance issues:

1   For firms to operate efficiently managers must have the freedom to take risks, make strategic decisions and take advantage of opportunities as they arise and though they should remain subject to effective monitoring mechanisms, they cannot submit ever decision to a shareholder vote.

2   A group of shareholders with a large total share of the equity might be more effective at monitoring management, but their powers must also be restrained to prevent them taking advantage of other shareholders.

3   Many investors prefer the advantages of liquidity and diversity in their portfolios to the time and resource commitment involved in monitoring.

4   Investors require accurate accounting information, but any performance measures can provide misleading information or distort incentives by encouraging managers to focus attention on inappropriate goals. Further, releasing some kinds of information can weaken a firm's competitive position (Blair, 1995).

The attenuation of the shareholders role in managing the business and the rise of professional management is associated with a growing recognition of the significance of the role and contribution of other stakeholder groups to the performance of the company. As Figure 2 illustrates with management assuming responsibility for the supervision of the physical capital

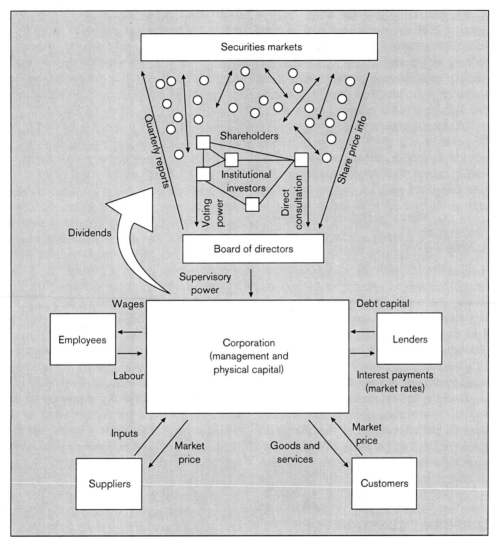

Figure 2 Revised 'Berle and Means' model with institutional investors.

Source: M.M. Blair, Ownership and Control: Rethinking Corporate Governance for the Twenty-first Century, The Brookings Institution, Washington, 1995.

of the corporation, each of the primary stakeholder groups stakeholders, lenders, customers, suppliers and employees have a relationship with the company in which they provide some resource vital for the company's survival and in return receive some value. Berle and Means, argue:

> Neither the claims of ownership nor those of control can stand against the paramount interest of the community . . . It remains only for the claims of the community to be put forward with clarity and force. Rigid enforcement of property rights as a

temporary protection against plundering by control would not stand in the way of the modification of these rights in the interests of other groups. When a convincing system of community obligations is worked out and is generally accepted, in that moment the passive property right of today must yield before the larger interests of society. Should corporate leaders, for example, set forth a program comprising fair wages, security to employees, reasonable service to their public and stabilisation of business, all of which would divert a portion of the profits from the owners of passive property and would the community generally accept such a scheme as a logical and human solution of industrial difficulties, the interests of passive property owners would have to give way. Courts would almost of necessity be forced to recognise the result, justifying it by whatever of the many legal theories they might choose. It is conceivable, indeed it seems almost essential if the corporate system is to survive, that the 'control' of the great corporations should develop into a purely neutral technocracy, balancing a variety of claims by various groups in the community and assigning to each a portion of the income streams on the basis of public policy rather than private cupidity.

(Berle and Means, 1932: 312)

In 1932, the same year their book was first published, Berle insisted 'You cannot abandon emphasis on the view that business corporations exist for sole purpose of making profits for their shareholders until such time as you are prepared to offer a clear and reasonably enforceable scheme of responsibilities to someone else' (Berle, 1932). He could not have foreseen that after 65 years of patient and deliberate effort by company managers to balance their responsibilities and objectives, that no 'clear or enforceable scheme' for them to do this has emerged, or that though the law has struggled to keep pace with industrial reality, the changes in the fundamental principles of company law could have proved so modest.

THE CORPORATE CONSTITUENCY

On the ground in the USA 38 state legislatures attempted to protect the companies in their local economies from hostile takeover by passing stakeholder laws that permitted or required directors to consider the impact of all their activities on constituencies other than shareholders including employees, customers, suppliers and the community (Hanks, 1994; Orts, 1992).[1]

Steven M.H. Wallman, an SEC Commissioner who helped draft the 'corporate constituency' law passed in Pennsylvania, defines the corporation's interest as 'enhancing its ability to produce wealth indefinitely . . . both profit from today's activities and expected profit from tomorrow's activities' (Wallman, 1991). This could provide the basis of a new interpretation of what it means for directors to act 'in the interests of the

corporation'. Defining the interests of the corporation in terms of maximising the wealth producing potential of the enterprise and linking the interests of the various constituencies to the interests of the corporation 'resolves much of the tension that would otherwise exist from competing and conflicting constituent demands' (Blair, 1995; Wallman 1991: 170).

Over half of the Standard & Poor's 500 corporations in the USA are listed in the state of Delaware which does not have a 'corporate constituency' statute, however in a case involving Paramount Communications the Delaware Supreme Court was understood to give the same freedom to management to judge the short terms and long term interests of the company, though in 1993 this ruling was altered in a case involving the same company, leaving it unclear if directors of companies incorporated in Delaware can consider the effects of takeover decisions on stakeholders other than just shareholders (Blair, 1995: 220–222).

Martin Lipton offers a precise legal interpretation, '. . . Under Delaware law the objective of the corporation is the *long-term* growth of shareholder value; assuming the board of directors has used due case (followed reasonable procedures) and did not have a conflict of interest, the board may prefer *long-term* goals over *short-term* goals, except when the decision is to sell control of the corporation or to liquidate it in which case the board must use reasonable efforts to get the best value obtainable for the shareholders. Under this standard the board has the right to invest for the *long-term* in people, equipment, market share and financial structure even though the financial markets do not recognise (or overtly discount) the future value and even though and board's strategy results in elimination of dividends and reduction in market price of the stock. Also under this standard, the board has the right to "just say no" to a premium takeover bid. However, the board does remain subject to shareholder control and the shareholders have the right at least once a year to replace at least some of the directors who have followed a strategy or taken a position disliked by the shareholders' (Blair, 1995: 222).

THE SHAREHOLDER THEORY OF THE FIRM

Though the law in the USA has inched towards acknowledging the rights of other stakeholders, at least in the extreme circumstances of company takeovers, for most of this century a 'property conception' of the company has predominated in the Anglo-Saxon world. This has received most robust expression in the Chicago School of law and economics, which treats the company as a nexus of contracts through which the various participants arrange to transact with each other. According to this theory assets of the company are the property of the shareholders, and managers and boards of directors are viewed as agents of shareholders, with all of the difficulties of enforcement associated with agency relationships, but without legal obligations to any other stakeholder. This view maintains 'the rights of creditors, employees and others and strictly limited to statutory, contractual and common law rights' (Allen, 1992; Aoki *et al.*, 1990).

Any broadening of the social obligations of the company was dangerous according to this school of thought, 'Few trends could so thoroughly undermine the foundations of our free society as the acceptance by corporate officials of a social responsibility other than to make as much money for their stockholders as possible' (Friedman, 1962). The difficulty is whether in trying to represent the interests of all stakeholders, company directors simply slip the leash of the only truly effective restraint that regulates their behaviour – their relationship with shareholders. In apparently seeking to become the arbiter of the general interest, all that occurs is that executives become a self-perpetuating group of princes: 'So long as the management has the one overriding duty of administering the resources under its control as trustees for the shareholders and for their benefit, its hands are tied; and it will have no arbitrary power to benefit from this or that particular interest. But once the management of a big enterprise is regarded as not only entitled but even obliged to consider in its decisions whatever is regarded as of social interest, or to support good causes and generally to act for the public benefit, it gains an uncontrollable power – a power which would not be left in the hands of private managers but would inevitably be made the subject of increasing public control' (Hayek, 1979).

These views were expressed with vigour by liberal economists, and enjoyed the support of some business leaders and senior politicians. More practically, such views reflected how USA and UK companies were driven in the period of the 1970s and 1980s, with an emphasis upon sustaining share price and dividend payments at all costs and freely using merger and takeover activity to discipline managers who failed in their responsibility to enhance shareholder value. The economic instability and insecurity created by this approach was criticised in a report by Michael Porter on America's failing capital investment system to the USA Council on Competitiveness (Porter, 1992).

Monks and Minnow have attempted a recent restating of the essential principles of the shareholder theory of the firm, which is more tolerant of the interests of other constituents, but insists they are best served by acknowledging the supremacy of the ultimate owner: 'It seems to make most sense to envision a hypothetical long-term share holder, like the beneficial owner of most institutional investor securities, as the ultimate party of interest. That allows all other interests to be factored in without losing sight of the goal of long term wealth maximisation. But without a clear and directly enforceable fiduciary obligation to shareholders, the contract that justifies the corporate structure is irreparably shattered. It is difficult enough to determine the success of a company's strategy based on only one goal – shareholder value. It is impossible when we add in other goals . . . The only way to evaluate the success of a company's performance is to consult those who have the most direct and wide-reaching interest in the results of that performance – the shareholders. The problem is one of effective accountability (agency costs). Only owners have the motive to inform themselves and to enforce standards that arguably are a proxy for the public interest' (Monks and Minnow, 1995).

It could be contested whether a focus upon shareholder interests really have been the key to good corporate performance and effective accountability in the recent past in the USA and UK. Also whether in an age of more active participation by consumers, employees and other economic groups, assuming that only shareholders are capable of effective monitoring sounds like wishful thinking. An irony is that shareholders, particularly the scattered army of individual shareholders, have not been particularly well looked after or informed in the recent past, even by companies espousing shareholder value views.

The arguments against the stakeholder view recently have been summarised by John Argenti (1997).

1 Companies have a relatively homogenous group of shareholders to relate to, but diverse stakeholders.
2 It is clear what shareholders expect, but not clear what stakeholders expect.

3   The pursuit of the profit motive is simple, but if all stakeholder interests are to be balanced, trade-offs will become increasingly complex.
4   There is a need for a single bottom line to provide a focus for managers.
5   There is difficulty in measuring and verifying values to other stakeholders.

As Andrew Campbell suggests this straightforward view of management underestimates the existing complexity of the task and restrictively confines the objectives of business to a single purpose, when in fact the 'market economy allows each company to define its own "deal" for each stakeholder group. This in turn encourages creativity' (Campbell, 1997). Why 'value' is only what ends up in the hands of shareholders in a mystery of financial economics. For example the 1997 annual report of Enterprise Oil plc includes among its central corporate objectives 'nurturing an environment in which the best people want to work towards delivering a strong growth in *values*' (Jungels, 1997).[2]

THE STAKEHOLDER THEORY OF THE FIRM

The Oxford dictionary definition of stakeholding records the first use of the term in 1708 as a bet or deposit, 'to have a stake in (an event, a concern etc.): to have something to gain or lose by the turn of events, to have an interest in; especially to have a stake in the country (said of those who hold landed property). Hence specifically a shareholding (in a company)'. A stakeholder theory of the firm has existed in various forms and has been based on different economic principles, since the origins of industrialism. The philosophical antecedents of stakeholder theory reach back into the nineteenth century, to the conceptions of the co-operative movement and mutuality (Clarke, 1984, 1991). Periodically such theory has become marginalised and forgotten, only to be reclaimed later in response to changing economic circumstances. Because of its fragmented development and marginal status, it has never been elaborated and explained as fully and coherently as the shareholder theory of the firm.

Edith Penrose in *The Theory of the Growth of the Firm* (1959) laid the intellectual foundations for stakeholder theory in her concept of the company as a bundle of human assets and relationships. The term stakeholder theory was first used in 1963 at the Stanford Research Institute, where stakeholder analysis was used in the corporate planning process by Igor Ansoff and Robert Stewart (Freeman and Reed, 1983). However Ansoff was cautious in his use of the concept: 'While . . . responsibilities and objectives are not synonymous, they have been made one in a "stakeholder theory" of objectives. This theory maintains that the objectives of the company should be derived by balancing the conflicting claims of the various "stakeholders" in the firm, managers, workers, stockholders, suppliers, vendors' (Ansoff, 1965).

Freeman provides a history of the USA use of the stakeholder concept (Freeman, 1993; Mintzberg, 1994).[3] In 1975 Dill argued: 'For a long time we have assumed that the views and initiatives of stakeholders could be dealt with as externalities to the strategic planning and management process: as data to help management shape decisions, or as legal and social constraints to limit them. We have been reluctant, though, to admit the idea that some of these outside stakeholders might seek and earn active roles with management to make decisions. The move today is from stakeholder influence to stakeholder participation' (Dill, 1975). The Wharton School in Pennsylvania began a stakeholder project in 1977 exploring the implications of the stakeholder concept as a management theory; as a process for practitioners to use in strategic management; and as an analytical framework (Freeman and Reed, 1983: 91).

CONCEPTUAL RIGOUR OF STAKEHOLDER THEORY

The stakeholder notion is deceptively simple. Definitions of who the stakeholders are range from the highly specific and legal to the general and social. The

Contractual stakeholders	Community stakeholders
Shareholders	Consumers
Employees	Regulators
Customers	Government
Distributors	Pressure groups
Suppliers	The media
Lenders	Local communities

Table 1   Contractual and community stakeholders.

Stakeholder	Expectations of stakeholder *from* the company	Nature of accountability *by* the company
Employees	Remuneration, employment security, conditions, training	Company reports, employment news, bargaining information
Owners	Dividends and share price appreciation	Annual report and accounts, merger and takeover information
Customers	Quality, service, safety, value for money	Sales literature, advertising, servicing
Bankers	Liquidity and solvency of company, value of security, cash generation	Cover ratios, collateral, cash forecasts
Suppliers	Stable and enduring relationship	Payment according to terms
Government	Compliance with law, jobs, competitiveness, accurate data	Reports to official bodies, press releases
General public	Safety of operations, contribution to the community	Safety reports, press reports
Environment	Benign operations, substitution of non-renewable resources	Environmental reports, compliance reports

Table 2 What do stakeholders want?

Source: Adapted from 'Organisational Legitimacy and Stakeholder information Provision', D.G. Woodward, F. Edwards and F. Birkin (1996), *British Journal of Management* 7 (4), 340.

Stanford Research Institute's definition of stakeholders was 'those groups without whose support the organisation would cease to exist' (Freeman and Reed, 1983: 91). Max Clarkson organised an academic conference on the subject at the University of Toronto in May 1993, the papers from which resulted in a special edition of the *Academy of Management Review* in January 1995, offering the following definition of stakeholder theory, 'The firm is a system of stakeholders operating within the larger system of the host society that provides the necessary legal and market infrastructure for the firms activities. The purpose of the firm is to create wealth or value for its stakeholders by converting their stakes into goods and services' (Clarkson, 1994).

Hill and Jones enlarge the standard principal–agent paradigm of financial economics, which emphasises the relationship between shareowners and managers to create a 'stakeholder agency theory' which constitutes in their view 'a generalised theory of agency'. From this conception managers can be seen as the agents for all of the other stakeholders (Hill and Jones, 1992).

Charkham offers a distinction between contractual and community stakeholders (Table 1) (Charkham, 1992).

Having identified who the stakeholders are the next question is to ask what do they want? It is possible for managers to seek more accurate information concerning the expectations of stakeholders *from* the company and to examine more closely the nature of accountability *by* the company towards stakeholders (Table 2).

ACCOUNTABILITY TO WHOM?

A related and unresolved problem is to work out how stakeholder interests may be more formally represented in the direction of companies, if that is desirable, the appropriate spheres of influence of the different parties and whether there is any need to change company law. In his review of the centrality of stakeholder models to the running of enterprises in Germany, France and Japan, Charkham argues: 'In one important respect the law does not need to be changed: namely the bodies to which the board is accountable. In the "other constituencies" debate, it is argued that management has a great many interests to consider other than the shareholders, such [as] employees, customers, suppliers, bankers and the community. Of course it does: it cannot hope to succeed unless it takes all these interests properly into account . . . Shareholders may come at the end of the queue for dividends (and for distribution if the company ceases to trade), but they are the anchormen.

If the board's accountability to them is lessened it [could] be altogether weakened: the distinction between "taking into account" and "being responsible to" must be maintained' (Charkham, 1994).

It was this critical distinction which let the Hampel Committee on Corporate Governance in the UK off the hook of more formally recognising stakeholder interests among the duties of company directors: 'A company must develop relationships relevant to its success. These will depend on the nature of the company's business; but they will include those with employees, customers, suppliers, credit providers, local communities and governments. It is management's responsibility to develop policies which address these matters; in doing so they must have regard to the overriding objective to preserving and enhancing the shareholders' investment over time . . . This recognises that the directors' relationship with the shareholders is different in kind from their relationship with other stakeholder interests. The shareholders elect the directors. As the CBI put it in their evidence to us, the directors are responsible *for relations with* stakeholders; but they are accountable to the shareholders. This is not simply a technical point. From a practical point of view, to redefine the directors' responsibilities in terms of the stakeholders would mean identifying the various stakeholder groups; and deciding the nature and extent of the directors' responsibility to each. The result would be that the directors were not effectively accountable to anyone since there would be no clear yardstick for judging their performance. This is a recipe neither for good governance nor for corporate success' (Committee on Corporate Governance, 1997).

Identifying and communicating with relevant stakeholder groups, deciding the nature of responsibilities to each, and being judged by a wider range of performance indicators that relate to stakeholder concerns is precisely what enlightened companies are striving to do as Wheeler and Sillanpaa illustrate (1997). A more basic question, which Hampel failed to ask, is what are the principal assets of the contemporary company?

THE PRINCIPAL ASSETS OF KNOWLEDGE BASE COMPANIES

The principles of corporate governance to which the Hampel Committee refers were established almost two centuries ago. Charles Handy in an essay on The Citizen Corporation explains why clinging to former certainties is no longer appropriate:

> The old language of property and ownership no longer serves us in the modern world because it no longer describes what a company really is. The old language suggests the wrong priorities, leads to inappropriate policies and screens out new possibilities. The idea of a corporation as the property of the current holders of shares is confusing because it does not make clear where power lies. As such, the notion is an affront to natural justice because it gives inadequate recognition to the people who work in the corporation, and who are, increasingly, its principal assets.
>
> (Handy, 1997)

This argument has particular resonance with regard to knowledge based companies and of course all companies are becoming more knowledge based. As Robert Grant insists, 'If knowledge is the pre-eminent productive resource and most knowledge is created by and stored within individuals, then employees are the primary stakeholders. The principal management challenge . . . is establishing mechanisms by which cooperating individuals can co-ordinate their activities in order to integrate their knowledge into productive activities' (Grant, 1997). Silicon Valley which has given the world Intel, Apple, Silicon Graphics, Netscape and a host of other high technology companies fully recognises this fact.

This triumph of technological innovation could only be achieved by attracting the brightest people to start-up companies with the most generous employees stock options in the history of corporate America. As Matt Ward of West Ward Pay Strategies puts it, 'Silicon Valley is the economic engine of the world and options the fuel'. The idea of employee stock options is catching on, according to Sanford C. Bernstein & Co the total value of employee stock options rose from $59 billion in 1985 to $600 billion in 1996, when 90 per cent of public companies in the USA had employee stock-option programmes. Before the recent meteoric rise in the value of Microsoft shares, a Wall Street analyst calculated that 2,200 of Microsoft's 11,000 employees each held options worth at least $1 million. Now Microsoft is facing legal action from employees who feel left out of this bonanza (*Fortune*, July 52–62, 1997). Of the 200

Companies	Stock awards (%)
Morgan Stanley	91.36
Merrill Lynch	40.26
Travelers	39.42
Warner-Lambert	35.00
Microsoft	32.95
J.P. Morgan & Co.	29.62
Lehman Brothers	28.25
US Airways	26.71
Sun Microsystems	25.99
Marriott	25.81
Bankers Trust	25.53
General Mills	25.41
MCI	24.39
Allied Signal	24.23
ITT Industries	24.14

Table 3 USA companies employee options and stock awards 1996.

Source: Pearl Meyer & Partners, *Fortune* July 1997.

largest USA companies, 15 had at least 24 per cent of their shares set aside for employee options and other stock awards in 1996 (Table 3).

STAKEHOLDER STRATEGIES IN PRACTICE

In practice, executives leading companies and managers operating them have increasingly utilised elements of the stakeholder approach. The growing emphasis upon customer relations, employee relations, supplier relations and indeed investor relations, is an indication of the way managers are grappling with the need to satisfy the interests of more complex constituencies than shareholder theory would suggest.

The defence of shareholder rights sits uneasily with how increasingly companies are managed. The Tomorrow's Company Inquiry launched by the RSA in 1992, way sponsored by 25 major UK corporations and captured much of the sense that business needs to fundamentally examine its objectives, relationships and performance measures if sustainable commercial success is to be achieved. Only by creating stronger relationships with employees, customers, suppliers, investors and the community will companies learn fast

enough and change fast enough, the *Final Report* of the RSA Inquiry argued citing extensive published evidence (RSA, 1995). Anthony Cleaver, then Chairman of IBM UK, in the preface to the *Final Report* of the Inquiry argued, 'Only by giving due weight to all key stakeholders can shareholder value be assured.' The report continued, 'Only through deepened relationships with, and between, employers, customers, suppliers, investors and the community will companies anticipate, innovate and adapt fast enough, while maintaining public confidence' (RSA, 1995: 1).

Kotter and Heskett studied 200 companies over 20 years and clearly correlated superior long term profitability with corporate cultures that express the company's purpose in terms of all stakeholder relationships (Kotter and Heskett, 1992). John Kay defines success in terms of value added, and – arguing that outstanding businesses derive their strength from a distinctive structure of relationships with employees, customers and suppliers – explains why continuity and stability in these relationships are essential for a flexible and co-operative response to change (Kay, 1993). He offers a hard-headed interpretation of how a stakeholder approach is an essential basis for industrial viability:

> Inclusion and shared values promote trust, co-operative behaviour and the ready exchange of information. These things also yield hard-nosed commercial advantages. Such values encourage closer working together, which is why the Japanese have achieved unmatched levels of component reliability, implemented just-in-time production processes and shortened model cycles. They help explain why the German and Swiss have secured exceptional standards of production engineering.
>
> (*Financial Times*, 17 January 1996)

Winners of the Baldridge award, which has been in place in the USA for seven years – and which, like other national and international quality models, including the European Foundation for Quality Management (EFQM), covers performance in all key relationships – show better than average financial returns (Garvin, 1991). The EFQM Quality Award for excellence adopts explicitly a stakeholder framework in its model and interestingly measures results in terms of 20 per cent customer satisfaction, 18 per cent people management and satisfaction, 6 per cent impact on society and 15 per cent business results in terms of continuing success in achieving financial and non-financial targets and objectives (Figure 3) (European Foundation for Quality Management, 1993).

A paradox is that companies driven by financial indices to satisfy shareholders often appear capable of doing so for limited periods of time. 'Companies that set profits as their number one goal are actually less profitable in the long run than people-centred companies' (Waterman, 1994). Of the 11 companies named as Britain's most profitable by *Management Today* between 1979–1989, four subsequently collapsed and two were acquired (Doyle, 1994). A BOC/London Business School survey *Building Global Excellence* commented on the preoccupation of UK managers with financial performance. The report commented: 'To be in a position to predict the future and discover you need to change

3–4 years before the crisis comes, today's managers need to switch their attention away from the *financial* health of their companies and start measuring the *strategic* health' (BOC/London Business School, 1994; Lazonick, 1992).[4]

In the USA, Kaplan and Norton's concept of the balance business scorecard was developed by a number of leading companies looking for a new performance measurement model including DuPont, General Electric and Hewlett Packard. 'The collision between the irresistible force to build long range competitive capabilities and the immovable object of the historical cost financial accounting model has created a new synthesis: the balanced scorecard. The balanced scorecard retains traditional financial measures. But financial measures tell the story of past events, an adequate story for industrial age companies for which investment in long term capabilities and customer

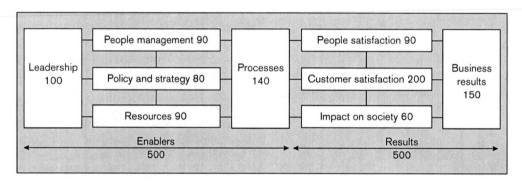

Figure 3 European quality award assessment model: people, processes and results.

Established focus on	Emerging focus on
One-way, passive communication	→ Multi-way, active dialogue
Verification as option	→ Verification as standard
Single company progress reporting	→ Benchmarkability
Management systems	→ Life cycles, business design, strategy
Inputs and outputs	→ Impacts and outcomes
Ad hoc operating standards	→ Global operating standards
Public relations	→ Corporate governance
Voluntary reporting	→ Mandatory reporting
Company determines reporting boundaries	→ Boundaries set through stakeholder dialogue
Environmental performance	→ Triple bottom line – economic, environmental and social – performance

Table 4 UNEP sustainability programme ten transitions for the future.

relationships were not critical for success. These financial measures are inadequate, however, for guiding and evaluating the journey that information age companies must make to create future value through investment in customers, suppliers, employees, processes, technology and innovation' (Kaplan and Norton, 1996).

Finally recent developments in reporting company impact on the environment reveal the emerging sophistication of environmental measures and how challenging it is for companies to enter into a dialogue in this area. For example the UN Environmental Programme (UNEP) for environmental and social/economic reporting proposes 50 quantitative indices, making it impossible for companies to argue that systematic disclosure of social information was impossible and indicators of sustainability too diffuse (Wheeler and Sillanpaa, 1997). The UNEP sustainability programme recommends ten transitions for the future (Table 4).

INTERNATIONAL INTERPRETATION AND EXPERIENCE OF STAKEHOLDER CONCEPTS

In Europe and Japan companies have traditionally adhered consciously to a stakeholder model, which it is often claimed is the basis of their industrial success and social stability. However more recently with the development of their equity markets and the increasing activity of international investors, particularly from the USA, some major European and Japanese companies for the first time have come under pressure to focus upon shareholder value.

Among the notable features of the German business sector is the relatively strong concentration of ownership of individual enterprises; the importance of small and medium sized unincorporated companies, with a close correspondence between owners and managers; and the limited role played by the stock market (OECD, 1995). More broadly the dominant feature of German commercial enterprises is the inside characteristic of their governance systems through which all interested stakeholders – managers, employees, creditors, suppliers and customers – are able to monitor company performance: 'it relies on continuous monitoring of managers by other stakeholders, who have a long-term relationship with the firm and engage permanently in the important

aspects of decision-making and in the case of dissatisfaction, take action the correct management decisions through internal channels. In the case of incorporated firms (Kapitalgesellschaften) stakeholder influence is exerted through a two-tier company board structure' (OECD, 1995: 85). Whether this system can survive in major German companies such as Mercedes Benz and Hoechst following their listing on the New York Stock Exchange and the insistent pressures they will face to yield shareholder returns, is open to question. At the other end of the scale, upto 700,000 of the family run Mittelstand, the locally based backbone of German enterprise, could be up for sale within the next ten years, as their post-war founders retire (*Financial Times*, 10 October 1997).

In Japan stakeholder conceptions are deeply embedded in corporate thinking and practice. Yoshimori highlights a company survey in which 97 per cent of companies agreed a firm exists for the interest of all stakeholders. Asked whether a CEO should choose to maintain dividends or lay off employees a similar number of companies agreed that job security was more important. Asked which stakeholder was most important as a source of support, 63 per cent of Japanese chief executives responded it was the employees and only 11.5 per cent suggested it was shareholders (Steadman *et al.*, 1995; Yoshimori, 1995). Japanese firms have favoured long term growth and sustained a policy of low dividend payments, with shareholders more concerned with total returns. However in 1993 company law in Japan was changed to strengthen the powers of shareholders and pressure for improved performance is coming from institutional investors, including from overseas. As institutional investors become more influential in Japan and the influence of banks diminishes, it is likely Japanese corporations will be under increasing pressure to alter their stakeholder orientations in favour of shareholder interest (OECD, 1996).

A STAKEHOLDER ECONOMY?

As countries traditionally associated with essentially stakeholding principles appear to be drifting away from them, the UK which under Mrs Thatcher launched a free market property rights counter revolution upon the world from 1979, has travelled in the opposite direction. Will Hutton provided a robust defence of stakeholder capitalism which helped provoke a public discussion still developing (Hutton, 1995; 1997a,b). Hutton's vision encompasses reframing the relationship between finance and business; reforming workplace relations; transforming the welfare state and the benefit system; reformulating macroeconomic policy; and reconstructing the democratic system. On a tour of the Far East in January 1996, UK Prime Minister Tony Blair briefly entered the debate with a speech on stakeholder economics, before quickly retreating to the safer ground of a stakeholder society (Plender, 1997). Mario Nuti (1997) remains sceptical of such an ambitious extension of the stakeholder principle and suggests 'once the set of a country's stakeholders coincides with the set of all citizens, the concept of stakeholders becomes completely redundant'. However he may be underestimating the appeal of an 'inclusive society' in economies that have felt the consequences of the cold draught of exclusion in poverty, crime and failing economic performance.

CONCLUSIONS

To many in business the stakeholder concept remains little more than a public relations exercise. However it is conceivable that a stakeholder approach may be not just a moral imperative, but a commercial necessity 'in a world where competitive advantage stemmed more and more from the intangible values embodied in human and social capital' (Plender, 1997: 2). In this context it is likely there will be further investigation by many companies of how stakeholder strategies may usefully be applied in business, and how stakeholding is interpreted in other countries.

NOTES

1 Hanks (1994) goes on to describe stakeholder theory as an 'idea whose time should never have come . . .'.
2 Apparently the plural caused problems for one of the company's non-executives.
3 Henry Mintzberg (1994) finds 'bizarre' Freeman's model of a 'stakeholder strategy formulation process', which Mintzberg suggests assumes managers can factor into the planning process the wants and needs of the different influencer groups, hence avoiding the messiness of politics. *The Rise and Fall of Strategic Planning*, Prentice Hall, Hemel Hempstead, 141–144.
4 Lazonick (1992) suggests that many corporate executives have been co-opted into this finance-oriented view

because they rose to the top of their organisations in an era that rewarded financial market performance more than innovation or growth. Today executive rewards and compensation packages are tied more than ever to share price performance and other financial indicators.

REFERENCES

Allen, W.T. (1992). Our Schizophrenic Conception of the Business Corporation, *Cardozo Law Review* 14 (2), 261–281; an interesting reinterpretation of this approach is, M. Aoki, B. Gustafsson and O. Williamson, *The Firm as a Nexus of Treaties*, London (1990).

Ansoff, I. (1965). *Corporate Strategy*, McGraw Hill, New York, 33.

Aoki, M., B. Gustafsson and O. Williamson (1990). *The Firm as a Nexus of Treaties*, London, Sage.

Argenti, J. (1997). Stakeholders: The Case Against, *Long Range Planning* 30 (3), 442–445.

Berle, A.A. (1932). For Whom Are Corporate Managers Trustees?, *Harvard Law Review* 45, 1365–1367.

Berle, A.A. and G.C. Means (1932). *The Modern Corporation and Private Property*, Commerce Clearing House, New York.

Blair, M.M. (1995). *Ownership and Control: Rethinking Corporate Governance for the Twenty first Century*, The Brookings Institution, Washington, DC.

BOC/London Business School (1994). *Building Global Excellence*, BOC/London Business School, London.

Campbell, A. (1997). Stakeholders: The Case in Favour, *Long Range Planning* 30 (3), 446–449.

Charkham, J. (1992). Corporate Governance: Lessons from Abroad, *European Business Journal* 4 (2), 8–16.

Charkham, J. (1994). *Keeping Good Company A Study of Corporate Governance in Five Countries*, Clarendon Press, Oxford, 336.

Clarke, T. (1984). Alternative Modes of Co-operative Production, *Economic and Industrial Democracy*, Sage, London 5 (1), 97–129.

Clarke, T. (1991). Democracy, Integration and Commercial Survival, In R. Russell and V. Rus (eds), *Handbook of Participation in Organisations*, Oxford University Press, Oxford.

Clarke, T. and R. Bostock (1994). International Corporate Governance: Convergence and Diversity, In T. Clarke and E. Monkhouse (eds), *Rethinking the Company*, Financial Times, Pitman, London.

Clarkson, M.B.E. (1994). *A Risk Based Model of Stakeholder Theory*, The Centre for Corporate Social Performance and Ethics, University of Toronto, Toronto, 21.

Committee on Corporate Governance (1997). *Preliminary Report*, The Stock Exchange, August.

Dill, W.R. (1975). Public Participation in Corporate Planning, *Long Range Planning*?, 57–63.

Doyle, P. (1994). Setting Business Objectives and Measuring Performance, *Journal of General Management* 20 (2).

European Foundation for Quality Management (1993). The *European Quality Award Application Brochure*.

Freeman, R.E. (1993). *Strategic Management: A Stakeholder Approach*, Pitman, Marshfield MA.

Freeman, R.E. and D.L. Reed (1983). Stockholders and Stakeholders: A New Perspective on Corporate Governance, *California Management Review*, XXV (3), 88–106.

Friedman, M. (1962). *Capitalism and Freedom*, University of Chicago Press, Chicago, 113.

Garvin, D.A. (1991). How the Baldrige Award Really Works, *Harvard Business Review* November–December, 80–93.

Grant, R.M. (1997). The Knowledge-Based View of the Firm: Implications for Management Practice, *Long Range Planning* 30 (3), 450–454.

Handy, C. (1997). The Citizen Corporation, *Harvard Business Review*, September–October, 26–28 .

Hanks, J.J. (1994). From the Hustings: The Role of States With Takeover Control Laws, *Mergers and Acquisitions* 29 (2), September–October.

Hayek, F.A. (1979). *Law, Legislation, Liberty, Volume 3: The Political Order of a Free People*, University of Chicago Press, Chicago, IL, 82.

Hill, C.W. and T.M. Jones (1992). Stakeholder-agency Theory, *Journal of Management Studies* 29, 131–154 .

Hutton, W. (1995). *The State We're In*, Jonathan Cape, London.

Hutton, W. (1997a). An Overview of Stakeholding, In G. Kelly, D. Kelly and A. Gamble, *Stakeholder Capitalism*, Macmillan, Basingstoke.

Hutton, W. (1997b). *The State to Come*, Vintage, London.

Jungels, P. (1997). Conflict or Compromise: An International Perspective, *GHN Non-Executive Forum* RSA 23 October.

Kaplan, R.S. and D.P. Norton (1996). *The Balanced Scorecard*, Harvard Business School Press, Boston, MA.

Kay, J. (1993). *The Foundations of Corporate Success*, Oxford University Press, Oxford.

Kotter, J.P. and J.L. Heskett (1992). *Corporate Culture and Performance*, The Free Press, New York.

Lazonick, W. (1992). Controlling the Market for Corporate Control: The Historical Significance of Managerial Capitalism, *Industrial and Corporate Change* 1 Oxford University Press, Oxford.

Mintzberg, H. (1994). *The Rise and Fall of Strategic Planning*, Prentice Hall, Hemel Hempstead, 141–144.

Monks, R.A.G. and N. Minnow (1995). *Corporate Governance*, Blackwell, Oxford, 41.

Nuti, M. (1997). Democracy and Economy: What Role for Stakeholders? *Business Strategy Review* 8 (2), 14–20.

OECD (1995). *OECD Economic Surveys Germany*, OECD Paris.

OECD (1996). *OECD Economic Surveys Japan*, OECD, Paris.

Orts, E.W. (1992). Beyond Shareholders: Interpreting Corporate Constituency Statues, *The George Washington Law Review* 61 (1), 14–135.

Peacock, A. and G. Bannock (1991). *Corporate Takeovers and the Public Interest*, Aberdeen University Press, Aberdeen.

Penrose, E. (1959). *The Theory of the Growth of the Firm*, Oxford University Press, Oxford.

Plender, J. (1997). *A Stake in the Future: The Stakeholding Solution*, Nicholas Brealey, London.

Porter, M. (1992). Capital Disadvantage: America's Failing Capital Investment System, *Harvard Business Review* September–October, 65–82.

RSA (1995). *Tomorrow's Company Inquiry Final Report*, Royal Society of Arts.

Steadman, M.E., T.W. Zimmerer and R.F. Green (1995). Pressures From Stakeholders Hit Japanese Companies, *Long Range Planning* 28 (6), 29–37.

Tricker, R.I. (1994). The Board and the Company of the Future, In R.I. Tricker (ed), *International Corporate Governance*, Prentice Hall, Singapore.

Wallman, S.M.H. (1991). The Proper Interpretation of Corporate Constituency Statues and Formulation of Director Duties, *Stetson Law Review* 21, 163–192.

Waterman, R. (1994). *The Frontier of Excellence—Learning from Companies that put People First*, Nicholas Brealey, London.

Wheeler, D. and M. Sillanpaa (1997). *The Stakeholder Corporation: A Blueprint for Maximising Stakeholder Value*, Pitman Publishing, London.

Yoshimori, K. (1955). Whose Company Is It? The Concept of the Corporation in Japan and the West, *Long Range Planning* 28 (4), 33–44.

S
I
X

PART SEVEN

Theories of convergence

INTRODUCTION TO PART SEVEN

The *outsider* market-based system of dispersed ownership and the primacy of share holder value that prevails in the United States and the United Kingdom has become the dominant force in international corporate governance. Here principal/agent problems are assumed to be the central interest of corporate governance. In Europe a relationship-based system of corporate governance has prevailed, reflecting the rich cultural diversity of the continent, and different history and values. These *insider* systems of corporate governance are more dependent on loans from banks than the equity market, and tend to have the support of close business networks. Finally there are family-based corporate structures of the Asia Pacific, again reflecting different cultural traditions and aspirations.

The greatest contemporary theoretical and policy debates in corporate governance are whether there is global convergence towards the Anglo-Saxon market-based *outsider* model of corporate governance. This trend appeared irresistible in the late 1990s with the success of the new economy in the United States. However with the failure of Enron and the fall in the NASDAQ, the benefits of the American system are less self-evident. Advocacy of the convergence thesis came from the most influential quarters including the G7, OECD, and leading Western business and law schools. International competition, the globalization of capital markets, and deeper integration of markets have all contributed to the perceived need to meet certain governance conditions it is claimed. Michael Useem (Chapter 15) highlights the impact of the internationalization of finance. Institutional investors are now discovering a wider world of higher returns and lower risks. Company executives are learning that foreign investors are able to provide more capital at lower cost. The globalization of equity markets is leading firms to restructure their operations to enhance shareholder returns.

Mauro Guillen (Chapter 16) insists corporate governance models cannot be seen in isolation from the rest of the institutional underpinnings of the economy in question. Corporate governance systems are embedded in legal traditions, interact in complex ways with other institutional features, and are affected by national political dynamics. He concludes longitudinal evidence suggests little convergence in recent decades. In a similar vein Rhodes and Apeldoorn (Chapter 17) argue against analyses that minimize the role of domestic institutions, and understand the contemporary transformation of European institutions simply in terms of globalization around a neo-liberal convergence. Rather than the abandonment of structures the delivered efficiency and prosperity in the past, they perceive considerable scope for diversity continuing in European corporate governance. Finally Douglas M. Branson (Chapter 18) argues that the 'one size fits all' approach of convergence advocates is culturally and economically insensitive. The dominant form of ownership throughout the world remains *family* ownership, and other forms of embedded capitalism in which the economy is perceived as subservient to the society, rather than the opposite.

'Corporate Leadership in a Globalizing Equity Market'

from Academy of Management Executive (1998)

Michael Useem

THE RISE OF GLOBAL INVESTING

Skillful work with shareholders is a virtue born of necessity. The concentration of ever more stockholding in ever fewer hands has given institutional investors unprecedented influence on the firm. When professional stock analysts and money managers favor a company, its prospects are brighter, and when not, more in doubt. To assure investor favor and assuage doubt, executives must be capable of delivering the strategy story to the stock analysts and, ultimately, share value to the money managers.[1]

Still another executive capacity is now becoming essential as well: the ability to lead the company in a world of international stockholding. Cross-border investing is in its youth but growing fast. Companies with a demonstrated commitment to the international investment community will enjoy, as a result, an edge in the growing competition for global capital. And managers who work well with worldwide investors will bear an edge in executive advancement.

Since institutional shareholders are comparing investment opportunities worldwide, companies and their executives are judged less against their domestic neighbors and more against the best firms and executives worldwide. Attracting and retaining cross-border stockholders therefore requires adapting and applying international best practices. Either firms begin to measure up to the best global performers or risk disinvestment.

SHAREHOLDING IS INCREASINGLY INSTITUTIONAL

Shares of US companies are already more often found in the portfolios of institutions than individuals. Of the shares of the 1,000 largest companies ranked by market capitalization in 1985, 57 percent were owned by individuals. Today, nearly 60 percent is managed by institutions (Figure 1).

When mutual funds, pension systems, bank trusts, and other institutional investors acquire stock, they are typically doing so on behalf of individuals. Households, not institutions, are the ultimate beneficiaries for most institutional investing. But the difference lies in who ponders which stocks to buy, hold, or sell. In earlier years, individuals decided; now, professional money managers do so.

When millions are buying and selling shares, they rarely meet one another let alone the company executives in whom they are entrusting their family wealth. To the individual stockholder, other market players are as remote as the functionaries of Franz Kafka's castle. By concentrating large assets in few hands, however, institutional investing allows a personalizing of the impersonal, at least among those who routinely trade in blocks of 10,000 shares or more.

Preeminent among them is the manager of Fidelity's Magellan fund, the giant of the giants with $60 billion at his disposal. Peter Lynch managed Magellan from 1977 to 1990, Jeffrey Vinik from 1992 to 1996, and Robert Stansky now. Lynch averaged annual returns of 29 percent for 14 years, a legendary

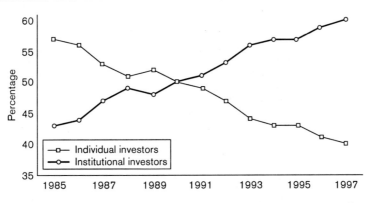

Figure 1 Percentage of shares of 1,000 largest US companies held by individuals and institutional investors, 1985–97.
Source: Business Week; Conference Board.

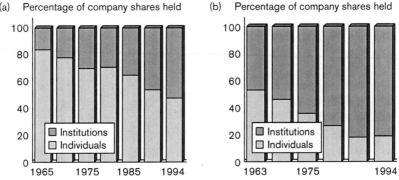

Figure 2 Individual and institutional holdings of (a) US (1965–94) and (b) UK company equity, 1963–94.
Source: (a) Securities Industry Association; (b) Stapledon, 1996.

achievement, bar successor Vinik averaged a mere 17 percent, and his successor Stansky hopes to do far better.

Robert Stansky is one of 9,000 money managers whose account holders always expect more. For insight on returning more, the money managers turn to some 5,500 equity analysts with 2,200 institutional investors and another 2,400 equity analysts with 200 stockbrokers. These are the people and organizations that have come to define the world of American investor capitalism. They know each other and the company executives in whom their assets are entrusted.[2]

Comparable trends are evident in most other economies. Some are more advanced, as in the UK, where better than 80 percent of British equities are already held by institutions (Figure 2). Others are less so, as in Brazil where families still predominate.

Each national setting displays its own unique ownership demography: *keiretsu* holdings are striking in Japan, banks in Germany, foreigners in France. But for most, the vector points in the direction of fading households, in 1950, individuals owned 61 percent of Japanese stock; by 1990, they are down to 23 percent (Figure 3). In 1970, households held 28 percent of German stock and 41 percent of French stock; by 1992–93, they retain only 17 percent of German equity and 34 percent of French.[3]

Company managers almost everywhere, as a result, face not many millions of anonymous shareholders but just several thousand identifiable money managers. These institutional owners are more demanding and less patient than individual holders; they look for company competitiveness and clamor for change when firms fall short.

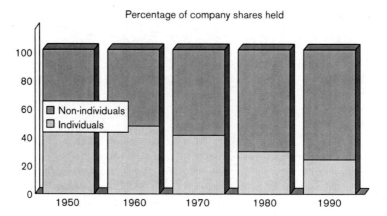

Figure 3 Individual and non-individual holdings of Japanese company equity, 1950–90.

Source: Tokyo Stock Exchange.

SHAREHOLDING IS INCREASINGLY INTERNATIONAL

The gathering of company shares in a small number of institutional hands dates to the 1960s. The internationalization of company shareholding, however, commenced in earnest only in the 1990s, as part of the wholesale globalization in all forms of private financing. It has been facilitated by the privatization of state enterprise, deregulation of domestic stock markets, and cross-listings of stocks on foreign exchanges. It has been driven above all by financial advantages that accrue to investors and companies alike.

Globalization of private finance

American equity holdings abroad multiplied more than five-fold between 1990 and 1997, from $110 billion to $600 billion (Figure 4). Illustrative of the global expansion, Asea Brown Boveri's American operation managed an employee retirement fund in 1991 of $600 million that included no foreign equities. By 1997, the fund had moved more than half of its assets into non-US stock.[4]

The growth of cross-border stock holdings is also evident in the sharp rise of assets in global and international US equity funds. Global funds are those investing at least some assets abroad; international funds place at least 75 percent offshore. Between 1990 and 1997, the assets of global and international funds rose from $28 billion to more than $300 billion (Figure 5).

All forms of foreign investment have been sharply ascendant during the 1990s, but equity investing has outpaced most. Joint ventures, new plants and other forms of direct investment in emerging economies, for instance, quadrupled between 1990 and 1996, while stock holdings rose more than ten-fold. Equity investing constituted just 11 percent of all private investing in emerging economies in 1990 – but 23 percent by the mid-1990s (Figure 6).

Privatization of public enterprise

Massive conversion of state-owned enterprises into publicly held companies during the 1990s added millions of new shares to the global equity market. The revenue from privatizations in emerging economies rose from less than $5 billion annually in the late 1980s to more than $20 billion in recent years (Figure 7). Because of the vast scale of many of the enterprises sales, local investors often lacked the capacity to absorb the new issues. In 1996, as a result, those privatizing Italy's energy firm, ENI, targeted a quarter of its shares abroad; of Germany's telecommunications monopoly, Deutsche Telekom, a third to international buyers; and of Russia's big natural-gas company, Gazprom, all to foreign investors.[5]

The winds of worldwide privatization are deflected here and there. The governments of Venezuela and Mexico are still resisting entreaties to dispose of their crown jewels, the national oil companies. But little of commercial value among state owned enterprise

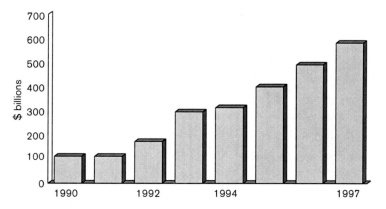

Figure 4 Value of foreign company equity among US holders, 1990–97.

Source: New York Stock Exchange.

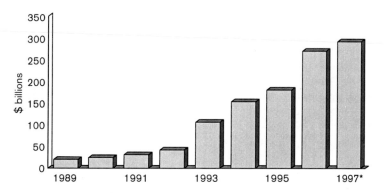

Figure 5 US mutual fund investment in foreign equities, 1989–97.

Source: Investment Company Institute.

Note

* March: assets in international and global mutual funds.

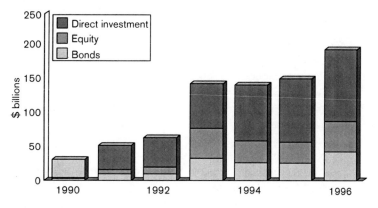

Figure 6 Net bond, equity, and foreign direct investment in developing countries, 1990–96.

Source: World Bank.

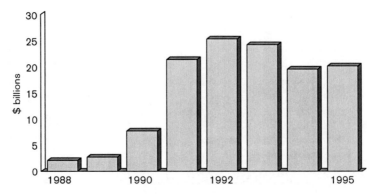

Figure 7   Revenues from developing country enterprise privatizations, 1988–95.

Source: World Bank.

elsewhere remains sacrosanct. Even China committed in 1997 to privatizing a third of its state-owned enterprises. Symptomatic of the climate for change, the Communist Youth League planned in 1998 to place two-thirds of the equity of its travel operation – China CYTS Tours Co. – on the Shanghai stock market. Hoping to raise $45 million in the public offering, this arm of the communist party intended to use the new capital to purchase tourist trains and an amusement park.[6]

DEREGULATION OF DOMESTIC STOCK MARKETS

The globalization of equity investments has been aided as well by the deregulation of many domestic stock markets. This has typically entailed an easing of restrictions on foreign ownership of brokerage firms and domestic stock. It often includes prescriptions on financial reporting and proscriptions on insider trading.

Taiwan opened its securities market in 1988, for instance, to allow foreign securities firms to take minority ownership in Taiwanese securities firms and even to establish their own local once for both domestic and overseas transactions. It also required that companies report results quarterly, prohibit self-dealing, and treat acquirers fairly.[7]

Malaysia now permits foreign money managers to own up to 70 percent of a local joint venture for managing Malaysian investment funds. Japan began opening domestic pension funds to foreign management in 1996 – Fidelity now manages $100 million of Honda's $4 billion retirement fund – and plans to have it fully open by 1999. Mexico is freeing its recently privatized pension system for international management, and Citicorp, Bank of Boston, Aetna, and American International Group are among those setting up shop in Mexico City.[8]

Cross-border stock exchange listings

The internationalization of stock holdings is also facilitated by the widening corporate practices of listing shares abroad. In 1990, 96 non-US firms had listed on the New York Stock Exchange (NYSE), but by 1997 the number had reached 345, including British Airways, Daimler Benz, Sony, Telefonos de Mexico, and Tommy Hilfiger (Hong Kong). New York's turnover in foreign shares rose five-fold (Figure 8).

The NYSE is more than a passive beneficiary. It actively recruits foreign firms, and with some 3,000 listed companies in 1997, it is eyeing not only another 700 US firms that could meet its listing requirements but also 2,300 foreign enterprises that could qualify as well. Although NYSE would increase its capitalization by a tenth if it successfully recruited its yet unlisted domestic prospects, it knows its real future resides abroad: If it attracts all of the qualified non-US companies, it would enlarge the value of its listed shares by fully two-thirds.[9]

The cross-border advantage

The ultimate engine behind the globalization of equities is the financial advantage that foreign diversification can bring to investors and companies alike.

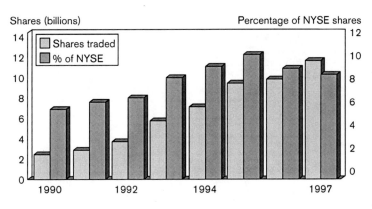

Figure 8 Non-US stock trading on New York Stock Exchange, 1990–97.

Source: New York Stock Exchange.

When carefully crafted, both sides stand to gain from the growth of international ownership, and it is for this reason that each will continue to press for global dispersion.[10]

Had US investors in the period from 1969 to 1993 diversified their actual portfolios more fully among seven major countries, their returns, according to one study, would have ranged 10–50 percent higher than those in fact obtained from their largely US holdings. Diversifying a US portfolio with a targeted array of foreign stocks, other research shows, can shrink variability in annual returns, a standard measure of risk, by 20 percent or more.[11]

Global diversification is advantageous for company executives as well. By bringing foreign buyers into a company's stock, managers can enhance their firm's market value. This can be seen in the aftermath of a 1988 decision by Nestlé, the Swiss food-products company, to abolish a special class of stock then available only to Swiss residents. The Swiss shares could not be purchased anonymously since proof of citizenship was required, but their holders otherwise enjoyed the same voting rights and dividends stream as the owners of Nestlé's unrestricted stock. The Swiss-only shares, however, traded at half the price of the unrestricted shares. Since half of Nestlé's equity resided in the restricted shares, the differing prices had the effect of increasing the firm's cost of capital by 3 to 4 percent. When Nestlé finally opened the restricted shares to worldwide ownership in 1988, it enlarged its market value by 10 percent.[12]

Similarly, when company managers list their firm abroad, they often enjoy a significant increase in market worth. A recent assessment of forty studies of stock price movements when company-shares are listed abroad concludes that US companies benefit comparatively little by listing in Tokyo, London or elsewhere. But non-US companies average a 12 percent annualized gain in stock price during the first week after they list in the US, lowering their cost or capital, depending upon the company and country, by 1 to 3 percent. Similar results emerge from a study of 128 non-US companies listing on the NYSE from 1985 to 1996: Daily trading in these stocks increased by 42 percent after the listing (trading in even the home market rose by 24 percent), and share prices during the six months after the listing averaged 6 percent more than the six months before.[13]

Company managers in emerging economies also enjoy higher price-earnings ratios when their government imposes fewer restrictions on foreign investing in their economies. Study of eighteen national markets from Argentina to Thailand between 1986 and 1992 shows that stock P/E ratios are generally higher in less constrained equity markets.[14]

Global mutuality

As a result of these developments, stock markets are increasingly driven more by international trends, less by domestic economics. Study of 20 emerging markets from 1976–1992, including those of Brazil, India, and Mexico, reveals a significant tightening of the linkage between local end worldwide stock returns. The same is true for advanced economies. Analysis of 16 developed stock markets, ranging from France and Germany to the US and UK finds an

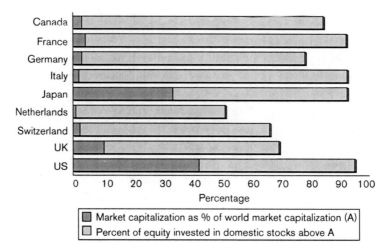

Figure 9 Domestic market capitalization and percent of equity in domestic stocks, 1995.

Source: Cooper and Kaplanis (1995).

average stock price correlation in 1967–70 of 0.30, but in 1986–1994 of 0.55. The radical gyrations of most major stock markets in the wake of a one-day decline of 10 percent – and later rebound – in Hong Kong's market index in late October, 1997, illustrate the rising interdependence among the various markets.[15]

Still, the globalization glass is nowhere near even half full, and even greater market interdependence can be expected as it further fills. US market value in 1995 represented 42 percent of world capitalization, but American investors still kept 95 percent of their holdings at home. The typical US pension fund allocated just 16 percent of its equity assets – only 9 percent of its total assets – to foreign stocks. The Japanese market is 33 percent of the world total, but Japanese investors have retained 92 percent in Japanese companies. Dutch investors have more aggressively looked beyond their borders, keeping only 51 percent of their assets in Netherlands companies. But given that Holland's stocks constitute only 1 percent of world equity, even, this home bias is huge. The domestic skews for these and other major economies, displayed in Figure 9, reveal how far the globalization of equity holdings has yet to go.[16]

Implications for managers

For corporate executives, then, access to the globalizing equity market can be enhanced by listing their own stocks abroad and reducing restrictions on investors at home. In taking steps to make their ownership more widely available – both through individual company actions and by joining other companies to promote domestic reforms – executives can boost their firms' market value.

But in doing so, company managers are also helping to create a shareholder world that looks radically different from what their predecessors had seen just a decade earlier. Rather than gazing on legions of small domestic holders whose dissatisfaction with poor performance could be disregarded, company managers now see a world community of professional investors whose dissatisfaction cannot be ignored. Whether American or Zambian, company leadership increasingly requires a capacity to understand and respond to the concerns of global money managers, who are far less tolerant of languishing results than their predecessors and far more capable of demanding stellar performance.

INTERNATIONAL INVESTOR ACTIVISM

The transformation of equity holdings from individual to institutional and the subsequent movement toward international is generating a first wave of global investor activism. Pioneered by American public retirement systems, activism means that disgruntled holders advise companies what to do when they do not like what they see.

This is a modification of the traditional Wall Street rule of simply selling if you do not like what management is doing. Active investors press companies for improved performance through a host of tactics, ranging from voting against management proposals to demanding independent directors (Figure 10). The globalization of equity markets means that company managers everywhere will come under increasing pressure from both domestic and foreign activism as investors learn to exercise the political muscle residing in their accumulating wealth.

At the forefront is the California Public Employees' Retirement System (Calpers) with an investment portfolio of $110 billion. Calpers pioneered American activism during the early 1990s and is now carrying the flag abroad. In 1994, Calpers announced that it was expanding its international holdings from 13–20 percent of its assets, and in 1996 stated that it would press companies in four target countries – Britain, France, Germany, and Japan – for improved performance and better governance. Calpers already had a toe in the water: In 1992 it openly opposed a proposed limitation of shareholder voting rights by the French food company BSN. In 1995, it voted against the election of two directors to the board of Japan's Nomura Securities Company, former presidents who had been implicated in a scandal over payments to preferred clients. Calpers is now urging other institutional investors to exercise their voting rights in the UK, and in France it is pressing for a reduction of cross-ownership among companies and equal voting rights for shareholders. 'Globalization is inexorable,' warns Calpers president William Crist. 'No one could stop it even if they wanted to.'[17]

The US government has added its own weight behind the export of American activism. In a 1994 policy directive, the Department of Labor now requires trustees of private pensions to cast informed votes on proxy ballots – which include director elections and resolutions on management and governance practices – not only for American firms but also for all foreign companies in their portfolios. An influential European policy center had called in 1995 for similar behavior on the continent; urging shareholders to 'exercise their voting rights in an informed and independent manner.' Such vigilance, the center said, should 'be adapted to the growing internationalism of shareholding and not be limited to national borders.'[18]

Impact of international investor activism

The impact of the cross-border activism is already evident in scattered contests for control of the executive suite. In Britain, a group of investors led by Chicago-based Harris Associates forced chairman Maurice Saatchi to resign in 1994 from the British-based advertising firm that he had founded but allowed to founder. In France, investors unhappy with the strategy of France's Cie. de Suez helped force its chairman, Gerald Worms, to resign in 1995, focusing widespread executive attention on big investors and *'le corporate governance.'*[19]

In Italy, foreign investors forced out Olivetti's long-time chairman, Carlo de Benedetti, in 1996 after his company reported accumulated losses of $2.8 billion. International investors held 70 percent of Olivetti's stock, and in response to their demands, the company added four new directors to its board, including British and French executives. In Holland in 1997, the US Teamsters union challenged the

Institutional investors press companies to . . .

- Redesign the company to be more competitive
- Improve short-term and long-term performance
- Retain effective strategies, abandon failing strategies

Institutional investors press companies by . . .

- Occasionally voting against management proposals
- Sometimes voting against company directors
- Sometimes demanding different managers
- Often telling companies to alter structure and improve performance
- Frequently meeting with company executives
- Frequently asking for quarterly performance of units and products
- Almost always seeking more information on company plans
- Increasingly demanding strong and independent boards of directors

Figure 10 Activist investors press companies for improved performance.

practice by the supervisory board of the Dutch supermarket company, Ahold, of reappointing its own directors without shareholder vote.[20]

Institutional investors outside the US still rarely adopt the most aggressive tactics of Calpers and its American fellow travelers, but more are moving in that direction. Netherlands's Algemeen Burgerlijk Pensioenenfonds (ABP), the largest privatized European retirement system with $129 billion in assets, is working with other Dutch institutions to form an investors' forum for pressing companies to reform their boards and improve performance. The Amsterdam Stock Exchange has urged that Dutch enterprises focus more on shareholder value, less on the company; more on the 'Anglo-Saxon' model of giving priority to shareholders, less on the 'Rhine' model of putting the company first.[21]

In Germany, fund-management group Union Investment GmbH in 1995 openly challenged the management of Bayerische Vereinsbank, declaring that the bank's return on equity and its stock price are unacceptably low. In France, shareholders aggressively questioned managements at Alcatel-Alsthom SA, Société Nationale, Elf Aquitaine, and Renault SA. In Switzerland, Martin Ebner, who controls BK Vision AG, a Swiss investment fund and the largest shareholder in the Union Bank of Switzerland, demanded a radical remake of the bank, including consolidation of its retail operations and reduction of the board by half. Ebner campaigned in 1996 for the proxy defeat of bank chairmen Robert Studer and managed to mobilize 37 percent of the shareholder vote against him.[22]

In India, foreign investors holding 34 percent of the Industrial Credit and Investment Corporation of India – one of the country's largest investment banks – became critical of its poorly managed operations and subpar shareholder return. They joined disgruntled domestic institutions that held 41 percent of the stock to push in 1997 for governance changes similar to those recommended in 1992 by a British panel, the Cadbury Committee, including a separation of the roles of board chair and chief executive.[23]

International standards

As an indirect form of investor activism, global institutions are pressing for world standards for corporate disclosure and governance. American and British international equity managers, reports one survey, strongly support efforts to create more uniform transnational disclosure policies, accounting principles, and governance practices, and several bodies are acting to foster such consistency:

- The US Financial Accounting Standard Board is working with counterpart groups in Canada, Mexico, and Chile to harmonize accounting standards in the wake of the 1994 North American Free Trade Agreement.
- The International Accounting Standards Committee and the International Organization of Securities Commissions are working together to develop common accounting standards by the end of the 1990s for companies that are listed cross-nationally or are seeking to raise capital outside their home country.
- The International Corporate Governance Network, an association of stock exchanges and industry groups, is developing guidelines for governance worldwide and methods for global share voting.
- The International Working Group on Transnational Communications of the Conference Board is fostering improved and more uniform cross-border distribution of company information to investors.

Improved transnational dissemination of corporate information should ultimately benefit not only investors but also the disclosing companies themselves. A study of 750 US companies in 1985–89 reveals that firms with better disclosure attract more stock analysts, the analysts are able to make more accurate forecasts of the companies' earnings, and both factors in turn bolster stock price.[24]

Implications for managers

The rising tide of international investor activism is placing private enterprise on notice. Money managers are becoming more vigilant, securities markets more reform minded, and governance standards more uniform. Although company managers may be tempted as short-term measures to erect defenses against the shareholder activism, such as poison pills and staggered boards, an enduring and more productive response calls for greater focus on shareholder value, improved disclosure of information, and stronger governing boards. Pre-emptive leadership is valued, for it is generally easier for companies to make changes before angry institutions demand them.

BUILDING RELATIONS WITH INVESTORS WORLDWIDE

Institutional investing has personalized the domestic equity market, and globalized investing is now achieving the same in the international equity market. US investors and executives are meeting with their counterparts abroad, and foreign investors and executives are encountering their counterparts in the US. The globalization of equity markets means that the ongoing dialogue between company executives and money managers is increasingly multilateral.

American managers abroad

US executives have learned during the past decade to meet frequently with domestic money managers and stock analysts to explain their vision and strategy. While little technical information can be selectively shared at such road shows – federal regulations require that all shareholders receive any material information – these gatherings allow investors to assess the quality of the executive talent and management vision. Conversely, executives hear what animates investors and learn whether their firm's business plans appear credible. Both sides have an opportunity to kick the tires, measure the other, and argue the future. When American chief executives present their strategies to groups of stock analysts, research confirms that institutional interest and stockholding goes up.[25]

American executives are increasingly taking their cases directly to investors in London, Paris, Zurich and other overseas financial centers, to meet current investors and to cultivate new ones. Investors consider direct contact with management vital: A survey in 1996 of 62 American and European institutional investors with a combined $2.5 trillion under management found that meetings with management are considered the best single source of company information. Personal contact has been vital to the rise of investor capitalism within the US, and will become even more so for international investing because of the difficulty of obtaining reliable information through other means.[26]

Foreign managers abroad

Non-US companies are pursuing much the same agenda, traveling to New York and other foreign financial centers to carry their case personally to those overseeing institutional assets wherever they reside.

The number of Japanese companies sending officers to meet with investors abroad more than doubled between 1993 and 1996. Executives of one Japanese food producer, Sagami Chain Co., presented their five-year sales and earnings forecasts and offered explicit comparisons of the firm's performance with those of fourteen competitors during 1996 meetings with investors around the Pacific Rim and then in New York, London, Edinburgh, Geneva, Frankfurt, and Paris. During the same period, foreign ownership of Sagami Chain stock rose seven points to 19 percent.[27]

Similarly, many Russian executives have beaten a path to institutional doors abroad, up from zero before mass privatization. During the early 1990s, when the nascent market economy began forcing companies for the first time to seek their financing in New York rather than Moscow, the newly privatized managers initially tended to offer old answers to new questions. American stock analysts have rarely met a company statistic they do not want, but when they asked the Russian executives for data they normally expected, the Russians responded warily, declaring some to be state secrets. After several years' experience with foreign road shows, however, Russian executives have learned that international investors tolerate few secrets of any kind.[28]

By way of illustration, Perm Uralsviazinform, a regional telephone company, and nine other Russian companies (including the Red October Chocolate Candy Factory) met in 1997 with 50 money managers in New York. Perm Uralsviazinform is already not only a telecom but also a credit card operator, bank owner, and radio/TV broadcaster, but it needed still more capital for further expansion. Not enough could be found at home and it decided to list its stock in New York. The investors attending the New York meeting grilled the firm's chief financial officer, Aleksandr Vokhmin, and other company representatives about the Russian habit of paying bills late and showering shares on insiders.[29]

Later, telecom executive Aleksandr Vokhmin met privately with New York money managers specializing in emerging economies, including director of the Biltmore Emerging Markets fund, Scott Sadler, who had already placed $4 million of his $160 million in Russian enterprise. For Sadler, such personal meetings are a welcome source of information. The financial data coming from emerging market companies are, in his view, too often simply 'not credible.' Thus, 'looking someone in the eye' can be the only way to understand his or her potential. In meeting with company executives like Vokhmin, Sadler seeks to discern their 'management capabilities' and 'motivations,' and if he likes what he sees, he may plunge in.[30]

Foreign disclosure is less regular or reliable in many countries than in the US, and this places a special premium on personal contact. 'The biggest single peril of foreign investing,' warns William Wilby, director of global equities at Oppenheimer Management Corporation in New York, 'is the credibility and trust of management,' and there are few better ways to appraise both than to meet the executives in question. Still, it is a competitive fray requiring long-term commitment. To increase its shareholding among US investors to match the 22 percent of its auto sales in the US, Volvo has repeatedly sent its executives across the Atlantic to explain its strategy and advocate its stock. 'We have to make a bridge to the US,' explains Volvo's director of investor relations, 'so analysts feel they are getting information that is as good as their European competitors are getting.'[31]

Implications for managers

Just as the concentration of institutional shareholding has already led to a world of personalized relations between company managers and money managers within the US, the globalization of institutional investing is placing a premium on personalizing relations between executives and investors across national boundaries. The challenge of creating those ties across nations and even continents is far greater than in the past because of the travel distances and cultural differences. But company managers are wise to create them now since such relationships may be even more critical for communicating the company's strategy and promise to foreign investors. Conversely, if company managers are to understand the concerns of big holders abroad, there is no better way than through direct contact with them.

DEVELOPING LEADERSHIP FOR A GLOBALIZING EQUITY MARKET

The globalizing equity market calls for new leadership skills. These skills are neither natural nor widespread.

Until a decade ago, few American executives worried about their relations with institutional owners. And until recently, few company executives anywhere worried about their foreign investors. The rapid expansion of institutional cross-border investing, however, places a premium on executive talents that make for effective company leadership across national boundaries.

In identifying those talents, it is useful to distinguish two facets of leadership, the personal and the organizational. The two facets are diagrammed in the upper rectangles of Figure 11. The lower rectangle displays the powers of office that executives acquire the moment they step in the door – the authority to revise budgets, assign people, and give raises. These inherent office powers are only a platform and leadership can be defined as rising above the vested authority in both personal and organizational ways. The personal includes the application of unique expertise and qualities of character. The organizational includes changing the firm and developing its employees. Leadership, then, can be seen as leveraging personally and organizationally what one is given in order to achieve far more with it.

Personal leadership with international investors

Developing personal leadership for executive work with international investors can usefully draw on the experience of American companies in preparing their managers for working with domestic institutions. Career success under the now well established US conventions depends above all on an executive's ability to focus on shareholder value. Career success under the emerging rules will depend upon an executive's capacity to deliver superior returns to international investors – where superior is no longer defined domestically (Figure 12).[32]

To deliver the value expected demands a nuanced understanding of the models and minds of investors on Well Street, the City of London, and other world financial centers. For this there is no substitute for regular dialogue through rapid shows, executive visits to money managers, and investors visits to the company. The point is to learn how investors perceive and react to earnings surprises, what information they want about the company and its leadership, and with which other firms they compare the

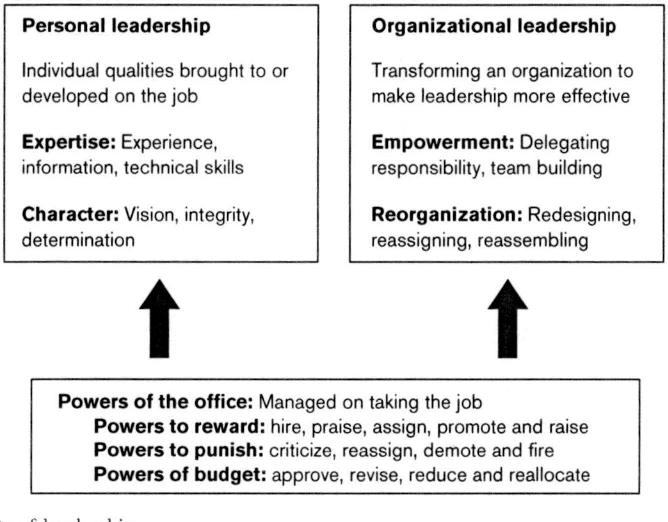

Personal leadership	Organizational leadership
Individual qualities brought to or developed on the job	Transforming an organization to make leadership more effective
Expertise: Experience, information, technical skills	**Empowerment:** Delegating responsibility, team building
Character: Vision, integrity, determination	**Reorganization:** Redesigning, reassigning, reassembling

Powers of the office: Managed on taking the job
Powers to reward: hire, praise, assign, promote and raise
Powers to punish: criticize, reassign, demote and fire
Powers of budget: approve, revise, reduce and reallocate

Figure 11 Two facets of leadership.

Personal leadership	Organizational leadership
Developing executives to operate more effectively with international investors.	Transforming a company to make it more effective with international investors.
Expertise: Building executive knowledge of investor concerns and forging personal familiarity with investors.	**Empowerment:** Arranging for heads of business unit to meet with stock analysts and money managers.
Character: Fostering executive capacity to communicate the company's strategy to international stock analysts and money managers.	**Reorganization:** Creating autonomous business units whose contribution to share holder value is more apparent.

Figure 12 Developing leadership with international institutional investors.

company's shareholder returns and prospects. Anticipating the strategic moves of global competitors is critical, as is understanding how investors evaluate those moves compared with one's own.[33]

Company executives also require a capacity to present the company's strategy to a constitutionally skeptical audience. Since investors now have a world of stocks from which to pick, a persuasive selling of a firm's strategy is essential. Moreover, since many investors are driven by annual if not quarterly concerns, persuading them of the company's long-term objectives is a foundation for their loyalty in the short-term. In the eyes of international investors, several classic virtues of leadership should be much in evidence, including accuracy, credibility, and integrity. When such

qualities abound, money managers like Biltmore's Scott Sadler can see past other shortcomings.

Organizational leadership with international investors

Effective leadership with international investors also requires revamping the firm to collaborate better with the investors. Stock analysts and money managers appraise not only the company and its top management team but also its major operating divisions. Among the questions they ask are whether the whole is greater than the sum of its parts, and whether specific product segments and national operations are ascendant or in decline. They want to learn about the divisions not only from the chief executive but also from those most directly responsible for the businesses. Analysts, for instance, often ask Ford Motor Company for data on its European auto production and ask to meet with those accountable for it.

Organizational leadership also requires the remaking of the firm to highlight its units' contributions to total shareholder return. This often means transforming the company from functional divisions such as production and marketing to strategic business units centered on distinct classes of products, services, or customers. Such redesign permits clearer management focus on measurable results for investor value.[34]

International institutions tend to be less risk averse than company managers and domestic owners in many countries, and as firms reach out for global holders, leadership also calls for increasing a company's willingness to take strategic risks. Movement in this direction is already evident among Japanese firms successfully attracting offshore investors. A study of 70 of Japan's 200 largest industrial firms during the early 1990s, for example, identified those that had listed their shares abroad and the fraction of the companies' equity that is not Japanese owned (it averaged nine percent). Companies with more overseas listings and more foreign ownership, other factors being equal, are found to invest more in research and development, and those with more foreign listings are less diversified – the kinds of higher risk profiles that international investors prefer.[35]

Global investors also like to see top management performance incentivized around shareholder return. This is most often achieved through stock-option based compensation. In response to US investor pressure, American firms have moved far along this path, with well over half of top management compensation now based on long-term company performance, most in the form of stock options (Figure 13). European firms are not nearly as far forward on this pay frontier, but they too are introducing stock-based compensation into their pay packages (Figure 14), Some nations, such as China and India, have discouraged or prohibited stock options in the past, but in many countries state barriers of contingent compensation are falling with rising cross-border holdings.

The ultimate adverse incentive is executive dismissal. In an era of global shareholder power, executives who build a relationship with investors worldwide and then deliver value to them are rewarded. But if they destroy value, their place at the helm is now at risk. This is evident in the impact of a sharp decline in a company's stock price on executive tenure. Whether the US, Japan, or Germany, the likelihood of a CEO's exit in the wake of a stock free fall is increased by as much a half (Figure 15). A study of Japanese companies stunned by a sharp reversal of fortune reveals that those whose top ten shareholders control a major fraction of the firm's stock dismiss the president and bring in new directors more often than other firms. Other evidence indicates that the probability an American board will dismiss its top executive has been rising in recent years, and boards worldwide will be increasingly likely to take such action in the years ahead.[36]

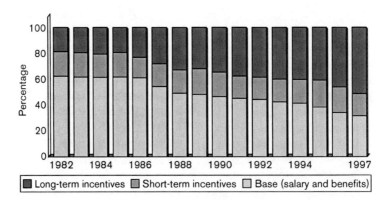

Figure 13 Fixed and variable compensation for executives of large manufacturing firms, 1982–97.

Source: Hewitt Associates annual surveys.

Note: Data for top 7 executives at 45 large industrial companies.

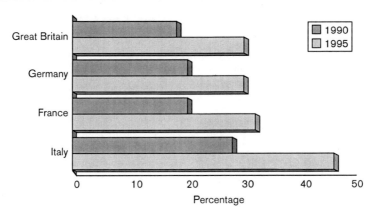

Figure 14 Percentage of European firms offering stock options to chief executives, 1990 and 1995.

Source: Watson Wyatt Data Services.

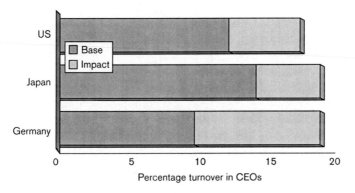

Figure 15 Likelihood of CEO turnover after 50 percent decline in stock price, US, Japan and Germany, 1980–88.

Source: Kaplan (1994a,b, 1997).

CORPORATE CONVERGENCE

The multidivisional structure has spread far and wide among large corporations, regardless of national setting. So too have key technologies of production. This is not the case, however, for such elementary features of governance as the composition of company boards. As stock analysts and money managers study their international prospects, they still see a welter of securities laws, reporting requirements, and board structures.

Governance systems and investor-corporate relations display as much variation from country to country as almost any feature of business organization.

The boards of virtually all large, publicity traded US firms include a solid majority of outsiders. The boards of virtually all large, publicly traded Japanese firms include almost no outsiders. German and Dutch governance is built around a two-tier governance structure; British and Swiss governance is designed around a single-tier, management-dominated structure. Some systems give formal voice to labor, others none: German law requires that labor representatives serve on the board, while French law places labor observers on the board, and American law mandates nothing.[37]

The days of divergent governance systems presiding over convergent organizational forms, however, are likely to be numbered as seasoned international investors urge a common model. When investors first enter the markets abroad, they are reluctant to press for better governance for fear of what they still do not know about local practices. But as they become comfortable with, foreign markets and uncomfortable with their shortcomings, they begin to turn up the heat. The process of corporate convergence will be prolonged, with many fits and starts. But given the accumulating assets and powers of the institutional holders and their movement onto the world stage, the process appears inevitable.

GLOBAL COMPETITIVENESS

The rise of global institutional investing is likely to foster a host of organizational changes in companies worldwide, as summarized in Figure 16. These are already seen among many American companies that have been pressed by institutional investors to change, or that have preemptively restructured before being forced to do so. For instance, American firms with large holding's by mutual funds and public pensions are, compared with others, observed to invest more in research and development and to bring more new products to market. Though some observers have worried about a potentially adverse impact of large investors on company performance, especially the dangers associated with excessive focus on the short-term, the US evidence suggests that institutional investors on balance enhance rather than undercut corporate performance.[38]

Comparable changes are likely to follow wherever international investors are taking major ownership stakes, and the rise of a global equity market will thus press companies worldwide to operate more productively. Institutional owners are increasingly comparing companies with the best performers anywhere, and if firms are to attract the investors they require for a fair pricing of their stock, they will have to be competitive with the best in their class.

- ■ Replacement of functional divisions by strategic business units
- ■ Disposal of unrelated business lines and focus on the core
- ■ Expansion of incentive compensation based on contribution shareholder value
- ■ Expanded R&D, joint venturing and outsourcing
- ■ Strengthened governing boards and more independent directors

---

Figure 16 Organizational changes that company managers are likely to make in response to increased holdings by international institutional investors.

CRISIS AND CONFIDENCE

The economic crises and market declines in Indonesia, Korea, Malaysia, Thailand, and other emerging economies in 1997–98 have naturally made investors skittish about the vagaries of cross-border holdings. *Wall Street Journal* columnist Roger Lowenstein warned investors that the 'shareholder in New Delhi or even Amsterdam doesn't have the paramount place in law and in culture that he holds in Kansas City,' and that whatever the merits of portfolio diversification, 'it hardly follows that the long-term investor need put shillings in Somalia.'[39]

Yet in their never ending search for superior returns, investors who return home for respite are sure to sally forth again. When the Mexican peso lost almost half of its value against the U.S. dollar in its infamous 1994–95 meltdown, the Mexican stock market also plummeted as anxious foreign investors fled for safer ground. But three years later, the Mexican economy had more than recovered – its growth rate in 1997 estimated at 7 percent – and the Mexican stock exchange's main index (IPC) had risen from a low of 1,448 just after the peso collapse to 5,000 by the end of 1997. Foreign owners drove much of the rise: They held 18 percent of Mexico's publicly-traded stock in 1991, 26 percent in 1994, and 30 percent by 1997. The Mexican comeback may not predict other recoveries, but it does suggest that although institutional investor horizons contract with crisis, institutions nonetheless soon return when confidence is restored.[40]

Some company managements may be unprepared to lead the changes required to restore that confidence, but international investors are acquiring the wherewithal to insist on the change anyway. Transparency became a mantra among many Thai companies when better disclosure emerged as a precondition in 1997 for bringing anxious foreign investors back. Teera Phutrakul, director of Thailand's Association of Investment Management Companies, described the executive embrace of the new rules: 'They'll strip down to their underpants for due diligence.'

The emergence of a global capital market is thus becoming a major force for global competitiveness. International investors are pressing companies to be as good as the best worldwide, and top managements of many are transforming themselves to become just that.[41]

NOTES

1 M. Useem, *Investor Capitalism: How Money Managers Are Changing the Face of Corporate America*. New York: Basic Books/HarperCollins, 1996; C. Brancato, *Institutional Investors and Corporate Governance: Best Practices for Increasing Corporate Value*. Chicago, IL: Irwin, 1997; M.J. Roe, *Strong Managers, Weak Owners: The Political Roots of American Corporate Finance*. Princeton, NJ: Princeton University Press. 1994.

2 *Investor Relations Newsletter*, 'Quantifying the Investment Community,' February, 1997: 2.

3 E. Berglof, 'Corporate Governance,' in B. Steil, ed., *The European Equity Markets*. London: Royal Institute of International Affairs, 1996; J. Franks, 'Corporate Ownership and Control in the U.K., Germany, and France,' *Journal of Applied Corporate Finance* 9, 1997: 30–45; J. Franks and C. Mayer, 'Corporate Ownership and Control in the U.K., Germany, and France,' in *Studies in International Corporate Finance and Governance Systems*, D.H. Chew, ed. New York: Oxford University Press, 1997; G.P. Stapledon, *Institutional Shareholders and Corporate Governance*. New York: Oxford University Press, 1996; C. Mallin, 'Investors' Voting Rights,' in *Corporate Governance: Responsibilities, Rights, and Remuneration*, K. Keasey and M. Wright, eds. London: Wiley, 1997; C. Mallin, 'The Role of Institutional Investors in the Corporate Governance of Financial Institutions,' Nottingham, UK: Nottingham Business School, 1997; C. Mallin, 'The Power and Influence of Institutional Investors in the UK,' Nottingham, UK: Nottingham Business School, 1997; Federation of European Stock Exchanges. *Share Ownership Structure in Europe*. Brussels: Federation of European Stock Exchanges, 1995; World Bank, *Private Capital Flows to Developing Countries: The Road to Financial Integration*. Washington, DC: World Bank, 1997: 97–98; Conference Board, *Institutional Investment Report: International Patterns of Institutional Investment*. New York: Conference Board, 1997.

4 J. Cochrane, J. Shapiro, and J. Tobin, 'Foreign Equities and U.S. Investors: Breaking Down Barriers Separating Supply and Demand,' New York; New York Stock Exchange, 1995; World Bank, *Private Capital Flows to Developing Countries*, op. cit., 99–101, 121–123; B. Rehfeld, 'Worldly-Wise Asset Allocation,' *Institutional Investor*, January, 1997: 41–51; J. Chernoff, 'Worldwide Pension Assets to Grow at Explosive Pace,' *Pensions and Investments* 23, May 15, 1995: 3.

5 V.J. Racanelli, 'Demand Builds for New European Shares,' *Wall Street Journal*, October 22, 1996: A17; *Financial Times*, ' "Big Bang" Approach to State Sell-Off,' April 29, 1997: 20.

6 Investor Relations, 'Communist Capitalism,' December, 1997: 19.

7 B.W. Sernkow, *Taiwan's Capital Market Reform*. New York: Oxford University Press, 1994, 147–154; restrictions on foreign equity investing in developing markets at the end of 1992 are summarized in Stijn Claessens and Moon-Whoan Rhee, 'The Effect of Equity Barriers to Foreign Investment in Developing Countries,' in J.A. Frankel, ed., *The Internationalization of Equity Markets*. Chicago, IL: University of Chicago Press, 1994.

8 M.C. Anderson, 'Fidelity Takes on Japan,' *Institutional Investor*, February, 1997: 115: *Economist*, 'Malaysian Finance: Thinking Big,' February 22, 1997: 85; J. Millman and C. Torres, 'Mexico to Allow 12 Companies to Offer Pension-Fund Services.' *Wall Street Journal*, January 29, 1997, A7; Anderson, 1997; *Economist*, 1997a; Millman and Torres, 1997.

9 R. Lambert, 'NY Exchange Sees Wider Horizons,' *Financial Times*, September 24, 1997: 4.

10 K.J. Engebreston, 'A Multi-Asset Class Approach to Pension Fund Investments,' *Government Finance Review* 11, February, 1995: 11–14.

11 K. Lewis, 'Consumption, Stock Returns, and the Gains from International Risk-Sharing.' Cambridge, MA: National Bureau of Economic Research, 1996; R.M. Stultz, 'Globalization of Capital Markets and the Cost of Capital.' *Journal of Applied Corporate Finance* 8, Fall, 1995: 30–38.

12 Stulz, op. cit.

13 G.A. Karolyi, 'What Happens to Stocks That List Shares Abroad? A Survey of the Evidence and Its Managerial Implications,' New York: New York Stock Exchange, 1996; K. Smith and G. Sofianos. 'The Impact of an NYSE Listing on the Global Trading of Non-U.S. Stocks.' New York: New York Stock Exchange, 1997.

14 S. Claessens and M.-W. Rhee, 'The Effect of Equity Barriers to Foreign Investment in Developing Countries,' in J.A. Frankel, ed., *The Internationalization of Equity Markets*. Chicago, IL: University of Chicago Press, 1994.

15 G. Bekaert and C.R. Harvey, 'Emerging Equity Market Volatility,' *Journal of Financial Economics* 43, 1997: 29–77; I. Cooper and E. Kaplanis, 'Home Bias in Equity Portfolios and the Cost of Capital for Multinational Firms,' *Journal of Applied Corporate Finance* 8, 1995: 95–102: J.A. Frankel, ed., *The Internationalization of Equity Markets*. Chicago, IL: University of Chicago Press, 1994.

16 Cooper and Kaplanis, op. cit.; Rehfeld, op. cit.; World Bank, *Private Capital Flows to Developing Countries*, op. cit, 99–101.

17 California Public Employees' Retirement System, 'Calpers Adopts International Governance Program.' Sacramento, CA: California Public Employees' Retirement System, 1996; J. Cossette, 'Making Waves,' *Investor Relations*, October, 1997. 27–31.

18 P.S. McGurn, 'DOL Issues New Guidelines on Proxy Voting, Active Investing,' *Corporate Governance Bulletin* July–August, 1994:1–7; Centre for European Policy

Studies, *Corporate Governance in Europe*, Brussels: Centre for European Policy Studies, 1995.

19 T. Kamm, 'Suez, Paribas Redefine French Business,' *Wall Street Journal*, May 13, 1996: A17.

20 *New York Times*, 'Olivetti Opens Board to Foreign Interests,' October 10, 1996: B5; *Economist*, 'Fair Shares,' February 15, 1997: 65; M.R. Sesit, 'Montedison Shareholders' Group Seeks to Split Company,' *Wall Street Journal*, May 13, 1996: A16B; Cossette, op. cit.

21 R. Bonte-Friedheim, 'Calpers Equivalent in Europe Dubbed "Consensus Company" with Soft Pitch,' *Wall Street Journal*, April 25, 1997; A9D: A. Schiffrin, 'Dutch Firms Debate Whether Employees or Shareholders Should Get Priority,' *Wall Street Journal*, November 1, 1996: A7D.

22 *Economist*, 'Fair Shares,' February 15, 1997; Cossette, op. cit.; *Bloomberg Business News*. 'UBS Says April "Good", Investors Not Sole Concern,' May 15, 1996; C. Arnold and K. Breen, 'Investor Activism Goes Worldwide,' *Corporate Board*, March–April, 1997: 7–11: M. Studer, 'Big Stockholder from a Small Bank Remains a Thorn in the Side of UBS,' *Wall Street Journal*, April 12, 1996: A8.

23 World Bank, *Private Capital Flows to Developing Countries*, op. cit., 318.

24 R. Bhushan and D.R. Lessard, 'Coping with International Accounting Diversity: Fund Managers' Views on Disclosure, Reconciliation, and Harmonization,' *Journal of International Financial Management and Accounting* 4, 1992: 149–164; L. Berton, 'All Accountants Soon May Speak the Same Language,' *Wall Street Journal*. August 29, 1995; A15; *Economist*, 'Global Accounting's Roadblock,' April 27, 1996: 79–80, Cossette, op. cit.; C.K. Brancato, 'Coping with Cross Borders,' *Corporate Agenda*, October, 1997: 5; M.H. Lang and R.J. Lundholm, 'Corporate Disclosure Policy and Analyst Behavior,' Accounting Review 71 (October, 1996): 467–492; J. Blitz, 'Italy Plans Shake-Up of Corporate Governance,' *Financial Times*, December 8, 1997: 18.

25 J.F. Byrd, M.F. Johnson, and M.S. Johnson, 'Investor Relations and the Cost of Capital.' Ann Arbor, MI: University of Michigan, School of Business Administration, 1993.

26 *Investor Relations*, 'Foreign Affairs,' December, 1996: 29–30.

27 J.S. Hirsch, 'Some Mutual Funds Go Back to Full Throttle to Emerging Markets,' *Wall Street Journal*, November 12, 1996: Al, 4; *Investor Relations*, 'Information Gap Widens.' December, 1996: 7.

28 D. Colarusso, 'Mission from Moscow: Find the Money,' *New York Times*, April 20, 1997: F5.

29 J. Blasi, M. Kroumova, and D. Kruse, *Kremlin Capitalism: Privatizing the Russian Economy*. Ithaca, NY: Cornell University Press, 1997.

30 Colarusso, op. cit.

31 C. Torres, 'Investing Overseas Isn't for the Fainthearted,' *Wall Street Journal*, June 27, 1996: R12; Stewart, op. cit. American companies are matching Volvo's efforts in reverse, working the premise that the global composition of their shareholders should resemble the international distribution in their sales. General Motors, for instance, with just 5 percent of its stock held internationally but new production facilities under construction in Argentina, Brazil, China, Poland, and Thailand, launched a campaign in 1996 to bolster it shareholding abroad to match its expanding foreign sales.

32 Useem, op. cit.; Brancato, op. cit.; M. Useem, E. Bowman, C. Irvine and J. Myatt, 'U.S. Investors Look at Corporate Governance in the 1990s,' *European Management Journal* 11, June, 1993: 175–189; W. Mahoney, *The Active Shareholder*. New York: Wiley, 1993,

33 M.A. Hitt, B.B. Tyler, C. Hardee and D. Park, 'Understanding Strategic Intent in the Global Marketplace,' *Academy of Management Executive* 9, 2, 1995: 12–29.

34 M. Useem, *Executive Defense: Shareholder Power and Corporate Reorganization*. Cambridge, MA: Harvard University Press, 1993.

35 P.H. Phan, and T. Yoshikawa, 'Agency Theory and Japanese Corporate Governance: A Test of the Convergence Hypothesis.' Toronto ON: Faculty of Administrative Studies, York University, 1996.

36 J.-K. Kang and A. Shivdasani, 'Corporate Restructuring During Performance Declines in Japan,' *Journal of Financial Economics* 46. 1997: 29–65; W. Ocasio, 'Political Dynamics and the Circulation of Power: CEO Succession in U.S. Industrial Corporations, 1960–1990,' *Administrative Science Quarterly* 39, 1994: 285–312.

37 J. Charkham, *Keeping Good Company: A Study of Corporate Governance in Five Countries*. New York: Oxford University Press, 1994; Heidrick & Struggles, *The Global Outside Director*. Chicago, IL: Heidrick & Struggles, 1993.

38 M. Useem, op, cit., 1993, 2996; R.E. Hoskisson and M.A. Hitt, *Downscoping: How to Tame the Diversified Firm*. New York: Oxford University Press, 1994; R. Kochhar and P. David, 'Institutional Investors and Firm Innovation: A Test of Competing Hypotheses,' *Strategic Management Journal* 17, 1996: 73–84; G.S. Hansen and C.W.L. Hill, 'Are Institutional Investors Myopic? A Time-Series Study of Four Technology-Driven Industries,' *Strategic Management Journal*, 12, 1991: 1–16; M. Porter, *Capital Choices: Changing the Way America Invests in Industry*. Washington, D.C: Council on Competitiveness, 1992.

39 R. Lowenstein, ''97 Moral: Drop Global-Investing Bunk,' *Wall Street Journal*, December 18, 1997: Cl.

40 S. Fidler, 'Mexican Finance and Investment: On the Crest of a Wave,' *Financial Times*, December 16, 1997, I; Bolsa Mexicana de Valores at <http://www.bmv.com.mx>

41 P. Waldman, 'Crisis Management: "Asian Values" Concept is Ripe for Revision as Economies Falter,' *Wall Street Journal*, November 28, 1997: Al, 4; Alan Murray, 'Asia's Financial Foibles Make American Way Look Like a Winner,' *Wall Street Journal*, December 8, 1997: Al, 13.

"Corporate Governance and Globalization: Is There Convergence Across Countries?"

from Advances in International Comparative Management (2000)

Mauro F. Guillén

INTRODUCTION

A corporate governance system is the "set of incentives, safeguards, and dispute-resolution processes used to order the activities of various corporate stakeholders" such as owners, managers, workers, creditors, suppliers, and customers (Kester, 1996: 109). Corporate governance provides a framework for the division of labor and of financial results in the firm. Corporate governance plays a key role in any economy. A well-functioning corporate governance system can contribute to economic efficiency, and perhaps even social equity. A poorly conceived system can wreak havoc on the economy by misallocating resources or failing to check opportunistic behaviors. Moreover, different corporate governance systems are associated with peculiar managerial decision-making criteria and temporal orientations (Bühner *et al.*, 1998; Kester, 1996; Lazonick and O'Sullivan, 1996).

Most conceptual analyses of corporate governance to date make comparisons between the shareholder centered models of the United States or the United Kingdom, and the stakeholder-centered models of Japan or Germany (Bühner *et al.*, 1998; Lazonick and O'Sullivan, 1996; Macey and Miller, 1995; Roe, 1993). Other researchers also propose the French and Scandinavian systems as separate models due to their different legal origins (La Porta *et al.*, 1998). Corporate governance patterns continue to differ markedly across

countries in spite of decades of economic globalization and 20 years of intense financial globalization. The literature has documented great cross-national differences in terms of such essential aspects of corporate governance as the importance of large stockholders, the legal protection of shareholders, the extent to which relevant laws are enforced, the treatment of stakeholders such as labor, suppliers or the community, the reliance on debt finance, the structure of the board of directors, the way in which executives are compensated, and the frequency and treatment of mergers and takeovers, especially hostile ones. Concentrated, not dispersed, ownership is still the rule rather than the exception throughout the world, and so is family control of even the largest corporations or business groups in most countries (Becht and Röell, 1999; La Porta *et al.*, 1998, 1999; Loredo and Suárez, 1998; Shleifer and Vishny, 1997; Thomsen and Pedersen, 1996).[1]

This chapter focuses on the question of whether globalization is reducing the diversity in corporate governance practices across countries or not. The effects of globalization on corporate governance have important social, economic, and political as well as managerial implications. Intuitively, globalization is a process related to increasing cross-border flows of goods, services, money, people, and information. Globalization appears to be associated with a disjunction of space and time (Giddens, 1990: 64, 1991: 21), a shrinking of the world (Harvey, 1989; Mittelman, 1996). The global economy – driven by increasing technological scale, alliances between firms, and information flows (Kobrin, 1997: 147–148) – is one "with the capacity to work as a unit in real time on a planetary scale" (Castells, 1996: 92). It is also one in which national economies become more interdependent in terms of trade, finance, and macroeconomic policy (Gilpin, 1987: 389).

While only a few skeptics doubt the existence of a process of globalization, there is little agreement as to what the consequences are (for reviews, see Guillén, 2001b; Waters, 1995). Some management scholars (Prahalad, 1997) and sociologists (Meyer *et al.*, 1997) argue that convergence in organizational patterns is taking place as a result of globalization. Other researchers see globalization as promoting diversity in the world as opposed to homogeneity (Guillén, 2001a,b; Macey and Miller, 1995). Among others, the argument is made that companies in different countries will tend to adopt corporate governance practices consistent with free capital markets and geared toward maximizing shareholder value. The increase in foreign direct and portfolio investment – with the concomitant rise of powerful multinational corporations and institutional investors – are commonly cited as pressures tending toward convergence. Companies and countries that do not bend to this trend are predicted to decline in terms of global competitiveness (Bishop, 1994; Charkham, 1995; Ibbotson and Brinson, 1993; Loredo and Suárez, 1998; OECD, 1998a; Useem, 1996). As recently as 1999, the World Bank and the OECD have joined forces to "improve global corporate governance practices" with the creation of the Global Corporate Governance Forum, an initiative that may increase the pressure on developing countries to reform their corporate governance systems, although it has thus far only recommended increasing transparency rather than uprooting long-standing practices (O'Sullivan, 1999; Sargent, 1999: 3).

Examining the impact of globalization on organizational patterns such as corporate governance systems is a delicate task because scholars do not agree as to when globalization started and to what extent it has made inroads (Guillén, 2001b). While some scholars date the beginning of globalization with the first circumnavigation of the Earth or the rise of the European-centered world economy in the early sixteenth century, others would rather wait until the turn of the twentieth century, World War II, the oil crises of the 1970s, the rise of Thatcher and Reagan, or even the collapse of the Soviet Union in 1989. This chapter focuses on trends in corporate governance since the mid-1970s. The proponents of the convergence thesis and its detractors coincide in observing that little convergence, if any, took place prior to 1973. Hence, they both focus on the rise in foreign trade, foreign direct investment, and cross-border portfolio investment since the late 1970s as factors potentially shaping corporate governance practices.

Surprisingly, the extant literature has not produced longitudinal evidence documenting changes in corporate governance practices for a number of countries large enough to tell whether there is convergence in the world or not. This chapter is the first to systematically compare the arguments for and against convergence in corporate governance, and to provide longitudinal empirical evidence on patterns of corporate governance for both rich and emerging countries. The chapter focuses on aggregate trends at the country level of analysis since the mid-1970s or the early 1980s (depending on the indicator) rather than on concrete events affecting specific companies. I start by presenting the arguments for and against convergence. Then I present longitudinal quantitative evidence, including the influence of foreign investment from different home countries, the presence of institutional investors, the distribution of listed corporate equity by type of shareholder, the debt-equity ratios of nonfinancial firms, the adoption of long-term incentives in CEO remuneration, and the occurrence of hostile takeovers. The evidence presented shows that little convergence has taken place since 1980 although some countries have adopted certain isolated features of the shareholder-centered model In the conclusion, I propose to intensify our research efforts on cross-national patterns of corporate governance from a comparative approach that takes national diversity and its consequences seriously into account.

ARGUMENTS FOR CONVERGENCE

Proponents of the "globalization thesis" about convergence in corporate governance systems see the rise of foreign direct and portfolio investment as a force tending toward homogeneity. However, they do not agree on the outcome of such a process of convergence. Some scholars and observers argue that globalization will cause corporate governance practices to converge on the American shareholder-centered model whereas others sustain that there will be convergence half way between the shareholder and stakeholder models. A third group of convergence proponents argues that it is hard to predict the final outcome of convergence. Let us analyze each argument in turn.

Convergence on the shareholder-centered model

Early students of corporate governance argued that secure shareholder rights and the sharp separation of (dispersed) ownership from (managerial) control were inevitably more "efficient" and "modern" than alternative models such as those underpinning family firms, conglomerates, bank-led groups, or worker cooperatives, and would accordingly become widespread (Berle and Means, 1932; Kerr *et al.*, 1964). These models developed historically in the United Kingdom and the United States, the two dominant world powers of the nineteenth and twentieth centuries, and spread to other countries that adopted English common law, largely the former colonies of the British Empire (La Porta *et al.*, 1998). Given the dominance of American business from the end of World War II to at least the 1970s, one would have expected the American corporate governance model – dispersed ownership, strong legal protection of shareholders and indifference to other stakeholders, little reliance on bank finance, relative freedom to merge or acquire – to have been adopted as the best practice throughout the world.

The globalization of financial investment and money-managing starting in the early 1980s has spurred another round of arguments predicting a convergence on the American model because it is based on market principles. Most financial experts and money managers would prefer companies throughout the world to observe shareholder rights, maximize shareholder value, and be transparent in their reporting of corporate activities and results (Useem, 1996). The rise of globally diversified mutual funds seems to create "pressures for the standardization of information on companies" (Ibbotson and Brinson, 1993: 321; see also Shleifer and Vishny, 1997: 757).[2]

Convergence on a hybrid model

A second group of convergence proponents seized on the rise of Germany and Japan as formidable manufacturing powers from the 1960s to the 1980s to argue that there is a trend toward a hybrid model combining features from both the shareholder and the stakeholder models (Fleming, 1998; OECD, 1998a). The OECD's report on corporate governance – written by six prominent managers or directors from the United States, France, Britain, Germany, and Japan – states that "as regulatory barriers between national economies fall and global competition for capital increases, investment capital will follow the path to those corporations that have adopted efficient governance standards . . . . Philosophical differences about the corporation's mission continue, although views appear to be converging" (1998a: 83). Unlike the first group of convergence proponents, however, the experts assembled by the OECD point out that convergence is not toward the US approach but toward a middle ground between the shareholder-and stakeholder-centered models.

The argument about convergence on a hybrid model is based on the premise that no single model is optimal along each and every dimension. "It is not productive to argue whether any system of governance is inherently superior to others . . . systems are 'path specific' " (OECD, 1995: 29). Therefore, this second group of convergence proponents argues that market forces will eventually encourage firms and countries to select features from existing models as they strive to remain competitive.

Convergence on an undefined model

The third group of proponents of convergence argues that it has become exceedingly difficult to predict whether the US model or a hybrid will ultimately predominate. Thus, Matthew Bishop, writing in 1994 for *The Economist* magazine, admits that "predicting trends in corporate governance is a tricky business. Five years ago the long-termism of the Japanese and Germans seemed the best course; and the turmoil caused by hostile bids in America and Britain seemed the opposite. Now things look different." After a detailed analysis of cross-national differences, Jonathan Charkham (1995: 363) leaves it up to the reader to decide which is the "best" model, assuming that the best or most efficient will eventually prevail.

ARGUMENTS AGAINST CONVERGENCE

There are at least three arguments in the extant literature that provide a rationale against the prediction that corporate governance practices are converging or will converge across countries. First, corporate governance systems are tightly coupled with path-dependent regulatory traditions in the areas of banking, labor, tax, and competition law that are unlikely to be modified in the near future. Second, corporate governance systems do not exist in isolation of other institutional features directly related to the ways in which firms formulate their strategy to compete in the global economy. Third, global pressures on corporate governance practices are mediated by domestic politics in ways that make convergence across countries rather unlikely.

The legal case against convergence

The legal argument against convergence in corporate governance notes that corporate law is intimately related not only to social custom but also to other legal areas, such as banking, labor, tax, and competition law. Such complex systems of laws and regulations evolve in a path-dependent way and are resistant to change (Bebchuk and Roe, 1999; Bühner et al., 1998). As Columbia law professor Mark Roe (1993) explains in detail, the American model of corporate governance emerged from a specific legal and law-making tradition prone to limiting the activities of banks, privileging managerial over worker rights, taxing the dividends obtained from cross-holdings of shares, and specifying tight constraints on collaborative arrangements between firms in the same industry. In Germany and Japan, by contrast, a different set of banking, labor, tax, and competition laws and regulations supports models of corporate governance that facilitate routine interactions between owners and managers, and extensive collaborative ties between financial institutions and firms or between firms themselves. In particular, executive compensation systems are unlikely to converge across countries because the tax treatment of perquisites, pension funds, and long-term incentives is so different. Similarly, the patterns of stockholding across different institutional actors such as financial intermediaries, nonfinancial firms, and households are also unlikely to converge because of competition and tax regulations specifying who can own what.

Economists La Porta, Lopez-de-Silanes, Shleifer, and Vishny argue in a series of influential papers (La Porta et al., 1998, 1999) that diversity in corporate governance around the world results from attempts

by stockholders to surmount poor legal investor protection (see also Bühner et al., 1998: 147, prop. 1). Thus, ownership concentration is a frequent way in which investors try to gain power in order to protect their interests. Using detailed data from nearly 50 countries, La Porta and colleagues (1998) identify four legal traditions – French (which includes the French, Spanish, and Portuguese spheres of colonial influence), German (Central Europe and Japan), Scandinavian, and Common Law (the former British colonies) – which help explain patterns of variation. Thus, legal traditions with relatively weak investor protection (German, Scandinavian, French) have more concentrated ownership than the common-law countries. In another paper, La Porta and colleagues (1999) establish that in 27 wealthy countries, both the largest 20 firms in terms of market capitalization and the 10 firms with capitalization just above $500 million do not tend to have dispersed ownership, but are under the control of families, the state, or financial institutions, in that order of importance (see also Guillén, 2001a: chap. 3; Orrù et al., 1997).

Like La Porta and colleagues, Roe (1993: 1989) concludes that "the American governance structure is not inevitable, that alternatives are plausible, and that a flatter authority structure does not disable foreign firms." Rather than using agency costs or contract theory or judicial doctrine to explain this or that feature as mitigating or reflecting managerial deviation from the maximization of shareholders' wealth, he continues, "we must consider the role of politics, history, and culture" (1993: 1997). To those variables now we turn.

The institutional case against convergence

An institutional approach indicates that it is futile to attempt identifying the best practice or model in the abstract (Guillén, 1994; Whitley, 1992, 1999). Rather, countries and their firms are socially and institutionally equipped to follow different competitive strategies in the global economy. One such institutional equipment is the pattern of corporate governance prevalent in the country, which facilitates specific competitive strategies and temporal orientations (Bebchuk and Roe, 1999; Bühner et al., 1998; Kester, 1996; Kim and Hoskisson, 1996; Lazonick and O'Sullivan, 1996).

Thus, German, French, Japanese, and American firms are justly famous for their competitive edge, albeit following different strategies for different industries and market segments that are closely intertwined with their corporate governance systems. Germany's educational and industrial institutions – dual-apprenticeship system, management-union cooperation, dual-board corporate governance system, and tradition of hands-on engineering or *Technik* – enable companies to excel in high-quality, engineering-intensive industries such as advanced machine tools, luxury automobiles, and specialty chemicals. The participation of labor on the supervisory boards of German corporations is a key mechanism compelling firms to look for smart ways of employing the skills of their expensive though extremely productive and sophisticated workers (Hollingsworth *et al.*, 1994; Murmann, 1998; Soskice, 1998; Streeck, 1991, 1995). The French model of elite engineering education has enabled firms to excel at large-scale technical undertakings such as high-speed trains, satellite-launching rockets, or nuclear power. French boards of directors tend to span the private and state-owned sectors of the economy, which play a key role in those industries (Storper and Salais, 1997: 131–148; Ziegler, 1995, 1997). The Japanese institutional ability to borrow, improve, and integrate ideas and technologies from various sources allows its companies to master most categories of assembled goods such as household appliances, consumer electronics, and automobiles (Cusumano, 1985; Dore, 1973; Westney, 1987). In order to do so Japanese corporations rely on the stability and close ties afforded to them by the *keiretsu* structure of corporate governance (Gerlach, 1992; Kim and Hoskisson, 1996). Last, the American cultural emphasis on individualism, entrepreneurship, and customer satisfaction enables her firms to become world-class competitors in goods or services that are intensive in people skills, knowledge, or venture capital, such as software, financial services, or biotechnology (Porter, 1990; Storper and Salais, 1997: 174–188). Undoubtedly, the capital market driven, shareholder-centered model of corporate governance fits this situation best.

Sociologists and political scientists have long noted the strong association between the stakeholder-centered model of corporate governance and social-democratic policymaking in Central European countries with extensive welfare states and strong labor market institutions (Hollingsworth *et al.*, 1991; Soskice, 1998; Streeck, 1991, 1995). It is important to underline that most of the empirical evidence available demonstrates that this alternative is viable, even in the face of globalization. Noting the association between openness to the global economy and the size of the state, and using cross-national data for the advanced industrial democracies since 1960, Geoffrey Garrett (1998: 1–2, 11, 107, 132–133, 157–158) empirically demonstrates the viability of social-democratic policymaking even with increasing exposure to globalization in the forms of cross-border trade and capital mobility. He also proves that it is possible to win elections with redistributive and interventionist policies, and that better economic performance in terms of GDP growth and unemployment is obtained, though with higher inflation than in the *laissez-faire* countries (United States, Britain). Garrett (1998: 157) concludes that "big government is compatible with strong macroeconomic performance," and that markets do not dominate politics.

Political scientist Evelyne Huber and sociologist John Stephens (1999) advance an interesting argument about the linkage between the stakeholder-centered view of the firm and macroeconomic policies and performance. They begin by noting that countries with generous welfare states have generally done at least as well as countries with less generous welfare states in terms of unemployment and economic growth. They maintain that a configuration of mutually consistent and reinforcing generous welfare state programs and coordinated production regimes (high union density, low wage dispersion, active worker participation in the governance of the firm) allow countries to compete in world markets on the basis of high wages and high-quality products – the so-called "high road" to international competitiveness (see also Hollingsworth *et al.*, 1991; Soskice, 1998; Streeck, 1991, 1995).

One finds a similar diversity of patterns among newly industrialized countries in Asia, Latin America, and Southern Europe. The distribution of organizational forms and corporate governance systems across these countries has grown more diverse over time, not less. In some countries cooperatives and small family firms thrive (Spain, Taiwan), while in others it is large business groups that predominate (Korea, Indonesia, Mexico, Turkey). Institutional scholars have documented with case studies and systematic quantitative evidence that organizations and patterns of corporate control diverge as countries develop and become more embedded in the global economy (Aguilera, 1998; Biggart and Guillén, 1999; Guillén, 2001a; Orrù *et al.*, 1996). Moreover, such diversity is related in complex ways to each country's role in the global economy. Korea has made a dent in international competition in a way that is intimately related to the indigenous patterns of social organization and corporate governance underpinning the rise of large, capital-intensive, and diversified conglomerates known as *chaebol*. Thus, the Koreans export mass-produced automobiles, consumer electronics, chemicals, and steel. The Taiwanese *guanxiquiye* networks of small family firms, by contrast, are thriving in the global economy on the basis of their adaptability and flexibility. Taiwan is known for its exports of machine tools, auto parts, and electronic components. And the Spanish worker-owned cooperatives and family firms have succeeded by leveraging relationships with foreign multinationals and managing not to fall prey to the lending practices of the country's all powerful banks. They are known internationally for their components and branded consumer products (Guillén, 2001a; Orrù *et al.*, 1996).

The institutional approach to the study of trends in corporate governance is useful to understand why the empirical literature has thus far failed to establish a clear link between corporate governance and economic performance using conventional multiple regression techniques. Quantitative studies have reported that differences in corporate governance across advanced industrial economies are not significantly associated with differences in financial or sales performance at the company level, after controlling for industry and firm size (Thomsen and Pedersen, 1996). Other researchers have found no evidence that differences in corporate governance systems affect GDP growth over the long run (La Porta *et al.*, 1998). One may interpret these results as proof that corporate governance does not matter for economic performance. A second possibility is, however, that the different corporate governance systems enable firms and countries to excel at different kinds of activities in the global economy. The institutional argument against convergence would support such an interpretation.

The political case against convergence

The third counterargument about corporate governance and globalization observes that economic and financial globalization are shaped and contested by political interests. The literature on the diffusion of corporate governance and organizational forms in general is replete with detailed studies of how domestic political conditions affect outcomes (Djelic, 1998;

Fligstein, 1990; Orrù *et al.*, 1996). Domestic politics mediate in the relationship between external trends or shocks and outcomes. There is no a priori theoretical reason why the impact of globalization on corporate governance should be any different, as scholars (Macey and Miller, 1995; O'Sullivan, 1999) and policymakers (Binns, 1998) have recognized.

Examples from the vast literature on the historical transformation of corporations and corporate governance suffice to make the point. Djelic (1998) provides compelling historical evidence that, under pressure from Marshall planners and advisors, German and French politicians, industrialists, and labor leaders resisted the direct implementation of American corporate governance and industrial organization blueprints during the 1950s. Domestic actors were able to shape and mold American models to their own goals and priorities. Outcomes also depended on the mutual accommodations found by governments, employers, and unions. Guillén (1994) analyzes how domestic coercive and normative factors affected the transfer of models of management throughout the twentieth century, with no one country adopting a given model for the same reasons or with similar outcomes. Aguilera (1998) notes that even most similar cases such as Spain and Italy have diverged considerably over time because of regulatory and policy choices made a long time ago, whose effects endure because actors become entrenched in them.

Even in the United States, trends and changes in corporate governance have typically taken place in the midst of fierce political battles. Fligstein (1990) documents how the transitions from the manufacturing to the marketing and to the financial conceptions of corporate control over the twentieth century were punctuated by political and legislative struggles. A raging debate erupted in the 1990s between, on the one hand, managers, economists, and legal experts celebrating the efficiency of the separation of ownership from control (Easterbrook and Fischel, 1991; Romano, 1993), and, on the other, institutional investors and economists charging that the system is deeply flawed because it gives managers way too much discretion (Jensen, 1993). The outcome of this struggle is yet to be determined (O'Sullivan, 1999; Useem, 1996) as American managers and boards reacted to the rise of institutional investors and financial deregulation with a mixture of defensive measures (e.g. poison pills) and adaptive actions (e.g. managerial incentives). What seems clear is that top managers have both been harmed and benefited by this struggle. Although the rate of CEO forced succession has increased, average CEO compensation was in 1999 roughly 419 times greater than for the average manufacturing worker, up from a multiple of 44 in 1965 (O'Sullivan, 1999).

The data and analysis by La Porta and colleagues (1998, 1999) provide further credence to the argument that political forces will shape and perhaps derail the homogenizing effects of globalization. They argue that the internationalization of capital markets is not enough to unsettle the existing ownership structures, which are "primarily an equilibrium response to the domestic legal environments that companies operate in" (La Porta *et al.*, 1999: 512). Given that concentrated ownership produces a centralization of power, La Porta and colleagues (1999: 513) are "skeptical about the imminence of convergence of corporate ownership patterns, and of governance systems more generally, to the Berle and Means model."

The creation of the single market among the European Union (EU) member countries illustrates how politics mediate in the relationship between globalization pressures and corporate governance outcomes. The process of European integration has so far failed to generate enough momentum to bring about a convergence in corporate governance laws and practices. In a revealing paper, Lannoo (1999: 270) observes that European legislators have fought "very hard" over the last 25 *years* "to bring some harmonization to standards for corporate control in the EU," but that their efforts have been thwarted by "irresolvable disagreements among member states". Instead, he maintains, "either industry or the European Commission should take the initiative to come up with a European-wide code of best practice, in the light of the improbability that any significant harmonization of corporate governance standards will occur at the European level." However, Susan Binns (1998), of the European Commission, notes that researchers are "still searching for economic evidence that one approach [to corporate governance] produces better results than another," and concludes that it is better to leave "these issues for regulation at the national level," albeit avoiding "too much divergence in national rules and practices."

Systems in which banks are successful players in corporate governance are unlikely to evolve toward the market-based system if only because banking interests will be opposed (O'Sullivan, 1999). Quantitative research on banking suggests that universal banks active in all sorts of financial services from commercial banking to investment banking and stock trading – a key component of the German corporate governance system – achieve "a better risk-return trade-off, due to superior monitoring and information collection capacity" than banks in market-based financial systems such as the American or the British (Steinherr and Huveneers, 1994: 271). It is not unusual for universal banks to be among the best managed and most profitable in the world, even when shareholders' return is the performance measure (Guillén, 2001a: chap. 7; Guillén and Tschoegl, 1999; *The Banker*, July 1998: 20). Scholars arguing against convergence observe that if universal banks with strong ties to industry are so profitable in some countries they are unlikely to implement reforms detrimental to their interests.

CONVERGENCE OF CORPORATE GOVERNANCE SYSTEMS: THE EVIDENCE

Data

A key problem besetting the cross-national study of corporate governance is the dearth of empirical indicators for the relevant dimensions. Table 1 summarizes the indicators used by selected cross-national studies to capture differences in corporate governance. Previous studies vary in terms of the range of indicators used, the nature of the indicator (quantitative or qualitative), and the number of countries included. With the only exception of the recent papers by La Porta and colleagues (1998, 1999) and Shleifer and Vishny (1997), the extant literature on cross-national corporate governance practices is generally based on evidence drawn from a small number of countries. Moreover, previous studies tend to rely on qualitative indicators to a much greater extent than quantitative ones. No previous study has provided longitudinal indicators of the various dimensions of corporate governance.

The choice of empirical indicators for this chapter was based on three criteria. First, the previous literature was consulted to develop a list of relevant aspects and indicators capturing the multidimensional character of corporate governance (see Table 1). Second, only indicators that speak to the tenets of the globalization thesis about convergence in corporate governance, and to the legal, institutional, and political cases against convergence were considered. Third, only

Dimension	Useem (1984)	Charkham (1995)	Shleifer and Vishny (1997)	La Porta et al. (1998, 1999)	Bühner et al. (1998)	OECD (1998a)	Loredo and Suárez (1998)	O'Sullivan (1999)	Guillén (2000)
Ownership structure	—	Yes	Yes	Yes*	Yes*	Yes	—	Yes*	Yes*
Impact of foreign investment	—	—	—	—	—	—	—	—	Yes*
Role of the banks	—	—	Yes	—	Yes	—	—	Yes	Yes*
Role of institutional investors	—	Yes	Yes	—	—	Yes	—	Yes*	Yes*
Role and nature of the board of directors	Yes	Yes	—	Yes	Yes	Yes	Yes*	—	—
Interlocking directors	Yes*	Yes	—	—	Yes	—	—	—	—
CEO pay components	—	—	—	—	—	—	—	—	Yes*
Market for corporate control (hostile takeovers)	—	—	Yes	—	Yes	—	—	—	Yes*
Number of countries	2	5	4	27–49	3	14	8	3	6–43

Table 1 Dimensions of corporate governance in selected cross-national empirical studies.

Note
* Quantitative indicator used.

quantitative indicators available for at least two points in time were included.

Six indicators met these criteria. The first two assess to what extent pressures toward convergence on the Anglo-Saxon model are present. The first indicator is the stock of foreign direct investment by firms under the influence of various corporate governance systems in their home countries, while the second is the presence of institutional investors in each country, which measures pressures toward convergence on a transparent and shareholder-friendly model like the Anglo-Saxon system. The remaining four indicators capture specific dimensions of corporate governance as reflected in the extant literature: the proportion of listed corporate equity held by different types of shareholders, which gives an indication of the various groups with a claim on the corporation; the balance between debt and equity financing struck by nonfinancial firms, which speaks to the influence of banks in corporations; the adoption of long-term incentives in CEO remuneration, which is indicative of attempts by shareholders to align the interest of the CEO with their own; and the occurrence of hostile takeovers, which indicates the existence of a market for corporate control. These six indicators cover essential dimensions of corporate governance as identified in the existing empirical literature (Table 1). Unfortunately, data on two of the dimensions reflected in Table 1 – the role and nature of the board of directors and the prevalence of interlocking directors – are not available for a sufficiently large number of countries and for at least two points in time.

It is also important to note two further features of the data. First, they are always aggregated at the national level of analysis, which may conceal some interesting within-national differences. For example, not all firms in Japan find themselves under the governance structure of a *keiretsu*, and not all German companies have a bank as a main shareholder. Second, given that measurement of the various dimensions was performed independently, convergence of corporate governance may be assessed for each dimension individually, without assuming that all dimensions have to evolve in unison.

The tabular data are presented for individual countries grouped · according to the legal tradition underpinning its corporate governance system. The influential classification developed by La Porta and colleagues (1998) was followed to group countries. It distinguishes among the Anglo-Saxon, French, German, and Scandinavian legal traditions. Taken together, these four categories account for virtually every capitalist country in the world. Classifying countries in groups of legal traditions facilitates assessing the evidence presented. In particular it makes it easier to see if trends over time are toward convergence or divergence.

Results

The globalization thesis argues that the spread of foreign multinationals will force a convergence of corporate governance models. While it may be true that multinationals are a homogenizing force, it is not at all clear why it should produce a worldwide convergence of corporate governance on the American model as opposed to another model or a hybrid. The reason is that the impact of foreign investment originating from countries with an Anglo-Saxon legal tradition and a shareholder-centered corporate governance system is waning. Table 2 presents some telling statistics. Following La Porta and colleagues' (1998) classification of countries in terms of legal tradition, it turns out that the proportion of the world's stock of outward foreign investment accounted for by the Anglo-Saxon countries is *falling*, from 66 percent in 1980 to just over 50 percent in 1997. Meanwhile, the combined shares of the countries influenced by the German, French, or Scandinavian legal traditions has grown from 34 to 49 percent over the same time period. It seems, therefore, that if there is convergence in corporate governance it may not be on the shareholder-centered model characteristic of the

Country	Foreign direct investment outward stock (% of world total)	
	1980	1997
Anglo-Saxon legal tradition	65.57	49.55
Australia	0.43	1.48
Canada	4.53	3.89
Hong Kong	0.03	3.88
India	0.00	0.02
Ireland	—	0.16
Israel	0.01	0.16
Malaysia	0.08	0.44
New Zealand	0.25	0.19
Nigeria	0.00	0.36
Pakistan	0.01	0.01
Singapore	1.84	1.23
South Africa	1.09	0.34
Thailand	0.00	0.11
United Kingdom	15.33	11.67
United States	41.97	25.63
French legal tradition	15.58	21.07
Argentina	0.01	0.03
Belgium	1.15	2.72
Brazil	0.12	0.25
Chile	0.01	0.16
Colombia	0.03	0.04
Egypt	0.01	0.01
France	4.50	6.40
Greece	—	0.02
Indonesia	—	0.12
Italy	1.40	3.53
Mexico	0.03	0.09
Netherlands	8.03	6.02
Peru	0.00	0.00
Philippines	0.03	0.03
Portugal	0.02	0.15
Spain	0.23	1.38
Turkey	—	0.01
Venezuela	0.00	0.10
German legal tradition	16.20	23.57
Austria	0.10	0.42
Germany	8.22	9.21
Japan	3.74	8.04
South Korea	0.03	0.51
Switzerland	4.10	4.43
Taiwan	0.02	0.97
Scandinavian legal tradition	1.96	4.32
Denmark	0.39	0.73
Finland	0.14	0.57
Norway	0.36	0.91
Sweden	1.07	2.11
Total four legal traditions	99.31	98.51
World Outward FDI Stock ($bn)	524.6	3,541.4

Table 2 The origin of foreign direct investment by type of home-country corporate legal tradition, 1980 and 1997.

Source: UNCTD (1998); La Porta *et al.* (1998: 1130–1131).

United Kingdom or the United States but rather on some kind of hybrid.

Also contrary to the predictions of the globalization thesis, institutional investors such as insurance companies, pension funds, and investment companies have a very unequal presence across countries. Moreover, the differences across countries are growing, not shrinking. Table 3 presents the available data for over 20 rich countries plus Mexico, South Korea, the Czech Republic, Hungary, and Poland. The influence of institutional investors – as measured by their financial assets held in shares of companies as a percentage of GDP – is the highest in the United Kingdom (at 112 percent), followed by the United States (62 percent; see Useem, 1996), and a handful of relatively small countries within the 30–50 percent range (Australia, Netherlands, Switzerland, and Sweden). Most countries shown in the table have ratios below 20 percent, and over half of them do not even reach 10 percent. Between 1990 and 1995 the influence of institutional investors barely grew in many countries (Greece, Italy, Portugal, Spain, Austria, Germany, Norway), and actually decreased in a few others (Mexico, Turkey, Japan, South Korea). Overall, differences in the presence of institutional investors across countries are widening, as revealed by the standard deviations, which have increased from 41 to 48 in the case of total financial assets, and from 16 to 26 in the case of assets held in shares.

Patterns of stockholding are proving to be remarkably resilient. Table 4 presents the breakdown for countries belonging to each of the four legal traditions. The Anglo-Saxon tradition differs sharply from the German and Scandinavian ones. Moreover, the differences are not getting smaller over time. It is only in the case of France that one observes a clear shift toward a greater presence of institutional investors, but this is coming at the expense not of banks but of households. Thus, large stockholders (banks and other financial institutions, and nonfinancial firms) continue to be the norm in countries whose legal tradition does not protect shareholder rights above and beyond those of other stakeholders. As hypothesized by La Porta and colleagues (1998, 1999) and Bühner and colleagues (1998: 147, prop. 1), large organizational actors are major shareholders in countries that did not adopt the common law provisions of the Anglo-Saxon tradition.

The role of banks as providers of funds to industry is another key aspect in which countries differ from one another. Figure 1 presents the debt-equity ratios of nonfinancial firms over the last three decades. Only the trend lines for such small countries as Austria, Belgium, Finland, and Norway show a convergence on the Anglo-Saxon pattern of relatively balanced debt and equity. German, Italian, Japanese, South Korean, and French nonfinancial firms show few signs of convergence over the last two decades. Figure 2 shows the unweighted means and standard deviations for each year between 1975 and 1995. Mean debt-equity ratios dropped during the mid-1980s from about 270 to about 160 percent, and the standard deviation from 160 to 100 percent, approximately. Since 1987, however, neither the mean nor the standard deviation have dropped any further in spite of the rapid increase in trade, foreign direct investment, and capital mobility across borders. Thus, there is little evidence that the patterns of financing by nonfinancial firms are changing as a result of globalization.

In the shareholder-centered model of corporate governance, there is a tendency to introduce incentives to align the interests of the managers with those of the shareholders. The adoption of long-term incentives to encourage CEOs to maximize shareholder wealth is extremely heterogeneous across countries. Not surprisingly, only the Anglo-Saxon countries have a strong tendency to use such incentives (Table 5). Among those in the French legal tradition, only France, Brazil, and the Netherlands have adopted such incentives. In the case of France, O'Sullivan (1999) reports that CEOs, and not shareholders or directors, are behind the adoption. Countries in the German or Scandinavian legal traditions remain oblivious to the trend toward long-term incentives in CEO pay, although there are indications that shareholders are reasserting their influence (O'Sullivan, 1999). As with the presence of institutional investors, differences in the use of long-term incentives have grown slightly between 1988 and 1998, as revealed by the increase in the standard deviation.

Perhaps the clearest indicator that corporate governance models are not converging has to do with the market for corporate control. The shareholder-centered model has historically been more susceptible to hostile takeover activity. During the 1980s shareholder activism and financial deregulation in the United States and United Kingdom contributed to a sharp rise in hostile takeovers (O'Sullivan, 1999;

Country	Total financial assets (% GDP)		Financial assets held in shares (% GDP)	
	1990	1995	1990	1995
Anglo-Saxon legal tradition				
Australia	47.5	75.9	18.5	38.0
Canada	58.6	87.9	11.7	21.1
United Kingdom	114.5	162.3	75.6	112.0
United States	127.4	170.8	29.3	61.5
French legal tradition				
Belgium[a]	44.8	59.4	8.5	11.3
France	52.9	75.3	11.6	16.6
Greece[b]	6.5	23.0	0.7	1.4
Italy	13.3	20.6	2.1	3.5
Mexico[c]	8.6	3.9	1.4	0.8
Netherlands	133.4	158.4	18.7	36.4
Portugal[d]	9.2	35.3	0.2	2.5
Spain[e]	16.3	38.3	1.8	2.3
Turkey	0.6	0.7	0.1	0.0
German legal tradition				
Austria[f]	24.5	35.2	1.2	3.2
Germany	36.5	46.1	3.3	5.5
Japan	81.7	77.4	18.8	13.9
South Korea	48.1	57.7	9.1	7.5
Switzerland[g]	120.2	78.1	19.2	39.1
Scandinavian legal tradition				
Denmark	57.4	66.8	11.5	18.7
Finland	33.2	50.0	5.6	10.0
Norway	36.0	42.6	5.0	6.8
Sweden	85.7	114.8	24.0	40.2
Transition economies				
Czech Republic[h]	—	24.0	—	11.5
Hungary	—	4.5	—	0.1
Poland[i]	—	1.6	—	0.4
Unweighted mean[j]	52.59	67.30	12.63	20.56
Standard deviation[j]	41.31	47.85	16.46	26.37

Table 3 Financial assets of institutional investors (insurance companies, pension funds, and investment companies).

Source: OECD, *Institutional Investors: Statistical Yearbook* 1997.

Notes
a Exc. pension funds in 1995.   b Exc. insurance and investment companies.
c Exc. pension funds.   d Exc. insurance companies in 1995.
e Exc. non-autonomous pension funds.   f Exc. pension funds in 1990.
g Exc. pension funds in 1995.   h 1994 data for 1995.
i Exc. pension funds for 1995.   j Exc. the transition economies.

Table 4 Listed corporate equity by type of shareholder (in percentages).

Type of shareholder	USA			UK[c]			Germany			France			Sweden		Japan[d]		
	1986	1993	1996	1976	1993	1996	1985	1993	1996	1982	1993	1996	1993	1996	1983	1993	1996
Households	51	49	49	28	18	21	17	17	15	38	19	23	16	19	27	24	20
Financial sector	51	46	47	60	61	68	15	29	30	24	8	30	23	30	42	44	42
Banks	—	—	6	—	1	1	—	14	10	—	3	7	1	1	—	22	15
Pension funds[a]	—	31	28	—	51	50	—	7	12	—	1	9	8	14	—	18	12
Investment funds[b]	—	11	12	—	7	8	—	8	8	—	2	11	14	15	—	3	-
Other financial firms	—	4	1	—	2	9	—	-	-	—	2	3	-	-	—	1	15
Nonfinancial firms	15	-	-	5	2	1	51	39	42	22	59	19	34	11	25	24	27
State	0	-	-	3	1	1	10	4	4	0	4	2	7	8	0	1	1
Foreign	6	5	5	4	16	9	8	12	9	16	11	25	9	32	5	7	11
Other	-	-	-	-	2	-	-	-	-	-	-	-	10	-	-	-	-
Total	100	100	100	100	100	100	100	100	100	100	100	100	100	100	100	100	100

Source: OECD (1995: 17, 1998b: 16); Berglof (1988).

Notes

- not applicable.

— not available.

a Includes insurance companies.

b Includes mutual funds.

c UK figures are for end of 1994 instead of the end of 1996.

d For Japan, pension and investment funds are included under other financial institutions.

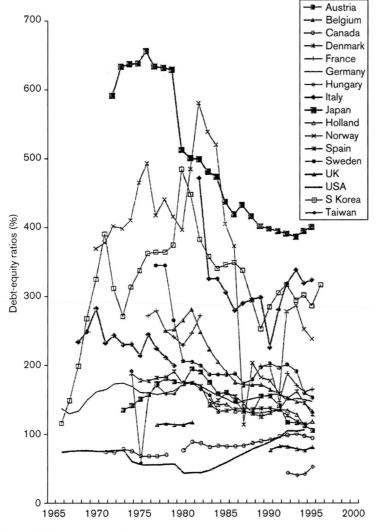

Figure 1 Debt-equity ratios for nonfinancial firms.

OECD, 1998b). The occurrence of hostile takeovers, however, is not a worldwide phenomenon, but one largely confined to the Anglo-Saxon countries, both in terms of targets and acquirers (Table 6). Companies in the United States and United Kingdom alone accounted for 94 percent of worldwide hostile targets in terms of transaction value in 1980–1989, and 79 percent in 1990–1998. American and British acquirers were responsible for roughly 80 percent of worldwide hostile takeovers during the 1980s and 1990s.

Among countries in legal traditions other than the Anglo-Saxon, only France stands out for its relatively high (and rising) level of hostile takeover activity targeting its companies. French companies, however, have become less likely to launch hostile bids. Italian, German, Norwegian, and Swedish acquirers have become more active in the 1990s than in the 1980s, but their absolute level of activity is still very low compared to the Anglo-Saxon countries, even after the decline of hostile activity in the United States and the United Kingdom during the 1990s. Hostile takeover activity remains stagnant at relatively low levels or has decreased in such countries as the Netherlands, Spain, Switzerland, and Japan, and even in some countries influenced by the Anglo-Saxon tradition, for example, Ireland and Malaysia. The rest of the world remains largely unaffected by hostile takeovers. Compared to the 1980s, differences across

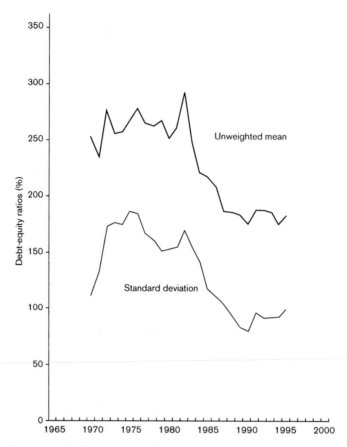

Figure 2 Mean and standard deviation of debt-equity ratios, selected countries, 1975–1995.

countries in the incidence of hostile takeovers have dropped slightly during the 1990s (from a standard deviation of 11.74 to 9.60), but remained approximately the same in terms of the home country of the acquirer firm.

DISCUSSION

The literature on corporate governance and globalization contains important theoretical disagreements. Scholars, however, have found very little evidence suggesting convergence. Except for the cases of France and, to a lesser extent, Belgium, the Netherlands, and the Scandinavian countries, there are no discernible shifts in stockholding, debt-equity ratios, long-term incentives in CEO pay, or hostile takeovers. Moreover, changes in the composition of foreign direct investment suggest that if there is convergence, it may not be on the shareholder-centered model but on a hybrid. One should keep in mind, however, that the trend toward globalization will continue and that it may be too early to tell the extent to which national corporate governance models are resistant to it. At any rate, it seems safe to conclude that, given the trends over the last 20 years, the wholesale convergence of corporate governance systems across countries is unlikely in the near future. Convergence along selected aspects or dimensions is more likely, although it has thus far affected only a handful of countries.

The lack of convergence in indicators of corporate governance in the face of growing globalization is consistent with the findings of previous studies focusing on other economic and organizational variables. The varieties of capitalism research tradition in

Country	Long-term incentives as % of total remuneration		
	1988	1993	1998
Anglo-Saxon legal tradition			
Australia	0	1	2
Canada	14	16	14
Hong Kong	0	0	12
Malaysia	—	—	12
New Zealand	—	—	0
Singapore	0	0	12
South Africa	—	—	10
United Kingdom	15	15	17
United States	28	34	36
French legal tradition			
Belgium	0	0	6
Brazil	0	0	11
France	15	16	14
Italy	0	4	6
Mexico	0	0	0.1
Netherlands	0	0	9
Spain	0	0	0
Venezuela	0	0	0
German legal tradition			
Germany	0	0	0
Japan	0	0	0
South Korea	0	—	0
Switzerland	1	4	3
Scandinavian legal tradition			
Sweden	0	0	0
Unweighted mean[a]	4.06	5.00	7.89
Standard deviation[a]	8.17	9.32	9.17

Table 5 Long-term incentives in CEO pay.

Source: Towers Perrin, *Worldwide Total Remuneration*, various years.

Note
a Excludes countries with missing data, that is, Malaysia, New Zealand, South Africa, and South Korea.

political science has contributed innumerable case studies and quantitative analyses demonstrating that, in spite of globalization, there is little convergence in terms of economic policymaking across countries (Garrett, 1998, 1999; Hollingsworth *et al.*, 1991; Soskice, 1998; Streeck, 1991, 1995). Comparative organizational sociologists have also presented qualitative and quantitative evidence to the effect that firms pursue different modes of economic action and adopt different organizational forms depending on the institutional and social structures of their home countries even as globalization increases (Biggart and Guillén, 1999; Guillén, 2001a; Orrù *et al.*, 1996). Taken together, the empirical evidence provided by sociologists and political scientists supports well the case for diversity, or at least resilience, in cross-national organizational patterns in the midst of globalization. This chapter adds to this growing body of comparative literature by documenting little convergence in patterns of corporate governance even with growing globalization. As Thomsen and Pedersen (1996) observe, there is no clear relationship between differences in corporate governance and differences in firm-level performance across countries. These findings invite further theoretical work to specify how exactly corporate governance practices affect firm strategy, and, in turn, how differences in strategy due to corporate governance translate into levels of performance. As the extant literature suggests, future theoretical work may aim at conceptualizing how different governance practices enable firms to pursue different strategies leading to comparable levels of high performance in the global economy (Bühner *et al.*, 1998; Kim and Hoskisson, 1996; Lazonick and O'Sullivan, 1996).

The absence of discernible convergence as a result of globalization invites a reconsideration of the effects of increasing cross-border economic activities. The social science literature on globalization provides two useful ways of addressing this apparent problem. First, the reason why globalization does not seem to produce convergence in corporate governance may have to do with the fact that increasing economic exchange across borders does not necessarily force actors to adopt similar patterns of behavior. Social scientists have underlined that what is perhaps most distinctive about globalization is that it intensifies our consciousness of the world as a whole, making us more aware of each other, and perhaps more prone to be influenced by one another, although not necessarily more like each other (Albrow, 1997: 88; Guillén, 2001a; Robertson, 1992: 8; Waters, 1995: 63).

The second way to better understand the effects of globalization on an organizational variable is to reconsider the nature of globalization itself, without denying its existence. A variety of social scientists have argued

Country	Transaction value (% of world total)			
	Targets		Acquirers	
	1980–1989	1990–1998	1980–1989	1990–1998
Anglo-Saxon legal tradition	96.9	89.0	90.4	88.4
Australia	1.5	2.6	2.9	2.1
Canada	1.1	6.1	4.6	4.9
Hong Kong	0.3	0.8	0.2	0.0
India	0.0	0.0	0.0	0.0
Ireland	0.1	0.2	0.0	0.2
Israel	0.0	0.0	0.0	0.0
Malaysia	0.1	0.1	0.1	0.1
New Zealand	0.0	0.1	0.0	0.4
Nigeria	0.0	0.0	0.0	0.0
Pakistan	0.0	0.0	0.0	0.0
Singapore	0.0	0.1	0.0	0.1
South Africa	0.0	0.1	0.0	0.2
Thailand	0.0	0.0	0.0	0.0
United Kingdom	18.4	18.2	18.6	17.5
United States	75.3	60.7	63.9	63.0
French legal tradition	2.1	6.5	5.0	6.5
Argentina	0.0	0.0	0.0	0.0
Belgium	0.0	0.0	0.0	0.1
Brazil	0.0	0.0	0.0	0.0
Chile	0.0	0.0	0.0	0.0
Colombia	0.0	0.0	0.0	0.0
Egypt	0.0	0.0	0.0	0.0
France	1.9	5.4	2.9	3.6
Greece	0.0	0.0	0.0	0.0
Indonesia	0.0	0.0	0.0	0.0
Italy	0.0	0.7	0.3	2.5
Mexico	0.0	0.0	0.1	0.0
Netherlands	0.1	0.0	1.6	0.1
Peru	0.0	0.0	0.0	0.0
Philippines	0.0	0.0	0.0	0.0
Portugal	0.0	0.2	0.0	0.2
Spain	0.0	0.1	0.0	0.1
Turkey	0.0	0.0	0.0	0.0
Venezuela	0.0	0.0	0.0	0.0
German legal tradition	0.7	2.1	2.7	3.1
Austria	0.0	0.1	0.0	0.1
Germany	0.2	1.8	0.2	2.2
Japan	0.5	0.0	0.4	0.0
South Korea	0.0	0.0	0.0	0.1
Switzerland	0.0	0.1	2.1	0.7
Taiwan	0.0	0.0	0.0	0.3

(*Continued*)

Country	Transaction value (% of world total)			
	Targets		Acquirers	
	1980–1989	1990–1998	1980–1989	1990–1998
Scandinavian legal tradition	0.1	1.3	0.3	1.1
Denmark	0.0	0.0	0.0	0.0
Finland	0.0	0.1	0.0	0.0
Norway	0.0	0.6	0.0	0.4
Sweden	0.1	0.6	0.2	0.7
Unweighted mean	2.32	2.30	2.28	2.32
Standard deviation	11.74	9.60	10.06	9.88
World total (million $)	805,440	423,652	805,440	423,652

Table 6 Announced hostile corporate takeovers.

Source: SDC Platinum (Securities Data Company).

Note: Dollar figures have been adjusted for inflation using the US's GDP deflator (1992 = 100).

and documented with empirical evidence that globalization is far from being a uniform process or an inexorable trend. Rather, it seems to be a more fragmented, incomplete, discontinuous, and contingent process than the proponents of convergence generally admit because it affects different sectors of the economy and regions of the world in different ways and to different degrees (Hirst and Thompson, 1996). Social and political theorists as well as historians and anthropologists have elaborated a comprehensive theoretical and empirical critique of the presumed convergent consequences of globalization that may provide the foundation for a better understandings of its impact on cross-national organizational patterns (Albrow, 1997: 86, 144, 149, 189; Cox, 1996: 28, 30 n. 1; Friedman, 1994: 210–211; Giddens, 1990: 64, 175, 1991: 21–22; McMichael, 1996: 177, 190–197, 234–235; Mazlish, 1993: 4; Robertson, 1992: 27, 145).

CONCLUSION: TOWARD A COMPARATIVE ANALYSIS OF CORPORATE GOVERNANCE

The three arguments against convergence in corporate governance – legal, institutional, political – provide enough reason to cast serious doubt on the idea that there is convergence in corporate governance, whether on the shareholder-centered model or a hybrid. Globalization seems to encourage countries and firms to be different, to look for a distinctive way to make a dent in international competition rather than to converge on a best model. In a global context, corporate governance must support what a country and its firms can do best in the global economy. Globalization seems not to be about convergence to best practice, but rather about leveraging difference in an increasingly borderless world. This argument and the empirical findings reported in this chapter are consistent with previous research on how different corporate governance systems enable firms to pursue different strategies (Bühner et al., 1998; Kester, 1996; Lazonick and O'Sullivan, 1996).

The complexity of both globalization and corporate governance certainly invites additional research. We are in great need of further theoretical work to clarify how corporate governance affects competitiveness and the well-being of various groups in society. We also need better data and on more countries. Better indicators will facilitate making comparisons on specific dimensions as opposed to looking for wholesale convergence of entire corporate governance systems. Given the infancy of our efforts to understand the impact of globalization on corporate governance, it seems sensible to ask for more studies using a comparative approach. We need to engage in comparative work in the dual sense of using multiple methods of data collection and analysis, and of applying our theoretical and empirical tools to a variety of research settings defined at various levels of analysis

(Cheng, 1989, 1994a,b; Skocpol, 1984; Smelser, 1976; Tilly, 1984). The differences and similarities across such settings ought to give us a handle on the patterns according to which the effects of globalization change from one setting to another.

ACKNOWLEDGMENTS

The author thanks the University of Pennsylvania's Research Foundation for funding. He is also grateful to Work Study research assistants Anne Chun, Yi Jun, and Gina Mok for their constancy and precision. Gerald Davis, Michael Useem, Edward Zajac, two anonymous referees, and the editor, Joseph Cheng, provided useful comments.

NOTES

1 One exception to the large literature on cross-national differences in corporate governance is Corbett and Jenkinson (1996), who document that there are only small differences in the financing patterns of firms across countries.
2 It is not at all clear, however, that financial and money managers would prefer to see a wholesale convergence in patterns of corporate governance across the world. The reason lies in that different corporate governance systems are associated with peculiar competitive strategies and responses to the business cycle (Bühner et al., 1998; Kester, 1996; Kim and Hoskisson, 1996; Lazonick and O'Sullivan, 1996). Accordingly, the chances that stock markets in the world are uncorrelated with each other increase with the diversity in patterns of corporate governance. Uncorrelated stock markets "enrich the menu" for diversification because they provide greater opportunities for global portfolio investment, one of the key ways in which financial managers achieve superior performance over the long run (Financial Times, 1995: 447–453; Siegel, 1998: 139, 286; Malkiel and Mei, 1998: 23; Ibbotson and Brinson, 1993).

REFERENCES

Aguilera, R.V. (1998). *Elites, corporations and the wealth of nations: historical institutional patterns in Italy and Spain.* Ph.D. Dissertation, Department of Sociology, Harvard University.

Albrow, M. (1997). *The global age.* Stanford, CA: Stanford University Press.

Bebchuck, L.A. and Roe, M.J. (1999). A theory of path dependence in corporate ownership and governance. *Stanford Law Review, 52,* 127–170.

Becht, M. and Röell, A. (1999). Blockholdings in Europe: an international comparison. *European Economic Review, 43,* 1049–1056.

Berglof, E. (1988). Capital structure as a mechanism of control: a comparison of financial systems. In M. Aoki, B. Gustafsson, and O. Williamson (Eds), *The firm as a nexus of treaties.* Newbury Park, CA: Sage.

Berle, A. and Means, G. (1932). *The modern corporation and private property.* New York: MacMillan.

Biggart, N.W. and Guillén, M.F. (1999). Developing difference: social organization and the rise of the auto industries of South Korea, Taiwan, Spain, and Argentina. *American Sociological Review, 64,* 722–747.

Binns, S.M. (1998). A preliminary reply to the preliminary report. www.ecgn.ulb.ac.be/ecgn/docs/html/PreliminaryReply.htm

Bishop, M. (1994). Watching the boss: a survey of corporate governance. *The Economist,* January 29.

Bühner, R., Rasheed, A., Rosenstein, J. and Yoshikawa, T. (1998). Research on corporate governance: a comparison of Germany, Japan, and the United States. In J.L.C. Cheng and R.B. Peterson (Eds), *Advances in international comparative management, 12,* 121–155. Stamford, CT: JAI Press.

Castells, M. (1996). *The rise of the network society.* Cambridge, MA: Blackwell.

Charkham, J. (1995). *Keeping good company: a study of corporate governance in five countries.* Oxford: Oxford University Press.

Cheng, J.L.C. (1994a). Toward a contextual approach to cross-national organization research: a macro perspective. In S.B. Prasad (Ed.), *Advances in international comparative management, 4,* 3–18. Greenwich, CT: JAI Press.

Cheng, J.L.C. (1994b). On the concept of universal knowledge in organizational science: implications for cross-national research. *Management Science, 40,* 162–168.

Corbett, J. and Jenkinson, T. (1996). The financing of industry, 1970–1989: an international comparison. *Journal of the Japanese and International Economies, 10,* 71–96.

Cox, R.W. (1996). A perspective on globalization. In J.H. Mittelman (Ed.), *Globalization: critical reflections,* 21–30. Boulder, CO: Lynne Rienner Publishers.

Cusumano, M. (1985). *The Japanese automobile industry: technology and management at Nissan and Toyota.* Cambridge, MA: Harvard University Press.

Djelic, M.-L. (1998). *Exporting the American model.* New York: Oxford University Press.

Dore, R. (1973). *British factory – Japanese factory.* Berkeley, CA: University of California Press.

Easternbrook, F. and Fischel, D. (1991). *The economic structure of corporate law.* Cambridge, MA: Harvard University Press.

Financial Times (1995). *FT global guide to investing.* London: FT Pitman Publishing.

Fleming, R.W. (1998). Worldwide changes in corporate governance. *The Corporate Board*, November–December, 1–4.

Fligstein, N. (1990). *The transformation of corporate control.* Cambridge, MA: Harvard University Press.

Friedman, J. (1994). *Cultural identity and global process.* London: Sage.

Garrett, G. (1998). *Partisan politics in the global economy.* New York: Cambridge University Press.

Garrett, G. (1999). *Trade, capital mobility and government spending around the world.* Working Paper, Department of Political Science, Yale University.

Gerlach, M.L. (1992). *Alliance capitalism: the social organization of Japanese business.* Berkeley, CA: University of California Press.

Giddens, A. (1990). *The consequences of modernity.* Stanford, CA: Stanford University Press.

Giddens, A. (1991). *Modernity and self-identity.* Cambridge, MA: Polity Press.

Gilpin, R. (1987). *The political economy of international relations.* Princeton, NJ: Princeton University Press.

Guillén, M.F. (1994). *Models of management: work, authority, and organization in a comparative perspective.* Chicago: The University of Chicago Press.

Guillén, M.F. (2001a). *The limits of convergence: globalization and organizational change in Argentina, South Korea, and Spain.* Princeton, NJ: Princeton University Press.

Guillén, M.F. (2001b). Is globalization civilizing, destructive or feeble? A critique of six key debates in the social-science literature. *Annual Review of Sociology, 27*, 235–260.

Guillén, M.F. and Tschoegl, A.T. (1999). *At last the internationalization of retail banking? The case of the Spanish banks in Latin America.* Working Paper. The Wharton School.

Harvey, D. (1989). *The condition of postmodernity.* Oxford: Blackwell.

Hirst, P. and Thompson, G. (1996). *Globalization in question.* London: Polity.

Hollingsworth, J.R., Schmitter, P.C., and Streeck, W. (1994). Capitalism, sectors, institutions, and performance. In J. Hollingsworth, P. Schmitter, and W. Streeck (Eds), *Governing capitalist economies: performance and control of economic sectors*, 3–16. New York and Oxford: Oxford University Press.

Huber, E. and Stephens, J.D. (1999). *Welfare state and production regimes in the era of retrenchment.* Occasional Papers No. 1, School of Social Science, Institute for Advanced Study, Princeton, NJ.

Ibbotson, R.G. and Brinson, G.P. (1993). *Global investing.* New York: McGraw-Hill.

Jensen, M. (1993). The modern industrial revolution, exit, and the failure of internal control systems. *Journal of Finance, 48*, 831–880.

Kerr, C., Dunlop, J.T., Harbison, F. and Myers, C.A. [1960] (1964). *Industrialism and industrial man.* New York: Oxford University Press.

Kester, W.C. (1996). American and Japanese corporate governance: convergence to best practice? In S. Berger and R. Dore (Eds), *National diversity and global capitalism*, 107–137. Ithaca, NY: Cornell University Press.

Kim, H. and Hoskisson, R.E. (1996). Japanese governance systems: a critical review. In J.L.C. Cheng and R.B. Peterson (Eds), *Advances in international comparative management, 11*, 165–189. Greenwich, CT: JAI Press.

Kobrin, S.J. (1997). The architecture of globalization: state sovereignty in a networked global economy. In J.H. Dunning (Ed.), *Governments, globalization, and international business*, 146–171. New York: Oxford University Press.

La Porta, R., Lopez-de-Silanes, F., and Shleifer, A. (1999). Corporate ownership around the world. *Journal of Finance, 54*, 471–517.

La Porta, R., Lopez-de-Silanes, F., Shleifer, A. and Vishny, R.W. (1998). Law and finance. *Journal of Political Economy, 106*, 1113–1155.

Lannoo, K. (1999). A European perspective on corporate governance. *Journal of Common Market Studies, 37*, 269–294.

Lazonick, W. and O'Sullivan, M. (1996). Organization, finance, and international competition. *Industrial and Corporate Change, 5*, 1–49.

Loredo, E. and Suárez, E. (1998). Corporate governance in Europe: is convergence desirable? *International Journal of Management, 15*, 525–532.

Macey, J.R. and Miller, G.P. (1995). Corporate governance and commercial banking: a comparative examination of Germany, Japan, and the United States. *Stanford Law Review, 48*, 72–112.

McMichael, P. (1996). *Development and social change: a global perspective.* Thousand Oaks, CA: Pine Forge Press.

Malkiel, B., and Mei, J.P. (1998). *Global bargain hunting.* New York: Simon and Schuster.

Mazlish, B. (1993). An introduction to global history, In B. Mazlish and R. Buultjens (Eds), *Conceptualizing global history*, 1–24. Boulder, CO: Westview Press.

Meyer, J.W., Boli, J., Thomas, G.M., and Ramirez, F.O. (1997). World society and the nation-state. *American Journal of Sociology, 103*, 144–181.

Mittelman, J.H. (1996). The dynamics of globalization. In J.H. Mittelman (Ed.), *Globalization: critical reflections*, 1–19. Boulder, CO: Lynne Rienner Publishers.

Murmann, J.P. (1998). *Knowledge and competitive advantage in the synthetic dye industry, 1850–1914: The coevolution of firms, technology, and national institutions in Great Britain, Germany, and the United States.* Book manuscript. Evanston, IL: Kellogg Graduate School of Management, Northwestern University.

OECD (1995). Financial markets and corporate governance. *Financial Market Trends, 62*, 13–35.

OECD (1998a). *Corporate governance: improving competitiveness and access to capital in global markets*. Paris: Organization of Economic Cooperation and Development.

OECD (1998b). Shareholder value and the market in corporate control in OECD countries. *Financial Market Trends, 69*, 15–37.

Orrù, M., Biggart, N.W., and Hamilton, G.G. (1997). *The economic organization of East Asian capitalism*. Thousand Oaks, CA: Sage.

O'Sullivan, M. (1999). *Corporate governance and globalisation*. Working Paper, INSEAD.

Porter, M.E. (1990). *The competitive advantage of nations*. New York: Free Press.

Prahalad, C.K. (1997). Corporate governance or corporate value-added? In D.H. Chew (Ed.), *Studies in international corporate finance and governance systems: a comparison of the U.S., Japan, and Europe*, 46–56. New York: Oxford University Press.

Robertson, R. (1992). *Globalization: social theory and global culture*. London: Sage Publications.

Roe, M.J. (1993). Some differences in corporate structure in Germany, Japan, and the United States. *Yale Law Journal, 102*, 1927–2003.

Romano, R. (1993). *The genius of American corporate law*. Washington, DC: American Enterprise Institute Press.

Sargent, J. (1999). World bank, OECD introduce global corporate governance forum. *The ISS Friday Report*, October 1, 3–4.

Shleifer, A. and Vishny, R.W. (1997). A survey of corporate governance. *Journal of Finance, 52*, 737–783.

Siegel, J.J. (1998). *Stocks for the long run*. New York: McGraw-Hill.

Skocpol, T. (Ed.) (1984). *Vision and method in historical sociology*. New York: Cambridge University Press.

Smelser, N.J. 1976. *Comparative methods in the social sciences*. Englewood Cliffs, NJ: Prentice-Hall.

Soskice, D. (1998). Divergent production regimes: coordinated and uncoordinated market economies in the 1980s and 1990s. In H. Kitschelt, P. Lange, G. Marks, and J.D. Stephens (Eds), *Continuity and change in contemporary capitalism*, 101–134. New York: Cambridge University Press.

Steinherr, A. and Huveneers, C. (1994). On the performance of differently regulated financial institutions: some empirical evidence. *Journal of Banking and Finance, 18*, 271–306.

Storper, M. and Salait, R. (1997). *Worlds of production: the action frameworks of the economy*. Cambridge, MA: Harvard University Press.

Streeck, W. (1991). On the institutional conditions of diversified quality production. In E. Matzner and W. Streeck (Eds), *Beyond Keynesianism: The socio-economics of production and full employment*, 21–61. Hants, England: Edward Elgar Publishing.

Streeck, W. (1995). *German capitalism: Does it exist? Can it survive?* Discussion Paper 95/5. Cologne: Max Planck Institut für Gesellschaftsforschung.

Thomsen, S. and Pedersen, T. (1996). Nationality and ownership structures: the 100 largest companies in six European nations. *Management International Review, 36*, 149–166.

Tilly, C. (1984). *Big structures, large processes, huge comparisons*. New York: Russell Sage Foundation.

Useem, M. (1984). *The inner circle: large corporations and the rise of business political activity in the U.S. and U.K.* New York: Oxford University Press.

Useem, M. (1996). *Investor capitalism: How money managers are changing the face of corporate America*. New York: Basic Books.

Waters, M. (1995). *Globalization*. New York: Routledge.

Westney, D.E. (1987). *Imitation and innovation: The transfer of western organizational patterns to Meiji Japan*. Cambridge, MA: Harvard University Press.

Whitley, R. (1992). *Business systems in East Asia: Firms, markets, and societies*. London: Sage.

Whitley, R. (1999). Firms, institutions and management control: The comparative analysis of coordination and control systems. *Accounting, Organizations, and Society, 24*, 507–524.

Ziegler, J.N. (1995). Institutions, elites, and technological change in France and Germany. *World Politics, 47*, 341–372.

Ziegler, J.N. (1997). *Governing ideas: strategies for innovation in France and Germany*. Ithaca, NY: Cornell University Press.

'Capital Unbound? The Transformation of European Corporate Governance'

from Journal of European Public Policy (1998)

Martin Rhodes and Bastiaan van Apeldoorn

When Europe's leaders met at Maastricht in 1991, the last thing they intended was that monetary union should be a vehicle for spreading Anglo-Saxon capitalism. But that will be the most dramatic effect of the single currency . . . There will be more equities and corporate bonds. And as it grows, the capital market will exert its influence on all other sectors of the European economy. It will increase the pressure on companies to perform. Pursuit of shareholder value, hostile take-overs and better corporate governance – all will become increasingly prominent features of the European landscape.

(*Financial Times*, 'The Lex Column', 30 March 1998)

INTRODUCTION

The above quotation is typical of the excitement and anticipation with which the mainly 'Anglo-Saxon' financial press awaits the full implementation of the European single market and monetary union. In combination with the irresistible forces of globalization, these final phases of European integration are expected to rein in the powers of national governments to set taxes, establish labour relations and influence the framework of corporate governance at will. Already restrained by the capacity of firms to shift production, tax burdens and corporate identity on a global scale, in a fully integrated European economy, national jurisdictions will become increasingly standardized as they compete for international investment. A strong stream of academic analysis agrees with this popular prognosis: advocates of the 'strong globalization' thesis like Teeple (1995: 5) argue that 'the neo-liberal agenda is the social and political counterpart to the globalization of production, distribution and exchange', marking an epochal change in the development of capitalism from one dominated by national capital tied to the nation state to one dominated by global capital escaping national regulation and control.

But for those familiar with another stream of political economy – one which takes a comparative approach and highlights the character and origins of national distinctiveness – the idea that capital is finally 'unbound', and will produce a process of transnational convergence on an 'Anglo-Saxon' or 'neo-liberal' model, is counter-intuitive. Zysman (1994), for instance, argues that 'historically rooted trajectories of growth' created by national institutional networks are not susceptible to rapid transformation or demise. Fligstein and Freeland (1995) characterize these trajectories in terms of the timing of entry into industrialization and the institutionalization of that process; the role of states in regulating property rights and rules of co-operation and competition; and the social organization of national élites. They further argue that, together, these combinations of institutions and rules create 'stable organization fields' and national systems that are resistant to convergence. There is, then, a puzzle: on the one hand we have a view of sweeping transformation, but on the other a picture of relative calm. Both cannot be correct.

This article sets out to tackle this conundrum. After examining the diversity of European 'capitalisms' below, we consider the arguments and evidence concerning their contemporary transformation. We first examine the institutions, rules and organizations of West European capitalism by focusing on 'corporate governance', construed broadly to include not just the regulation of the activities of firms but the web of relations that surround their operation, between 'stakeholders', shareholders, employees and the state. We then seek to develop a tentative understanding of the forces – both domestic and international – that may be changing these systems of governance and suggest a thesis of partial transformation in formerly stable systems. But there is also the question of what kind of socio-economic order, or 'model of capitalism', is emerging within the supranational regime of the European Union (EU). Rather than creating a pan-European, neo-liberal regime, we argue that, alongside other forms of internationalization, the creation of the single European market integrates elements of 'Anglo-Saxon' corporate governance and economic organization with established national institutions, norms and rules, thereby allowing for continued national diversity within a framework of 'embedded neo-liberalism'.

CAPITALISM VERSUS CAPITALISM IN WESTERN EUROPE

The diversity of West European capitalisms

Various attempts have been made to categorize capitalist systems, providing important insights into institutional distinctions and the way they affect the functioning and performance of firms. Albert (1993) draws a distinction between 'Atlantic' (Thatcherite/neo-American) and 'Rhenish' (German or Rhineland) capitalism. While the former prioritizes individual success and short-term financial profits, the latter promotes collective achievement, consensus and long-term results. The principal differences derive from contrasts in corporate governance: while the key characteristics of the Atlantic model are arm's-length relations between sources of finance and firms, the supremacy of shareholder interests and few restrictions on predatory behaviour (via mergers and acquisitions), those of the 'Rhenish' model derive from the concept of 'stakeholder' capitalism – that is, the location of the firm and its management within a

network of interests, including banks and workers. Although Vitols (1997) warns against romanticizing the German company as a 'stakeholder community', the purpose of corporate governance is often a much more 'collective' one than in the Anglo-American systems, given the stability of contractual relationships and widespread antipathy to 'hostile' takeover activity – although not, it should be noted, to the accumulation of 'hostile stakes', as in Germany where companies, with the assistance of banks, frequently use this method to gain control of competitors (Jenkinson and Ljungqvist, 1997).

We cannot adequately present here the different characteristics of these systems, or acknowledge the important differences that exist within these broad 'capitalist families'. Tables 1 and 2 therefore summarize the characteristics of these systems, the first outlining the 'external' environment of firms, the second the system of 'corporate governance'.

As Gourevitch (1996) argues, the microstructures of industries and firms are shaped by regulatory policies which structure incentives to use different organizational forms. These, in turn, have a substantial effect on the efficiency of economies. In this respect, we can attribute 'advantages' and 'disadvantages' to the characteristics of these different models. In the *Anglo-Saxon, market-oriented systems*, advantages are thought to derive from the dynamism imparted by the external threat to poorly performing managers from hostile take-overs and the incentives provided by performance-related compensation. The sovereignty of shareholders is assumed to provide another check on management since the large shareholders can, in principle, replace it (although if managers are also the largest shareholders, this constraint is clearly reduced). These systems may also have a comparative advantage in fast-moving consumer markets (e.g. retailing and banking) or more high-risk areas of innovation such as pharmaceuticals and biotechnology (see Vitols, 1997), while in Europe, Britain may be establishing some comparative advantage with its higher level of labour market flexibility. These advantages may be offset, however, by the lower levels of education and skills in the British workforce, certainly by comparison with Germany, and, although to a lesser extent, France; by the absence of long-term contractual relationships with suppliers of capital and workers which may encourage short-term, quick profit-oriented strategies; by the faster pace of mergers and acquisitions – frequently of a 'hostile'

Institutional context	Market-oriented Anglo-Saxon	Network-oriented	
		Germanic	Latin
Role of the state	Shift towards a minimal state since the 1980s	A regulatory rather than interventionist state	Extensive public ownership (now declining)
Co-operation between social partners	Conflictual until the 1980s; now minimal contact (Ireland maintains corporatism)	Extensive at the national level till late 1960s. Revived in the 1980s/1990s	Social pacts in Italy and Portugal in 1980s/1990s; problematic in Spain and Greece
Labour organization	Union membership high till 1980s; fragmented organization	Union membership density high; strong centralized unions	Union density generally low: significant decline outside public sector
Education and training	Fragmented training system; poor skills provision	High level of participation in vocational and professional training	Lower levels of participation in fragmented training systems
Labour market flexibility	Poor internal flexibility owing to poor skills; high external flexibility	High skills allow internal flexibility, external flexibility more restricted	Lower internal flexibility (lower skills); external flexibility also restricted
National innovation system	Low levels of R&D; weak regional innovation support system	Higher levels of R&D; regionalized innovation support systems	France excepted, R&D national and regional support weak
Finance for innovative small firms	Explosion of venture capital companies, but regionally concentrated	Venture capital weak; access to regional banks for small firm finance	Venture capital weak; access to regional banks for small firm finance

Table 1 Characteristics of market and network-oriented systems: external environment.

character – which may distract management from long-term corporate strategy, without necessarily adding to firm productivity or viability;[1] and by the priority given to 'shareholder value' at the expense of employees which means not just lower employee remuneration as a proportion of net value added, but also less institutionalized and, arguably, less productive industrial relations.

The *network-oriented systems* of the European continent also have advantages and disadvantages, and here the Germanic and Latin systems need to be distinguished. For while the former provides a generally productive environment for firms – with high levels of education and research and development (R&D) support and patient capital – the latter are much less well endowed in all these respects. Among the advantages attributed to Germanic network-oriented, 'contractual' governance are: the benefits of close and long-term relationships between firms and strategic capital suppliers (banks with board

Corporate features	Market-oriented Anglo-Saxon	Network-oriented	
		Germanic	Latin
Employee influence	Limited; Japanese FDI promotes shop-floor collaboration, 1980s/1990s	Extensive through works councils on organization of work and training	Strong shop-floor influence until early 1980s; now minimal
Role of banks	Banks play a minimal role in corporate ownership	Universal banks play an important role in corporate finance and control	Bank holdings and participation in France and Spain only
Role of stock exchange	Strong role in corporate finance; 70 per cent of top 100 companies in UK listed	Publicly listed corporate firms limited; stock exchanges small	Stock exchanges relatively undeveloped; closed ownership
Shareholder sovereignty	Widely dispersed share ownership; dividends prioritized	Number of freely traded shares limited; dividends less prioritized	Shareholder sovereignty recognized but shareholders' rights restricted
Family-controlled firms	General separation of equity ownership and management control	Family ownership important in small and medium-sized firms	Family ownership and control extensive, exercised through holdings
Market for corporate control	Scope for hostile take-overs 'corrects' management failure	Take-overs restricted; managers under direct stakeholder influence	Take-overs restricted; little external challenge to management
Management boards	One-tier board system: includes executive and non-executive managers	Two-tier board system: supervisory and executive responsibilities separate	Administrative board combines supervisory and executive duties
Managerial labour market	Incentives (e.g. stock options) align management with shareholders	Performance-linked compensation limited: 'equality' important	Incentives more important (e.g. stock options in France)

Table 2 Characteristics of market and network-oriented systems: corporate governance.

Sources: Rhodes and van Apeldoorn (1997: 174–5); Moerland (1995a,b); De Jong (1995).

representation are thought to monitor managerial behaviour in a more constructive way than the Anglo-Saxon 'market' for corporate control, but the stability of long-term shareholdings in providing 'patient' capital is probably more important); a better institutionalized and similarly longer-term relationship between management and employees; and an advantage in market sectors which require 'depth competencies' (e.g. high-quality mechanical engineering, long-term relationship banking) (Vitols, 1997).

More negatively, these systems are proving less successful in new sectors requiring greater flexibility in organization, labour relations and financial supply (e.g. venture capital for high-technology 'start-ups'); the strong 'insider' role of capital suppliers (the famous *Hausbanken* in the German case) may create an information gap to the disadvantage of 'outsider' smaller investors, compounded by a traditional lack of transparency in corporate governance (Moerland, 1995a); and the absence of an active external market for corporate control means that managerial failure may not be corrected, especially where managers have been least subject to shareholder influence and where ownership has been separated from control by complex cross-shareholdings and pyramidal groups. The latter is especially true of the Latin countries where covert and cosy relationships are often consolidated by membership of a relatively closed élite (e.g. the network of graduates of the prestigious French École Nationale d'Administration in France and the restricted club – *salotto buono* – of leaders of the largest Italian companies and financial organizations) and where the role of banks as monitors has certainly been less important: France and Italy are neither bank-centred nor market-oriented, given the absence in both countries of strong and independent financial intermediaries (France is, after Italy, the country where the ownership share of financial institutions is lowest, owing in part to legal obstacles to bank equity ownership) (Goldstein, 1996; Sarcinelli, 1997).

GLOBALIZATION AND SYSTEM TRANSFORMATION

Given the continued diversity of West European capitalisms, the argument that globalization has swept away the national distinctiveness of both firms and their national systems of innovation and support is untenable. We broadly agree with the analysis of Forsyth and Notermans and their colleagues (1997) which suggests that the shift to a disinflationary macroeconomic policy regime and deregulation of the financial sector cannot be explained primarily by the globalization of business and financial markets in the 1970s and 1980s, but has had more to do with the need to forestall a cumulative inflationary dynamic across the industrial nations. Their argument that the

liberalization of financial regulation has not led to convergence in national financial systems is also well taken. Nevertheless, as we argue below, important tensions are now emerging between national systems and the 'extra-national' sphere of multinationals and global finance and within national systems between the protagonists of liberalizing change and the defenders of the status quo. Bit by bit, globalization – and the new domestic pressures and coalitions it generates – are beginning to transform the traditional relationships between governments, banks, companies and unions that have underpinned national socio-economic orders, even if 'convergence' may not be the end result.

While Gill (1995) links globalization to neoliberalism in arguing that the impact of the latter will vary 'according to the size, economic strength, form of state and civil society, and prevailing national and regional institutional capabilities, as well as the degree of integration into global capital and money markets' (1995: 415), Boyer (1996) and Gourevitch (1996) have suggested more precise ways of understanding the mechanisms behind such change. For Boyer, diverse systems may find 'by chance or necessity' solutions to common problems; or international consulting firms, international bodies or multinationals may diffuse the same business principles and economic policies across national borders, while also defining or enforcing the rules of the game within a given international regime. Gourevitch mentions the internalization of external pressures, internally generated pressure, producer-led reform, and the role of the bureaucracy and political parties. Adapting the insights of all three approaches, we argue that several dynamics are at work in which domestic and international forces interact in destabilizing traditional 'contractual' relations:

- competitive pressures on producers who consequently seek to modify their domestic contexts, depending on whether they prioritize local or global markets;
- the liberalization and integration of financial markets, which has also modified the behaviour of banks, making them in certain cases the advocates of further, liberalizing domestic change;
- the growing role of international actors – multinationals, investment banks, pension funds, international authorities – in advocating domestic regulatory change in countries where they are active;

■ and the equally potent role of non-economic domestic actors (politicians, bureaucrats and technocrats) in internalizing external pressures.

Here we examine the combined impact of these forces in three critical areas where a significant shift in power between actors is occurring:

■ in corporate governance, especially in terms of the balance of power between 'stakeholders' and shareholders;
■ in the relationship between and respective weight of the 'public and the private' in these systems;
■ and in the balance between capital and labour in the 'networked' (and especially the 'Germanic') firm.

'Stakeholders' versus 'shareholders' in corporate governance

Fligstein and Freeland (1995: 36) have argued that 'while the American industrial structure is firmly in the grasp of the finance conception of control, the rest of the world has steadfastly resisted importing such a notion of governance . . . in large part because of state and élite resistance.' While they are correct to emphasize the resistance of European countries to the wholesale adoption of Anglo-American practice, this should not blind us to the fact that the nature of their capitalist élites is changing, making them much more amenable than hitherto to the finance conception of control – and especially the associated notion of 'shareholder value'.

Recent evidence suggests that network systems will increasingly accommodate the 'Anglo-Saxon' characteristic of channelling capital flows to corporations through investment funds, pension funds and insurance companies, while managers will identify more closely with stock price behaviour as more companies seek stock market quotation and managers' remuneration is tied more closely to performance (e.g. through stock options). Funded pensions are spreading as continental countries find them a solution to the demographic problem of an ever-climbing ratio of retirees to the employed and they will take their 'Anglo-Saxon' values with them. While the Anglo-Saxon market for corporate control seems to be becoming less ferocious (as corporate raiding, hostile take-overs and asset stripping lose favour),

management in 'network' countries is becoming increasingly subject to the influence of shareholders, the result of a combination of growing shareholder pressure and new EU regulations (see following matter). This has important implications not just for the balance between 'stakeholder' and shareholder power in the network systems but also for the behaviour of companies.

German companies are leading the way in adopting both the rhetoric and practice of 'shareholder value' – in large part because their continued expansion requires access to international capital: as Viag chairman Georg Obermeier has stated, 'We need international capital markets and therefore we inevitably need to meet international standards' (which means greater transparency through the use of global accounting standards and an end to cross-subsidization and the use of hidden reserves to disguise bad earnings figures) and 'less social consensus, although it is important, and more value added. This is the trend change in Germany' (*Financial Times*, 14 January 1998). Thus, large German companies (Deutsche Bank and Daimler Benz) have introduced stock option schemes for senior management,[2] while others are also modifying their internal rules regarding the rights of shareholders and transparency: Continental has abolished the rule limiting voting rights to 5 per cent or more of equity capital, while Bayer has raised the return on shareholders' funds from 14 to 20 per cent. Deutsche Bank has introduced International Accounting Standard (IAS) accounting and Veba, the energy and telecommunications group, has shifted to Generally Accepted Accounting Principles (GAAP) (Marsh, 1996). In both France and Germany, one of the consequences of the growing number of Anglo-Saxon institutional investors on shareholder rosters means that managers are increasingly oriented towards restructuring and a more aggressive exploitation of market opportunities.

This last point alerts us to the fact that, while the increasingly international reach of these companies clearly plays a role in their transformation, so too does the penetration of their domestic markets by foreign actors with a different set of corporate values. Germany, France, Italy and the other continental economies have all witnessed an increase in the domestic presence of foreign – especially American – investors, attracted by the opening up of European markets and the lucrative business generated by privatization programmes. While the nature of privatization differs from country to country (in some, like France and Italy, companies are often secured from foreign take-over by continued government stakes or shareholder pacts between core investors), its net effect has been to undermine traditional relationships. As Schmidt (1997) notes in the French case, privatization has helped to ensure the internationalization of French capital through the participation of foreign firms in the hard core of investors and on the boards of directors. Foreign financial services companies have also expanded in the European market, bringing more aggressive business methods with them and influencing the business practices of European companies, given that, until recently, financial intermediaries in most European countries have been as hidebound and conservative as their stock markets. American business culture is being spread throughout Europe by the growing presence of US institutional investors, consultancy firms and credit agencies like Standard & Poors – which exercise considerable influence over the direction and nature of investment – not to mention the arrival of a new generation of executives trained in US business schools or with formative career years in US companies.[3] Goldman Sachs, for example, is becoming a major operator, if not *the* major operator, in mergers and acquisitions (M&A) in a number of European countries. In France, in 1996, it beat the Parisian company Lazard Frères into second place in the French M&A business league (Jack, 1997) and has also been a key player on the protagonists' side in recent hostile take-over bids. In Germany (where M&A activity has accelerated in recent years) (Müller-Stewens and Schäfer, 1997), Goldman Sachs has close links with Daimler Benz and Deutsche Bank and played a key role in Krupp Hoesch's debt-financed bid for Thyssen in 1996, which, though it failed (owing to widespread antipathy towards such practices), led to the negotiated merger of these groups in 1997. Both steel groups are now striving for a clearly defined return on capital – 12.5 per cent for Thyssen, 15 per cent for Krupp – and have been downsizing (US style) to achieve it (*Financial Times*, 5 November 1997).

As already mentioned here, one obvious way that the foreign lobby is influencing corporate governance is by encouraging the spread of shareholder sovereignty in the 'network' systems. Lobbying by domestic shareholder groups for greater management transparency and responsiveness (German investment funds have been particularly active) has

been backed by foreign shareholders and fund managers frustrated by the interlocking élite relationships that still dominate these systems.[4] More generally, the shift towards greater reliance on equity markets and the desirability of international alliances are forcing even the most secretive private companies to become more open. Even in Italy, where corporate culture is at its most opaque, companies are being forced to become more transparent: attempts by companies like Fiat to forge the international alliances they need to grow are forcing them to consider transformation from family-owned conglomerates to public ones; in 1996, Olivetti was forced to report quarterly figures in response to a 1996 shareholders' revolt that also toppled chairman Carlo De Benedetti. As one observer has commented, alongside the dismantling of the Italian public sector, a combination of both internal and external pressures is forcing the 'privatization' of the Italian private sector (Betts, 1997). As discussed in the following section, politicians and technocrats are also gradually responding to these pressures, introducing new legislation to open up the club-like character of continental corporate control.

The changing balance between public and private sector power

The privatization of state-owned firms and utilities and the parallel liberalization of previously closely controlled markets are turning previously mixed economies into regulated market economies, implying a considerable boost in the scale and power of once public but now private sector companies. One result has been the emergence of a major cleavage between private sector actors who have embraced the new world of the liberalized market and those companies which retain a public sector character and a more 'social' orientation. Political struggles along this divide promise to become one of the major determinants of the future shape of national capitalisms in western Europe.

Take France, for example, where large parts of the extensive public industrial and financial sector (built up by the Socialist government in the early 1980s) are now being privatized. While certain large corporations will remain under state control – especially non-commercial financial institutions such as the mutual banks, the Caisse d'Épargne savings bank network,

Crédit Agricole and the Post Office – the way that they operate may have to change substantially as the result of an onslaught by the expanding commercial sector on their special lending rights and subsidies. Long seen as a central part of a 'socially oriented' banking system, these institutions are now seen as the source of 'competitive distortions'. Private sector French banks have increasingly attacked the allegedly unfair way that the state has repeatedly bailed out Crédit Lyonnais, the highly loss-making French public sector bank (which has received FF49 billion of aid to date). And backed by the powerful Jean-Claude Trichet, the governor of the Bank of France and head of the state regulatory Banking Commission, they and their political allies have been waging war on the 'uncompetitive practices' of those financial institutions which remain protected by the state. The Caisse d'Épargne is a key target (for it is not obliged to pay dividends on its shares and has exclusive rights to offer the *Livret A*, a tax-exempt savings product), as are Crédit Mutuel (which exclusively runs the *Livret Bleu*, a state-run savings account which has higher than market rates) and Crédit Agricole which has a monopoly right to collect deposits from notaries in rural areas. The commercial banks claim that this special status distorts competition and enables the savings bank network to undercut them and reduce their interest rates to uncompetitive levels.

Meanwhile, in Germany a similar cleavage has opened up between the private sector banks (grouped in the German Banking Association) and public sector banks, again over allegedly unfair competition. An example is the accusation levelled against WestLB and five other *Länder*-backed public sector banks (*Landesbanken*) for receiving capital injections in the form of housing development funds (and – at least in the case of WestLB – for operating internationally in the same way as the large German universal banks), using their triple A rating (gained because of their *Länder*-guaranteed status) to borrow and lend at lower rates of interest (Kregel, 1997). However, both Bonn and the *Länder* also regard public banks as important agents of regional policy, while the *Landesbanken* are deeply embedded in local political and economic structures and play a critical role in the network of regional and local savings banks (*Sparkassen*). While the large commercial banks (especially the 'Big Three' – Deutsche Bank, Dresdner Bank and Commerz Bank) have sought to be more competitive, both domestically and

internationally, have reduced the size of their equity stakes in non-financial companies, and have set out to become global players by buying 'Anglo-American' investment banks (Deutsche Bank-Morgan Grenfell, Dresdner-Kleinwort Benson), the savings and co-operative banks play a major role in under-pinning the financial strength and adaptability of Germany's *Mittelstand* of medium-sized firms, creating a dual system of industrial finance (see Deeg, 1997).

In both countries, the European Commission has been drawn into the dispute. In December 1997, French mutual banks were put under investigation by the Commission after complaints by commercial rivals about distortions in the financial sector: the probe is focusing on the Crédit Mutuel *Livret Bleu* operations and Crédit Agricole. In the German case, Helmut Kohl's attempts to secure special protection for the German public bank network in the Amsterdam Treaty led to a compromise in which the local authority-linked financial infrastructure system will remain safe (as long as it does not infringe competition policy guidelines), but a more general ring-fencing of the sector was refused. As a result, the Commission is now probing the activities of WestLB.

The changing balance of power in industrial relations

The potential effect of globalization on employee influence and solidarity in the 'networked' (and especially 'Germanic' firm) is far-reaching. Quite apart from the issue of non-wage labour cost competition – with all that this implies for wider issues of social welfare policy – there is the pressure that the changing nature of the global corporation will place on the tradition of social consensus. First, German employers – like their counterparts in other 'organized' capitalist countries such as Denmark and Sweden – have been decentralizing bargaining to the level of the firm to tailor costs more precisely to its needs. Solidarity among workers may consequently be diminished. In addition, as 'networked' firms 'go global' and embrace new methods of business organization and new forms of finance, the traditionally greater share of net value added that they distributed to workers in the past will be challenged by the growing power of institutional shareholders – both domestic (including newly liberated pension funds) and foreign: until now, for Europe as a whole, the wage share in value added has been stable, generally reflecting the rise and fall in the business cycle (high at the troughs, low at the peaks), and significantly higher than in the Anglo-American systems (Young, 1997).

Moreover, even if it does not actually relocate all parts of its production, conception and design process, the increasingly internationalized firm can use its locational power (i.e. the threat of exit) to modify contractual relations at home, making it potentially a major agent in eroding the differences between 'shareholder' and the 'stakeholder' economies. German firms – including Daimler Benz, Bosch, BMW as well as multinationals with a wider scope such as Ford and GM Europe – have increasingly used locational threats to weaken the power of unions and force concession bargaining (see Mueller, 1996).[5] German companies and unions are now agreeing patterns of flexible working that were unthinkable just five years ago, and many of these are reached locally with company works' councils, thereby circumventing national accords. But the national union IG Metall is also sometimes involved. This was the case in a recent example of concession bargaining from Osram, the German light bulb manufacturer which is part of the Siemens group. A deal with the union was forced after the company threatened to shift production from Augsburg to Bari in southern Italy, where labour costs are some 40 per cent lower. In the productivity deal that saved the plant for Augsburg, the union agreed that the new production line there would be kept running for 160 hours a week, 18 hours longer than the previous maximum for the plant. Ford's loss-making German operations have struck a deal with 34,000 employees, whereby it saves $120 million and gains greater flexibility in organizing work levels in return for keeping jobs and investment in Germany and compensates for a drop in overall take-home pay with more time off. Following a 1997 deal in the chemical industry, companies can cut wages by up to 10 per cent in a downturn in return for not laying off workers (*Financial Times*, 17 June 1997).

More generally, certain employers' associations and large companies are testing both the will of the government and of labour in key areas of labour regulation. In September 1996, Daimler Benz, Siemens and Mannesmann cut sick pay unilaterally by 20 per cent, provoking widespread labour unrest (although many other large companies opposed this action as destructive to what they still see as the broadly positive German system of consensual industrial relations). In August 1996, Werner Stumfe, the head of Gesamtmetall (which represents 8,500 German engineering companies), launched an attack on the influence of trade unions on management boards in large German companies, arguing that it prevented competitive restructuring and was deterring foreign investment. Gesamtmetall renewed its attack in November 1997 and called for a new system of working hours, more profit-related pay, special treatment for loss-making companies, greater all-round flexibility in collective sector-wide wage bargaining and the introduction of varied working time arrangements. In January 1998, Hans Olaf Henkel, the head of the German Industry Federation, also attacked centralized wage bargaining and advised companies to start breaking their wage contracts.

THE TRIUMPH OF ANGLO-SAXON CAPITALISM?

Globalization – and the new domestic pressures and coalitions that it generates – are thus beginning to transform the traditional relationships between government, banks, companies and unions that have underpinned national socio-economic orders. But in none of these areas is a clear process of neo-liberal convergence occurring. We argue that there are several reasons why neo-liberal convergence is not occurring and is very unlikely in the future.

- first, there is a power argument: in the same way that the rhetoric and practice of Anglo-American corporate governance are being adopted to bolster the power of certain élites, those same élites will resist any changes that might go too far in undermining their own positions, as will those who will clearly lose from the modification of traditional rules and norms;
- second, there is an argument about path dependence and the lock-in effects of historical development which, as discussed by Fligstein and Freeland (1995), create formidable pressures for continuity;
- third, there is an efficiency argument: as argued by Gourevitch (1996), the efficiency and competitiveness of economies are linked to the microstructures of industries and firms whose incentives to use different organizational forms are shaped by

particular national regulatory policies: continued competitiveness will depend on the adjustment rather than abandonment of those structures and policies.

Two further reasons stem from the external environment:

- external pressures (international competition, the shift to a new macropolicy regime under European monetary union) are as likely to reinforce existing relationships as they are to break them down (we argue that this is most clearly the case with social partnership and corporatism);
- and finally – the subject of our final section – the creation of a new regulatory environment for European capitalism which links supranational and national rules is one in which considerable scope for national variety is allowed.

Beginning with 'shareholder' value: while the rhetoric and practice of a new style of 'corporate governance' are becoming important in the network systems, there is widespread resistance to the full-scale adoption of Anglo-Saxon rules and norms and to the unravelling of traditional 'contractual' relations. Numerous examples of such resistance can be found, especially in Germany, including opposition to hostile take-over bids, as with the widespread chorus of disapproval voiced by national and local politicians, business and labour representatives to the abortive Krupp Hoesch bid for Thyssen in 1996; and the joint 1996 position paper presented by a broad business coalition opposed to an agenda for reform promoted by the opposition SPD (including measures to reduce the influence of large private banks via shareholdings in non-banks and the exercise of proxy powers, and the anti-competitive practice of cross-shareholdings with competing companies) (Vitols and Woolcock, 1997). To the continued importance of stable, long-term shareholdership in the German system and of the large banks in the insider system of corporate control (see Deeg, 1997), one can add the centrality of large and powerful actors, such as the Italian investment bank Mediobanca, or the financial groups Paribas and Indo Suez in France, in governing the tight network of relations that span their countries' cross- and circular shareholdings and interlocking boards. These are key features of these systems and a major defence against outsider influence and

far-reaching corporate change – even if in recent years these linkages have been unravelling, owing to the turbulence created by privatization and the greater independence of those companies with foreign partners. But in neither France nor Italy does this amount to their abandonment, nor does it suggest a radical shift towards Anglo-Saxon corporate governance.

But under the aegis of pro-reform élites, an onslaught *is* occurring on the worst abuses of power which can result from the 'club-like' character of continental capitalism. New codes of governance influenced by Anglo-Saxon practice have been introduced in the wake of the 1995 Viénot Committee of the French employers' federation, the CNPF (and parallel proposals from the Senate's Marini Committee), and the 1995 take-over code drawn up by the Advisory Committee of the Deutsche Börse AG. These have been influenced in part by the recommendations of the 1994 Cadbury Report in the UK, which became semi-compulsory for British listed companies, and concern the rights of minority shareholders and the monitoring of accounts and remuneration packages. In Spain, the Aznar conservative government set up a commission in 1997 to overhaul that country's arcane and opaque corporate governance system, while in Italy legislation designed by the Treasury's Draghi committee is revising the rules of Italian capitalism and challenging the old interlocked vested interests of family firms and financial holding companies. Again, policies to open up the corporation and elevate shareholder's interests to a higher level will not necessarily overturn the existing system or align it with Anglo-Saxon practice. But one of the key elements of continental capitalism – the closed, backroom conduct of corporate affairs – is clearly under siege.

Second, although there has been an onslaught on 'public purpose' banking in Germany and France, for example, led by increasingly internationalized and market-oriented finance capital, it seems likely that a new equilibrium will be found, in part because of the willingness of the European Commission to protect the local financial infrastructure of the network systems that has a 'social purpose', but also because of the obvious efficacy of these forms of finance for small and medium-sized firms. Here, the power and efficiency arguments go hand in hand with path dependency to explain continuity. It is true that the international and domestic financial environment has been transformed by the emergence of global markets in short-term securities and cross-border equity trade, by rapid innovation in new financial instruments like derivatives (swaps, futures and options), and by the appearance of actors with transnational investments (insurance companies, mutual investment funds and pension funds). In response, national authorities have had to surrender traditional control over banking and financial markets, and monetary instruments like credit control, and replace them with regulatory frameworks that permit international capital flows. Once cosy relations between central banks and domestic financial communities are being undermined. But, on the other hand, as Vitols (1997: 249) notes, the importance of institutional interdependence is preventing these changes from generating full financial system convergence, for different types of production regime make varying demands for varying types of capital; while companies that rely on cheaper labour and less new equipment are less likely to require long-term debt capital than those relying on greater quantities of new equipment and long-term planning, the greater stability of industrial organization in these latter companies (owing, e.g. to tighter forms of labour market regulation) may also produce stability in industrial finance.

This brings us back to industrial relations. Although the long-term linkages between productive systems and financial systems will not necessarily cement in place a similar linkage between productive systems and labour relations, it does seem that both path-dependence and the efficiency argument will ensure that employers will not rush to abandon arrangements that have served them well in the past. Indeed, in the German case, the posturing and rhetoric of certain companies and employer organizations have simply hastened arrival at a new compromise rather than precipitating a crisis. While there has been a perceptible shift in the balance of power between capital and labour, neither the destruction of co-operative labour relations nor the abandonment of social partnership is imminent: on the contrary, as elsewhere, new forms of social partnership will prove essential for macro-economic policy innovation and micro-economic adjustment. Thus, other corporate leaders in Germany have lined up alongside trade unions to defend the merits of centralized wage bargaining (although most insist that the system needs reform to ensure its survival) and, together, German employers and trade unions are likely to find a more flexible version of the present system. Dieter

Hundt, the president of the BDA (the German employers' federation), has said that his organization is working towards a 'sensible reform' and wants its members to stick by their wage agreements; meanwhile, IG Metall leader Klaus Zwickel says that a raft of different agreements could be concluded centrally and then companies could choose from those 'building blocks' according to their needs (*Financial Times*, 29 January 1998).

This type of reform would introduce into the German system the kind of centrally negotiated bargaining flexibility that is being adopted in many European industrial relations systems. Contrary to common prediction, these have actually preserved in most cases either the principal elements of their centralized bargaining systems (e.g. Finland, Denmark, Norway and Austria) or (as in the case of the Netherlands since the mid-1980s) have revived and made corporatist policy-making and wage regulation more flexible. Only Sweden has seen a radical departure from its previously centralized model (arguably owing more to the conflict between employers and unions over new labour laws and wage earner funds from the late 1970s than any globalization effect), while incomes policies and wider corporatist bargains are now well established in Portugal, Italy and Ireland.

The persistence or modification of social partnership can be attributed to the fact that pressures for the dismantling of contractual social relations have been accompanied by equally powerful pressures for their preservation. On the one hand, decentralization in formerly centralized industrial relations systems has been induced by the introduction by multinationals of 'alien' elements into national bargaining arenas and by cross-class 'flexibility' alliances between employers and workers in export sectors, while employers in all systems are searching for greater company and plant-level flexibility. The creation of the single market and movement towards monetary union are also placing new pressures on wage-cost competition, given constraints on competitive devaluation. But there are also pressures in favour of centralization – as well as high levels of national (and European) employment protection. For also in response to competitive pressures, the diffusion of new forms of 'best practice' management and work organization implies the creation or maintenance of co-operative labour relations and a high-trust firm environment. Well-designed systems of labour market rules remain essential in this context, while both cost competitiveness and stability require a means of preventing wage drift and inflationary pressures. This has focused the attention of governments on revitalizing incomes policies. Rather than disrupting these forms of concertation, the movement to full monetary union is likely to lock the bargaining partners even more closely together (Rhodes, 1998).

THE EUROPEAN DIMENSION: A CONVERGENT OR FRAGMENTED CORPORATE SPACE?

On the basis of the above, we argue that globalization is not demanding a global neo-liberal order, nor for that matter is market integration in Europe demanding the destruction of national distinctiveness. For globalization and market integration not only involve the state as an agent in the process of opening borders, liberalizing markets and promoting the flow of finance and trade, but also, of necessity, in channelling, constraining and legitimizing market power. The spread of market ideology (neo-liberalism) hits its functional limits when the dependence of the market on national institutions is revealed. Quite apart from ideological resistance, at that point a purely neo-liberal strategy becomes dysfunctional; for the effective functioning of market mechanisms still requires purposive state intervention – and in many countries social concertation and corporatism – in *re*regulating the domains of welfare, taxation, innovation, employment and education.

In the European context, there has been a convergence of philosophy and strategy among the EU's most powerful business and political actors on what we call 'embedded neo-liberalism' (see Apeldoorn, 1998), the result of a conflict between three incompatible views of state–market relations in the 1970s and 1980s: *pan-European social democracy*, promoted by social democratic political forces and the European trade union movement as a strategy to protect the European 'social model' – the mixed economy and extensive social protection – against globalization; *neo-liberalism*, as the ideological outlook of global financial capital (based primarily in the City of London), but also of some (mainly British) multinationals, according to which the European region must be exposed to what are seen as the beneficial forces of globalization; and *neo-mercantilism*, oriented

instead towards a strong regional economy through industrial policy and the promotion of Euro-champions (if necessary protected by European tariff walls) as a bulwark against global competition. *Embedded neo-liberalism* (most clearly advocated by the German multinationals) is premised on a strong belief in the free market and supports neo-liberal policies of deregulation and flexibilization, but recognizes that the market must be embedded in a regulatory framework fostering both competitive business and social consensus.

By the early 1990s, Europe's most powerful businesses, grouped in the European Roundtable of Industrialists, had overcome their earlier division between neo-liberals and neo-mercantilists, and advocated an 'embedded neo-liberal' compromise. At the same time, politicians across Europe were moving towards a compromise of their own in introducing a social component (albeit a rather weak one) into the European constitutional settlement at Maastricht, as well as stressing the need to preserve national prerogatives via the subsidiarity clause. For this reason, the Maastricht compromise represented neither a triumph for Thatcherite neo-liberalism nor the construction of a neo-mercantilist Europe, but rather a complex synthesis. Monetary union – the central part of the treaty – and its convergence criteria most clearly reflect the neo-liberal orthodoxy. But aspects of the Rhenish 'network' model can be found in the Maastricht chapters on 'Trans-European {infrastructure} Networks' and 'Research and Technological Development' (reflecting a German-style industrial policy or *Ordnungspolitik*) and in the appended Social Protocol and Agreement which sets out procedures for bargaining between European trade unions and employers.

One of the reasons for the acknowledgement of subsidiarity at Maastricht was the battle waged in the 1980s and early 1990s over attempts to introduce a uniform system of corporate governance – part and parcel, in fact, of the broader conflict outlined above. Harmonization had been advocated from various quarters, but the most powerful arguments were either based on the need for lower transaction costs via standardization or on the need simultaneously to avoid a convergence spiral (triggered by corporations moving their headquarters to countries with more lenient governance systems) and remove the *de facto* entry barriers to capital created by continued differences in rules on take-overs and share ownership (see Schaede, 1995). But, in fact, the directives regulating European corporate space have either been blocked by national disagreements over surrendering national sovereignty or have been issued in a form which allows a degree of national diversity. Moreover, there remain many gaps in the European regulatory framework preventing a full liberalization of financial services and cross-border investment.

The existence of national disagreement on the constitution of a European corporate space should not surprise us since, as Fligstein and Mara-Drita (1996) argue, the regulation of property rights and competition is more central to the state's claim on sovereignty than rules of exchange, and it is the liberalization of the latter rather than the former in the single market project that has gained the greatest degree of élite consent. Moreover, many of the directives which affect this area of sovereignty have been poorly conceived, translating particular national models into draft European legislation: thus, while the UK model was adopted for proposals on take-over rules (the Thirteenth Company Law Directive), the Germanic two-tier board structure strongly influenced the EU draft on internal governance mechanisms (the Fifth Directive), provoking predictable rejections from élites in both the Anglo-Saxon and network economies (Schaede, 1995). Similarly, both the proposal for a European Company Statute and the Tenth Company Law Directive on cross-border mergers remain blocked – mainly because of disputes over their employee participation components but also because, like the Fifth and Thirteenth Directives, they ignore the fundamental interdependence between corporate law and corporate finance in national systems (Berglöf, 1997).

In the case of the Company Statute, the struggle between a pure neo-liberal and an embedded neo-liberal view of the market continues, for, true to their global orientation, the large British multinationals are opposed to a European statute altogether, advocating a mix of national and international governance, and a harmonization of rules for company behaviour through the International Accountancy Standards Committee. The latter view may ultimately prevail. For attempts to reduce the diversity of accounting standards within the EU via the Fourth Directive on Company Accounts (1979) and the Seventh Directive on Consolidated Accounting (1983) produced little in the way of harmonization and the adoption of mutual recognition seems to have reduced the

priority given to it. As recent German developments suggest, as national standards decline within the EU they are more likely to be replaced by international IAS or US GAAP rules than European standards (Leftwich, 1997). In February 1998, the German government introduced a bill to regulate a *de facto* reality and allow quoted companies to use international accounting standards as part of its plan to broaden its country's capital markets.

Alongside the other institutional and political impediments outlined above, regulatory gaps and inconsistencies prevent the adoption or imposition of a single European capitalist model – neo-liberal or otherwise. Finance again provides a clear example. The first step towards the creation of a free European financial area began in 1988 with the Capital Movements Directive. As in other sectors, rather than a shift in governance to the European level, a two-tier structure has been created. While the Commission is responsible for removing national barriers and controls, the main policy instruments – and responsibility for domestic market regulation – remain with the member states. The governing principle here is mutual recognition rather than harmonization. Under the Second Banking Directive of 1989, for example, banks of one country can offer a full range of services in another. But while a financial institution must comply with the market rules of the country in which it operates, responsibility for regulating that institution lies with its home country. Moreover, a full surrender of national influence is unlikely in the near future. Some countries enjoy derogations, preventing access to various parts of their financial sectors, while tax differences affecting many financial products remain extensive and most directives allow governments to apply local conduct-of-business rules to foreign firms.

In financial services – an area of regulation with far-reaching consequences for European corporate governance – EU directives have already altered business conduct by introducing new standards of capital adequacy and risk assessment and increasing transparency. Old practices – insider trading, the monopoly status of traditional brokers, unregulated 'gentleman's' agreements on conduct – have been swept away, and parochial stock exchange activities have been revolutionized by organizational change, computerization and, in the German case, a centralization of securities, futures and options trading and a privatization of the Frankfurt exchange. The 1996

Investment Services Directive (ISD) and its sibling, the Capital Adequacy Directive (CAD), set new minimum standards for markets and traders and will help to remove some of the vestiges of 'nationalism' from Europe's stock markets. But as with the Capital Movements and Second Banking Directives, scope for some national diversity is maintained. While it is no longer possible for governments and stock exchanges to prevent competition across their borders – for investment firms regulated in their own countries can acquire a 'passport' to operate in others and trade on foreign exchanges using remote access – host countries cannot take away the passport of 'visiting' companies (which may have been awarded in a country with more relaxed standards) and capital adequacy standards will remain diverse, given that a *minimum* rather than a uniform level is required.

At the same time, governments may continue to protect their home markets in numerous ways, as evidenced by the problems of insurance companies in gaining access to Germany and mortgage issuers in penetrating France. The regional differences between Europe's personal insurance markets are still too great for any real cross-border synergies in the insurance market, while European monetary union on its own will fall short of providing the economic and legislative harmonization required to sell life assurance and pensions across borders: in some countries (e.g. Belgium) one can only claim back tax on life policies when they have been bought from local suppliers – a privilege enshrined in law by the European Court of Justice in the early 1990s. Equally, VAT rules are still unharmonized (in part because of the difficulties in bringing corporate tax rates together) and bankruptcy laws remain nationally specific. The 1985 Undertaking for Collective Investment in Transferable Securities Directive does not prevent countries from protecting their home financial services markets, by restricting pension funds products, for example, to resident fund managers (a market which the UK is currently campaigning to liberalize). Equity markets are still fragmented by a maze of different rules and regulations: thus in Denmark, Sweden, France and the UK, it is not possible for companies from another member state to launch a public offering using a prospectus drawn up in accordance with the EU's Prospectus Directive (*Financial Times*, 26 January 1998). In sum, Europe is set to remain a regulatory mosaic, regardless of the greater uniformity that is also being created by pan-European rules.

CONCLUSION

Whether embedded neo-liberalism will prove to be a stable *European* model of capitalism remains to be seen. What seems clear, however, is that the EU will not recapture the public governance that is being eroded at the national level, since European integration will continue to be primarily a process of *market* integration. This supremacy of the market is 'softened', however, in so far as the single market is still embedded at the national level by old institutions as well as by new European institutions although the former are clearly still more important. In this respect, the embeddedness of neo-liberal Europe is located primarily at the national level in terms both of economic organization and social legitimacy.

If the Anglo-Saxon model of finance gains more ground on the European continent once European monetary union sweeps away the remaining national barriers to economic integration, the 'strong globalization' thesis may then prove correct in predicting that the social and political structures of European national capitalisms may also be eroded and move towards the more minimal provisions of market-oriented systems. Nevertheless, as we have explained, there are good reasons to expect that systems of corporate governance will converge only at the margins, while the external support networks of the Germanic – and, to a lesser extent, the Latin – firms will be remodelled rather than abandoned. This is because these systems still gain competitive advantage from their 'network' resources and because the complex relationships that underpin them are highly resistant to radical change. That said, the stability of these systems will ultimately depend on the outcome of the political struggles between stakeholders and shareholders, companies and their employees, and private and publicly oriented capital, and on their ability to accommodate the forces of global capitalism without also abandoning their own institutions of national economic governance.

NOTES

1 To quote Young (1997: 48–9): 'output per employee in the entire manufacturing sector has risen by about 7 per cent more in Europe than it has in the USA during the past decade . . . {this} raises the issue of what restructuring is about if the USA does it, Europe does not do it, and Europe has the higher labour productivity growth'.

2 It is worth noting that another 'network' system – Japan – is travelling a similar path in terms of executive remuneration. The Japanese parliament removed the legal obstacles to stock options in 1997.

3 There has recently been a proliferation of such people in the new structure created by the merger of Mercedes Benz and Daimler Benz in January 1997.

4 To date, however, the tactics used by large US pension funds in the USA to shake up management in the companies where they invest have not been widely employed in Europe: it was expected that Calpers (the California Public Employees' Retirement Funds), which has large holdings in both the UK and France, would adopt such tactics there but so far it has behaved much more cautiously. Calpers has, however, lobbied actively to support changes in French and British corporate governance systems.

5 Similar developments have occurred in other European countries, including, most notably, Sweden, where the relocation debate has been as vigorous as in Germany. Here the problem seems to be less labour costs and corporate tax rates (which are low) than very high personal tax rates, which makes it hard for companies like Ericsson and Astra to retain and attract personnel for their large R&D operations. Ericsson has been threatening for some time to transfer the headquarters of its transport and cable networks business from Stockholm to the UK.

REFERENCES

Albert, M. (1993) *Capitalism Against Capitalism*, London: Whurr Publishers.

Apeldoorn, B. van (1998) *Transnational Capitalism and the European Integration Process*, doctoral thesis, Florence: European University Institute.

Berglöf, E. (1997) 'Boardrooms: reforming corporate governance in Europe', *Economic Policy*, April: 93–123.

Betts, P. (1997) 'Boxed-in capitalism', *Financial Times*, 17 April.

Boyer, R. (1996) 'The convergence hypothesis revisited: globalization but still the century of nations?', in S. Berger and R. Dore (eds), *National Diversity and Global Capitalism*, Ithaca: Cornell University Press, pp. 29–59.

Deeg, R. (1997) 'Banks and industrial finance in the 1990s', *Industry and Innovation* 4(1): 53–74.

De Jong, H.W. (1995) 'European capitalism: between freedom and social justice', *Review of Industrial Organization* 10: 399–419.

Fligstein, N. and Freeland, R. (1995) 'Theoretical and comparative perspectives on corporate organization', *Annual Review of Sociology* 21: 21–43.

Fligstein, N. and Mara-Drita, I. (1996) 'How to make a market: reflections on the attempt to create a single market in the European Community', *American Journal of Sociology* 102(1): 1–33.

Forsyth, D.J. and Notermans, T. (1997) 'Macroeconomic policy regimes and financial regulation in Europe, 1931–1994', in D.J. Forsyth and T. Notermans (eds), *Regime Changes: Macroeconomic Policy and Financial Regulation in Europe from the 1930s to the 1990s*, Providence and Oxford: Berghahn Books, pp. 17–68.

Gill, S. (1995) 'Globalization, market civilization, and disciplinary neoliberalism', *Millennium: Journal of International Studies* 24(3): 399–423.

Goldstein, A. (1996) 'Privatisation and corporate governance in France', *Banca Nazionale del Lavoro, Quarterly Review* 199: 455–88.

Gourevitch, P.A. (1996) 'The macropolitics of microinstitutional differences in the analysis of comparative capitalism', in S.Berger and R. Dore (eds), *National Diversity and Global Capitalism*, Ithaca: Cornell University Press, pp. 239–59.

Jack, A. (1997) 'French banks lose out in M&A', *Financial Times*, 15 January.

Jenkinson, T. and Ljungqvist, A. (1997) 'Hostile stakes and the role of banks in German corporate governance', *Nota di Lavoro* No.65, Milan: Fondazione Eni Enrico Mattei.

Kregel, J.A. (1997) 'Corporate governance of banks: Germany', *Banca Nazionale del Lavoro, Quarterly Review*, March: 67–82.

Leftwich, R. (1997) 'Obstacles to a global accounting deal', *Financial Times*, 19 May.

Marsh, D. (1996) 'Reinventing German capitalism', *German Politics* 5(3): 395–403.

Moerland, P.W. (1995a) 'Alternative disciplinary mechanisms in different corporate systems', *Journal of Economic Behavior and Organization* 26: 17–34.

Moerland, P.W. (1995b) 'Corporate ownership and control structures: an international comparison', *Review of Industrial Organization* 10: 443–64.

Mueller, F. (1996) 'National stakeholders in the global contest for corporate investment', *European Journal of Industrial Relations* 2(3): 345–66.

Müller-Stewens, G. and Schäfer, M. (1997) 'The German market for corporate control: structural development, cross-border activities and key players', in G. Owen and A. Richter (eds), *Corporate Restructuring in Britain and Germany*, London: Anglo-German Foundation for the Study of Industrial Society, pp. 30–40.

Rhodes, M. (1998) 'Globalization, labour markets and welfare states: a future of competitive corporatism?', in M. Rhodes and Y. Mény (eds), *The Future of European Welfare: A New Social Contract?*, London: Macmillan.

Rhodes, M. and van Apeldoorn, B. (1997) 'Capitalism versus capitalism in western Europe', in M. Rhodes, P. Heywood and V. Wright (eds), *Developments in West European Politics*, London: Macmillan, pp. 171–89.

Sarcinelli, M. (1997) 'Bank governance: models and reality', *Banca Nazionale del Lavoro, Quarterly Review*, March: 249–79.

Schaede, U. (1995) 'Toward a new system of corporate governance in the European Union: an integrative model of the Anglo-American and Germanic systems', in B. Eichengreen, J. Frieden and J. von Hagen (eds), *Politics and Institutions in an Integrated Europe*, Berlin and New York: Springer Verlag, pp. 93–119.

Schmidt, V. (1997) 'Privatization in France'. Paper presented at the American Political Science Association National Meetings, 28–31 August, Washington, DC.

Teeple, G. (1995) *Globalization and the Decline of Social Reform*, New Jersey and Toronto: Humanities Press and Garamond Press.

Vitols, S. (1997) 'Financial systems and industrial policy in Germany and Great Britain: the limits of convergence', in D.J. Forsyth and T. Notermans (eds), *Regime Changes: Macroeconomic Policy and Financial Regulation in Europe from the 1930s to the 1990s*, Providence and Oxford: Berghahn Books, pp. 221–56.

Vitols, S. and Woolcock, S. (1997) 'Developments in the German and British corporate governance systems'. Discussion paper, Workshop on Corporate Governance in Britain and Germany, May, University of Birmingham.

Young, R.M. (1997) 'Restructuring Europe: an investor's view', in G. Owen and A. Richter (eds), *Corporate Restructuring in Britain and Germany*, London: Anglo-German Foundation for the Study of Industrial Society, pp. 41–60.

Zysman, J. (1994) 'How institutions create historically rooted trajectories of growth', *Industrial and Corporate Change* 3(1): 243–83.

"The Very Uncertain Prospects of 'Global' Convergence in Corporate Governance"

from Cornell International Law Journal (2001)

Douglas M. Branson

INTRODUCTION

In the area of corporation law, the United States legal academy periodically falls in love with its own ideas. In the early 1990s, for example, scholars wrote about, and subsequently oversold, institutional investor activism as a means of holding corporate managers and boards of directors accountable.[1] In the 1980s, takeover bids and the market for corporate control occupied center stage.[2]

Scholars partaking in the corporate social responsibility movement of the 1970s thought government intervention was necessary to keep managers and boards responsible, whether in the form of federal minimum legal standards for corporate actors,[3] federal chartering of large publicly held corporations,[4] mandatory corporate social accounting and disclosure,[5] or installation of public interest directors.[6]

Today the academy has become much enamored with the notion of "global" convergence in corporate governance. That is to say, in the opinion of a number of the elites in the United States corporate law academy, the governance structure and practices of larger corporations all over the world soon will take on a resemblance one to another.[7] The telecommunications revolution, the ease of international jet travel, and pressure from law makers, stock exchanges, pension funds, and others, combine to motivate and enable those who control larger corporations to become conversant with corporate governance structures and practices. Those who control large corporations feel considerable pressure to adopt the best of such practices and structures gleaned from a global inventory.

Assuming that such a convergence is taking place, the further question is toward what point are those global corporate governance vectors converging? According to United States scholars writing on the subject, with little dissent, the agreement is that the convergence will be on a set of governance parameters that will replicate the American model of corporate governance.[8] The only debate involves questions such as whether convergence will be "formal," in the sense of adoption of United States style corporate legal regimes throughout the world, or "functional," in the sense of a worldwide accord as to best practices.[9]

Increasingly, corporate directors are familiar with governance developments in other nations. An Australian company director knows not only what the Bosch Report in Australia[10] may dictate for her company but may also be familiar with the Cadbury Code in the United Kingdom,[11] the American Law Institute's *Principles of Corporate Governance and Structure*,[12] and the General Motors 29 Points in the United States.[13] The Cadbury, Hampel,[14] and Greenbury[15] Reports in the United Kingdom have influenced corporate law reform proposals in Germany[16] and in France.[17] In that manner, to a degree at least, life has begun imitating art: corporations are modeling their corporate governance practices based upon blueprints drawn up by academics, regulators and directors interested in the notion of corporate self-regulation.

But it is a limited phenomenon. There is no massive "global" convergence in corporate governance. At best the evidence is of some incomplete transatlantic convergence with an outlier here and there.

In other cultures and economies great resentment exists toward United States economic imperialism and Americanocentric notions of the United States as the universal nation that, as unstated premises, underlie much of the global convergence scholarship. The "Millennium" or "Seattle" round of trade negotiations under the aegis of the World Trade Organization (WTO), with mass anti-WTO demonstrations, and the Washington, DC protests at the annual meetings of the World Bank and the International Monetary Fund, tell us further that there is significant opposition to globalization of anything, whether led by the United States or otherwise.[18]

The section on *Global convergence in corporate governance advocacy* of this chapter reviews the United States global convergence scholarship. The section on *The failure of attempts at export of legal institutions, harmonization, and globalization* develops the theme that United States corporate regulation has never traveled well internationally as well as the complementary theme that prior attempts at harmonization on an international scale have failed badly. Those themes raise the question why convergence advocates believe that United States style corporate governance will travel any better.

The section on *Cultural insensitivity: lack of a culture fit for the global convergence model of governance* points out the relative insularity and cultural insensitivity of the United States scholarship. Convergence advocates posit convergence based upon their study of capitalism in the United States, the United Kingdom, Germany and perhaps Japan.[19] They ignore most of the world's remaining 6 billion people, the largest nations on earth (the People's Republic of China, India, Indonesia), and the culture beneath law and economic systems that is as or more important than law or capitalism itself. Cultural diversity militates against convergence.

The section on *Different views of the deus ex machina: Anglo-American "ascendent" economics versus "embedded capitalism"* pursues the similar theme of economic, rather than cultural, insensitivity. A rich literature, ignored by the global convergence advocates, exists on capitalism in contrasting cultures. While most (but not all) nation states may now be said to have a capitalistic economic system, comparisons to

US and UK style capitalism are inapt. Worldwide the prevailing form of capitalism is said to be an "embedded capitalism" that serves and is integrated into the social order rather than the stand alone, highly individualistic Reagan–Thatcher style of capitalism that, for convergence advocates, constitutes the platonic form for capitalism everywhere. There are many cultures and many kinds of capitalism – family capitalism, managed capitalism, bamboo capitalism, crony capitalism, even the gangster capitalism of modern day Russia – and most of them may be ill-suited for United States style corporate governance.

Another worldwide phenomenon is backlash, chronicled in the section on *Backlash against American economic imperialism and globalization in any form as a force countering any "global" convergence in corporate governance.* From France to Indonesia and from South Africa to Sweden there is a backlash against passing off United States culture, including its economic and legal culture, as universal ("one size fits all") culture that presents the obvious solution to national and regional problems. Coupled with the anti-American backlash is the growing world unrest with globalization, at the least in the bulldozer-like form it takes in the thinking of multinational corporations and international organizations such as the World Bank, the International Monetary Fund or the World Trade Organization, all of which the world perceives as being controlled or dominated by the United States. These powerful emerging forces of backlash militate against anything that could be said to be "global" convergence in corporate governance.

Perhaps the best argument against global convergence in corporate governance is its irrelevancy if, indeed, some convergence is taking place. The recent growth of huge multinationals is the most striking worldwide economic development of the late 1990s and the early 21st century. United States style and traditional forms of corporate governance, which respond to the Berle–Means separation of ownership from control and the ensuing agency cost problem, simply are not responsive to the problems the growth of large multinationals portend. Worker exploitation, degradation of the environment, economic imperialism, regulatory arbitrage, and plantation production efforts by the growing stable of gargantuan multinationals, whose power exceeds that of most nation states, is far higher on the global agenda than is convergence in governance. The section on *The simple irrelevancy of United States style corporate governance to the pressing problem of the new century: the growth and regulation of large multinational corporations* develops those ideas.

The conclusion is that, simply put, most United States scholars have a fundamental misunderstanding of what globalization is and what may be expected of it. They share the view of United States multinationals and much of the community of international organizations that globalization means elimination of all barriers and differences – the promotion of homogeneity across the face of the earth – "globalization as a bulldozer." Instead, globalization is a technological and telecommunications revolution, a phenomenon of the information age, which will not necessarily erase all differences and barriers between nations and cultures.

Globalization thus portends convergence but it will not be global. Further, what convergence does occur may not be United States dominated but may occur around several disparate loci. Most importantly, the growth of large multinational corporations renders the convergence advocacy relatively insignificant in the larger scale of things.

GLOBAL CONVERGENCE IN CORPORATE GOVERNANCE ADVOCACY

Introduction

In 1993, the author published the first United States treatise on corporate governance.[20] The editors conducted a copyright search to insure the title's availability. This manuscript was apparently the first, on this side of the Atlantic at least, to lay claim to the title "Corporate Governance."

Today there is a flood of corporate governance scholarship, much of it comparative. In March 2000 alone, on the Social Science Research Network, authors posted abstracts and/or drafts of eight comparative corporate governance articles, ranging from *Corporate Governance Lessons from Russian Enterprise Fiascoes*,[21] and *Corporate Governance in Post-Privatized Slovenia*,[22] to *Japanese Corporate Governance: The Hidden Problems of the Corporate Law and Their Solutions*.[23] Other papers do not include "Corporate Governance" in the title but do deal with some aspect of corporate governance, pursuing a comparative theme.[24]

None of that corporate governance scholarship postulates a global convergence. Indeed, some of it demonstrates a decided lack of convergence, such as the failure of a Westernized corporation law in Russia[25] or the conscious choice in post-privatized Slovenia for extensive labor involvement in governance and a statutory scheme along the lines of German co-determination,[26] or the empirical demonstration that in Australia at least American style boards comprised of independent directors do not increase corporate profitability.[27]

Undaunted, United States scholars continue to predict the hegemony of United States governance. Some of these predictions take the form of bald assertions, with little analysis or citation. For example, in France family style capitalism is the overwhelmingly dominant form.[28] The French government promotes dispersed ownership and United States style market capitalism as a means of strengthening an economy that has been in a protracted slump, but without great success.

Nonetheless, the very scholar who makes those observations asserts that "technological changes and the globalization of the economy are pushing corporate governance worldwide towards a United States style market capitalism."[29] In the same vein, after discussing the potential influence of culture on shareholder manager relationships, he concludes:

> Yet, like economic destiny, corporate governance is no longer entirely under the control of any nation state. Indeed, corporate law scholars debate whether a transformation in the world business environment has [already] caused a "convergence" of corporate governance whereby cultural factors are losing their influence.[30]

Global convergence based upon European developments

A more analytical treatment reviews several manifestations of global convergence in European and European Union harmonization efforts.[31] Thus the Frankfurt and London stock exchange agreed to (and later abandoned) a merger that also involved a 20 percent participation by the French.[32] The European Union (EU) has pushed hard for standardization of the accounting rules used in its 15 member states.[33] The Paris based Organization for Economic Cooperation and Development (OECD) has promulgated a Code of Conduct for Multinational

Corporations.[34] Large multinational corporations such as DaimlerChrysler list their shares both on European and United States stock exchanges.[35] The SEC has been working with the International Organization of Securities Commissions (IOSCO) to develop international standards for nonfinancial statement disclosure.[36]

Given that evidence and its largely United States-European bias, it seems a stretch to conclude that "[c]ross border alliances among businesses are leading to the articulation of a new global corporate governance template which uses existing tools to build a new corporate world order."[37] The statement seems disproportionately outsized for the evidence presented which is, after all, only of EU and transatlantic developments.

Convergence in the quest for equity capital

Professor John Coffee, an eminent scholar always in the forefront of new thought, predicts global convergence through "the backdoor," so to speak, as foreign firms seek stock exchange listings in the United States and thus make themselves subject to United States style corporate governance norms.[38] Foreign issuers arrive on United States shores because of the strength of United States capital markets. In turn, the strength of United States capital markets stems from the protection United States law extends to minority investors in United States enterprises.[39]

Foreign issuers come to United States shores, however, because that is where the money is, not because of the protection United States law may once have given to minority share interests. And the United States supply of capital is not inexhaustible and is not exclusive. There is money elsewhere in the world, lots of it in fact, in Frankfurt, London, Zurich, Johannesburg, Riyadh, Milan, Sydney and Singapore, to name a few international banking centres. In fact, in February 2000, perhaps aware of strong capital markets in East Asia, seven United States high tech firms listed their common shares on the Hong Kong Stock Exchange.[40]

The protection of minority shareholdings in United States publicly traded ventures is also yesterday's, or the day before yesterday's, news. The odds of a minority shareholder obtaining a hearing on her complaint in the United States corporate court, the Delaware Chancery Court, are overwhelmingly against the plaintiff investor.

Delaware has crafted a number of procedural obstacles to prevent an investor from ever arguing the merits of her case, let alone obtaining relief.[41]

Under the other principal United States corporate law regime, the Revised Model Business Corporation Act, the drafters of that statute have adopted a number of even more draconian measures designed to insure that minority shareholders' complaints never see the light of day. These measures include a universal demand rule that never excuses demand on the board of directors as "futile,"[42] and an absolute prohibition on court review of directors' actions refusing a demand to commence litigation.[43]

The reputation of the United States legal system for protection of minority investors in corporations is no longer grounded in reality. It is probably not a sustainable reputational advantage for the United States corporate governance regime. Arguably, then, neither the United States's largely historical protection of minority investors nor the existence of an inexhaustible pool of capital will induce the spread of United States style corporate governance.[44]

Convergence by bald assertion: "The end of history for corporate law"

A recent paper by two elites in the United States academy is a chauvinistic Statement of the Americanocentric convergence thesis.[45] These two scholars contend that in the United States the supreme, or platonic, form of corporate governance structure has evolved. Both logic and competitive pressures to adopt the ideal United States shareholder-oriented model of corporate governance are irresistible and will result (or already have resulted) in its dominance around the globe. Thus, the authors posit an "end of history for corporate law," that is, an end for continued evolution of corporate law or of advocacy of competing governance models. The ideal has been achieved.

The evidence these two scholars set out in support of their thesis largely consists of bald assertions. Thus, "[r]ecent years ... have brought strong evidence of a growing consensus on [convergence] issues among the academic, business, and governmental elites in leading jurisdictions."[46] Continuing, "at the beginning of the twenty-first century we are witnessing rapid convergence on the standard shareholder-oriented model as a normative view of corporate structure and governance. We should also expect this normative convergence to produce substantial convergence in the practices of corporate governance and in corporate law."[47]

After asserting on very little, if any, evidence that competing governance models (labor, stakeholder, team production, family capitalism) no longer have any role to play, the authors tell us that "[t]he shareholder-oriented model has emerged as the normative consensus,"[48] and that in the competition engendered by international product and financial markets, "[i]t is now widely thought that firms organized and operated according to the shareholder-oriented model have had the upper hand."[49]

The preference of international equity markets and institutional investors for the shareholder model also lead to the conclusion that "[o]ver time, then, the standard [American] model is likely to win the competitive struggle . . . ."[50] Ergo, "no important competitors to the standard model of corporate governance remain persuasive today."[51]

Globally, then, we will witness the dominance of the United States model, with the "appointment of larger numbers of independent directors to boards of directors, reduction in overall board size, development of powerful board committees dominated by outsiders (such as audit committees, compensation committees, and nominating committees), closer links between management compensation and the value of the firm's equity securities, and strong communication between board members and institutional shareholders."[52]

On and on, the authors progress through a series of categorical statements to the preordained conclusion that

> [t]he triumph of the shareholder-oriented model of the corporation over its principal competitors is now assured, even if it was problematic as recently as twenty-five years ago. Logic alone did not establish the superiority of this standard model or of the prescriptive rules that it implies . . . [T]he standard model earned its position as the dominant model of the large corporation the hard way, by out-competing during the post-World War II period the . . . alternative models of corporate governance . . . [53]

Thus, apparently we are told, in Asia or Africa, in South America or the former Russian republics, as well as in Europe, and everywhere else on the globe, there is only one way – the American way.

A critique of the global convergence advocacy scholarship

This section makes five points, two of them briefly and three in more detailed sections that follow. They are: (1) the existing convergence scholarship engages in a high degree of pontification, with little evidence in support of assertions made and seemingly consciously unmindful of authority to the contrary; (2) the existing scholarship is highly inbred, ignoring work of scholars at lesser known institutions or in other fields and citing almost exclusively work by a few scholars at a handful of elite institutions; (3) when the convergence scholars do assemble evidence in support of their thesis the sample is an extremely narrow one from which to postulate "global" anything; (4) the advocacy of the United States model as global demonstrates an extreme lack of cultural understanding and sensitivity, ignoring countless cultures and billions of persons for whom United States style corporate governance would never be acceptable; and (5) implicit in this advocacy scholarship is the assumption that only one economic model, that which places efficiency and profit in the ascendancy, is acceptable. The reality is that in most of the world other economic models, grouped generically under "embedded capitalism," govern human and fictional beings' (corporations') lives, goals and aspirations.

A high degree of pontification

In much of this scholarship we are told we must accept major and minor premise as well as conclusion because the authors say so. For example, a major premise in *The End of History for Corporate Law* is that models advocating a role for labor representation in corporate governance are now dead letters,[54] as are the more far ranging "stakeholder models" along similar lines,[55] because the authors say so.

Yet a substantial body of corporate law scholarship to the contrary, much of it recent, exists, in the United States alone. Recent titles include *The Place of Workers in Corporate Law*,[56] *Organized Labor as Shareholder Activists: Building Coalitions to Promote Worker Capitalism*,[57] and *The Human Capital Era: Reconceptualizing Corporate Law to Facilitate Labor-Management Cooperation*.[58]

Along the lines of the broader stakeholder model, one respected scholar alone has authored *New*

Directions in Corporate Law: Communitarians, Contractarians, and the Crisis in Corporate Law,[59] *Theories of the Corporation,*[60] and *Redefining Corporate Law.*[61] A recent, and well-received, volume of essays largely devotes itself to the stakeholder model and variants thereon.[62]

Statutory drafters around the world also continue attempts to impose responsibilities on workers and stakeholders, if not through their direct participation in governance, then as a matter of corporate law.[63] How global convergences advocates ignore this evidence of divergence, or at least divergence from their opinions, is explainable only as a matter of hubris.

Inbred scholarship

When many of the global convergence advocates do cite to authority the leading scholars in an area are not cited unless, of course, those scholars are in the select inner circle of elites. In *End of History for Corporate Law*, the only works cited on labor participation in governance are by one of the co-authors himself.[64] In another recent piece of global convergence scholarship by two elites, in 58 footnotes the co-authors cite to their own works 33 times. In two or three other instances they cite to publications by other scholars, but in works one or the other co-author has edited.[65]

A narrow, and unrepresentative, sample for postulation of "global convergence"

It is surprising just how teetering the thin base upon which the convergence hypothesis rests is. The convergence advocates presume that the US and UK corporate law and corporate governance regimes are identical, or nearly so, which of course they are not. United States corporate law has become relentlessly enabling while increasingly British company law has become prescriptive, with countless substantive commands and minimum requirements.[66] The two bodies of law have diverged but the convergence advocates never examine the differences.[67]

As has been seen, examination of the Japanese corporate law model waxes and wanes.[68] Thus it is that the advocates of the "global" convergence hypothesis focus on developments in the United States, the United Kingdom, France and Germany.[69]

Outliers (limited to brief mention) are the Czech Republic,[70] Italy,[71] the Netherlands,[72] Israel[73] and Korea.[74] That is the total sample from which it is argued that a worldwide, or "global," convergence on United States style corporate governance norms is occurring or, indeed, is a *fait accompli*.

The convergence advocates ignore the nature of economies, legal systems and corporate governance on the Pacific Rim or in South and Central America, even though the Pacific Rim (population 3.8 billion)[75] and South America (population 734 million)[76] are often thought to be the emerging economies of the 21st century. Convergence advocates construct competing models based upon a limited sample of, on the one hand, the United States (population 270 million), and, on the other hand, the UK (population 59 million), Germany (82 million) and France (59 million).[77] They then declare the United States the winner of the competition. Last of all, they project that winning model over a world inhabited by 6 billion people, with an endless variety of cultures, economic and legal systems, and goals and aspirations.

There is an extreme skepticism and indeed distrust born of such advocacy by United States based scholars of the notion that United States style principles are universal truths. The former Prime Minister of Singapore, speaking of the potential twilight of Occidental style capitalism and the rise of Asia and the Pacific Rim as economic powers, described the uniqueness of Asian institutions:

> for America to be displaced, not in the world, but only in the Western Pacific . . . is emotionally very difficult [for American policy makers] to accept. The sense of cultural supremacy of the Americans will make this adjustment most difficult. Americans believe their ideas are universal – [for example] the supremacy of the individual and free, unfettered expression. But they are not – they never were.[78]

Convergence advocates' use of outliers, while laudable, may also be suspect. One advocate of convergence cites the great number of foreign listings on United States stock exchanges as evidence of forthcoming convergence.[79] The advocate points to a number of Israeli high tech firms that have listed shares on the NASDAQ.[80] Yet the greatest numbers of "foreign" listings on NASDAQ and the New York Stock Exchange remains listings by Canadian corporations.[81] Canadian firms' listings combined with one outlier group hardly constitute robust evidence of "global" convergence.

THE FAILURE OF ATTEMPTS AT EXPORT OF LEGAL INSTITUTIONS, HARMONIZATION, AND GLOBALIZATION

Failed attempts at export

United States corporate law has traveled very few places.[82] The drafters of the Russian corporation law took United States legislation as one starting point,[83] but even the drafters now admit that the Russian statute has been a failure, perhaps due as much to weak enforcement as to weak principles of law.[84]

By contrast, at least historically, British company law and company institutions have traveled very well.[85] On the Pacific Rim, for instance, Australia, New Zealand, Hong Kong, Singapore, Malaysia, Sri Lanka and India have British company law.[86] South Africa, which has a Roman Dutch civil law, also has British company law. So, too with former British colonies: Zimbabwe (Southern Rhodesia), Zambia (Northern Rhodesia), Malawi, Tanzania, Kenya, and Egypt have British company law. The reach of British company law has not been confined to former colonies. Namibia, the former German Southwest Africa, has a civilian legal system but British company law. Ghana is similar.[87]

The prevalence of British company law may be due to path dependency, but not completely. With its highly regulatory content, protection of minorities, and other features, British company law apparently adapts well to less developed countries (LDCs) and newly industrializing countries (NICs) better than does open ended "enabling" United States corporation law.

The relative lack of portability for United States corporate law then should give some pause to global convergence advocates. If United States corporate law has fared so poorly, why posit that United States style corporate governance will travel so much better?

Harmonization and standardization failures

Attempts to harmonize corporate law, especially its governance aspects, in the EU have been a dismal failure. The Draft Fifth Company Law Directive seeks to impose German-style co-determination on the member states and corporations chartered by them.[88] The British have strenuously opposed mandated labor participation in governance while other EU member states are lukewarm about the prospect. The Draft Fifth Directive is permanently stalled.[89]

The EU has also proposed a pan-European company, the Societas Europea, but that proposal has also stumbled badly because of its incorporation of co-determination features.[90] The staff of the Council of the EU recently announced an effort to simplify and retrench on less controversial elements of company law harmonization as well.[91]

EU efforts have gone beyond harmonization and promotion of the four freedoms which are at the core of the Union.[92] Those efforts have exceeded any mandate the Council and the Commission may have had, proceeding in the direction of uniform laws and standards throughout the Union. That overzealousness had produced a backlash, making legitimate harmonization more difficult to achieve.

Professor Paul Stephan has extensively analyzed harmonization and standardization efforts on an international scale.[93] His work points to several reasons such efforts are fated to achieve only minimal success, at best.

Lack of political accountability and rent seeking as obstacles to global convergence

In the international sphere, promotional efforts on behalf of harmonization are apt to encounter skepticism at the national level. The authors of such international efforts lack the political accountability of elected and appointed officials at national and local levels.[94] "In free and democratic societies, we insist on . . . a right to investigate and criticize lawmakers . . . [i]nternational lawmakers largely face weaker constraints on their behavior."[95] When faced with international or "global" proposals akin to law, the nation state may view the proposals with a greater degree of skepticism: "The domestic decisionmaker, even if a bureaucrat, still bears some political accountability for its choices; the international lawmaker does not. What underlies the skeptical position is a belief that the more accountable decisionmaker should receive the benefit of the doubt."[96]

International unification and harmonization efforts also encounter skepticism because they lack the transparency of local lawmaking: "interest groups tend to have somewhat lower costs of expressing their preferences to executives engaged in international lawmaking than in conveying their wishes to domestic legislators, and . . . the general public had higher monitoring costs with respect to international lawmaking."[97]

Lack of transparency in turn can result in a greater rate of rent seeking in efforts such as the one to promote global corporate governance. Economic rents are returns in excess of what is necessary to keep a given resource, including a human resource, from transferring to some other occupation.[98] Thus, "rents are earned only by owners of resources that cannot be augmented rapidly and at low cost to meet an increased demand for the goods [or services] that are used to produce."[99] In every jurisdiction, there exist various kinds of rent seekers who will attempt to foil efforts at harmonization or globalization.

The cadre of lawyers who specialize in corporate law, earning rents from their ability to explain the nuances of the status quo and to manipulate existing regulatory structures, may oppose simplification and harmonization efforts. In every jurisdiction, too, there exists a more elite inner circle of attorneys and advisers who earn economic rents as the gatekeepers trusted by legislators and government ministers when harmonization and globalization efforts reach the level of the nation state. They may foil such efforts unless the way is clear for their rent-seeking to continue.[100] Finally, bureaucrats will decrease transparency and engage in turf protection because they will feel threatened by harmonization-unification and the end of their ability to engage in rent seeking.[101]

Change in corporate law and attempted imposition from above of "global" standards of corporate governance will at some point be slowed, if not stopped, by some of the same obstacles other international efforts at unification or harmonization of economic laws and structures have encountered.[102] The lack of transparency perceived to exist in some such efforts, the lack of political accountability, the pretentious and condescending "we know better" tone of much of the convergence advocacy, and rent-seeking (as well as perceptions that rent seeking is occurring at the global level) all may impede convergence.

The myth of globalization

Introduction

The creation of the large multinational corporate organization in ways that will open up channels of communication about corporate governance, leading to convergence, and which many of the convergence advocates cite as prime evidence of their thesis, is the exception and not the rule. The Daimler-Chrysler or Deutsche Bank-Bankers Trust combinations are not representative of what empirical evidence demonstrates is occurring. In an important new book, *The Myth of the Global Corporation* (Myth),[103] the authors demonstrate that globalization is not taking place, or at least not occurring along the lines the legal elites assert.

"Good" globalization versus "Bad" globalization

Good, healthy globalization would be characterized by technology diffusion as well as other types of decentralization. Large multinational corporations (MNCs) would be transferring research and development (R&D) efforts to satellite operations in a meaningful way. Some of those receiving satellites would be located in newly industrializing countries (NICs) and perhaps in less developed countries (LDCs) as well. MNCs would be engaged in significant direct foreign investment (DFI). Forming subsidiaries and joint ventures in countries around the globe, MNCs would be making significant investments in plant and other production facilities, in modernization efforts, and in human resources so as to be able to decentralize financial, marketing and other "nerve center" aspects of their businesses. Simultaneously, MNCs would be shaking free from their roots and national origins, converging on a global model of governance and operation.

But "[t]he global corporation is mainly an American myth";[104]

The . . . idea[] that mobile corporations freed from political interference are now somehow arbitraging diverse national structures and forcing an involuntary process of convergence or an inevitable trend toward openness . . . marks a road to discord. On the surface, there is indeed a certain process of homogenization at work in a world where Americans drive BMWs, Germans listen to Sony CD players, and Japanese eat McDonald's hamburgers. But below the surface, where the roots of leading MNCs remain lodged, our research indicates durable sources of resistance to fundamental economic convergence.[105]

Contrary to what global convergence advocates state, and "however lustily they sing from the same hymnbook when they gather together in Davos or Aspen, the leaders of the world's great business enterprises continue to differ in their most fundamental strategic behavior and objectives."[106]

Lack of widespread direct foreign investment or technology diffusion

Worldwide DFI has expanded dramatically, from US$500 billion in the early 1980s to US$2.0 trillion in the early 1990s.[107] Yet, as the authors of Myth demonstrate, DFI remains concentrated in developed nations that are members of the OECD, or in a truncated version of that list. Japan still closes its border to significant DFI.[108] EU domestic content requirements discourage inward investment in EU member countries.[109] The spreading of wealth and the globalization that high absolute DFI numbers might portend is not occurring.

Tracking the volume of international royalty and license fee transactions, as well as other statistics, the economist authors of Myth ask, "Is a global technology base emerging?"[110] They conclude that hard evidence suggests it is not: "MNCs move R&D abroad far more slowly than production, sourcing, marketing, and other business activities . . . MNCs conduct relatively little R&D outside the home country."[111] Japanese foreign affiliates have "low R&D intensity."[112] Thus, "[d]evelopment of new technology remains centralized in the home market operations of MNCs."[113] The roots for future globalization, or for high quality globalization, are not being put down.

The resiliency of incorporating nation states and their cultures

Even in the transnational mergers which global convergence advocates feature prominently in their writing, the authors find that one culture (belief system) extinguishes the other, rather than convergence taking place.[114] National differences persist – are "hard wired into core corporate structures" and "embody distinctive and durable ideologies or, as some analysts now prefer to call them, belief-systems."[115] Thus, the authors note "an array of evidence documenting striking differences between the behavior of most continentally based firms and their counterparts in Great Britain."[116] Governance and financial structures "differ markedly" among major nations.[117] German firms differ markedly from firms in Scandinavia, France or the Benelux countries.[118] In fact, differences between German firms and firms in other countries seem especially persistent.[119]

Japanese firms operate in foreign wholesale rather than retail markets, use intrafirm investment to a great extent, and display "a comparatively low level of integration in local markets."[120] In turn, Korea, Taiwan, Hong Kong and Singapore each reflects great and persistent differences one from another in governance, finance, and other aspects of business.[121]

The strongest determinant of these differences is national origin:

[S]triking differences in firm behavior persist. These differences correlate most obviously with corporate nationality, not with sectoral characteristics or investment maturity . . . . Those differences . . . are systemic. Across firms, sectors, and in the aggregate, only one set of behavioral variations shines through – national ones.[122]

Continuing their conclusion, the authors of Myth remark that:

The evidence . . . suggests a logical chain that begins deep in the idiosyncratic national histories behind durable domestic institutions and ideologies and extends to firm-level structures of internal governance and long-ter[m] financing. Those structures, in turn, are then linked to continuing diversity in patterns of corporate R&D operations in the complex connections between corporate FDI and IFT [intrafirm trading] strategies . . . . [T]he basic linkage . . . [is that] [d]istinctive national institutions and ideologies shape corporate structure and vitally important policy environments in home markets. The external behavior of firms continues to be marked by their idiosyncratic foundations.[123]

"The Myth of Globalization" tells us what is, namely that "national roots remain a vital determinant" and that multinationals' "corporate cores remain national in a meaningful sense."[124] The next question is to ask is, "Why is that so?"

CULTURAL INSENSITIVITY: LACK OF A CULTURE FIT FOR THE GLOBAL CONVERGENCE MODEL OF GOVERNANCE

Cultural traits implicit in the United States governance model

Convergence advocates rely heavily, really exclusively, on the United States model of corporate governance. That model, of course, is centered on a board of directors the majority of whom are independent, that is, free of significant financial or perhaps even social contacts with the corporation's senior managers.[125] Indeed, a respectable school of thought is that all directors save one or two should be independent, non-executive directors.[126]

In turn, that independent board has a new and more focused mission. United States corporate law once provided that the "business and affairs of the corporation should be managed by a board of directors." Later, intermediate and less imperative versions of that mandate provided that the business and affairs could be managed by others "under the supervision" of a board of directors.[127] Today, one authoritative source for United States law provides that the senior executives are to manage the business and affairs of the corporation.[128] In turn, the board's role is to select, monitor, evaluate, and, if necessary, remove, the senior executive officers, including principally the chief executive officer or managing directors.[129]

The United States model contemplates a significant role for highly individualistic behavior. For example, if a director of a United States corporation disagrees with action taken she should clearly voice her objection. United States law commonly provides that a director is presumed to consent to action taken unless her dissent is recorded in the minutes of the meeting or filed in writing immediately thereafter.[130] The United States scheme contemplates a significant role for shareholder litigation. Individual shareholders who are aggrieved by corporate managers' acts should rise up, retain attorneys, and bring suit to hold those managers accountable.[131]

Lessons in diversity: the United States model in other cultures

The People's Republic of China and the overseas Chinese

For example, a scheme that places significant reliance on highly individualistic forms of behavior does not mesh well, or at all, with the Confucian value system of the Chinese. The People's Republic of China is, of course, the most populous nation on earth. Through the Chinese diaspora, an additional 40 million Chinese have emigrated to other East Asian nations, where as of 1990 their family enterprises added $200 billion to various states' gross annual domestic products.[132] Overseas Chinese number over 40 million,[133] playing significant roles in the economies of Taiwan, Singapore, Indonesia, the Philippines, Malaysia and Thailand.[134] These roles far exceed their number in their adopted countries. In the Philippines, for example, overseas Chinese control 47 percent of the 68 locally owned publicly held companies.[135] In 1990, Chinese accounted for 2.1 percent of the population but 75 percent of the private domestic capital in Indonesia.[136]

Although Confucianism lacks either a deity or an organized church, Confucian values permeate the lives of Chinese peoples everywhere.[137] From a very early age, "[i]n the school context, Confucianism is taught by the study of the main writings and the discussion of their implications. The child is encouraged to memorize the classics and to build relationships based on the Confucian principles."[138] Central to those relationships is a high degree of abnegation of self and tolerance and patience for others.[139] One has to question how a corporate governance model that entails a certain degree of confrontation and a high degree of individualistic behavior fits with beliefs that "an individual must fit into and conform with the basic social order of his surrounding world."[140] That order is "strongly hierarchical" with each individual regarding himself "not only ... as part of nature but also part of the natural order ..."

one of the most important effects of Confucianism, and one of the principal determinants of social and economic behavior ... is the passivity induced by a system which places the individual in a powerfully maintained family order, itself inside a powerfully maintained state order, itself seen as part of a natural cosmic order, and all dedicated to the maintenance of the status quo.[141]

Core values in economic behavior include a "concern for reconciliation, harmony [and] balance" coupled with "practicality as a central focus."[142] It is doubtful whether individuals taught from an early age that "the shiny nail is the first to feel the sting of the hammer" will confront and forcibly remove underperforming CEOs or step forward to file derivative or class action lawsuits.[143]

The Republic of Indonesia[144]

Other societies remain highly feudal in character. In Indonesia, the world's third largest democracy and fourth most populous nation, for example, a strong sense of permanence in the socioeconomic order, which after all still has a network of ruling sultans, may prevent the development of the cadre of independent directors and the required behavior by them or sufficiently aggressive shareholders to make United States style corporate governance take hold. The perception is widespread that it is futile to challenge one who "has the power."[145]

The quasi-feudal nature of Indonesian society is an impediment to United States style corporate governance. In the 1998–99 Asian economic crisis, 38 Indonesian banks, many of them publicly held, were closed, as a result of extreme mismanagement that had permitted over US$90 billion in loan defaults.[146] Indonesian corporate law clearly provides for derivative actions by shareholders.[147] Yet not a single share-holder suit was filed. The absence of suit may be in part explained by the weakness of the Indonesian legal system but cultural factors are also at work in a situation which in the United States would have produced a firestorm of litigation.

Another concept of Indonesian society and the legal system might be inimical to introduction of United States style corporate governance. The political and legal systems are founded on the notion of *musyawarah* and *mufakat*, translated as "discussion and consensus."[148] The concept places upon parties to a proceeding or transaction a duty to avoid confrontation, including a duty even to avoid pushing issues to a formal vote. Duties based upon "discussion and consensus" are reflected not only in the customary law of Indonesia but in the company law itself. For example, "[t]he resolutions of the GMS [General Meeting of Shareholders] shall be adopted based on the principle of deliberation to reach a consensus."[149]

The world's dominant form of economic organization – family capitalism

A third example of the lack of cultural fit for the United States style corporate governance systems first requires a brief overview of the dominant form of capitalism in many countries – family capitalism. For example, overseas Chinese firms represent "molecular organization – heavily networked family firms" that tend toward vertical integration.[150] In South Korea, the *Chaebol* are "family dominated, but less centralized, grow extremely large, are elaborately and formally co-ordinated . . . [t]heir environment is also patrimonial . . . [and] has a similarly Confucian moral-based government."[151] Indonesia has a brand of family capitalism characterized by "long term mutually enriching alliances between local military forces and Chinese businessmen."[152]

Turning toward Europe, France's government yearns for finance capitalism with the dispersed type of share ownership it produces.[153] The truth is, however, that France's economic topography is populated by family firms, including family controlled publicly held firms.[154] The same may be said of Italy.[155]

While in some families a willingness may exist to appoint independent directors and permit them to constitute a majority of the board, as the United States governance model dictates, in many other families there will not be such a willingness to relinquish power. The same observations may be made with regard to the rigorous evaluation and possible removal of senior executive officers. The culture of family capitalism will pose an obstacle to that occurring with any frequency.

The teaching of years of comparative study is that it is the culture beneath the law and behind economic and other institutions that is as or more important than law itself, legal structures, and good governance practices. "At the heart of the matter is the manner in which culture, as a process, tends, cultivates and regulates particular types of economic outcomes."[156] With the nearly complete absence of any discussion of varying cultures, or of the role of culture, the United States global convergence advocates seem never to have learned those basic truths about comparative study.

DIFFERENT VIEWS OF THE DEUS EX MACHINA: ANGLO-AMERICAN "ASCENDENT" ECONOMICS VERSUS "EMBEDDED CAPITALISM"

Embedded capitalism

United States academic elites, including the global convergence advocates, seem to hold as universal a view of economies as free-standing machines with profit maximization as each firm's and the nation's goal, market forces supreme, and the society subservient to, or at least apart from, the economy. That mind set, heavily imbued as it is with the supremacy of the individual and *laissez-faire*, traces its roots to the writings of John Stuart Mill, Adam Smith, Karl Marx and, later, Max Weber and Frederick Hayek, who mistook the tendencies of 19th century English markets to be universal laws and did so based upon empirical observations of a very few western economies.[157]

Yet, outside of the former British Empire, and even to some extent within it, the world's economies are perceived as serving the society as whole. Citizens and national leaders see the economy as but an element of the larger society. The view is that for most capitalistic countries the proper form of capitalism is "embedded capitalism."[158]

Certain welfare economists believe that the natural state of things is a form of constrained, regulated capitalism rather than unfettered markets. A constrained market economy is the inevitable result of the interplay of capitalism and democracy. Through politics the majority (the "have nots") will elect representatives based upon platforms and programs that promise to temper or brake the Darwinian "survival of the fittest" that is the product of the unfettered market system and limit at least runaway economic success by the most fortunate in the society (the "haves").[159] In fact, relatively unfettered markets have existed only in two eras: Victorian times in England and the Thatcher-Reagan years in the United States and the UK.[160]

The individual versus the society

Stronger still, the market individualism of market leaning economies is simply intolerable in many societies. The economy is embedded in the social order and social cohesion, not rugged individualism, is the value in the ascendancy.[161] For example, "[l]ife in a collectivist and group-dominated society means that the Chinese self is not isolated in the same sense as the Western one."[162] In some cultures, firms are "independent legal entities which are well bounded and distinct from their environments."[163] By contrast, theorists have recognized Asian business firms' "form and operation as contingent, socially contextual phenomenon varying across cultures and historical periods."[164]

Convergence advocates might point to the unparalleled economic success of the United States in the 1990s as predictor that United States style corporate governance will vanquish any rivals. But United States economic success, with its concomitant supremacy of the individual, is viewed in much of the world as destructive of social cohesion and to be avoided rather than emulated.[165] To observers and opinion makers in many countries, the United States's high divorce, murder, and incarceration rates, categories in which the United States leads the world,[166] together with the obscene rates of United States corporate executive compensation,[167] symbolize the abandonment of social cohesion and the ascendancy of market style individualism and unbridled greed. There is no trend to homogeneity in world economics, as globalization advocates might assert. Modernization and Westernization are not converging trends, as the underlying premise of global convergence scholarship implies. For much of the world, modernization and Westernization have become diverging trends or, indeed, anathema to one another.[168] In the march of progress, many less affluent nation states regard themselves as ahead of, not behind, the United States.

In fact, in much of the world the belief is that, by emulating the United States and copying its economic thoughts and institutions, a sort of Gresham's Law[169] will prevail: bad capitalism (United States style) will drive out good capitalism (family capitalism, bamboo capitalism, guided capitalism).[170]

Impenetrable barriers to western economic ideas

In still another part of the world in a subset of nations powerful political and religious forces cause the rejection of all Western ideology:

> In China, Malaysia and Singapore, in Egypt, Algeria and Iran, in post-communist Russia and parts of the Balkans, in Turkey and India, the end of the Cold War has released powerful political movements which reject all westernizing ideologies . . . .

Only in the United States is the Enlightenment project of a global civilization still a living political faith. During the Cold War this Enlightenment faith was embodied in American anti-communism. In the post-communist era it animates the American project of a universal free market.[171]

Many of the Muslim nations of the world (Iraq, Iran, Saudi Arabia, Indonesia to an extent) are loathe to permit American influence of any kind to flourish within their borders. Some of that group actively block penetration of United States economic or other ideas.

United States global convergence advocates have the wrong view of capitalism and economies of the world. They have, it seems, fallen prey to the error of John Stuart Mill or Adam Smith, who also made sweeping (global) assertions based upon empirical observations of a few (a very few)[172] western economies.

BACKLASH AGAINST AMERICAN ECONOMIC IMPERIALISM AND GLOBALIZATION IN ANY FORM AS A FORCE COUNTERING ANY "GLOBAL" CONVERGENCE IN CORPORATE GOVERNANCE

There are two principal types of backlash inimical to any "global" convergence of corporate governance, especially governance patterned on the United States model. One form is a direct worldwide backlash against United States influence and domination in everything from product markets to ideas. The other is the growing backlash against globalization, a significant component of which is rooted in the notion that globalization is little more than a vehicle for Americanization.

Scholars who posit a convergence in corporate governance proceed on the premise that United States business, political and academic leaders can project American products and values to the last corner of the earth. As the following editorial from the *International Herald Tribune* (Paris) suggests, those leaders face significant backlash in creation of the new economy empire they predict:

It is impossible to pinpoint the moment when the successes of the United States in the 1990s moved from a topic of grudging admiration around the world to a constant source of annoyance . . . to a rationale of mistrust and resistance.

Perhaps the clincher was envy over the dramatic ascent of the Dow Jones industrial average from a little over 2,000 points at the start of the decade to more than 11,000 this year. Maybe it was the dawning realization that people around the globe are all flicking on the same Windows operating system in the morning, on their way to navigating an Internet dominated by U.S. innovations and businesses . . . .

Maybe it was when the United States, in the wake of the Asian economic crisis, began offering tutorials on American-style capitalism and insisting that the financial architecture of the world be rebuilt to U.S. building codes.[173]

It is not only protesters against the WTO in Seattle or at the IMF and World Bank annual meetings in Washington, DC,[174] but also a significant number of thoughtful persons around the globe who see globalization of anything, including corporate governance, as a Trojan horse for United States dominance:

One of the most frequent complaints about globalization is that it is equivalent to Americanization. There are widespread fears that in today's borderless, high tech world, national differences will be overwhelmed by American economic and cultural domination . . . .[175]

First and foremost, according to its critics, globalization serves the agenda of large United States based multinational corporations, for whom growth of sales and profits are ascendant over all other values:

Growth, [critics of globalization] argue, can be wasteful, destructive, unjust. The jobs created by globalization are often less sustaining and secure than the livelihoods abolished by it. Weak economies abruptly integrated into the global system do not become stronger, or develop a sustainable base; they just become more dependent, more vulnerable to the ructions of ultravolatile, deregulated international capital.[176]

Globalization, to their way of thinking, is the imposition from above by international institutions such as the WTO, IMF and World Bank, of a worldwide Darwinian regime that will make the rich richer and the world's poor no better off:

In many countries, the benefits of economic growth [wrought by globalization] are so unequally distributed that they intensify social and political tensions, leading to increased repression rather than to greater democracy. To the hoary trope that a rising tide lifts all boats, critics of corporate-led globalization retort that in this case it lifts only yachts.[177]

It is easy to dismiss the concerns of protesters in Seattle, Washington, Gothenberg, or Genoa as the poorly articulated, contradictory outcry of a disorganized mob, and many do.[178] From their ivory tower perches in the American academy, "global" convergence in corporate governance advocates do not even broach the subject of opposition to globalization, or any other form of backlash. They simply believe that any ideas with which they are associated, such as superior United States style corporate governance practices and structures, ultimately will prevail in some world wide market-place of ideas.[179] Backlash against United States influences and against globalization cannot be quantified but they are palpable nonetheless. In both forms, worldwide backlash poses a significant impediment to "global" convergence in corporate governance.

THE SIMPLE IRRELEVANCY OF UNITED STATES STYLE CORPORATE GOVERNANCE TO THE PRESSING PROBLEM OF THE NEW CENTURY: THE GROWTH AND REGULATION OF LARGE MULTINATIONAL CORPORATIONS

Background

The inexorable growth of large multinationals has been one of the least noticed phenomena of the 1990s and, in the new century, is only now receiving the critical attention it deserves. The growth of large multinational and truly international corporations poses a number of overlapping problems, such as the irrelevancy-impotency of the nation state, the resulting field of play for economic imperialism, and resulting opportunities to engage in regulatory arbitrage, leading to problems such as environmental degradation and "plantation production," especially in the new industrializing countries (NICs) and less developed countries (LDCs) of the world. Traditional corporate governance theory, structure, and practices deal with solving problems thought to be generated by the separation of ownership from control in large publicly held corporations. They are simply irrelevant to the problems posed by the growth of large, sprawling multinational entities.

The accelerating growth of large multinationals

The number and size of large multinational corporations have grown at geometric rather than arithmetical rates as of late. Predictions are that by the year 2010 the number of large multinationals will be several times the number that existed just a few years ago.[180] Domestic and transnational merger activity is at an all time high. Particularly in commodities areas (oil, aluminum), but also in automobile manufacture, telecommunications, food and other fields, senior corporate managers are engaged in a quest to be number one, two, or three in size – on a global rather than merely a domestic or continental (EU or NAFTA) scale.

The quest to be in a handful of the largest corporations in a given field, and on a global scale, is driving a headlong pursuit of size, manifesting itself in a worldwide merger movement. The recent acquisition by Alcoa Aluminum of Reynolds Metals Co. illustrates this trend.[181] Alcoa faced a situation in which three smaller foreign rivals combined to form an aluminum multinational with $21 billion in worldwide sales.[182] Alcoa's CEO felt that Alcoa had no choice but to make a bear hug offer for the world's third largest producer of aluminum products, Reynolds Metals. After the acquisition, Alcoa will rival the world's largest producer, with slightly less than $21 billion in annual sales.[183]

In another commodities field, oil, Exxon has acquired Mobil Oil in a $81.2 billion combination.[184] The British Petroleum Amoco merger represents a $48 billion transaction, which has been followed by a proposed BP Amoco PLC buyout of Atlantic Richfield Co. for $30 billion more.[185] In the summer of 1999, France's Fina Petroleum made an offer for Elf Acquitaine. France's other large international oil company. Reminiscent of the Bendix Martin Marietta "Pac Man" affair of the 1980s, Elf countered with a bid for Fina. Later in the summer the two corporations agreed on a friendly amalgamation that will result in the world's fourth largest oil company.[186]

Global oligopoly seems a near certain prospect for the world's automobile manufacturing industry. Chrysler and Daimler-Benz have combined[187] as have Ford and Volvo.[188] In March 1999, Renault S.A. of France took effective control of Nissan Motor Co.[189] General Motors Corporation has held talks with Fiat SpA.[190] These latter business combinations involve not only sheer size, but also portend an age of increasing transnational takeover and merger activity.[191]

Carlo De Benedetti's 1988 attempt to take over *Societe Generale de Belgique* was characterized as the first major transnational takeover, hostile or friendly, in the European Union.[192] By that time, of course, the United States had witnessed a crazy decade of merger activity, hostile takeovers, insider trading scandals and financial excesses.

Europe and the EU member states are awakening, if not catching the United States. In summer, 1999, Bank Nationale of France made two simultaneous $38 billion hostile offers, for Paribas and for Belgium's Societe Generale.[193] Deutsche Bank in Germany and Bankers Trust in the United States have combined.[194] Recently, in telecommunications, Mannesmann A.G., the largest German wireless company, has acquired Orange PLC, Britain's third largest wireless corporation, in a $33 billion transaction.[195] Vodafone Airtouch, PLC then made an offer for Mannesmann.[196]

The size of the acquisitions has become truly staggering. In the 1980's the RJR Nabisco transaction featured in *Barbarians at the Gate* was thought to have set a record for the size of the deal, a record that would endure, at $24 billion.[197] The recent MCI World Wide Communications proposed acquisition of Sprint is a $115 billion transaction.[198] The America Online (AOL) Time Warner combination is a $165 billion transaction.[199] The Vodafone offer for Mannesmann, A.G. is valued at $180 billion.[200]

An illustrative new multinational

A recent business combination of two multinationals frames the issues nicely. Unilever, a Netherlands based food and consumer products company, is a mid-size multinational which has 138 subsidiaries in 71 countries worldwide: 11 in North America, 15 in Latin America, 23 in Africa and the Middle East, 23 on the Pacific Rim, 55 in the European Economic Union, and 11 in the remainder of Europe.[201] Its worldwide sales are approximately $44 billion.[202] It employs 2.25 million people of whom 550,000 work on corporate owned plantations.[203]

In May 2000, Unilever made overtures to a smaller United States based food multinational, Best Foods Co. With $10 billion or so in worldwide sales, Best has 62 subsidiaries operating in 110 different countries, many on the Pacific Rim.[204] Combined, after the $20.3 billion acquisition, with elimination of some overlap, the two multinationals will have over 200 subsidiaries in over 120 countries, with Best Foods' strong presence in Asia complementing nicely Unilever's presence in the Americas and the European Union. The combined entity is now the world's second largest food company, after Nestle of Switzerland, with Kraft Foods of the United States ranking third.[205]

A corporate organization such as the combined Unilever-Best organization illustrates nicely four inter-related regulatory problems: (1) power, size and the resulting irrelevancy-impotency of the nation state; (2) increased economic imperialism; (3) regulatory arbitrage; and (4) the related "plantation production" problem.

The regulatory setting in the multinational corporate sphere

The power and size of multinationals and the irrelevancy of the nation state

In the 1990s the case for regulation clearly departs from the 50 plus year search by law professors and reformers to fill the vacuum created by the separation of ownership from control Berle and Means hypothesized in 1932.[206] Berle's and Means's analysis implicitly assumes a large but not all powerful corporation operating, by and large, subject to the dictates of a single nation state which, in theory, possesses sufficient power to regulate should it desire to do so. Later reforms of the corporate social responsibility movement, such as federal chartering of corporations[207] or federal minimum standards,[208] hypothesized a lack of a will to regulate brought on by charter mongering, the "race to the bottom" engaged in by the states.[209] Those proposals still assumed, however, the power of the nation state, in the form of the federal government, to bend corporations to its will if it wished to do so.

Today, however, large corporate empires sprawl across the globe. The power of the corporation may not only exceed that of any host but also that of the incorporating state. With a combined $54 billion in sales, the Unilever-Best entity has an annual turnover that exceeds the gross domestic product (GDP) of all but about 50 nations, including Ecuador, the United Arab Emirates, Kuwait and Kenya, ranking just behind the Republic of Ireland whose GDP is $59.9 billion.[210] Often the nation states in which subsidiaries operate and in which externalities are most felt do not have the power (or the will) to regulate.[211] This scenario brings renewed call for the domiciliary state of the parent corporation to assert itself.[212]

In turn, incorporating nation states may refuse to take adequate action because of the fear that large multinationals may reincorporate elsewhere. Indeed, a multinational could move to an offshore incorporating jurisdiction (the Netherlands Antilles, the Cook Islands, Grand Cayman) in which secrecy prevails and the threat of meaningful regulation is nil.[213]

Observations as to sheer power and size have led many scholars to predict or proclaim the irrelevancy of corporate law and of the identity of the incorporating state.[214]

Economic imperialism

On quaint Fort Street, in Victoria, British Columbia, Canada, a United States Banana Republic Store and a Burger King have displaced a Scots Tartan store and a tea shop that had been on Fort Street for decades. The main street of a middle size town in Malaysia will be lined with United States franchised fast food outlets: a Kentucky Fried Chicken, an A and W Root Beer and a Burger King. Can a GAP store be far behind? The United States based McDonalds is everywhere, its stores and its billboards despoiling the urban and the rural landscapes of countries around the globe.

In their attempts to homogenize the world, United States multinationals often attempt to march in under the banner of free trade. Monsanto has attempted to shoehorn its genetically engineered seed products into the European Union, over the objections of French farmers.[215] Prodded by multinational United States based producers, the United States trade representative argues for the introduction into European markets of beef fattened using human growth hormones.[216]

This is the new economic imperialism. That imperialism views the eradication of all barriers as tantamount to globalization. That imperialism wants a world without borders so that the same products and services dominate market after market. That imperialism uses globalization as a bulldozer to crush resistance to achievement of those goals by the multinational corporations that are the progenitors of economic imperialism.

Regulatory arbitrage by multinationals

The need to regulate, based upon the global scenario, is buttressed by a refinement, the notion of "regulatory arbitrage."[217] A multinational may locate activities in nation states in which the regulation poses the least, or no, obstacle to the activity in which the multinational wishes to engage. For example, the multinational may locate a polluting facility in a former Soviet Republic in which environmental law or enforcement is not only lax but non-existent. The same multinational might locate a "knockoff" manufacturing facility in a nation with a large market for the product and little or no protection for intellectual property, such as the People's Republic of China. With labor intensive manufacturing the multinational may seek out a developing nation eager for employment at any cost and locate a facility there. Through time, the multinational may shift activities from country to country, depending upon the regulatory obstacles that spring up in the multinational's path, usually as the standard of living and expectations rise.[218]

A combined Unilever-Best, with 200 separate operations already existent in 120 countries around the globe, and on every continent save Antarctica, illustrates the potential for regulatory arbitrage open to managers of a far flung multinational.

The plantation production problem

Multinationals may move activities to host nations in which working conditions are substandard to atrocious and in which wages paid do not rise even to the level of a living wage. Over decades a manufacturer might move a facility from Korea to Malaysia to Indonesia to Vietnam. Newly industrializing countries (NICs) of Africa could be next in the parade of host states. In other instances, a manufacturer may move manufacture or assembly activities from facility to facility in the same country, as in the *maquiladora* phenomenon that has occurred in Mexico and has accelerated under NAFTA.[219]

Host states often welcome roving multinationals, despite the exploitation of their citizens involved. In competition for economic growth, other states that may be prone to regulate at least more extreme forms of worker exploitation do not do so, fearing a competitive disadvantage. Among nation states a collective action problem exists that may be solved by international organizations such as the World Bank or the World Trade Organization. Within the WTO, however, the NICs and the LDCs resist, perceiving WTO efforts to regulate plantation production as a ploy by wealthier states to keep NICs and LDCs in their place.[220] Given the economic disparities among nations around the globe, the plantation production problem seems an intractable one,[221] certainly not susceptible to traditional corporate governance analysis.

The irrelevance of traditional corporate governance to the multinational sphere

In 1932 Adolph Berle and Gardiner Means published their empirical findings with regard to the publicly held corporation.[222] Berle and Means found that with modern communications, well-organized stock exchanges and a proliferation of investors the owners of incorporated business had become dispersed and their shareholdings had become, for the most part, atomized. The modern corporation represented a new form of property. Those who owned the property, the shareholders, no longer controlled it. Instead, self-perpetuating boards of directors and senior corporate managers controlled the property. Berle and Means hypothesized and then proved the existence of the fabled "separation of ownership from control."[223]

Due to what we today call collective action problems, even when shareholders detect that corporate managers are underperforming, or performing in other undesirable ways, shareholders find it very difficult to unite and then reassert themselves. Collective action problems include the difficulty in many public corporations of identifying who fellow shareholders are in the first place and then the costs of communicating with them. The latter costs include regulatory costs, most specifically the cost of complying with the SEC's rules governing proxy solicitation, which permit the corporation and its managers to sue the activist shareholder for mere slips of the pen in their communication with others. Another collective action problem is the "free rider" problem. A certain number of fellow shareholders may support the activists in spirit, but not financially, or in other meaningful ways. They will watch closely, but only as bystanders who "free ride" on the efforts of their activist brethren.

Traditional corporate governance analysis deals with what regulatory or market forces should fill the "vacuum" created by the separation of ownership from control. Most "reforms" propose insertion of substitute monitors, who will supply the monitoring the dispersed shareholder no longer can provide. Substitute monitors include governmental (Ralph Nader's proposed Federal Chartering Agency), reinvigorated shareholders (expanded SEC shareholder proxy proposal rule), auditors and enhanced audits (corporate social accounting), public interest directors, or activist institutional investors.

Another approach is to use those and other devices such as performance based compensation to re-align managers' interests with shareholders's interests. Economists would posit that any agent, whether it be the property manager for an absentee landlord or the senior executive of a major corporation with dispersed shareholders, has a different agenda than does the owner and will not take care of the property in the same manner as the owner would if she were present. Thus agents may engage in shirking (laziness, playing excessive amounts of golf) or opportunistic (self serving, self dealing) behavior. The central problem of corporate law, and especially corporate governance, is to reduce these agency costs.[224]

The current vogue in United States style corporate governance emphasizes use of boards of directors comprised of truly independent directors.[225] Instead of managing the corporation's business and affairs, those independent directors have a changed mission. Their focus should be to hire, evaluate, and, if necessary, replace the corporation's senior executive officers.[226] Independent directors, assisted by a committee structure (audit, nominating and compensation committees),[227] reduce agency costs and represent the substitute monitor yearned for since Berle and Means published their book.

In the multinational sphere, however, the evils imagined result from managers over performing, relentlessly pursuing profit through economic imperialism, excessive regulatory arbitration, degradation of the environment and plantation production. The United States style corporate governance model, which convergence advocates say should or already does dominate on global fronts, contemplates an underperforming or self dealing manager, not an over performing one. Put another way, in the international sphere, the senior managers and dispersed owners share an interest in financial returns that is less hampered, or not hampered at all, by an agency cost problem. Their interests are in alignment rather than out of alignment, as traditional corporate governance theory hypothesizes. Why this is so is a matter for conjecture. Perhaps it is because of the larger stakes and the absence of significant obstacles, the "easy pickings" as it were in the multinational sphere.

Professor Lawrence Cunningham labels what traditional United States style corporate governance analysis and debate deals with as "vertical" corporate governance.[228] Assessments are made along a vertical line running up from shareholders through boards of directors and other monitors (such as auditors) to senior executive managers. The alignment, or lack of alignment, of various groups' interests along that vertical line is a central subject for discussion.

The large multinational corporation poses a completely different set of potential problems. Economic imperialism, degradation of the environment, regulatory arbitrage, and plantation production are problems of "external" corporate governance.[229] How a large multinational corporation interacts with the multitudinous societies and nation states in its far flung empire is a subject on which corporate governance, of the type the United States global convergence advocates know and write about, has very little if anything to say.

The self-anointed corporate governance experts, elite as they may be in the United States corporate law academy, are not cognizant of the real issues of the twenty first century. Their advocacy of "global" convergence, and that along the lines of United States style corporate governance, is not based upon "global" developments, is culturally chauvinistic, and is anachronistic. With the looming menace of gargantuan multinationals roaming the earth, events have moved swiftly past the elites' "global" convergence advocacy. As described above, in the larger scheme of things, "global" convergence in corporate governance is simply beside the point.

CONCLUSION

Convergence in corporate governance may occur in discrete areas, such as financial accounting or disclosure standards. That convergence is far more likely to be regional rather than "global." In East Asia, for example, the ten SEAN states, perhaps lead by Singapore, could encourage direct foreign investment in the region, although at present there is no evidence of such a development beginning, let alone occurring.

Seldom will one see scholarship and advocacy that is as culturally and economically insensitive, and condescending, as is the "global" convergence advocacy scholarship that the elites in United States academy have been throwing over the transom. Those elites have oversold an idea that has little grounding in true "global" reality.

Instead those academics should turn their not inconsiderable talents to the issues of the new century. The astounding growth of huge multinational corporations, the impotence or lack of will among nation states to regulate them, the role of international organizations in the regulation of multinationals, and the relevance or lack of relevance of traditional corporate governance regimes – not "global" convergence in corporate governance – are the corporate law issues to which we must devote our time and our thoughts in the twenty first century.

ACKNOWLEDGMENTS

The author wishes to thank John Farrar, Professor of Law, Bond University, Queensland, Professorial Associate, University of Melbourne and the University of Hong Kong, Brian R. Cheffins, S.J. Berwin Professor of Law, Cambridge University, and Bernie Black, Professor of Law, Stanford University for their comments. The views expressed herein are those of the author alone.

NOTES

1 See, for example, Bernard S. Black, (1992), Agents Watching Agents: The Promise of Institutional Investor Voice, 39 *UCLA L. Rev.* 811; John C. Coffee, Jr (1991), Liquidity Versus Control; The Institutional Investor as Corporate Monitor, 91 *Colum. L. Rev.* 1277 cf. Edward B. Rock, (1991), The Logic and (Uncertain) Significance of Institutional Shareholder Activism, 79 *Geo. L.J.* 445 (explaining the only likely players will be a small subset of a subset of institutional investors, namely, some but not all of the public employee pension funds in the pension fund sector); Roberta Romano (1993), Public Pension Fund Activism in Corporate Governance Reconsidered, 93 *Colum. L. Rev.* 795.

2 Leading pieces include Frank H. Easterbrook and Daniel R. Fischel (1981), The Proper Role of a Target's Management in Responding to a Tender Offer, 94 *Harv. L. Rev.* 1161; Ronald Gilson (1982), Seeking

Competitive Bids Versus Pure Passivity in Tender Offer Defense, 35 *Stan. L. Rev.* 51; see also Ronald J. Gilson (1982), The Case Against Shark Repellent Amendments: Structural Limitations on the Enabling Concept, 34 *Stan. L. Rev.* 775. The insight that a market exists for corporate control was developed by Dean Henry Manne. Henry G. Manne (1965), Mergers and the Market for Corporate Control, 73 *J. Pol. Econ.* 110.

3 For example, William L. Cary (1974), Federalism and Corporate Law: Reflections upon Delaware, 83 *Yall L.J.* 663, 700–01.

4 For example, Ralph Nader *et al.* (1976), *Constitutionalizing the Corporation: The Case for the Federal Chartering of Giant Corporations*; Donald E. Schwartz (1972), Federal Chartering of Corporations: An Introduction, 61 *Geo. L.J.* 71; Note, Federal Chartering of Corporations: A Proposal, 61 *Geo. L.J.* 89 (1972).

5 For example, Douglas M. Branson (1976), Progress in the Art of Social Accounting and Other Arguments for Disclosure on Corporate Social Responsibility, 29 *Vand. L. Rev.* 539.

6 For example, Herman Schwartz (1965), Governmentally Appointed Directors in a Private Corporation–The Communications Satellite Act of 1962, 79 *Harv. L. Rev.* 350; Symposium. The Corporate Machinery for Hearing and Heeding New Voices, 27 *Bus. Law,* 195, 197–208 (1971).

7 For example, Lawrence A. Cunningham (1999), Commonalities and Prescriptions in the Vertical Dimension of Global Corporate Governance, 84 *Cornell L. Rev.* 1133, 1145–1146; Brian R. Cheffins (1999), Current Trends in Corporate Governance: Going from London to Milan via Toronto, 10 *Duke J. Comp. & Int'l L.* 5, 6; John C. Coffee, Jr (1999), The Future as History: The Prospects for Global Convergence in Corporate Governance and Its Implications, 93 *Nw. U.L. Rev.* 641; Jeffrey N. Gordon (1999), Pathways to Corporate Convergence? Two Steps on the Road to Shareholder Capitalism in Germany, 5 *Colum. J. Eur. L.* 219; Henry Hansmann and Reinier Kraakman (2001), The End of History for Corporate Law, 89 *Geo. L.J.* 439; Edward B. Rock (1996), America's Shifting Fascination with Comparative Corporate Governance, 74 *Wash. U. L.Q.* 367; see also Lucian Arye Bebchuk and Mark J. Roe (1999), A Theory of Path Dependence in Corporate Ownership and Governance, 52 *Stan. L. Rev.* 127. For other convergence pieces, see Mary E. Kissane (1997), Global Gadflies: Applications and Implications of U.S. Style Corporate Governance Abroad, 17 *N.Y.L. Sch. J. Int'l & Comp. L.* 621; Gustavo Visentini (1998), Compatibility and Competition Between European and American Corporate Governance: Which Model of Capitalism?, 23 *Brook. J. Int'l L.* 833.

8 But see William W. Bratton and Joseph A. McCahery (1999), Comparative Corporate Governance and the Theory of the Firm; The Case Against Global Cross Reference, 38 *Colum. J. Tran'l L.* 213; Roberta Romano (1993), A Cautionary Note on Drawing Lessons from Comparative Corporate Law, 102 *Yale L.J.* 2021, 2036 (expressing reservations about basing corporate law change on differences in short term national productivity rates and terming "a dubious proposition" that "German and Japanese corporate governance arrangements should be emulated by U.S. firms").

9 For example, Coffee, see note 7, at 679–80; Ronald J. Gilson (Dec 5. 1998), Globalizing Corporate Governance; Convergence of Form or Function (unpublished manuscript), *cited* in Coffee, see note 7, at 649 n. 27; Hansmann and Kraakman, see note 7, at 459 n. 35.

10 Australian Institute of Company Directors *et al.*, Corporate Practices and Conduct (2nd edn 1993).

11 Committee on the Financial Aspects of Corporate Governance, The Code of Best Practice (London 1992).

12 American Law Institute, Principles of Corporate Governance: Analysis and Recommendations (1994).

13 General Motors Board of Directors, GM Board Guidelines on Significant Corporate Governance Issues (rev. ed. 1995).

14 Committee on Corporate Governance, Committee on Corporate Governance: Final Report (London 1998).

15 Directors Remuneration: Report of a Study Group Chaired by Sir Richard Greenbury (1995).

16 For example, Thomas J. Andre, Jr (1998), Cultural Hegemony: The Exportation of Anglo-Saxon Corporate Governance Ideologies to Germany, 73 *Tul. L. Rev.* 69, 78–79, 109–16.

17 For example, James A. Fanto (1998), The Role of Corporate Law in French Corporate Governance, 31 *Cornell Int'l L.J.* 31, 87. But see ibid. at 87 n.286 ("A cynic might also suggest that since U.S. scholars and practitioners produced their 'Principles of Corporate Governance' and their U.K. counterparts their 'Cadbury Report,' the French felt obligated to do the same, without acknowledging that they were simply following the Anglo-Saxon model . . . .").

18 And that opposition continues. For example, undated flier posted in Forbes Quadrangle, University of Pittsburgh, April, 2000 (on file with author):

> Mobilization for Global Justice, Washington, D.C. In April the World Bank and the international Monetary Fund will hold their annual spring meetings in Washington. As usual, their agenda includes making the world safer for corporations – and more dangerous for people and the planet. So join us as we call for justice! Sunday, April 16, Non-violent direct action. Shut down the meetings! . . . For more information: www.a16.org.

Ibid.; see also Mark Helm Apr. 10, 2000, Seattle Protesters Target D.C. – Aiming to Disrupt Next

Week's World Bank-IMF Joint Meeting, *Pittsburgh Post-Gazette*, at A5.

19 Since the economic crisis hit Asia, many United States scholars have deleted Japan from their already artificially narrow sample of corporate governance jurisdictions. Rock (1991), see note 7, at 380–81 ("The tone of comparative corporate scholarship has changed over the last few years as the U.S. economy has bounced back and Germany and Japan have lagged."). The picture was radically different a few years earlier, with many comparisons being made between Japanese and United States corporate governance styles. For example, J. Mark Ramseyer (1987), Legal Rules in Repeated Deals: Banking in the Shadow of Defection in Japan, 20 *J. Legal. Stud.* 91, 97–114; J. Mark Ramseyer (1993), Takeovers in Japan; Opportunism, Ideology, and Corporate Control, 35 *UCLA L. Rev* 1; Mark J. Roe (1993), Some Differences in Corporate Structure in Germany, Japan and the United States, 102 *Yale L.J.* 1927. See generally William S. Dietrich (1991), In the Shadow of the Rising Sun The Political Roots of American Economic Decline.

20 Douglas M. Branson (1993), *Corporate Governance*.

21 Merritt B. Fox and Michael A. Heller (2000), Corporate Governance Lessons from Russian Enterprise Fiascoes, 75 *N.Y.U. L. Rev.* 1720, available at Social Science Research Network Electronic Paper Collection, abstract_id 203368 (1999).

22 Rado Bohinc and Stephen M. Bainbridge (1999), Corporate Governance in Post-Privatized Slovenia, available at Social Science Research Network Electronic Paper Collection, abstract_id 199548.

23 Zenichi Shishido (1999), Japanese Corporate Governance: The Hidden Problems of the Corporate Law and their Solutions, Columbia Law School Working Paper No. 153, available at Social Science Research Network Electronic Paper Collection, abstract_id 163377. Other papers included Marcello Bianchi and Luca Enriques (2001), Corporate Governance in Italy After the 1998 Reform: What Role for Institutional Investors?, available at Social Science Research Network Electronic Paper Collection, abstract_id 203112; Cheffins (1999), see note 7; Curtis J. Milhaupt (1999), Privatization and Corporate Governance: Strategy for a Unified Korea, available at SSRN Electronic Paper Collection abstract_id 203548; Committee on Corporate on Corporate Governance, Code of Best Practice for Corporate Governance (KOREA).

24 E.g., Laurence Bloch and Elizabeth Kremp (1999), Ownership and Voting Power in France, available at Social Science Research Network Electronic Paper Collection, abstract_id 200632; Laura N. Beny, (1999), A Comparative Empirical Investigation of Agency and Market Theories of Insider Trading, available at Social Science Research Network Electronic Paper Collection, abstract_id 193070; Utpal Bhattacharya and Hazem Daouk (1999), The World Price of Insider Trading, available at Social Science Research Network Electronic Paper Collection, abstract_id 200914; Jeffrey Lawrence and G.P. Stapledon, Is Board Composition Important? A Study of Listed Australian Companies, available at Social Science Research Network Electronic Paper Collection, abstract_id 193528.

25 See, for example, Fox and Heller, see note 21.

26 Bohinc and Bainbridge, see note 22, at 1–2.

27 Lawrence and Stapledon, see note 24, at 27.

28 Bloch and Kremp, see note 24, at 18.

29 Fanto, see note 17, at 32.

30 Ibid. at 33.

31 Cunningham, see note 7, at 1148–52.

32 Ibid. at 1151–52; see also Edmund L. Andrews, July 8, 1998, London and Frankfurt Stock Exchanges Form Alliance, *N.Y. Times*, at D4; Alan Cowell, Nov. 20, 1998, French Agree to a European Stock Exchange, *N.Y. Times*, at C6. But see Erik Portanger and Vanessa Fuhrmans, Nov. 2, 2000, How It Became a Foggy Day on the London Exchange, *Wall St. J.* at C1.

33 Cunningham, see note 7, at 1148.

34 Ibid. at 1171; see OECD. The OECD Guidelines for Multinational Enterprises, at http://www.oecd.org/daf/investment/guidelines/index.htm (last modified Apr. 5, 2001).

35 Cunningham, see note 7, at 1170.

36 Ibid.

37 Ibid. at 1194.

38 See generally Coffee (2000), note 7 (stating that functional convergence in corporate governance is arriving at the level of securities regulation and stock exchange requirements). On February 21–23, Professor Coffee expounded on a similar theme in delivering the Julius Rosenthal Foundation Lectures at Northwestern University School of Law, entitled "The Public Corporation in the Global Era." John C. Coffee. Jr (Feb. 21–23, 2000), Address at the Julius Rosenthal Foundation Lecture Series, Northwestern University School of Law (brochure on file with author).

39 Coffee, see note 7, at 644, 698.

40 See International Developments: Seven NASDAQ Stocks to be Available in Hong Kong in Pilot Program, 31 SEC, REG & L. REP. (BNA) 1654 (Dec. 20, 1999) (noting Hong Kong listings for Microsoft, Intel, Cisco, Dell Computer, Amgen, Applied Materials and Starbucks Coffee).

41 For example, if the investor corresponds with the corporation in any way, she may be deemed to have made a demand on the board of directors and thus have tacitly conceded the independence of the board for purposes of dealing with the demand. Spiegel v. Buntrock, (Del. 1990) 571 A.2d 767. If the corporation refuses the demand, a court may not review the board's decision

that the minority shareholder's suit is not in the corporation's best interests. Levine v. Smith (Del. 1991) 591 A.2d 194. Pursuit of another avenue to a court hearing, that demand is excused because a critical mass of the corporation's directors are not disinterested, has also been made extremely difficult in Delaware. Aronson v. Lewis (Del. 1984) 473 A.2d 805. Under the substantive law of Delaware, corporate directors are free to discriminate among shares of the same class, including minority held shares, because Delaware requires only "fair" treatment, not "equal" treatment of shares. Nixon v. Blackwell (Del. 1993) 626 A.2d 1366.

42 Model Bus. Corp. Act §7.40 (1993).

43 Ibid. § 7.44(a). See generally Douglas M. Branson (1993), Recent Changes to the Model Business Corporation Act: Death Knells for Main Street Corporation Law, 72 *Neb. L. Rev.* 258 (explaining in their attempt to compete with the American Law Institute Corporate Governance Project, model act drafters adopted a governance and litigation model inappropriate for small and mid sized corporations).

44 Stock market demutualization, with resulting private ownership of the London Stock Exchange, the New York Stock Exchange, or the NASDAQ, as well as others, may blunt governance initiatives by those organizations, further undercutting Professor Coffee's thesis of convergence by the backdoor. E.g., Roberta S. Karmel (2001), The Future of Corporate Governance Listing Requirements, 54 *Smu L. Rev.* 325, 326, 348–52.

45 Hansmann and Kraakman, (1992), see note 7. The title The End of History derives from either Francis Fukuyama (1998), The End of History and the Last Man or Francis Fukuyama, The End of History.

46 Hansmann and Kraakman, see note 7, at 440.

47 Ibid. at 443.

48 Ibid. at 449.

49 Ibid. at 450 (citation omitted).

50 Ibid. at 451.

51 Ibid. at 454.

52 Ibid. at 455. This is, of course, the American Law Institute model. American Law Institute, see note 12; see Branson, (1998), see note 20, at 227–45.

53 Hansmann and Kraakman, see note 7, at 468.

54 Ibid. at 444–46.

55 Ibid. at 447–49.

56 Kent Greenfield (1998), The Place of Workers in Corporate Law, 39 *B.C. L. Rev.* 283.

57 Marleen A. O'Connor (1997), Organized Labor as Shareholder Activist: Building Coalitions to Promote Worker Capitalism, 31 *U. Rich. L. Rev.* 1345.

58 Marleen A. O'Connor (1993), The Human Capital Era: Reconceptualizing Corporate Law to Facilitate Labor-Management Cooperation, 78 *Cornell L. Rev.* 899; see also O'Connor (1991), Restructuring the Corporation's Nexus of Contracts: Recognizing a Fiduciary Duty to Protect Displaced Workers, 69 *N.C. L. Rev.* 1189; David Millon (1998), Default Rules, Wealth Distribution, and Corporate Law Reform: Employment at Will Versus Job Security, 146 *U. Pa. L. Rev.* 975.

59 David Millon (1993), New Directions in Corporate Law: Communications, Contractarians, and the Crisis in Corporate Law, 50 *Wash. & Lee L. Rev.* 1373.

60 David Millon (1990), Theories of the Corporation, 1990 *Dukl L.J.* 201.

61 David Millon (1991), Redefining Corporate Law, 24 *Ind. L. Rev.* 223.

62 Lawrence E. Mitchell (1995), *Progressive Corporate Law.*

63 In the United States, over 30 jurisdictions have adopted non-shareholder constituency statutes, directing or permitting corporate directors to take into account interests of stakeholders other than shareholders. E.g., Brason, supra note 20, § 8.03; Stephen M. Bainbridge (1992), Interpreting Nonshareholder Constituency Statutes, 19 PEPP. L. REV. 971, 985–86; Timothy L. Fort (1997), The Corporation As Mediating Institution: An Efficacious Synthesis of Stakeholder Theory and Corporate Constituency Statutes, 73 *Notrf Damf L. Rev.* 173, 173–74. In many foreign jurisdictions, the stakeholder model has struck a responsive note. For example, recent Korean (enacted) and Indonesian (in progress) codes of best practices have chapters devoted to directors' and managers' responsibilities to stakeholders. Committee on Corporate Governance (Korea), Code of Best Practice for Corporate Governance, Part IV (1999); National Committee on Corporate Governance (Indonesia), Code of Good Corporate Governance, Chapter 6 (2000) ("Stakeholders").

64 Hansmann and Kraakman (1996), see note 7, at 446 n.9 (citing Henry Hansmann, The Ownership of Eneterprise) Henry Hansmann (1993), *Probleme von Kollektivent-scheidungen and Theorie der Firma – Folgerungen fur die Arbeitnehmermitbestimmung,* in Okonomische Analyse Des Unternehmscreohts 287–305 (Claus Ott and Hans-Bernd Schafer eds., 1993); Henry Hansmann (1993), Worker Participation and Corporate Governance, 43 *U. Toronto L.J.* 589, 589–606.

65 See, for example, Bebchuk and Roe, note 7, at 136 n.13, 137 nn.17–18, 138 nn.19–20, 22.

66 See, for example, Douglas M. Branson (1983), Countertrends in Corporate Law: Model Business Corporation Act Revision, British Company Law Reform, and Principles of Corporate Governance and Structure, 68 *Minn. L. Rev.* 53, 73–88; Douglas M. Branson (2000), Teaching Comparative Corporate Governance: The Significance of "Soft Law" and International Institutions, 34 *Ga. L. Rev.* 669, 682–84.

67 Although one result of both legal systems is the same, that is, a pattern of dispersed share ownership and a

large number of publicly held corporations per given amount of population, see Coffee, note 7, at 644 (nothing that "while the United Kingdom has thirty-six listed firms per million citizens and the United States has thirty. France, Germany, and Italy have only eight, four and five, respectively") (citation omitted), convergence advocates do not ask why that is so because they presume, without examination or research, that United States corporation law and British company law are largely identical.

68 See note 19; see also Bebchuk and Roe, note 7, at 164; Coffee, note 7, at 653, 680; Cunningham, note 7, at 1142. Today, most references to Japanese style corporate governance are made in passing.

69 See Bebehuk and Roe, note 7, at 133 (focusing on the United Kingdom), 136, 140–41, 150 (focusing on Germany); Coffee, note 7, at 644, 653, 663–64 (focusing on Germany); Ibid. at 644, 653, 656 (focusing on France); Ibid. at 644–53 (focusing on the United Kingdom); Cunningham, see note 7, at 1136–39 (focusing on the United Kingdom); Ibid. at 1140–42 (focusing on Germany); Ibid. at 1141–42 (focusing on France); Hansmann and Kraakman, see note 7, at 445–46 (focusing on Germany); ibid. at 446–47 (focusing on France); Ibid. at 447–48 (focusing on the United Kingdom).

70 Coffee, see note 7, at 697.

71 Bebchuk and Roe, see note 7, at 165, 169; Coffee, see note 7, at 644, 649, 663–65.

72 Cunningham, see note 7, at 1140–41; Hansmann and Kraakman, see note 7.

73 Coffee, see note 7, at 675–76.

74 Hansmann and Kraakman, see note 7, at 451.

75 Primedia Reference, Inc., The World Atmanac and Book of Facts 1999, at 863 (1998). The population of Asia alone was estimated to be 3,527,969,000 in 1998. Ibid.

76 See Ibid. at 862–63.

77 Ibid. at 863.

78 Interview with Lee Kuan Yew (1996), 13 New Persp. Q. 4.

79 Coffee, see note 7, at 673 n. 107 (citing Amir N. Licht, (1998) Regulatory Arbitrage for Real: International Securities Regulation in A World Interacting Securities Market, 38 Va. J. Int'l L. 563, 566 (noting that as of Dec. 31, 1996, foreign listings totaled 416 on the NASDAQ and 305 on the New York Stock Exchange)).

80 Coffee, see note 7, at 675.

81 Ibid.

82 Alfred F. Conard (1976), Corporations in Perspective 75–76 (stating that United States corporate laws have been "peculiarly inept for export."). But see Brian R., Cheffins, (1989), U.S. Close Corporation Legislation: A Model Canada Should Not Follow, 35 McGili L.J. 160, 161 ("U.S. corporate legislation considerably

influenced the thinking of Canadian corporate law reformers in the 1960s and 1970s.").

83 Bernard Black and Reinier Kraakman (1996), A Self-Enforcing Model of Corporate Law, 109 Harv. L. Rev. 1911, 1935–36, 1946–49.

84 E.g., Bernard Black et al. (2000), Russian Privatization and Corporate Governance: What Went Wrong?, 52 Stan. L. Rev. 1731, 1752–57; see also Fox and Heller, supra note 21, at 1762–64.

85 Cheffins, see note 7, at 6 ("The work which has been done in the United Kingdom has spurred reviews of corporate governance in markets around the world and has provided a yardstick against which investment frameworks in other countries are measured.").

86 Robert I. Tricker, 1990 Corporate Governance: A Ripple on the Cultural Reflection, in Capitalism in Contrasting Cultures 187 (Stewart R. Clegg and S. Gordon Redding eds).

87 Transplant of other countries' laws is highly, but not completely, path dependent. Thus, receiving countries may, to some degree, pick and choose from alternatives when a legal system is being transplanted. See, e.g., David Berkowitz et al. (2000), Economic Development, Legality, and the Transplant Effect, CID Working Paper No. 39, at 4, 11 (on file with the author) (analyzing forty-nine countries with "transplanted" legal systems).

88 See Proposal for a Fifth Directive, Foundation Article 54(3)(g) of the EEC Treaty Concerning the Structure of Public Limited Companies and the Powers and Obligations of Their Origins, 1983 O.J. (C240) 2. The draft contains two alternative but mandatory structures for providing employee representation in corporate governance. See Ibid.

89 Terence L. Blackburn (1993), The Societas Europea: The Evolving European Corporation Statute, 61 Fordham L. Rev. 695, 700 735–36.

90 Ibid. at 700–01.

91 See Caroline De Vos (1999), The SLIM IV Project of the European Commission: Harmonization Thought Deregulation of European Company Law, Working Paper 1999_16, Financial Law Institute, University of Gent, available at Social Science Research Network Electronic Paper Collection, abstract_id 192136.

92 See George A. Bermann (1998), Comparative Law in the New European Community, 21 Hastings Int'l & comp. L. Rev. 865, 867 ("The experience of the last forty years also shows that pursuit of a 'neutral' harmonization or convergence of national law has consistently been subordinate to the Community's pursuit of its own distinctive, policydriven legislative agenda."); George A. Bermann (1993), A Commenaryt on the Harmonization of European Private Law, 1 Tul. J. Int'l & Comp. L. 47, 48–52 (stating that the European Union has moved beyond regulating member states and

regulation of their economies into defining rights and obligations of citizens of member states *vis-à-vis* one another). The four freedoms are the freedom of movement for goods, workers, services, and capital. Treaty Establishing the European Economic Community, Mar. 25 1957, 298 U.N.T.S. 11, 18, 36–42; see also Idid. art. 2 (establishing the European Economic Community). Preservation of the four freedoms remains a central objective of the now European Union. Peter J. Groves, (1995), *European Community Law* 7–8.

93 Paul B. Stephan (1999), The Futility of Unification and Harmonization in International Commercial Law, 39 *Va. J. Int'l L.* 743 [hereinafter Stephan, Futility of Unification]; Paul B. Stephan (1997), Accountability and International Lawmaking: Rules, Rents and Legitimacy, 17 *Nw. J. Int'l L. & Bus.* 681 [hereinafter Stephan, Rules, Rents and Legitimacy]; Paul B. Stephan (1999), The New International Law – Legitimacy, Accountability. Authority, and Freedom in the New Global Order, 70 *U. Colo. L. Rev.* 1555 [herinafter Stephan, New International Law].

94 This is because "[n]o mechanism exists for voters to pass judgment on the international lawmakers. At best they can vote for the domestic governments that in turn choose the drafters of international agreements." Stephan, Futility of Unification, see note 93, at 752.

95 Stephan, Rules, Rents and Legitimacy, see note 93, at 682.

96 Ibid. at 732.

97 Ibid. at 699.

98 Richard G. Lipsey and Peter O. Steiner (3rd ed. 1972), *Economics* 341–42.

99 Richard A. Posner (2nd ed. 1977), *Economic Analysis of Law 9* Examples of rent seeking include "the very high incomes earned by a few singers, athletes, and lawyers . . . due to the scarcity of the resources they control – a fine singing voice, athletic skill and determination . . ." Ibid.

100 A related impediment to change in legal institutions may be a network externality. A legal institution gains value only after a critical mass of others has also decided to adapt to the new way. An "actual" network market would be for fax machines: one machine is useless, a community of them gives rise to an entire new industry. See, for example, Mark A. Lemley and David McGowan (1998), Legal Implications of Network Economic Effects, 86 *Cal. L. Rev.* 479, 488. Network economic effects pose an impediment to refinements or more radical change of corporate law. Ibid. at 562–86. Network externalities, even if not expressed in those terms, may be excuses that rent seekers utilize to prolong adherence to the "old" ways.

101 Stephan, Rents, Rules and Legitimacy, see note 93, at 706 (nothing that, other things being equal, bureaucrats rent seek through efforts to enlarge their budgets).

102 Indeed, the elite and somewhat closed circle of global convergence advocates may be perceived as rent seekers themselves, engendering skepticism as a "one size fits all" corporate governance scheme is peddled from country to country around the globe. Rent seeking does occur at the international, as well as the local level. Stephan. Rents, Rules and Legitimacy, see note 93, at 708–09; Stephan, Futility of Unification, see note 93, at 793 ("An essential element of the critique of technocratic lawmaking at the international level rests on the premise that interest groups can influence the process . . . [t]hese [local] concerns about international lawmaking seem plausible precisely because a substantial body of evidence suggests that such rentseeking takes place with some frequency at the national level."). Indeed, the convergence advocates may actually be rent seekers, judging from the amount of academic resource and reputation they have invested in the "global" convergence hypothesis.

103 Paul N. Doremus, *et al.* (1998) *The Myth of the Global Corporation.*

104 Ibid. at 143.

105 Ibid. at 146. In fact, the authors of Myth surprised themselves: "Neither liberal nor radical approaches to understanding multinational corporate behavior . . . led us to expect the degree of continuing diversity we found at the level of the firm." Ibid. at 141.

106 Ibid. at 144.

107 Ibid. at 74.

108 Ibid. at 77.

109 Ibid. at 78.

110 Ibid. at 84.

111 Ibid. at 85 (citation omitted); *see also* ibid. at 134 ("MNCs still retain the bulk of their innovative capabilities in their home markets, and technology that does flow overseas tends to stay within multinational networks").

112 Ibid. at 93.

113 Ibid. at 109.

114 Ibidd. at 15.

115 Ibid.

116 Ibid. at 12.

117 Ibid. at 23.

118 See, for example, Ibid. at 13.

119 Convergence advocates seem to see what they want to see. They see in some agitation for change in Germany and in the Daimler and Deutsche Bank mergers harbingers of German participation in global convergence in corporate governance. See, for example, Coffee, note 7, at 664, 676–82; Cunningham, see note 7, at 1169. Based upon systematic evidence, the authors of Myth see a picture of persistent difference and resistance to change rooted in national origin. The German economy is characterized by codetermination of the supervisory board of large firms, a large role played by universal banks which vote fifty percent or more of the

shares in all large German firms, and a pattern of cross share holdings. The result is an absence of hostile takeovers, a comfortable safety net for managers in the event of serious managerial mistakes or unanticipated market shocks because of the availability of backup resources from the banks, stable research and development budgets and wider fluctuations in earnings than would be tolerated in other countries. Doremus *et al.*, see note 103, at 33–42.

120 Ibid. at 116.

121 Stewart R. Clegg and S. Gordon Redding, Introduction to Capitalism in Contrasting Cultures, see note 86, at 14.
     [I]t would be mistaken to regard these countries [Japan and the "little dragons" of Hong Kong, Taiwan, South Korea and Singapore] as essentially similar in their patterns of economic success. They have quite distinct foundations which are sufficiently different as to counter any too easy reliance on a view of a single "post-Confucian" way. Ibid.

122 Doremus *et al.* see note 103, at 139.

123 Ibid.

124 Ibid. at 145.

125 For example, see note 52 and accompanying text.

126 SEC's Williams Calls for Independent Boards, Warns of Federal Intervention Into Government, *Sec. Reg. and Law Rep.* No. 437, Jan. 25, 1978, at A22 (noting argument by Chairman of U.S. SEC that all directors save one should be independent); Branson, see note 20, §5.03 (concluding that Delaware Supreme Court opinions constitute a de facto requirement of a high degree of director independence).

127 In 1974 the American Model Business Corporation Act shifted to language that "[a]ll corporate powers shall be . . . managed under the direction of [] a board of directors, . . ." Model Bus. Corp. Act § 35. (1975). *See generally* Branson, see note 20, §5.02.

128 See American Law Institute, see note 12, §3.01.

129 Ibid. §3.02.

130 Model Bus. Corp. Act §8.24(d).

131 American Law Institute, see note 12, Part VII, "Remedies" (seventeen sections dealing with derivative actions by shareholders).

132 S. Gordon Redding (1990), *The Spirit of Chinese Capitalism 3.*

133 Ibid. at 3, 18.

134 Ibid. at 2, 17.

135 Ibid. at 29.

136 Ibid. at 25.

137 There has been very little assimilation into the ambient culture by overseas Chinese. See, for example, Ibid. at 57 (noting little assimilation in Malaysia, the Philippines, or Indonesia). Other nations such as Japan and Korea are said to be influenced by "post-Confucian" values. The Post-Confucian thesis is attrib-

uted to Herman Kahn, (1979), World Economic Development: 1979 And Beyond. Kahn proposed "that the success of organizations in Japan, Korea, Taiwan, Hong Kong and Singapore was due in large part to certain key traits shared by the majority of organization members which were attributable to an upbringing in the Confucian tradition." Stewart R. Clegg *et al.*, "Post-Confucianism", Social Democracy and Economic Culture, in *Capitalism in Contrasting Cultures*, see note 86, at 38.

138 Redding, see note 132, at 48.

139 'The Confucian ideal is that family, clan, and head of state take precedence over the individual." Ibid. at 63. In a series of interviews with Chinese business men, a representative answer demonstrated the Chinese principle of tolerance: "[B]e tolerant – it creates less worries. Try to put the lawyers out of business." Ibid. at 87.

140 Ibid. at 58. In the Confucian context, "the individual has a built-in sense of the legitimacy of the superior-subordinate relationship . . . it is an extension of a natural order. The open challenge of formal authority is rare." Ibid. at 61.

141 Ibid. at 52.

142 Redding, see note 132, at 76.

143 In the United States model, by contrast, the 1990s witnessed an unprecedented number of forced removals of CEOs of major United States corporations. See, for example, Doremus *et al.*, see note 103, at 26 (noting the ouster of chief executive officers at, inter alia, IBM, Kodak and Westinghouse).

144 In 1999–2000, the author was a USAID consultant to the Indonesian Ministry of Justice on corporate law revision and corporate governance reform in Indonesia.

145 See, for example, Kfith Lovfard (1999) *Suharto: Indonesia's Last Sultan* 123–24 ('for the vast majority of Indonesians, and particularly the Javanese, . . . there was a strong sense that he had control of the power and that whatever they did to oppose it would be futile'); see also Clegg and Redding, Introduction to *Capitalism in Contrasting Cultures*, see note 86, at 23 ("[T]he feudal nature of traditional Chinese social relationships has in some important local respects survived intact into the present day: the 'war-lords' have changed, but practices of the fief have remained remarkably constant.").

146 Loveard, see note 145, at 380.

147 New Company Law of Indonesia ("Undang-undang Tentang Perseroan Terbatas"), Law Number 1 of the Year 1995, Articles 85 and 98 (authorizing suit against a director or commissioner who "has caused losses to the Company due to his fault or negligence.") [hereinafter Company Law of Indonesia].

148 Loveard, see note 145, at 114.

149 Company Law of Indonesia, see note 147, Article 74(1).

150 S. Gordon Redding and S. Tam (1985), Networks and Molecular Organizations. An Exploratory View of Chinese Firms in Hong Kong, in K.C. Mun and T.S. Chan, *Perspectives in International Business* 192–242.

151 S. Gordon Redding and Richard D. Whitley, Beyond Bureaucracy. Towards a Comparative Analysis of Forms of Economic Resource Co-ordination and Control, in *Capitalism in Contrasting Cultures*, see note 86, at 101.

152 See generally Richard Robinson (1986), *Indonesia, The Rise of Capital*; see also Lovfard, see note 145, at 21, 33–35, 201.

153 Fanto, see note 17, at 69–71.

154 Bloch and Kremp, see note 23, at 18 ("Families seem to play an important role in ownership and voting power, both in unlisted firms and in the CAC 40 firms.").

155 See Family Firms in Italy: The Generation Game, Economist, March 4, 2000, at 65.

156 Clegg *et al.*, see note 137, at 32.

157 John gray (1998), *False Dawn: The Delusions of Global Capitalism* 169–70.

158 This phenomenon is a testament to what Granovetter has termed the "embeddedness of economic actions": "the argument [is] that the behavior and institutions to be analyzed [in economic analysis] are so constrained by ongoing social relations that to construe them as independent is a grievous misunderstanding." Mark Granovetter (1985), Economic Action and Social Structure: The Problem of Embeddedness, 91 *Am. J. Soc.* 481, 481–82.

159 Karl Polanyi (1944), *The Great Transformation* 119 (noting that Burke and Bentham, among others, "refused to defer to zoological determinism . . . [and] rejected the ascendency [sic] of economics over politics proper").

160 Gray, see note 157, at 14–16 (noting that truly free market economy only existed in Anglo-Saxon societies in mid Victorian England (1840–70)).

161 Ibid. at 26 ("In the normal course of things markets come embedded in social life. They are circumscribed in their working by intermediary institutions [such as labor unions and professional associations] and encumbered by social conventions and tacit understandings."), 182 ("As in other economic cultures, Chinese capitalism comes embedded in the networks and values of the larger society.").

162 Redding, see note 132, at 95; see also Thomas A. Acton, Ethnicity and Religion in the Development of Family Capitalism: Seui-Seung-Yahn Immigrants from Hong Kong to Scotland, in *Capitalism in Contrasting Cultures*, see note 86, at 391 ("'Economy' and 'culture' have been seen by westerners as two great independent variables or value systems while Asian cultures see them as closely intertwined or one (economy) deeply embedded in the other").

163 Redding and Whitley, see note 151, at 80.

164 Ibid.; see also Ibid. at 79 ("Anglo-Saxon conceptions of the legally bounded form as the basic unit of economic action are inadequate to explain the economic actions and structures of [Korean] chaebol and Chinese family businesses").

165 Gray, see note 157, at 101, 115–16.

166 One of every 193 United States adults is incarcerated or under restraint. The United States's rate of incarceration is four times that of Canada, five times that of the UK, and fourteen times that of Japan. Gray, see note 157, at 116; see also Graham Searjeant, Economically, Jails Cost More Than Corner Shops, The Times (London), Dec. 11, 1995, at 38 ("Why do we look to America for economic and social models, from deregulation and institutional investor power to workfare schemes, if they produce this kind of society?")

167 In 1989, US CEOs earned 160 times the pay of the average worker, while in Japan the figure was 16 and in Germany 21. Graef S. Crystal (1991), *In Search of Excess: The Overcompensation of American Executives* 205–09. In 2000, compensation consultant Graef Crystal says "it is 'north of 400 times and heading rapidly to 500 times.'" Kathleen Day, Aug. 27, 2000, Soldiers for the Shareholder, *Wash. Post*, at H1.

168 Gray, see note 157, at 121.

169 Sir Thomas Gresham explained that "bad money drives out good." Lipsey and Steiner, see note 98, at 592.

170 Gray, see note 157, at 78–79.

171 Ibid. at 101.

172 See notes 66–78 and accompanying text (noting that convergence advocates base their postulate of globalization on observations of the United States, on the one hand, and the United Kingdom, Germany and France, with brief mention of outliers from time to time).

173 David E. Sanger (1999), U.S. Is the "800 pound Gorilla" – Global Power Encounters Envy and Mistrust, *Int'l Herald Trib.*, July 19, at I.

174 On disruption of the WTO meeting in Seattle, see for example Sam Howe Verhovek & Steven Greenhouse, Dec. 1, 1999, National Guard is Called to Quell Trade-Talk Protests, *N.Y. Times*, at A1; Timothy Egan, Dec. 2, 1999, Black Masks Lead to Pointed Fingers in Seattle, *N.Y. Times*, at A1; Sam Howe Verhovek, Dec. 2, 1999, Seattle is Stung, Angry and Chagrined as Opportunity Turns to Chaos, *N.Y. Times*, at A16; Michael Kazin, Dec. 5, 1999, Saying No to WTO. *N.Y. Times*, at 17; Timothy Egan, Dec. 5, 1999, Free Trade Takes on Free Speech, *N.Y. Times*, at 1; John Burgess and Steven Pearlstein, Dec. 1, 1999, Protests Delay WTO Opening, *Wash. Post.* at 1; Tom Hayden *et al.*, Dec. 5, 1999, The Battle in Seattle: What Was That All About. *N.Y. Times*, at B1. Disruption of the IMF and World Bank annual meetings is chronicled in, inter alia, John Burgess, Activists Aim to Halt Meeting

of World Bank and the IMF, *Int'l Herald Trib.*, Jan. 27, 2000, at 17; David Sanger, Global Storm: Loan Agencies Under Siege, *N.Y. Times*, Apr. 16, 2000, at 1; John Kifner and David E. Sanger, Financial Leaders Meet As Protests Clog Washington, *N.Y. Times*, Apr. 17, 2000, at 1; John Burgess, Globalization and Its Discontents, *Wash. Post*, Apr. 13, 2000, at A1; Helene Cooper and Michael M. Phillips, Protests Hit World Bank/IMF Sessions, *Wall St. J.*, Apr. 17, 2000, at A2.

175 Reginald Dale, "Americanization" Has Its Limits, *Int'l Herald Trib.*, Jan. 25, 2000, at 9.

176 William Finnegan, After Seattle, *New Yorker*, Apr. 17, 2000, at 40, 42.

177 Ibid.; see also Michael M. Phillips, Can World Bank Lend Money to Third World Without Hurting Poor?, *Wall ST. J.*, Aug. 14, 2000, at A1 (explaining that World Bank finance of open pit coal mines in India has worsened rather than bettered the lives of local citizens, and subsistence farmers have been displaced by expansion of mines).

178 E.g., Thomas L. Friedman, Senseless in Seattle, *N.Y. Times*, Dec. 1, 1999, at A23 (noting "a Noah's ark of flat-earth advocates, protectionist trade unions and yuppies looking for their 1960's fix"); Global Whipping Boy: The Wrong-headed Take to the Streets to Protest the WTO, *Pittsburgh Post-Gazette*, Dec. 5, 1999, at E2 (noting a "kaleidoscope of interests that feel victimized by changes in the way the world functions . . . [t]hey are on the wrong side of the issue, on the wrong side of history and on the wrong side of the political tide . . . [s]o, the losers took to the streets with a vengeance"); Stephen Schwartz, Seattle Has Gone "Wobblie" Before, *Wall St. J.*, Dec. 3, 1999, at A14 ("[In] 'the 47 states and the Soviet of Washington' . . . it should come as no surprise that the Seattle street fighters attempt to obstruct a WTO summit that aims to improve the economic situation of the developing countries."); Francis Fukuyama. The Left Should Love Globalization, *Wall St. J.*, Dec. 1, 1999, at A26 ("It is ironic that the left should rebel against globalization, since globalization is one of the most progressive forces in the world today.")

179 See notes 45–53 and accompanying text.

180 Eric W. Orts (1998), The Future of Enterprise Organization, 96 *Mich. L. Rev.* 1947, 1962 ("In the late twentieth century, the exponential growth of multinational or transnational corporate enterprise qualifies as one of the most important historical developments."). Looking to the past, multinationals accounted for 18 percent of the world's manufacturing output and 7.5 percent of total global output in 1992. Martin Wolf, The Heart of the New World Economy, *Fin. Times* (London), Oct. 1, 1997, at 16.

181 See Robert Guy Matthews *et al.*, Aug. 20, 1999, Fitness Test: Alcoa-Reynolds Union Bears Stamps of Deal Rocking Commodities, *Wall St. J.*, at Al (noting the

"latest in a string of recent deals that have seen one commodity giant gobble up another" and "mergers reflect the confluence of three important trends: industry consolidation, convergence of once-distinct lines of products or services, and globalization."); Matthew *et al.*, Commodity Crunch: Alcoa-Reynolds Deal Shows the Logic of Merger Dynamics-From Aluminum to Oil, Survival of the Fittest is Now the Order of the Day, *Wall St. J.* (Europe), Aug. 20, 1999, at 1.

182 See Nikhil Deogun and Robert Guy Matthews, Reynolds Metals Yields to Alcoa's Bid, *Wall St. J.*, Aug. 20, 1999, at A3 (describing Alcoa's reaction to three way merger of Canada's Alcan Aluminum, Ltd., France's Pechiney, SA and Switzerland's Alusuisse Lonza Group.). But see Anita Raghavan and Nikhil Deogun, Alcan's Merger Plan May Be in Jeopardy, *Wall St. J.*, Apr. 12, 2000, at A3 (noting antitrust opposition by Commission of the European Union).

183 Deogun and Matthews, see note 182.

184 Steve Liesman and Alexei Barrionuevo, 1999, Exxon and Mobil Shareholders Approve the $81.2 Billion Merger, *Wall St. J.*, May 28, at A4.

185 John R. Wilke and Steve Liesman, BP Amoco's Arco Buyout Faces Hurdles, *Wall St. J.*, Nov. 2, 1999, at A2.

186 Thomas Kamm and Bhushan Bahree, Sept. 14, 1999, French Oil Giants Agree to $48.7 Billion Merger, *Wall St. J.*, A15. Later, the Chevron acquisition of Texaco for $38 billion relegated the combined French entity to fifth place worldwide. See, for example, Neela Banerjee and Mary Williams Walsh, Texaco Hopes Chevron Can Polish Fading Star, *Int'l Herald Trib.*, Oct. 18, 2000, at 15.

187 Keith Bradsher, Effective Today, Chrysler and Daimler-Benz Are One, *N.Y. Times*, Nov. 12, 1998, at C4.

188 Edmund L. Andrews, Jan. 30, 1999, Ford-Volvo: A Deal for All Sweden, *N.Y. Times*, at C1.

189 Peter Landers, How Cable and Wireless Pulled Off an Upset in Japanese Takeover, *Wall St. J.*, Nov. 10, 1999, at A1.

190 Deborah Ball, Mar. 24, 2000, Fiat and GM Are Holding Talks About Alliance, *Wall St. J.*, Mar. 13, 2000, at A3; Keith Bradsher, New Terrain Drives Global Auto Industry to Merge, *Int'l Herald Trib.*, at 1.

191 The drug industry is another example of a sector headed toward oligopoly. See, for example, Stephen D. Moore *et al.*, Smith Kline and Glaxo Agree to Merger, *Wall St. J.*, Jan. 17, 2000, at A3 (noting that the $75.7 billion English-Swiss corporate combination will create the world's largest drug company); Robert Langreth, Pfizer, Warner-Lambert Agree on Terms, *Wall St. J.*, Feb. 7, 2000, at A3 (noting that the $84 billion transaction will create the world's second largest drug company).

192 See William C. Symonds *et al.* (1989), De Benedetti's Grab for a Big Piece of Belgium, *Bes. Wk.*, Feb. 1, 1988, at 42. The De Benedetti bid may have helped hurry

along the EU's efforts on the transnational merger front. See generally Nathalie Basaldua, Towards the Harmonization of EC-Member States' Regulations on Takeover Bids: The Proposal for a Thirteenth Council Directive on Company Law, 9 *Nw. J. Int'l L. and Bus.* 487, 491 ("Certainly the best known example [of a takeover bid] in Europe is the hostile bid in January 1988 for Societe Generale de Belgique . . . by the Italian entrepreneur, Carlo de Benedetti").

193 See Advertisement, Bank National Popular (BNP), *Int'l Herald Trib.* (Paris), July 26, 1999, at 7 ("Shareholders of Societe Generale and Paribas – Only 5 Days Left to Maximize Your Investment – Tender Your Shares to BNP."); Thomas Kamm and Deborah Ball, Aug. 17, 1999, Bank Merger Speculation Grows-Europeans Expect Cross Boarder Deals, *Wall St. J.* (Europe), at 1.

194 Christopher Rhoads, Deutshe Bank's Bet Looks to Be Paying Off: In Buying Bankers Trust, German Lender Boosts Investment-Bank Profit, *Wall St. J.*, Nov. 18, 1999, at A16.

195 William Boston and Anita Raghavan, Mannesmann Agrees to Buy U.K.'s Orange For Cash, Stock, *Wall St. J.*, Oct. 21, 1999, at A15.

196 Gautam Naik and Anita Raghavan, Vodajone to Sweeten Mannesmann Offer, *Wall St. J.*, Nov. 17, 1999, at A3.

197 Bryan Burrough and John Helyar (1990), *Barbarians at the Gate: The Fall of rjr Nabisco* 480.

198 Rebecca Blumenstein, MCI Says Sprint Unit's Losses May Weigh on Firm, *Wall St. J.*, Nov. 9, 1999, at B9.

199 See Saul Hansell, America Online Agrees to Buy Time Warner for $165 Billion; Media Deal Is Richest Merger, *N.Y. Times*, Jan. 11, 2000, at A1.

200 Philip Shishkin and William Boston, Vodafone Wins EU Clearance to Acquire Mannesmann in Record $180 Billion Deal, *Wall St. J.*, Apr. 13, 2000, at A14.

201 Unilever Annual Accounts 1999 at 41–43 (2000) (noting Principal Group Companies and Fixed Investments as of December 31, 1999).

202 Unilever Charts 1989–98 at 2 (2000).

203 Ibid. at 10.

204 Joyce Gannon, Bestfoods: A Big Company You Never Heard Of, *Pittsburgh Post-Gazette*, Sept. 16, 1999, at A11.

205 Shelly Branch, Mammoth Deals Are Expected to Spur More Consolidation in the Food Industry, *Wall St. J.*, June 27, 2000, at A3.

206 See generally Adolf A. Beri F and Gardnier C. Means, (1991), The Modern Corporation and Private Property; Arthur R. Pinto and Douglas M. Branson, (1999), *Understanding Corporate Law* 83, 90.

207 Nader *et al.*, see note 4, at 26–70; Schwartz, see note 4; Note, see note 4.

208 The leading piece was by the late Professor William J., Cary, Federalism and Corporate Law Reflections Upon Delaware, 83 *Yale L.J.* 663, 666 (posting a "race to the bottom" in states' competition for incorporations).

209 The opposing view was that competition for charters produced an efficient mix of legal rules, resulting in a "race to the top" rather than "a race to the bottom." Barry D. Baysinger and Henry N. Butler (1985), Race for the Bottom v. Climb to the Top: The ALI Project and Uniformity in Corporate Law 10 *J. Corp. L.* 431, 433; Daniel R. Fischel (1982), The "Race to the Bottom" Revisited: Reflections on Recent Developments in Delaware's Corporation Law 76 *Nw. U.L. Rev.* 913, 920–22.

210 See, e.g. Central Intelligence Agency, The World Factbook 1999, at http://cia.gov/cia/publications/factbook/fields/gdp.html (last visited Feb. 28, 2001).

211 Eric W. Orts (1995), The Legitimacy of Multinational Corporations, in *Progressive Corporate Law* 258–60 (Lawrence E. Mitchell ed., 1995) (noting that "multinational corporations often seem like ghosts escaping the various national and international laws that reach out impotently to claim them" and "[s]pread out among various countries, the operations of multinational corporations are often above the law of any particular country."); see also Kenichi Ohmae *The End of the Nation State: The Rise of Regional Economies* 39.

212 In response to which are heard replies that even domiciliary states lack the power or the will to regulate. Robert B. Reigh (1991), *The Work of Nations: Preparing Ourselves for 21st Century Capitalism* 136–53 (posting "[t]he coming irrelevancy of corporate nationality"); Orts, supra note 211, at 253 (citation omitted).

> Even when the international context is explicitly considered [by American legal academics in their writings] . . . discussion often degenerates into a neomercantilist debate over comparative models of corporate law. This debate is neomercantilist because it advances the assumption that multinational corporations will necessarily act as faithful instruments of the nation-states in which their parents are incorporated, rather than recognizing the more complex reality that multinationals are in fact becoming more and more "stateless."

Ibid.

213 A vexing conundrum has been precisely why so few, if any multinationals have moved to an offshore incorporating state. Scholars have raised the possibility of a "bandit" multinational moving off shore but it seems not to have occurred. Eric Hobsbawm (1996), *The Age of Extremes: A History of the World* 1914–1991, at 278 ("[a] suitably complex and ingenious combination of the legal loopholes in the corporate and labour laws of kindly mini-territories-for-instance, Curacao, the Virgin Islands and Liechtenstein-could do wonders for a firm's balance-sheet").

214 See note 30; see also Enrico Colombatto and Jonathan R. Macey (1996), A Public Choice Model of International Economic Cooperation and the Decline of the Nation State, 18 *Cardozo L. Rev.* 925.

215 Sam Lowenberg, For American Businesses Lobbying the European Union Has Become a Priority, *Am. Legal Times*, Nov. 8, 1999, Dec. 27, 1998, at 1 (noting that Monsanto hired former US Trade Representative to lobby EU and to overcome French opposition to genetically engineered seed products); Bill Lambrecht, World Recoils at Monsanto's Brave New Crops, *St. Louis Post-Dispatch*, at A1; Sam Lowenberg, Cultivating Allies in Genetic Food Fight, *Legal Times*, Dec. 13, 1999, at 14.

216 In retaliation, the United States put punitive tariffs on Roquefort cheese, French mustard, and other luxury foods, sparking destruction of a McDonald's in France and elevation of the French farmer who led the raid to the status of anti-globalization folk hero. Suzanne Daley, French Turn Vandal into Hero Against U.S., *N.Y. Times*, July 1, 2000, at A1; Suzanne Daley, French See a Hero in War on "McDomination," *N.Y. Times*, Oct. 12, 1999 at A1.

217 See Orts, note 211, at 250 ("Multinational flexibility allows firms to perform regulatory arbitrage, that is, to shift operations among countries to take advantage of differing legal requirements, for example, lower labor costs due to absence of minimum wage laws or unions, more flexible antitrust or tax law, or weaker environmental law.") (emphasis in original) (citing Joel P. Trachtman (1993), International Regulatory Competition, Externalization, and Jurisdiction, 34 *Harv. Int'l L.J.* 47).

218 Nike is an example a multinational that has engaged in regulatory arbitrage over time. As wages and expectations rise and requirements for better working conditions are adopted by host nations, Nike has moved its athletic shoe manufacturing facilities – from Korea to Thailand, then to Indonesia, and, currently, to Vietnam.

219 Maquiladoras assemble motor vehicle parts, electric capacitors, stuffed animal toys, apparel, televisions sets, electric motors, and a host of other products, often for multinationals, using low cost labor in tilt up construction facilities that may change products on a sixty or ninety-day basis. See generally, Khosrow Fatemi (1990), *The Maquiladora Industry: Economic Solution or Problem?* Kathryn Kopinak (1996), *Desert Capitalism: Maquiladoras in North America's Western Industrial Corridor*, Leslie Sklair, (1989), *Assembling for Development: The Maquila Industry in Mexico and the United States*.

220 Compare Jonathan Peterson, Leadership Struggle Reflects Growing Schism in WTO Trade *L.A. Times*, July 21, 1999, at C.I., with Tyrone Beason, Oct. 26, 1999, WTO in Seattle: Herman Bids to Put Labor on Agenda – Clinton Administration Official Promotes Worker Rights, *Seattle Times*, at E1.

221 In addition to the potential for oppression of less developed countries, law making in the international context brings another set of problems. The bureaucrats, trade representatives, and others who make law in the international sphere lack accountability to any electorate. See notes 94–97 and accompanying text. See generally Stephan, Rules, Rents and Legitimacy, supra note 93, at 681. Critics "assert that the establishment of NAFTA and the World Trade Organization (WTO) will mean that state and federal legislatures no longer may decide what kind of environmental safeguards or standards of consumer and worker protection we will have." Ibid. at 681.

222 Berle and Means, see note 206.

223 Ibid. at 112–116.

224 The seminal piece is Jensen and Meckling (1976), Theory of the Firm: Managerial Behavior, Agency Costs and Ownership Structure, 3 *J. Fin. Econ.* 305, see also Eugene F. Fama (1980), Agency Problems and the Theory of the Firm, 88 *J. Pol. Econ.* 288.

225 See American Law Institute, see note 12, §3A.01 ("The board of every large publicly held corporation should have a majority of directors who are free of any significant relationship with the corporation's senior executives . . . .").

226 Ibid. §3.02(a)(1) ("The board of directors of a publicly held corporation should perform the following functions: (1) Select, regularly evaluate, fix the compensation of. and where appropriate, replace the principal senior executives . . . .").

227 See Ibid. §§3A.03, 04, 05.

228 Cunningham, see note 7, at 1134 ("Internal governance mechanisms are classified as vertical when they address the relationship between those in control of the corporation and all other constituents (including shareholders, workers, lenders . . .).").

229 Ibid. ("External corporate governance" defined).

PART EIGHT

Critique of shareholder value

INTRODUCTION TO PART EIGHT

The view of the inevitability of convergence was part of the rally call of those who believed equity markets and the pursuit of shareholder value are the basis of contemporary corporate governance. During the 1990s, there was considerable pressure to adopt a shareholder value orientation as the central policy of corporations almost as an article of faith. European executives began to feel it increasingly necessary to emphasize the importance of shareholder value in their companies if they were to be taken seriously in international capital markets. Lazonick and O'Sullivan (Chapter 19) offer an analysis of the rise of shareholder value as the driving force of US corporate governance, tracing the transformation of US corporate strategy from the retention of earnings and reinvestment in the business through the 1970s, to one of downsizing of labour forces and corporate activities in order to enhance earnings to shareholders in the last two decades. This raises questions concerning whether shareholder value management orientations can contribute to sustainable enterprise. (In this regard Lazonick and O'Sullivan, accurately anticipate the dramatic fall in US equity markets that occured in 2001/2002.)

The rhetoric of shareholder value has become prominent in Germany, France and Sweden in recent years, and has been incorporated in the OECD principles of corporate governance. Lazonick and O'Sullivan confront the questions, what does shareholder value mean, and is it an appropriate principle of corporations in the advanced economies? Engelen (Chapter 20) explores further why, despite the resilience of national institutions and practices in corporate governance, an idealized model of shareholder activism, liquid equity markets, and shareholder value continue to seize the imagination of European policy makers. He identifies three claims for shareholder value: the prudential claim for shareholder control and the market allocation of capital as being of superior efficiency; the functional claim for shareholder control resting on the contribution of risk-carrying capital; and the moral claim based on the liberal doctrine of ownership that grounds exclusive rights in property title-holders. Engelen recognizes that public equity markets are used for specific purposes, but the overwhelming majority of productive investment is financed from the retained earnings of the companies themselves. He argues conceptions of property rights do not recognize the complex relations and interdependencies that actually exist in industry.

'Maximizing Shareholder Value: A New Ideology for Corporate Governance'

from Economy and Society (2000)

William Lazonick and Mary O'Sullivan

INTRODUCTION

Over the past two decades the ideology of shareholder value has become entrenched as a principle of corporate governance among companies based in the United States and Britain. Over the past two or three years, the rhetoric of shareholder value has become prominent in the corporate governance debates in European nations such as Germany, France and Sweden. Within the past year, the arguments for 'maximizing shareholder value' have even achieved prominence in Japan. In 1999 the OECD issued a document, *The OECD Principles of Corporate Governance*, that emphasizes that corporations should be run, first and foremost, in the interest of shareholders (OECD, 1999).

But what does 'maximizing shareholder value' mean? Is it an appropriate principle for the governance of corporations in the advanced economies in the twenty-first century? Does the implementation of this principle improve the competitive performance of corporate enterprises? Would the reform of the continental European and Japanese systems of corporate governance based on the principle of maximizing shareholder value bring sustainable prosperity to these economies?

In the so-called Anglo-Saxon economies of the United States and Britain, the exclusive focus of corporations on shareholder value is a relatively recent phenomenon, having risen to prominence in the 1980s as part and parcel of the Reaganite and Thatcherite revolutions. The decade-long boom in

the US stock market and the more recent boom in the US economy have impressed European and Japanese corporate executives with the potential of shareholder value as a principle of corporate governance, while American institutional investors, investment bankers and management consultants have incessantly promoted the virtues of the approach in Europe and Japan.

There is, however, in both Europe and Japan, considerable misinformation about why shareholder value has become so prominent in the governance of US corporations over the past two decades and the actual impact of its implementation on the performance of US corporations and the US economy. Therefore, as a precondition for considering the arguments for 'maximizing shareholder value' in those nations in which it is not yet an entrenched principle of corporate governance, it is imperative that we understand the evolution and impact of the quest for shareholder value in the United States over the past two decades. Such is the purpose of this chapter.

THE ORIGINS OF 'SHAREHOLDER VALUE'

The arguments in support of governing corporations to create shareholder value came into their own in the United States in the 1980s. As has been the case throughout the twentieth century, in the 1980s a relatively small number of giant corporations, employing tens or even hundreds of thousands of people dominated the economy of the United States. On the basis of capabilities that had been accumulated over decades, these corporations generated huge revenues. They allocated these revenues according to a corporate governance principle that we call 'retain and reinvest'. These corporations tended to retain both the money that they earned and the people whom they employed, and they reinvested in physical capital and complementary human resources. Retentions in the forms of earnings and capital consumption allowances provided the financial foundations for corporate growth, while the building of managerial organizations to develop and utilize productive resources enabled investments in plant, equipment and personnel to succeed (Ciccolo and Baum, 1985; Corbett and Jenkinson, 1996; Hall, 1994).

In the 1960s and 1970s, however, the principle of retain and reinvest began running into problems for two reasons, one having to do with the growth of the corporation and the other having to do with the rise of new competitors. Through internal growth and through merger and acquisition, corporations grew too big with too many divisions in too many different types of businesses. The central offices of these corporations were too far from the actual processes that developed and utilized productive resources to make informed investment decisions about how corporate resources and returns should be allocated to enable strategies based on 'retain and reinvest' to succeed. The massive expansion of corporations that had occurred during the 1960s resulted in poor performance in the 1970s, and outcome that was exacerbated by an unstable macroeconomic environment and by the rise of new international competition, especially from Japan (Lazonick and O'Sullivan, 1997; O'Sullivan, 2000b: ch. 4).

Japanese competition was, of course, particularly formidable in the mass-production industries of automobiles, consumer electronics and in the machinery and electronic sectors that supplied capital goods to these consumer durable industries. Yet these had been industries and sectors in which US companies had previously been the world leaders and that had been central to the prosperity of the US economy since the 1920s.[1] Japan was able to challenge the United States in these industries because its manufacturing corporations innovated through the development and utilization of integrated skill bases that were broader and deeper than those in which their American competitors had invested (Lazonick, 1998). Compared with American practice, Japanese skill bases integrated the capabilities of people with a broader array of functional specialities and a deeper array of hierarchical responsibilities into processes of organizational learning. In particular, the hierarchical integration of Japanese skill bases extended from the managerial organization to shop-floor production workers and subsidiary firms that served as suppliers and distributors. In contrast, US companies tended to use their managerial organizations to develop and utilize technologies that would enable them to dispense with shop-floor skills so that 'hourly' production workers could not exercise control over the conditions of work and pay. US companies also tended to favour suppliers and distribution who would provide goods and services at the lowest price the same day, even if it meant that they were not engaged in innovation for tomorrow (Lazonick and O'Sullivan, 1997).

As, during the 1970s, major US manufacturing corporations struggled with these very real problems of excessive centralization and innovative competition, a group of American financial economists developed an approach to corporate governance known as agency theory. Trained, as virtually all American economists are, to believe that the market is always superior to organizations in the efficient allocation of resources, these economists were ideologically predisposed against corporate – that is, managerial – control over the allocation of resources and returns in the economy. Agency theorists posited that, in the governance of corporations, shareholders were the principals and managers were their agents. Agency theorists argued that, because corporate managers were undisciplined by the market mechanism, they would opportunistically use their control over the allocation of corporate resources and returns to line their own pockets, or at least to pursue objectives that were contrary to the interests of shareholders. Given the entrenchment of incumbent corporate managers and the relatively poor performance of their companies in the 1970s, agency theorists argued that there was a need for a takeover market that, functioning as a market for corporate control, could discipline managers whose companies performed poorly. The rate of return on corporate stock was their measure of superior performance, and the maximization of shareholder value became their creed (see, e.g. Baker *et al.*, 1988; Fama and Jensen, 1983; Jensen, 1986; Jensen and Meckling, 1976; Ross, 1973; Scharfstein, 1988).

In addition, during the 1970s, the quest for share-holder value in the US economy found support from a new source – the institutional investor.[2] The transfer of stockholding from individual households to institutions such as mutual funds, pension funds and life insurance companies made possible the takeovers advocated by agency theorists and gave shareholders much more collective power to influence the yields and market values of the corporate stocks they held. During the 1950s and 1960s, there were legal restrictions on the extent to which life insurance companies and pension funds could include corporate equities in their investment protfolios, while mutual funds played only a limited, although growing, role in the mobilization of household savings. In the 1970s, however, a number of changes occurred in the financial sector that promoted the growth of equity-based institutional investing. Partly as a consequence of Wall Street's role in the buying and selling of companies during the conglomeration mania of the 1960s, from the early 1970s there was a shift in the focus of Wall Street financial firms from supporting long-term investment activities of corporations (mainly through bond issues) to generating fees and capital gains through trading in corporate and government securities. To expand the market for securities trading, Wall Street firms convinced the Securities and Exchange Commission (SEC) to put an end to fixed commissions on stock exchange transactions. At the same time, developments in computer technology made it possible for these firms to handle much higher volumes of trade than had previously been the case.

Meanwhile, the oil-induced inflation of the 1970s created a problem for US financial institutions in managing their financial assets to generate adequate returns, thus leading to the financial deregulation of the American economy. As investors in stock and bonds, mutual funds had advantages over other institutional investors such as life insurance companies and pension funds in generating higher returns on household savings because they were not subject to the same stringent regulations concerning the types of investments that they could make. Moreover, even without the mutual funds as competitors, the inflationary conditions of the 1970s meant that, under current regulations, pension funds and insurance companies could no longer offer households positive real rates of return. The regulatory response ERISA – the Employee Retirement Income Security Act (1974) – which, when amended in 1978, permitted pension funds and insurance companies to invest substantial proportions of their portfolios in corporate equities and other risky securities such as 'junk bonds' and venture funds rather than just in high-grade corporate and government securities.

During the 1970s the US banking sector also experienced significant deregulation. With the inflationary conditions boosting the nominal rates of interest on money-market instruments, through a process that became known as 'disintermediation', money-market funds emerged to offer savers much higher rates of returns than the regulated banks could offer them. Beginning in 1978, the government sought to help the banks compete for depositors by deregulating the interest rates that commercial banks and savings banks could pay to depositors and charge on loans. In this deregulated environment, however, savings and loans institutions (S&Ls), a type of savings bank whose assets were long-lived, low-yield mortgages, found that, unless they could invest in higher-yield assets, they could not compete for household deposits. The regulatory response was the Garn-St. Germain Act of 1982 that permitted the S&Ls to hold junk bonds and to lend to inherently risky new ventures, even while the government continued to guarantee the accounts of S&L depositors.

FROM 'RETAIN AND REINVEST' TO 'DOWNSIZE AND DISTRIBUTE'

The stage was now set for institutional investors and S&Ls to become central participants in the hostile takeover movement of the 1980s. An important instrument of the takeover movement was the junk bond – a corporate or government bond that the bond-rating agencies considered to be below 'investment grade'. In the early 1970s, the main sources of junk bonds were 'fallen angels' – previously investment-grade bonds the ratings of which had been downgraded – or 'Chinese paper' – low-grade bonds that had been issued as part of the conglomerate mania of the 1960s – as distinct from newly issued bonds (see Bruck, 1989: 27, 37–38, 44; Taggart, 1988). The innovation of Michael Milken, an employee at the Wall Street investment bank of Drexel, Burnham, and Lambert, was to create a liquid market in junk bonds by convincing financial institutions to buy and sell them (Bruck, 1989: ch. 1). In the early 1970s, when Milken initiated this new financial market, it was mainly the mutual funds, faced by a slumping stock market, which were willing and able to become players.

But, over the next decade, financial deregulation brought, first, pension funds and insurance companies and, then, S&Ls into the junk-bond market. From the late 1970s, it became possible to issue new junk bonds, most of which were used at first to finance management buyouts of divisions of corporations, a mode of undoing the errors of the conglomerate movement of the 1960s that left the new independent companies with huge debt burdens. By the early 1980s, and especially after the Garn-St. Germain Act of 1982 enabled S&Ls to enter the market, it became possible to use junk bonds to launch hostile takeovers of even the largest corporations (Gaughan, 1996: 302). Milken orchestrated most of these hostile takeovers by gaining commitments from institutional investors and S&Ls to sell their shareholdings in the target company to the corporate raider, when the target company was taken over, to buy newly issued junk bonds that enabled the company to buy the raider's shares.

The result was (until, beginning in late 1986, the arbitrageur Ivan Boesky and then Milken as well as others were indicated and eventually imprisoned for insider trading) the emergence of a powerful market for corporate control – something of which the agency theorists of the 1970s had only dreamed. The ideology of the market for corporate control lent powerful support to the claim that such takeover activity was beneficial to the corporations involved and indeed to the US economy as a whole. Takeovers, it was argued, were needed to 'disgorge the free cash flow' from companies (Jensen, 1989). The exchange of corporate shares for high-yield debt forced liquidity on the acquired or merged companies. These takeovers also placed managers in control of these corporations who were predisposed towards shedding labour and selling off physical assets if that was what was needed to meet the corporation's new financial obligations and, indeed, to push up the market value of the company's stock. For those engaged in the market for corporate control, the sole measure of corporate performance became the enhanced market capitalization of the company after the takeover.

If the attempts to engage in corporate governance reform on the principle of creating shareholder value had been confined to the takeover movement of the 1980s, the rise of shareholder value as a principle of corporate governance might have met a rapid demise in the US with the stock-market crash of 1987. Instead the US stock market made a rapid recovery,

and since that time has had the longest bull-run in its history. During the 1990s, it would appear US corporations have been extremely adept at 'creating shareholder value'.

Increasingly during the 1980s, and even more so in the 1990s, support for corporate governance on the principle of creating shareholder value came from an even more powerful and enduring source than the takeover market. In the name of 'creating shareholder value', the past two decades have witnessed a marked shift in the strategic orientation of top corporate managers in the allocation of corporate resources and returns away from 'retain and reinvest' and towards 'downsize and distribute'. Under the new regime, top managers downsize the corporations they control, with a particular emphasis on cutting the size of the labour forces they employ, in an attempt to increase the return on equity.

Since 1980, most major US corporations have been engaged in a process of restructuring their labour forces in ways that have eroded the quantity of jobs that offer stable employment and good pay in the US economy.[3] Hundreds of thousands of previously stable and well-paid blue-collar jobs that were lost in the recession of 1980–82 were never subsequently restored. Between 1979 and 1983, the number of people employed in the economy as a whole increased by 377,000 or 0.4 per cent, while employment in durable good manufacturing – which supplied most of the well-paid and stable blue-collar jobs – declined by 2,023,000, or 15.9 per cent (US Congress, 1992: 344).

Indeed, the 'boom' years of the mid-1980s saw hundreds of major plant closures. Between 1983 and 1987, 4.6 million workers lost their jobs, of which 40 per cent were from the manufacturing sector (Herz, 1990: 23; more generally, see Patch, 1995; Staudohar and Brown, 1987). The elimination of well-paid and stable blue-collar jobs is reflected in the decline of the proportion of the manufacturing labour force that is unionized from 47.4 per cent in 1970 to 27.8 per cent in 1983 and to 18.2 per cent in 1994 (US Bureau of the Census, 1976: 137; US Dept of Commerce, 1975: 375; 1995: 444).

Not only were blue-collar workers affected by the mounting predilection of US corporate managers towards downsizing during the 1980s and 1990s. The 'white-collar' recession of the early 1990s saw the elimination of the positions of tens of thousands of professional, administrative and technical employees – salaried white-collar workers who were considered to be members of 'management'. Even in this recession, however, it was blue-collar workers who bore the brunt of displacement.

Overall, the incidence of job loss in the first half of the 1990s stood at about 14 per cent, even higher than the quite substantial rates of about 10 per cent in the 1980s. The rate of job loss for 1981–83, a period with a slack labour market, was about 13 per cent. As the labour market tightened during the mid-1980s, the rate of job loss fell. As the economy went into recession from 1989, the job-loss rate increased again to a level similar to that in the recession of the early 1980s, notwithstanding the fact that the recession of the late 1980s was much milder. Moreover, even as the economy moved into a recovery from 1991, the job-loss rate rose to ever higher levels, a trend that continued through 1995, despite an acceleration of economic growth (see Figure 1).

Leading the downsizing of the 1980s and 1990s were many of America's largest corporations. In the decades after Second World War, the foundations of US economic development were the willingness and ability of the nation's major industrial corporations to allocate their considerable financial resources to investment strategies that created the good jobs that many Americans began to take for granted. In 1969, the fifty largest US industrial corporations by sales directly employed 6.4 million people, equivalent to 7.5 per cent of the civilian labour force. In 1991, these companies directly employed 5.2 million people, equivalent to 4.2 per cent of the labour force (Lazonick and O'Sullivan, 1997: 3). And since 1991 the downsizing of these companies has gone forward

at a steady pace. By the early 1990s even US firms known for their no-lay-off commitments – IBM, DEC, Delta – had undergone significant downsizing and lay-offs of blue-and white-collar workers (Weinstein and Kochan, 1995: 16).

The American Management Association (AMA) conducts a survey every year of lay-offs by major US companies.[4] A striking finding of this survey is that job elimination has continued to be pervasive among US corporate enterprises leading to substantial reductions in their workforce(s), notwithstanding the considerable improvement in the business cycle during the 1990s. Moreover, notwithstanding the downward trend since 1994–95 in the proportion of companies reporting job elimination, the most recent Challenger, Gray and Christmas estimates of announced staff cuts by major US corporations suggests that another upsurge in lay-offs by US corporations is in the offing (see Figure 2). The AMA survey shows, moreover, that job cutting is much more prevalent among larger employers than smaller ones. Almost 60 per cent of companies that employed more than 10,000 people laid off some of their workforce in 1996–97 (American Management Association Surveys various years). In the boom year of 1998 the number of announced staff cuts by major US corporations was greater than for any other year in the 1990s.

The costs of job loss to displaced workers have been substantial. They have a large probability – around 35 per cent on average – of not being employed two years after displacement. On average, displaced workers, when re-employed, receive real weekly earnings that are some 13 per cent less than before they lost their original jobs (about 9 per cent for workers displaced from full-time jobs who are re-employed on full-time jobs) (Farber, 1997). And these are estimates only of the wage effects of losing a job.

There are, of course, other costs to workers of downsizing. Prominent among them is growing worker insecurity at the prospect of losing a job, and the anxiety that these expectations breed. A commonly used, although imperfect, proxy for a change in job security is a change in job tenure. From 1983 to 1998 there was a slight decline in the median years of tenure of employed wage and salary workers with their current employer from 5 years to 4.7 years. But the average for male and female workers masks significant differences by gender. For male workers aged 25 years and over, median tenure fell from 5.9 years to 4.9 years from 1983 to 1998. A decline in tenure was particularly

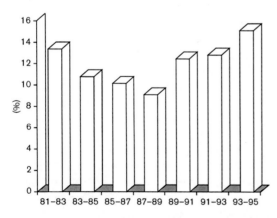

Figure 1 Rate of job-loss in the US: annual average number of jobs lost as a proportion of the labour force.

Source: Farber (1997).

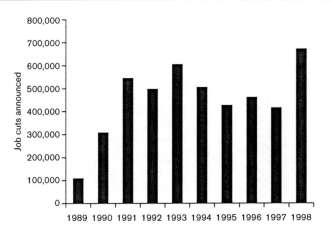

Figure 2 Announced staff cuts by major US corporations 1989–98.

Source: Challenger, Gray, and Christmas Inc. (www.challengergray.com).

pronounced for men aged 55 to 64, falling from 15.3 years to 11.2 years between 1983 and 1998. It is especially striking that these overall declines were registered within the context of a general trend towards an ageing of the male workforce. Among men, in all age groups, the fall in tenure was sufficiently great to outweigh the positive impact of ageing on tenure. In contrast, women aged 25 years and over enjoyed an increase in median tenure from 4.2 years to 4.4 years, although some of this effect was a result of the ageing of the female workforce. Most age groups within the female working population experienced the increase in median tenure, with the notable exception of women aged 55 to 64 years, whose median tenure fell from 9.8 years in 1983 to 9.6 years in 1998.

As proxies for job security, job tenure figures must be used with caution. With lay-offs occurring on a large scale, the proportion of workers with long tenure could rise, not because workers as a group are enjoying greater employment security, but because workers with lower seniority are being laid off. In the aircraft and parts industry, for example, a sharp rise in median tenure from 6.3 in 1991 to 9.6 in 1998 at a time of widespread lay-offs seems to be, at least partly, attributable to this effect (US Bureau of Labor Statistics various years).

While US corporate managers became focused on downsizing their labour-forces in the 1980s and 1990s, they also became focused on distributing corporate revenues in ways that supported the price of their companies' stocks. During the 1950s, 1960s and 1970s the pay-out ratio (the ratio of dividends to after-tax adjusted corporate profits) varied from a low of 37.2 per cent in 1966 (when increases in dividends lagged increased profits) to a high of 53 per cent in 1974 (when profits fell by 19 per cent while dividends went up by 8 per cent). But averaged over any five-year period during these three decades, the pay-out ratio stayed remarkably stable, never going above 45.9 per cent (1970–74) and never falling below 38.8 per cent (1975–79). The stability is even greater over ten-year periods – 47.9 per cent for the 1950s, 42.4 per cent for the 1960s and 42.3 per cent for the 1970s (see Figure 3). These pay-out ratios were high by international standards, manifesting the extent to which US corporations returned value to stockholders even before the rise of the institutional investor.

Compared with the 1960s and 1970s, an upward shift in corporate pay-out ratios occurred in the 1980s and 1990s. In 1980, when profits declined by 17 per cent (the largest profits decline since the 1930s), dividends rose by 13 per cent, and the pay-out ratio shot up 15 points to 57 per cent. Thereafter, from 1980 through 1998, the pay-out ratio fell below 44 per cent only twice, in 1984 and 1985, and even then not because dividends fell but because the increase in dividends did not keep up with the increase in profits. There was no five-year period within the period 1980 to 1998 during which the pay-out ratio did not average at least 44 per cent, and over the nineteen years it averaged over 49 per cent (O'Sullivan, 2000b: fig. 6.4; US Congress, 1999: 431).

Since the mid-1980s, moreover, increases in corporate dividends have not been the only way in

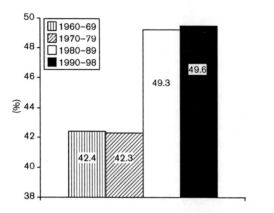

Figure 3 US corporate pay-out ratio (1960–98): corporate dividends as a percentage of corporate profits after tax with inventory valuation and capital consumption adjustments.

Source: US Congress (1992; 403; 1999: 431).

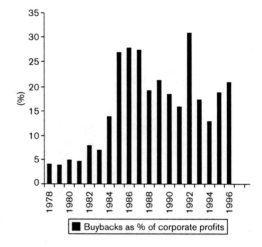

Figure 4 Buybacks as a share of US corporate profits 1978–96.

Source: Securities Data Corporation.

which corporations have distributed earnings to stockholders. Prior to the 1980s, during a stock-market boom, companies would often sell shares on the market at inflated prices to pay off debt or to bolster the corporate treasury. In general, although equity issues have never been an important source of funds for investment in the development and utilization of the productive capabilities of US corporate enterprises, they tended to issue more equities than they repurchased, But, during the 1980s, the net equity issues for US corporations became negative in many years, largely as a result of stock repurchases.

In 1985, when total corporate dividends were $84 billion, stock repurchases were $20 billion, boosting the effective pay-out ratio from under 40 per cent, based on dividends only, to 50 per cent with the addition of stock repurchases. In the quarter following the stock market crash of 1987, there were 777 announcements by US corporations of new or increased buybacks ('The buyback monster', *Forbes*, 17 November 1997). In 1989, when dividends had risen to $134.4 billion, stock repurchases had increased to over $60 billion, increasing the effective pay-out ratio to over 81 per cent. With close to $70 billion in stock repurchases in 1994, the effective pay-out ratio was about 66 per cent. In 1996, stock repurchases were $116 billion, for an effective pay-out ratio of 72 per cent ('The hidden meaning of stock buybacks', *Fortune*, September 1997). Although for any one year the announced buyback plans tend

to be lower than actual repurchases, the continuing high levels of announced buyback plans since 1996 suggest that US corporate enterprises continue to favour buybacks as a respectable use for their cash; US corporations announced plans to buy back $177 billion of stock in 1996, $181 billion in 1997, and $207 billion in 1998 (see Figure 4).

For many major US corporations stock repurchases have now become a systematic feature of the way in which they allocate revenues and a critically important one in terms of the amount of money involved. General Electric is a good example. From 1994 to 1998, its cumulative dividend growth was 84 per cent compared with 29 per cent for the population of S&P 500 firms. Moreover, during the same period, the cumulative amount of cash that GE spent on share repurchases at $14.6 billion rivalled the $15.6 billion paid out in cumulative dividends. Together these two outflow of cash amounted to an extraordinary 74.4 per cent of GE's cumulative cash from operations from 1994 to 1998. Notwithstanding the enormous amounts that the company has already spent on repurchases, in December 1997, GE's Board of Directors increased the authorization to repurchase company stock to a massive $17 billion (GE 10K 1998). It is perhaps not coincidental that since 1981, when the current CEO, Jack Welch, took office, GE has set the tone for downsizing among corporations.

Why and how did this shift in the orientation of top managers from retain and reinvest to downsize and distribute occur? Corporate governance for most US corporations from their emergence in the late nineteenth and early twentieth century through the 1970s was based on the strategy of retain and reinvest. Top managers tended to be integrated with the business organizations that employed them and governed the corporate enterprises that they controlled accordingly. One condition that supported this integration of top managers into the organization was the separation of share ownership and managerial control. In the absence of hereditary owners in top management positions, career employees who worked their way up and around the managerial hierarchy could realistically hope to rise to top management positions over the course of their careers. Into the 1970s the salaried compensation of top managers was largely determined by pay structures within the managerial organization.

Forces were at work from the 1950s that increasingly segmented top managers of US corporations from the rest of the managerial organization. Top managers of many US corporations began receiving stock options in 1950, after tax changes made this form of compensation attractive. During the 1950s and 1960s, with the stock market generally on the rise, gains from the exercise of these options and the holding of stock became increasingly important components of the incomes of top managers. When, in the early 1970s, the stock market turned down, many corporate boards transformed worthless stock options into increases in salaried remuneration, on the grounds that these managers could not be blamed for the general downturn in the stock market. In effect, the *expectations* of gains from stock options that had been formed during the general rise in the stock market in the 1950s and 1960s came to be considered, along with salaries, as part of the basic compensation of top managers. Thus began a trend that during the 1970s favoured the pay of top managers over the pay of everyone else in the corporation (see Figures 5 and 6). During the 1980s and 1990s the explosion in top management pay has continued unabated, with stock-based rewards playing an ever more important role (Hall and Liebman, 1997). On average, the pay packages of CEOs of US corporations were forty-four times those of factory workers in 1965, but 419 times in 1998 (*Business Week*, 20 April 1998, 19 April 1999).

From the 1950s, therefore, US corporate managers developed and ever-growing personal interest

in boosting the market value of their companies' stock. Yet even though US companies had relatively high payout ratios by international standards in the 1950s, 1960s, and 1970s, during these decades US top managers remained oriented towards a strategy of retain and reinvest rather than simply using corporate revenues to increase dividends or repurchase stock to boost stock prices. The fact is that, given the dominance that these corporation exercised over many of their product markets, the pursuit of retain and reinvest

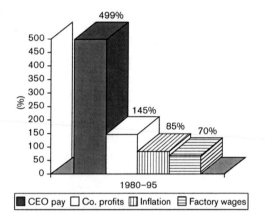

Figure 5 CEO pay versus factory wages in major US corporations 1980–95.

Source: http://www.aflcio.org/paywatch.

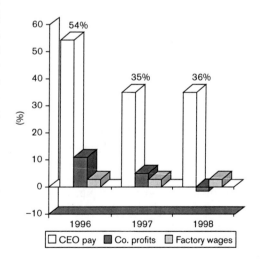

Figure 6 CEO pay versus factory wages in major US corporations 1996–98.

Source: http://www.aflcio.org/paywatch.

strategies permitted lots of different stakeholders to gain. Workers could get paid higher wages and have better employment stability and working conditions; suppliers and distributors could make more profits, some of which could potentially be passed on to their workers; consumers could get lower prices on the goods that they purchased; the dividends to stockholders could be maintained or even increased; and there could still be substantial funds left over for the corporation to reinvest either within the United States or, as was increasingly the case in these decades, abroad.

Such was the happy situation facing US corporation in their era of unchallenged dominance in the post-Second World War decades. It was this environment of growth that spawned the belief among many top managers of US corporations that a good manager could manage anything – a belief that the major business schools of the time were happy to propound and that provided a rationale for the conglomeration movement of the 1960s. But in the much more difficult economic environment of the 1970s and early 1980s, this belief in the omnipotence of top management began to be shattered. Indeed, the over-extension of the corporate enterprises into too many different lines of business had helped to foster the strategic segmentation of top managers from their organizations. At the same time, the innovative capabilities of international competitors made it harder to sustain the employment of corporate labour-forces, unless the productive capabilities of many if not most of these employees could be radically transformed. Under these conditions, US corporate managers faced a strategic crossroads: they could find new ways to generate productivity gains on the basis of retain and reinvest or they could capitulate to the new competitive environment through corporate downsizing.

If the changed competitive environment of the 1970s and 1980s made it more difficult for top managers of US corporations to be successful through a strategy of retain and reinvest, increased segmentation within their own organizations made it more difficult for them to understand what type of innovative strategies they should pursue and the capabilities of their organizations to implement these strategies. In addition, by the 1980s the deregulated financial environment and the rise of the institutional investor as a holder of corporate stocks encouraged top managers to align their own interests with external financial interests rather than with the interests of the productive organizations over which they exercised control. Manifesting this alignment was the explosion in top management pay, while the other side of the same paycheck was the shift in the strategic orientation of top management from retain and reinvest to downsize and distribute. With the co-operation of top corporate managers, shareholder value had by the 1990s become a firmly entrenched principle of US corporate governance.

SHAREHOLDER VALUE AND ECONOMIC PERFORMANCE

Shareholders and top managers have certainly benefited under the rule of shareholder value (see Table 1). But how has the US economy as a whole performed? Again, as in the case of hostile takeovers and the market for corporate control, financial economists, versed in theories of the inherent economic superiority of market resource allocation over corporate resource allocation, have provided the theoretical rationale for corporate governance in the interests of shareholders with its emphasis on downsize and distribute.[5] Financial economists contend that, when the corporate enterprise maximizes shareholder value, everyone – workers, consumers, suppliers and distributors – will, as a result, be better off. These financial economists posit that shareholders are the 'owners' or 'principals' in whose interests the corporations should be run. They recognize, however, that, in the actual running of the corporation, shareholders must rely on managers to perform certain functions. The proponents of shareholder value have argued, often with justification, that the managers who control the allocation of corporate resources and returns are self-serving in the exercise of this control. As a result, such managers do not adequately 'create value for shareholders'.

When corporations are run to maximize shareholder value, these financial economists argue, the performance of the economy as a whole, not just the interest of shareholders, can be enhanced. In making this claim, advocates of maximizing shareholder value rely on arguments that portray any residual revenues – profits – that the corporation generates as rewards for critical economic functions that, allegedly, shareholders perform and without which these residuals would not be possible. In one version of the argument, shareholder returns are regarded as incentives for waiting and risk bearing; in another version, as rewards for shareholder monitoring of managers.

	1950–59	1960–69	1970–79	1980–89	1990–98
Real stock yield	17.7	8.3	−1.7	11.7	14.3
Stock price yield	14.8	7.5	1.4	12.9	14.8
Dividend yield	4.9	3.2	4.1	4.3	2.6
Change in CPI	2.1	2.4	7.1	5.6	3.1
Real bond yield	1.3	2.7	1.2	5.8	4.9

Table 1 US corporate stock and bond yields 1950–98: per cent, annual averages.

Source: US Congress (1992: 366, 378, 397; 1999: 399, 412, 436).

According to the logic of shareholder value theory, if corporate managers cannot allocate resources and returns to maintain the value of the shareholders' assets, then the 'free cash flow' should be distributed to shareholders who can then allocate these resources to their most efficient alternative uses. Since in the modern corporation, with its publicly listed stock, these shareholders have a market relation with the corporation, the economic argument for making distributions to shareholders in an argument concerning the efficiency of the replacement of corporate control over the allocation of resources and returns with market control.

Shareholder value advocates, moreover, point to the stock-market boom throughout the 1990s and the prosperity of the US economy in the late 1990s as proof positive of the economic benefits that the pursuit of shareholder value has delivered. Theory, they argue, has been borne out by practice. Specifically, proponents of 'creating shareholder value' through downsizing and distributing argue:

- US corporations that have engaged in such restructuring have become more efficient, as reflected in enhanced profitability and higher market valuations of their assets.
- The release of labour and capital from major corporations has provided, moreover, the basis for the flourishing of new ventures in industrial districts such as Silicon Valley based on the highly dynamic and internationally competitive US information technologies sector.
- In effect, the dismantling of corporate control over the allocation of resources and returns in the economy has enabled labour and capital markets to reallocate those resources to start-up companies that are fast, flexible and innovative and that are driving the current boom in the US economy.

- In cross-national comparative perspective, such restructuring of existing corporations and the creation of such dynamic new ventures are precisely what are missing in Japan and the advanced nations of Europe.
- Nothing could do more to jumpstart these economies than to import American-style institutional investing and corporate restructuring so that the mechanisms of the market can redirect the allocation of labour and capital to their most profitable uses.

The current boom conditions in the US economy, and the undoubted success of Silicon Valley in the information-technology sector, would seem to provide powerful support to those who argue that the pursuit of shareholder value is the path to sustainable prosperity. Besides the booming stock market, it is common to cite the relatively low rates of unemployment that the United States has achieved in the late 1990s, with an emphasis on the fact that, in February 1999, for the first time since the early 1950s, the official US unemployment rate was lower than the official Japanese unemployment rate.

There are, however, many problems with this rosy view of the power of shareholder value is reshaping corporate governance and, indeed, the organization of the economy to deliver sustainable prosperity. In both theory and practice, the arguments for maximizing shareholder value ignore significant problems of US economic performance in the era of 'downsize and distribute' as well as important historical foundations of the current stock-market and economic booms. A consideration of these problems of economic performance and foundations of the current booms raises serious questions about the future sustainability of US prosperity in a shareholder-value regime.

PROBLEMS OF US ECONOMIC PERFORMANCE

Declining employment security, falling job tenures and the significant costs of job loss that many, if not most, Americans have experienced in the 1990s reflect a longer-run trend, dating back to the 1970s, towards a persistent worsening of the distribution of income in the United States. The flexibility of US labour markets may have enabled the US economy to achieve reasonable rates of unemployment in the 1990s, but only at the cost of creating an economy based on low wage rates and incomes for most of the working population. To make ends meet, moreover, most families need incomes from two adults who have to work long hours. Indeed, during the 1990s, the yearly working hours of the average American surpassed those of the average Japanese.

The problem of income inequality in the United States reflects not only significant differences in levels of wages and salaries but also significant inequalities in the distribution of wealth, among which is the distribution of stockholdings. The top half of 1 per cent of all US households in terms of the size of their stockholdings owns, directly or through institutional investors, almost 37 per cent of all outstanding corporate equities whereas 80 per cent of US households own less than 2 per cent (Poterba and Samwick, 1995: 328). The high rates of returns on corporate stocks that have been achieved in the era of shareholder value have served only to exacerbate income inequality in the United States.

During the 1980s and 1990s, while US financial economists have been confidently advocating the creation of shareholder value, US labour economists have been unable to explain the worsening income distribution. In our view, the impacts of the tendency of US corporations to downsize and distribute are only part of the story of the worsening income distribution. Even corporations that *favour* a strategy of downsizing and distributing must, if they are to persist, also engage in strategies that require them to retain and reinvest. Another part of the story of worsening income inequality is what we call the 'skill-base hypothesis': the strategic focus of *innovative* US corporations on those types of activities in which innovation can be generated by investing in 'narrow and concentrated' skill bases of highly educated personnel. In the post-Second World War era that extended through the 1970s – decades when US corporate governance favoured strategies of 'retain and

reinvest' – US blue-collar or 'hourly' workers were well paid and provided with stable employment, even though by world standards they were poorly educated and trained. During this period there was a general improvement in the distribution of income that contrasts with the worsening of the income distribution since that time. The corporations that employed these workers had achieved market dominance by developing managerial organization and fostering managerial learning, and shared some of the gains of this dominance with production workers, whose co-operation was required on the shop-floor.

But in the 1970s and 1980s, the lack of investment in shop-floor skills proved to be the Achilles heel of US corporations in international competition, and especially in competition with Japanese companies that had innovated by investing in broader and deeper skill bases than US companies. In response to the historical legacy of the US economy in neglecting investment in shop-floor skills in the face of competitive challenge from abroad, the retention and reinvestment strategies of US corporation in the 1980s and 1990s focused on activities in which they could innovate and compete by investing in the capabilities of only the most highly educated personnel. Indeed, in engaging in these activities and investing in these employees, US corporations are able to drawn on an international pool of highly educated labour. This labour comes to the United States in search of high-paid employment, often by way of one or more university degrees from world-class universities and departments in the US system of higher education. The skills-base bias of US corporate investment and the availability of a well-educated international labour supply have meant, moreover, that corporate America has had little interest in upgrading the quality of education available to most Americans. This is evidenced by the highly unequal and, by international standards, generally inferior system of mass education in the United States.

FOUNDATIONS OF THE CURRENT PROSPERITY

It is common in the late 1990s for Americans to tout the innovation and prosperity of Silicon Valley as an outcome of the corporate restructuring of the past two decades that has made both capital and labour free to move into new ventures. This view, however, ignores historical accumulations of resources and capabilities in districts such as Silicon Valley that have made the current prosperity possible. In effect, the prosperity of Silicon Valley in the 1990s owes more to the post-war 'military industrial complex', in which 'retain and reinvest' corporations such as IBM, Hewlett Packard, Motorola and Xerox were central, rather than it does to a resurgence of entrepreneurship – something that has always been in abundant supply in the United States. The success of these corporations in developing and utilizing technologies was in turn highly dependent on massive government procurement contracts and research initiatives. In historical perspective, the current re-allocation of labour and capital to new ventures in the United States is, therefore, just the most visible tip of the military-industrial complex – a developmental iceberg that took the American economy decades to put in place. Given the focus of US corporations on downsizing and distributing, as well as the US government's retreat from investments in basic research, there are questions about whether the American economy is currently generating the new technological infrastructure that can provide foundations for sustainable prosperity in the twenty-first century.

If there are questions about the foundations and future of productive investment in the United States, there are also questions about the sources and availability of American savings. Corporate policies of 'downsize and distribute' have provided the underlying impetus to the stock-market boom of the 1990s, but the sustained and rapid rate of increase in stock prices is the result of a massive flow of funds into the stock market through equity-based mutual funds. Since the 1960s US households have been increasing the proportion of their financial assets that are invested in pension and mutual funds. From 1982 to 1994 pension and mutual funds alone accounted for about 67 per cent of the net growth of the total financial assets of households (Edwards, 1996: 16–27).

Reflecting their growing importance in managing the savings of US households, pension and mutual funds' shares of corporate equities have increased dramatically. Pension funds held 24 per cent of US corporate stock in 1997, with private pensions accounting for 13.8 per cent and public pensions for 10.2 per cent, compared with 0.3 per cent in 1945. Over the same period, mutual funds increased their share of US corporate stock from 1.5 per cent to 16.2 per cent. A substantial proportion of the recent upsurge in the share of mutual funds is attributable to their growing popularity for pension provision; at the

end of 1996, retirement-plan assets represented 35 per cent of all mutual fund assets. In contrast to the growing importance of institutional investors, the share of corporate stocks held directly by individuals has fallen from 93 per cent in 1945 to 42.7 per cent in 1997 (US Board of Governors, Federal Reserve various years). Institutional share ownership is even higher in the largest US corporation than in the population of corporate enterprises as a whole. In 1987, the institutional share of the equity of the top 1,000 US corporations was 46.6 per cent; by 1995 it had increased to 57.2 per cent (Brancato, 1997).

The shift of stockholdings to institutional investors had by no means exhausted itself by the mid-1990s. During the last half of the 1980s, the net new cash flow into equity mutual funds ranged from a high of about $21.9 billion in 1986 to a low of minus $16.2 billion in 1988. During the early 1990s, however, the flow of new money into mutual funds picked up speed, and during 1993–95 net additions to mutual funds averaged about $125 billion per year. In 1996 and 1997 the net additions to equity mutual funds rose to the unprecedented levels of $217 billion and $227 billion respectively. In the first seven months of 1998, the pace of inflows remained vigorous. However, in conjunction with the downturn in the US stock market in August 1998, the inflow of cash slowed down sufficiently to bring the net inflow for the year to $159 billion, which represented a 30 per cent fall compared with 1997. Yet, as the market regained its vigour in late 1998 and especially in early 1999, inflows revived again (Investment Company Institute).

The origins of this 'new' money are not well documented. What is clear, however, is that the savings rate of US households, already low by international standards in the 1980s, has plunged further in the 1990s. An older generation of Americans – the ones who were able to accumulate significant savings, pensions and other assets during the era of 'retain and reinvest' – appear to be reallocating their financial resources to capture the returns of the booming stock market. But what if, as appears to be the case, the younger generations, living in an era of 'downsize of distribute', will not have the same opportunities as the older generations for the accumulation of financial assets? And, indeed, what if the returns to the financial assets of older generations, who have become increasingly reliant on the stock market for returns on their savings to fund their consumption expenditures, cannot be sustained?

IS THE CURRENT PROSPERITY SUSTAINABLE?

We must consider the possibility that the US stock-market boom is encouraging US households to live off the past while corporations have less incentive to invest for the future. The current consumption-driven boom seems to be closely tied to the stock-market boom. For the first time in US history, the returns to the savings of American households are directly dependent on the sustainability of high yields on corporate stock. What will happen to US consumption, and to the US (and world) economy, if the US stock market should turn down, and stay down?

Yet the stock-market boom has not made capital available to industry. The persistent and massive flow of funds into stock-based mutual funds in the 1990s has bid up stock prices, increasing the market capitalizations of corporations. But, as we have seen, net corporate equity issues have been negative over the course of the 1990s because of corporate stock repurchases, while the main impact of the stock-market boom on capital markets has been to raise consumption.

No one knows the 'real' limits to the current stock-market boom. What we can say is that, unlike the speculative stock-market booms that occurred in the late 1920s in the United States, and in the late 1980s in Japan, in which corporations sold stock at high price – earnings ratios to increase their cash reserves or pay off debt, the current US boom is being supported by corporate cash distributions. What is the continuing capacity of US corporations to support stock prices through 'downsize and distribute' strategies?

A proponent of shareholder value would argue that vibrant new ventures are replacing the stodgy old corporations that are being downsized. But even if one were to accept the claim that the stock-market boom has induced entrepreneurs to set up new ventures with their eyes on the prospect of not-too-distant and very lucrative initial public offerings, are new ventures sustainable if they are governed by the principle of shareholder value? One important effect of the stock-market boom on new ventures has been to make them dependent on the performance of the stock market even before these enterprises themselves have gone public. Most new ventures finance themselves by the willingness of employees to accept shares in the company in lieu of immediate remuneration. But should the stock market turn down, and with it the expectations for gains on the sale of shares

in a successful IPO also go down, many new ventures will find that the financial commitment required to secure the personnel to develop and utilize the enterprise's productive resources are beyond their financial means or those of the venture capitalists who support them.

Indeed, it is not just new ventures that are looking to stock-market gains to pay employee compensation. In 1998, for example, the widespread use of stock options to attract and reward employees meant that Intel spent more than twice as much on stock repurchases than on R&D (Intel 10K 1999). During the same year, Microsoft's stock repurchases were almost equal to its in-house spending on R&D (Microsoft 10K 1999). We have no precedent for examining how, given such remuneration schemes, strategically central corporations such as these would be affected by a stock-market collapse. However, it is worthwhile remembering that Intel and Microsoft were once new ventures that transformed themselves into going concerns by establishing themselves as key suppliers to IBM. IBM was a US corporation that epitomized governance according to the principles of 'retain and reinvest', while Intel and Microsoft became dominant in their sectors by governing themselves according to the same principles. The experience of the United States suggests that the pursuit of shareholder value may be an appropriate strategy for running down a company – and an economy. The pursuit of some other kind of value is needed to built up a company and an economy.

ACKNOWLEDGEMENTS

Funding for the research in this paper was provided by the Jerome Levy Economics Institute and by the Targeted Socio-Economic Research Program of the European Commission (Contract no. SOE1-CT98-1114).

NOTES

1 An important analysis of US loss of competitive advantage in a number of major industries can be found in Dertouzos *et al.* (1989).
2 The following paragraphs on the transformation of the US financial sector are based on Lazonick and O'Sullivan (1997); see also Lazonick (1992) and O'Sullivan (2000: ch. 5).

3 The following paragraphs on downsizing of labour and distribution of earnings are drawn from O'Sullivan (2000: ch. 5).

4 The AMA survey is sent to human resources managers in AMA member companies every year. AMA's corporate membership consists of 9,500 organizations which together employ 25 per cent of the American workforce. Over 85 per cent of surveyed firms gross more than $10 million annually, which puts them among the top 5 per cent of US corporations.

5 For an elaboration of shareholder theory and a critique, see O'Sullivan (1999).

REFERENCES

Baker, G., Jensen, M. and Murphy, K. (1988) 'Compensation and incentives: practice vs. theory', *Journal of Finance* 43: 593–616.

Brancato, C. (1997) *Institutional Investors and Corporate Governance: Best Practices for Increasing Corporate Value*, Chicago: Irwin Professional.

Bruck, C. (1989) *The Predators' Ball*, London: Penguin.

Ciccolo, J. Jr. and Baum, C. (1985) 'Changes in the balance sheet of the U.S. manufacturing sector, 1926–1977', in B. Friedman (ed.) *Corporate Capital Structures in the United States*, Chicago, IL: University of Chicago Press.

Corbett, J. and Jenkinson, T. (1996) 'The financing of industry, 1970–1989: an international comparison', *Journal of the Japanese and International Economies* 10(1): 71–96.

Dertouzos, M., Lester, R. and Solow, R. and the MIT Commission on Industrial Productivity (1989) *Made in America: Regaining the Productive Edge*, Cambridge, MA: MIT Press.

Edwards, F. (1996) *The New Finance: Regulation and Financial Stability*, Washington, DC: AEI Press.

Fama, E. and Jensen, M. (1983) 'Separation of ownership and control', *Journal of Law and Economics* 26: 301–25.

Farber, H. (1997) 'The changing face of job loss in the United States', *Brookings Papers: Microeconomics*, Washington, DC: Brookings Institution.

Gaughan, P. (1996) *Mergers, Acquisitions, and Corporate Restructurings*, New York: Wiley.

Hall, B. (1994) 'Corporate restructuring and investment horizons in the United States, 1976–1987', *Business History Review* 68(1): 110–43.

—— and Liebman, J. (1997) 'Are CEOs really paid like bureaucrats?', *NBER Working Paper Series* no. 6213.

Herz, D. (1990) 'Worker displacement in a period of rapid job expansion, 1983–1987', *Monthly Labor Review* May.

Jensen, M. (1986) 'Agency cost of free cash flow, corporate finance, and takeovers', *American Economic Review* 76: 323–9.

—— (1989) 'Eclipse of the public corporation', *Harvard Business Review* 67(5): 61–74.

—— and Meckling, W. (1976) 'Theory of the firm: managerial behavior, agency costs, and ownership structure', *Journal of Financial Economics* 3: 305–60.

Lazonick, W. (1992) 'Controlling the market for corporate control', *Industrial and Corporate Change* 1(3).

—— (1998) 'Organizational learning and international competition', in J. Michie and J. Smith (eds) *Globalization, Growth, and Governance: Creating and Innovative Economy*, Oxford: Oxford University Press.

—— and O'Sullivan, M. (1997) 'Investment in innovation, corporate governance, and corporate employment', *Jerome Levy Economics Institute Policy Brief* No. 37.

O'Sullivan, M. (2000a) 'The innovative enterprise and corporate governance', *Cambridge Journal of Economics* 24: 393–416.

—— (2000b) *Contests for Corporate Control: Corporate Governance and Economic Performance in the United States and Germany*, Oxford: Oxford University Press.

OECD (1999) *OECD Principles of Corporate Governance*, Paris: OECD.

Patch, E. (1995) *Plant Closings and Employment Loss in Manufacturing: The Role of Local Conditions*, New York: Garland.

Poterba, J. and Samwick, A. (1995) 'Stock ownership patterns, stock market fluctuations, and consumption', *Brookings Papers on Economic Activity* 2: 295–372.

Ross, S. (1973) 'The economic theory of agency: the principal's problem', *American Economic Review* 63: 134–9.

Scharfstein, D. (1988) 'The disciplinary role of takeovers', *Review of Economic Studies* 55: 185–99.

Staudohar, P. and Brown, H. (1987) *Deindustrialization and Plant Closure*, Lexington, MA: Lexington Books.

Taggart, R. (1988) 'The growth of the "junk" bond market and its role in financing takeovers', in A. Auerbach (ed.) *Mergers and Acquisitions*, Chicago, IL: University of Chicago Press.

US Board of Governors, Federal Reserve (various years) *Flow of Funds Accounts, Flows and Outstandings*, Washington, DC: US Government Printing Office.

US Bureau of Labor Statistics (various years) *Employment and Earnings*, Washington, DC: US Government Printing Office.

US Bureau of the Census (1976) *Historical Statistics of the United States from the Colonial Times to the Present*, Washington, DC: US Government Printing Office.

US Congress (various years) *Economic Report of the President*, Washington, DC: US Government Printing Office.

US Department of Commerce (various years) *Statistical Abstract of the United States*, Washington, DC: US Government Printing Office.

Weinstein, M. and Kochan, T. (1995) 'The limits of diffusion: recent developments in industrial relations and human resource practices', in R. Locke, T. Kochan and M. Piore (eds) *Employment Relations in a Changing World*, Cambridge, MA: MIT Press.

'Corporate Governance, Property and Democracy: A Conceptual Critique of Shareholder Ideology'

from Economy and Society (2002)

Ewald Engelen

INTRODUCTION

Recent comparative studies have taught at least two things (Goodin, 1998; Hall and Taylor, 1996; Immergut, 1998; Thelen, 1999): first, that there is no 'one best way', but rather several 'functionally equivalent' ways to solve co-ordination, information and enforcement problems, implying that there are many 'varieties of capitalism' instead of one self-enclosed capitalist system (Berger and Dore, 1996; Boyer and Drache, 1996; Crouch and Streeck, 1997; Hall and Soskice, 2001; Hirst and Thompson, 1999; Hollingsworth and Boyer, 1997; Hollingsworth *et al.*, 1994; Kitschelt *et al.*, 1999; Whitley, 1999); second, that convergence is not imminent. 'Path dependency', 'lock in', 'institutional inertia' refer to the phenomenon that there are (and will be) clear and distinct national institutional trajectories, even in the midst of powerful global pressures to change and adapt to what is perceived as the norm (Roe, 1994, 1996; Visser and Hemerijck, 1998). Labour relations, social arrangements, fiscal systems, mechanisms of economic governance, governance conventions, the statistical apparatus of the state: the institutions of the warfare/welfare state have different histories and react differently to the tensions and contradictions of ongoing integration (Ferguson, 2001; Skocpol, 1992; Tilly, 1990; Weiss, 1998). In other words, the forces of integration are refracted differently in various but often functional equivalent institutional settings, resulting in different outcomes (Streeck, 1998: 440).

Institutional clusters differ with regard to their resilience to change. National systems of corporate governance appear to be a much easier target of homogenizing forces than welfare arrangements, fiscal systems or industrial relations (Deeg, 1999: 73ff.; Streeck, 1997). However, one's assessment depends upon what is included in the institutions of corporate governance, for corporate governance can be conceptualized in either of two ways. In the 'small' or 'narrow' conception, corporate governance refers to the articles in corporate law that regulate the establishment of joint stock corporations. In the 'broad' one, corporate governance encompasses labour relations, the pension system as well as co-determination laws and practices.

Economists, legal theorists and accountants who argue that liquid stock markets are the most efficient way to allocate capital, and want legal restrictions torn down, usually adhere to the narrow view (Jensen 1988, 2000; Jensen and Ruback, 1983; Scherer, 1988). Moreover, as the notion of efficiency suggests, they generally rely on 'one best way' that is a close look-alike of the American institutions of corporate governance.[1]

Their adversaries – many of whom belong to the growing community of comparative researchers – usually adopt the broad view and emphasize the resilience of national corporate governance traditions, either by creating 'Chinese walls' between different models of corporate governance (Albert, 1992; Dore, 2000; Pollin, 1995), or by stressing the strong interlock between corporate law, mechanisms of economic governance, industrial relations, managerial practices, business systems, schooling and training systems, and the market behaviour of individual firms (Lane, 1990, 1995; Whitley, 1992, 1999; Whitley and Kristensen, 1996, 1997).

The model-based criticism of convergence is not very convincing, primarily because it uses a static picture to depict a dynamic world. A good case can be made for a tendency towards convergence in corporate governance that crosses the artificial boundaries between the Anglo-American and German models, first, because US insurers, investment funds and pension funds might turn into the same type of large, involved and responsible 'block holders' that are known from the German context (Roe, 1994), and, second, because recent legal changes in Germany – initiating a transition from a 'pay-as-you-go' pension system to a funded one (Lamping and Rüb, 2001), removing fiscal constraints on the disentanglement of corporate cross holdings and facilitating access to international capital markets – seem destined to 'deepen' the German stock market and to boost shareholderism (Deeg, 1999: 87ff.; Ferguson, 2001: 318).

The interlock-based criticism is stronger. Since it starts from a disaggregated view of capitalist economies – using theoretical correlations between specific institutions to explain national 'varieties of capitalism' – it allows for theoretical predictions about the disposition as well as direction of change of these economies. Whitley, for one, argues that German and Japanese firms have a much lower tendency to change than American or British ones, as the level of institutional embeddedness is much higher in Germany and Japan than in the US or the UK (Whitley, 1999: 117–36). This is borne out by the fact that Japanese 'transplants' have had a huge impact on management practices, organizational models, market orientation and even economic governance in the US and the UK,[2] whereas the converse has occurred only rarely (Whitley and Kristensen, 1997). In Germany, US transplants have adopted German practices, whereas German transplants in the US have recreated German-like environments within the 'host' country (Boyer et al., 1998).

Nevertheless, changes in business orientation are emerging, even in German and Japanese firms. A recent research programme by the German Max Planck Institute has constructed an elaborate distributive model to operationalize the effects of market integration on the orientations of large German firms (www.mpi-fg-koeln.mpg.de). Using the financial data of 59 large German firms – listed and unlisted ones – Beyer and Hassel conclude that the growing financial internationalization of German firms has resulted in a stronger emphasis on the management of investor's relations and a slight increase in dividend pay-outs. Given the novelty of most of the deregulatory legislation, Beyer and Hassel expect these tendencies to increase. However, no spillovers to neigbouring institutions – labour relations, co-determination, etc. – are visible yet. Beyer and Hassel offer three explanations: time lag, less institutional interlock than usually presumed[3] and a development towards institutional *hybridization*, of which they prefer the last, adding the rider that 'the relationship between corporate governance regimes and labour relations is not conceptualised thoroughly enough yet to be able to draw a firm conclusion' (Beyer and Hassel, 2001: 20; see also Lane, 2000).

Even though Whitley could point out that distributive shifts in the earnings of large German firms are not illustrative for the German economy as a whole, as the German economy consists of two 'industrial orders' – one of large autonomous firms and one of 'co-ordinated industrial districts' populated by highly integrated small and medium-sized firms with a distinct 'artisinal orientation' (Herrigel, 1996) – the shifts themselves are real and must be accounted for (see Van Apeldoorn, 2001).

UNPACKING SHAREHOLDER IDEOLOGY

The focus of this chapter is on the ideological dimension of institutional change. I take it that the internationalization of product and capital markets is a political event. However, once taken, political decisions can be as binding as the 'laws of nature'. Moreover, they have real effects. In game-theoretical terms, they change the pay-off matrix, shake up existing equilibriums and force agents to find new ones. By enlarging the exit options of some agents and limiting those of others, the internationalization of markets has enhanced the power positions of some compared to others (Engelen, 2000: 86, 2001: 138). Power positions are largely determined by the ability to make credible threats of non co-operation. These abilities, in turn, are related to the unequal possession of direct and indirect resources such as knowledge and legitimating worldviews. Hence, focusing on the ideological dimension is far from futile (Bader, 1991: 268; see also Edelman, 1977, 2001).

In general, theories of collective action emphasize that the behaviour of organizations is the result of objective behavioural opportunities, on the one hand, and their subjective perceptions, on the other (Bader, 1991; Tarrow, 1998; Tilly, 1978). As cognitive frameworks colour these subjective perceptions and tend to replicate themselves over time by changing the objective opportunity structure through the actions of agents whose perceptions they in part form, ideological criticisms of these perceptions can have real effects too, as has been recognized by a growing number of comparative researchers (Hall, 1986; Hall and Taylor, 1996; Roe, 1994; Visser and Hemerijck, 1997).

The main driving forces behind the internationalization of capital markets are liberalization policies and the spread of new information-processing techniques, in that order, allowing investors to expand the scope of their investment strategies and making capital available on a global scale, where formerly it was partitioned nationally (Hirst and Thompson, 1999). The recent changes of the investment strategy of the ABP, the Dutch civil service pension fund and the third largest pension fund worldwide are a case in point. It was privatized in 1996 and the legal requirement to keep over 70 per cent of its capital in Dutch government bonds was gradually lifted, allowing the fund to put ever-larger sums in stocks. Recently – partly because of the integration of the Dutch, Belgium and French stock exchanges in Euronext, partly because of diversification rules and the need for liquidity – the ABP has started to Europeanize and even globalize its investment strategy. As a result the ABP has begun to sell off most of its stocks of small and medium-sized enterprises, turning them into easy prey for corporate raiders and severely restricting their ability to raise capital.

The ideological legitimation underlying these decisions is threefold. *Prudential* claims stress the efficiency of shareholder control through liquid stock markets. In this view, the large corporation has resulted in the substantial gains in wealth as well as in 'principal agency' problems, in particular between managers and owners, which ask for institutional solutions to realign these interests. Liquid stock markets

are such an instrument; by providing investors with cheap exit options; stock markets serve as a whip to urge managers to make the most of the assets entrusted to them. If they fail, shareholders will look for a new management term to run their business for them. Thus, in a nutshell, the argument is that stock markets make for an efficient 'market for corporate control' (Jensen, 2000; Shleifer and Vishny, 1997). As the prudential claim of shareholderism has already received considerable critical attention (see Lazonick, 2000; Lazonick and O'Sullivan, 2000a,b; O'Sullivan, 2000a,b), I leave it largely unaddressed.

The second claim is *functional*. According to this argument, stock markets serve as one of two ways to allocate scarce capital, the other being allocation by banks (Berglöf, 1997; Pollin, 1995; Porter, 1992). As markets are the most efficient mechanisms to discover costs and future rewards (Hayek, 1949), allocation by stock markets is more efficient than allocation by banks. However, stock markets can function only if individual investors are better rewarded for putting their money through the exchange system than for putting it in the banker's vault, as it is perceived to be the case (Ferguson, 2001: 313). This 'equity premium' is usually legitimated by the riskiness of the business of investing. Since shareholders provide risk-carrying capital and since all other claims on corporate earnings are covered by contracts, shareholders are rightfully rewarded with the 'residual earnings' of the firm. And, as shareholders prefer higher to lower residual earnings, the promise to invest in those firms that have yielded the highest earnings yesterday spurs management to do so tomorrow.

The *moral* claim is based on property rights. Following liberal legal doctrine, stocks and shares are equivalent to ownership titles, which give the owner full and absolute disposition rights over the object of ownership. As in the 'residual earnings' argument, ownership claims are ultimately rooted in the moral principle of reward according to contribution, as they clearly are in Lockean theory: ownership is rightful if (and only if) the object of ownership is the result of a mix of effort and natural resources or has been obtained by legitimate transaction (Locke, 1988).[4]

DEBUNKING THE FUNCTIONAL CLAIM

According to the functional claim, the providers of capital ought to have the ultimate say in corporate governance because they carry the risk of investment. Do they?

The shares of joint stock corporations are traded on either of two kinds of equity markets, the *private* or the *public* equity market. The private equity market is a generic term for each private placement, either at highly organized and specialized venture capital firms, families (family firms), Keiretsu-like corporate networks (cross holdings) or at an informal market consisting of small, anonymous investors and professional investment partnerships. In the US, for example, the private equity market is divided into four smaller markets: the venture capital market, the 'Angel capital' market, the 'rule 144A' market and an informal market.

In these markets, providers of capital are generally strongly involved, well informed, practise close monitoring and are located in proximity to their investments. As a rule, professional venture capital firms tend to restrict their 'span of control' to a maximum of a two hours' drive or a one-hour airplane ride (Kenney, 2000; OECD, 1998: 265). Hence the orientation of the typical investor is over-whelmingly *entrepreneurial*, rather than *speculative*. This is reflected in the way the fees of venture capital firms are structured. Normally they claim a so-called 'initiation fee' of 1 per cent, an annual 'management fee' of 2 per cent, but the main rewards are the 'realized capital gains' that can be pocketed when the firm goes 'public' and their equity stake can be sold. A so-called 'liquidation fee' of 15–20 per cent is meant to minimize risks. In other words, in these markets even speculative motives are channelled in an entrepreneurial direction by linking the main reward (realized capital gains) to long-term business success (Kenney, 2000).

Investing in the private equity market does raise exit problems. As a well-organized market for property titles is lacking, exit comes as one of three 'liquidity events', as they are called: through a private transaction, through an initial public offering (IPO), or through bankruptcy, in which case the investor reaps his 'liquidation fee' (Kenney, 2000; OECD, 1998: 265). In the first case, the firm is still privately held. In the third case, the firm ceases to exist. Only in the second case does its equity change legal status and become public.

The *public equity market* too consists of several sub-markets. The first distinction is between a primary, a secondary and a tertiary market. The primary market is reserved for IPOs. In most cases, large issuing parties set up road shows to sell as many shares as possible to banks, insurers, pension funds and trusts. This is called 'syndication'. They, in turn, will try to sell most of their shares to large customers and will sell the remainder to the public at large; this is the secondary and most visible of the public equity markets. The tertiary market refers to the over-the-counter exchange of large packages of shares between institutional investors (Guttmann, 1998: 647).

Focusing on the secondary market as the prototypical stock market, a further distinction is between first-tier and second-tier public equity markets. The NYSE belongs to the first tier, whereas the National Association of Securities Dealers (NASDAQ) belongs to the second tier. The secondary status of the NASDAQ is reflected in its entry criteria. To be listed on the NYSE, firms must be able to show a record of profitability for at least three consecutive years, must have a total market value and tangible assets of $18 million or more, must have minimally 1.1 million outstanding shares and at least 2,000 shareholders. To enter the NASDAQ firms need $4 million assets, $1 million market value and only 300 shareholders (Henwood, 1998: 17).

Firms turn towards public equity markets for one of the three reasons: to buy out the initial founders or venture capitalists (IPOs), to raise capital for new acquisitions or to finance (managerial) employee shareowner plans (ESOPs). Equity capital is hardly ever used to finance production, R&D or new production facilities. The overwhelming majority of productive investments is financed from retained earnings. According to O'Sullivan, debt and equity amounted to a mere 3.2 and 3.1 per cent of total corporate investment over the 1982–87 period (O'Sullivan, 2000a: 79). Henwood cites US census data that show that manufacturing corporations financed most of their investment from retained earnings over the period 1970–84, on average by 71.1 per cent.[5] There are good reasons for that. Not only do public offerings imply a loss of managerial autonomy, they are also prohibitively costly. The transaction costs – ranging from advertising to brokerage and, especially, legal advice – can reach 10 per cent or more of the sum involved.

This is not to suggest that the financial economy is but an epiphenomenon of the real economy. The growing importance of the financial economy has to do with functional connections between loan and bond markets, on the one hand, and equity markets, on the other. Since market integration forces firms to expand their activities and since it is generally cheaper to take over production facilities than to build them, firms turn increasingly to loan and bond markets to finance these takeovers. They do so via so-called 'convertible bonds', that is, redeemable obligations which, at the end of the term, can either be cashed for the nominal amount or converted into stocks. Access to the bond and loan market is determined by the share price, which is seen as a proxy for financial health by the financial community. The higher the share price, the cheaper external capital becomes, and vice versa.

Stock markets matter for moral reasons too. Even though most productive investments are financed from retained earnings, the case can still be made that some shareholders *should* have greater control, since the advantages of control by large block holders would outweigh the disadvantages of speculation, as is suggested by Roe (1994). This claim is based on the intuition that the orientation of the investor – *speculative, integrative* or *entrepreneurial* – changes with the size of his stake, as does his involvement and expertise. A small stake would betray a speculative orientation and an interest in price gains only, whereas a large stake means an integrative or entrepreneurial orientation and an interest in managerial strategy. Following this intuition, Roe proposes to lift legal restrictions on large block holdings to enhance the efficiency as well as the fairness of American corporate governance. The linchpin of his argument is that the combination of 'strong managers' and 'weak owners' is the effect of a prolonged history of political fund busting that had nothing to do with functional requirements. Hence, if only the legal restrictions on financial concentration were raised, committed ownership would spring up.

Roe's argument is based on the expectation that the ownership structure of corporations – dispersed or closely held – influences the size of the holdings of the median investor and hence his orientation. Large corporations generally have a more dispersed ownership structure than small or medium-sized enterprises. Since most governments have put legal ceilings on the total sum institutional investors may invest in any one corporation, the chance that the threshold for effective control will be reached is small, turning even institutional investors willy-nilly into speculative owners. However, most institutional investors – banks, insurers, mutual funds, pension funds – have a risk profile that forces them to diversify

their holdings, running against the grain of committed ownership.[6] In other words, committed ownership is limited not only by legal restrictions but also by functional ones.

There are exceptions to this 'rule'. Many large corporations are controlled by one large block holder, whether the state, a family fund, a holding, a foreign 'owner' or, via cross holdings, a Keiretsu-like cluster of firms. Hence a better proxy for committed ownership appears to be the degree of 'free float'. Most stock exchanges try to fine-tune their indices to real market trends by correcting the market capitalization of firms with the amount of shares that are actually traded. As the means are available to determine the degree of free float, if only by approximation, this could be used as a threshold for determining which corporations should adopt which regime of corporate governance. If the free float is relatively small, holdings will be long term and strategic, serving primarily integrative goals. If the free float is large, on the other hand, commitment will be low and speculative orientations will dominate. Only in the first instance is there a case for shareholder control, not only because their interests will over-whelmingly be long term and contributory, but also because their holdings will be relatively concentrated, allowing them to overcome the paradoxes of collective action dispersed ownership raises. In the second instance, however, there is no case for control rights. As investors' shares are too small to get any leverage over management and as their number is too large to co-ordinate their actions, small shareholders lack not only the will to control management but also the knowledge and expertise.

In almost every study of corporate governance, whether by proponents or opponents of shareholderism, it is taken for granted that stock markets do allocate scarce resources. Implicit in this assumption is the moral argument that shareholders deserve their earnings and hence their controlling rights because they contribute crucial production factors. I agree that the principle of reward according to contribution has *prima facie* moral validity. If taken seriously, it serves as a measuring rod to distinguish speculative investors from contributory ones. Only those shareholders whose financial involvement with the firm is contributory can rightfully claim control rights. What is a real contribution is of course controversial. Here an intelligent mix of the length of possession, the percentage of shares in possession and the type of information on which buy and sell decisions are based might do the trick. In general, the more capital markets are transparent and liquid, the more the orientation of investors will be speculative rather than entrepreneurial and the more their knowledge will be financial rather than economic. So the 'real' contributory investor is only to be found in the private equity market, for it is here that new activities arise, that liquidity is limited and hence risk is greatest. And it is this characteristic, which, in an ideologically powerful move, is projected on each and every investor – on giant pension funds as well as small households and everything in between.

DEBUNKING THE MORAL CLAIM

According to the Lockean conception of ownership, property refers to the full and absolute discretionary power of an 'owner' over an external 'object' which the title identifies (MacPherson, 1973, 1978: 1–13; Singer, 1988). Property thus consists of a set of consolidated rights, which can have only one bearer, who is identifiable via formal titles only. Moreover, these rights are seen as rigid and permanent; they function as 'shooting guns' that protect the owner from intruders by granting him an absolute right to exclude (Singer, 1996: 70–1). Liberal legal doctrine thus reproduces the myth of a sharp demarcation between 'ownership' (*dominium*) and 'power' (*imperium*), and – by analogy – between 'economy' and 'polity'. In the economy, 'owners of the means of production' contract with one another only if it is mutually advantageous. Wielding power, on the other hand, is the exclusive prerogative of the state (Bader and Benschop, 1989: 256; Schwa, 1975).

This conception of property must be rejected for five reasons. First, ownership should not be conflated with the object in question. Rather, ownership describes and prescribes a certain set of social relations surrounding the object that is supposedly 'owned'. Ownership constitutes a relationship between the owner and other agents and demarcates *relational rights* instead of *absolute* ones. In that sense, ownership does not so much concern things or objects as relations. Property does not say so much 'this is mine' as 'I can do this with it and not that, whereas you can do that and not this'. Its atomistic premises blind liberal legal doctrine to the social dimension of ownership (Bader and Benschop, 1989: 254–5, 345; Cohen, 1978; MacPherson, 1973: 127–9, 1978; Singer, 1996).

Second, specific legal rights always reflect historical societal constellations and the class relations and ownership structures of which they consist. Groups differ over time and from each other in their ability to use the state's power to acknowledge their possessions, whether peacefully produced or brutally conquered, as 'rightful property' (Campbell and Lindberg, 1990; Campbell, *et al.*, 1991; Hill, 1996; Ziegler, 2000). Ownership is never neutral, as liberal legal theorists maintain (Bowles and Gintis, 1986; Gaventa, 1980). In practice, property rights never completely determine concrete ownership relations and the interdependencies they underpin, and hence leave much leeway for political contestation. The appeal to ownership does not end distributive conflicts, but invites the question: who is the owner (Bader and Benschop, 1989: 255–7; Renner, 1949; Scott, 1997: 23–4, 37–8; Singer, 1988)?

Third, ownership is not the same as *private* ownership. The subjects of appropriation are manifold, as are the modes of ownership, and range from 'natural subjects' to 'legal subjects' and even to families, tribes, communities and states. According to the exclusionary logic of liberal legal doctrine, every mode of ownership is 'private', in the sense of exclusive. Therefore the relevant contrast is not between 'private' or 'public' ownership – for both share this exclusionary logic – but between an exclusive (or liberal) model of ownership and an inclusive (or anarchistic, libertarian-socialist and democratic) one (MacPherson, 1973: 136). As liberal legal doctrine conceptualizes property exclusively as individual or 'private' rights, it obfuscates such alternatives (Bader and Benschop, 1989: 257–8).

Fourth, property rights can never be absolute in practice. Liberal legal doctrine hides a reality in which property rights are restricted by all sorts of 'constraints'. For example, actual property rights consist of a 'bundle' of rights – use rights, control rights, transmission rights, disposition rights, transaction rights, etc. (Hohfeld, 1916; Honoré, 1961; Kay, 1997) – which do not automatically accrue to the 'owner'. In complex societies, a growing number of 'objects of ownership' simply do not fit the liberal mould; a state of affairs that is further complicated by the rise and transformation of the welfare state (Reich, 1978; Grey, 1980). Rights and obligations are widely distributed, emptying the notion of the 'owner' of most of its defining content.

Fifth, most legal traditions recognize not only 'formal' ownership titles as constituting legally enforceable claims, but also 'informal' rights and responsibilities that are the result of reciprocal expectations. In many legal traditions workers possess ownership rights, such as control and co-determination rights, as *workers* and not as *investors*. The Dutch and German Co-determination and Works Council Acts are a case in point, as well as the co-governance rights of labour unions in Dutch and German corporatism. The same holds for (local, regional and national) governments, communities and other 'stakeholders'; they too possess ownership rights – co-determination rights and income rights – whether or not their involvement with the firm is proprietary in the liberal sense.

Since ownership claims take many different forms, the liberal legal doctrine must be rejected. According to 'legal pluralism', property consists of a 'bundle' of rights, which accrue conditionally to different agents. Moreover, these rights and obligations can and do have different legal sources. A pluralist conception of property is therefore theoretically more plausible, empirically more adequate and morally superior, especially when dealing with the corporation. As the number of legally recognized 'owners' increases, so do the interests that will have to be accommodated within the firm, thus allowing for institutionalized constraints upon the short-term maximization of shareholder value, ensuring a higher quality of corporate decision-making and preventing negative externalities.

How to do that?

CORPORATE DEMOCRACY

Democracy means that collective decisions should be made by those whose interests are at stake, in a manner that is proportional to their interest (Beetham, 1994; Dahl, 1985, 1989). As such, the democratic principle is a transposition of the early-modern ideal of individual autonomy, understood as the ability to live according to self-proclaimed rules, to a modernity of societal differentiation, specialization, professionalization and increasing interdependencies (Elias, 1993; Weber, 1972). As a result, autonomy can no longer be seen as the autarchy of 'rugged individualists', but must be phrased in participatory terms; the autonomy of modern subjects requires equal political rights as a starting point, implying that the burden of proof lies with those who propose otherwise (Beetham, 1994; Dahl, 1985, 1989).

In the case of economic organizations, though, these proofs are rather convincing. Since corporations operate on competitive markets, decisions stand under severe time constraints. Hence corporate

decision-making should be the exclusive prerogative of the manager – owner. A variant of this argument has it that corporate democracy can work only in small firms, and, as large corporations make for economies of scale, corporate democracy automatically implies economic regression.

There are obvious reasons to think that small organizations are better suited for democracy than large ones, which have to do with the trade-off between effectiveness and inclusiveness. Inclusiveness complicates decision-making. As the number of participants increases, more negotiations result in 'deadlock'. This tension is part and parcel of the democratic tradition. Effectiveness, or 'getting what you want', is the supreme value for democratic theories that argue for representation, division of power and other limiting procedures, whereas inclusiveness and direct democracy are central to the participatory strand associated with Rousseau. The problem is that you cannot seem to have them both: inclusiveness makes for ineffective decision-making, whereas effectiveness requires a limited number of participants (Scharpf, 1970, 1997: 151ff., 1999: 6ff.).

Following Rousseau, the solution is generally sought in small size. The smaller the firm, the less complex the issues at stake, the less time democracy takes, the more employees have intimate knowledge and the more they will participate. Since the trade-off between effectiveness and inclusiveness appears to be a function of scale and since economic concentration results in political inequalities, it follows that for democracy's sake small firms must prevail (Blumberg, 1968; Dahl, 1985; Gould, 1988; Pateman, 1970).

Is economic regression the price for corporate democracy? No, for there is no reason why a small-scale economy is automatically economically backward. Innovation, for example, is more a matter of diversity, interaction and experimentalism than of scale and concentration (Cooke and Morgan, 1998; Piore and Sabel, 1984; Sabel and Zeitlin, 1985; Whitley, 2000). The minimally required amounts of means and people can be organized in different ways, of which the large integrated firms is only one (Whitley, 1999). Of course not all products of processes are equally suited for alternative ways of organizing 'inter-firm co-ordination'. If products are homogeneous, product cycles long and capital intensity high, large integrated firms tend to dominate. Hence, sophisticated proposals for corporate democracy must accept at least a modicum of economic concentration, as Hirst, for one, does (Hirst, 1994: 128).

However, the presumed ineffectiveness of inclusive decision-making is not a conclusive argument against corporate democracy in large firms either, for effectiveness is not a matter only of speed but also of quality. As inclusive decision-making makes for better decisions, it is preferable to include as many views as possible and to try to minimize deadlock by creating fair procedures, inviting participants to focus on what they agree upon, rather than autocratically waving them away. We know from German co-determination that co-decision making by works councils improves the quality and availability of knowledge, prevents short-sightedness and short-termism, puts managers under a beneficial pressure to legitimatize their decisions, and generates loyalty and involvement among workers (Rogers and Streeck, 1995; Streeck, n.d., 1995).

Moreover, corporate democracy does not mean that the firm must be turned into a city council or a national parliament. Intelligent models of democracy allow for a 'division of democratic labour' to accommodate constraints of time, expertise and motivation, for democracy is not the same as granting each and everyone a complete say on every topic (Barber, 1984). People do not differ only with regard to the time they have available, but also with regard to their willingness to spend that time on participatory activities. Moreover, it would be foolish to sacrifice superior expertise on the moral touchstone of political equality; the judgment of experts should prevail over those of ignoramuses, even in a democracy (Budge, 1996; Catt, 1999; Dahl, 1970; Dahl and Tufte, 1974).[7]

should be left as much as possible to those whom it concerns most, namely the workers on the shopfloor. By using informal modes of participation for these kinds of decisions, for example, quasi-autonomous work teams, time demands can be kept as limited as possible (Engelen, 2000: 45–73). Much the same is true for tactical decisions, with the rider that, for some tactical decisions, notably those of market strategy and production processes, capital providers, suppliers and customers should be included. Shares and contracts give them only exit options. As these topics require a regular exchange of local knowledge, voice mechanisms – such as works councils and a supervisory board that contains both suppliers and consumer advocates – are superior.

Arguably, the hardest nut to crack is that of strategic decision-making. However, a closer look reveals that speed is an absolute necessity in times of crisis only.[8] Decisions concerning restructuring, mergers and acquisitions, and divestment seem to allow for a much larger degree of prudence and hence democratic inclusiveness (Naschold, 1971: 88). The Dutch mergers and acquisitions regulations, for example, deliberately slow down the process to give unions and other agents the opportunity to assess the social and economic consequences. Moreover, most regimes of corporate governance oblige joint stock corporations to call a general shareholders meeting as soon as the identity of the firm is at stake. In short, there is no a priori reason to suppose that corporate democracy would be worse than corporate autocracy, even in large firms.

UNPACKING STRATEGIC DECISION-MAKING

Collective decision-making can be analysed along three dimensions, related to the *objects*, the *phases* and the *forums* of decision-making. The first dimension has to do with the idea that constraints upon democratic control vary between different types of decisions. Three types of decision are usually distinguished: *operational*, *tactical* and *strategic* decisions. The first have to do with human resource management in a broad fashion. The second are related to work content and work conditions. The third deal with the objectives and orientations of the firm in general (Archer, 1995: 104).

As operational decisions have less impact on the environment of the corporation, there is virtually no case for outside control. Instead, decision-making

FROM AGENDA SETTING TO IMPLEMENTATION

Collective decision-making consists of three *phases*. First comes agenda setting: the phase when problems are isolated, defined and analysed, solutions listed and ranked, and the order of deliberation determined. There are several ways to do that. When issues are controversial and negotiations fraught by distrust, it is better to have the agenda set by an independent external agent that can be trusted to act as an 'honest broker' by all (Scharpf, 1997: 145). Under more advantageous conditions, consensual agenda setting is preferable, as is practiced, for instance, under Dutch co-determination law where the chair of the (central) works council consults the chairperson of the board to set the agenda for their regular meetings.

Second comes decision-making itself. Here the questions are: which decision rule should be used? Should decision-making be consensual, unanimous or majoritarian, either simple or qualified? Consensual decision-making implies trust and hence symmetry. One way to reach symmetry is to decouple distributive issues from problem solving (Bader, 1991: 336ff.; Scharpf, 1997: 166ff.). In Japanese bureaucracies, for example, salary raises and promotion decisions are based on seniority to shift the attention of workers away from distributive matters towards problem solving (Scharpf, 1997: 132). Another example is the way in which wage bargaining is kept at a distance from the intra-organizational prerogatives of works councils in Dutch and German labour relations.

Further questions have to do with the chairperson. Is he an outsider or an insider, and, if an insider, from which constituency? Does he have a casting vote, a normal vote or no vote at all? And the most important question of all, of course, is: who has access? Here the design of the voting procedure is at stake: who is allowed to vote? Who is eligible for election? Which thresholds must be overcome? Will it be a proportional system or a district system? Of course these issues are well known from empirical political science (Gallagher, et al., 1992; Lijphart, 1984). However, the political scientist has eyes for the institutions of high politics only, while the issue of designing decision-making procedures that are both effective and inclusive is encountered much more widely.

The third phase concerns implementation. Ideally, implementation is simple and straightforward: just do what we have agreed upon. However, this implies that all agents will act according to plan, even if they have voted against it. As implementation can be costly, the anticipated distribution of costs feeds back into the decision-making phase, causing delays and other complications (Scharpf, 1997: 117–18). One solution to ensure faithful implementation is to construct a complex structure of different moments of control – ex ante, in situ and ex post – to ensure that parties are unable to defect and do follow up on their promises.

In the debate on sustainable production and consumption, for instance, an important role is given to outside pressure, especially by consumers and institutional investors. State regulation in these matters is rejected as if it were 'encroaching socialization', although the official line is that as of yet there are no clear-cut criteria for sustainability. However, that argument is spurious, as systems of 'rolling rule regimes'

prove (Fung and Wright, 2001; Sabel et al., 2000). States can put legal thresholds under firm behaviour, pressuring them to develop standards, by isolating best practices and turning them into new legal norms, as has been done, for instance, by the Californian state authorities with car emission norms (Vogel, 1995, 1997).

The real problem, it seems, is the ineffectiveness of these standards. Since governments lack the ability and expertise to turn abstract requirements into concrete practices, methods and technologies, and do not possess the means to monitor and control their implementation as the sites that must be controlled are simply too numerous, legislation cannot be the end of story but must be supplemented with the recruitment of local advocates (Cohen and Rogers, 1995; Fung and Wright, 2001). A co-ordinated utilization of the different levels of corporate democracy – works councils, supervisory boards and general shareholders meetings – might do the trick, if combined with legal protection for 'whistleblowers' (Bovens, 1999), a high-trust environment on the shopfloor and newly appointed internal ombudsmen in corporations with more than 500 workers, for example.

Co-ordination, however, presupposes strong organized interests who possess the means to do the co-ordinating. Currently environmentalists are poorly organized and too heterogeneous. In other policy fields the level of organizational concentration is much higher. Politics, with its well-developed part system, is of course a case in point. But so is the field of labour relations, at least in the Netherlands. There a decade-long, incremental process of concentration has resulted in three large labour federations, which participate in numerous corporatist advisory councils and executive boards. The crucial question is: can such processes be manipulated and are they reproducible?

Contrary to neo-pluralist assumptions (Dahl, 1956; Hirst, 1989; Lijphart, 1968), civil society is not prior to the state. As neo-corporatist studies have shown, state and civil society have shaped each other's perceptions, abilities and resources (Schmitter, 1974; Schmitter and Lehmbruch, 1979; Streeck and Schmitter, 1985). The theory of neo-corporatism is very clear on this point: societal interests strive for state protection, while the state tries to pacify strong societal agents by turning them into joint producers of governance (Streeck, 1994). Making governing powers available to unarticulated and unorganized groups usually has a crystallizing effect, helping them to turn 'noises' into powerful and well-organized 'voices' (Offe, 1995). This means that it is not beyond the means of the state to speed up the concentration process among environmental organizations, creating legitimate negotiating partners for firms, labour unions and the state, and enabling them to shoulder the burden of co-ordination across the different levels of corporate democracy.

As current debates on the declining legitimacy of labour unions demonstrate, legitimacy can be lost as well as won. Especially for neo-corporatist regimes this proves to be a problem. How to get rid of labour union oligarchs who have lost most of their constituency but are still seated in corporatist councils? A promising way around this issue is the idea of 'associational vouchers', allowing voters to put associations of their liking on a list of become eligible for public funding and giving them 'vouchers' to allocate these funds among them. In this way excluded voices stand a better chance of getting public funding, whereas electoral competition ensures their democratic legitimacy (Schmitter, 1994, 1995). The objection that this entails too much volatility to allow for the trust building of corporatism can be overcome by temporizing mechanisms and numerical thresholds as are used in state financing of political parties (Von Beyme, 1985).

SUPERIORITY THROUGH COMPLEXITY

With regard to the *forums* of decision-making, the third dimension of collective decision-making, the key distinction is between *simple* systems of corporate governance and *complex* ones. A complex system allows for a much more sophisticated architecture of interrelated rights and responsibilities, enabling the legislator to give each interest its optimal forum and each forum its optimal jurisdiction. As the American regime of corporate governance has only two political forums – the board of directors and the general shareholders meeting – there is not much opportunity for a division of democratic labour, turning the claim that democracy is incompatible with effective management into a self-fulfilling prophecy.

The Dutch and German regimes of corporate governance, however, consist of a works council and a supervisory board, alongside a board of directors and a general shareholders' meeting. Moreover, Dutch corporate law provides for a differentiated system of corporate governance. Joint stock corporations with either fewer than 100 workers, less than €11.25 million in corporate equity or not eligible under the Dutch Works Council act are free to install a distinct board of supervisors voluntarily. Firms with a size that surpasses these criteria *have* to install a board of supervisors, which is self-appointing and is legally compelled to weight the interests of all stakeholders. The board of supervisors has the right to dismiss directors, authorizes the annual report and has to be kept informed by the board of directors of all matters that touch upon the identity of the firm.

However a two-tiered board is not a priori superior to a one-tiered board, particularly in democratic terms, as Hirst (1994: 146–51) and Hutton (1995: 302) maintain. As the Dutch experience proves, there is nothing democratic about a self-appointing board of supervisors. To become so, amendments along German lines are needed, where workers have direct access to the board of supervisors, with up to half the seats reserved for worker representatives and, in some cases, to the board of directors as well (Lane, 1990; Müller-Jentsch, 1995; Streeck, 1992: 137–68). Although the increasing habit of appointing external as well as internal directors in British and American boards indicates a tendency towards a practice that is more or less the functional equivalent of a two-tiered board (Scott, 1997: 5), there are good reasons to suspect that a more formal distribution of tasks among the different layers of the board is still functionally superior.

In a recent empirical study of the working of the boards of large British corporations, Stiles and Taylor (2001) point out that boards have strategic, controlling and institutional roles to fulfil. However, these roles can and do conflict. Strategic deliberations presuppose a high level of involvement, reciprocal trust and a good working knowledge of the firm. Effective control presupposes independence, distance and sanctions. The institutional role, moreover, requires a good working relationship with key external constituencies. Hence there is a tension between co-operation based on a high level of trust between directors and management, on the one hand, and control based on good relationships with outside interests, on the other. Although Stiles and Taylor state explicitly 'that there seems little enthusiasm for moving towards a German–Japanese model of governance' (2001: 126), there are good theoretical reasons to suppose that this tension is better resolved in a two-tiered board, where the strategic, controlling and institutional roles are distributed over the executive and supervisory board, making for more effective control, better relations with constituencies and – especially in the German case – with more constituencies than is possible in a one-tiered board.

Finally, there is the role of works councils to consider. In general, co-determination rights consist of information rights ('ear'), advisory and consultation rights ('voice') and co-decision and veto rights ('muscle') (Rogers and Streeck, 1995: 10–11). Dutch works councils have *advisory* and *consultation rights* over all board decisions that touch upon the continuity of the firm, such as mergers and acquisitions, divestitures, plant closures and relocations, production slow-downs and speed-ups, diversifications, reorganizations, corporate restructurings, substantial investments and loans. They have *co-decision rights* over all issues of human resource management in its broadest sense, ranging from pension arrangements and work time schedules to schooling and training facilities. And they have *information rights* to compensate for the structural information asymmetries of hierarchical organizations, as well as a so-called *right of initiative* to give them agenda setting powers (Visser, 1995).

CONCLUSION

If combined in an intelligent manner, complex regimes of corporate governance allow for a division of democratic labour that can be both effective and inclusive. Since the Dutch regime is a contingent patchwork of liberal, corporatist and social democratic institution building, it is clearly in need of democratic empowerment. Despite legal guarantees, Dutch works councils have been unable to overcome the structural power asymmetries that worker representatives in capitalist firms encounter. Because of weak rights in the strategic domain, works councils have failed to become equal negotiating partners. The same holds for the tactical domain. And they have proven to be too rigid to adapt adequately to changes in the labour market as well as to new social issues such as sexism, multiculturalism and environmentalism. Notwithstanding good intentions, most works councils take on intra-organizational issues only. This is due to a lack of resources

and manpower, caused by the budget constraints of supporting trade unions, to address a growing range of topics.

Strengthening corporate democracy is not easy, for the growing internationalization of markets enables firms to shift the locus of decision-making continuously to evade national co-determination laws. However, as of 1996, a European council has become obligatory to cover this 'representation gap'. Recent assessments show that most multinationals – even British ones – have installed some form of workers' consultation. As of yet their rights do not amount to much. But a new round of legislative evaluation is sure to set in motion a second wave of law making, expecting to enhance the information and consultation rights of European works councils.

Second, the increasing decentralization of collective bargaining in the Netherlands could enhance the importance of works councils and enlarge their ability to trade wage concessions for more control over tactical and strategic matters. Whoever has more to offer can become a more attractive negotiating partner.

Third, the Dutch government has recently granted works councils direct access to the supervisory board in exchange for more shareholder control over the proxy system. As with all legal changes, these too entail changes as well as dangers. Whether the first or the second will prevail depends crucially on the strategic intelligence of labour union officials, as labour unions are as yet the only organized interests that can link shopfloor to trading floor and parliament to firm. To do so they need a 'mission statement' that is both realistic and utopian. 'Corporate democracy' might be the one.

NOTES

1 Or, more precisely, to their popular image. See Roe (1994) and Scott (1997) for an effective attempt to debunk these images.

2 Backed up by the enormous publicity success of *The Machine that Changed the World* (Womack *et al.*, 1990).

3 This explanation is squarely at odds with Whitley's scepticism regarding the destabilizing effects of the 'financialization' of national systems of corporate governance. Whitley's argument against this particular type of globalization theory is based on the notion of institutional integration. The higher the level of institutional integration, the less it is likely that financialization will have much impact upon nationally based business systems: 'changing

specific practices will be easier, where it does not involve challenging the entire national patterns of labour-market organisation and highly institutionalised systems of interest-group organisation' (Whitley, 1999: 114–15). According to Whitley, radical change is less imminent in Japan, as it is an institutionally highly integrated country, than in the UK, which is clearly less integrated in the above-given sense. Compared with the many examples history provides of rapid institutional changes, whether intended or not, Whitley clearly overstresses the degree of functional cohesiveness of existing institutional arrangements, as he himself seems to acknowledge when he allows for the possibility of radical consequences of incremental but cumulative institutional change (Whitley, 1999: 206).

4 Locke added, of course, that 'as good and as many' needed to be left over for others, for appropriation to be legitimate. Monetarization took care of that proviso (MacPherson, 1962: 211ff.).

5 The growing use of the bond market for corporate finance – a record $512 billion in the first quarter of 2001 – does not undermine the importance of internally generated funds, as it reflects only the increasing replacement of 'securitized loans' (obligations) for traditional bank loans, notably by multinationals.

6 See, for instance, the tendency among Dutch pension funds and insurers to increase their trading activities. In 1996 Dutch pension funds held their shares for three years on average. As their risk profile has changed during the maturation process – from long-term obligations to short-term ones – the average length of possession has decreased to two years in 1999 and seventeen months in 2000. American funds have an even higher circulation; they change their entire portfolio twice or thrice a year (Windolf and Nollert, 2001: 68).

7 It is noteworthy that, in circles of transaction cost theorists too, 'division of decisional labour' is proposed as a solution to the twin problems of information overload and informational impoverishment in complex 'private hierarchies' (Williamson, 1985: 133–5; Scharpf, 1997: 175).

8 The ability to define a situation as critical enables agents to sidestep democratic procedures – hence the importance of procedural checks on the definition powers of powerful agents.

REFERENCES

Albert, M. (1992) *Kapitalisme contra Kapitalisme*, Amsterdam/Antwerpen: Uitgeverij Contact.

Apeldoorn, B. van (2001) 'The rise of shareholder capitalism in continental Europe? The commodification of corporate control and the transformation of European corporate governance', *Wassenaar* 23–5 April.

Archer, R. (1995) *Economic Democracy: The Politics of Feasible Socialism*, Oxford: Clarendon Press.

Bader, V.M. (1991) *Kollektives Handeln: Protheorie sozialer Ungleichheit und kollektiven Handelns, II*, Opladen: Leske & Budrich.

—— and Benschop, A. (1989) *Ungleichheiten: Protheorie sozialer Ungleichheit und kollektiven Handelns, I*, Opladen: Leske & Budrich.

Barber, B. (1984) *Strong Democracy: Participatory Politics for a New Age*, Berkeley, CA: The University of California Press.

Beetham, D. (1994) 'Key principles and indices for a democratic audit', in D. Beetham (ed.) *Defining and Measuring Democracy*, London: Sage, pp. 25–43.

Berger, S. and Dore, R. (1996) *National Diversity and Global Capitalism*, Ithaca, NY: Cornell University Press.

Berglöf, E. (1997) 'Reforming corporate governance: redirecting the European agenda', *Economic Policy* 24: 93–123.

Beyer, J. and Hassel, A. (2001) 'The market for corporate control and the financial internationalization of German firms', paper presented at the 13th Annual Meeting on Socio-Economics, Amsterdam, 28 June–1 July.

Beyme, K. von (1985) *Political Parties in Western Democracies*, Aldershot: Gower.

Blumberg, P. (1968) *Industrial Democracy: The Sociology of Participation*, London: Constable.

Bovens, M. (1999) *The Quest for Responsibility: Accountability and Citizenship in Complex Organizations*, Cambridge: Cambridge University Press.

Bowles, P. and Gintis, H. (1986) *Democracy and Capitalism*, London: Routledge & Kegan Paul.

Boyer, R. and Drache, D. (eds) (1996) *States against Markets: The Limits of Globalization*, London: Routledge.

——, Charon, E. and Jürgens, U. (1998) *Between Imitation and Innovation: The Transfer and Hybridization of Productive Models in the International Automobile Industry*, Oxford: Oxford University Press.

Budge, I. (1996) *The New Challenge of Direct Democracy*, Oxford: Polity Press.

Campbell, J.L. and Lindberg, L.N. (1990) 'Property rights and the organizations of economic activity by the state', *American Sociological Review* 55: 634–47.

——, Hollingsworth, J.R. and Lindberg, L.N. (eds) (1991) *Governance of the American Economy*, Cambridge: Cambridge University Press.

Catt, H. (1999) *Democracy in Practice*, London and New York: Routledge.

Cohen, J. and Rogers, J. (1995) 'Secondary associations and democratic governance', in E.O. Wright (ed.) *Associations and Democracy*, London: Verso, pp. 7–98.

Cohen, M. (1978[1927]) 'Property and sovereignty', in C.B. MacPherson (ed.) *Property: Mainstream and Critical Positions*, Toronto: University of Toronto Press, pp. 156–75.

Cooke, P. and Morgan, K. (1998) *The Associational Economy: Firms, Regions, and Innovation*, Oxford: Oxford University Press.

Crouch, C. and Streeck, W. (eds) (1997) *Political Economy of Modern Capitalism: Mapping Convergence and Diversity*, London: Sage.

Dahl, R. (1956) *A Preface to Democratic Theory*, New Haven, CT: Yale University Press.

—— (1970) *After the Revolution, Authority in a Good Society*, New Haven, CT: Yale University Press.

—— (1985) *A Preface to Economic Democracy*, Berkeley, CA: University of California Press.

—— (1989) *Democracy and Its Critics*, New Haven, CT: Yale University Press.

—— and Tufte, E. (1974) *Size and Democracy*, Stanford, CA: Stanford University Press.

Deeg, R. (1999) *Finance Capitalism Unveiled: Banks and German Political Economy*, Ann Arbor, MI: The University of Michigan Press.

Dore, R. (2000) *Stock Market Capitalism: Welfare Capitalism: Japan and Germany versus the Anglo-Saxons*, Oxford: Oxford University Press.

Edelman, M. (1977) *Political Language: Words that Succeed and Policies that Fail*, New York: Academic Press.

—— (2001) *The Politics of Misinformation*, Cambridge: Cambridge University Press.

Elias, N. (1993) *The Civilization Process: The History of Manners, State Formation and Civilization*, Oxford: Blackwell.

Engelen, E. (2000) *Economisch Burgerschap in de Onderneming: Een Oefening in Concreet Utopisme*, Amsterdam: ThelaThesis.

—— (2001) 'Globalisation and multi-level governance in Europe: realist criteria for institutional design, or: how pessimistic should one be?', in P. Hirst and V.M. Bader (eds) *Associative Democracy: The Real Third Way*, London: Frank Cass, pp. 131–56.

Ferguson, N. (2001) *The Cash Nexus: Money and Power in the Modern World 1700–2000*, New York: Basic Books.

Fung, A. and Wright, E.O. (2001) 'Deepening democracy: innovations in empowered participatory democracy', *Politics and Society* 29(1): 5–41.

Gallagher, M., Laver, M. and Mair, P. (1992) *Representative Government in Western Europe*, New York: McGraw-Hill.

Gaventa, J. (1980) *Power And Powerlessness: Quiescence and Rebellion in an Appalachian Valley*, Urban, IL: University of Illinois Press.

Goodin, R. (1998) 'Institutions and their design', R. Goodin (ed.) *The Theory of Institutional Design*, Cambridge: Cambridge University Press, pp. 1–53.

Gould, C. (1988) *Rethinking Democracy: Freedom and Special Co-operation in Politics, Economy and Society*, Cambridge: Cambridge University Press.

Grey, T. (1980) 'The disintegration of property', *Nomos* 22: 147–52.

Guttmann, R. (1998) 'Die strategische Rolle der Pensionfonds', *Prokla* 28(4): 643–50.

Hall, P.A. (ed.) (1986) *Governing the Economy: The Politics of State Intervention in Britain and France*, Oxford: Polity Press.

—— and Soskice, D. (eds) (2001) *Varieties of Capitalism*, Oxford: Oxford University Press.

—— and Taylor, R. (1996) 'Political science and the three new institutionalisms', *Political Studies* 44: 936–57.

Hayek, F.A. (1949) *Individualism and Economic Order*, Chicago, IL: University of Chicago Press.

Henwood, D. (1998) *Wall Street: How It Works and for Whom*, London: Verso.

Herrigel, G. (1996) *Industrial Constructions: The Sources of German Industrial Power*, Cambridge: Cambridge University Press.

Hill, C. (1996) *Liberty against the Law: Some Seventeenth-Century Controversies*, Harmondsworth: Penguin.

Hirst, P. (ed.) (1989) *The Pluralist Theory of the State: Selected Writings of G.D.H. Cole, J.N. Figgis, and H.J. Laski*, London: Routledge.

—— (1994) *Associative Democracy: New Forms of Social and Economic Governance*, Oxford: Polity Press.

Hirst, P. and Thompson, G. (1999) *Globalization in Question*, Oxford: Polity Press.

Hohfeld, W. (1916) 'Some fundamental legal conceptions as applied in juridical reasoning', *Yale Law Review* 23: 16ff.

Hollingsworth, J.R. and Boyer, R. (eds) (1997) *Contemporary Capitalism: The Embeddedness of Institutions*, Cambridge: Cambridge University Press.

——, Schmitter, P. and Streeck, W. (eds) (1994) *Governing Capitalist Economies: Performance and Control of Economic Sectors*, Oxford: Oxford University Press.

Honoré, A. (1961) 'Ownership', in A. Guest (ed.) *Oxford Essays in Jurisprudence*, Oxford: Oxford University Press, pp. 107–47.

Hutton, W. (1995) *The State We're In*, London: Cape.

Immergut, E. (1998) 'The theoretical core of the new institutionalism', *Politics and Society* 26(1): 5–34.

Jensen, M. (1998) 'Takeovers: their causes and consequences', *Journal of Economic Perspectives* 2: 21–48.

—— (2000) *A Theory of the Firm: Governance, Residual Claims and Organizational Forms*, Cambridge: Harvard University Press.

—— and Ruback, R. (1983) 'The market for corporate control', *Journal of Financial Economics* 11: 5–50.

Kay, J. (1997) 'The stakeholder corporation', in G. Kelly, D. Kelly and A. Gambel (eds) *Stakeholder Capitalism*, London: Macmillan, pp. 125–41.

Kenney, M. (ed.) (2000) *Understanding Silicon Valley: The Anatomy of an Entrepreneurial Region*, Stanford, CA: Stanford Business Books.

Kitschelt, H., Lange, P., Marks, G. and Stephens, J. (eds.) (1999) *Continuity and Change in Contemporary Capitalism*, Cambrdige: Cambridge University Press.

Lamping, W. and Rüb, F.W. (2001) 'From the conservative welfare state to "something uncertain else": German pension politics in comparative perspective', paper presented at the 13th Annual Meeting on Socio-Economics, Amsterdam, 28 June–1 July.

Lane, C. (1990) *Management and Labour in Europe: The Industrial Enterprise in Germany, France and Britain*, Aldershot: Edward Elgar.

—— (1995) *Industry and Society in Europe: Stability and Change in Britain, Germany and France*, Aldershot: Edward Elgar.

—— (2000) 'Globalization and the German model of capitalism – erosion or survival?', *British Journal of Sociology* 51(2): 207–34.

Lazonick, W. (2000) 'From innovative enterprise to national institutions: a theoretical perspective on the governance of economic development', <www.insead.fr/cgep>

—— and O'Sullivan, M. (2000a) 'Maximizing shareholder value: a new ideology for corporate governance', *Economy and Society* 29(1): 13–35.

—— and —— (2000b) 'Perspectives on corporate governance, innovation and economic performance', <www.insead.fr/cgep>

Lijphart, A. (1968) *The Politics of Accommodation; Pluralism and Democracy in the Netherlands*, Berkeley, CA: The University of California Press.

—— (1984) *Democracies: Patterns of Majoritarian and Consensus Government in Twenty-one Countries*, New Haven, CT: Yale University Press.

Locke, J. (1988) *Two Treatises of Government*, student edn, Cambridge: Cambridge University Press.

MacPherson, C.B. (1962) *The Theory of Possessive Individualism: Hobbes to Locke*, Oxford: Oxford University Press.

—— (1973) *Democratic Theory: Essays in Retrieval*, Oxford: Oxford University Press.

—— (1978) 'The meaning of property', in C.B. MacPherson (ed.) *Property: Mainstream and Critical Positions*, Toronto: University of Toronto Press, pp. 1–13.

Müller-Jentsch, W. (1995) 'Germany: from collective voice to co-management', in J. Rogers and W. Streeck (eds) *Works Councils: Consultation, Representation and Cooperation in Industrial Relations*, Chicago, IL: University of Chicago Press, pp. 53–78.

Naschold, F. (1971) *Organisation und Demokratie: Untersuchungen zum Demokratisierungspotential in komplexen Organisationen*, Kohlhammer: Stuttgart.

OECD (1998) *Fostering Entrepeneurship*, Paris: OECD.

Offe, C. (1995) 'Some skeptical considerations on the malleability of representative institutions', in E.O. Wright (ed.) *Associations and Democracy*, Verso: London, pp. 114–32.

O'Sullivan, M. (2000a) *Contests for Corporate Control: Corporate Governance and Economic Performance in the United States and Germany*, Oxford: Oxford University Press.

—— (2000b) 'The innovative enterprise and corporate governance', *Cambridge Journal of Economics* 24: 393–416.

Pateman, C. (1970) *Participation and Democracy*, Cambridge: Cambridge University Press.

Piore, M. and Sable, C. (1984) *The Second Industrial Divide: Possibilities for Prosperity*, New York: Basic Books.

Pollin, R. (1995) 'Financial structures and egalitarian economic policy', *New Left Review* 214: 26–61.

Porter, M. (1992) 'Capital disadvantage: America's failing capital investment system', *Harvard Business Review* September–October: 65–82.

Reich, C.A. (1978) 'The New property', in C.B. MacPherson (ed.) *Property: Mainstream and Critical Positions*, Toronto: University of Toronto Press, pp. 179–98.

Renner, K. (1949) *The Institutions of Private Law and their Social Function*, London: Routledge and Kegan Paul.

Roe, M. (1994) *Strong Managers, Weak Owners: The Political Roots of American Corporate Finance*, Princeton, NJ: Princeton University Press.

—— (1996) 'Chaos and evolution in law and economics', *Harvard Law Review* 109: 641–65.

Rogers, J. and Streeck, W. (1995) 'The study of works councils: concepts and problems', in J. Rogers and W. Streeck (eds) *Works Councils: Consultation, Representation and Cooperation in Industrial Relations*, Chicago, IL: University of Chicago Press, pp. 3–26.

Sabel, C. and Zeitlin, J. (1985) 'Historical alternatives to mass production; politics, markets and technology in nineteenth-century industrialization', *Past and Present* 108: 133–76.

——, Fung, A. and Karkkainen, B. (2000) *Beyond Backyard Environmentalism*, Boston, MA: Beacon Press.

Scharpf, F. (1970) *Demokratietheorie zwischen Utopie und Anpassung*, Konstanz: Universitätsverlag.

—— (1997) *Games Real Actors Play: Actor-Centered Institutionalism in Policy Research*, Boulder, CO: Westview Press.

—— (1999) *Governing in Europe: Effective and Democratic?*, Oxford: Oxford University Press.

Scherer, F. (1988) 'Corporate takeovers: the efficiency arguments', *Journal of Economic Perspectives* 2(1): 69–82.

Schmitter, P. (1974) 'Still the century of corporatism?', *Review of Politics* 36: 85–131.

—— (1994) 'Interests, associations and intermediation in a reformed post-liberal democracy', in W. Streeck (ed.) *Staat und Verbände: 25 Jahrbuch Politisches Vierteljahres Schrift* 160–71.

—— (1995) 'The irony of modern democracy and the viability of efforts to reform its practice', in E.O. Wright (ed.) *Associations and Democracy*, London: Verso, pp. 167–83.

—— and Lehmbruch, G. (eds) (1979) *Trends towards Corporatist Intermediation*, London: Sage.

EIGHT

Schwab, D. (1975) 'Eigentum', in O. Brunner, W. Conze and R. Koselleck (eds) *Geschichtliche Grundbegriffe: Historisches Lexikon zur politisch-sozialen Sprache in Deutschland*, Stuttgart: Klett-Cotta, pp. 65–115.

Scott, J. (1997) *Corporate Business and Capitalist Classes*, Oxford: Oxford University Press.

Shleifer, A. and Vishny, R.W. (1997) 'A survey of corporate governance', *Journal of Finance* 52(2): 737–83.

Singer, J. (1988) 'The reliance interest in property', *Stanford Law Review* 40: 611–75.

—— (1996) 'Property and social relations: from title to entitlement', in G. van Maanen and A. van der Walt (eds) *Property Law on the Threshold of the 21st Century: Proceedings of an International Colloquium 'Property Law on the Threshold of the 21st Century'*, Antwerpen and Apeldoorn: Maklu, pp. 69–90.

Skocpol, T. (1992) *Protecting Soldiers and Mothers: The Political Origins of Social Policy in the United States*, Cambridge, MA: Harvard University Press.

Stiles, P. and Taylor, B. (2001) *Boards at Work: How Directors View thier Roles and Responsibilities*, Oxford: Oxford University Press.

Streeck, W. (n.d.) 'Democracy and efficiency', unpublished manuscript.

—— (1992) *Social Institutions and Economic Performance*, London: Sage.

—— (1994) 'Staat und Verbände: Neue Fragen, neue Antworten?', in W. Streeck (ed.) *Staat und Verbände: 25 Jahrbuch Politisches Vierteljahres Schrift* 7–34.

—— (1995) 'Works councils in Western Europe: from consultation to participation', in J. Rogers and W. Streeck (eds) *Works Councils: Consultation, Representation and Cooperation in Industrial Relations*, Chicago, IL: University of Chicago Press, pp. 313–48.

—— (1997) 'German capitalism: does it exist? can it survivie?', in C. Crouch and W. Streeck (eds) *Political Economy of Modern Capitalism*, London: Sage, pp. 33–54.

—— (1998) 'The Internationalization of Industrial Relations in Europe: Problems and Prospects', *Politics and Society* 26(4): 429–459.

—— and Schmitter, P. (eds) (1985) *Private Interest Government: Beyond Market and State*, London: Sage.

Tarrow, S. (1998) *Power in movement: Social Movements and Contentious Politics*, Cambridge: Cambridge University Press.

Thelen, K. (1999) 'Historical institutionalism in comparative politics', *Annual Review of Political Science* 2: 369–404.

Tilly, C. (1978) *From Mobilization to Revolution*, New York: McGraw-Hill.

—— (1990) *Coercion, Capital and European states, Ad. 1990–1992*, (*Studies in Social Discontinuity*), Oxford: Blackwell.

Visser, J. (1995) 'The Netherlands: from paternalism to representation', in J. Rogers and W. Streeck (eds) *Works Councils: Consultation, Representation and Cooperation in Industrial Relations*, Chicago, IL: University of Chicago Press, pp. 79–114.

—— and Hemerijck, A. (1997) *A Dutch Miracle: Job Growth, Welfare Reform and Corporatism in the Netherlands*, Amsterdam: Amsterdam University Press.

Vogel, D. (1995) *Trading Up: Consumer and Environmental Regulation in a Global Economy*, Cambridge, MA: Harvard University Press.

—— (1997) 'Trading up and governing across: transnational governance and environmental protection', *Journal of European Public Policy* 4: 556–71.

Weber, M. (1972) *Wirtschaft und Gesellschaft: Grundriss der verstehenden Soziologie*, Tübingen: J.C.B. Mohr.

Weiss, L. (1998) *The Myth Of the Powerless State: Governing the Economy in a Global State*, Cambridge: Polity Press.

Whitley, R. (ed.) (1992) *European Business Systems: Firms and Markets in their National Contexts*, London: Sage.

—— (1999) *Divergent Capitalisms*, Oxford: Oxford University Press.

—— (2000) 'The Institutional Structuring of Innovation Strategies: Business Systems, Firm Types and Patterns of Technical Change in Different Market Economies', *Organization Studies* 21(5): 855–886.

—— and Kristensen, P.H. (eds) (1996) *The Changing European Firm: Limits to Convergence*, London and New York: Routledge.

—— and —— (eds) (1997) *Governance at Work: The Social Regulation of Economic Relations*, Oxford: Oxford University Press.

Williamson, O.E. (1985) *The Economic Institutions of Capitalism: Firms, Markets, Relational Contracting*, New York: The Free Press.

Windolf, P. and Nollert, M. (2001) 'Institutionen, Interssen, Netzwerke: Unternehmungsverflechtung im internationalen Vergleich', *Politisches Viertel-Sahres Schrift* 42(1): 51–78.

Womack, J.P., Jones, D.T. and Roos, D. (1990) *The Machine that Changed the World: The Story of Lean Production*, New York: HarperCollins.

Ziegler, J.N. (2000) 'Corporate governance and the politics of property rights in Germany', *Politics and Society* 28(2): 195–221.

PART NINE

Post-Enron theories

INTRODUCTION TO PART NINE

The sense that the rest of the world simply needed to learn from the robust, market-oriented corporate governance regimes of the Anglo-Saxon *outsider* model were abruptly dispelled with the series of US corporate crashes commencing in 2001 at Enron, and continued with WorldCom, Tyco International, Adelphia Communications, Global Crossing, Qwest Communications, Computer Associates, Arthur Andersen and others. The collapse of Enron, the largest bankruptcy in US history at that time, led to thousands of employees losing their jobs *and* their life savings tied up in the energy company's stock. Federal indictments charged Enron executives with devising complex financial schemes to defraud Enron and its shareholders through transactions with off-the-books partnerships that made the company look profitable.

Gordon (Chapter 21) contends that the Enron experience challenges some core beliefs and practices that have underpinned the academic analysis of corporate law and governance since the 1980s. They throw doubt on the interlocking set of institutions that constitute 'shareholder capitalism', based on assumptions about the connection between stock market prices and the underlying economic realities; the reliability of independent auditors and financial standards and extensive disclosure in monitoring financial performance. He further questions the utility of stock options in aligning management and shareholder interests, and the value of employee share ownership both as an incentive device and as part of retirement planning.

Coffee (Chapter 22) highlights how Enron exposed the way in which increased market incentives and legal deregulation had led auditors to acquiesce in aggressive accounting methods that often bordered illegality while analysts remained positive in spite of the warning signs. The changes in executive compensation in the 1990s designed to align executive interests with those of shareholders, provided an irresistible incentive to managers to inflate earnings, even if this was not sustainable, as they could bail out before the inevitable reality confronted the shareholders. At a time when the average tenure of CEOs of US corporations was diminishing to between three and four years, the temptation of immense stock options caused many executives to spike the share price, cash in their options, and move on quickly. Meanwhile the markets responded slowly, if at all, to the mounting evidence of overvaluation. He suggests that the explosion of financial irregularity in the US in 2001–2 was the natural consequence of trends and forces that were developing for some time, and were by-products of the prevailing system of corporate governance.

"What Enron Means for the Management and Control of the Modern Business Corporation: Some Initial Reflections"

from The University of Chicago Law Review (2002)

Jeffrey N. Gordon

On October 16, 2001, Enron Corporation, a Houston-based energy trading and distribution company famous for its advocacy of energy deregulation, announced a $1.01 billion nonrecurring charge related to "losses associated with certain investments . . . and early termination during the third quarter of certain structured finance arrangements with a previously disclosed entity."[1] Chairman and CEO Ken Lay reassured investors about the strength of the company's core businesses, said he was "very confident in [Enron's] strong earnings outlook" and "reaffirmed" that the company was "on track to continue strong earnings growth." Nevertheless, the write-offs produced a third-quarter loss of more than $600 million and surprised Wall Street. Moreover, *The Wall Street Journal* reported that $35 million of the losses derived from business dealings with partnerships managed by the company's CFO, Andrew S. Fastow.[2]

The bad news, the reported conflict of interest, an ensuing SEC investigation, and the fall in Enron's stock price from the mid-$30s to the low $20s, triggered a crisis of confidence in the company. Enron's energy trading business, its crown jewel, depended crucially on solid finances, since parties dealing with Enron were loath to assume significant counterparty credit risk: a serious chance that Enron could not perform on a contract to buy or sell energy meant that parties no longer would trade with the firm. In desperation, Enron turned to a merger with its crosstown rival, Dynergy, to save the day. Then, on November 8, Enron released a bombshell. The quarterly earnings statement restated (i.e. reduced) previously reported earnings back to 1997 by $586 million, a 20-percent reduction in profits over the period, "mostly due to improperly accounting for its dealings with partnerships run by some company officers."[3] The quarterly statement revealed more about Enron's troubled financial relationship with officer-managed partnerships.

The third-quarter report was devastating. The ramifications led Dynergy to call off the merger. On December 2, barely six weeks after the crisis first broke, Enron filed for bankruptcy. The turnabout was remarkable. By some turnover measures, Enron had been the seventh largest company in the United States. Barely a year before, its stock had crested at $90 per share, yielding a market capitalization of approximately $80 billion. The company was invariably mentioned in "most admired" lists of US companies; its CEO was lionized in Houston and a nicknamed confidant of the President of the United States.

Enron's collapse triggered investigations by a "special committee" of the Enron board, the SEC, the

Justice Department, nearly a dozen congressional committees, and various shareholder plaintiffs' attorneys. The Enron board's special committee investigation suggested that a substantial fraction of the company's reported profits over a four-year period had been the result of accounting manipulations.[4] Early targets included Enron's senior officers, the accountants at Arthur Andersen, the Enron board and its various special oversight committees, and the law firm Vinson & Elkins, which helped put together the controversial transactions. Not only had Enron apparently filed false and misleading disclosure documents, but also insiders allegedly sold stock and exercised options while publicly restating their faith in the company. By contrast, rank-and-file employees were unable to sell their Enron stock locked into 401(k) retirement plans. This particular element – privileged insiders walking away with hundreds of millions of dollars in stock-related profits while ordinary employees were losing a substantial chunk of life savings – added to the political saliency of the events.

The Enron case plays on many different dimensions, but its prominence is not merely part of popular culture's obsession with *scandal du jour*. Rather, the Enron situation challenges some of the core beliefs and practices that have underpinned the academic analysis of corporate law and governance, including mergers and acquisitions, since the 1980s. These amount to an interlocking set of institutions that constitute "shareholder capitalism," American-style, 2001, that we have been aggressively promoting throughout the world. We have come to rely on a particular set of assumptions about the connection between stock market prices and underlying economic realities; the reliability of independent auditors, financial standards, and copious disclosure in protecting the integrity of financial reporting; the efficacy of corporate governance in monitoring managerial performance; the utility of stock options in aligning managerial and shareholder interests, and the value of employee ownership as both an incentive device as well as a retirement planning tool.

In particular, I want to assert that Enron raises at least the following problems for the received model of corporate governance:

First, it provides another set of reasons to question the strength of the efficient market hypothesis, because Enron's stock price reached dizzying heights despite transparently irrational reliance on its auditors' compromised certification.

Second, it undermines the corporate governance mechanism, the monitoring board, that has been offered as a substitute for unfettered shareholder access to the market for corporate control. In particular, the board's capacity to protect the integrity of financial disclosure has not kept pace with the increasing reliance on stock price performance in measuring and rewarding managerial performance.

Third, it suggests the existence of tradeoffs in the use of stock options in executive compensation because of the potential pathologies of the risk-preferring management team.

Fourth, it shows the poor fit between stock-based employee compensation and retirement planning. More generally, it raises questions about the shift in retirement planning towards defined contribution plans, which make employees risk-bearers and financial planners, and away from defined benefit plans, which impose some of the risk and fiduciary planning obligations on firms.[5]

THE EFFICIENT MARKET HYPOTHESIS

Although the efficient market hypothesis is a useful null hypothesis about the workings of a well-developed capital market, sophisticated application in policy settings requires awareness of its limits as well as its power. The 1987 stock market crash, which in retrospect still seems like a random quantum fluctuation, and the recent dot.com exuberance, which looks like a classic bubble, both give ample evidence of those limitations. Even if it is the case that the prevailing stock price is the best available estimate of expected future cash flows, "best" may not be very good in some cases. But Enron seems to demonstrate those limits in a new way. If the dot.com boom, for example, was a sectoral gold rush, Enron's price escalation (hitting a multiple of sixty on trailing earnings) showed how markets can ignore the handwriting on the wall for a single firm. It seemed barely possible that the Internet was about to become the prime medium for transactions in the United States and that the firms that staked their claims first would achieve increasing (and enormous) returns to scale. The failure of markets to assess adequately the earnings prospects at Enron is a more granular failure and thus more troubling. How can the market price so widely diverge from intrinsic value despite the firm-specific scrutiny that market institutions, including a battalion of securities analysts, bring to bear on such a widely held stock? Even if Enron lacked candor – indeed, actively misled – about its true financial condition, wasn't enough known to sophisticated market participants about the company's murky finances so that efficient markets never should have placed such a high value on Enron's stock?

The argument has a few steps. First, it was known and widely discussed in the analytic community that Enron's financial structure was highly complex and that the bodies were buried in off-balance sheet entities that were described cryptically in Enron's disclosure documents. No one on the outside really understood Enron's financial condition, but they also knew they did not know. As one analyst put it, Enron was a "faith" stock. Yet such willful obscurity ordinarily leads to skepticism rather than belief. Enron could have disclosed more but did not. It reveled in information asymmetry. What were we to infer from this: that it had a secret, nonpatentable elixir for money-making (that investment banks would not have already shopped to every other large firm)? Or rather that full disclosure would have been embarrassing? George Akerlof just won a Nobel Prize for providing the answer to that question.[6] In other words, in an efficient market, Enron should have been a "lemons" stock instead of a "faith" stock.

Not so simple, you might say: Enron's accountants at Arthur Andersen certified that the financial statements "fairly presented" the overall financial picture of the company, and the reputational capital of a Big Five accounting firm credibly bonds Andersen's certification. Andersen's failure was a surprise, you might say. But, in fact, it seems to have been a foreseeable failure. That Andersen had a lot to lose from a bad audit is insufficient. No one who observed the firm-threatening bridge loans made in leveraged transactions in the 1980s by investment bankers eager for a success fee can believe that there is necessarily a link between what is rational for the firm and what actions may be taken by the firm's self-interested agents. Much depends on the way the firm manages the internal moral hazard problems. On the basis of what we knew before the Enron collapse, the credibility of Andersen's certification had been severely compromised, first because it had permitted its independence as a firm to be fatally undermined, and second, because the internal governance of Andersen was insufficient to control potentially aberrant behavior by its partners.

Much has already been said about the problems raised by letting accounting firms cross-sell various consulting services to their audit clients.[7] As one of my colleagues pithily put it, "The batter ought to worry about the umpire who is selling life insurance to the pitcher." But the issue bears close examination for what it says about the credibility of Andersen's certification.

The most important guarantor of an accountant's independence is that its firing is highly salient. This is a material event: it must be disclosed on a Schedule 8-K and even if the accountant breathes not a word about the precipitating facts (and the accountant may shout from the rooftop), it will trigger scrutiny and inquiry. Firing the accounting firm is thus a "high visibility sanction" that may well cause more harm to the sanctioning company (and its officers and directors) than to the accountant, and therefore it cannot credibly be threatened to bring into line an accountant who disagrees with management about an important accounting matter. Indeed, too vigorous an effort to force a particular accounting treatment may well trigger an accountant's resignation, also a material event.

This picture changes dramatically when the accounting firm begins to cross-sell consulting services. It is not that the accountant now has more at stake in the relationship and thus would lose more if fired by the company. Nor is it simply that the accountant may now have a particular reason to please, or at least not alienate, the client who may buy additional services, and may even hope that cooperation on difficult accounting questions will be appreciated as part of a total client relationship. Rather, it is that the client now has available a repertoire of "low-visibility sanctions" to discipline the accountant's behavior. If the accountant is resistant, a contract may be withheld or not renewed (or if the accountant is cooperative, the reverse). But unlike the firing, these disciplinary measures will not be disclosed. (Even if the total amount of the accountant's consulting services is disclosed, the investor will not have a full picture of the accountant-issuer relationship, because the disclosure will not reveal the set of potential contracts.) Thus the issuer now has credible threats against an accountant who disagrees with management on an important issue. Moreover, the issuer now knows the accountant's type: No accounting firm that prizes its independence above all else would put itself in a position where that independence is so readily undermined. To push the argument further: this may be why there are two polar equilibria in the bundling of auditing and consulting services. Accountants cannot afford to compete on their relative independence. The willingness to expose oneself to low-visibility sanctions – the sacrifice of inherent independence – offers such a competitive advantage in attracting audit clients that there will be a race to the bottom.

There is a related cultural factor associated with consulting that also tends to undermine the credibility of the accountant's certification. The press often has referred to the bundling of auditing and glamorous information technology consulting. But the more common, and more insidious, bundle may be auditing plus tax planning, because of the carryover mindset from "tax planning" into "accounting planning." Tax planners provide value by structuring a company's transactions so as to minimize tax, applying a formalist's approach to the constraints of the tax law against a background interpretive norm of "reasonable basis." If a close, ingenious reading of the Code and the regulations permits a reshaping of economic reality to minimize taxes, then excelsior. Whatever the ultimate social desirability of such gamesmanship, at least it serves the narrow shareholder interest of maximizing after-tax income, that is, increasing the cash in the corporate till. But this tax planning approach all too readily carries over to "accounting planning," in which the accountant aggressively construes accounting rules to maximize reported income irrespective of less illuminating disclosure to the ultimate client, the shareholders. Accounting rules, like tax rules, become the subject of professional manipulation, despite a potentially distorted portrayal of the underlying economic reality. The ingenious evasion wins a merit badge and perhaps additional compensation.[8] Thus "independent" accountants become part of the management "team." Moreover, the balance sheet is disaggregated, as each successive transaction is evaluated on a stand-alone basis against the accounting rules, myopically applied. So in addition to the low-visibility sanctions, consulting can create a culture that undermines the capacity of the accountant to make the arm's length judgment about public financials that must "fairly present" the underlying economic realities taken as a whole.

Yet all of this is known to sophisticated investors. The sharply diminished value of Andersen's certification for a company like Enron with complicated accounting, abundant consulting opportunities, and obvious accounting planning should have been impounded in Enron's price from the get-go. Apparently, it was not.

There is a second compromising element of the value of Andersen's certification, the weakness of its internal governance mechanisms in controlling the behavior of the firm's partners – the internal agency problem.[9] The previous paragraphs addressed the independence of Andersen as a firm, but of course services were delivered by specific agents of the firm, its Houston partners. It now seems that the compensation of the Houston partners was significantly tied to their client billings both for auditing services and for consulting services. Enron might have been a relatively small client for Andersen, the firm, but it was the largest client for its Houston office, and, for the Enron relationship partners, perhaps their only significant client. The forces that would undermine the independence of the firm are much magnified in the case of the relationship partners. In a multi-office, multi-national firm like Andersen, it may be economically rational to treat each office as a profit center and to tie a significant portion of partner compensation to own-billings or office-billings. But the consequent threat to the partner's independence and the resulting risk to Andersen's reputation are foreseeable and seem virtually to compel an appropriate internal monitoring mechanism. The disparity between the value of the Houston partners' share of Andersen's reputation and the value to them of a continued (or more lucrative) Enron client relationship sets up an obvious moral hazard problem. This problem is compounded by the interaction with the first compromising factor. That is, the low-visibility sanctions associated with the bundling of audit and consulting services have particular compromising force at the relationship partner level because of the impact of lucrative consulting contracts on relationship partner compensation.

There are at least two obvious ways to monitor. First, an internal "inspector general" might provide disinterested internal review of important accounting judgments made by the Houston partners, an internal auditor's audit. Second, partners might rotate among offices (for the same reason that bank officers frequently rotate). Neither of these mechanisms, nor any other, seems to have been used by Andersen. Indeed, it seems that the Houston office could reject accounting judgments from Chicago headquarters with impunity.[10]

But this absence of internal controls was no secret. It was widely known, one presumes, to accounting sophisticates, and thus the consequent undermining of the credibility of Andersen's certification should have been impounded in Enron's price. Yet throughout the period that Enron was assembling its deceptive array of off-balance-sheet partnerships and special purpose entities, its stock soared.

How are we to interpret the gradual fall in Enron's stock price during 2001, in absolute and market-adjusted terms, despite steadily increasing reported earnings during the period? The stock price hovered around $80 per share in January and February, drifting down to $60 in March and April, falling to $50 in the summer and to $40 by early fall. Yet the company was reporting favorable operating results, including substantial increases in quarterly earnings per share, an 18 percent increase for the first quarter, a 32 percent increase for the second quarter. Perhaps there was information leakage from the partnership participants, who possessed nonpublic deal documents that could have revealed the potential fragility of Enron's accounting alchemy, or perhaps the pressure of skeptical short sellers was having an effect. This provides only limited vindication of the efficient market hypothesis because of the slow correction of the initial overpricing. Indeed, the pattern is consistent with an undersupply of arbitrage in the presence of "noise traders," one of the by-now classic explanations of the limitations on market efficiency.[11]

In short, Enron disturbs the efficient market hypothesis. The only compelling reason not to assume the worst about Enron's deliberately obscure financial statements was because of Andersen's certification, yet the market "knew" that the certification had little value.[12]

BOARD-CENTERED CORPORATE GOVERNANCE

The efficient market hypothesis has been one of the underpinnings of the argument for shareholder choice in the decision whether to accept a hostile takeover bid at a premium to the market price. (It is by no means a necessary step to that conclusion, however, since the possibility of a gap between prevailing market price and intrinsic value hardly resolves the question of whether management has markedly better information and superior evaluative skills so as to outweigh the agency problems.) Those who argued most strenuously against unfettered shareholder access to hostile bids, for management's right to "just say no," have offered the visible hand of robust corporate governance instead of the market in corporate control as a solution to the agency problems of large public corporations. That is, the appropriate remedy for the problem of the potentially self-interested or incompetent managerial team is said to be the monitoring board. The major features are independent directors, specialized committees (especially an audit committee) consisting exclusively of independent directors to perform crucial monitoring functions, and clear charter of board authority. Some have argued additionally for stock-based compensation for directors, better to align their interests with shareholders.

Enron is an embarrassment for this position. Its board was a splendid board on paper, fourteen members, only two insiders. Most of the outsiders had relevant business experience, a diverse set including accounting backgrounds, prior senior management and board positions, and senior regulatory posts. Most of the directors owned stock, some in significant amounts, and almost all had received stock options or phantom stock as part of the director compensation package. The Audit Committee had a state-of-the-art charter, attached to the 2001 Proxy Statement for all to admire, which made it the "overseer of the Company's reporting process and internal controls" and gave it "direct access to financial, legal, and other staff and consultants of the Company" and the power to retain other accountants, lawyers, or consultants as it thought advisable. But if the report of the Enron Special Investigation Committee is accurate, the board was ineffectual in the most fundamental way, the Audit Committee particularly somnolent if not supine. It turns out that the independence of virtually every board member, including Audit Committee members, was undermined by side payments of one kind or another.[13] Independence also was compromised by the bonds of long service and familiarity.

Obviously one bad board does not an argument undo, but it does reveal a certain weakness with the board as a governance mechanism. Much is made of the heuristic biases of investors that undercut the reliability of stock market prices, but Enron reveals that the heuristic failings of small groups may be even more pronounced. The gap between what the Enron board knew and could have/should have known is far greater than the valuation gap between intrinsic and market values that typically emerges from competitive markets (one-third, Fisher Black famously suggested). Things at Enron appeared to be going so well, and management told such a convincing story, that a tell-tale sign of trouble – the proposal to suspend the corporate ethics code to permit conflicted transactions by a senior executive, an extraordinary request – did not stir the antennae. Skepticism, suspicion, and healthy scrutiny were inconsistent with the board's culture. Yet this sort of cognitive dissonance, which is probably widespread at corporations that appear successful, is also probably very common even at corporations in some trouble. Boards always seem to think that hostile bids undervalue the firm.

The Enron board failure also may reveal a certain tension in the current modes of director compensation and selection. Recruitment of directors who are qualified to be board members of a large public company may require substantial compensation, especially for directors on time-consuming or high-profile committees such as the audit committee. Yet high levels of compensation may compromise director independence, since a director's sharp questioning of senior management may lead to subtle pressures against his/her renomination. Moreover, stock-based director compensation may enhance the board's vigor as a shareholder agent but also increase its ambivalence about uncovering embarrassing facts that will reduce the share price. Finally, directors' independence can be compromised by both "soft conflicts," such as significant charitable contributions to an institution where a director may have a strong affiliation, or more direct conflicts, such as consulting arrangements. Both of these sorts of conflicts open the door to low-visibility sanction, this time against director independence. The failure to renominate a director is high-visibility, and, much as the accountant firing, may stir inquiry, whereas the making or not of a charitable contribution, or entering into or not of a consulting arrangement are much lower visibility and thus in practice may undercut independence even more.

One possible way to mitigate some of these tensions is to change the nominating and compensation practices for what might be called "trustee" directors in large public corporations. Even where the nominating committees consist of nominally independent directors, the CEO often plays a significant backstage role. Perhaps the members of the audit committee,

for example, should, in ordinary course, be "self-nominated," that is, the committee should have the power to designate the managerial nominees for directors who will be expected to serve on the audit committee (except that a proxy contestant should have the power to make an initial designation of its own audit committee nominees). This would provide a useful safeguard of independence.[14] Compensation for audit committee members should be different, a flat fee (or time-charged) rather than incentive-based. Audit committee members are in a real sense the board's and thus the corporation's compliance officers. To protect both the reality and appearance of their willingness to ferret out bad facts, they should not receive compensation closely tied to the corporation's profits or stock price. Finally, charitable contributions or other side payments related to a director's service should simply be eliminated, if not for all directors, then certainly for audit committee members and perhaps other "trustee" directors.

A group of "trustee directors" subject to different nomination and compensation rules differs, to be sure, from the usual US pattern of generalist, nonconstituency directors. For example, employee-designated directors are a decided rarity in US public corporations, found most prominently in an employee-owned firm like United Air Lines. The board's most important decisions typically involve matters of overall business strategy or executive leadership in which "trustee"-type considerations may not loom large, and arguably a single-minded focus on shareholder value assures the best outcomes. But a trustee director class would not disrupt the functioning of the board. In all probability, they would have the same general attitudes toward shareholder value as other directors, since ultimately they are elected by and accountable to the shareholders generally, not a particular constituency. The members of this class would be strengthened to function on behalf of shareholders in circumstances where independence from management may be crucial.

The "trustee director" approach may seem more attractive when compared to other approaches in light of Enron-type board failure. One alternative is to raise legal liability for directors for breach of the duty of care, or more particularly, breach of the duty of managerial oversight. This could be done in several different ways: expanding the circumstance in which liability might be attached,[15] narrowing the scope of director liability exculpation statutes to increase exposure to significant monetary loss, or, to similar effect, curtailing the availability of corporate indemnification or directors' and officers' liability insurance. Another alternative is to create mechanisms that more potently "forfeit" the reputational "bond" that directors allegedly post as a guarantee of good performance. For example, in cases of significant board oversight failure, the SEC could bring a proceeding to bar the directors from serving on other public boards or institutional investors could work privately to establish such a practice. (A lesser sanction would be a disclosure requirement associated with director nomination of a party who had served on the board of a company sanctioned by the SEC for a serious disclosure violation.) Each of these alternatives depends upon accurate *ex post* determination of board failure followed by application of appropriate sanctions, monetary or reputational. It is a familiar move in the debate to observe that such measures may have the perverse effect of discouraging board service by the well-qualified, especially for corporations facing significant business challenges.

By contrast, the "trustee director" approach is structural: it aims to affect the overall performance of the board by buttressing the particularly important role that certain directors must perform without changing the applicable legal duties. It represents the next stage in the evolution of board governance of the large public corporation, in which firms and managers must anticipate the pressures (and temptations) of competitive capital markets.

An "audit committee" for public corporations is itself a relatively recent innovation, a product of the 1970s corporate governance movement.[16] In light of the increasing reliance on stock prices as the measure of both managerial performance and compensation, the audit committee has become an increasingly important institutional complement for the control of the associated moral hazard problems. If relatively small changes in earnings, or the growth rate of earnings, have significant impact on the stock price, and if management receives a significant portion of its compensation through stock options, the temptations are obvious. Indeed, the increasingly widespread practice of "earnings management" was the basis for the SEC's very recent efforts to strengthen the role and accountability of audit committees.[17] The Enron case reemphasizes the importance of audit committee independence and vigilance and suggests possible structural weaknesses in its present conception.

Audit committees would be strengthened if their members were "trustee directors."

STOCK-BASED EXECUTIVE COMPENSATION AND EMPLOYEE COMPENSATION

Stock-based compensation has emerged as a major tool in the employment contracts, express and implied, for both senior managers and employees. The overly high-powered incentives of executive stock option mega-grants may have contributed to Enron's downfall.

Stock options have become an increasingly important element in executive compensation. In part, this has developed from appreciation of the need to align managers' and shareholders' incentives to solve genuine problems of legitimately different perspectives. This has "finance" elements and "real" elements. On finance: managers and shareholders start with different attitudes toward firm-specific risk. Managers generally make large firm-specific human capital investments in their firms and thus are risk-averse; shareholders in public firms generally are reasonably well diversified (or at least have the opportunity to be) and thus are generally risk-neutral. Managers therefore might well choose projects with lower expected returns but less variance than shareholders otherwise would prefer. Executive stock options can solve this mismatch by compensating executives for the additional risk of the shareholder-preferred projects.

Stock options also can give managers particular incentives to undertake difficult measures that may even reduce the riskiness of the firm but that may be personally stressful. For example, competition inevitably means that large firms should exit from some losing businesses, close plants, redeploy assets and make other moves that will disrupt the lives of employees and other stakeholders, but that also will increase the value of the firm. Stock options have become a dominant mode of performance-based pay for senior managers. Options are favored in part because of a peculiar mismatch between accounting and tax consequences: the grant of stock options is not booked as an "expense" that reduces accounting earnings, yet, when exercised, options produce a tax deduction for the firm equal to the difference between the market value of the stock and the exercise price of the option. Stock options also can serve a coordinating function among the senior management team, promoting team efforts to increase the value of the "firm" and mitigating the tendency to aggrandize one's own particular "division" of the firm. These are examples of the "real" motives for stock options.

Stock options also have emerged as particularly important in contemporary mergers and acquisitions practice because of the power that courts and legislatures have given to target boards to refuse a hostile bid. As I have argued previously, stock options have become the currency with which stockholders have bought back the endowment that courts and legislatures have so generously conferred on management.[18] This works through the senior executive employment contract. At the outset of the contract the senior executive is given a pile of stock options that will vest over perhaps a ten-year period, a golden handcuff, you might say. But there is a crucial "acceleration clause" that provides for immediate vesting of the options in the event of a change in control. An executive who fought fiercely in the 1980s to preserve position, perquisites, and power is now quite willing to sell.

In each case, executive stock options are used to solve a problem of incentive compatibility. But frankly, no one really knows what is the optimal level of option grant: what level of stock option compensation will make an executive risk-neutral like the shareholders, or willing to bite the bullet on layoffs, or willing to accept a premium bid? Indeed, it is likely that each problem may have a different solution as to number, term, and exercise price. The optimal level also may vary depending upon the utility curve of the particular executive, which may be affected, for example, by outside wealth. So at best, the actual grant must trade off among a number of objectives. Nor is it realistic to think that the market in executive services functions very well in setting the level of option grants, particularly because the present accounting treatment of options makes them nominally costless to the corporation. But as option grants become increasingly larger, two pathologies may arise that seem to have been at work in Enron: first, the fraudster, and second, the risk-preferring executive. (The more commonly identified problem, shareholder dilution, is merely distributive, not a potential threat to the existence of the firm.)

Stock options have value, of course, only if at exercise they are "in the money," meaning the stock price is above the exercise price. If option grants are very large and exercisable in the relatively near term, then a positive swing in the stock price can make the senior executives immediately very rich. Even if the stock price falls back, the well-timed executive option exercise is a life-changing experience. More formally, the Black-Scholes option pricing model instructs us that the value of the executive's stock option will be increasing both in the value of the underlying security and the variance (since stock options are issued "at the money"). So managers with a rich load of options have incentives to get the stock price high by any means necessary, fraud included. In particular, they have incentives to increase the riskiness of the firm, including projects that offer lower expected returns but higher variance. This will reduce the value of the firm for risk-neutral shareholders but has the potential to increase the value of managers' firm-related investments in cases where the gain in option holdings exceeds the loss to human capital. Managers become risk-preferring. Both pathologies, fraud and costly risk-taking, appear to have occurred in Enron. Enron became a hedge fund, taking leveraged bets in exotic markets that if successful would produce a huge, disproportionate bonanza for its executives. In particular, for a management team that had profited from previous option exercises, the downside seemed a problem only for the shareholders.

EMPLOYEE STOCK OWNERSHIP AND RETIREMENT PLANNING

The Enron case exposes the weirdness of brigading employee stock ownership, used principally for incentive purposes, with employee retirement planning. First, employer stock is a strange tool for delivering incentives to employees. For all but senior management, the action of any individual employees will have negligible impact on the stock price. Even a major contribution to enhancing the profitability of a division is likely to go unnoticed in the consolidated results of a large public company. More precisely tailored pay-for-performance measures, bonuses, commissions, promotions, and other rewards for delivering specific results are bound to be far more effective in providing incentives.[19] Too stringent a focus on ownership of employer stock for its incentive effects may lead to employee disillusionment when strong individual efforts are not rewarded by a stock price increase. Rather, ownership of employer stock may serve other organizational goals. The stock price, which reflects the public market's evaluation of the company, is a salient benchmark of the company's success. Management can use this focal point to rally the troops, to explain the need for difficult economic decisions, to build a sense of a common enterprise and common culture. The stock is a common currency within the company. Unlike a grand title or corporate power, it is infinitely divisible. Every employee can have some; it is "commons" stock. Employer stock can also serve as a form of profit-sharing that does not require a cash outlay by the company and which receives favorable accounting treatment.

The tie-in to retirement planning makes employer stock particularly odd as an incentive device. Employer stock is typically placed into a contributory pension plan, for example, a 401(k) plan or an Employee Stock Ownership Plan, which places strict limits on the employee's ability to sell the stock, and even after sale, locks up the proceeds until the employee's retirement. Thus the employee is required to take a very long view towards the benefits of employer stock appreciation.[20] Consumption is postponed for a long time. In theory, there should be substitution among various savings vehicles, so employer stock appreciation in a retirement account should reduce other savings, increasing the amount available for consumption, but the mental arithmetic seems not to work that way in practice. Note that this pattern also is very different from the incentives granted to senior managers – stock options and other stock-based compensation that begin to vest and become exercisable as quickly as one year after their grant. In other words, the wealthier senior managers whose declining marginal utility should make them more likely candidates for incentives that pay off in the long run receive short-fused stock-based incentive compensation. If that is the right payoff horizon for incentivizing senior management, then the retirement planning link to stock-based incentives for line employees postpones the payoff long past the point of incentive compatibility.

The limited value of employer stock as an incentive device in these circumstances is, of course, the much less serious half of the retirement plan problem. Enron employees were heavily invested in employer stock in their 401(k) plans. An estimated $1.3 billion of the plan's $2.1 billion in pension assets consisted of now-worthless Enron stock.[21] To a significant extent, this was the result of the peculiar accounting and tax incentives that reduced Enron's cost of pension contributions if it used its own stock combined with the pension plan rules that limited employee sales of Enron-contributed stock until age fifty. Presumably, those tax incentives could be redirected to reward greater diversification. But employee choices to remain undiversified also accounted for a significant portion of these losses. The extent to which Enron's employees – probably much higher on the financial sophistication curve than most – chose to take on so much uncompensated firm-specific risk is stunning.

Enron shows why we might regret the diminishment of the defined benefit pension plan and the shifting of retirement planning risk onto employees.[22] Defined benefit plans, which promise a fixed payout based on an employee's longevity with the firm and his/her final salary, are collateralized by funding requirements set by the Employee Retirement Security Act of 1974 (ERISA) and managed by fiduciaries who operate under a prudent investor standard that emphasizes the value of diversification. Defined contribution plans generally, and 401(k) plans specifically, are the fastest-growing part of the private retirement planning universe.[23] Employees contribute a before-tax portion of their salaries, and employers often match, especially with employer stock, but all of the risk associated with the individual's management of his/her retirement savings is borne individually. Ironically, the problem until recently was that individuals typically underweighted equities, preferring instead less risky bonds and other fixed-income investments. Such conservatism meant that they would not attain retirement income targets. The Enron experience of a poorly diversified 401(k) plan, too much in employer equity, is of course just the opposite. It seems likely that the failures of individuals retirement portfolio management will cluster around these two poles.

Since pension plans are voluntary for the employer, reform needs to avoid imposition of significant new costs. But the devolution to individuals of both the responsibility for retirement-plan planning and the investment risk of their choices seems unwise.

CONCLUSION

The Enron matter will prove to be a very important event in the history of American shareholder capitalism. Many of the important institutions were subjected to a stress test at a particular firm and the outcome was poor. The real concern is that the gross overreaching at Enron is symptomatic of troubling if not egregious behavior elsewhere. Already, reform seems on the way, in the possible restructuring of accounting firms and the establishment of a new accounting self-regulator; in clearer standards under GAAP about the treatment of specialized financing vehicles; in new elements of mandatory disclosure; in efforts to redefine director independence. But Enron also reminds us that there is a problem that cannot be solved, but can only be contained, in the tension between imperfectly fashioned incentives and self-restraint.

ACKNOWLEDGMENTS

I appreciate discussion and comments from Jack Coffee, Ron Gilson, Victor Fleischer, Vic Khanna, Ed Iacobucci, Jon Macey, David Schizer, some Columbia alums who wish to remain anonymous, and participants at the *University of Chicago Law Review* Symposium.

NOTES

1 Enron Corporation, press release, *Enron Reports Recurring Third Quarter Earnings of $0.43 per Diluted Share; Reports Non-Recurring Charges of $1.01 Billion After-Tax; Reaffirms Recurring Earnings Estimates of $1.80 for 2001 and $2.15 for 2002 and Expands Financial Reporting* (Oct 16, 2001) available online at <http://www.enron.com/corp/pressroom/releases/2001/ene/68-3QearningsLtr.html> (visited Feb 19, 2002). For a contemporary history of Enron's collapse, see Kurt Eichenwald with Diana B. Henriques, (Feb 10, 2002), Enron's Many Strands: The Company Unravels; Enron Buffed Image to a Shine Even as It Rotted from Within, *NY Times* A1 (Feb 10, 2002).

2 John R. Emshwiller and Rebecca Smith, (Oct 17, 2001), Enron Jolt: Investments, Assets Generate Big Loss, *Wall St J* C1.

3 John R. Emshwiller *et al.*, (Nov 9, 2001), Enron Reduces Profit for 4 Years by 20%, Citing Dealings with Officers' Partnerships, *Wall St J* A3.

4 See Report of Investigation by the Special Investigation Committee of the Board of Directors of Enron Corporation 4–5, 14–15 (Feb 1, 2002), available online at<http://newsfindlaw.com/hdocs/docs/enron/sicreport/ indexhtml> (visited Feb 19, 2002).

5 For a wide-ranging account of the Enron collapse, see William W. Bratton, Enron and the Dark Side of Shareholder Value, 76 *Tulane L Rev* 1275–1361, June 2002.

6 George Akerlof, (1970), The Market for Lemons: Quality Uncertainty and the Market Mechanism, 84 *Q J Econ* 488, 489–92 (using the car market as an example to model the economic costs of dishonesty in the marketplace).

7 See generally John C. Coffee, Jr., (May 2001), The Acquiescent Gatekeeper: Reputational Intermediaries, Auditor Independence and the Governance of Accounting at 16–17, Columbia Law School Center for Law and Economics Studies Working Paper No 191 available online at <http://papers.ssrn.com/id=270944> (visited Feb 19, 2002) (suggesting that auditors also selling non-audit services to corporate clients can no longer be gatekeepers whose revenues from clients are too small for an auditor to risk its reputation in agreeing to an accounting irregularity).

8 The Enron Special Committee report confirms Andersen's role in helping to structure Enron's off-balance-sheet entities despite the obvious disclosure deficit that was created.

9 This section benefited particularly from conversations with Jon Macey.

10 For accounts of the cultural and monitoring failures at Andersen, see Ken Brown and Jonathan Weil, (Mar 12, 2002), How Andersen's Embrace of Consulting Altered the Culture of the Auditing Firm, *Wall St J* C1; Ianthe Jeanne Dugan, (Mar 14, 2002), Did You Hear the One About the Accountant? It's Not Very Funny, *Wall St J* A1.

Andersen's internal monitoring failure is one of the genuine puzzles about Enron. After all, Andersen's business, its core competence, if you will, is anticipating internal agency problems, especially in the financial realm, and figuring out how to minimize the consequent risks through internal monitoring systems. How is it that this shoemaker failed to make shoes for itself? One benign explanation is that Andersen, the firm, failed to realize its evolution from a partnership of accounting professionals, "certified public accountants" constrained by a strong sense of professional ethics, to a profit-maximizing business organization using high-powered incentive compensation schemes. The internal monitoring systems that might suffice in the case of the former are woefully inadequate in the case of the latter. In the course of pursuing consulting business and in devising compensation systems designed to maximize partner incomes, Andersen underwent a "norms shift" that required a matching change in the internal monitoring system. Perhaps the partners were unable to look at themselves hard enough in the mirror (or to hold a mirror to the firm).

This observation may have implications for the large law firm, another organization of professionals, "lawyers," which in general is moving towards incentive-based compensation. The internal monitoring system may have been appropriate for a small organization of "partners" who were compensated on a lock-step system and who may have highly valued a sense of professional identity, but will not be appropriate for a profit-maximizing large firm using high-powered incentive compensation schemes. Not only will the sense of "professional ethics" change, but such an environment will put greater pressure on such constraints. Law firms, like accounting firms, may find themselves at significant risk in the absence of strenuous internal monitoring.

11 For a summary, see Andrei Shleifer, *Inefficient Markets: An Introduction to Behavioral Finance* 28–52 (Oxford 2000).

12 The suggestion that Enron's $90 stock price could be justified as the weighted average of investor expectations (e.g. a 50 percent chance that Enron was worth $180 a share, a 50 percent chance that it was worth nothing) is consistent with the usual lemons equilibrium. Purchasers who are unable to determine whether the good is high or low quality assume they are purposefully being kept in the dark; they offer the low-quality price, not an average-quality price. (More technically, the value of Enron was not a "normally distributed random variable." At the very least, the "low-quality" outcome should have been much more heavily weighted than the "high-quality" outcome.) Note also that the $90 stock price reflected a price-earnings multiple of sixty. It is hard to imagine $90 per Enron share as the expected value of a probability distribution that gave significant weight to a low-quality outcome.

13 See Joanne S. Lublin, (Feb 1, 2002), Inside, Outside Enron, Audit Committee Is Scrutinized, *Wall St J* C1.

14 For another mechanism to protect director independence, see Ronald J. Gilson and Reinier Kraakman, (1993), Investment Companies as Guardian Shareholders: The Place of the MSIC in the Corporate Governance Debate, 45 *Stan L Rev* 985, 990–96 (proposing to institute publicly traded financial intermediaries that would make huge investments in small portfolios).

15 See *In Re Caremark International Inc Derivative Litigation*, 698 A2d 959, 967–70 (Del Ch 1996) (describing circumstances in which liability is currently attached).

16 See *Principles of Corporate Governance: Analysis and Recommendations* § 3.05 Reporter's Notes (ALI 1994).

17 See generally Gregory S. Rowland, (2002), Note, Earnings Management, the SEC, and Corporate Governance: Director Liability Arising from the Audit Committee Report, 102 *Colum L Rev* 168. Former SEC Chairman Arthur Levitt focused on audit committees as a governance response to earnings management in 1998. This led to a report of the Blue Ribbon Committee on Improving the Effectiveness of Corporate Audit Committees in 1999 and subsequent standard setting by the stock exchanges and rulemaking by the SEC, effective in 2000. See *The Blue Ribbon Committee*, available online at <http://www.nyse.com/content/ publications/ NT00006286.html> (visited Mar 23, 2002).

18 See Jeffrey N. Gordon, (2000), Poison Pills and the European Case, 54 *U Miami L Rev* 839, 841.

19 For a related view, see Saul Levmore, (2001), Puzzling Stock Options and Compensation Norms, 149 *U Pa L Rev* 1901, 1905–08 (comparing the incentive effects of stock options and bonuses).

20 See generally Jeffrey N. Gordon, *Employee Stock Ownership in Economic Transitions: The Case of United Airlines*, in Klaus J. Hopt *et al.*, *Comparative Corporate Governance: The State of the Art and Emerging Research* 387, 433–34 (Oxford 1998).

21 Theo Francis and Ellen Schultz, Enron Faces Suits by 401 (k) Plan Participants, *Wall St J* C1 (Nov 23, 2001). Of course, these figures overstate the employees' true loss since the value of Enron stock was pumped up by the accounting manipulation.

22 For some discussion of the risks of defined-contribution, Enron-type plans for employees, see Jeffrey N. Gordon, (1998), Individual Responsibility for the Investment of Retirement Savings: A Cautionary View, 64 *Brooklyn L Rev* 1037, 1038 (discussing the poor assessment by individuals of the risks that arise from the volatility of stocks versus bonds); Jeffrey N. Gordon, (1997), Employees, Pensions, and the New Economic Order, 97 *Colum L Rev* 1519, 1541–45 (noting employer obligations to employees under defined-benefits plans, and the undermining of those plans in the current economic trade-liberation order).

23 See Council of Economic Advisors, *Economic Report of the President* 71 (2002), available online at <http:// w3.access.gpo.gov/eop/> (visited Apr 18, 2002) (including a chart comparing the growth in numbers of defined-contribution plan participants with the growth in numbers of defined benefit plan participants).

"What Caused Enron? A Capsule Social and Economic History of the 1990s"

from Cornell Law Review (2004)

John C. Coffee Jr

The sudden explosion of corporate accounting scandals and related financial irregularities that burst over the financial markets between late 2001 and the first half of 2002 – Enron, WorldCom, Tyco, Adelphia and others – raises an obvious question: Why now? What explains the concentration of financial scandals at this moment in time? Much commentary has rounded up the usual suspects and placed the blame on a decline in business morality,[1] an increase in "infectious greed,"[2] or other similarly subjective trends that cannot be reliably measured. Although none of these possibilities can be dismissed out of hand, approaches that simply reason backwards, proceeding from the observation that the number of scandals has increased to the conclusion that a decline in business morality has therefore occurred, merely assume what is to be proven.

Alternatively, others have blamed these scandals either on a few "rogue" managers who somehow fooled the capital markets, or on negligent, inattentive boards of directors.[3] No doubt, there were some rogues and some particularly bad boards. Yet the most reliable evidence, when properly read, suggests that Enron and related scandals were neither unique nor idiosyncratic; rather, pervasive problems arose that undercut existing systems of corporate governance. Thus, a focus on the deficiencies of any individual board of directors cannot explain the sudden surge of governance failures. As no plausible theory suggests that board performance has generally deteriorated over recent years, one must look beyond the

board, in particular to those who provide or control its informational inputs, to explain this concentration of scandals.

Still another unsatisfactory response to the concentration of recent scandals has been to posit that a wave of recriminations, soul-searching, and scapegoating necessarily follows the collapse of any market bubble.[4] Clearly, a large frothy bubble did burst in 2001.[5] As a historical matter, bubbles do tend to produce scandals and prophylactic legislation,[6] but this loose generalization leaves unanswered the critical questions: What caused this bubble and how does the growth of a bubble relate to the apparent breakdown of a once-confident system of corporate governance?

This chapter seeks to move beyond the "few bad apples" or "rogue managers" explanation, or the cynical assumption that scandals are inevitable and cyclical, to identify common denominators across the range of recent cases. Although this chapter does not seek to explain what happened in any individual case (including Enron) or to generalize from any specific case to reach broader conclusions about corporate governance, it does suggest that the explosion of financial irregularity in 2001 and 2002 was the natural and logical consequence of trends and forces that had been developing for some time. Ironically, the blunt truth is that recent accounting scandals and the broader phenomenon of earnings management are by-products of a system of corporate governance that has indeed made corporate managers more accountable to the market. Yet sensitivity to the market can be a mixed blessing, particularly when the market becomes euphoric and uncritical. To the extent that the market becomes the master, governance systems that were adequate for a world in which market focuses were weaker need to be upgraded in tandem with market developments to protect against manipulation and distortion by self-interested managers. This, in turn, takes us back to the central role of gatekeepers.

Above all, the fundamental developments that destabilized our contemporary corporate governance system were those that changed the incentives confronting both senior executives and the corporation's outside gatekeepers. In contrast, little reason exists to believe that the behavior of boards deteriorated over recent years. Thus, a focus on gatekeepers and managers provides a better perspective for analyzing both what caused these scandals and the likely impact of the recent congressional legislation passed in their wake.[7] Accordingly, this chapter will initially relate the recent scandals to changes in managerial and gatekeeper compensation over the last two decades. Yet, although the incentives of managers and gatekeepers clearly changed over the 1990s because of exogenous changes in legal rules and market conditions, this is not the entire story. Bubbles – here defined to mean a state of market euphoria in which investors lose their normal skepticism – also change the behavior of gatekeepers, managers, and shareholders. To some degree, responsibility must be allocated among three different groups: (1) gatekeepers; (2) managers; and (3) shareholders, particularly institutional investors. Initially, this chapter will focus on the special institution of corporate gatekeepers (on whom it argues modern corporate governance depends) and how their behavior may logically change during a bubble. Then, it will turn to managers and shareholders. This chapter's conclusions have policy implications and in particular provide a perspective on the likely impact of Congress's efforts to address these recent scandals in the Sarbanes–Oxley Act.

THE PRIOR EQUILIBRIUM: AMERICAN CORPORATE GOVERNANCE AS OF 1980

The world of corporate governance changed quickly and radically during the final two decades of the last century. If one turned back the clock to before 1980, one would find that the dominant academic commentary on the corporation of the pre-1980 era articulated a "theory of managerial capitalism" that essentially saw the public corporation as a kind of bloated bureaucracy that maximized sales, growth, and size, but not profits or stock price.[8] Academic writers such as Robin Marris and William Baumol viewed the firms of that era as pursuing an empire-building policy, which "profit satisfied," rather than profit maximized.[9] Professional managers balanced the interests of different constituencies and, at least according to some commentators, assigned no special priority to the interests of shareholders. Such a management strategy was motivated in large part by the desire of the corporation's managers to increase their own security and perquisites.[10] Conglomerate mergers, for example, achieved these self-interested ends by reducing the risk of insolvency, thereby protecting senior managers by providing them with a diversified but largely unrelated portfolio of businesses that could cross-subsidize each other and thereby mitigate the impact of the business cycle.[11] Also, with greater size came greater cash income to managers and a reduced risk of corporate control contests or shareholder activism.

Some academic writers in this era – most notably Oliver Williamson – did not view the conglomerate as necessarily inefficient; rather, Williamson argued that internal capital markets could be as efficient as external ones.[12] Still, both sides in this debate concurred that managers were effectively insulated from shareholder demands and could treat shareholders as just one of several constituencies whose interests were to be "balanced."[13] Some criticized, while others defended, this lack of accountability, but few denied that managers possessed broad discretion in how they ran the business corporation.

During the 1980s, the advent of the hostile takeover profoundly destabilized this equilibrium. While hostile takeovers predated the 1980s, it was only during that decade, beginning in 1983,[14] that they first began to be financed with junk bonds. Junk bond financing made the conglomerate corporate empires of the prior decade vulnerable and tempting targets for the financial bidder, who could reap high profits in a bust-up takeover.[15] In turn, this gave managers of potential targets a stronger interest than they had in the past in their firm's short-term stock price because, despite the availability of defensive tactics, a target firm could seldom remain independent if its market price fell significantly below its breakup value for a sustained period.

Less noticed at the time, but possibly even more significant from today's perspective, was the change in the nature of executive compensation. Leveraged buyout firms, such as Kohlberg Kravis Roberts, entered the takeover wars, seeking to buy undervalued companies, often in league with these firms' incumbent management. Alternatively, they sometimes installed new management teams to turn the company around. Either way, the goal of the leveraged buyout firms was to create strong incentives that would link management's interest to the firm's stock market value. Thus, firms began compensating senior managers with much greater ownership stakes than had customarily been awarded in the past.

Ironically, the principal actors who destabilized the existing corporate equilibrium were institutional investors and Congress. Institutional investors encouraged greater use of stock options to compensate both managers and directors in order to increase their sensitivity to the market.[16] Congress unintentionally hastened this process by placing a ceiling on the cash compensation that senior executives could be paid. First, in 1984, Congress levied a punitive excise tax on "excess parachute payments" in order to discourage "windfall" compensation paid in connection with change of control transactions.[17] Then, in 1993, Congress enacted 162(m) of the Internal Revenue Code, which basically denies a tax deduction to a publicly held corporation for annual compensation paid to its chief executive officer, or to any of the next four most highly paid officers, where the amount paid to any such individual officer exceeds $1 million.[18] Predictably, once restricted in the cash compensation they could pay, corporate planners shifted to greater use of equity compensation, where fewer prophylactic rules governed.[19] Although this shift towards equity compensation accelerated in the 1990s, it began in the 1980s as a by-product of the takeover movement.

THE OLD ORDER CHANGETH: THE NEW GOVERNANCE PARADIGM OF THE 1990s

The two principal forces that initially changed American corporate governance over the 1990s have already been identified: the takeover movement and the growing use of equity compensation. Other forces that crested during the 1990s – including the heightened activism of institutional investors, a deregulatory movement that sought to dismantle arguably obsolete regulatory provisions, and the media's increasing fascination with the market as the 1990s progressed – reinforced the impact of the initial forces as each made managers more sensitive to their firm's market price. In so doing, however, these forces also induced managers to take greater risks to inflate their stock price.

The dimensions of this transition are best revealed if we contrast compensation data from the early 1990s with that from a decade or so later. As of 1990, equity-based compensation for chief executive officers of public corporations in the United States constituted approximately five percent of their total annual compensation; by 1999, this percentage had risen to an estimated 60 percent.[20] Moreover, between 1992 and 1998, the median compensation of Standard and Poor's (S&P) 500 chief executives increased by approximately 150 percent, with option-based compensation accounting for most of this increase.[21] The critical point is that in the 1990s, senior executive compensation shifted from being primarily cash-based to primarily stock-based. With this change, management's focus shifted from the relationship between the firm's market price and the firm's break-up value, which the advent of the bust-up takeover compelled them to watch, to the likely future performance of their firm's stock over the short run. Far more than the hostile takeover, equity compensation induced management to obsess over their firm's day-to-day share price.

Not only did market practices change during the 1990s, but deregulation facilitated both the use of equity compensation and the ability of managers to bail out at an inflated stock price. Prior to 1991, 16(b) of the Securities Exchange Act of 1934 required a senior executive of a publicly held company to hold the underlying security for six months after the exercise of a stock option.[22] Otherwise, 16(b) compelled the executive to surrender any gain from sale to the corporation as a "short swing" profit.[23] In 1991, the Securities and Exchange Commission (SEC) reexamined its rules under 16(b) and broadly deregulated.[24] In particular, the SEC relaxed the holding period requirements under 16(b) so that the senior executive could tack the holding period of the stock option to the holding period for the underlying shares. Thus, if the stock option had already been held six months or longer, the underlying shares could be sold immediately upon exercise of the option. As qualified stock options by their terms usually must be held several years before they become exercisable, this revision meant that most senior executives were free to sell the underlying stock on the same day that they exercised the option; thus, they could exploit a temporary spike in the price of the firm's shares. This quickly became the prevailing pattern. Although it was not the goal of deregulation to encourage bailouts, this was an unintended consequence that might have been foreseen.

Even prior to the 1990s, earnings management was a pervasive and longstanding practice.[25] Its goal, however, had traditionally been to smooth out fluctuations in income in order to reduce the volatility of the firm's cash flows and present a simple, steadily ascending line from period to period.[26] Thus, management perfected techniques such as "cookie jar reserves" to save earnings for a rainy day.[27] During the 1990s, however, the nature of earnings management changed, with managers shifting their focus from moderating earnings swings to advancing the moment of revenue recognition.[28] Accounting scandals rose commensurate with this shift toward premature recognition.[29]

At least in part, the increased willingness of managers to recognize income prematurely – in effect, to misappropriate it from future periods – appears linked to the need to satisfy the forecasts of security analysts covering the firm. By the mid-1990s, even a modest shortfall in earnings below the level forecasted could produce a dramatic market penalty as dissatisfied investors dumped the firm's stock.[30] Yet one must face a circularity problem before blaming earnings management failures on management's fear of a market overreaction to a modest shortfall below predicted earnings. Typically, the security analyst's chief source of information about the company is its senior management. If management doubted its ability to meet the analyst's projection, why did it not encourage the analyst to make a less aggressive forecast in the first instance? The most logical answer again involves the growing importance of equity compensation. Aggressive forecasts drove the firm's stock price up and enabled management to sell at an inflated price. Premature revenue recognition then became a means by which managers satisfied aggressive forecasts that they had themselves encouraged in order to achieve high market valuations.

High market valuations were not, however, simply the product of aggressive forecasting. Beginning in 1995 and continuing until March 2000, the stock market in the United States entered its longest, most sustained bull market in US history.[31] In such an excited environment, aggressive forecasting produces a predictable market reaction. Moreover, in a bubble, investors, analysts, auditors, and other gatekeepers may relax their usual skepticism amidst the market euphoria that a sustained bull market generates.

Accounting scandals have had a long history over the last half-century.[32] Viewed from a distance, Enron and the related scandals of 2001 and 2002 are probably most comparable to the Savings and Loan (S&L) crisis of the late 1980s, an episode that similarly resulted in draconian legislation.[33] Both episodes reveal that perverse managerial incentives were the driving force behind managers' acceptance of high risks on behalf of their firms that they did not fully bear themselves. After the S&L crisis, investigators quickly identified a classic "moral hazard" problem. Because the government guaranteed banks' financial obligations to depositors, these depositors had little reason to monitor management, and accordingly bank promoters were able to leverage their firms excessively. In the case of the Enron-era scandals, the impact of executive stock compensation may have played a similar explanatory role. This comparison leads to a tentative generalization: Perverse incentives, not declines in ethics, cause scandals.[34]

Still, an alternative hypothesis also remains plausible. Namely, that a market bubble better explains the failure of those monitors who should have restrained management. Because both explanations can account for the pervasive gatekeeper failures that have accompanied recent financial and accounting scandals, a synthesis seems necessary. Such a synthesis requires, however, that we focus more closely on what defines and motivates the professional gatekeeper.

THE CHANGING POSITION OF THE GATEKEEPER DURING THE 1990s

Although commentators often use the term gatekeeper,[35] its meaning is not self-evident. As used in this article, the term refers to intermediaries who provide verification and certification services to investors.[36] These services may include verifying a company's financial statements (as the independent auditor does), evaluating the creditworthiness of the company (as the debt rating agency does), assessing the company's business and financial prospects vis-a-vis its rivals (as the securities analyst does), or appraising the fairness of a specific transaction (as the investment banker does in delivering a fairness opinion). Attorneys may also act as gatekeepers when they pledge their professional reputations to a transaction, as the counsel for the issuer typically does in delivering its opinion in connection with an initial public offering (IPO).[37] However, as later discussed, the more typical role of attorneys serving public corporations is that of the transaction engineer, rather than that of a reputational intermediary. Thus, the auditor and the attorney are located at the opposite poles of a continuum: each can act as a reputational intermediary, but the attorney tends to function as the engineer and the auditor more often as the certifier or reputational intermediary.

Characteristically, the professional gatekeeper assesses or vouches for the corporate client's own statements about itself or a specific transaction. This duplication is efficient because the market recognizes that the gatekeeper has less incentive to deceive than does its client and thus regards the gatekeeper's assurance or evaluation as more credible than the client's statements. To be sure, the gatekeeper's role as watchdog is arguably compromised by the fact that it is typically paid by the party that it is supposed to monitor. Still, the gatekeeper's relative credibility stems from the fact that it is, in effect, pledging reputational capital that it has built up over many years of performing similar services for numerous clients. In theory, a gatekeeper would not sacrifice such reputational capital for a single client or a modest fee. Nonetheless, here as elsewhere, logic and experience conflict: Despite the seemingly clear logic of the gatekeeper rationale, experience during the 1990s suggests that professional gatekeepers will acquiesce in managerial fraud, even though the apparent reputational losses would seem to dwarf the gains to be made from an individual client.[38] In this light, the deeper question underlying Enron and related scandals is not: Why did some managers engage in fraud? Rather, it is: Why did the gatekeepers let them?

Initially, the gatekeeper's reasons for resisting fraud and not acquiescing in accounting irregularities seem obvious. In theory, a gatekeeper generally has many clients, each of whom pays it a fee, which is modest in proportion to the firm's overall revenues. Arthur Andersen had, for example, 2,300 separate audit clients.[39] On this basis, the firm had little incentive to risk its considerable reputational capital for any one of them.

During the 1990s, many courts wholeheartedly subscribed to this logic. For example, in *DiLeo* v. *Ernst & Young*,[40] Judge Easterbrook, writing for the Seventh Circuit, outlined precisely the foregoing theory:

> The complaint does not allege that [the auditor] had anything to gain from any fraud by [its client]. An accountant's greatest asset is its reputation for honesty, followed closely by its reputation for careful work. Fees for two years' audits could not approach the losses [that the auditor] would suffer from a perception that it would muffle a client's fraud … [The auditor's] partners shared none of the gain from any fraud and were exposed to a large fraction of the loss. It would have been irrational for any of them to have joined cause with [the client].[41]

Of course, the modest fees in some cases were much less than the $100 million in prospective annual fees that Arthur Andersen explicitly foresaw coming from Enron.[42] Yet, this difference in fees fails to explain Arthur Andersen's apparent willingness to accept high risk. Even if Arthur Andersen saw Enron as a potential $100 million client, it must be remembered that Arthur Andersen generated over $9 billion in revenues in 2001 alone and thus its expected Enron revenues would total only around 1 percent of its aggregate revenues.[43] Hence, a fuller explanation seems necessary to understand gatekeeper failure.

The auditing profession during the 1990s

Once among the most respected of all professional service firms (including law, accounting, and consulting firms), Andersen became involved in a series of now well-known securities frauds – Waste Management Inc., Sunbeam, McKesson HBOC Inc., Baptist Foundation of Arizona, and Global Crossing – that culminated in its disastrous association with Enron.[44] Those who wish to characterize the recent corporate scandals as simply the work of a few "bad apples," naturally wish to present Arthur Andersen as an outlier or "outlaw" firm unrepresentative of the profession. This theory, however, simply cannot be supported with objective data. The available evidence on the overall experiences of the Big Five[45] accounting firms suggests that Andersen was not significantly different from its peers and experienced the same, or even a lesser, rate of earnings restatements.[46] All in all, the more logical inference to draw from the "accounting irregularity" scandals of 2001 and 2002 is that erosion occurred during the 1990s in the quality of financial reporting.

Indeed, this is the area where the data is the clearest. During the 1990s, earnings restatements, long recognized as a proxy for fraud, suddenly soared. One study, conducted in 2001 by George Moriarty and Philip Livingston, found that the number of earnings restatements issued by publicly held corporations averaged 49 per year from 1990 to 1997, increased to 91 in 1998, and then skyrocketed to 150 and 156 in 1999 and 2000, respectively.[47] A later, more complete study conducted by the General Accounting Office (GAO) in October 2002 examined all financial statement restatements (not just earnings restatements) and found a similarly sharp spike in 1999 that has continued through 2002.[48] Figure 1 from the GAO Report displays this trend.[49]

When we compare Moriarty and Livingston's figure of 49 restatements in 1996 with the GAO's estimate of 250 for 2002, it shows that the number of restatements increased by approximately 270 percent over the five years ending in 2002.[50]

Not all restatements, however, are equal. Some may involve small, infrequently traded companies, or involve only trivial accounting adjustments, or trigger only modest stock price reactions. Others may be on a scale with those issued by Enron or WorldCom. For our purposes, it is useful to focus more precisely on financial restatements issued by companies listed on the NYSE, Amex, and Nasdaq, thereby excluding smaller companies with limited trading. Between 1997 and 2001, the proportion of NYSE, Amex and Nasdaq companies that restated their financial statements almost tripled, increasing from less than 0.89 percent in 1997 to approximately 2.5 percent in 2001.[51] The GAO Report further predicted that the number of restating companies would reach nearly 3 percent in 2002.[52] Overall, the GAO Report found that from January 1997 to June 2002, approximately "[ten] percent of all listed companies announced at least one restatement."[53] Equally revealing was that the size (in terms of market capitalization) of the typical restating company rose rapidly over this period,[54] and in 2002, companies listed on the NYSE or Nasdaq accounted for over 85 percent of all restatements identified in that year.[55]

What drove this sudden spike in restatements? Restatements are generally resisted internally because public corporations fear stock price drops, securities class actions, and SEC investigations that usually follow in the wake of financial statement restatements. Indeed, the GAO Report found that stock prices of restating companies over the 1997–2001 period suffered an immediate market-adjusted decline of almost 10 percent on average, measured on the basis of the stock's three-day price movement from the trading day before the announcement through the trading day after the announcement.[56] From 1997 to 2002, restating firms lost over $100 billion in market capitalization during this

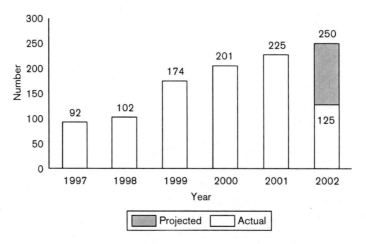

Figure 1   Total number of restatement announcements identified, 1997–2002.

three-day trading period alone.[57] Given these significant and adverse stock price effects, it is implausible to read the sharp increase in restatements at the end of the 1990s as the product of any new tolerance for, or indifference to, restatements. Perhaps, as some audit firms have argued, some portion of the change can be attributed to recent SEC activism about "earnings management,"[58] which became an SEC priority as of 1998.[59] But this explanation does not seem capable of accounting for most, or even many, of these restatements. Corporate issuers are not likely to voluntarily expose themselves to large stock price declines and potential securities fraud liability simply to please the SEC; nor would the market react with such surprise to "technical" or other modest accounting adjustments.

Not only did the number of earnings restatements increase over this period but the magnitude of the market reaction to these restatements grew as well.[60] This suggests that during this period, managers became progressively willing to take greater risks. Moreover, as the 1990s wore on, earnings restatements were increasingly issued by large, mature, publicly held firms, rather than by smaller, less experienced companies. Managerial behavior within the largest firms, therefore, appears to have changed over this period.

Data from the earlier noted GAO Report also supports this thesis that managerial behavior changed.[61] Although there are many reasons for a company to restate its financial statements (e.g. to adjust costs or expenses or to recognize liabilities), one particular reason drove the issuance of restatements during the period from 1997 to 2002. The GAO Report found that revenue recognition issues accounted for almost 38 percent of the 919 announced restatements that it identified over the 1997–2002 period.[62] In effect, attempts by management to prematurely recognize income appear to have been the most common cause of restatements. Earlier in the decade, corporate management may have hid "excess earnings" in "rainy day reserves" to smooth out undesired fluctuations in the firm's earnings in order to minimize the appearance of volatility. By the end of the decade, however, these same firms robbed future periods for earnings they could immediately recognize. In short, "income smoothing" gave way to increasingly predatory behavior.

Interestingly, during this period restatements involving revenue recognition produced disproportionately large losses.[63] Seemingly, the market especially feared revenue recognition restatements because they signaled that reported earnings could not be trusted. Nonetheless, revenue recognition restatements remained the most common form of restatement.[64] Overall, the interests of management and shareholders became increasingly misaligned, and gatekeepers were caught in the middle.

Security analysts during the 1990s

The pattern of increasing auditor acquiescence in accounting irregularities during the 1990s was not unique. Much the same pattern can be discerned in the behavior of securities analysts over the same period. Securities analysts were, if anything, more conflicted than auditors. While much of the evidence here is anecdotal, it is striking nonetheless.

As late as October 2001, shortly before Enron declared bankruptcy, 15 of the 16 securities analysts covering the company maintained "buy" or "strong buy" recommendations on its stock.[65] Yet, months earlier, as of December 31, 2000, Enron already had a stock price that was seventy times its earnings and six times its book value.[66] Further, it had earned an 89 percent return for the year despite a 9 percent decrease over the same period for the S&P 500 index.[67] Such a profile should have alerted any half-awake analyst to the possibility that Enron was seriously overvalued. Yet the first brokerage firm to downgrade Enron to a "sell" rating in 2001 was Prudential Securities, which did not engage at the time in investment banking activities.[68] Prudential also had the highest proportion of sell ratings among the stocks it evaluated.[69] Thus, even if Prudential also woke up late, it is revealing that the least conflicted were the first to awake.

How close then are the similarities between analysts and auditors? Much like auditors, analysts are also "reputational intermediaries" whose need to retain and please investment banking clients may often dominate their desire to be perceived as credible and objective. One statistic that inevitably arises in any assessment of analyst objectivity is the curious fact that the ratio of "buy" to "sell" recommendations has recently been as high as 100 to 1.[70] In truth, this particular statistic may not be as compelling as it initially sounds because there are obvious reasons why "buy" recommendations will normally outnumber "sell" recommendations, even in the absence of conflicts of interest.[71] A more revealing statistic shows the rapid shift in the ratio of "buy" to "sell" recommendations that took place in the 1990s, which shift parallels the earlier noted increase in accounting restatements during the 1990s. According to a study by First Call, the ratio of "buy" to "sell" recommendations actually increased from 6 to 1 in the early 1990s to 100 to 1 by 2000.[72] Again, it appears that something happened in the 1990s that compromised the independence and objectivity of the gatekeepers on whom our private system of corporate governance depends.[73] Even before Enron, the most sophisticated market participants had come to understand the extent of these conflicts in the case of analysts and had ceased to rely on "sell side" analysts.[74]

EXPLAINING GATEKEEPER FAILURE

A pattern of mounting irregularity in financial reporting became evident as the 1990s progressed. But what explains it? As a starting point, none of the watchdogs that should have detected Enron's collapse – auditors, analysts or debt rating agencies – did so before the penultimate moment. Yet, considerable evidence was available that should have alerted them to the pending collapse.[75] What plausible hypothesis can explain the collective failure of the gatekeepers? Two quite different, although complementary, hypotheses are available. The first is the "general deterrence" hypothesis and the second is the "bubble" hypothesis. The first is essentially economic in its premises, while the second is essentially psychological.

The deterrence explanation: the under-deterred gatekeeper

The general deterrence hypothesis focuses on the decline in the expected liability costs that faced auditors who were considering whether or not to acquiesce in aggressive accounting policies favored by managers. It postulates that, during the 1990s, the risk of auditor liability declined, while the benefits associated with acquiescence increased. As Economics 101 teaches, when both the costs go down and the benefits associated with the activity go up, the output of the activity will increase. Here, the activity that increased was auditor acquiescence.

Prior to the 1990s, auditors faced a very real risk of civil liability, principally from class action litigation.[76]

Why did the legal risks decrease during the 1990s? The obvious list of reasons includes:

1   The Supreme Court's 1991 decision in *Lampf, Pleva, Lipkind, Prupis & Petigrow* v. *Gilbertson*,[77] which significantly shortened the statute of limitations applicable to securities fraud;[78]
2   the Supreme Court's 1994 decision in *Central Bank of Denver, N.A.,* v. *First Interstate Bank of Denver*,[79] which eliminated private "aiding and abetting" liability in securities fraud cases;[80]
3   the Private Securities Litigation Reform Act of 1995 (PSLRA), which (a) raised the pleading standards for securities class actions to a level well above that applicable to fraud actions generally;[81] (b) substituted proportionate liability for "joint and several" liability;[82] (c) restricted the sweep of the RICO statute so that it could no longer convert securities fraud class actions for compensatory damages into actions for treble damages;[83] and (d) adopted a very protective safe harbor for forward-looking information;[84] and
4   the Securities Litigation Uniform Standards Act of 1998 (SLUSA), which abolished state court class actions alleging securities fraud.[85]

Although the rapid succession of these developments prevents us from calculating their individual impacts, their aggregate impact is easily susceptible to measurement. Here, the available data appears to show that the willingness of class action plaintiffs to sue secondary defendants declined during the latter half of the 1990s. Following the passage of the PSLRA in 1995, the SEC undertook a study of the legislation's apparent impact on securities litigation.[86] As its baseline, the SEC study began with the number of audit-related suits filed against the then Big Six accounting firms from 1990 to 1992.[87] For those three years, the relevant numbers were 192, 172, and 141, respectively.[88] In 1996, however, the first year following the passage of the PSLRA, the SEC found that, out of the 105 securities class actions filed in that year, accounting firms were named in only six cases, corporate counsel in zero cases, and underwriters in nineteen cases.[89] It thus concluded that "secondary defendants, such as accountants and lawyers, are being named much less frequently in securities class actions."[90]

Not only did the threat of private enforcement decline, but the prospect of public enforcement similarly subsided. In particular, there is reason to believe that, from some point in the 1980s until the late 1990s, the SEC shifted its enforcement focus away from actions against the Big Five accounting firms towards other priorities.[91] Although reasonable persons can debate whether the judicial and legislative shift towards deregulation in the 1990s was justified or excessive,[92] the collective impact of these changes was to appreciably reduce the risk of liability. Auditors were the special beneficiaries of many of these provisions. For example, the pleading rules and the new standard of proportionate liability protected them far more than it did most corporate defendants.[93] Thus, although auditors are still sued today, the settlement value of cases against auditors has significantly decreased.[94]

Correspondingly, the benefits of acquiescence to auditors rose during the 1990s as the Big Five learned how to cross-sell consulting services and to treat auditing services as a portal of entry into the lucrative client. Prior to the mid-1990s, few auditing firms provided significant consulting services to audit clients.[95] Yet, according to one recent survey, the typical large public corporation now pays its auditor for consulting services three times what it pays for auditing services.[96] Not only did auditing firms see more profit potential in consulting than in auditing, during the late 1990s, they also appeared to have begun to compete based increasingly on a strategy of "low balling," under which they offered auditing services at rates ranging from marginal to below cost.[97] The rationale for such a strategy was that the auditing function was best viewed as a loss leader through which firms could market more lucrative services.[98]

The argument that the provision of consulting services to audit clients eroded auditor independence is potentially subject to at least one important rebuttal. Those who defend the propriety of consulting services by auditors respond that the growth of such services made little real difference because the audit firm was already conflicted by the fact that the client paid fees for auditing services.[99] Put as bluntly as possible, the audit partner of a major client (such as Enron) has virtually a "one-client" practice. The partner will likely need to find employment elsewhere should he lose that client. In short, both critics and defenders of the status quo recognize that the desire to hold the client can compromise the audit partner.[100] From this premise, critics argue that a prophylactic rule prohibiting an auditing firm's involvement in consulting seemingly achieves little, because the auditor is already conflicted by the desire to receive fees.

Yet, even if this analysis is true to a degree, it overlooks the real-world difficulty faced by the client who wishes to fire its auditor. Under SEC rules, if a client fires an auditor or the auditor resigns because of a dispute over accounting principles, public disclosure is required.[101] To illustrate this point, let us suppose that a client becomes dissatisfied with an auditor who refuses to endorse the aggressive accounting policy favored by its management. Firing the auditor is an unattractive and costly step that invites potential public embarrassment and disclosure of the reasons for the auditor's dismissal or resignation, as well as potential SEC intervention. If the auditor is also a consultant to the client, however, the client can instead terminate the auditor in its role as a consultant or at least reduce its use of the firm's consulting services. This low visibility response neither requires disclosure nor invites SEC oversight, but it creates incentives for the audit firm to replace the intransigent partner. Thus, in effect, the client can bribe or coerce the auditor in its core professional role by raising or reducing its use of consulting services. As a result, the combination of auditing and consulting services within a single professional firm gives the client a disciplinary tool with which to both seduce and threaten the firm.

Of course, the argument that the client can discipline and threaten the auditor-consultant in ways that it could not discipline the simple auditor relies more on logic than actual case histories. Yet it does fit the available data. For example, a recent study by academic accounting experts based on proxy statements filed during the first half of 2001 finds that those firms that purchased more nonaudit services from their auditor (as a percentage of the total fee paid to the audit firm) were more likely to match the profile of a firm engaging in earnings management.[102]

The irrational market story

Alternatively, Enron's and Arthur Andersen's downfalls, and the host of other sudden stock declines in 2001 and 2002, can be seen as the consequence of a classic bubble that overtook the equity markets in the late 1990s and produced a market euphoria. Yet, what exactly links a market bubble with gatekeeper failure?

Arguably, the services of gatekeepers become less relevant to investors in a bubble, and they therefore experience a decline in both their leverage over their client and the value of their reputational capital. As a result, in an atmosphere of market euphoria, because investors generally rely less on gatekeepers, managers, in turn, regard them as more of a formality than a necessity.

While this hypothesis may be impossible to rigorously prove, it nonetheless seems consistent with modern behavioral economics. Gatekeepers provide a critical service only when investors are cautious and skeptical and therefore rely on the gatekeeper's services. Conversely, in a market bubble, investors largely abandon caution and skepticism. In such an environment, companies continue to use auditors because the SEC rules mandate it, or because no individual firm wants the notoriety of being the first to dispense with them, rather than because investors demand their use. As a result, gatekeepers have less relevance and, consequently, reduced leverage with their clients. Accordingly, if we assume that euphoric investors will largely ignore the auditor, the rational gatekeeper's best competitive strategy, at least for the short term, is to become as acquiescent and low cost as possible. Although this thesis assigns some causal responsibility to investors for their own losses, it does not absolve gatekeepers of responsibility. Even if shareholders care little about the auditor's reputation, it is still possible for an auditor to intervene effectively and prevent fraud by refusing to certify the issuer's financial statements, by withdrawing its certificate on a later discovery of the fraud, or by notifying the SEC.[103]

The key element in the foregoing explanation involves the reason that investors ceased to care about the gatekeeper's reputation. After all, the auditing profession arose out of investors' own concerns about fraud and irregularity, not because of regulatory requirements.[104] What then caused this concern to weaken? Modern behavioral economics supplies a plausible answer as it recognizes that individuals, including investors, have "bounded rationality" and do not pursue all information relevant to an optimal decision.[105] In particular, the Nobel Prize-winning research of Professors Daniel Kahneman and Amos Tversky has demonstrated that individuals typically make decisions by using heuristics – that is, rules of thumb – rather than by incorporating and processing all obtainable information.[106] Professors Kahneman and Tversky found that individuals pervasively use one

such rule of thumb – the "availability heuristic"[107] – that has special relevance to the context of securities markets. The availability heuristic asserts that individuals estimate the frequency of an event by recalling recent instances of its occurring, even if, when viewed from a longer-term perspective, these instances are normally rare or infrequent.[108] Hence, if the stock market has recently experienced extraordinary returns, it becomes predictable that individuals will overestimate the likelihood that such extraordinary gains will continue.[109] In effect, there is a status quo or persistence bias; investors expect what has recently occurred to continue. As a result, when the market soared in the early and mid-1990s, investors, operating on heuristics, came to assume that this pattern would continue.[110]

Thus, from the perspective of behavioral economics, bubbles are not irrational moments of speculative excess or frenzy, but rather the product of the predictable expectations of individuals who tend to assume that whatever has recently occurred will persist. To trigger this persistence bias, it is arguably only necessary that market returns have in fact been extraordinary for a few successive years, possibly because of real economic growth. This bias then causes investors to treat the market phenomenon as normal and likely to continue. Such an explanation also helps us understand why bubbles have reoccurred throughout history. To explain bubbles, one need not posit that investors are inherently gullible, but only that investors suffer from normal heuristic biases, which are created by a period of extraordinary market returns and which cause investors to expect such returns to continue.

Such heuristic biases are not, of course, the whole story. For the securities analyst, a market bubble presents a different and more serious challenge. During such times, those who recklessly predict extraordinary returns will outperform those who are cautious and prudent. Hence, in a bubble, extreme optimism for analysts becomes less of a heuristic bias than a competitive necessity. Put bluntly, it is dangerous to be sane in an insane world. As a result, the securities analyst who prudently predicted reasonable growth and stock appreciation during the 1990s was increasingly left in the dust by the investment guru who prophesized a new investment paradigm in which revenues and costs were less important than the number of "hits" on a website.

Institutional factors compounded this problem. As the IPO market soared in the 1990s, securities analysts became celebrities and valuable assets to their firms.[111] Indeed, securities analysts became the principal means by which investment banks competed for IPO clients, as the underwriter with the "star" analyst could produce the greatest first day stock price spike in an IPO.[112] As the salaries of such analysts soared, their compensation came increasingly from the investment banking side of their firms. Hence, just as in the case of the auditor, the analyst's economic position became progressively more dependent on favoring the interests of persons outside their profession – consultants in the case of the auditor and investment bankers in the case of the analyst – who had little reason to respect or observe the gatekeeper's professional standards or culture.[113]

Ultimately, as auditors increasingly sought consulting income and as analysts became more dependent on an investment banking subsidy, their common desire to preserve their reputational capital for the long run became subordinated to their wish to obtain extraordinary returns in the short run at the risk of that reputational capital. The value of gatekeepers' reputational capital may have also declined during the bubble as investors rationally reduced their reliance on gatekeeping services because of their biased assumption that extraordinary returns would persist. Under either hypothesis or both, it may often have become profitable for firms to risk their reputational capital by trading on it in the short-run, rather than by preserving it for the long-run. Indeed, during the 1990s, to the extent that the auditing function became a loss leader for multi-service accounting firms eager to sell more lucrative consulting services and to the extent that investment banking firms began to subsidize securities analysts, each profession became less self-supporting and more dependent on those who could profit from the liquidation of their reputational capital.

Allocating responsibility among gatekeepers, managers and investors

The foregoing explanations still fail to explain fully the mechanisms by which the gatekeepers sacrificed or liquidated their reputational capital, built up over decades, once the legal risks of doing so declined or a bubble developed. Here, an allocation of responsibility must be made among the various participants in corporate governance: managers, gatekeepers, and investors.

The role of managers

The pressure on gatekeepers to acquiesce in earnings management was not constant over time, but rather accelerated during the 1990s as managerial incentives changed. As noted earlier, executive compensation shifted during the 1990s from being primarily cash-based to primarily equity-based.[114] The clearest measure of this change is the growth in stock options. Over the last decade, stock options rose from 5 percent of shares outstanding at major U.S. companies to 15 percent, a 300 percent increase.[115] The value of these options rose for the 2000 largest corporations by an even greater percentage, and over a dramatically shorter period: from $50 billion in 1997 to $162 billion in 2000, an over 300 percent rise in three years.[116]

Such stock options created an obvious and potentially perverse incentive for managers to engage in short-term, rather than long-term, stock price maximization because executives can exercise their stock options and sell the underlying shares on the same day.[117] This ability was itself the product of deregulatory reform in the early 1990s, which relaxed the rules under 16(b) of the Securities Exchange Act of 1934 to permit officers and directors to exercise stock options and sell the underlying shares without holding the shares for the previously required six month period.[118] Thus, if executives inflated the stock price of their company through premature revenue recognition or other classic earnings management techniques, they could quickly bail out in the short-term by exercising their options and selling. Shareholders were left to bear the cost when the inflated stock could not maintain its price over subsequent periods. Given these incentives, it became rational for corporate executives to use lucrative consulting contracts, or other positive and negative incentives, to induce gatekeepers to engage in conduct that assisted their short-term market manipulations. As a result, the shift to stock options as the principal means of executive compensation, plus the removal of the legal impediment to exercising and selling them simultaneously, placed gatekeepers under greater pressure to acquiesce in short-term oriented financial and accounting strategies.

The role of investors

Investors cannot fairly be presented as entirely innocent victims in the recent epidemic of financial irregularities. During a bubble, investors may ignore, or at least overly discount, gatekeepers' conflicts of interest that might alarm investors in other circumstances. To be sure, biased analyst research and overstated earnings likely misled many investors, but investors also cheered on analysts who made the most optimistic predictions and disdained those who were more cautious. Even institutional investors, who own nearly 50 percent of the equity securities listed on the New York Stock Exchange and account for approximately 75 percent of its daily trading volume,[119] overlooked or recklessly ignored abundant evidence that should have alerted them. According to one estimate, at the peak of the market bubble large institutional investors held 60 percent of Enron stock.[120] Why didn't they see that Enron was overvalued, particularly once alarm bells began to sound? The most plausible explanation for the failure of institutional investors to respond to such signals begins with the premise that professional money managers are rationally motivated by the desire to perform no worse than their major institutional rivals. This pressure quickly leads to herding behavior.[121] According to this analysis, fund managers attract investor funds and maximize their fees based on their "quarterly reported performance relative to comparable funds or indices."[122]

To illustrate, suppose that a hypothetical fund manager suspects that Enron is overvalued. What should this manager do? If the manager sells the fund's investment in Enron, the manager and the manager's clients may do well, but only if the market agrees and Enron's stock price falls that quarter. Conversely, if the market persists in overvaluing Enron or actually climbs based on biased sell-side research, the fund manager becomes an unfortunately premature prophet and the manager's performance falls relative to rival managers. Hence, clients' funds flow out of the manager's account and into the accounts of rival fund; the funds managed by our hypothetical manager contract like an accordion. As a result, this manager may not profit significantly even when Enron ultimately does fail.

In such an environment, there is little incentive to be ahead of the crowd and considerable incentive to ride the bubble to its top in order not to underperform rival investment managers with a similar strategy. The result is a phenomenon known as "herding,"[123] because, by following the herd, the fund manager will not underperform most of his rivals. Put differently, it

is far worse to be individually wrong than collectively wrong. The fund manager can survive mistakes that others also make, as he can claim that the error was undetectable (i.e. "Who knew? Enron fooled us all!"). But the manager may suffer immense injury when he makes correct decisions that the market only belatedly recognizes. In turn, this may explain why institutions followed sell-side research that they knew to be biased during the bubble. Anticipating that others would follow it also, institutional investors took the safe course and followed the herd.[124]

The role of gatekeepers

This conclusion that even sophisticated investors will follow and rely on sell-side research that they know to be biased brings us back to the central role of gatekeepers. Up to a point, investors will follow gatekeepers' advice even when they do not trust it because they expect that such advice will influence the market. When the advice can no longer move the market, however, the bubble bursts. Earlier this article argued that gatekeepers performed poorly in the 1990s, at least in the case of auditors and analysts, because they faced a reduced legal threat and because they could increase their benefits by acquiescing in managerial misbehavior. But there are further nuances regarding the absence of competition and the principal–agent relationship that also contributed to this story.

The absence of competition

The Big Five (now Big Four) accounting firms obviously dominated a very concentrated market for auditing services.[125] As a result, smaller competitors could not expect to develop the international scale or marketable brand names that the Big Four possessed simply by quoting a cheaper price. Thus, high barriers chilled entry into this market. More importantly, in a market this concentrated, implicit collusion easily develops. For example, each of the Big Four could in parallel develop and follow a common competitive strategy without fear of being undercut by a major competitor. Under such conditions, it would be rational for each of the Big Four firms to pursue a strategy under which it acquiesced to clients' preferences for risky accounting policies in order to obtain more lucrative consulting revenues. The cost of such a strategy would be an occasional litigation loss and some public humiliation, but this cost would be acceptable so long as all of the Big Four firms behaved similarly. The costs of such a policy would become prohibitive, however, if the firm was so humiliated that it stood out in contrast to a rival firm intent on marketing its high integrity.

Indeed, in a very concentrated market, collusion in any form is not a necessary element in this explanation. Rather, in such a market, it becomes more likely that every firm will incur some scandals and will bear some litigation scars from highly public frauds and insolvencies. The only necessary assumption is that of high information costs: namely, that investors will find it difficult to distinguish among these firms, once all have been implicated in some scandals. In a less concentrated market, some dissident firm would predictably market itself as distinctive for its integrity. In a market of just four firms, however, this is much less likely.

Principal–agent problems

Auditing firms have always known that a large client could dominate an individual partner in a manner that might inflict liability on the firm. Thus, auditing firms were quick to develop internal monitoring systems that were far more elaborate than anything that law firms have yet attempted. Yet, within the auditing firm, this internal monitoring function is not all-powerful, because, in large part, this function is not itself a profit center. Once firms added consulting services as a major profit center, however, a natural coalition developed between the individual audit partner and the consulting divisions; each had a common interest in overruling the firm's internal monitoring division when its prudential decisions would prove costly to them. Finally, as the expected risk of liability fell during the 1990s, the influence of the internal monitoring staff logically declined correspondingly.

Cementing the marriage between the audit partner and the consulting division was the use of incentive fees. For example, if the internal division providing software consulting services for an accounting firm offered the principal audit partner an incentive fee of one percent of any contract sold to the partner's audit client, the audit partner would have an enhanced reason to acquiesce in risky accounting policies. Under the software consulting contract, the audit partner might receive as much or more compensation from incentive fees for cross-selling as from auditing fees, and thus the partner would have even more reason to value his client's satisfaction above his interest in the firm's reputational capital. More importantly, the audit partner also acquires an ally in the consultants, who similarly would want to ensure that they satisfied their mutual client. Together, the audit partner and the consultants would form a coalition that was potentially able to override the protests of their firm's internal monitoring unit. While case histories matching this exact pattern have not yet come to light, abundant evidence suggests that incentive fees can bias audit decision-making.[126] Interestingly, Enron itself presents a fact pattern in which the audit firm's on-the-scene quality control officer was overruled and replaced.[127]

IMPLICATIONS: EVALUATING CONGRESS'S RESPONSE

This chapter has presented a variety of explanations for the corporate governance failures of 2001 and 2002: (1) uncontrolled equity compensation that motivated executives to manipulate the market; (2) inadequate deterrence of gatekeepers; and (3) a broader phenomenon of a market bubble that implicates investors as well as gatekeepers. Which of the foregoing theories is most persuasive? Does it matter? Although they are complementary rather than contradictory, their relative plausibility bears on what reforms are most necessary or desirable. For example, the more one accepts the deterrence explanation, the more one might favor legislative changes aimed at restoring an adequate legal threat. In principle, these changes could either raise the costs or lower the benefits of acquiescence to auditors. Alternatively, to the extent one accepts the bubble hypothesis, the problem may be self-correcting; once the bubble bursts, gatekeepers may come back into fashion, as investors become skeptics and once again demand assurances that only credible reputational intermediaries can provide.[128] Of course, not all gatekeepers are alike. Thus, it may be that the deterrence solution works better for auditors, while analysts would benefit more from structural reforms aimed at increasing their independence.[129]

Viewed historically, the Enron crisis is only one of several modern accounting crises, extending from the Penn Central crisis in the 1970s to the S&L crisis in the 1980s.[130] The distinctive difference between the Enron crisis and the crises of the 1970s and the 1980s, however, is that in those eras only insolvency threatened management with ouster.[131] Thus, management in those earlier crises had a strong incentive to "cook the books" only as their corporation approached insolvency. Today, as the mechanisms of corporate accountability – takeovers, control contests, institutional activism, and more aggressive boards – have shortened management's margin for error, the incentive to engage in earnings management and accounting irregularities is much greater. Although the increasingly competitive business environment makes management's survival less certain, the instant wealth promised by stock options also gives rise to an incentive to cheat, even when management's survival is not in question. Together, the fear of ouster and the temptation of instant wealth increase the likelihood of fraud.

Congress's response: the Sarbanes–Oxley Act

Passed almost without dissent, the Public Company Accounting Reform and Investor Protection Act of 2002, popularly known as the Sarbanes–Oxley Act, essentially addresses the problem of accounting irregularities by shifting control of the auditing profession from the profession itself to a new body, the Public Company Accounting Oversight Board (the Board).[132] Conceptually, this is a familiar approach, as the Board's authority largely parallels that of the National Association of Securities Dealers (NASD) over securities brokers and dealers.[133] What is new, however, is that the Act explicitly recognizes the significance of conflicts of interest, as it bars auditors from providing a number of categories of professional services to their audit clients and authorizes the Board to prohibit additional categories of services if necessary.[134] Thus, to the extent that conflicts of interest compromised auditors, the Act responds with an appropriate answer.

There is less reason for optimism, however, if accounting irregularities stem from a lack of general deterrence or the increased incentive of corporate executives to "cook the books" to maximize the value of their stock options. The Act simply fails to address these problems. For example, the Act neither revises the PSLRA (except in a minor way),[135] nor does it

make gatekeepers who knowingly aided and abetted a securities fraud liable to investors in private litigation. Finally, the Act never addresses stock options or executive compensation, except to the extent that it may require the forfeiture of such compensation to the corporation if the corporation later restates its earnings.[136] In short, while the potential benefits from acquiescing in accounting irregularities appear to have been reduced for auditors, the expected costs to gatekeepers from accounting irregularities seemingly remains low because the level of deterrence that they once faced has not been restored.[137]

This same critique applies with even greater force to the recent efforts of the NYSE and Nasdaq to reform their listing standards. After much study, both bodies have proposed new independence standards that will require listed companies to have both majority independent boards and entirely independent audit, nominating, and compensation committees, and to utilize a tighter definition of independence.[138] Although such reforms and heightened independence requirements seem desirable, it does not appear that they would have affected the boards of Enron or WorldCom.[139] Nor does enhanced independence for board members sound like the most appropriate response if the deeper problem, as this chapter has suggested, is gatekeeper failure.

Thus, from this chapter's perspective, a relevant public policy agenda should address three goals that Sarbanes–Oxley failed to address: (1) increasing the legal threat to deter sufficiently gatekeeper acquiescence in managerial fraud; (2) reducing the perverse incentives created by the unconstrained use of stock options; and (3) addressing the structural conflicts that cause herding, analyst bias, and an excessive market bias towards optimism.

The unused lever: shareholder power

Initially, let us assume that the most difficult issue left by Sarbanes-Oxley involves the misaligned incentives of managers, caused by the sudden shift in the form of executive compensation during the 1990s. This is a fair premise because other problems, such as the need for greater deterrence, can be addressed by any of several means. For example, Congress could restore private aiding and abetting liability, thereby overruling Central Bank of Denver,[140] and increasing the expected costs to gatekeepers of acquiescence in financial irregularity. Such a reform may be unlikely in the current political environment, but it poses no conceptual problem.

In contrast, reforming executive compensation poses a more serious conceptual challenge. Why? The short answer is that neither Congress nor the SEC can legislate or formulate optimal executive compensation rules for all publicly held companies. One size simply does not fit all. What works for a dot-com company does not work for a public utility, and vice versa. Who then could propose and implement more specific reforms? One answer is the board of directors. Yet one has to be an extreme optimist to expect activism from boards on this issue. Boards are populated by fellow CEOs, who are not likely to be excited about restricting executive compensation or their own liquidity.

Thus, the more practical answer is to encourage institutional investors to address this problem. In 2003 shareholders placed a record number of proposals on corporate proxy statements for a shareholder vote at corporations' annual meetings.[141] The majority of these proposals dealt with executive compensation.[142] These propositions, however, are generally only precatory and can be ignored by managers.[143] Missing, therefore, is some next step that shareholders can take when a proposal receives majority support at the annual shareholder meeting and yet management ignores it. In theory, shareholders could commence a proxy contest, but the costs are prohibitive and the problems of shareholder collective action are considerable.[144]

What else could be done? Institutional shareholders have a preferred answer: they want to be able to nominate one or more minority directors on the corporation's own proxy statement in order to economize on the costs of shareholder activism. The SEC has begun to study this proposal,[145] but the business community is actively organizing against it.[146] Its central attraction is that it gives shareholders a next step, without threatening a full scale control contest, if management ignores their proxy proposal. If adopted, its real impact would not be a spate of minority directors suddenly elected to boards, but rather a significant number of negotiations between institutional shareholders and corporate managers over specific executive compensation issues. In effect, enhanced shareholder rights to nominate board members may be the procedural solution to the substantive problem of reforming executive compensation.

Curbing excessive optimism

Earlier, this chapter noted that serious principal–agent problems compromise the effectiveness of fund managers.[147] Therefore, if stock prices tend to be systematically inflated by biased research and if fund managers are reluctant to combat such inflation, a different champion must be found to bring the market back into equilibrium. In an unregulated market, that natural champion would be the short seller. Under US securities laws, however, the short seller is disfavored and heavily regulated.[148] Relaxing these regulations, while not politically popular, would be one way of creating a countervailing force to those that inflate stock prices. Ironically, in this particular regard, deregulation – that is, deregulation of the short seller – might be a legitimate response to Enron.[149]

CONCLUSION

This chapter has reviewed several different explanations for the surge in financial irregularities in the late 1990s. Chief among these are

1   The Gatekeeper Explanation. Professional "reputational intermediaries" faced less legal risk and had more reason to defer to their clients as the 1990s wore on. This combination of increased market incentives and legal deregulation may explain why auditors acquiesced and analysts became more biased, but it cannot stand alone as a comprehensive explanation. One still needs some further explanation of why managers and underwriters became more interested in bribing their gatekeepers than they were in the past.

2   The Executive Compensation Explanation. As executive compensation changed during the 1990s, it increased the incentive for managers to inflate earnings, even if the resulting stock prices were not sustainable, because management could bail out ahead of their shareholders. This explanation accounts for the increased incentive on the part of managers to induce gatekeepers to acquiesce in aggressive accounting. In particular, the fact that the plurality of financial statement restatements in the late 1990s involved revenue recognition issues supports this explanation.[150] Still, it must be stressed that the real problem here

is not equity compensation, or even excessive compensation, but rather excessive liquidity that allows managers to bail out at will. Only firm-specific answers, such as holding periods and retention ratios, seem likely to work effectively to solve this problem.

3   The Herding and Investor Bias Explanations. These explanations can help account for the market myopia underlying a bubble, but they lack quantitative support. Although it can be asserted that individual investors expect extraordinary returns to persist, this hypothesis is less credible when applied to institutions. Still, fund managers have their own reasons to herd and persist in buying stocks they consider overvalued. Ultimately, they fear being individually wrong much more than being collectively wrong, and this bias inclined them to "ride the bubble." As a result, the market did not respond to available evidence of overvaluation.

If weight is accorded to any of these explanations, then it becomes clear that the Sarbanes–Oxley Act, while useful, still addresses only one aspect of the first explanation for gatekeeper failure by curbing the ability of managers to seduce auditors with consulting income. A more relevant public policy agenda should also: (1) increase the legal threat to deter acquiescence in managerial fraud; (2) reduce the perverse incentives created by the unconstrained use of stock options; and (3) address the structural conflicts that cause herding, analyst bias, and an excessive market bias towards optimism. As discussed, enhanced shareholder rights to nominate board members may be the best procedural solution to the substantive problem of reforming executive compensation. Furthermore, deregulation of the short seller may be the most direct means to combat stock price inflation. Currently, however, these issues have gone unaddressed. Thus, to conclude, one can only paraphrase George Santayana: those who ignore conflicts of interest are destined to repeat history, cycle after cycle.[151]

NOTES

1   See William H. Widen, Enron at the Margin, 58 *Bus. Law.* 961, 962–63 (2003) ("The problem is that corporate and legal culture has lost all sense of right and wrong."). I hope that Professor Widen has overstated the matter, but I cannot prove him wrong.

2   Federal Reserve Chairman Alan Greenspan coined this colorful phrase, observing that: "'An infectious greed seemed to grip much of our business community.'" See Floyd Norris, Yes, He Can Top That, N.Y. Times, July 17, 2002, at A1.

3   Although some boards certainly did fail, this explanation again seems intellectually unsatisfactory. Admittedly, a special committee of Enron's own board has concluded that the Enron board failed to monitor adequately officers or conflicts of interest. See William C. Powers, Jr. *et al.*, Report of Investigation by the Special Investigative Committee of the Board of Directors of Enron Corp. 148–77 (2002), 2002 WL 198018. A Senate subcommittee has similarly assigned the principal blame to the Enron board. See Permanent Subcommittee on Investigations of Committee on Governmental Affairs, United States Senate, The Role of the Board of Directors in Enron's Collapse, S. Rep. No. 107-70, at 59 (2002). Nonetheless, such studies beg the larger question: Why did these boards fail now and not earlier?

4   See Larry E. Ribstein, Bubble Laws, 40 *Hous. L. Rev.* 77, 77–78 (2003) (blaming recent scandals on the latest turn in a "centuries-old cycle of capital market booms followed by busts and regulation").

5   Revealingly, the stock market bubble of the late 1990s burst in two stages, first in 2001 with the demise of the internet related stocks (the "dot-com" bubble) and then again in the late spring of 2002 as WorldCom and other crises further shook market confidence. The S&P 500 index fell 31 percent between the beginning of 2002 and July 23, 2002. See E.S. Browning, Nasdaq Stocks Sustain Biggest Loss of Year, *Wall St. Journal*, July 24, 2002, at C1. The Dow Jones Average similarly hit its low for the period January 1, 1998 to January 1, 2003, on October 9, 2002, when it closed at 7286.27. See E.S. Browning, Bears Claw Markets Yet Again, as Dow Industrials Fall Nearly 3 percent, Wall St. Journal, Oct. 10, 2002, at A1 (noting that 7286.27 was the Dow Jones's lowest finish since October 27, 1997). This low point was after the passage of the Sarbanes– Oxley Act in late July of 2002, suggesting that law alone did not return investor confidence.

6   Professor Stuart Banner has argued that, over the last 300 years, most major instances of legislation regulating the securities markets have followed a sustained price collapse on the securities market. See Stuart Banner, What Causes New Securities Regulation? 300 Years of Evidence, 75 *Wash. U. L.Q.* 849, 850 (1997).

7   See Sarbanes–Oxley Act of 2002, Pub. L. No. 107-204, 116 Stat. 745 (stating that this is "[an act to] protect investors by improving the accuracy and reliability of

corporate disclosures made pursuant to the securities laws, and for other purposes").

8 See for example, William J. Baumol, Business Behavior, Value and Growth (2d ed. Harcourt, Brace & World, Inc. 1967) (discussing oligopoly theory and the theory of economic development); Robin Marris, The Economic Theory of 'Managerial' Capitalism (1967) (discussing managerial capitalism and proposing an internal theory of the firm); see also Oliver E. Williamson, Managerial Discretion and Business Behavior, 53 *Am. Econ. Rev.* 1032, 1055 (1963) (suggesting that either corporations are operated according to a managerial, utility-maximizing model "or, if 'actual' profits are maximized, that reported profits are reduced by absorbing some fraction of actual profits in executive salaries and [a variety of perquisites]").

9 See Baumol, 8, *passim*; Marris, note 8, *passim*.

10 See Williamson, note 8, at 1055.

11 See Yakov Amihud & Baruch Lev, Risk Reduction as a Managerial Motive for Conglomerate Mergers, 12 *Bell J. Econ.* 605, 605–06 (1981); Alan J. Marcus, Risk Sharing and the Theory of the Firm, 13 Bell J. Econ. 369, 370 (1982); see also John C. Coffee, Jr., Shareholders Versus Managers: The Strain in the Corporate Web, 85 *Mich. L. Rev.* 1, 28–31 (1986) (providing an overview of the managerialist model of the firm).

12 See Oliver E. Williamson, Markets and Hierarchies: Analysis and Antitrust Implications 158–59 (1975); Oliver E. Williamson, The Modern Corporation: Origins, Evolution, Attributes, 19 *J. Econ. Literature* 1537, 1557–58 (1981) [hereinafter Williamson, The Modern Corporation].

13 See for example, Williamson, The Modern Corporation, note 12, at 1559 (noting the "evident disparity of interest between managers and stockholders").

14 The Congressional Research Service identified the year 1983 as the first occasion on which "junk bonds" were used to finance hostile takeovers. See Congressional Research Service, 99th Cong., The Role of High Yield Bonds [Junk Bonds] in Capital Markets and Corporate Takeovers: Public Policy Implications 23 (Comm. Print 1985).

15 See Coffee, note 11, at 2–7 (arguing that the characteristic pattern of takeovers began to shift in the early 1980s from synergistic acquisitions to bust-up takeovers); John C. Coffee, Jr., The Uncertain Case for Takeover Reform: An Essay on Stockholders, Stakeholders and Bust-Ups, 1988 *Wis. L. Rev.* 435, 444.

16 See Amy L. Goodman, The Fuss Over Executive Compensation, 6 Insights No. 1, at 2 (Jan. 1992) (noting that a survey of institutional investors conducted at the 1991 United Shareholder Association Conference revealed that such investors wanted executive compensation to be performance-based and to reflect management's accountability for company performance).

17 Concerned that target company executives were receiving unjustified "windfall" compensation in connection with "golden parachute" arrangements, Congress enacted the Deficit Reduction Act of 1984, which added 280G and 4999 to the Internal Revenue Code. See Deficit Reduction Act of 1984, Pub. L. No. 98-369, 98 Stat. 494 (codified as amended at 26 U.S.C. 280G, 4999 (2000)) (providing that the corporation could not take a deduction for any "excess parachute payment," 26 U.S.C. 280G(a), and levying a 20 percent nondeductible excise tax on any executive who received such a payment, ibid. 4999(a)). Parachute payments consisted of compensation contingent on a change in corporate control, and "excess" payments subject to disfavorable tax treatment were those that exceeded three times the executive's average taxable compensation from the corporation over the past five years. See ibid. 280G(b). Hence, if the corporation paid the executive an average compensation of $600,000 over that period, any payment in excess of $1,800,000, which was contingent on a change in control, would be subject to this special excise tax. For a more detailed explanation of the mechanics of this tax, see Bruce A. Wolk, The Golden Parachute Provisions: Time for Repeal?, 21 *Va. Tax Rev.* 125, 129–134 (2001).

18 See 26 U.S.C. 162(m). Two exceptions to this prophylactic rule are: (1) commissions, such as those from sales that are paid for income generated by the individual, and (2) performance-based compensation based on performance goals established by outside directors and approved by a majority of the shareholders. See ibid. 162(m)(4)(B)–(C). Stock options fall within the second exemption. See James R. Repetti, The Misuse of Tax Incentives to Align Management-Shareholder Interests, 19 *Cardozo L. Rev.* 697, 708 (1997). The effect of this provision was not to impose an absolute ceiling, because some firms decided to forego deductions in order to pay higher compensation to their executives. See Joann S. Lublin, Firms Forfeit Tax Break to Pay Top Brass $1 Million-Plus, *Wall St. J.*, Apr. 21, 1994, at B1.

19 See generally Robert Dean Ellis, Equity Derivatives, Executive Compensation, and Agency Costs, 35 *Hous. L. Rev.* 399 (1988) (investigating the consequences of the use of equity derivatives in pay-for-performance arrangements).

20 See Daniel Altman, How to Tie Pay to Goals, Instead of the Stock Price, N.Y. Times, Sept. 8, 2002, 3 (Business), at 4 (citing data collected by Harvard Business School Professor Brian J. Hall). Professor Hall in fact finds that the median equity-based compensation of top U.S.

executes at S&P 500 industrial companies rose from 0 percent in 1984 to 8 percent in 1990, and to 66 percent in 2001. See Brian J. Hall, Six Challenges in Designing Equity-Based Pay, 15 Accenture *J. Applied Corp. Fin.* 21, 23 (2003).

21 See Tod Perry & Marc Zenner, CEO Compensation in the 1990s: Shareholder Alignment or Shareholder Expropriation?, 35 *Wake Forest L. Rev.* 123, 145 (2000).

22 See 15 U.S.C. 78p(b) (1988).

23 See ibid.

24 See Ownership Reports and Trading by Officers, Directors and Principal Security Holders, Exchange Act Release No. 34-28869, 56 Fed. Reg. 7242 (Feb. 21, 1991) [hereinafter Ownership Reports] (codified at 17 C.F.R pts. 229, 240, 249, 270, 274) (adopting revised Rule 16b-3(d)(3), which permits an officer or director to combine the two holding periods).

25 See Arthur Levitt, The "Numbers Game," Remarks at the NYU Center for Law and Business (Sept. 28, 1998), http://www.sec.gov/news/speech/speecharchive/1998/spch220.txt (noting that "the problem of earnings management is not new").

26 See ibid. (discussing management's "zeal to . . . project a smooth earnings path").

27 See ibid. (suggesting that "companies try to meet or beat Wall Street earnings projections in order to grow market capitalization and increase the value of stock options").

28 The best evidence of this shift is that the leading cause of financial statement restatements in the late 1990s was revenue recognition errors. The General Accounting Office (GAO) has found that 39 percent (by far the largest category) of the financial restatements between 1997 and 2002 were the consequence of revenue recognition errors. See U.S. Gen. Accounting Office, Pub. No. 03-138, Financial Statement Restatements: Trends, Market Impacts, Regulatory Responses, and Remaining Challenges 5 (2002), available at http://www.gao.gov/new.items/d0.pdf [hereinafter GAO Report]. For a brief review of recent accounting scandals, which have been numerous, see Lawrence A. Cunningham, Sharing Accounting's Burden: Business Lawyers in Enron's Dark Shadow, 57 *Bus. Law.* 1421, 1423–30 (2002).

29 A 2001 article in the Wall Street Journal estimated that more than half of all accounting lawsuits involved "premature revenue recognition." See Holman W. Jenkins, Jr., Accounting For When Dreams Become Reality, *Wall St. J.*, June 13, 2001, at A21. Other experts, including both scholars and practitioners, have identified premature revenue recognition as one of the most common accounting frauds and have attributed its new prevalence to the widespread use of equity compensation. See Daniel V. Dooley, Financial

Fraud: Accounting Theory and Practice, 8 *Fordham J. Corp. & Fin. L.* 53, 58–59, 63–66 (2002); Manning G. Warren III, Revenue Recognition and Corporate Counsel, 56 *S.M.U. L. Rev.* 885 (2003). In late 1999, the SEC issued Staff Accounting Bulletin No. 101, 64 Fed. Reg. 68,936 (Dec. 9, 1999) (codified at 17 C.F.R. pt. 211), which attempted to control some of the more recent abuses of revenue recognition.

30 For the suggestion that management became obsessed with maximizing earnings in the 1990s, see Jeffrey N. Gordon, What Enron Means for the Management and Control of the Modern Business Corporation: Some Initial Reflections, 69 *U. Chi. L. Rev.* 1233, 1244–47 (2002) (noting the "obvious" temptations where relatively small changes in earnings have significant impact on the stock price, particularly where management receives a portion of its compensation through stock options).

31 On January 1, 1995, the Dow Jones Average stood at 3,838.48, up only modestly from the 3,756.60 figure at which it stood on January 1, 1994. See http://djindexes.com/downloads/xlspages/DJIA Hist Perf.xls (on file with Cornell Law Review). During 1995, it rose 33.45 percent, and by January 1, 2002, it had reached 10,073.40, peaking on March 19, 2002 at an all-time high of 10,635.25. See ibid. It fell that year to a low of 7,286.27 on October 9, 2002 and closed at 8,341.63, for a net decline in 2002, the year of Enron's bankruptcy, of 16.76 percent. See ibid.

32 For a review of recent accounting scandals, see Cunningham, note 28, at 1423–30.

33 The S&L crisis led directly to the Financial Institutions Reform, Recovery, and Enforcement Act of 1989 (FIRREA), Pub. L. No. 101-73, 103 Stat. 183 (1989), which imposes high fiduciary standards on directors of thrift and savings and loan institutions. See ibid. 901–920, 103 Stat. at 446–88. FIRREA also created a new regulatory body: the Resolution Funding Corporation. See ibid. 511, 103 Stat. at 394–406.

34 Although one could argue that a decline in ethics occurred, at least within the S&L industry, during the 1980s, economic misincentives better explain that scandal, the accounting irregularities scandals of the 1990s, the securities analyst crisis of 2002, and the current controversy involving mutual funds. Indeed, commentators have so overused the concept of ethical decline that it has lost much of its meaning and now seems merely a post hoc rationalization.

35 The term gatekeeper is not simply an academic concept. For example, the SEC recently noted that "the federal securities laws . . . make independent auditors 'gatekeepers' to the public securities markets." See Revision of the Commission's Auditor Independence Requirements, Exchange Act Release No. 33-7870, 65 Fed. Reg. 43,148, 43,150 (July 12, 2000) (codified at 17 C.F.R pts. 210, 240).

36 For a fuller, more theoretical consideration of the concept of the gatekeeper, see generally Stephen Choi, Market Lessons for Gatekeepers, 92 *Nw. U. L. Rev.* 916 (1998) (discussing the function of intermediary gatekeepers in different markets and how market failures lead to a decline in gatekeepers); Reinier H. Kraakman, Corporate Liability Strategies and the Costs of Legal Controls, 93 *Yale L.J.* 857 (1984) (discussing liability rules as a means to induce corporate participants to control corporate wrongdoing); Reinier H. Kraakman, Gatekeepers: The Anatomy of a Third-Party Enforcement Strategy, 2 *J.L. Econ. & Org.* 53 (1986) (examining liability imposed on private party gatekeepers who "disrupt misconduct by withholding their cooperation from wrongdoers").

37 Today, in most public, underwritten offerings of securities, issuer's counsel delivers an opinion to the underwriters – typically called a "negative assurance" opinion – stating that it is not aware of any material information required to be disclosed that has not been disclosed. See Richard R. Howe, The Duties and Liabilities of Attorneys in Rendering Legal Opinions, 1989 *Colum. Bus. L. Rev.* 283, 287. Such opinions are not truly legal opinions in that they do not truly state any legal conclusion, but rather pledge the lawyer's reputational capital to assure the underwriters that adverse material information is not being hidden by the issuer. In this sense, the lawyer functions as a gatekeeper, pledging his reputational capital and accepting the risk of liability if he has recklessly misstated. See also John C. Coffee, Jr., The Attorney as Gatekeeper: An Agenda for the SEC, 103 *Colum. L. Rev.* 1293, 1313 (2003) (discussing "negative assurance" opinions).

38 This observation hardly originated with this author. See for example, Robert A. Prentice, The Case of the Irrational Auditor: A Behavioral Insight into Securities Fraud Litigation, 95 *Nw. U. L. Rev.* 133 (2000) (applying a behavioral analysis to securities fraud and challenging traditional rational actor assumptions).

39 See Michelle Mittelstadt, Andersen Indicted in Enron Case, Dallas Morning News, Mar. 15, 2002, at 1A.

40 901 F.2d 624 (7th Cir. 1990).

41 Ibid. at 629; see also Melder v. Morris, 27 F.3d 1097, 1103 (5th Cir. 1994) (concluding that the plaintiffs failed to allege sufficient motive for an accounting firm to engage in securities fraud and stating that earning two years' fees from one client would not establish such motivation); *Robin* v. *Arthur Young & Co.*, 915 F.2d 1120, 1127 (7th Cir. 1990) (finding that a mere $90,000 annual audit fee would have been an irrational motive to commit fraud).

42 See for example, Robin, 915 F.2d at 1127 (involving $90,000 in annual audit fees).

43 Arthur Andersen's total revenues for its fiscal year ended August 31, 2001 were $9.3 billion. See Melissa Klein, Guilty Verdict Draws Mixed Reactions: Profession Mulls Post-Andersen Future, Accounting Today, July 8, 2002, at 1. In a February 6, 2001 email to David Duncan, the principal Enron audit partner for Arthur Andersen, from Michael Jones, another Arthur Andersen partner in Houston, the latter notes that the Enron audit team at Arthur Andersen believes "that it would not be unforeseeable that fees could reach a $100 million per year amount considering the multidisciplinary services being provided" by Andersen to Enron (copy on file with Cornell Law Review). Even on this basis, however, the prospective fees from Enron to Arthur Andersen would come to just over 1 percent of its $9.3 billion revenues in that year.

44 See for example, Elizabeth Douglass & Tim Rutten, Accounting Worried Global Crossing Exec, L.A. Times, Jan. 30, 2002, at A1; Mark Watts, Numbers Don't Add up for Big Five Group of Bean Counters, Sunday Express, Mar. 24, 2002, at P6.

45 The Big Five firms were Arthur Andersen LLP, Deloitte & Touche LLP, Ernst & Young LLP, KPMG LLP, and PricewaterhouseCoopers LLP. See In re IKON Office Solutions, Inc., 277 F.3d 658, 662 n.1 (3d Cir. 2002).

46 Compared to its peers within the Big Five accounting firms, Arthur Andersen appears to have been responsible for less than its proportionate share of earnings restatements. While it audited 21 percent of Big Five audit clients, it was responsible for only 15 percent of the restatements issued by Big Five firms between 1997 and 2001. See Allan Sloan, Periscope: How Arthur Andersen Begs for Business, Newsweek, Mar. 18, 2002, at 6. On this basis, it was arguably more conservative than its peers. Industry insiders have characterized Andersen as different from its peers only in that it marketed itself as a firm in which the audit partner could make the final call on difficult accounting questions without having to secure approval from senior officials at Andersen. Although this could indicate a weaker system of internal controls, that hypothesis seems inconsistent with Arthur Andersen's proportionately low rate of earnings restatements.

47 See George B. Moriarty & Philip B. Livingston, Quantitative Measures of the Quality of Financial Reporting, Fin. Executive, July–Aug. 2001, at 53, 54.

48 See GAO Report, note 28, at 4–5, 15–16.

49 Ibid. at 15.

50 This comparison does slightly mix apples and oranges, as Moriarty and Livingston include only earnings statement restatements, while the GAO Report focuses more broadly on all financial statement restatements. Compare Moriarty & Livingston, note 47 (discussing

only earnings statement restatements), with GAO Report, note 28 (examining financial restatements broadly). The differences are, however, likely to be modest because the vast majority of financial restatements involve earnings restatements.

51 See GAO Report, note 28, at 4.

52 See ibid.

53 Ibid.

54 Specifically, the median size by market capitalization of a restating company rose from $143 million in 1997 to $351 million in 2002. Ibid.

55 Of the 125 accounting irregularity restatements identified through mid-2002, 85 percent were listed on the Nasdaq and the NYSE. Ibid.

56 See ibid. at 5. The GAO Report also found a longer term market-adjusted decline of 18 percent over the period from 60 trading days before the announcement to 60 trading days after the announcement. See ibid. at 29.

57 See ibid. at 28.

58 Accounting firms have attempted to explain this increase in restatements by noting that the SEC tightened the definition of materiality in 1999. This explanation is not very convincing, however, because the principal SEC statement that redefined materiality was issued in mid-1999, one year after the number of restatements began to soar. See Staff Accounting Bulletin No. 99, 64 Fed. Reg. 45,150 (Aug. 19, 1999) (codified at 17 C.F.R. pt. 211). Further, Staff Accounting Bulletin No. 99 did not mandate restatements, but rather advised that any standard practice employed by auditors and issuers that assumed amounts under 5 percent were inherently immaterial could not be applied reflexively. See ibid. at 45,151.

59 The SEC's prioritization of earnings management as a principal enforcement target can be dated approximately to former SEC Chairman Arthur Levitt's speech on the subject in 1998. See Levitt, note 25.

60 According to Moriarty and Livingston, companies that restated earnings suffered market losses of $17.7 billion in 1998, $24.2 billion in 1999, and $31.2 billion in 2000. See Moriarty & Livingston, note 47, at 55. Expressed as a percentage of the overall capitalization (which ascended dramatically during this period), the market losses for 1998 through 2000 came to 0.13 percent, 0.14 percent and 0.19 percent, respectively.

61 See GAO Report, note 28, at 5.

62 See ibid. Revenue recognition was also the leading reason for restatements in each individual year over this period. See ibid.

63 While revenue recognition restatements accounted for only 38 percent of restatements over the 1997 to 2002 period, they were associated with $56 billion of the $100 billion in market capitalization that restating companies lost during this period. See ibid. at 28.

64 See ibid. at 5.

65 See The Watchdogs Didn't Bark: Enron and the Wall Street Analysts: Hearing Before the Sub Committee on Governmental Affairs, 107th Cong. 5 (2002) (statement of Sen. Thompson); see also The Fall of Enron: How Could it Have Happened?: Hearing Before the Subcommittee on Governmental Affairs, 107th Cong. 119 (testimony of Frank Partnoy, Professor of Law, University of San Diego School of Law) (testifying that "as late as October 2001 sixteen of seventeen of the securities analysts covering Enron rated it a 'strong buy' or 'buy'").

66 See Paul M. Healy & Krishna G. Palepu, The Fall of Enron, 17 *J. Econ. Persps.* 3 (2002).

67 See ibid.

68 See Lauren Young, Independence Day, SmartMoney, May 2002, at 28.

69 See ibid.

70 See Analyzing the Analysts: Hearing Before the Subcommittee on Capital Mkts., Ins., & Gov't Sponsored Enters. of the H.R. Comm. on Fin. Servs., 107th Cong. 120 (2001) [hereinafter Analyzing the Analysts] (statement of Paul E. Kanjorski, Member, House Subcomm. on Capital Mkts., Ins., & Gov't Sponsored Enters.) A study by First Call also found that less than 1 percent of the 28,000 stock recommendations issued by brokerage firm analysts during late 1999 and most of 2000 were sell recommendations. See ibid.

71 Sell-side analysts are employed by brokerage firms that understandably wish to maximize brokerage transactions. In this light, a buy recommendation addresses the entire market and certainly all of the firm's customers, while a sell recommendation addresses only those customers who own the stock (probably well under 1 percent) and those with margin accounts who are willing to sell the stock short. In addition, sell recommendations annoy not only the company that is adversely rated, but also institutional investors who fear that sell recommendations will spook retail investors, causing them to panic and sell, while the institution is locked into a large position that it cannot easily liquidate.

72 See Analyzing the Analysts, note 70, at 120.

73 Participants in the industry also report that the professional culture changed dramatically in the late 1990s, particularly as investment banking firms began to hire star analysts for their marketing clout. See Gretchen Morgenson, Requiem for an Honorable Profession, N.Y. Times, May 5, 2002, 3, at 1 (suggesting that the change in research culture dates from around 1996).

74 Although the empirical evidence is limited, research suggests that independent analysts (i.e. analysts not associated with the underwriter for a particular issuer) behave differently than, and tend to outperform in

terms of accuracy, analysts associated with the issuer's underwriter. The market in turn gave greater weight to the former's recommendations. See Roni Michaely & Kent L. Womack, Conflict of Interest and the Credibility of Underwriter Analyst Recommendations, 12 *Rev. Fin. Stud.* 653, 655–56 (1999).

75 See notes 66–67 and accompanying text (noting that Enron was trading at seventy times earnings and six times its book value and earned an 89 percent return for the year 2000). These are hallmarks of an overvalued company, and should serve to discourage investment unless firm-specific information suggests continued strong earnings growth.

76 See Private Litigation Under the Federal Securities Laws: Hearings Before the Subcommittee. on Sec. of Subcommittee on Banking, Hous., and Urban Affairs, 103rd Cong. 347 (1993) (statement of Jake L. Netterville, Chairman, Board of Directors of the American Institute of Certified Public Accountants) (noting that the six largest accounting firms' potential exposure to loss was in the billions). One major auditing firm, Laventhol & Horwath, did fail as a result of litigation and associated scandals growing out of the S&L scandals of the 1980s. See What Role Should CPAs Be Playing in Audit Reform?, Partner's Report for CPA Firm Owners (Apr. 2002) (discussing the experience of Laventhol & Horwath). The accounting profession's bitter experience with class action litigation in the 1980s and 1990s probably explains why it became the strongest and most organized champion of the Private Securities Litigation Reform Act of 1995. See Private Securities Litigation Reform Act of 1995, Pub. L. No. 104-67, 109 Stat. 737 (codified as amended at 15 U.S.C. 78u-3).

77 501 U.S. 350 (1991).

78 See ibid. at 359–61 (creating a federal rule requiring plaintiffs to file within one year of when they should have known of the violation underlying their action, but in no event more than three years after the violation). This one to three year period was typically shorter than the previously applicable limitations periods, which were determined by analogy to state statutes and often permitted a five or six year delay.

79 *Cent. Bank of Denver* v. *First Interstate Bank of Denver*, 511 U.S. 164 (1994).

80 See ibid. at 164.

81 See Private Securities Litigation Reform Act of 1995, Pub. L. No. 104-67 101, 109 Stat. at 737–749.

82 See ibid. 201, 109 Stat. at 758–62.

83 See ibid. 107, 109 Stat. at 758.

84 See ibid. 102, 109 Stat. at 749–56.

85 Securities Litigation Uniform Standards Act of 1998, Pub. L. No. 105-353, 112 Stat. 3227 (codified in scattered sections of 15 U.S.C.). For an analysis and critique of this statute, see generally Richard W.

Painter, Responding to a False Alarm: Federal Preemption of State Securities Fraud Causes of Action, 84 *Cornell L. Rev.* 1 (1998).

86 See Office of the Gen. Counsel, U.S. Sec. & Exch. Comm'n, Report to the President and the Congress on the First Year of Practice Under the Private Securities Litigation Reform Act of 1995 (1997), http://www.sec.gov/news/studies/lreform.txt [hereinafter Practice Under the Private Securities Litigation Act of 1995].

87 The Big Six firms were Arthur Andersen LLP, Deloitte & Touche LLP, Ernst & Young LLP, KPMG LLP, Price Waterhouse, and Coopers Lybrand. See In re IKON Office Solutions, Inc., 277 F.3d 658, 662 n.1 (3d Cir. 2002). The Big Six became the Big Five in 1998 when Price Waterhouse and Coopers Lybrand merged to form PricewaterhouseCoopers. Ibid.

88 Practice Under the Private Securities Litigation Act of 1995, note 86, at 21–22. The figures for the years 1990–1992 were reported to the SEC by the Big Six and include all class actions against them; thus, potentially some non-securities class actions could be included in this total. Nonetheless, the number of such nonsecurities actions seems likely to have been small. As the above SEC study further notes: "During the period 1991 through June 1996, accountants were defendants in 52 reported settlements (as opposed to complaints), . . . and law firms were defendants in 7. Thus, there seems to be a real decline in the number of lawsuits against secondary defendants." Ibid. at 22.

89 Ibid. at 21–22.

90 Ibid. at 4. As this study expressly noted, both the PSLRA and the Supreme Court's decision in Central Bank of Denver in 1994 that ended private "aiding and abetting" liability under Rule 10b-5 could have caused this decline. See notes 79–84 and accompanying text.

91 Several former SEC officials, including Stanley Sporkin, the longtime former head of the SEC's Division of Enforcement, have made this point to me. They believe that the SEC's enforcement action against Arthur Andersen, which was resolved in June 2001, was one of the very few (and perhaps the only) enforcement actions brought against a Big Five accounting firm on fraud grounds during the 1990s. See *SEC* v. *Arthur Andersen LLP*, SEC Litigation Release No. 17039 2001 SEC LEXIS 1159, (D.D.C. June 19, 2001). Although the SEC did bring charges during the 1990s against individual partners in these firms, the high cost and manpower required to bring suits against the Big Five, and the expectation that these defendants could zealously resist appears to have deterred the SEC from bringing suits against them. In contrast, during the 1980s, especially during Mr. Sporkin's tenure as head of the Enforcement Division, the SEC regularly brought enforcement actions against the Big Five.

NINE

92 Indeed, this author would continue to support proportionate liability for auditors on fairness grounds and agrees with the Second Circuit's interpretation of the PSLRA's heightened pleading standards. See for example, *Novak* v. *Kasaks*, 216 F.3d 300, 306 (2d Cir. 2000) (noting that "the PSLRA imposed stringent procedural requirements on plaintiffs pursuing private securities fraud actions").

93 At a minimum, plaintiffs today must plead with particularity those facts giving rise to a " 'strong inference of [fraudulent intent].' " See ibid. at 307. At the outset of a case, it may be possible to plead such facts with respect to the management of the corporate defendant (e.g. based on insider sales by such persons prior to the public disclosure of the adverse information that caused the stock drop), but it is rarely possible to plead such information with respect to the auditors (who by law cannot own stock in their client). In short, the plaintiff faces a "Catch 22" dilemma in suing the auditor in that it cannot plead fraud with particularity until it obtains discovery and it cannot obtain discovery under the PSLRA until it pleads fraud with particularity.

94 Although no systematic data exists, recent cases have noted that, after the enactment of the PSLRA in 1995, the odds facing plaintiffs in class actions have climbed, particularly when they are suing secondary defendants. In particular, because the plaintiff is obliged to prove "that a professional acted with knowledge and/or recklessness with regard to material misstatements and omissions, a successful outcome can never be regarded as a sure thing." See In re Rite Aid Corp. Sec. Litig., 269 F. Supp. 2d 603, 608 (E.D. Pa. 2003). Compare In re Ikon Office Solutions, Inc., 277 F.3d 658 (3d Cir. 2002) (affirming dismissal of securities class action against accountants in case where primary defendants had early settled for $111 million), with In re Ikon Office Solutions Inc., Sec. Litig., 194 F.R.D. 166 (E.D. Pa. 2000) (approving $111 million settlement by primary defendants). While there have been some large settlements in the wake of Enron, see In re Ikon Office Solutions, Inc., 194 F.R.D. 166, the SEC has also found that accountants today are less frequently named as defendants. See notes 86–90 and accompanying text.

95 Consulting fees paid by audit clients exploded during the 1990s. According to the Panel on Audit Effectiveness (the Panel), audit firms' fees from consulting services for their SEC audit clients increased from 12 percent of gross fees in 1990 to 32 percent in 1999. See Public Oversight Board, Panel on Audit Effectiveness, Report and Recommendations 112 (2000). For 1990, the Panel found that 79 percent of the Big Five firms' SEC audit clients received no consulting services from their auditors, and only 1 percent of those clients paid consulting fees exceeding their auditing fees. Ibid. Although the Panel found only marginal changes during the 1990s, later studies have found that consulting fees for large public corporations have become a multiple of the audit fee. See note 96 and accompanying text.

96 A 2003 survey by the Chicago Tribune finds that the 100 largest corporations in the Chicago area (determined on the basis of market capitalization) paid consulting fees to their auditors that were, on average, over three times their audit fee. See Janet Kidd Stewart & Andrew Countryman, Local Audit Conflicts Add Up: Consulting Deals, Hiring Practices in Question, *Chi. Trib.*, Feb. 24, 2002, at C1. The most extreme example cited in the study was Motorola, which had over a sixteen to one ratio between consulting fees and audit fees. See ibid.

97 See Lee Berton, Audit Fees Fall as CPA Firms Jockey for Bids, *Wall St. J.*, Jan. 28, 1985, at 33 (discussing lowballing in the United States); Andrew Jack, The FT500, *Fin. Times*, Jan. 20, 1994, at XLVI (discussing concerns about low-balling in the United Kingdom); Ann Shortell & Ann Walmsley, Toughening Up the Books, *Maclean's*, Feb. 10, 1986, at 48 (noting low-balling in Canada).

98 See Berton, note 97, at 33.

99 See, for example, Max H. Bazerman *et al.*, The Impossibility of Auditor Independence, 38 *Sloan Mgmt. Rev.* 89, 90 (1997); cf. Richard W. Painter, Lawyers' Rules, Auditors' Rules and the Psychology of Concealment, 84 *Minn. L. Rev.* 1399, 1436 (2000) (arguing that compensation-related incentives undermine auditor independence).

100 For a review of the empirical literature on this point, see Robert A. Prentice, The SEC and MDP: Implications of the Self-Serving Bias for Independent Auditing, 61 *Ohio St. L.J.* 1597, 1648–49 (2000) ("Most knowledgeable observers seem to believe ... that auditor independence and objectivity are affected by auditors' self-interest in that, for example, the more revenue coming from a client, the more the likely auditors are to give [in to] client pressure for improper accounting treatment.") (footnote omitted).

101 The General Instructions of Form 8-K, and Item 4 ("Changes in Registrant's Certifying Accountant") of Form 8-K, both found in the Securities and Exchange Act of 1934, require a reporting company to file a Form 8-K within five days after the resignation or dismissal of the issuer's independent accountant or the independent accountant of a significant subsidiary. See 17 C.F.R. 249.308; see also Sec. & Exch. Comm'n, Form 8-K, B, Item 4 (SEC 873, 2003), http://www.sec.gov/about/forms/form8-k.pdf. The company must then

provide the elaborate disclosures mandated by Item 304 of Regulation S-K, found in the Securities Act of 1933, relating to any dispute or disagreement between the auditor and the accountant. See 17 C.F.R. 229.304.

102 See generally Richard M. Frankel *et al.*, The Relation Between Auditors' Fees for Non-Audit Services and Earnings Management (MIT Sloan Working Paper No. 4330-02, 2002) (providing empirical evidence on the relation between auditor fees and earnings management), at http://www.ssrn.com/id = 296557. Similarly, "firms purchasing more [nonaudit] services were found more likely to just meet [or beat] analysts' expectations," which is the standard profile of the firm playing "the numbers game." See ibid. at 20.

103 Section 10A of the Securities Exchange Act of 1934 requires the auditor of a public company to notify the SEC where the auditor discovers an "illegal act [that] has or may have occurred," which "has a material effect on the financial statements of the issuer" where management and the board of the issuer has not done so itself within one day of notification by the auditor. See 15 U.S.C. 78j-1 (2000). Since its adoption in 1995 as part of the Private Securities Litigation Reform Act of 1995, Pub. L. No. 104-67, 109 Stat. 737, this provision has been seldom, if ever, employed.

104 The rise of the public accountant paralleled the rise of the publicly owned corporation, and was commensurate with the growing need of investors for objective financial information. This growth preceded the adoption of the federal securities laws in the 1930s. For example, the American Association of Public Accountants was formed in 1887, and in 1896, New York became the first state to certify public accountants who successfully passed a required state exam. See John L. Carey, The Rise of the Accounting Profession: From Technician to Professional 1896–1936, at 2, 6–7, 43–45 (1969); see also James Don Edwards, History of Public Accounting in the United States (1960).

105 For overviews of behavioral economics, see Christine Jolls *et al.*, A Behavioral Approach to Law and Economics, 50 *Stan. L. Rev.* 1471, 1476–89 (1998); Cass R. Sunstein, Behavioral Analysis of Law, 64 *U. Chi. L. Rev.* 1175 (1997). Herbert Simon, a Nobel Prize winner, coined the broadly accepted term "bounded rationality." See Jolls *et al.*, at 1477; Herbert A. Simon, Rationality as Process and as Product of Thought, 68 *Am. Econ. Rev.* pt. 2, at 1 (1978).

106 See Amos Tversky & Daniel Kahneman, Judgment Under Uncertainty: Heuristics and Biases, in Judgment Under Uncertainty: Heuristics and Biases 3 (Daniel Kahneman *et al.* eds., 1982).

107 See ibid. at 11–14; see also Jolls *et al.*, note 105, at 1477–78 (applying the "availability heuristic" to the field of law and economics).

108 See Tversky & Kahneman, note 106, at 11.

109 This is by no means the only way to explain bubbles without resorting to claims of mass delusion. An alternative theory is that institutional money managers have rational incentives to engage in "herding behavior," preferring a common wrong decision to a risky, correct one. See text and accompanying notes 123–27.

110 The deep-seated bias displayed by many individuals toward optimism in predicting future events probably aggravated this trend. See Jolls *et al.*, note 105, at 1524–25 (noting that people tend to think that bad events are far less likely to happen to them than to others); see generally Neil D. Weinstein, Unrealistic Optimism About Future Life Events, 39 *J. Personality & Soc. Psychol.* 806 *passim* (1980) (reporting the results of two studies that investigated the tendency of people to be unrealistically optimistic about future life events).

111 For the view that investment banking firms changed their competitive strategies on or around 1996 and thereafter sought the "popular, high-profile analyst" as a means of acquiring IPO clients, see Morgenson, note 73, 3, at 1 (citing Stefan D. Abrams, chief investment officer for asset allocation at Trust Company of the West).

112 One court has recently even taken judicial notice of the conflicted role of star securities analysts in landing IPOs for the investment banking firms that hired them away from smaller competitors. See In re Merrill Lynch & Co., Inc. Research Reports Sec. Litig., 273 F. Supp. 2d 351, 383–89 (S.D.N.Y. 2003). Judge Pollack quoted the Wall Street Journal, the Boston Globe and other publications, stating: "To bring a company public, a firm needs its analyst on board. It is the analyst that explains – and implicitly, trumpets – the investment merits of the offering." at 383. Judge Pollack also quoted an article which stated that analysts have become an important sales tool for the investment bankers to land their super-profitable deals. A top analyst and the credibility that he or she brings can be the difference between landing a deal or not – and the pay for the most sought-after analysts can top $5 million a year. Ibid. at 383–84 (internal quotation marks omitted). In particular, the court cited the case of Henry Blodgett, who according to press reports, was lured to Merrill Lynch with a high salary in order to attract IPOs. Ibid. at 386 (citing Jon Birger, New Executive Henry Blodgett; Merrill Lynch's Top Pick; Internet Analyst Lured from CIBC; On-Target Research Should Attract IPOs, Crain's N. Y. Bus., Mar. 22, 1999, at 11).

113 The idea that persons outside of the profession began to dominate professional gatekeeping is at the heart of a recent lawsuit initiated by the New York Attorney General against five chief executive officers of major U.S. corporations. See Patrick McGeehan, Spitzer Sues

Executives of Telecom Companies Over "Ill Gotten" Gains, N.Y. Times, Oct. 1, 2002, at C1.

114 See notes 20–21 and accompanying text.

115 See Gretchen Morgenson, Bush Failed to Stress Need to Rein in Stock Options, N.Y. Times, July 11, 2002, at C1 [hereinafter Morgenson, Bush Failed]; Gretchen Morgenson, Time for Accountability at the Corporate Candy Store, N.Y. Times, Mar. 31, 2002, 3, at 1 [hereinafter Morgenson, Time for Accountability].

116 See Morgenson, Bush Failed, note 115, at C7 (citing a study by Sanford C. Bernstein & Co.). Thus, if $162 billion is the value of all options in these 2,000 companies, aggressive accounting policies that temporarily raise stock prices by as little as 10 percent create a potential gain for executives of over $16 billion, a substantial incentive.

117 A variety of commentators, calling for minimum holding periods or other curbs on stock options, have made this point. These include Henry M. Paulson, Jr., chief executive of Goldman Sachs, and Senator John McCain of Arizona. See David Leonhardt, Anger at Executives' Profits Fuels Support for Stock Curb, N.Y. Times, July 9, 2002, at A1.

118 Rule 16b-3(d) expressly permits an officer or director, otherwise subject to the short-swing profit provisions of Section 16(b) of the Securities Exchange Act of 1934, to exercise a qualified stock option and sell the underlying shares immediately "if at least six months elapse from the date of acquisition of the derivative security to the date of disposition of the . . . underlying equity security." See 17 C.F.R. 240.16b-3(d) (2003). In 1991, the SEC engaged in a comprehensive revision of its rules under Section 16(b) to facilitate the use of stock options as executive compensation and to "reduce the regulatory burden" under Section 16(b). See Ownership Reports, note 24, at 7243. A premise of this reform was that "holding derivative securities is functionally equivalent to holding the underlying equity security for purpose of section 16." Ibid. at 7248. Hence, the SEC permitted the tacking of the option holding period onto the stock's holding period, thereby enabling officers and directors to exercise options and sell on the same day, so long as they had already held the option for six months.

119 See James D. Cox & Randall S. Thomas, Leaving Money on the Table: Do Institutional Investors Fail to File Claims in Securities Class Actions?, 80 Wash. U. L.Q. 855, 855 (2002).

120 See Healy & Palepu, note 66, at 22.

121 See ibid. at 26–27.

122 Ibid. at 26.

123 Professors David Scharfstein and Jeremy Stein coined the term herding over a decade ago. See David S. Scharfstein & Jeremy C. Stein, Herd Behavior and

Investment, 80 Am. Econ. Rev. 465, 465 (1990). However, the concept long predates this term and is implicit in Keynes's 1936 analysis of the stock market. See John Maynard Keynes, The General Theory of Employment Interest and Money (1936).

124 There is considerable evidence that fund managers do think in these terms. See generally Judith Chevalier & Glenn Ellison, Career Concerns of Mutual Fund Managers, 114 Q.J. Econ. 389, 416–20 (1999) (finding that younger fund managers hold less unsystematic risk and have more conventional portfolios).

125 See Watts, note 44, at P6.

126 One of the most notable recent accounting scandals involved the Phar-Mor chain of retail stores. There, an audit partner for Coopers & Lybrand was denied participation in profit sharing because he had insufficiently cross-sold the firm's services. The next year he sold $900,000 worth of business – most of it to Phar-Mor and its affiliates – but subsequently failed to detect $985 million in inflated earnings by Phar-Mor over the following three years. See Bazerman et al., note 99, at 89; Prentice, note 38, at 184.

127 Carl E. Bass, an internal audit partner, warned other Andersen partners in 1999 of Enron's dangerous accounting practices. See Robert Manor & Jon Yates, Faceless Andersen Partner in Spotlight's Glare, Chi. Trib., Apr. 14, 2002, 5, at 1. One Enron-related lawsuit alleged that David Duncan, the Andersen partner in charge of the Enron account, joined with Enron executives to have Mr. Bass removed from the Enron account within a few weeks of his warning. See ibid. This evidence suggests, if nothing else, that executives of a Big Five firm could overcome the internal audit function when the prospective consulting fees were high enough.

128 Federal Reserve Chairman Alan Greenspan has indeed suggested that market corrections will largely solve the problems uncovered in the wake of Enron. See Alan Greenspan, Corporate Governance, Remarks at the Stern School of Business, New York University (Mar. 26, 2002), www.federalreserve.gov/boarddocs/speeches/2002/2002032 62/default.htm. In his view, earnings management came to dominate management's agenda and as a result, "it is not surprising that since 1998 earnings restatements have proliferated." Ibid. Greenspan further stated that "this situation is a far cry from earlier decades when, if my recollection serves me correctly, firms competed on the basis of which one had the most conservative set of books. Short-term stock price values then seemed less of a focus than maintaining unquestioned credit worthiness." Ibid. He goes on to suggest that: "[a] change in behavior, however, may already be in train." Ibid. Specifically, he finds that "perceptions of the reliability

of firms' financial statements are increasingly reflected in yield spreads on corporate bonds" and that other signs of self-correction are discernible. Ibid.

129 This would certainly seem to be the premise of the recent "global settlement" between the SEC, the New York Attorney General, and the major underwriting firms, as its principal focus is on structural relief that will increase the professional independence of securities analysts. See Stephen Labaton, 10 Wall Street Firms Reach Settlement in Analyst Inquiry, N.Y. Times, Apr. 29, 2003, at A1.

130 For an overview of these crises, see Cunningham, note 28; note 32 and accompanying text.

131 As noted earlier, the takeover became a mechanism that could threaten managers at large public corporations with ouster only after or in conjunction with the development of junk bonds, which were first used to finance a hostile takeover in 1983. See note 14 and accompanying text. In contrast, the S&L crisis of the 1980s was distinctive in that the S&Ls did not typically trade in liquid public markets; rather, control was transferred by the sale of control blocks. Hence, a controlling shareholder was by definition immune from a takeover and thus could only be threatened with ouster by the approach of insolvency.

132 See 15 U.S.C. 7211(a) (2003). Section 101(c) of the Act enumerates the broad powers of the Board, including the authorty to "establish . . . auditing, quality control, ethics, independence, and other standards relating to the preparation of audit reports for issuers . . ." Sarbanes–Oxley Act of 2002, Pub. L. No. 107-204, 101(c), 116 Stat. 745.

133 See 15 U.S.C. §78o-3 (regarding the creation and activities of registered securities associations).

134 Section 201 of the Act, amending 10A of the Securities Exchange Act of 1934, specifies eight types of professional services which the auditor may not perform for an audit client and authorizes the Board to prohibit additional services if it determines that they may compromise auditor independence. See 201(a), 116 Stat. at 771–72 (codified at 15 U.S.C. 7231).

135 Note, however, that section 804 of the Act does extend the statute of limitation for securities fraud suits, thereby reversing a 1991 Supreme Court decision that shortened the time period. See ibid. 804, at 801 (codified at 28 U.S.C. 1658) (setting the statute of limitations for securities fraud); see also *Lampf, Pleva, Lipkind, Prupis & Petigrow* v. *Gilbertson*, 501 U.S. 350, 359–61 (1991) (creating the former federal rule requiring plaintiffs to file within one year of when they should have known of a particular securities violation underlying their action, but in no event more than three years after the violation).

136 Section 304 of the Act requires the forfeiture of certain bonuses "or other incentive-based or equity-based compensation" and any stock trading profits received by a chief executive officer or chief financial officer of an issuer during the twelve-month period following the filing of an inflated earnings report that is later restated. See 304, 116 Stat. at 778 (codified at 15 U.S.C. 7243). This does cancel the incentive to inflate earnings and then bail out, but ambiguities abound as the enforcement methods applicable to this provision are unspecified and the provision applies only if the earnings restatement is the product of "misconduct." See ibid.

137 Prior to the 1990s, private litigation was a genuine and arguably an excessive constraining force on auditors. See note 76 and accompanying text.

138 For a brief overview of these reforms, see Amy Borrus *et al.*, Reform: Business Gets Religion, Bus. Wk, Feb. 3, 2003, at 40, 41 (noting that corporations have adopted these reforms with little resistance, but also noting that some "governance gurus fear that companies are checking the boxes rather than taking changes to heart").

139 Ironically, one survey by Yale School of Management Professor Jeffrey Sonnenfeld has found that when it comes to the standard measures of good governance – the independence, attendance, and financial acumen of directors – the "least admired" companies do about as well as the "most admired" companies. See Jerry Useem, From Heroes to Goats and Back Again? How Corporate Leaders Lost Our Trust, Fortune, Nov. 18, 2002, at 40, 48.

140 See 511 U.S. 164, 164 (1994).

141 See Terry Gallagher, The Sarbanes–Oxley Act of 2002: One Year Later, Corp. Governance Advisor, July–Aug. 2003, at 18.

142 See (noting that "more than 50 percent of the record number of shareholder proposals during this proxy season dealt with executive compensation issues").

143 Most state statutes permit shareholders to amend the bylaws of the corporation. See for example, Del. Code Ann. tit. 8, 109(a) (2003) (providing that "after a corporation has received any payment for any of its stock, the power to adopt, amend or repeal bylaws shall be in the stockholders entitled to vote"). This power, however, conflicts with the universal provision, which most states have adopted, giving the board of directors control of the business and affairs of the corporation. See for example, ibid. 141(a) (providing that the "business and affairs of every corporation organized . . . shall be managed by or under the direction of a board of directors"). The law in this area remains unsettled. See generally John C. Coffee, Jr., The Bylaw Battlefield: Can Institutions Change the Outcome of Corporate Control Contests?, 51 *U. Miami L. Rev.* 605 (1997) (discussing

legal theories in connection with the questions raised by the allocation of power between boards and shareholders). For contrasting recent decisions, compare *International Brotherhood of Teamsters General Fund* v. *Fleming Cos.*, 975 P.2d 907, 908 (Okla. 1999) (upholding a bylaw adopted by shareholders against the claim that it impermissibly invaded the authority accorded to the board under Oklahoma law), with *Invacare Corp.* v. *Healthdyne Technologies Inc.*, 968 F. Supp. 1578, 1582 (N.D. Ga. 1997) (invalidating a mandatory bylaw adopted by a shareholder because it invaded the authority given to board under Georgia law).

144 See Lucian Arye Bebchuk & Marcel Kahan, A Framework for Analyzing Legal Policy Towards Proxy Contests, 78 *Cal. L. Rev.* 1071, 1080–81 (1990) (discussing the collective action problem in context of shareholder voting).

145 See Notice of Solicitation of Public Views Regarding Possible Changes to the Proxy Rules, Exchange Act Release No. 34-47, 778, 68 Fed. Reg. 24530 (May 1, 2003) (soliciting public comment regarding revisions to rules relating to shareholder proposals and director nomination processes). On July 15, 2003, the SEC's staff indicated that it would propose changes in its proxy rules in order to facilitate direct shareholder nomination of "watchdog" directors under some circumstances. See Div. of Corp. Fin., Sec. & Exch. Comm'n, Staff Report: Review of the Proxy Process Regarding the Nomination and Election of Directors 30–31 (2003).

146 See Phyllis Plitch & Lynn Cowan, Investors, Stirred Up by Scandals, Rally for Corporate Democracy, *Wall St. J.*, July 9, 2003.

147 See notes 120–24 and accompanying text.

148 Increasing economic evidence suggests that short sale constraints can cause stocks to be overvalued. See generally Charles M. Jones & Owen A. Lamont, Short-Sale Constraints and Stock Returns, 66 *J. Fin. Econ.* 207 (2002) (presenting a study of the costs of short selling stock). The best known of the legal constraints on short selling is the up-tick rule, which permits short sales only at a price higher than the previous price (an up-tick) or at the previous price if the last different price was lower. See 17 C.F.R. 240.10a-1 (2003). Securities Exchange Act Release No. 13091 outlines the purposes of the up-tick rule. See Short Sales of Securities, Exchange Act Release No. 34-13,091, 41 Fed. Reg. 56,530, 56,535 (Dec. 28, 1976) (codified at 17 C.F.R. 240.10a-1). Today, the advent of decimalization of securities prices has weakened the impact of the up-tick rule. Further, recent commentators have argued that the tax laws impose the primary constraints on short selling. See, for example Michael Powers *et al.*, Market Bubbles, Wasteful Avoidance, and Tax and Regulatory Constraints on Short Sales (2003) (unpublished manuscript, on file with author) (detailing both tax and regulatory constraints on short selling).

149 The SEC has recently shown some willingness to reconsider and liberalize its rules regarding short sales. See Securities Exchange Act Release No. 34-48709, 2003 SEC LEXIS 2594 (Oct. 28, 2003). In that Release, the SEC has proposed a new Regulation SHO that would permit short sales to be effected at a price one cent below the consolidated best bid; however, the Release would also tighten the restrictions on "naked" short sales. Thus, its actual provisions may have offsetting effects. More importantly, SEC proposed in this Release to relax its short sale rules for certain liquid securities for a two-year pilot period in order to test the effects of less regulated short selling on market volatility, price efficiency, and liquidity. Although these proposals do not appear to be Enron-related, the fact remains that the short seller should be as motivated to serve as a private attorney general, eagerly seeking to detect fraud, as the plaintiff's attorney.

In recommending some relaxation of the constraints on the short seller, this author does not mean to suggest that the prohibition against market manipulation should be relaxed, but only that the more prophylactic rules, such as the up-tick rule, should be revised, and that tax penalties should be eased.

150 See notes 61–62 and accompanying text.

151 See George Santayana, 1 The Life of Reason; or, the Phases of Human Progress 284 (1st ed. New York, Charles Scribner's Sons, 1905).

Index

eBooks – at www.eBookstore.tandf.co.uk

A library at your fingertips!

eBooks are electronic versions of printed books. You can store them on your PC/laptop or browse them online.

They have advantages for anyone needing rapid access to a wide variety of published, copyright information.

eBooks can help your research by enabling you to bookmark chapters, annotate text and use instant searches to find specific words or phrases. Several eBook files would fit on even a small laptop or PDA.

NEW: Save money by eSubscribing: cheap, online access to any eBook for as long as you need it.

Annual subscription packages

We now offer special low-cost bulk subscriptions to packages of eBooks in certain subject areas. These are available to libraries or to individuals.

For more information please contact webmaster.ebooks@tandf.co.uk

We're continually developing the eBook concept, so keep up to date by visiting the website.

www.eBookstore.tandf.co.uk